ALSO BY SHIRLEY CHRISTIAN

Nicaragua: Revolution in the Family

BEFORE LEWIS
AND CLARK

BEFORE LEWIS AND CLARK

The Story of the Chouteaus, the French Dynasty

That Ruled America's Frontier

SHIRLEY CHRISTIAN

FARRAR, STRAUS AND GIROUX

New York

Farrar, Straus and Giroux
19 Union Square West, New York 10003

Grateful acknowledgment is made to the following for permission to reprint the illustrations: © Shirley Christian for the image of Pierre Laclède Liguest's house; © Collection of The New-York Historical Society for the image of Cheveux Blancs; © Smithsonian American Art Museum, Washington, D.C. / Art Resource for the images of Clermont II and George Caitlin's painting of The Bluffs; the Illinois Historic Preservation Agency for the image of the Pierre Ménard home; the Joslyn Art Museum, Omaha, Nebraska, for the engraving of Karl Bodmer's painting of the S.B. Yellow Stone; and the Missouri Historical Society, St. Louis, for all other images.

Library of Congress Cataloging-in-Publication Data
Christian, Shirley, date.
    Before Lewis and Clark : the story of the Chouteaus, the French dynasty
that ruled America's frontier / Shirley Christian.— 1st ed.
        p.   cm.
    Includes bibliographical references and index.
    ISBN 0-374-11005-0 (alk. paper)
    1. Chouteau family.   2. Pioneers—Missouri—Saint Louis—Biography.
3. French Americans—Missouri—Saint Louis—Biography.   4. Businessmen—
Missouri—Saint Louis—Biography.   5. Saint Louis (Mo.)—Biography.
6. Missouri River Valley—Biography.   7. Frontier and pioneer life—Missouri
River Valley.   8. Missouri River Valley—History.   I. Title.

F474.S253A225 2004
977.8'6600441—dc22

                                                                    2003064176

Designed by Jonathan D. Lippincott
Map and family tree designed by Jeffrey L. Ward

www.fsgbooks.com

1   3   5   7   9   10   8   6   4   2

Contents

❋

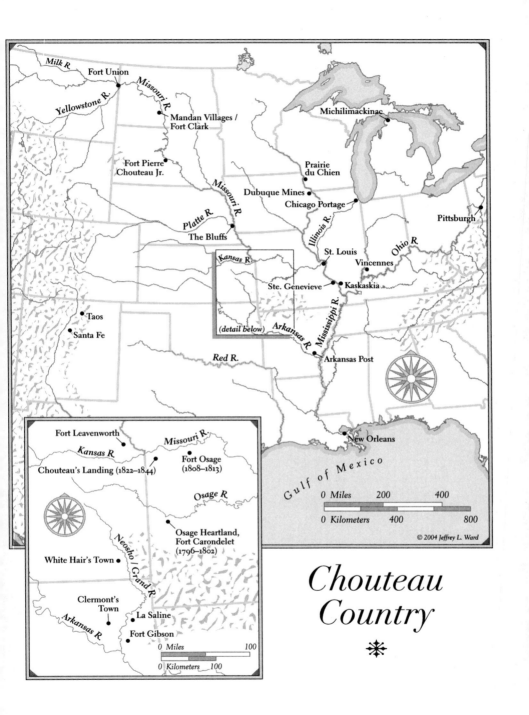

Milk R.   Fort Union

Yellowstone R.   Missouri R.

Mandan Villages /
Fort Clark

Fort Pierre
Chouteau Jr.

Missouri R.

Platte R.   Missouri R.

The Bluffs

Kansas R.

Michilimackinac

Prairie
du Chien

Dubuque Mines

Chicago Portage

Illinois R.

St. Louis

Vincennes

Ohio R.

Pittsburgh

Ste. Genevieve   Kaskaskia

(detail below)   Arkansas R.   Mississippi R.

Taos

Santa Fe

Red R.

Arkansas Post

Gulf of Mexico

New Orleans

0 Miles   200   400

0 Kilometers   400   800

© 2004 Jeffrey L. Ward

Detail inset

Fort Leavenworth

Kansas R.   Missouri R.

Chouteau's Landing (1822–1844)

Fort Osage
(1808–1813)

Osage R.

Osage Heartland,
Fort Carondelet
(1796–1802)

White Hair's Town

Neosho / Grand R.

Clermont's
Town

La Saline

Arkansas R.

Fort Gibson

0 Miles   100

0 Kilometers   100

Chouteau
Country

❈

Marie Thérèse
Bourgeois *m.*
(1733–1814)

René Augustin
Chouteau
(1723–1776)

René
Chouteau (?)
(1749–?)

Auguste
Chouteau *m.*
(1750–1829)

Marie Thérèse
Cerré
(1769–1842)

Marie Thérèse
Chouteau
(1788–1796)

Catherine Emilie
Chouteau
(1790–1792)

Auguste Aristide
Chouteau
(1792–1833)

Gabriel Sylve
(Cerré) Chou
(1794–1887)

Marie Thérèse
Bourgeois *not m.*
(1733–1814)

Pierre Laclède
Liguest
(1729–1778)

Pierre
Chouteau *m.*
(1758–1849)

Pélagie
Kiersereau
(1767–1793)

Marie Pélagie
Chouteau *m.*
(1760–1812)

Sylvestre
Labbadie
(1737–1794)

Auguste Pierre
(A.P.) Chouteau
(1786–1838)

Pierre (Cadet)
Chouteau Jr.
(1789–1865)

Pélagie
Chouteau
(1790–1875)

Paul Liguest
Chouteau
(1792–1861)

Pierre
Chouteau *2nd m.*
(1758–1849)

Brigitte
Saucier
(1778–1829)

François Gesseau
Chouteau
(1797–1838)

Cyprien
Chouteau
(1802–1879)

Louis Pharamond
Chouteau
(1806–1831)

Charles B.
Chouteau
(1808–1884)

Frederick
Chouteau
(1809–1891)

Emilie S.
Labbadie
(1778–1844)

Sylvestre
Labbadie Jr.
(1779–1849)

Marie Pélagie
Labbadie
(1781–1833)

Marie Thérèse
Labbadie
(1787)

Joseph
Papin
(1780–1850)

Marguerite
Papin
(1781–1808)

Alexandre LaForce
Papin
(1782–1849)

Marie Thérèse
Papin
(1784–1840)

Marie Louise
Papin
(1785–?)

Hypolite Le
Papin
(1787–184.

Julie
Gratiot
(1782–1852)

Victoire
Gratiot
(1785–1860)

Charles
Gratiot Jr.
(1786–1855)

Marie Thérèse
Gratiot
(1788–1815)

Henry
Gratiot
(1789–1836)

Laclède-Chouteau Family Tree

※

T. Eulalie Chouteau (1797–1835)	Marie Louise Chouteau (1799–1832)	Emilie A. Chouteau (1802–1843)	Henry Pierre Chouteau (1805–1855)	Edward René Chouteau (1807–1846)

Marie Louise Chouteau (1762–1817)	*m.*	Joseph M. Papin (1741–1811)				Victoire Chouteau (1764–1825)	*m.*	Charles Gratiot (1752–1817)

Anne Sophie Labbadie (1788–1790)	Dominique Auguste Labbadie (1789–1794)	Anne Sophie Labbadie (1791–1862)	Pierre Labbadie (1793–1794)	Marie Antoinette Labbadie (1795–1818)

Pélagie Papin (1790–1798)	Sophie Papin (1791–1808)	Pierre Millicour Papin (1793–1849)	Sylvestre Vilray Papin (1794–1828)	Emilie Papin (1796–1849)	Pierre Didier Papin (1798–1853)	Theodore Dartigny Papin (1799–1851)

Emilie Anne Gratiot (1793–1862)	Isabelle Gratiot (1796–1878)	Marie Brigitte Gratiot (1798–1803)	J. P. "Bunyon" Gratiot (1799–1871)	Paul B. Gratiot (1800–1855)

Note: For most of the information contained in the Family Tree, the author is indebted to the work of Mary B. Cunningham and Jeanne C. Blythe in their book *The Founding Family of St. Louis* (St. Louis: Midwest Technical Publications, 1977). The dates of death of two members of the family, Brigitte Saucier Chouteau and Charles Gratiot Jr., were corrected to conform to the information the author found in surviving family letters.

BEFORE LEWIS
AND CLARK

Among a People of Strange Speech

When Meriwether Lewis and William Clark descended on the shores of the Mississippi River at the end of 1803 to organize their "Voyage of Discovery" up the Missouri River and beyond, they knew next to nothing about the Louisiana Purchase region, which would eventually form all or part of fifteen states. But William Clark, thanks to the path opened in the Illinois country by an older brother some twenty years earlier, knew an important person in the little French Creole village of St. Louis, whose inhabitants were then living amiably under Spanish rule. The name of the man was Chouteau, which neither Clark nor Lewis could spell.

Because St. Louis and the Upper Louisiana territory had not yet been transferred to the United States, Lewis and Clark set up camp opposite the mouth of the Missouri River on the east bank of the Mississippi to await the official completion of the Louisiana Purchase. From Camp Dubois, named for the river that emptied into the Mississippi at the spot, they rowed southerly across to St. Louis—as breaks in the winter ice permitted—and commenced the work of gathering information and filling out their crew and supply needs.

Seen from the river, St. Louis was a collection of fewer than two hundred stone and timber houses and other buildings sitting atop a perpendicular limestone bluff extending for two miles along the Mississippi. The best of the houses were built of stone, and some of them included large gardens enclosed by high stone walls. Their styles were a blend of those of Quebec, the Caribbean, and New Orleans. The principal thoroughfare and two other streets ran parallel to the river about forty feet above the usual water level. Only one cross street, present-day Market Street, connected Rue Royale to the riverfront. It had been quarried down to the level of the river. A sand towpath ran close to the water's edge for the use of cordellers who pulled flatboats and other craft up the river. At high water, the towpath was completely submerged.

St. Louis occupied a place on the North American continent just before the forested midlands gave way to open prairies and eventually the arid plains. The settlement had been carved out of a great stand of trees—oak, black walnut, ash, hickory, pecan, cottonwood. The forests stretched far south into the hills and low mountains of the region the French called Aux Arcs. Hemp grew wild and thick among the trees. To the west, along the Missouri River, intermittent open prairies and fertile valleys marked the landscape.

The population of what was called the "district" of St. Louis, which included the villages of Carondelet and St. Ferdinand in addition to the town of St. Louis, was estimated at 2,780, including 500 slaves and a few free mulattos. The remainder were whites of primarily French or French-Canadian ancestry. The nearby district of St. Charles had about 1,400 whites and 150 blacks. In addition, some 1,200 settlers lived on small farms ringing the district, most of them Americans who had emigrated from east of the Mississippi during the previous decade, including Daniel and Rebecca Boone and their large clan.

These lands surrounding St. Louis were "beautiful beyond description," in the words of a first-time visitor. They contained "marrow and fatness" and produced "all the conveniences, and even many of the luxuries of life," including fruit, grains, vegetables, mutton, fowl, beef, pork, butter, and cheese. Grape vines imported from France and Germany were flourishing, and it was also possible to make wine from the so-called summer grape native to the area. Buffalo were already becoming scarce, but tasty black bears, elk, and antelope still roamed the hills to the south. In short, the region was so fertile that the inhabitants had it in their power "to live as they please, and to become opulent with little labor."

The "West's first tourists" quickly found their way to the elegant mansions of Auguste and Pierre Chouteau, half brothers whose parents had come up the Mississippi from New Orleans forty years earlier and founded St. Louis. Making a comfortable living trading furs and skins from surrounding Indians and then shipping them to Europe via New Orleans and Montreal, the Chouteaus were the leading figures in the future metropolis.

Each of their homes, filled with large families and frequent guests, had two full stories plus a dormer floor. Double-height porticos supported by pillars stretched partially around the houses, which, together with buildings for slaves and horses, took up a square block each on the principal street. Auguste's house measured about 95 by 55 feet, which would have represented about 10,000 square feet of living space on two floors. Each property was enclosed by solid stone walls with portholes, giving the houses the appearance of castles. They were remarkable sights in such a small town.

Auguste, courtly and fifty-three years old, was a steady, trustworthy man of outward moderation who had years earlier given up travels among the Indian tribes in favor of overseeing the accounts and bringing up a young family. He was the "Mr. Shoto" who had entertained William Clark at a ball during his previous visit, in 1797, where Clark enjoyed "all the fine girls & buckish Gentlemen." The festivities during that visit had been such that it was nearly daylight when Clark got to his bed in the home of the Chouteaus' youngest sister, Victoire, and her husband, Charles Gratiot. On that occasion Clark had walked around the town and found it to be "in a Thriveing state, a number of Stone houses built & on the stocks, tho all in the french stile."

Forty-five-year-old Pierre Chouteau was the far more outgoing of the two brothers. Almost universally known as Cadet, a French designation for the second brother in a family, he was ambitious, zealous, and explosive—but charming and hospitable. The departing Spanish administration considered him a brave and daring man of unsurpassed skill for maintaining peace with, and among, Indian tribes. He was the right man to lead a force "against whatever enemies happen to present themselves."

Pierre opened his home to Lewis and Clark during their stays in St. Louis. He and his twenty-five-year-old second wife, Brigitte, provided the travelers with housing far more luxurious than the spartan camp their men erected across the river. Meriwether Lewis, who did most of the information gathering among the knowledgeable citizens of St. Louis, enjoyed Pierre's hospitality more than did William Clark, who had principal responsibility for the camp and men.

Pierre and Auguste Chouteau had been brought up to be equally at home in the drawing room and the Indian lodge. Little is known about their physical appearances except for a surviving portrait of Auguste, showing some middle-age softness, a pronounced widow's peak, and the beginnings of a receding hairline. The only portrait representing Pierre is a composite made long after his death, based on the recollections of some of his descendants. It depicts a commanding man with lines about a thin face and a firmly set jaw. Both had short hair and were clean-shaven. They wore the finery of satin, linen, and lace that men of their era favored for formal occasions.

Despite the trappings of French style and sophistication, the brothers had been students of Indians and Indian ways since their adolescent years, especially of the Osages, the dominant tribe along the Lower Missouri River. Pierre had wintered among them for many years, and he displayed a curiosity and knowledge of nature that easily matched that of the man who had sent Lewis and Clark on this journey. It soon gave him great pride to be able to supply a number of the specimens sent to President Jefferson by Meriwether Lewis.

Most likely, Auguste had been schooled in New Orleans before the family came upriver when he was fourteen, but Pierre's formal education was severely constrained in a village that did not even have a schoolmaster until 1774, by which time Pierre was sixteen. Nevertheless, both Chouteau brothers were tutored and well-read in the classical tradition. Not only did they know double-entry bookkeeping and how to chart rivers and survey lands, but they also wrote literate, well-composed letters with good penmanship.

They treasured books, sometimes asking business associates in Europe, New Orleans, or Montreal to buy a recent book for them. On trips up and down the rivers on keelboats and barges, there was time to absorb literature, history, philosophy, and the latest on science and geography. Descartes, Bacon, Voltaire, and Locke were among the writers and thinkers in their libraries, along with Defoe's *Robinson Crusoe*, Fielding's *Tom Jones*, and Cervantes's *Don Quixote*.

They and the other people of St. Louis also liked to have fun. They enjoyed billiards, cards, horse races, and, most of all, dancing to the music of fiddlers. They partied every Saturday evening and began again on Sunday as soon as high mass was finished in the little wooden church, continuing their social gatherings for the rest of the day and evening.

Protestants from the East at first thought such activities bordered on licentiousness, but they were soon won over to the joyful ways of the French Creoles, who told them that "men were made for happiness." To those "educated in regular and pious habits," it was suggested that such amusements "appear unseasonable and strange, if not odious and seem prophetic of some signal curse on the workers of iniquity." But one American new to St. Louis was surprised to find that "the French people on those days avoid all intemperate and immoral excesses, and conduct themselves with apparent decorum." He found them to be people "void of superstition . . . prone to hospitality, urbanity of manners, and innocent recreation," who were as confident of being faithful to their religion "as the most devout puritans in Christendom."

Another early visitor to the French settlement found "scarcely any distinction of classes." The virtues of the inhabitants included "honesty and punctuality in their dealings, hospitality to strangers, friendships and affection amongst relatives and neighbours." Women were seldom abandoned and seldom seduced, he observed. By contrast to their virtues, however, this visitor said the people of St. Louis "are devoid of public spirit, of enterprise or ingenuity, and are indolent and uninformed."

Lewis, who was twenty-nine years old, and Clark, thirty-three, were the honored guests at balls graced by the beautiful and charming daughters of Charles and Victoire Gratiot, the handsome sons of Pierre Chouteau, and the numerous young adults in the families of the two other Chouteau sisters, the Papins and Labbadies. Whatever conflicts might arise between people speaking different tongues were easily dispelled amid rustling taffeta, gleaming silver, and flickering candles reflected on polished walnut floors. Enveloped in this flirtatious Gallic setting, the soon-to-be explorers found themselves almost giddy with delight. House slaves served wines and brandies from France, rum from the Caribbean. Tables were laden with food.

Implicitly, amid all the gaiety, a deal was being struck under which the Chouteaus would do all they could to help Lewis and Clark succeed on their daunting voyage. The Americans, in turn, would help assure for the Chouteaus an influential position with the new power in the region, just like the one the family had enjoyed under the French and Spanish. In this new and distant outpost of the young republic, the Chouteaus and Lewis and Clark would need each other.

It was thanks to the virtual nonstop wars in Europe during the second half of the eighteenth century that the United States had been able to acquire the Louisiana Purchase lands stretching from the Gulf of Mexico nearly to the border of modern Canada. After a century under French control, the Louisiana lands had been ceded to Spain in 1763 as the result of France's loss to England in the French and Indian War. But thirty-seven years later, in 1800, Napoleon Bonaparte reached agreement with Spain to reclaim France's American empire. He promptly laid plans to reassert power in the New World. However, Napoleon's dreams suffered a mortal setback when the army he sent in 1802 to put down the slave rebellion in present-day Haiti was nearly wiped out by a combination of yellow fever and the unexpectedly competent black army led by former slave Toussaint L'Ouverture.

Thus, Robert R. Livingston and James Monroe, Jefferson's representatives, found themselves in the right place at the right time when they opened negotiations with the French government in Paris in the spring of 1803. They had the relatively modest goal of acquiring New Orleans and West Florida, plus shipping rights on the Mississippi. Instead, and to their surprise, they were offered almost all of France's remaining domain on the American continent. Livingston and Monroe quickly agreed to pay $15 million for the vast territory that Jefferson was already making plans to explore even had it remained a Spanish or French possession.

Under the agreement between Napoleon and Spain, France was to have taken control of Louisiana in late 1802, but Napoleon's financial and military problems prevented that happening before the territory was sold to the United States. Thus, the transfer from Spain to France occurred at New Orleans on November 30, 1803, and twenty days later the transfer was made from France to the United States. The new American authorities in New Orleans then sent Captain Amos Stoddard upriver, where he was to take possession of St. Louis, the seat of the territorial lieutenant governor, and to serve as acting governor until a permanent governor was named.

Looking to save money, the French authorities at New Orleans asked Stoddard to act on their behalf as well, once he reached St. Louis, by taking ceremonial possession of St. Louis and the surrounding lands from Spain in the name of France before passing it to himself as the representative of the United States. At the same time, the French prefect in New Orleans, Pierre Clement de Laussat, sent a note to Pierre Chouteau asking him to inventory and appraise all the buildings and houses at St. Louis, other than fortifications, that had belonged to the Spanish monarchy.

It would take Stoddard several months to reach St. Louis and carry out his assignment there. While he was making his way upriver in January and February, Lewis and Clark were busy gathering information about the town of St. Louis, the surrounding countryside, and the tantalizing Missouri River, with its promise of untold riches and access to the Pacific. Lewis regularly wrote Jefferson with the results of their intelligence gathering.

Neither Lewis nor Clark spoke French, and the Chouteau brothers did not speak English. Nevertheless, the Chouteaus, probably with their bilingual brother-in-law, Charles Gratiot, or one of Pierre's older sons at their side, were key contacts. Lewis began by asking questions about the inhabitants of St. Louis and the surrounding region, some of which he submitted in writing to Auguste Chouteau. He wanted to know about the geography, the nature of the population, how much immigration was occurring from the United States, and about the Indian tribes in the region.

By that point, the Chouteaus and their associates had certainly been as far up the Missouri River as the mouth of the Kansas, eventual site of Kansas City, and probably to the Platte, near today's Omaha–Council Bluffs. They had traveled the width and breadth of what became the state of Missouri, also parts of Iowa, into the northeast corner of today's Oklahoma, and for an unknown distance along the Kansas and Arkansas rivers across the eventual state of Kansas. They were familiar with the Mississippi River for most of its length, had regularly been sending boats up the Illinois River and through the Chicago Portage to Lake Michigan, across the lake to Michilimackinac (near present-day Mackinac), then onward across Canada via the Ottawa River to Montreal and the St. Lawrence. Charles Gratiot had traveled to Europe by that long, slow route on business for his brothers-in-law and others.

In addition to the Osages, the Chouteaus traded with the Sac and Fox Indians, the Omahas, the Kansas, the Iowas, Miamis, Pawnees, Quapaws, and probably some others. They also drew on information from independent traders who had ventured farther afield, and from Indians, particularly the Osages, who roamed over many hundreds of miles to hunt buffalo, possibly as far as the area around Santa Fe and Taos in New Mexico. Because they were so deeply involved in trade with the Osages, the Chouteaus had not taken part in an effort launched from St. Louis ten years earlier to penetrate the Upper Missouri region for fur trading. That expedition, which was a huge financial loss for the backers, did not achieve its goal of reaching the Mandan Indian villages near present-day Bismarck, but it did get as far as the Arikara villages near the South Dakota–North Dakota line.

Although Lewis had bought supplies in the East, he did some more shopping in St. Louis and Cahokia. Making the rounds of the merchants, Lewis bought mosquito nets, shirts, flour, salt pork, ground corn, nails, and whiskey. He also picked up flags and red and blue ribbons for the Indians. The Chouteaus secured seven French *engagés* to man the oars of one of the two pirogues the explorers were taking up the Missouri River to the Mandan villages.

Strolling around Pierre Chouteau's garden one day, Lewis took note of two exotic plants, which Pierre told him were the Osage apple and the Osage plum, and he gathered cuttings of both to send to Jefferson. He described the pale yellow plums as having "exquisite flavor," but did not suggest eating the Osage apple, which later became known as the Osage orange, or the hedge apple. A bumpy green object that looks like neither apple nor orange, it has never since been judged to be edible.

Lewis wrote Jefferson that "Mr. Peter Choteau" had obtained the cuttings for the plants from a place about three hundred miles west of the village of the Big Osages, one of the branches of the tribe. The Big Osages were then situated on the Osage River in present-day Vernon County, Missouri, so the location from which Pierre Chouteau took the cuttings was probably in central Kansas. "So much do the savages esteem the wood of this tree for the purpose of making their bows, that they travel many hundred miles in quest of it," Lewis wrote Jefferson.

Pierre showed Lewis some specimens that he believed to be bones from a prehistoric mammoth, which he had found some years earlier when he attempted to explore a salt lick on the south side of the Osage River some distance west of the Osage villages. Lewis recounted that Pierre had been forced to turn back by water discharging into the lick from a nearby spring. "The specimens obtained by Mr. Couteau [*sic*] were large but much mutilated," Lewis noted.

A highly controversial issue was also on Lewis's agenda during his days in St. Louis. It arose out of President Jefferson's ignorance of the fact that the newly acquired territory had a long history in which many Indian tribes possessed reasonably defined territories, and a relatively small number of whites had also been there for many decades and coexisted peacefully with the tribes. Jefferson was already thinking of using lands west of the Mississippi to resettle Indians from the East, moving them out of the way of advancing white settlers. He thought the whites living west of the Mississippi should move east of the river. But as soon as Lewis broached Jefferson's idea during his rounds in St. Louis, it raised great alarm, particularly among the Chouteaus and other leading Frenchmen. There is no surviving record of the words Auguste Chouteau used in reaction to Lewis's proposal, but he quickly acted to organize his neighbors to oppose the concept, which suggests that he was deeply angered.

Lewis advised Jefferson that any effort at resettlement was going to run into strenuous opposition. If they were resettled, he said, the French would likely want to live in the adjacent Indiana Territory for its proximity to areas of the Indian fur trade, but the territorial laws of Indiana forbade the further importation of slaves. As Lewis saw it, the French might be faced with having to choose between moving to the South and keeping their slaves or giving up the slaves in order to live closer to their trading partners, the Indians of the Missouri and Upper Mississippi.

"I fear that the slaves will form a source of some unwillingness in the French to yeald [sic] to the wishes of the government," Lewis wrote Jefferson.

> They appear to feel very sensibly a report which has been circulated among them on this subject, that the Americans would [force them to] emancipate their slaves immediately on taking possession of the country, this however false, is sufficient to show the Opinions and disposition of the people on that subject; there appears to be a general objection not only among the French, but even among the Americans not slave holders, to relinquish the right which they claim relative to slavery in it's present unqualifyed shape . . . thus the slaves appear to me in every view of this subject to be connected with the principal difficulties with which the government will have to contend in effecting this part of it's policy.

Lewis may have been mistaken in assuming that the issue revolved so much around the right of slave ownership. The French in St. Louis and the surrounding area used slaves to make their daily lives comfortable, employing the slaves as household servants and for a limited amount of farming, mainly to supply food to their own households. However, they made their real money by trading with Indians for furs and pelts. It was those long-standing trading arrangements that could be easily upset by resettlement, not only by forcing the white traders to move across the Mississippi but also by bringing immigrant farming tribes into traditional hunting and trapping grounds of the western tribes.

Further, although the Chouteaus were not heavily engaged in farming, they wanted to protect their large landholdings, many of which dated back four decades to the founding of St. Louis and had been recognized as legal by French and Spanish authorities. It was highly unlikely that they could acquire anything comparable at that late date in the country east of the Mississippi. Thinking in dynastic terms, they wanted to pass those holdings to their children and grandchildren, whom they expected to benefit by selling land in parcels to the settlers likely to pour into the territory now that it was part of the United States.

Between the Chouteau brothers and their kin, the lands included many square blocks that would eventually be covered with skyscrapers, other major structures, and parks in the commercial heart of modern St. Louis. In addition, family members held rural properties ranging in size from a few hundred acres to a few thousand acres within a hundred-mile radius of St. Louis.

Even with the discord over the resettlement question, the French and the Americans found many areas in which to serve each other's interests. Pierre made an offer to Clark to lead a delegation of Osage chiefs and principal men to Washington to meet with President Jefferson. For Pierre, who had not previously traveled to the United States or the former English colonies, this was an opportunity to make himself known to the leaders of his new country.

It was also a unique opportunity for Jefferson's government to have a major Indian tribe brought to its center of power by the man whom the Osage leaders trusted more than any other white man. In dealing with Indian tribes, the Chouteaus had always operated on the premise that they could be most effective if they appeared to the Indians to be rich and powerful, which partly explained their insistence on impressive homes and substantial trading posts. They reasoned that showing the Indians the growing cities and relatively large population of the United States would awe the tribal leaders and help convince them to accept American authority.

Lewis was at Camp Dubois when Clark informed him of the offer to take the Osages east, and Lewis quickly responded:

Nothing has given me more pleasure than the proposition he has made to you on the subject of the Osages . . . I wish him not only to bring in some of those Chiefs (the number hereafter to be agreed on) but wish him to attend them to the seat of the government of the U'States provided he can make it convenient to do so; I presume the Chiefs would come more readily provided Mr. Chouteau would make them a promise to that effect; I am as anxious as Mr. C. can be that he should set out on this mission as early as possible.

Pierre probably waited until March, and warmer weather, to set off for the Osage villages to gather the delegation. Making the journey to the main Osage villages meant a grueling trip by horseback unless the Missouri River was already thawed. Even with the river thawed, it would have been a slow trip upriver, probably making less than ten miles a day. Near present-day Jefferson City, he would have left the Missouri to follow the Osage River into the tribal heartland.

On the return trip to St. Louis, while traveling downstream on the Missouri, the party was attacked by a band of Sac and Fox warriors, and five of the Osages were killed. This sour beginning to the great adventure of traveling to Washington reflected some of the issues in intertribal rivalries about which the American government was just beginning to learn. The Sacs and Foxes, historically friends of the British, were old and bitter enemies of the Osages, who were historically friends of the French. Jealousy that their worst enemies were being honored with a visit to Washington undoubtedly played a role in the attack by the Sacs and Foxes.

Meanwhile, Captain Stoddard arrived at Cahokia, the village opposite St. Louis to the southeast, on February 24, 1804. Carlos Dehault Delassus, the Spanish lieutenant governor of Upper Louisiana, was ill, and Stoddard's men had been delayed by ice on the Mississippi, so the formal ceremonies of transfer were postponed a few more days.

In the first days of March, a single company of about forty American artillerymen reached Cahokia by boat and remained there, on the American side, awaiting final arrangements for the transfer. On March 8, Delassus issued a public notice that at "either 11 o'clock or noon" the next day he would surrender Upper Louisiana to Stoddard as "agent and commissioner of the French Republic."

Most of the inhabitants of St. Louis were waiting in the streets when the United States troops crossed over on March 9 and climbed the future Walnut Street to Rue Royale. Amos Stoddard and Meriwether Lewis and leading citizens of the town were gathered in front of Government House, a small one-story structure with a porch extending around three sides. A chimney rose through the pitched roof, and simple wooden posts supported a wide roof overhanging the porch. The building sat catercornered to Auguste Chouteau's mansion. At the next corner to the north was the square where farmers and tradespeople came to sell produce and other food items.

Although the French of St. Louis had received the Americans with great cordiality, they quietly regretted the missed opportunity to reclaim their own nationality. During the years of Spanish rule, they had remained a French society except for the use of the Spanish language in official documents. Spain had always appointed French-speaking governors, and two or three of the governors, including the popular Delassus, were of French birth. Except for the handful of Spanish officials and soldiers posted in St. Louis, not more than a dozen Spaniards had settled in the area during Spanish rule, and they usually adopted French ways and married Frenchwomen.

Nevertheless, when the French of St. Louis learned of the retrocession of their land to France, they had hoped their colony was destined for a more dynamic future under a French regime. Now they were uneasy, realizing that this change of power would bring far more change to their lives than had occurred when the territory passed back and forth between France and Spain. The sympathetic Stoddard commented later that "they seemed to feel as if they had been sold in open market."

Delassus formally received and welcomed Stoddard at Government House, then proceeded with the ceremony of transfer. Tears rose in Delassus's eyes when he told the crowd that in obedience to the desires of "the great Napoleon," he was delivering this country to the Americans. Expressing his love for the territory, he said he intended to remain and live among them.

"The flag under which you have been protected for a period of nearly thirty-six years is to be withdrawn," he said. "From this moment you are released from the oath of fidelity you took to support it." The

Spanish troops at the fort on the hill began to fire in salute, which continued at intervals until completed. Stoddard and Delassus signed the transfer document, with Meriwether Lewis, Antoine Soulard, who was the surveyor general, and Charles Gratiot as witnesses.

Deferring to French sentiment, Stoddard allowed the Tricolor to fly over St. Louis for twenty-four hours before raising the flag of the United States. As Stoddard prepared to lower the French flag, Charles Gratiot interpreted for the benefit of the largely French-speaking crowd.

You are now "divested of the character of subjects, and clothed with that of citizens," Stoddard told them. "You now form an integral part of a great community, the powers of whose government are circumscribed and defined by charter, and the liberty of the citizen extended and secured." He said they might soon expect the establishment of a territorial government, to be followed eventually by statehood, and that one of the first objectives of the United States government would be to "ascertain and confirm your land titles," touching on the issue uppermost in the minds of many in St. Louis.

"It is confidently expected that you will not be less faithful to the United States than you have been to his Catholic majesty," he told them. "Your local situation, the varieties in your language and education, have contributed to render your manners, laws, and customs, and even your prejudices, somewhat different from those of your neighbors, but not less favorable to virtue—These deserve something more than mere indulgence; they shall be respected."

As the Stars and Stripes floated to the breeze for the first time on land west of the Mississippi River, Gratiot urged his relatives and friends to cheer. But, as a daughter of Gratiot's recalled years later, the cheers were faint and few, some people still shedding tears of regret for France's lost empire.

Despite this underlying nostalgia, the social circles of St. Louis took Stoddard into their fold. The very evening after the flag raising, the Chouteaus, Delassus, and other St. Louisans honored him with a public dinner and ball, and all eyes seemed focused on the future. The next month, on April 7, Stoddard returned the courtesies with a dinner and ball at his rented house, with Lewis and Clark and many townspeople attending. This was another of those St. Louis affairs that began on Saturday evening and went through to Sunday morning.

Stoddard's party may have been where he discovered that French Creole women were "less guarded than their female neighbors on the east side of the Mississippi" in conversing with men and expressing opinions, which might lead "a prudish observer to believe that there existed a laxity in their morals." But he said that Frenchmen did not consider their women any more exempt from propriety than other women. Calling the women "small and attractive" and their homes "remarkably neat and cleanly," he said it was normal for them to be consulted by men in many areas of their mutual interest, such as purchases of land and items for the home.

The party cost Stoddard $622.75, as much a shock to his New England grain as the charm and openness of the women.

While Delassus waited for boats to be built to transport him and the Spanish troops to New Orleans, he prepared for Stoddard a list of those in the community who had served him in some official capacity, and he included his assessment of them. Of the thirty-eight men on the list, he reserved his highest praise for Pierre Chouteau, writing:

> Mr. Pierre Chouteau, a very zealous officer, he was commandant of Fort Carondelet, at the Osage Nation . . . So long as this officer had the trade of this nation, he so managed them, and his authority was such as to induce them whenever they killed any one, to bring in the ring-leaders. He is respected and feared, and I believe loved by this nation (the Osages) . . . I saw him here with a party of 200 Indians make himself respected and obeyed, and manage them with firmness and mildness. I think he is the most suitable officer of this post, to be employed in that nation and others of the Missouri.

In their search for ways to assure the loyalty of the Chouteaus and other prominent Frenchmen to the United States, Lewis and Stoddard offered some of the young men appointments to the new military academy at West Point. There were a number of youths in the French families who were about the age of recent high school graduates, including Pierre Chouteau's eldest son, Auguste Pierre, and a cousin, Charles Gratiot Jr., both of them turning eighteen in 1804. Auguste

Chouteau had married relatively late, and his first two children were girls who died in childhood. A son, Auguste Aristide, was then a rebellious twelve-year-old at a boarding school in Montreal. Another son, Antoine, born to an Indian mother when Auguste was in his late teens, had died at the age of about twenty-eight a few years before the Americans arrived.

Lewis and Clark had undoubtedly made an impression on the young men in St. Louis, perhaps setting a standard they wanted to emulate. In a portrait a few years later, Auguste Pierre, known in his mature years as A. P. Chouteau, was wearing his hair in the same style as Meriwether Lewis, combed forward all the way around from the crown. Though never as famous as Lewis and Clark, A. P. Chouteau would himself grow into a heroic figure of the American frontier, a man as revered by Indians as his father had been.

Military men were highly regarded among the Chouteaus and other French families in the territory. Most of the adult men, including both Chouteau brothers, held positions in the militia under the Spanish regime. Auguste Chouteau was routinely addressed as "Colonel" for his Spanish militia rank, and Pierre Chouteau was known as "Major." They thus welcomed the offer of an education at the new academy for some of their young men.

There was also potential benefit to the American government from the West Point appointments, because the young Frenchmen had skills and travel experiences in the West that were lacking among other cadets. According to historian Donald Chaput, who researched the early Missouri appointments to West Point, "Being reared on the frontier, these young men could be of great value as leaders of military units expected to deal with Indian problems. Additionally, they would possess first-hand knowledge to answer questions about transportation and travel in the Louisiana Territory."

On March 28, 1804, Meriwether Lewis wrote recommendations to West Point for Charles Gratiot Jr.; A. P. Chouteau; and Auguste Bougainville Loramier,* a son of Louis Lorimier, the leading

*The Lorimier family changed the spelling of its last name to Loramier about the time the son was admitted to West Point, and his name is listed that way in the West Point records.

citizen of nearby Cape Girardeau, whose wife was a Shawnee Indian.

West Point was then enrolling its fourth class of cadets after a slow start in the aftermath of the Revolutionary War. The first group of twelve cadets had begun classes in 1801 under the temporary direction of Lieutenant Colonel Louis de Tousard, a French officer who had fought in the American Revolution under General Lafayette. At the end of the year, President Jefferson appointed Major Jonathan Williams, a nephew of Benjamin Franklin, as permanent superintendent. Only two members of that first class graduated, and after four years there was a total of just ten West Point graduates. The army itself had shrunk at the beginning of the 1800s from a Revolutionary War–era high of 400,000 soldiers and militia to fewer than 3,000 men and about 175 officers.

But the West Point class of 1806, entering in 1804, represented a big jump to fifteen admissions. There were no fixed admission or graduation dates for the early cadets, who normally graduated two years after entering. Nor were there requirements of age or ability for the cadets. They had to make their own arrangements for food and lodging. Under Williams, there were just two teachers, who placed a strong emphasis on mathematics, artillery, and fortifications. No Greek or Latin was taught, but French, the language of science and military art at that time, was added to the curriculum the following year. Cadets who completed the two-year program were assigned to either engineering or artillery.

The War Department wrote Stoddard on May 16, 1804, that if the parents of the three youths nominated by Lewis "should be inclined to have those young men appointed Cadets I the Artillerists . . . at the Military Academy they will receive appointment accordingly and may come forward as soon as they find it convenient."

There was a flurry of activity in the first half of May in St. Louis and at Camp Dubois as final preparations were made for two historic trips. The dogwoods and fruit trees had long since shed their springtime blossoms along the riverbanks, and the men of the Lewis and Clark expedition were eager to be under way. They were waiting for Lewis to complete arrangements with Pierre Chouteau, who had returned to

St. Louis with the delegation of Osage chiefs he was to lead to Washington. The success of that visit was of great importance to all sides.

Wanting to assure a warm reception and hospitality for Pierre Chouteau and the Indian leaders, Clark wrote a letter to his brother-in-law, Major William Croghan, and gave it to Pierre to deliver in person when the party passed through Virginia. Clark informed Croghan that Pierre Chouteau was

> a gentleman deservedly esteemed among the most reputable and influential citizens of upper Louisiana. Mr. Choteau's [sic] zeal to promote the public welfare has induced him, at the instance of our government to visit the Osage Nation since the session of this country to the United States. He has brought with him the great chief of that nation and many other chiefs of the first consideration and respectability among them, and is now on his [way] to the City of Washington in charge of those Chiefs, with a view to effect a treaty between the United States and that nation.
>
> The promptitude and fidelity with which Mr. Choteau [sic] has fulfilled the wishes of the government on this occasion, as also the personal dangers to which he has been exposed in the course of this transaction, intitle him in an eminent degree to the particular attention and best services, not only of yourself but of his fellow citizens generally.

Clark praised the efforts made by Pierre Chouteau and "his Lady and family" on behalf of himself and Lewis during the winter and spring. "During our residence in this country on our several visits to St. Louis, in the course of the winter and spring, we have made the house of this gentleman our home."

On May 14, 1804, Clark and forty men set out from Camp Dubois in a fifty-five-foot keelboat and two pirogues, crossed to the mouth of the Missouri, and began their upriver trip toward St. Charles. There, they would await Lewis, who was coming later by land from St. Louis. Clark wanted some extra time to test the way he had loaded the vessels. "I . . . proceeded on under a jentle [sic] brease up the Missourie to the upper Point of the 1st Island 4 Miles and camped," he noted. It rained most of that night but stopped at about 7 a.m. the next day, so the group took off again and camped that evening at a Mr. Fifer's landing opposite an island.

> The barge ran foul three several [sic] times on logs, and in one instance it was with much difficulty they could get her off; happily no injury was sustained, tho' the barge was several minutes in eminent danger; this was ca[u]sed by her being too heavily laden in the stern. Persons accustomed to the navigation of the Missouri and the Mississippi also below the mouth of this river, uniformly take the precaution to load their vessels heavyest in the bow when they ascend the stream in order to avoid the danger incident to running foul of the concealed timber which lyes in great quantities in the beds of these rivers.

In St. Louis, Lewis completed last-minute arrangements. He appointed Amos Stoddard his agent, with power to pay bills, receive Indian delegations, and handle other matters that arose. If Stoddard should be away, then Charles Gratiot, with his indispensable language skills, was to act in his place.

Lewis also wanted to see Pierre Chouteau and the Osages off to Washington before turning his own sights toward St. Charles to meet Clark. On the day before Pierre and the Osages departed, Lewis put together a packet of items he had collected for Jefferson, mostly from the Chouteaus and their relatives, which Pierre was to deliver to the President.

There were some specimens of silver ore, lead ore, and an "elegant Specimen of Rock Chrystal," all from Mexico, probably meaning the Santa Fe/Taos area, which Lewis said the Osages had collected during war excursions and had given to Pierre Chouteau. There were specimens of lead ore from the Osage River and the Breton Mine on the Meramec River, both in the future state of Missouri.

He also sent what may have been a giant hair ball, described as a mass taken from the stomach of a buffalo, which was apparently formed by the animal continually licking itself, then swallowing. A horned lizard from the Osage plains along the Arkansas River, five hundred to six hundred miles west of St. Louis, had been supplied by Charles Gratiot. A salt specimen from the Great Saline on the

Arkansas River (Salina in present-day northeastern Oklahoma) was provided by Auguste Chouteau.

A chart of the Mississippi, from the mouth of the Missouri to New Orleans, had been "compiled from the observations of Mr. August [sic] Chouteau, made with a Marinors Compass, distance being computed by his own estimate and that of many other French traders, accustomed to ascend and descend this River, the same being drawn by Mr. Soulard, late Surveyor General of Upper Louisiana." Finally, there was a rough map of part of Upper Louisiana compiled by Lewis and Clark from information collected from inhabitants of St. Louis and the Osages.

Amos Stoddard also wrote a letter to be delivered to Secretary of War Henry Dearborn that reflected the racial questions already building within the new nation. "This letter will be handed to you by Louis Lorimier Jr., the brother of the one of the same sir [sic] name, whom Captain Lewis and myself have recommended for a cadet," Stoddard began.

> So extremely solicitous was he to go on with Mr. Chouteau, that his father at last consented. His father has applied to me to recommend him as a cadet—in reply I told him, that I believed he would be considered as rather too old for the military school. But my real objection was, that he exhibited too much of the Indian in his color. This circumstance may make his situation among the cadets at the school rather disagreeable—a situation of which he is not aware, as in this country the mixture of blood in him does not prevent his admission into the first circles. He is certainly very active, and at the same time rather dissipated, tho perhaps not more so than the generality of young men of his age; he is now seventeen.
>
> As his father is one of the most respectable men in this country . . . I did not feel myself at liberty to refuse his request. The young man will exhibit his real character before you; and should you not think proper to appoint him, I believe his father will not regret the expence of his journey to the Atlantic States.

Clark reached St. Charles at noon on May 16 to be greeted by French and Indian spectators gathered on the bank. "The Village contns about 100 houses, the most of them small and indefferent [*sic*] and about 450 inhabitents chiefly French, those people appear pore, polite & harmonious," he reported. The next day, Clark held a court-martial for two men who had been absent without leave the night before. On May 18 Clark had the loading of the vessels examined "and changed so as the bow of each may be heavyer loded than the stern." Two keelboats arrived from Kentucky loaded with whiskey and some other items. The night of May 18–19 brought three hours of rain and violent winds, but the sky cleared about 8 a.m.

On May 19, barely back from his harrowing trip to collect the Osage leaders, Pierre Chouteau set out for Washington with his son Auguste Pierre, his nephew, Charles Gratiot Jr., the two Loramier boys, and fourteen Osages, twelve of them chiefs or tribal elders and two of them boys. From Washington the newly appointed cadets would continue to West Point. At that time of year it seems likely that the group would descend the Mississippi to the mouth of the Ohio, then ascend the Ohio to Pittsburgh. They were seen passing through Pittsburgh on Saturday, June 16. From there they continued to Washington by stagecoach or on horseback.

On May 20 Lewis bid "an affectionate adieu" to Pierre's wife, Brigitte, then departed with Stoddard, Auguste Chouteau, David Delaunay, Charles Gratiot, Sylvestre Labbadie Jr., and several others for St. Charles "in order to join my friend companion and fellow labourer."

About 1:30 p.m. the travelers had their journey interrupted by the approach of a violent thunderstorm from the northwest. They took shelter in a small cabin for an hour and a half and, according to Lewis, "regailed ourselves with a could collation which we had taken the precaution to bring with us from St. Louis." The rain didn't stop, so they continued anyway, arriving at St. Charles about 6:30 p.m. in the midst of driving rain and thunderstorms.

The next day, May 21, the group shared a big midday meal as the guests of a Mr. Ducett while hoping the rain would let up. It did not, so the voyagers decided to get under way. As the rain continued to pour down, the small flotilla inched up the river, and the people clustered on the bank cheered them on their long way.

With both groups of travelers gone, Amos Stoddard returned to St. Louis and sat down to respond to a letter from his mother, who had expressed concerns for his safety "among a people of strange speech." He assured her that people in the Louisiana Territory were very friendly toward him. "About two thirds of the people in this country are from the States—many of them from New England, particularly from Connecticut; the other third are French. I now speak of those who dwell in Louisiana; very few French are intermixed with those on the east side of the Mississippi. I, however, find the French people very friendly—I even speak part of their language—and they consider it a duty as well as a pleasure to make themselves agreeable to the United States."

TWO

The First Generation: Pierre Laclède Liguest

✳

Two sets of voyagers left St. Louis in May 1804. Lewis and Clark headed into an unknown world of excitement and promise and danger. Pierre Chouteau, with his eldest son and the other young Frenchmen and the Osage leaders, stepped off into the unknown world of a new country, a new tongue, and a culture that had been thrust upon them over a matter of months. The Missouri's waters on which Lewis and Clark were setting forth were known for their unpredictable turbulence and swift currents, at times terrifying. Pierre Chouteau's mission was to guide his group safely across the Appalachians and through the political turbulence of Washington. The French-Osage group would undoubtedly have felt more secure on the Missouri.

Lewis and Clark were carrying out the vision of Thomas Jefferson. Pierre Chouteau was carrying out the vision of Pierre Laclède, the father whose name he could not carry.

The privileged position of the Chouteaus and their in-laws, built up over four decades, from which Lewis and Clark were beneficiaries, was the legacy of Laclède, father of Pierre Chouteau and his three sisters, stepfather and loving mentor of Auguste Chouteau. During the years in which the English-speaking colonies in the East were debating their political course and fighting for their independence, Laclède was starting from nothing at the confluence of the continent's two mightiest rivers to build a successful future for his family on the basis of a respectful business relationship with their Indian neighbors. By 1804 Laclède's vision and judgment had opened the door to great opportunity for his descendants. Even amid the rawness of the frontier, he imbued in his children and stepson the sense that they were entitled to rule. From the depths of his own education, and from the treasured books that came up the river with him, he managed to foster learning and inquiring minds in the next generation. Finally, he taught his son and stepson to astutely play whatever hand was dealt them.

Pierre Laclède's story began in the valley of the Aspe, a stream fed by the melting snows of the Lower Pyrenees near the French-Spanish border. It was a pretty waterway, winding through gorges where the mountains closed in, then crossing green pastures with flocks of sheep and shepherds and carts drawn by oxen or donkeys. The clear, rapidly flowing stream was about twenty-five yards wide and strong enough to turn a mill. Laclède was born to modest privilege in a back bedroom of a turreted three-story house surrounded by trees and gardens in the village of Bedous, about thirty-five miles south of Pau, in what was then called the Béarn region. The village and the house were overshadowed by the ragged skyline of the Pyrenees, the highest peaks often covered with snow. Though not large enough to be considered a château, the house was the most substantial in the village.

Magdeleine d'Espoeys d'Arance and Pierre de Laclède, a lawyer accredited to the provincial parliament of Navarre, baptized their second son on November 22, 1729, at the church of St. Michel in the parish of Bedous, giving him the name Pierre de Laclède de Liguest. The second surname was considered a "personal suffix"—a custom of the area to distinguish him from his father and ancestors of the same name.

At the time of Laclède's birth, the part of France around his home had been torn by intermittent warfare for more than a century. The wars were fought over religion and politics and, later, over differences with nearby Spain. It was therefore logical that his parents would send their younger son to study military affairs. Laclède was graduated in 1748 from the Académie d'Armes de Toulouse, receiving two prizes for his performance as a student: a sword with a vermeil hilt as first place and a sword with a silver hilt for second place.

He was erect, with a commanding presence, standing about five feet eight and a half or nine inches, moderately tall for the time. He had an olive complexion, a broad forehead with a prominent nose, and what were described as "piercing and expressive eyes." He was said to be of a "brave and adventurous disposition."

His schooling and early life experiences produced a man with knowledge of agriculture and milling, well versed in civil engineering, and in a general way well educated. Having been reared on the Spanish border, he is believed to have known Spanish in addition to French. Despite Pierre's good education and skills, his older brother, Jean de Laclède, had the right to inherit the family's property and its privileged status in the provincial gentry. So in 1755, when Pierre was twenty-six years old, he set out for New France in search of opportunity. According to family history, he sailed from Bordeaux with a small "colony" of people. His destination: New Orleans.

The colonial empire to which Laclède was traveling predated only barely the English efforts to colonize the eastern seaboard of North America. The French had made their first permanent settlement at Port Royal, now Annapolis Royal, Nova Scotia, in 1605; they laid the foundations of Quebec in 1608, a year after the first permanent English settlement at Jamestown, Virginia. Before the arrival of the French, only Spain among the European powers had established operating colonies on the North American continent, first Mexico, then St. Augustine in Florida. From Quebec the French gradually pushed westward and downward while the English were extending their settlements up and down the East Coast. The great attraction to the French of the vast interior of the continent was furs and skins, which drove French exploration and settlement as surely as if they had been gold.

French traders in Canada had heard Indians talk of a great river farther to the west that flowed neither north nor west, which they conjectured must empty into the Gulf of Mexico. Father Jacques Marquette, a Jesuit missionary, and Louis Jolliet, a fur trader, were sent to explore the region, starting from the north. On June 16, 1673, they reached the Mississippi at the mouth of the Wisconsin River, then floated downriver past the Missouri and the Ohio rivers as far as the mouth of the Arkansas. On their return, they discovered a shortcut to Lake Michigan by following the Illinois and Des Plaines rivers to a portage at what is today Chicago, which took them to the lake. At first the French called the Mississippi the Colbert River in honor of Louis XIV's finance minister, an advocate of naval power and mercantilism.

In 1677, René-Robert Cavelier de La Salle began a ten-year exploration of the entire length of the Mississippi. He reached the mouth on April 7, 1682, claimed formal possession in the name of the King of France of all the land drained by the Mississippi and its tributaries, and gave it the name Louisiana. In 1699, France established a settlement on the Bay of Biloxi and in 1718 founded New Orleans, where a colonial government was instituted in 1721.

France and Spain were jockeying for position in the Mississippi Valley and the region farther west. By the mid–sixteenth century, the Spanish explorers de Soto and Coronado had separately penetrated present-day Kansas, Oklahoma, and Arkansas. In the early eighteenth century, the French made repeated explorations into present-day Oklahoma, Texas, western Louisiana, and Alabama. The Spanish built a fort in western Kansas, and the French reacted by building Fort Orléans in the center of Missouri in 1723, which was largely abandoned within ten years. In 1744 the French built another post, known as Fort Cavagnial, farther west on the Missouri, near a village of the Kansa Indians, two and a half miles upriver from the eventual site of Fort Leavenworth. It lasted for about twenty years.

As early as 1700, French explorers knew that there were potentially rich mines on the west side of the Mississippi in present-day Missouri. Indians were probably already extracting lead at the site, but the French expected to find silver as well. By 1716, dispatches from Louisiana to Paris were boasting of vast wealth, setting off financial speculation in Paris. This frenzied interest led to the construction of Fort de Chartres in 1720, almost directly across the river, to protect and store the ore. But by the time the fort was completed, it had become clear that the mines held no silver. In Paris, what became known as the Mississippi Bubble soon burst.

Neither France nor Spain succeeded in developing substantial population centers in North America. By the beginning of the eighteenth century, when the population of the English colonies exceeded a quarter of a million, the widely scattered French settlements had only 6,000 to 7,000 people, and the Spanish numbers in North America were insignificant. By the outbreak of the French and Indian War, in 1754, the population of the English colonies had grown to 2 million, but in all of New France, scattered over territory many times the size of the English colonies, there were fewer than 100,000 non-Indians. A Spanish census of the former French colonies nearly half a century later, in 1800, found that Lower Louisiana had only 41,700 whites and 38,800 blacks, plus several hundred mulattos; Upper Louisiana, including St. Louis, had just 9,020 whites and 1,320 blacks.

One of the enduring tales from the reign of Louis XV is that he cleaned the streets of Paris by shipping ne'er-do-wells off to the colonies. John Joseph Mathews, historian of the Osage nation, says that this "riffraff" concentrated around the French posts on the Mississippi and Missouri rivers and became known as *bohèmes*. Most were men who took Indian wives, and they and their sons ended up as boatmen or other laborers in the fur trade. Families and men of education and capital, such as Laclède, did not come to New France to the extent that the English moved to the colonies on the Eastern Seaboard. Those of means or education who came to New France usually raised sugarcane in the future Haiti or Lower Louisiana with slave labor.

The French and Indian War, which was the American phase of the Seven Years' War between England and France in Europe, broke out about the time Laclède arrived in New Orleans. Despite his military credentials, Laclède had no plans to serve with the French forces. He tried agriculture, but floods and hurricanes hindered him. He invested the capital he brought from France in business in New Orleans, but trade and commerce were suffering during the war. So Laclède volunteered for military service and was assigned to duty on the staff of Colonel Antoine de Maxent, a wealthy New Orleans merchant then serving the French crown. Great regard developed between Maxent and Laclède, who dropped both "de's" from his name and signed himself simply Pierre Laclède Liguest after arriving in the New World. Maxent was older and had influence with colonial authorities, which he was willing to use to help his young friend. He introduced Laclède into the circles of other prominent people in New Orleans.

During this time, Laclède also met Marie Thérèse Bourgeois Chouteau, who found herself in the difficult position of being a young, abandoned mother in the mid–eighteenth century. It is easy to imagine that she and Laclède fell deeply in love. They were willing to flaunt the conventions of the time and place—which did not allow her to divorce her renegade husband—in order to live shared lives and bring their own family into the world.

Marie Thérèse Bourgeois had been born in New Orleans on January 14, 1733, the daughter of Nicolas Charles Bourgeois, a native of Paris, and Marie Joseph Tarare, a native of Cambray in France. She was wed at fifteen to René Augustin Chouteau, a twenty-five-year-old man with seemingly few positive traits. Her husband was variously described in the few documents that exist about him as "eating house keeper," "liquor dealer," and "pastry cook." The only significant reference to him in official documents of the time was a slander suit filed by another baker, Bernard Shiloc, who alleged that Chouteau came into a billiards hall and accused him of putting poison in pastries.

Chouteau was born in l'Hermenault, La Rochelle, France, where he was baptized on September 2, 1723, the son of René Chouteau and Marie Sarazin. No record has been found of when he arrived in New Orleans, but his marriage to Marie Thérèse Bourgeois is placed at September 20, 1748. The couple baptized a son, whose name was listed only as René, on September 9, 1749. There is confusion as to whether this son was Auguste Chouteau or whether the first son died and a second son, Auguste, was born a year later. The Auguste Chouteau who became a founder of St. Louis was sometimes identified as René Auguste, further contributing to the confusion. Auguste's birth date is listed in family records as September 26, 1750, but no baptismal record has been uncovered. Years later, in his will, Marie Thérèse's husband stated that he had had two sons by his wife, leading researchers to conclude that one of the boys died after he left her to return to France.

Family tradition passed down the story that René Chouteau was abusive toward his wife and that she left him and moved in with friends or relatives after he had inflicted what became a permanent scar on her face. But research has established that Chouteau returned to France* during this time, after which Marie Thérèse styled herself "Widow Chouteau." She was so listed on a census and was known for the rest of her life as Madame Chouteau. To the young mother with no husband and no means—her own father had died when she was a child—the arrival in her life of Laclède, who had some capital and was attractive, educated, generous, and well connected, must have seemed little short of miraculous. The only portrait in existence of Madame Chouteau shows a stern-looking woman in her later years, so it is not possible to say whether she was a beautiful young woman. There is no known surviving portrait of Laclède. A painting purchased by the Missouri Historical Society in the 1920s from descendants of his brother in France turned out, after expert examination, to be the portrait of someone from a later generation of the Laclède family, probably a descendant of the older brother.

Laclède and Madame Chouteau followed a policy of never admit and never explain. That gave them cover for dealing with both civil and religious authorities, who had no inclination to question a man of Laclède's standing. Thus, the four children they had together were all baptized at St. Louis Cathedral in New Orleans as having been born "of the legitimate marriage of René Chouteau and Thérèse Bourgeois, his wife." Their son, who was christened Jean Pierre but known throughout his life as Pierre, was born on October 10, 1758. He was

---

*The late John Francis McDermott, a respected historian and Laclède descendant who knocked down a number of family myths during his long research career, found ship registers proving that Chouteau left his wife and returned to France, not returning to New Orleans until well after the family had moved upriver with Laclède. That does not rule out abuse as a factor in the separation, but the abuse story also could have reflected the desire of observant Roman Catholic descendants to put a more positive spin on the situation. McDermott's research on this topic is explored at length in his unpublished manuscript, "Laclède and the Chouteaus: Fantasies and Facts," in Box 48/f. 1, McDermott Mississippi Valley Research Collection, Bowen University Archives and Special Collections, Lovejoy Library, Southern Illinois University at Edwardsville.

followed by Marie Pélagie, born October 12, 1760; Marie Louise, born December 4, 1762; and Victoire, born March 23, 1764.

While Laclède and Madame Chouteau were building their family, Laclède and his sponsor, Maxent, were laying plans to open a new French outpost deep within the North American continent, far up the Mississippi River at the mouth of the Missouri. On the strength of their service in the war against England, which was then winding down after France's bitter loss on the Plains of Abraham in Quebec, they went to the territorial governor, M. D'Abbadie, and obtained a license for what was later termed "exclusive trade with the savages of the Missouri and with all of the [Indian] nations residing west of the Mississippi for the term of eight years."

This would not be the first French post in what was then referred to as the "Illinois Country" or "Upper Louisiana." There were already small settlements at Cahokia and Kaskaskia and around Fort de Chartres on the east side of the Mississippi in present-day Illinois, plus Arkansas Post, the dividing point between Upper and Lower Louisiana. Fort de Chartres, originally a wooden stockade dating from 1720 and rebuilt as a massive stone fortress in 1760, was the center of French administration of the Illinois country. Kaskaskia was the largest settlement, with about sixty-five families, plus some slaves. There were corn mills and sawmills along the Kaskaskia River, which emptied into the Mississippi. The village of Ste. Genevieve, in present-day Missouri, founded near the lead mines sometime before 1750, was the only French settlement on the west bank of the Mississippi.

The Laclède-Maxent license, with its emphasis on the Missouri River tribes, would push the French presence and influence farther west as well as north. The granting of the license to Maxent and Laclède reflected D'Abbadie's concerns about the languishing state of trade coming from the colony. Until then, Indian trade was wholly or partly in the hands of post commanders, who often interfered to get more profit for themselves. At times it had been open to all licensed traders; at other times certain traders had been given exclusive privileges.

To carry out this new venture, the firm of Maxent, Laclède and

Dée was organized. Maxent provided or raised most of the capital. Merchandise for trade was ordered from Europe. Laclède organized the expedition, obtained boats, and recruited workers. Nothing is known of Dée, whose name disappeared from the firm in a short time.

Unbeknownst to Laclède and Maxent, however, Louis XV of France was then in the process of giving up all his sovereignty on the North American continent. In two secret treaties settling the Seven Years' War, one in November 1762 and the other in February 1763, he had signed over the Louisiana territory west of the Mississippi to his cousin, King Carlos III of Spain, and the portion east of the Mississippi to England. New Orleans, even though on the east side, was included in the territorial grant to Spain. This grant was supposedly being made to compensate Spain for the suffering it had incurred as a result of siding with France in the war and in exchange for transferring Florida to British control. Like Louis XIV before him, Louis XV found himself unable to successfully wield power on two continents. He chose to concentrate his resources in Europe, the real prize to him. France also was disappointed that Louisiana had provided so little revenue, having expected more in the way of precious metals. Instead, Louisiana had been a constant drain on French finances.

Whether or not he himself knew of the dramatic changes on the horizon, the new French director general and commandant at New Orleans, D'Abbadie, issued the trade license to Maxent and Laclède on July 6, 1763.

In August 1763 Laclède's flotilla left New Orleans. Young Auguste Chouteau, not yet fourteen, accompanied his stepfather. Madame Chouteau remained behind with her three younger children to await the birth of Victoire in March of the following year.

The Laclède group of at least thirty men, including a few slaves, made eight miles a day going up the river. Some of those ascending with Laclède had come with him from France. Jean B. Ortes, who was born in the same region as Laclède, testified years later that he came with Laclède at age eighteen from France, then moved up the Mississippi with him as well. Their boats were low hulls, somewhat resembling barges of later times. There were no cabins or accommodations for the crew. Bales and barrels of goods, materials, and tools filled the hulls. At the center of each boat was a stubby, strong mast, well braced. Tied to the mast was a rope several hundred feet long, the cordelle. Men known as cordellers walked along the shore in single file with the end of the rope in their hands, dragging the boats. In shallow water, the men got onto the boats and used poles to force the vessels upstream. When they were lucky, the wind blew upstream, and sails could be used.

The banks of the river were heavily overgrown. In advance of the cordellers went men with axes, clearing the path of fallen trees and vines. *Chasseurs de bois* left the boats in the morning and hunted in the woods for game for meals. At night the boats were tied to the bank, and a tent was pitched for Laclède. The men slept on the ground or on the cargo.

Through August, September, and October, the expedition toiled along the riverbanks. On November 3 the voyagers finally sighted Ste. Genevieve, where the news was waiting that would dramatically change Laclède's plans. Word had reached the New World that France was ceding to England the country east of the Mississippi. It would be some months yet before Laclède would learn of the rest of the agreement: that the country on the west side of the Mississippi, where he was to set up his trading post, was passing out of French hands as well.

Until he could build a secure structure at his destination, Laclède needed a safe, dry place to store the trade merchandise he had brought with him. There was not enough available storage space in Ste. Genevieve, but French troops at Fort de Chartres, a few miles upriver, had sighted his expedition. An officer arrived with greetings from the commandant, who offered Laclède a place to stay and store his goods, at least until the English garrison took over.

Laclède pushed on to Fort de Chartres and docked at the landing. The stone walls of the fort, eighteen feet high, rose like a medieval mirage out of prairies surrounding it on three sides. The massive doors to what was then called "the most convenient and best built fort in North America" were no more than eighty paces from the riverbank. A four-acre area was enclosed within the fort's walls, which had been built of limestone quarried from nearby bluffs and hauled to the site by raft and oxen.

Laclède's boatmen carried the goods into a stone warehouse ninety feet long. The fort enclosure also contained a government house, barracks, coach house, chapel, guardhouse, powder magazine, and bakery, all of stone with doors of wood and iron. Cannon in the bastions covered approaches to the fort. Laclède bought a house for himself and Auguste from Jean Girardin, one of the French troops, and settled in for the winter.

On his arrival, however, Laclède saw that there was great confusion inside the fort, as well as in the adjacent settlement, which was home to some forty families. Pierre Joseph Neyon de Villiers, the commandant, without knowing when the English would arrive to take control, was calling in the French garrisons from outlying posts and making plans to depart for New Orleans. He urged the settlers to "follow their flag" by joining him. "But the real motive of Monsieur de Neyon was to take with him a numerous train and to descend the Mississippi in triumph, to make the government believe that all these people followed him for the great esteem which they had for his person," Auguste Chouteau later claimed.

Observing all of this, Laclède decided to capitalize on the situation by expanding his plans. Instead of just establishing a trading post at the mouth of the Missouri, he would create an entire community. The people of French Illinois had traditionally considered the English to be their mortal enemies, and religious heretics as well. So Laclède began to encourage farmers, shopkeepers, craftsmen, and their families to join him in creating a new community on the west side of the river, which he still believed was to remain French. Eventually, some decided to go with Laclède, and others followed the commandant downriver.

In December, with ice already forming on the Mississippi, Laclède set out with young Auguste to explore the country on the west bank north of Ste. Geneviève in search of the right place for the new settlement. They went as far as the mouth of the Missouri, studying topography and the quality of land extending inland from the river. After reaching the Missouri, they returned down the bank of the Mississippi a few miles until Laclède made scratches into some trees and told Auguste that as soon as navigation reopened, this was the place to which he must return and begin the clearing work for the settlement. The spot that Laclède had chosen would eventually become the financial and commercial heart of St. Louis.

The English were slow, even hesitant, to occupy the Illinois country. It was partly the result of the difficult logistics of moving men around a wilderness with virtually no roads and hardly any paths even along the riverbanks. It was also because the Indian leader Pontiac — the scourge of the English and a fervent loyalist of the French through countless battles at their side — was organizing the large confederacy of Indian tribes under his influence to revolt against British control of the areas around the Great Lakes. Eventually Pontiac expanded his plans to include the prevention of British occupation of the posts in the Illinois country as well.

Because of these delays, on January 30, 1764, Commandant D'Abbadie in New Orleans forwarded final orders to Neyon de Villiers at Fort de Chartres to go ahead and evacuate the posts and the territory and report to New Orleans with his troops and as many settlers as chose to come. He was instructed to leave a garrison of forty men under Captain Louis St. Ange de Bellerive, who was coming from Vincennes, in the future Indiana, to await the English forces, whenever they should arrive.

Meanwhile, in early February 1764, with jagged edges of ice still clinging to the shores of the Mississippi, young Auguste Chouteau left Fort de Chartres with thirty men to go to the site Laclède had selected for the settlement, where he and the men were to build storage and lodging. Cordellers pulled their boat along the riverbank for sixty miles before striking out across the waters. In the memoir he wrote in old age about the founding of St. Louis, Auguste Chouteau said that they reached the site on March 14, but it is possible that his memory was off by a month. McDermott claims the date was February 14, which seems more likely, given the short distance they had to cover.

The men went to work the day after their arrival. Included in the group were two millers, several carpenters, various farmers, a gun-smith, a church chorister, traders, and a blacksmith. After clearing land that now lies within the park surrounding the Gateway Arch, the workers put up a large storage shed, then built small cabins for them-selves. In the spring, a few families arrived from the east bank to begin preparing the soil for crops,. In the fall, after harvesting their crops on the other side, a few additional farm families came.

"Immediately where the Town stands was very heavily timbered; but back of the Town, it was generally prairie, with some timber grow-ing, but where the timber did grow, it was entirely free from under-growth, and the grass grew in great abundance everywhere," one of the settlers recounted. Soon after arrival they fenced a common field, which was later extended to take in a pond; part of the fence was picket, some of it horizontal tree trunks.

"In the early part of April, Laclède arrived among us," recalled Au-guste Chouteau. "He . . . fixed the place where he wished to build his house, laid a plan of the village which he wished to found . . . and or-dered me to follow the plan exactly, because he could not remain any longer with us. He was obliged to proceed to Fort de Chartres, to re-move the goods that he had in the fort, before the arrival of the En-glish, who were expected every day to take possession of it."

After the birth of Victoire, Madame Chouteau and the smaller chil-dren left New Orleans and traveled upriver to Fort de Chartres. Even with the probable help of slaves, it was a struggle to spend two to three months on a simple wooden boat with a boy five years old and three girls ages three, fifteen months, and newborn. Before they arrived, the word—or at least the rumor—of the ceding of the west side of the river to Spain would have reached the area.

On April 18, 1764, Commandant D'Abbadie at New Orleans wrote in his journal: "The rumors of the cession of this colony to Spain have the appearance of truth." On April 21 Louis XV sent him a letter stating that France had given up its sovereignty in North America and divided her colonies between England and Spain. D'Ab-badie was instructed to deliver the province to Spanish authority. This letter did not reach New Orleans until September 10, but by then the news had reached the colony unofficially and spread to Upper Louisiana as well.

Pontiac did arrive at Fort de Chartres, in April, with about four hundred warriors of the Huron, Miami, Chippewa, Ottawa, Potawatomi, and Missouri tribes. He told Commandant Villiers he was there to protect the French from the English and urged him and Captain St. Ange to join him in the revolt. Under instructions to give up the post, they declined Pontiac's offer. The Indian leader remained in the area until July, leaving for Detroit after news arrived that a British expedition coming from the south had been stopped by Indians in Lower Louisiana.

In June, Villiers and the French troops finally departed Chartres for New Orleans, followed by a fleet of twenty-one boats carrying eighty settlers. As planned, Villiers left forty men with St. Ange to await the British. The colonists who descended the river with Villiers had been promised land if they would move to New Orleans. Given their fear of the English, they were easy to convince. But when the group reached New Orleans, the local French government was in disarray because of the expected arrival of the Spanish forces. Frustrated at being ignored, many of those families, remembering Laclède's offer, returned up the river to St. Louis, or even decided to risk returning to their old homes and living under the despised English. Laclède was not deterred by the news that the site of his new settlement was going to be under Spanish rather than French domain; perhaps he thought he and his followers could live in peace under another Catholic monarchy. It is also probable that many of those engaged in building the future St. Louis believed that the Spanish would never assume control and the area would remain French.

To young Auguste fell the task of performing the first survey and platting the young town. "The Main Streets were all of them laid out to be thirty six feet French measure wide, and all the cross streets were laid out to be thirty feet French measure wide . . . the blocks were generally laid out to be two hundred and forty feet fronting on the main streets, and running back three hundred feet to the other main streets—and the grants to the town lots were always intended to be

bounded by the said plan or plot above mentioned, so as not to en-
croach upon the streets," he recalled. A space was always left between
the lots and the river for a towpath or road.

The next year, 1765, many families came to the new settlement
from the east side of the Mississippi, plus several families from Ste.
Genevieve and New Orleans, accepting building lots assigned to
them by Laclède. Those coming from the other side often brought all
that they possessed that was movable, even dismantling parts of their
houses and bringing doors, windows, and planking. Many were driven
by a feeling that they had to escape ahead of the English arrival.

Most of the new houses were built of upright posts set in the
ground in the French style known as *poteaux en terre*; a few were
stone. Each house usually had a galerie, or porch, on two or more
sides, with the roof extending over the porch. The site was thickly covered with timber, so each settler had to clear his land first. The only
landmark to guide each new owner in finding his location was the distance from Laclède's trading post, which was the initial point of the
village. Everything else was measured from there.

Not until October of 1765 did English troops arrive on the east side of
the Mississippi to take command of Fort de Chartres. A force of a
hundred Highlanders came by way of Pittsburgh and the Ohio River
after two previous British expeditions had turned back because of fears
of Pontiac. After handing over the fort, Captain St. Ange marched up
the river and went across to the new settlement, where he was received at Laclède's house. He took with him twenty soldiers, plus
some arms, stores, and munitions. After St. Ange's move, additional
French settlers followed him from the east bank.

Spain, which was occupied putting down a rebellion by French
loyalists in New Orleans, still had sent no troops or any other authority to the Upper Louisiana country. Laclède had been the de facto authority for the village, and after St. Ange's arrival, the inhabitants
vested the former French commandant with the functions of temporary governor.

At first the new settlement was known simply as Laclède's Village,
but at some early point Laclède named it St. Louis. Some assumed it

was named in honor of Louis XV, the reigning monarch of France, but historians later concluded that it was done in honor of Louis IX, a thirteenth-century monarch who was canonized and was known as the special protector of towns and cities against the encroachments of feudal lords.

THREE

Haughty Children of the Middle Waters

᛭ ❉

As young Auguste and the other settlers were at work in October 1764 trying to complete the most necessary structures before winter came, about 400 men, women, and children of the nearly extinct Missouri tribe, including some 150 warriors, appeared and threw the tiny colony into alarm. The Missouris were then little more than a remnant of a tribe. Although related to the powerful Osages, the Missouris' numbers had been dramatically reduced by disease and warfare with other tribes. Starving and destitute, they had turned to the white man to help them survive.

"Although they did not appear to have any evil intentions toward us, they were none the less a heavy charge on us, from their continual demands for provisions, and from their thefts of our tools—telling us, always, that they wished to form a village around the house we intended building, of which it would be the center," Auguste Chouteau recalled. At the same time, the colonists who had come from the east side of the Mississippi, fearing the Indians, made a hasty retreat back across the river, reducing the colony to the thirty to thirty-five men who had arrived with Auguste. Facing a tense situation, Auguste sent a messenger to Fort de Chartres to bring Laclède.

Once Laclède arrived, the Indian leaders went into council with him. In Auguste Chouteau's recollections of the events, the Indians pleaded with Laclède to take pity on them. Like ducks and bustards, they said, they were looking for open water on which to rest and procure an easy subsistence, and they could not find any place more suitable than around the new settlement. The next day, the council reconvened for Laclède's reply.

"I will reply to you in a few words, and I will say, that if you followed the example of the ducks and the bustards in settling yourselves, you followed bad guides, who have no foresight," Laclède told them,

> because if they had any, they would not put themselves into open water, so that the eagles and birds of prey could discover them easily, which would never happen to them if they were in a woody place, and covered with brush. You Missouris will not be eaten by eagles; but these men who have waged war against you for a long time past, who are in great numbers against you, who are few, will kill your warriors, because they will offer resistance, and will make your women and children slaves.

He warned them that followers of Pontiac were still at Fort de Chartres and might come to attack the Missouris. The tribe weighed his words and agreed to leave, but they asked for provisions and powder and balls to allow them to hunt for food as they went back up the Missouri River. The white settlers did not have much food surplus, but Laclède agreed to provide the departing Indians some means of subsistence.

During the fifteen days the Missouris were at the settlement, Auguste put the Indian women and children to work digging out the cellar of the building that would initially house the Chouteau family as well as Laclède's business. "I gave them, in payment, vermilion, awls and verdigris. They dug the largest part of [the cellar], and carried the earth in wooden platters and baskets, which they bore upon their heads," he remembered. The vermilion and verdigris were used by Indian women to dye porcupine quills and other decorative items for clothing; sometimes the men used vermilion to paint their clean-shaven heads. The awls could be used to make holes in leather and wood.

Despite the early rebuff that the unfortunate Missouris received from Laclède and the people of the settlement, both the Osages and the Missouris soon became regular visitors. The Missouris got into the habit of spending their summers with the French. They came in canoes, bringing their wigwams, which they set up near the village. The Indian women helped to build houses and to plant crops. The Osages began to come several times a year in small groups. The Sacs and Foxes also came, bringing maple sugar and pecans to trade to the colonists. In about 1769, a band of Peoria Indians built a village near St. Louis.

Thus began a friendly and businesslike relationship with all of the Indians in the Missouri country. The relationship, even with its ups and downs, was crucial to Laclède's plan to establish himself and his family and build a fortune. Settling far from a coast and far from larger white communities, he had no option but to continue the interdependence that Native Americans and French had practiced for a century.

Above all, it was the Osage Indians on whom the success of Laclède's vision of building a substantial trading enterprise would rest. Since the earliest days of Europeans in the New World, the French, the Osages, and the Missouri River had been intertwined. Unlike the English and the Spanish, the French saw the continent as a network of rivers, which they plied like today's superhighways and dreamed of dominating. Central to that network were the Mississippi and the Missouri. From the time they found the mouth of the Missouri, in 1673, Frenchmen had been thinking of ways to ascend it in the search for what they called the Western or Southern Sea—the Pacific Ocean. Like Thomas Jefferson more than a century later, they believed that the Missouri, with its more powerful waters, was the main river of the two, flowing from its then unknown headwaters in today's Montana all the way to the Gulf of Mexico.

Searching for the source of the Missouri and its possible connection to the Pacific, a Frenchman named Pierre Gaultier de Varennes, sieur de La Vérendrye, traveled out of Canada in 1739 as far as the Mandan villages near present-day Bismarck, North Dakota. About three years later, his two sons traveled as far down the Missouri as the future site of Fort Pierre, South Dakota, where they left a lead plate to prove their feat.

Somewhere up the Missouri, and perhaps by following the Platte as well, the French also hoped that they might find the way to Santa Fe, thereby strengthening their ownership claim to the lands between the Missouri River and Santa Fe as well as opening trade with the Spanish and the Indians in the Southwest. In 1739, the year La Vérendrye reached the Mandan villages, Frenchmen traveled to New Mexico for the first time. It was accomplished by ascending the Missouri, going up the Platte, then going south by land through Comanche country to Taos and Santa Fe. Most of that first party eventually returned by descending the Canadian and Arkansas rivers.

These early goals required the French to have peace with the Indians who dominated that vast sweep of prairies and plains between the Mississippi and the Rocky Mountains, particularly the Osages. Since at least the late seventeenth century, the Osages had represented the balance of power in the country that stretched far to the west and southwest from the site of St. Louis. A warring society, they were the gatekeepers to the region, sitting astride the middle of the continent. When whites first came to the region, the widely roaming Osages were claiming, or exerting their influence over, all the lands between the Missouri and Arkansas rivers and from the Mississippi to the Rocky Mountains.

There were numerous other tribes, most of them smaller than the Osages, but they were either allies of the Osages or were intimidated by them. The latter included the Apaches and the Comanches, so feared by whites, on the western and southern flanks of the Osages. The Comanches, whom the early French and Spanish called the Padoucas, became, along with the Apaches, a buffer between the Spaniards and the French. The Osages, in turn, helped to keep the Comanches confined to their domain.

Because of the need the French had for help from the Osages and fraternal tribes in keeping the Comanches in line, the French began pampering the Osages and giving them gifts to keep them happy. This was occurring long before Pierre Laclède, his family, and his followers appeared at the mouth of the Missouri River. As a result, the Osages quickly realized that they had a lot of leverage over their French allies.

"This necessitous pampering was the beginning of the haughty insolence which characterized the . . . [the Osages] for a century and a half," according to the Osage historian John Joseph Mathews. "They received fusils in trade with the French and horses in trade with the Kiowas and [Kansas] and by theft from the Pawnees and the Padoucas and the Apaches. They had the musket first among the tribes of the lower Missouri because they had the power to open the water tradeways of the Missouri."

But the Osages were not the most pliant of peoples, and they were not always susceptible to French charms and gifts. The early French found them to be "sly, treacherous, and given to breaking their word." They were also considered haughty, spoiled, and thieving—handsome giants with a Roman manner. To sum up the significance of the Osages, the early French used the word *méfiance*, meaning that the Osages were suspicious or untrustworthy, a term employed to characterize any tribe strong enough to frustrate French plans.

For their part, the Osages were not especially impressed with the French at first. Repulsed by the hairiness of these men—the first whites they had seen—they called them the Heavy Eyebrows. Osage men shared the common Indian dislike of body hair and removed their own slight facial and body growths with mussel-shell tweezers. They shaved their heads, leaving a Mohawk-like roach or scalp lock, which they allowed to grow long and then plaited into two braids.

The Osages had known the French for nearly a century before they had their first encounter with the English at Braddock's defeat in Pennsylvania in 1755. The Osages, of course, were fighting alongside the French. It was in the hands of the enemy English soldiers that the Osages first saw sabers or swords, so they came to call the English the Long Knives, a name they later transferred to Americans.

By the time Laclède obtained his trading license, the Spanish, French, and English were all going to great effort and considerable expense to win over tribes with trade and gifts. Both sides, white and Indian, were nervous about the state of their relations. It was a period of intense jockeying among the three European powers to gain the best position on the continent, for which they were willing to bribe, woo, or do whatever else was necessary to win loyalty and cooperation from the Indians.

Despite their initial distrust of each other, once a relationship of mutual benefit was established, the Osages remained faithful to the French for as long as Gallic power lasted in America, and loyal to the Chouteaus and other French Americans long after the Louisiana Purchase. They refused to learn any white man's language except French. The connection to the French endured nearly two centuries, and the connection to the Chouteau family continued through four generations, until the United States government sent the Osages to their final tribal lands in today's Osage County, Oklahoma.

The name Osage was supplied by the first French to come into contact with the tribe. It is the corruption of Wazhazhe, the Osages' own name for themselves. The Osages also called themselves Ni-u-kon-ska, "Children of the Middle Waters." Informally, they called themselves The Little Ones, which was odd, given their enormous heights.

Archeologists believe they came down from the north as part of the Siouan linguistic family. They were probably the southwesternmost of the larger Siouan tribes, the vanguard of their downward migration. They had linguistic and cultural links to—or were once part of the same tribe as—the Kansas, Omahas, Poncas, Iowas, Otoes, and Missouris.

A major element in Osage history was a flood at some unrecorded time. "When the waters rose, so the story went, some of the Osages escaped by fleeing to higher ground; others stayed put 'under the bluff.' The chiefs concluded that the heavens wished the tribe to divide and disperse. The 'stayers' acquired the name Down-Below People, destined to be diminutivized by Frenchmen as Petit Ouazhaghi, or Little Osages. The 'fleers' to the uplands, comprising several groups, eventually to reunite into one unit, became the Up-Above People—to the French the Grand Ouazhaghi or Big Osages," explained Patrick Brophy, another historian of the Osages.

Despite the wide roaming they did to hunt, steal horses, and make war, the Osages lived in several semipermanent villages, to which they returned after every hunting season and from their wars. In their villages, they lived in rectangular huts as long as sixty feet. All their villages were within the present boundaries of the state of Missouri from at least the late seventeenth century throughout most of the eighteenth century. Their traditional home area was near the headwaters of the Osage River in modern Vernon County, Missouri. Following the split that produced the Big and Little Osage tribes, further fragmentation occurred in which disaffected groups broke away from the main tribes and created new Osage villages, still within the present boundaries of Missouri, sometimes near the old group and sometimes at considerable distance. However, starting at the end of the eighteenth century and into the nineteenth century, a combination of new internal disputes and United States government policies pushed their villages into present-day Kansas and Oklahoma, which they had traditionally used only as hunting grounds.

The Osage homelands were fields of plenty, though given to wild climatic changes. In John Joseph Mathews's nearly poetic description, they lived "at the contact line between the prairie-plains and the woodland, in a region where the Arctic air found no barriers to its savage rush and would periodically meet the dog-breath air from the Gulf to spawn disaster." Food was abundant in the Osage country: white-tailed deer, wild turkeys, prairie chickens, wapiti, buffalo, skunks, fish, lotus, pawpaws, haws, grapes, persimmons, hickory nuts, walnuts, hackberries, pecans, and acorns. They cultivated maize, squash, beans, pumpkins, and wild potatoes.

European and eastern travelers to the Osage prairies inevitably expressed awe at the physical appearance of the Osages. One found them to be "so tall and robust as almost to warrant the application of the term gigantic . . . Their shoulders and visages are broad." Another thought they might be "the tallest race of men in North America, either of red or white skins; there being very few indeed of the men, at their full growth, who are less than six feet in stature, and very many of them six and a half, and others seven feet." Still another called them "the finest looking Indians I have ever seen in the West," looking like "so many noble bronze figures."

Except for the men painting their shaved heads with vermilion, the Osages were not given to fanciful dress or adornment. They stuck to "stern and simple" garb long after many tribes had begun to mix the clothing styles of white people with tribal dress.

To one visitor in 1835, "the sight of these half nude men, with shaven skull, with warlike appearance, that strange harmony of movements and of songs, made a savage exaltation pass within my mind."

Father Jacques Marquette and the trader Louis Jolliet were probably the first white men to come into contact with the Osages. It occurred during the latter part of June 1673, as they made their exploratory voyage down the Mississippi. In two canoes, with five paddlers, they traveled down the Wisconsin River to the Mississippi, then to the Missouri, and up the Missouri to the Marmaton and Osage rivers, where Marquette mapped the locations of the Big and Little Osage villages. Returning to the Mississippi, they eventually descended as far as the Arkansas River before returning north.

In the early 1700s several other French explorers encountered the Osages, beginning with Étienne Veniard de Bourgmont, a *coureur de bois,* or independent trapper, from Canada who became commandant of Fort Detroit in 1706. When some Indians of the Missouri tribe came to the post in 1712 to help the French fight off an attack by Fox Indians, Bourgmont fell in love with a woman in the group and left his post to follow her back to the Missouri River. He married his Indian sweetheart and explored the region by its rivers. In 1714, according to his diary, he followed the course of the Osage River from its mouth at the Missouri, near today's Jefferson City, Missouri, during which voyage he would have encountered the Osages, the more numerous kinsmen of his wife's Missouri tribe.

After a few years Bourgmont returned to French service, took part in the capture of Pensacola in May 1719, then traveled to France. There, the directors of the Company of the Indies were showing increasing interest in the Missouri River region. Various other French officers in the New World were also urging steps to assert French authority over the length of the Missouri and were extolling its potential for trade.

Meanwhile, Charles Claude du Tisné, member of a well-to-do French family, visited the Osages and other tribes by way of the Missouri River. In the spring of 1719 he set out from Kaskaskia and ascended the Missouri to the Osage River, then traveled up it eighty leagues to the Osage villages. Tisné traded merchandise to the Osages in exchange for horses they had stolen from other tribes, and for some skins.

In 1722 Bourgmont left Paris after being given the title of commandant of the Missouri and the assignment of building a fort on the river. Arriving in New Orleans in June, he left there in February 1723 for the Osage villages on the Missouri, where he arrived the following November and proceeded to erect Fort Orléans on the north bank of the river in present-day Carroll County, Missouri. Then he turned to the task of putting together an alliance of the Comanche, Missouri, Osage, Kansa, Otoe, and Omaha tribes. All agreed to live in peace and friendship with one another, and with the French. Fort Orléans, however, lasted only a few years, disappearing long before Laclède ascended the Mississippi to live and trade among the Indians.

Bourgmont's contacts with the Indians also resulted in an invitation for a delegation of chiefs to visit France. He convinced four Osages, five Missouris, including a daughter of the principal chief, and four Illinis, including a chief named Chicagou [*sic*], to go with him to Europe. But when the travelers reached New Orleans, the Company of the Indies, which was paying the costs, told Bourgmont to pare the party down to one representative of each tribe. The smaller group included the Missouri princess, one Otoe, one Osage, one Missouri chief, one Illini, plus Chicagou and the ambassador of the Metchegamias (Michigans). The group reached France on September 20, 1725, and proceeded to captivate Paris. The Indians were presented to the fifteen-year-old king, Louis XV, received by other royalty, and given clothes. They performed war dances at the opera and were likely bedded by rich women and ladies of the court.

Even before the first white men arrived in their lands, the Osages had been profoundly affected by white influences. The horse, a Spanish import, had already reached the Plains tribes and had begun to change the tribes' ways of hunting and waging war. It had replaced the dog as the Osages' beast of burden and had provided the Indian men with rapid transportation. Brophy notes that archaeology does not provide many clues to Osage life before the white man came, because "the earliest known Osage sites seem to contain far more European than native material."

When their first direct contacts with exploring white men occurred, the Osages were immediately attracted to the possibility of acquiring European manufactured goods, including hand tools, small mirrors, dyes, and, later, guns and gunpowder. They were eager to obtain anything made of metal. The tribe soon took the initiative to seek out the whites in pursuit of trade. They began traveling to the settlements around Kaskaskia after its founding in 1703. By the time of Laclède's arrival, in 1763, the Osages had been regularly visiting Fort de Chartres to trade, crossing the Mississippi a short distance above Ste. Genevieve at Isle au Bois. Traders from the fort ascended the Mississippi in canoes, then traveled by way of the Missouri to the Osage village on the Osage River.

So eager were the Osages to obtain trade goods that they intensified their hunting activities for furs and skins and even abandoned their age-old taboo against hunting beaver so as to have something attractive to offer the whites in exchange for European goods. In addition, by the mid-1700s the growing number of traders and *coureurs de bois* on the rivers made it possible for the Osages and other tribes to obtain some of the coveted items by robbery.

To a much greater extent than the English or even the Spanish, the French incorporated Indians into their lives and society. In the words of Mathews, "The French fraternized with the tribes, learned their languages, ate their food, married their women, and in general treated them in harmony with the new thought being born in scintillating France concerning the importance of the common man."

Frenchmen regularly took Indian wives for long or short-term relationships, and many children were born of those unions. There were few white women in the vast area through which the *coureurs de bois* and the Indians roamed, which encouraged marriages contracted in what was often described as "the manner of the country" or "the Indian way." Such marriages could involve true affection, or they could be the result of business dealings between traders or trappers and Indian leaders who routinely offered young women of the tribes to the white men, with little concern for the feelings of the women.

Perrin du Lac, a Frenchman who traveled among the Kansa Indians, close kin of the Osages, said that accepting the daughter of a headman was considered a prerequisite for negotiating for furs. It was fairly common for men of a tribe to sell young Indian women, typically fifteen-year-old virgins, to white men. Sometimes these were girls from the men's tribe or sometimes they were girls who had been captured in warfare with other tribes.

Being Roman Catholics, the Frenchmen often had their children by Indian women baptized by priests who occasionally traveled through the tribal areas. "The *coureurs de bois* would believe that their living with Missouria [*sic*] and Osage women was not a sin to be confessed, since obviously these women were pagans, but the offspring of such cohabitation were quite another category; they were souls to be saved and to do nothing about the saving of them would be a mortal sin," Mathews observed.

As a result, baptismal records of many such births have survived, substantiating information on the relationships of the Frenchmen and the "robe mates" and "blanket mates" with whom they shared the cold nights and rigors and uncertainties of life on the rivers and prairies. Those men included both Pierre and Auguste Chouteau before they married French wives in St. Louis, and later various of their sons and grandsons.

A number of early white travelers to the area described in their journals and reports the almost brutal treatment to which Indian women were routinely subjected within their tribes. They did the heavy work of feeding, housing, and clothing the tribe, and whatever farming was done as well. The men hunted, held a lot of meetings, went to war, and played games. Some visitors concluded that the Indian women generally received better treatment at the hands of white men and thus may not have objected to being offered to them like virtual commodities.

One white visitor to the Osage country noted: "The countenances of the Osage squaws . . . after true savage fashion, were bent towards the earth, from the burden of skins or other articles imposed upon their shoulders, and secured in its position by a strap of leather over the temples."

Adultery and promiscuity were fairly common. An Osage man, for example, was considered to have rights to his wife's sisters. It was also considered acceptable for a man to have various unrelated wives—if he could afford to pay their fathers for them in horses, robes, blankets, or other things of value. Some travelers observed that this meant it was mainly the chiefs and principal men of the tribe who had more than one wife other than his wife's sisters. Mathews, basing much of his writing on the oral history of the tribe, claimed that when "traders and officials and the explorers and the royal adventurers lured women to their robes by presents, these women were chiefly widows whose chances of remarriage were not too bright, or girls of the second class whose immediate ancestors had mated in the sumac or the tall grasses under the Moon Woman."

Some travelers noted that Indian men were sometimes ready to of-fer white traders a little private time with their female companions in exchange for a shirt or some manufactured item, thinking it cheaper to share a woman than to give up pelts or skins in order to obtain Eu-ropean goods. Such customs were not confined to the Osages. When Lewis and Clark stopped at the Mandan villages along the Upper Mis-souri in January 1805, Clark recorded that the tribe held a buffalo dance lasting three nights at which the young men offered their wives to the older men—including those in the expedition—for sex, "all this to cause the buffalow [sic] to come near so that they may kill them."

In a reaction common among early-nineteenth-century visitors from the East, the writer Washington Irving, when he visited the area in 1832, characterized St. Louis and the tiny settlements farther west as a "mongrel" society made up of "mongrel Indians, and mongrel Frenchmen." Nevertheless, this interaction between the French and Indians created what the contemporary historian James E. Davis has called "a middle ground society" in which "French, Indians, and their offspring lived, mingled freely, borrowed from each other, got along, occasionally spatted, and fashioned a hybrid world."

As Davis said, this culture "spawned no battles of extermination and cultural annihilation." Instead, it "cemented ties and mutual re-spect." That was possible, in part, because the French had more toler-ant attitudes toward Indians and Indian ways, but also because the French were trying to live off the land, along with the Indians, instead of farming it. The Indians felt less threatened by French civilization than by the English.

By the time French rule ended in the Missouri Valley, in 1769,* the Osages had had three-quarters of a century of contact with Europeans. They had learned to like guns, clothing, horses, and liquor, which they obtained for their skins and furs. But the French, despite their willingness to share the blanket and the campfire with the Osages, had been unsuccessful in controlling plundering raids along the Arkansas River valley by rebellious young braves. The French had been able to do nothing in reprisal but deny the availability of merchandise, which made the Osage leaders contrite and caused them to promise better behavior, usually without results.

Laclède and the Chouteaus inherited the mantle of seeking a peaceful, profitable relationship with the Osages. Eventually the frustrated United States government would find itself endlessly turning to them, as the Osages' best white friends, for help and guidance. But before the Americans, it was the turn of the Spanish to spend nearly four decades trying in vain to live profitably and peacefully with the Osages.

---

*Officially, the French gave up the region to the Spanish in 1764, but a rebellion against Spanish authority in New Orleans effectively prevented the Spanish from asserting control of the Upper Louisiana region until 1769.

FOUR

The Business of St. Louis

✳

The founders of St. Louis were not fleeing injustice, nor were they driven by religious sentiments or political ideals. Neither did they aspire to become gentleman farmers overseeing vast plantations worked by slaves. They simply wanted to make money and provide well for themselves and their families. The business of St. Louis, and of Laclède and the Chouteaus, was to be the fur trade, which Laclède was able to successfully launch the very first year. In addition, he put a roof over the heads of his family and created the beginnings of a community.

"Religion was a business left to the priest—when there was one in the neighborhood," explained John Francis McDermott, historian of the Mississippi Valley French.

> Those citizens who were religious had apparently a confidence in their God which sufficed; those who were not inclined toward religion tended to ignore it. Neither found reason to make a fuss about it. These Creoles were engaged in making a living and in enjoying life . . . There was no chance to bicker locally over religion or with the religious in the home-country. Unlike the New Englanders in their first century, the Creoles had no special concern about their self-importance. They were evidently not under the necessity of justifying themselves to themselves; they were not so sure that God had destined them above all others; they did not spend their time writing about themselves.

Well before Laclède set up business in St. Louis, Louis XIV had made the wide-brimmed beaver hat the fashion rage among European men by perching it atop his chestnut curls and parading around in high heels. But John Jacob Astor, who was to amass from the fur trade America's first multimillion-dollar fortune, was still in diapers in the German village of his birth. The fur trade was then dominated from Canada, where most of the twelve thousand whites were in the fur trade in some form by the end of the seventeenth century. In the Mississippi and Missouri basins, the business had been very modest, operated by individuals with little capital. Laclède brought a determination to change that, to build a large, well-organized business, and to impose his leadership.

Three British fur companies with long histories were operating from the north. The Northwest Company, headquartered in Montreal, with operations extending into the colonies of the future United States, grew out of the French Canada trade. The Hudson's Bay Company was the oldest of the three firms, with a charter dating from 1670. The third, founded after the Northwest Company was well along, was the Mackinaw Company, headquartered at Michilimackinac. It operated mainly around the shores of Lake Michigan and westward to the Upper Mississippi and in Canadian territory east of Lake Huron.

Laclède and those who soon joined or followed him in the fur trade would lead the way in exploring the midsection of the continent, building on the knowledge gained by Marquette and Jolliet and others of their countrymen over the previous century. Decades before most of the official exploration by the United States, they created what Hiram M. Chittenden, the leading historian of the American fur trade, called "the avenues of commerce" in the region. Taking on physically daunting voyages into the unknown for months at a time long before the steamboat would shorten those trips to a few weeks, the traders and trappers established the routes of travel in the region that survived to the twenty-first century.

"*They* were the 'pathfinders' of the West, and not those later official explorers whom posterity so recognizes," Chittenden declared.

Laclède and other fur traders also set a course for friendly and knowledgeable relations with Indians that would never be matched by the white men who followed them into the West. "It was only in these early years that the white man and the Indian truly understood each other," concluded Chittenden. "Very rarely has any Indian agent or army officer, however wide their experience, displayed that intimate acquaintance with the tribes and knowledge of the native character, that was possessed by the trader and trapper."

If the traders brought to the Indians "corrupting vices and desolating disease they also brought to the Indian his first lessons in the life that he was yet to lead. They mingled with his people, learned his language and customs, understood his character, and, when not impelled by business rivalry, treated him as a man and as a brother."

At first Laclède relied on Indians coming to St. Louis to exchange their buffalo skins and furs for the merchandise he shipped upriver from New Orleans. Soon he reached outward and sent traders—including eventually his son, his stepson, and his son-in-law—to Indian villages to be on hand for the first chance at peltries when the tribes came back from hunting expeditions.

In the early years, in May and June, tribes in large parties descended to St. Louis not only from the Missouri and Mississippi rivers but also from the Wabash, the Ohio, and as far away as the Straits of Mackinac to "declare the furs." In 1768, twenty-eight tribes were listed in Spanish records as coming to St. Louis to trade. The atmosphere during their visits was hospitable and festive. After Captain Pedro Piernas was appointed lieutenant governor for Upper Louisiana in 1769, it became traditional for him to provide the visiting tribes with bread and corn, purchased by the Spanish royal treasury, for the duration of their stay. They hunted their own meat. When the tribes prepared to depart, the lieutenant governor was expected to give them some kind of gift. Alcoholic beverages were preferred. Spanish authorities, from the time they took power in Upper Louisiana, were opposed to giving the tribes alcohol, but they had to deal with a system already put in place by the French, and to an even greater extent by the English, with which Laclède and the other St. Louis traders were competing.

As Piernas informed Governor Alejandro O'Reilly in New Orleans in 1769, "Most of the tribes, with the exception of some remote and distant tribes of the Misuri [sic] are accustomed to the use of brandy, and prefer a small portion of it to any other present of merchandise even of four times its value. If the savages are treated with kindness, reasonably, and with consideration, they are reasonable when in their right mind. But when drunk they are importunate, beggars, insatiable, and tiresome."

Out of this early well-meaning hospitality and gift giving by white traders and authorities emerged a dependence on the part of the Indians that led them to expect more and more gifts and more and more alcohol. Eventually, instead of merely trading their skins and furs for merchandise, the Indians wanted merchandise on credit before going out to hunt, or they insisted on guns and ammunition with which to hunt. If the hunt went badly, they might be unable to pay off their debts that year and have to carry some over to the next. Years later, after the territory passed to the United States, accumulated debts to the traders were often paid off only after the tribe ceded lands to the government for cash, which partly went to pay off debts to traders.

For the traders in St. Louis, there were three ways of obtaining skins and furs. The first involved direct trade with the Indians. The tribes came to St. Louis in late spring, or traders went to the villages of the tribes. No money exchanged hands, not even gold. The traders offered the Indians manufactured goods, usually from Europe, in exchange for furs. Typically, the items offered by the traders were blankets, measured in *points* (French for "stitch") according to size and quality, plus pots and pans, knives and other cutting utensils, needles, dyes, beads, buttons, and silver or metal adornments made into bracelets, necklaces, and other objects to be worn. As the fur trade grew more competitive, guns and gunpowder became part of the traders' merchandise.

When Laclède was starting out, many of these items offered to the Indians were considered by the traders to be little more than "trinkets" having minimal value. The traders often referred to them in such terms when ordering from suppliers in New Orleans, London, and Montreal. As time passed, however, and the Indians learned to distinguish the quality of the goods of one trader from that of another, and to demand the best, the traders became insistent on quality from their agents and suppliers. They sometimes switched suppliers, or threatened to do so, to obtain better blankets, for example. The largest cost to the traders of most of these items involved the time and distance in getting them delivered.

But if white men did not think they were giving Indians anything of much value, neither did the Indians place a high value on what they traded for the European goods. Indian men could get hundreds of bison robes from a fun-filled afternoon of doing what they most enjoyed: chasing buffalo with wild abandon. Before fur traders came into buffalo country, Indians would chase and kill the animals if for no other reason than to get their tongues, a delicacy for the dinner table. They used skins for clothing and housing, but those requirements could be satisfied with far fewer skins than the number of buffalo the braves were capable of killing in a short time. Having a market for the skins was a bonus.

Further, the hard, dirty work of preparing the robes for trade fell to the Indian women and did not much concern the men when they went to trade away the robes. Even beaver pelts got most of their value from the work of the women in cleaning them, shaving them, and then wearing them next to their bodies all winter to make them soft and shiny from body oil. As Chittenden observed, "In the early intercourse of the white man with the Indian, each gave to the other something that he valued lightly, and received in return something that he valued highly, and each felt a keen contempt for the stupid taste of the other."

The fur companies also employed some of their own hunters and trappers, who killed buffalo and caught beaver and gathered other furs that came their way. These men worked for wages. And the companies obtained other furs from so-called free hunters and trappers, generally known by their French name, *coureurs de bois*. They worked on their own account and sold the pelts at trading posts, occasionally taking them directly to St. Louis. They usually took part of their payment in supplies for new expeditions, plus tobacco and liquor.

In addition to being the main items of commerce in Upper Louisiana, skins and furs were also the principal currency. Almost no currency or coins circulated in the area until at least 1804, and even after the transfer of the territory to the United States it was not unusual for people to make large purchases or contracts in peltries. Taxes in the early years under the United States were payable in "shaven deer-skins at the rate of 3 pounds to the dollar."

At the time Laclède founded St. Louis, accounting books were kept in livres, the currency of France. A livre was worth 18½ American cents, slightly less than the franc, which replaced it after the French Revolution. Actual payments were calculated in peltries, as were estates and other items related to the assets of a person. Marriage contracts commonly stated how many deerskins or other peltries each party was bringing to the marriage. The earliest known conversion rates at St. Louis were forty cents of the livre for each pound of the finest furs, thirty cents for medium grade, and twenty cents for inferior.

The parties to all transactions kept careful records of each side's credits and debits over an extended period, so that many debts and payments were canceled on the basis of what one owed or had coming from the other, without the necessity of actual payment changing hands in the form of peltries or anything else. This was the standard for doing business between the traders in St. Louis and their merchant suppliers in New Orleans and elsewhere. Running accounts were kept open and not settled for years.

Historians have concluded that the fur trade out of St. Louis was profitable from the beginning. They base that conclusion in part on the fact that keelboats and barges were regularly going up the Mississippi from New Orleans loaded with merchandise for the Indian trade. Also, Spanish government records show that large numbers of Indians quickly began coming to St. Louis to trade. So Laclède and other traders had merchandise from Europe as well as willing customers among the Indians, which would have created the potential for profit.

By tracing an invoice of fur-trade merchandise from Europe to St. Louis, then to the wilderness, and back the same route in the form of peltries and eventually items of clothing in Europe, Chittenden found that a profit of several hundred percent was likely for the European merchants. However, it took four years for that round-trip to be completed. For the St. Louis traders, who had to bear the risk of losses or damages to the trading goods and pelts on the high seas or rivers, the profits were not quite so grand, although Chittenden thought them to be quite substantial.

These profits were also a mixed blessing in St. Louis because the result was that during the early days, almost the entire workforce wanted to be in the fur trade. Raising crops had little appeal. The new community often had to get food from Ste. Genevieve and elsewhere. In other French settlements, from Quebec to New Orleans, Laclède's town soon became known as Paincourt, or short loaf, for being chronically short of food.

As Lieutenant Governor Piernas explained to Governor O'Reilly, the "sole and universal trade" in the territory then being called Spanish Illinois consisted of furs. This was despite the fact that "the country of Ylinoeses is, in general, healthy and fertile, its climate delightful, and suitable for all sorts of plants, fruits, and grains. In some parts it is mountainous, and in others level. It contains vast prairies fit for the pasturage of cattle, and cleared level plains for farming. With but little cultivation those fields produce copious harvests, especially wheat, maize, cotton, and all sorts of vegetables." But the territory also abounded in game, and hunting was "the chief occupation of its inhabitants; for from the flesh they obtain their food, and from the skins their profits."

The profit picture for Laclède, however, was complicated by the fact that Maxent, his partner, had provided the capital that went into the family's move upriver, the founding of the settlement, and the merchandise with which to open the fur trade, all of which, in turn, took several years to produce results. Laclède was also the man to whom most of the people in the community turned when in need. He was a soft touch for those who had put their faith in him and had crossed the river to build their homes in the new settlement. He was lenient in extending credit, often without collateral, and people often did not, or could not, repay him. So even if the fur trade by itself made an operating profit for him, he was faced with other demands that overwhelmed his fur-trade income.

Laclède had also counted on having the exclusive right to the trade with the Indians of the Missouri River region, in line with the license he and Maxent had been given by the last French governor at New Orleans. Instead, he found himself surrounded by competitors. Merchants of the older settlement at Ste. Genevieve, sixty miles down the Mississippi from St. Louis, had been accustomed to trading in the Missouri River country before the arrival of Laclède, and they did not intend to withdraw.

In April 1765 a boat loaded with merchandise for the Missouri River Indian trade, coming from two merchants at Ste. Genevieve, was seized at the request of Laclède on the grounds that it violated his exclusive trading license. The boat was brought to St. Louis, the goods inventoried and stored. Then the two merchants filed suit before the Superior Council in New Orleans, which decided against Laclède two years later and ordered his firm to pay 6,485 livres, 8 sols—equal to $1,297—to the owners of the goods.

Laclède, at the time he requested the seizure, was not aware that his exclusive trading privileges had been canceled in the process of the transfer of the colony from France to Spain. During the Spanish assumption of power, confused by a revolt against them by local French in New Orleans, the new authorities took the step, first, of halting all trade with the Indians for a time, then resuming it but canceling Laclède's exclusive license. Laclède's partner, Maxent, in New Orleans, made a strong complaint to Governor Antonio de Ulloa, claiming that this had cost both him and Laclède dearly and demanding compensation for their losses.

There is no indication that the Spanish authorities acceded to that request, but on the same date that Maxent filed his complaint, May 8, 1769, Maxent and Laclède ended their partnership, a decision for which they left no explanation. Laclède agreed to buy out Maxent for 80,000 livres* payable over four years beginning in 1771. In return, Laclède received merchandise and accounts payable of 22,000 livres, furs and skins valued at 25,000 livres, twelve slaves valued at 14,000 livres, a house, mill, barns, and land valued at 12,000 livres, and cattle, horses, pigs, farming and blacksmith tools, and household furniture and goods. In short, everything with which Laclède had es-

*Equivalent to $16,000.

tablished his family and business in Upper Louisiana came from Maxent. Now he was even more in debt to Maxent to be able to continue in business.

In addition to his business debts, Laclède felt the pressure of providing security for a family that he could not openly claim as his. Four years after the village of St. Louis was begun, construction was completed on a family house, and Laclède was able to move Madame Chouteau and the children out of the combined home-business headquarters and into their real home. Concerned about the uncertain legal situation of his family, Laclède took the step of having the house, four slaves, the child of one slave, and a piece of farmland deeded to the five children, including eighteen-year-old Auguste, with Madame Chouteau receiving the gift on their behalf. Among other things, this protected the family in the event of his death, because under both French and Spanish law only legitimate children could inherit. If he had no legitimate heirs, his estate, at his death, would pass to his brother or other relatives in France. The action also protected the family home from claims by business creditors. The notarized deed he signed kept up the fiction that René Chouteau was the father of all of the children, declaring that:

> Pierre Laclède Liguest, merchant of the Illinois . . . in consideration of the faithful service which he has received from Mr. Auguste Choutaud [sic], during the several years in which he has worked for him as his Clerk, in order to give evidence to the said Chouteaud [sic] as well as to Pierre Choutaud, Pélagie Choutaud, Marie Louise Choutaud, and Victoire Choutaud, brothers and sisters, children of dame Marie Thérèse Bourgeois and of Sieur René Choutaud, the said Sieur Choutaud, father, absent from the post, and the said dame Marie Thérèse Bourgeois, his wife here present . . . [deeds to them]: a piece of ground one hundred and twenty feet front by one hundred and fifty feet in depth, situated in the post of St. Louis, which the said Sieur Laclède did acquire heretofore from the Domaine of the King by title of a Concession accorded to him. The said land faces a wide street which adjoins the land of one named Bissonet . . . on which land is built a house of stone, which the said Sieur Laclède had built, and is fifty feet long by thirty-four feet wide, covered with shingles,

distributed into several low rooms, all well floored and ceilinged, quite new and in good condition. Besides a negress named Louisa, aged about twenty-two years, and another negress about the same age with her child, a boy about two years old; an Indian girl named Manoy aged about twelve or thirteen years of age, an Indian girl named Thérèse about fourteen years old; and a piece of land about two arpents* front by forty arpents in depth situated on the Grand Prairie of St. Louis . . .

As everything was agreed upon, and there being no impediment, Dame Choutaud accepting for her said children, said that she was familiar with the place, having seen and visited it.

Madame Chouteau stated in the notarized document that she would use the house after her children were grown and that on her death it would pass to them. If all of them should die before she did, and without heirs, it would go to Laclède's family heirs in France. This was signed and notarized before two witnesses on May 4, 1768.

After his buyout of Maxent, Laclède was able to secure continuing supply arrangements with merchants in New Orleans whose goods were still regularly sent upriver to him. The barges returned downriver with the furs and skins acquired in trade from Indians. Occupied with business details from his headquarters in St. Louis, and with frequent travels to New Orleans, Laclède soon turned to his trusted stepson, Auguste, to be his representative out in the field among the Osages. By the time he was eighteen, Auguste was active with the tribe, regularly wintering in its lodges near the headwaters of the Osage River.

"Young Chouteau lived with the Little Ones with a species of joy of living and treated them with respect and kept his promises, and they trusted him. His personality was such that he could reconcile the exigencies of the fur trade with his romantic attachment to them without arousing their suspicion," wrote Mathews, the Osage historian.

By 1775 Auguste's half brother, Pierre, then seventeen, had also begun living among the Osages for long periods, coming back to St. Louis each summer with the "returns" from the Osage hunting and

---

*Old French land measure. One arpent equaled about .85 acre.

trapping season. At least initially, the license was still issued in Auguste's name. Included in the list of licensed traders for Upper Louisiana that was reported to New Orleans on November 28, 1777, were Auguste Chouteau and his new brother-in-law, Sylvestre Labbadie, who had married Marie Pélagie Chouteau the year before. Both were issued licenses to trade with the Big Osages. Auguste, probably standing in for his stepfather, was the largest trader in terms of the amount of merchandise he acquired to take to the Indians. Auguste's license stated that he had taken or sent 10,000 deerskin pounds worth of goods for trade. The value of the merchandise taken to the Indians by all the seventeen listed traders was 55,800 deerskin pounds. Other lists of traders, covering 1778, show that Auguste was also trading among the Kansa Indians at the mouth of the Kansas River, the present-day site of Kansas City.

Both Chouteau brothers had quickly learned Osage ways and the tribe's language, as well as earning its respect and trust. As the years passed, Auguste would gradually establish himself as the inside man, working at the office in St. Louis, and Pierre would make his mark throughout his long life as the man for whom life among Indians, especially the Osages, was second nature.

The great regard the Osages felt for the Chouteau brothers did little to control the propensity of the fiery young bloods in the tribe to wreak havoc among whites and other Indians at the slightest provocation or misunderstanding. The violent acts they committed in the late eighteenth century, however, bore no relation to the massive warfare and attacks on wagon trains that would become part of white-Indian lore a century later. Mostly the Osages pillaged, stole horses, committed petty thievery, and only occasionally killed someone. Sometimes, whites did the killing.

Within a short time of assuming power, Spanish authorities in New Orleans were so bothered by what they called "depredations" by the Osages that they debated whether to rally other Indian tribes to lead a joint effort to annihilate the troublesome tribe. Some Spanish officials preferred a soft approach, forgiving murders and other acts of violence out of fear the Osages would turn to the British as allies. These officials always tried to bring the Osages in line by threatening to cut off trade goods or just begging and cajoling them. The same officials often tried to get the Osages to turn over for punishment, even execution, particular braves who had committed acts of violence against whites or other Indian tribes.

In the summer of 1772, for example, a number of Little Osage and Missouri warriors broke into Fort Prince Carlos, the Spanish military post near St. Louis, overcame the tiny guard of five soldiers, and stole all the munitions and provisions. They then went into St. Louis, terrorized the town, and planted a British flag. Since the Osages bore no love for the British, it seems likely that they planted the flag only because they knew it would anger the French and Spanish.

Governor Luis Unzaga in New Orleans insisted on a tough response, but he backed off almost as soon as the words poured forth from his pen. He wrote Captain Piernas in St. Louis: "There is no other remedy than their extermination since the tolerance which we have had with them, instead of attracting them, has made them insolent. It is clear that the time has arrived when this wrong demands this last sad remedy, but we are not in a position to apply it because [we] lack people and supplies, and lastly because of the expense."

It was far from the only time that whites, whether French, Spanish, English, or American, would declare that the Osages should be wiped out. Like Unzaga, those who called for the elimination of the tribe inevitably realized in the next breath that it was all but impossible. When the Big Osages arrived in St. Louis in August 1772 for their annual presents, Piernas complained to them about the crimes, and they were repentant and contrite.

A brief period of peace emerged in 1773 after the Missouris and Little Osages returned some stolen horses. The Osages also surrendered three tribal members who had murdered Frenchmen. But in March 1776 Osages struck a hunting party along the Arkansas River, killing two whites and losing four of their own. Other raids followed along the Arkansas River that summer. It was not only the whites who were facing violence from the Osages. By November 1777 the Big Osages, with 800 warriors under their principal chief, Clermont, were at war with the Otoes, Quapaws, Pawnees, Republics, and all the Missouri River Indian nations.

The next month, things worsened. Unhappy with the slow arrival of trading goods, the Big Osages sent out a party to look for traders, and the Osage party was attacked by a large number of Pawnees, with five of the seven Osages killed. After that, the Big Osages went in search of vengeance and took some scalps.

The Chouteaus, however, had won such a place in the Osage hearts that Laclède and Madame Chouteau did not worry about the safety of their young son when he set out on a journey of several weeks up the Missouri River to the Osage villages, where he regularly spent months before returning home. But it was becoming clear that the two Chouteau brothers, as they reached manhood, had a difficult task ahead if they were to build their fortunes by doing business with the petulant and recalcitrant Osages.

Even with uncertainties about whether the Osages could be counted on to be friendly or hostile, life in St. Louis was taking on the characteristics of a stable community. With the help of a notary and a lawyer who moved to the new settlement from the other side of the river, the civil government began on a de facto basis in Laclède's first home and business headquarters. After arriving from Fort de Chartres in 1765, Captain Louis St. Ange de Bellerive was asked to take charge. He and Laclède shared responsibility for the day-to-day functioning of the community. St. Ange issued titles and real estate deeds to settlers as he considered necessary, without anything being charged for the land. Later, Spanish authorities accepted those deeds as legal.

In 1774, at the request of Lieutenant Governor Piernas, a ten-by-twenty-foot jail was added to Laclède's business structure. A sergeant and a couple of soldiers were posted there in case they were needed to guard someone or otherwise maintain order. The jail construction, based on a budget that survived in the handwriting of Auguste Chouteau, cost 840 livres, 11 sols. That included stonework, iron, and eighteen barrels of lime for mortar. Generally, though, no one was imprisoned in early St. Louis. Anyone found to be undesirable was more likely to be escorted to the bank of the Mississippi, put in a boat, and sent to British Illinois.

Every decision having to do with public policy, however trivial, was made through a town meeting, not only under St. Ange but later under Piernas and successive Spanish lieutenant governors. Usually the gatherings occurred after mass on Sunday, the one day when people could be counted on not to be working. At the close of mass one Sunday, for example, the people were summoned to government hall to decide on the best way to provide drainage for the rainwater that settled along the backstreets of the village. They decided to dig a gutter or canal between the properties of two families in order to direct the extra water to the Mississippi, and they appointed five men to come up with the plan for doing it.

On Christmas Eve 1774 everyone in town turned out for the blessing of the first church bell, which was hung on a temporary scaffold outside the tiny log church that had been constructed four years earlier in the square block immediately west of the Laclède-Chouteau home. After the ceremony, the parishioners voted to erect a permanent church.

At the Laclède-Chouteau house that night, the warmly regarded St. Ange de Bellerive lay dying. On the day after Christmas, he dictated his will to Lieutenant Governor Piernas and witnesses. He made a point of stating that he owed Madame Chouteau for his lodging since August 1, 1773, less the 390 livres he had already paid her. Never having married, he willed that after his bills and other obligations were paid, 500 livres be contributed toward construction of the parish church. He bequeathed his Indian slave woman and her children to his niece, but he wanted the two children liberated when they turned twenty. He named Pierre Laclède his executor, "beseeching him to give this last proof of his friendship, delivering into his hands all the goods belonging to him, to be employed according to the aforesaid will." St. Ange died that very night, December 26.

By that time, the village of St. Louis had grown to include 115 houses stretching along the riverfront on three tiered streets: Rue Royale, Rue de l'Église, and Rue des Granges. There were nine cross streets on each side of the church block. The population stood at 444 whites and 193 slaves. One reason the inhabitants liked to have their homes close to the river was that most of them hauled their water up from the river in barrels. A few of the early settlers attempted to dig wells, but the underlying formation of the town was limestone, which lay just below the surface and prevented easy access to underground water.

On April 19, 1775, when the inhabitants assembled for Easter festival, they approved plans to build a church thirty feet by sixty feet and fourteen feet high, made from hewn posts set in the ground in the French style known as *poteaux en terre*. Of the seventy-eight male householders, thirty-three signed their names to the agreement; the remainder signified their consent with the letter X. The contract was awarded to Pierre Lupien, a carpenter, but he died in the fall, and Jean Cambas finished the church in the summer of 1776. The new parish curate, Father Bernard de Limpach, arrived in May, carrying documents transferring authority for the parish from the Diocese of Quebec to that of Cuba. He presented his credentials to the new lieutenant governor, Francisco Cruzat, plus Laclède and eleven other citizens.

St. Louis continued to be French in every essential way, except for the partial use of Spanish in official documents. French was the language of business, religion, and social life. Some of the governors and officers appointed by the Spanish were of French origin, and the others spoke French. Only by possession was the area Spanish.

Except for Laclède and the Chouteaus, most of the early settlers had come from the French communities on the east side of the Mississippi, having settled there from Canada or directly from France. Several were French military officers who had settled at Cahokia, Kaskaskia, or Fort de Chartres after completing their service. Their places of origin in France ranged from Paris to Cahors in the south, to Orléans and Brittany.

Except for those with access to the library of Pierre Laclède and perhaps a few other educated men, learning was not a high priority in eighteenth-century St. Louis. Throughout the days of Spanish rule, there was only one village schoolmaster, Jean B. Truteau [*sic*], and he also found time to dabble in the fur trade. Fewer than half the men in the settlement were literate.

Despite the reluctance of the populace to farm, the people of St. Louis managed a varied diet that included plenty of fruits and vegetables. Watermelon was native to the Mississippi Valley, and the French fell in love with it. The country around St. Louis produced excellent apples, which were eaten raw, used in pastries, and fermented for cider. The apples also found a ready market in New Orleans. When someone in the upper country wanted to send a special gift to someone in New Orleans, it was common practice to send apples. Bread was the single most important item of the diet. Distilled beverages and French wines and brandies were shipped from New Orleans. Tafia, or rum, came from the Caribbean. Bear oil, from the plump bears in the surrounding forests, was a delicacy used as salad dressing, shortening, and seasoning.

Farming around St. Louis was concentrated in the common fields, or Grand Prairie, outside of town. Each house also had a small kitchen garden for peas, beans, cabbage, beets, carrots, and other vegetables. Early farming produced corn for bread, plus potatoes, turnips, pumpkins, and melons. After a few years, Laclède built a water mill, so the farmers added wheat for bread. The prairie provided an abundance of hay for domestic animals; the inhabitants had beef and milk in addition to poultry, eggs, wild game, and fish.

Even though the Illinois country on the east side of the Mississippi had been the breadbasket of the Louisiana Territory under French rule, little effort was made in St. Louis to produce crops for income. A rare example was the "goodly quantity" of hemp that Laclède shipped to New Orleans for sale in 1775. Native to the region, it grew to a height of eleven feet.

For amusement, there were billiards, cards, and pony races, for which the stakes were kept low. As early as 1767 the village already had two billiards establishments, and a third appeared in 1770, when a man named Louis Vigé went before the royal notary and agreed to lease from Jean Baptiste Vien a billiards table for three years for 600 livres, payable in peltries. Vigé promised to erect a building to house the billiards table.

On November 16, 1771, the village bell ringer went through St. Louis crying out the important news that a case of packs of playing cards had arrived and was to be auctioned immediately. The event quickly attracted nearly everyone in town. Among the eager buyers was the wife of the lieutenant governor and a woman known as La Giroflée, who was the first successful bidder and paid the highest price at the auction for three packs.

There was no racetrack in the early years; for horse races the inhabitants gathered on the Grand Prairie in back of town. The races were no more than a quarter of a mile in length, sometimes just a few hundred yards, because the only horses available around St. Louis were a breed of small Indian ponies, mostly natural pacers. Larger horses did not appear in St. Louis until after Americans took possession of the east side of the Mississippi, in 1778.

For a good many years after the founding of St. Louis, the only wheeled vehicles available were primitive carts made of two pieces of wood ten to twelve feet long, held together by two or more crosspieces, on the back of which a wicker body was placed; the front ends of the boards were rounded to serve as the shafts. The whole thing was placed on the axletree of the wheels. Laclède had transported his family up from Fort de Chartres in such a cart in 1764. The main use of these carts was to bring corn and hay from the Grand Prairie to the barns in back of the village. And the men sometimes used them to take their wives and children out for a bumpy pleasure ride.

Dress in St. Louis and the other settlements of French America combined a taste for bright colors, especially blue and red, with loose, comfortable attire for working days and fitted elegance for dress-up occasions. For work outside in the winter, the men usually wore knee-length belted and hooded outer garments of coarse wool, plus buckskin leggings and stocking caps. Underneath, there was probably a checkered shirt, which they wore with pantaloons in warmer weather, plus a handkerchief over their heads. Fewer details have survived of women's dress, but the women are believed to have covered their heads with caps or hats and made their dresses from the wide variety of fabrics regularly shipped upriver from New Orleans, including gingham, silk, linen, taffeta, and plain cotton.

Laclède's wardrobe included some coats and breeches of drill cloth and linen, which may have been his workday attire. He also had at least two dozen fine white linen shirts, ten dimity collars, waistcoats of white satin and blue silk trimmed with gold and silver braid, breeches of black satin, two pairs of red-striped breeches, and several pairs of silk stockings.

As in the case of the card auction, almost everyone turned out for nearly every occurrence in the early years. Even though there were obviously people considered to be of higher standing than others, it was the custom for everybody to participate on an equal basis in the joyful happenings of early St. Louis. Pierre Chouteau would later recall these years as one of the things that made his childhood and youth so happy.

Although Pierre remembered it as a time when people treated each other as equals, there was a major exception: the slaves, both African and Indian. The future state of Missouri was never a place where large numbers of slaves were put to work on plantations, but Laclède and the Chouteaus believed human bondage to be a normal state of affairs. Although considered personal property, slaves were recognized under French law as individuals with identities and souls to be saved. Slaves of Laclède and the Chouteaus figure by first name throughout their correspondence, often with reference to their work habits, their particular skills, and their family situations.

The first African slaves were introduced into the future states of Illinois and Missouri in 1719–20. Jesuit priests are believed to have brought sixteen to eighteen slaves from Lower Louisiana to the east side of the Mississippi in the area between Cahokia and Kaskaskia to work in agriculture. On the west side of the river, the earliest slaves were brought from Haiti by a Frenchman named Philip François Renault to work in the lead mines near what became Ste. Genevieve.

In 1724 Louis XV issued what was known as the Black Code — governing slaveholders' rights to their property in French Louisiana; protecting whites from slave conspiracy, rebellion, and insurrection; and requiring that all slaves be instructed and baptized into Catholicism. The Code, based on one promulgated by the Bourbon monarchy in 1685 for the West Indies, included requirements that masters properly house, clothe, and feed their slaves, that slave children not be sold away from parents until puberty, and that slaves not be worked before sunrise or after sunset. Masters could whip and bind their slaves, but the slaves could not be imprisoned, mutilated, or put to death without due process. Slave women were not to be sexually exploited, and interracial marriage was prohibited, but the number of mulatto slaves listed on bills of sale of the era suggests that this part of the Code was often ignored. The same regulations continued under Spanish rule, except that Spanish law did not forbid interracial marriage.

The French and Spanish had a broader definition of who might be enslaved than that which applied in the English colonies to the east. It included Indians as well as blacks, although the actual number of Indian slaves seems to have been relatively few. In at least some cases the enslavement of particular Indians came about when they were captured by another tribe in warfare and sold to whites. As noted in the will of St. Ange de Bellerive and the deed passing the house from Laclède to Madame Chouteau and the children, they were among those in St. Louis whose slaves included Indians. In 1769, however, Governor O'Reilly changed the policy when he declared that throughout Louisiana Territory all Indian slaves were henceforth free at the deaths of their masters, and all of their children were born free from the date of the publication of the emancipating ordinance.

✳

Laclède's natural tendency to be generous and paternal eventually placed him under the mounting pressure of trying to be too many things for too many people. He sustained a debt burden that could have been managed only by a more hardheaded, focused business-man, someone more inclined to say no than yes. In addition to his debts to Maxent, he was borrowing from at least four men in St. Louis in order to have operating capital for the fur trade. Also, the trading house had accumulated a lot of worthless or doubtful debt paper because of Laclède's leniency in extending credit or loans. His trips to New Orleans became more frequent as he attempted to arrange his affairs with Maxent, with whom he had fallen into arrears. Known as a man of trust, Laclède was also handling business interests in New Orleans of several other men from St. Louis.

He spent the winters of both 1776–77 and 1777–78 in New Orleans. Soon after he arrived on the second visit, in December of 1777, he dealt with the question of his arrears with Maxent, to whom he had apparently been unable to make all of the payments that were to have begun in 1771. To cover the accumulated debt, Laclède executed a deed of relinquishment to Maxent for the square of land and buildings in St. Louis where he had his trading house.

Finally, with the kind of premonition about his own mortality that people must have sensed more keenly before medical science could supply more precise evidence, Laclède took up his pen on December 31, 1777, and wrote a letter of instructions to his trusted stepson, Auguste Chouteau, who had been away from St. Louis when Laclède left. If Auguste got back to St. Louis ahead of Laclède, he was to "look over the accounts and make out bills for those that are due us and collect them." He said he had left the account book with "Madame your mother."

"I have also left with her the notes that many persons have given me in payment for merchandise from this same stock—so that, monsieur, it is in these bills and in the current accounts that lie today the funds which I have placed in reserve from what I have collected, and which I have joined to the fur trade and armament of ships which I have in partnership with you and Labaddie."

Then he told Auguste what to do in the event he should die before returning home. He tried to separate, in his explanation to Auguste, the old debt he had to Maxent from the more recent debts he had for operating capital, which had to be paid first.

"If, by the will of God, I die on this voyage, will you have the good will and the kindness to render me this service: After having collected all of the accounts in question due to our stock and armament, I pray you to pay out of my personal funds twelve hundred *piastres* to M. Thiery Desnoyer of St. Louis, which I owe him on my note with which I began to work last year." With profits and money left, he also directed payments to others, saying, "that which I have in the business for the last year comes from borrowing, and without which I should be today without any means of earning my living . . .

"This frank confession which I make of the situation in which I find myself in respect to persons to whom I am in debt will, I hope, convince these gentlemen that I have been faithful not to divert anything from the trade."

Nothing of what he had obtained from Maxent was in the stock and armament for the fur trade and boats, Laclède said, so he hoped that his former partner would "be just and fair, and not oppose the execution of what I recommend that you do . . . His uprightness, which I know to be clean and pure, permits me to hope that he will accept the recommendations I make to you."

He ended the letter with an eloquent admission of his difficulties.

"Goodbye, my dear sir, I desire to see you again, and to be able myself to settle my affairs, because it is very hard and painful, as I see, to have to die in debt. One bequeaths nothing but pain and trouble to friends when one dies poor.

"Such is my deplorable situation. One must suffer and not murmur."

What the French called Poste aux Arkansas was situated a few miles up the Arkansas River from its mouth at the Mississippi. It was the first establishment founded by whites in the Lower Mississippi Valley, dating from the arrival of part of La Salle's ill-fated Texas colony in 1686, and it had been operated continuously since then.

In 1778 the post consisted of a simple fort on the north bank of the Arkansas River about 200 yards from the water, with maybe ten run-down houses clustered nearby. The stockaded, quadrangular fort had exterior sides of about 180 feet, with one three-pounder cannon mounted in the flanks and faces of each bastion. Within the fort were a barracks, a commander's house, a powder magazine, and other facilities for the garrison, which consisted of a captain, a lieutenant, and about thirty soldiers. All the structures were in a dilapidated condition, barely habitable. The land had been cleared back to about 900 yards from the river, but the sandy soil did not allow the settlers to raise enough food for the fort and themselves. They lived by hunting and did not expect "anything beyond the mere necessaries of life, except whiskey," as one visitor observed.

There was one other thing in the area of the post: a branch warehouse owned by Pierre Laclède, who stopped there on his voyages up and down the Mississippi between St. Louis and New Orleans. Laclède was headed there on May 27, 1778.

As his barge ascended the river, the cordellers groaned under the weight of the huge inventory of merchandise he had acquired in New Orleans. The barge carried nearly a ton of sugar, 42 sacks of bullets, 52 cases of liquor, 332 blankets, 1,325 pounds of powder, 100 pounds of salt, 781 pounds of coffee, 60 tomahawks, 84 little mirrors, 1,000 rifle flints, two baskets of olive oil, two rounds of cheese weighing 117 pounds, two barrels of Malaga wine, and an endless list of fabrics, clothing, and household utensils. Tucked away in Laclède's personal trunk were a twelve-volume history of the Roman emperors, two flacons of mustard, three packets of ink in powder, and two pounds of chocolate. The vast array of goods, acquired during the winter he had spent in New Orleans, constituted his means of doing business, plus a few things to make life more pleasant, perhaps some of them intended as gifts for Madame Chouteau and the family.

Two leagues before reaching the post, however, Laclède died. No record has survived of the cause of his death, if anyone knew, or the way his last days were spent on the slow-moving vessel. Perhaps the cause was cancer, then hardly a word in anyone's vocabulary. Or heart disease. Or perhaps the mysterious "fever" that claimed so many lives in those days. He was forty-nine years old and probably feeling unwell five months earlier when he wrote his deeply apologetic letter to Auguste Chouteau with instructions on settling business affairs in the event of his death.

The boat continued to the Poste aux Arkansas, where the skipper, Tropé Ricard, went ashore and summoned the commander, Balthazar de Villiers. In accord with Spanish procedures, Villiers made an inventory of everything belonging to Laclède and put it under seal, and he and Ricard signed a statement about Laclède's death.

Then, choosing a spot along the bank, close by the lapping waters of the Arkansas River, they buried Pierre Laclède Liguest.

FIVE

Auguste and Pierre,
Greatly Loved and Greatly Feared

✳

Nearly two months after Pierre Laclède was buried, the boat laden with the last merchandise he had purchased completed its journey to St. Louis. At 9 a.m. on July 19, 1778, Tropé Ricard appeared before Fernando de Leyba, Spanish lieutenant governor, and turned over to him Laclède's locked trunk, covered by a band of white paper sealed at each end with red wax. Leyba took it to the home of Madame Chouteau, to whom word of Laclède's death had undoubtedly found its way in advance of the slow-moving boat.

Auguste Chouteau was summoned, and he led the way to "the room where Monsieur Laclède was lodged . . . before his departure," where the trunk was left, to be opened later when an inventory was taken of all of Laclède's possessions. Leyba placed his seal on the windows and doors with an imprint of red wax on each end of a band of white paper and then left everything in Auguste's care.

Six days later, Leyba, Auguste, and two witnesses met again; Auguste presented the cargo, and they compared it to the invoices. Everything was in order. On July 29 Leyba concluded that Laclède had died *ab intesta*, "moreover not having in this said post any relative or heirs who may pretend to have a right to his succession and nobody presenting himself in order to see to the surety of the rights and interests of the creditors of the said Laclède."

"This is why, before coming to make the removal of our said seals and to proceed to the inventory of his goods movable and immovable, titles, papers and instructions, we have judged it convenient to name as *syndic* to this succession three persons capable and knowing the affairs who will present themselves in order to regulate in consequence," Leyba said. Jean Baptiste Sarpy, a merchant whose family would subsequently intermarry with the Chouteaus, was named syndic, and Martin Duralde and Joseph Pereault were named his adjuncts with instructions to handle Laclède's estate "as they would do for their own interests."

On August 1 Leyba and the syndics went to the house of Madame Chouteau and summoned Auguste, who again led the way to Laclède's room. Aided by three men called to estimate the value of items, they went through Laclède's personal possessions one by one. The list began with four pairs of new shoes, which were estimated to be worth twenty-four livres in pelts or forty-eight livres in money. The list continued with breeches plain and fancy, linen shirts, dimity collars, silk stockings, waistcoats of linen and satin, braided and plain, a pair of silver buckles, and an old copper watch out of order and without hands. All of the articles were assigned a value in both pelts and money.

After a midday break, they returned to work, placing valuations on four geography maps, a curling iron, copper kettles, reams of writing paper, a three-volume dictionary of commerce, a dictionary of the arts in two volumes, and a language dictionary of the French Academy. Among his other books were practical volumes on commerce, engineering, experimental physics, fruit-tree cultivation, and geometry, but also poetry, theater criticism, horses, Locke's essays, Descartes' philosophy, and four volumes of *The Spectator*. In all, there were 215 books, most in French, but at least 24 in Spanish, and others in Italian and English. There were two bedsteads, one mattress, one straw sack, three barrels of glass beads, and an old hood of a fine military blanket. Together, these personal items were valued at 2,954 livres.

In a locked cupboard they found "papers relating to the succession of Mr. Laclède" and a ledger of the management of Maxent, Laclède & Company from November 11, 1763, to August 4, 1777. There were numerous other business documents and records, including a bundle of receipts and invoices for sales of slaves acquired from various people. The inventory continued for pages and pages.

Of particular note was "a sword with a silver hilt carrying the arms of the king and of the town of Toulouse" with an accompanying certificate dated June 30, 1748, affirming that it was "one of the swords of the prize won by the said Sieur Laclède which sword is furnished with a belt with buckles and ring of silver of which sword no estimation is carried in the uncertainty of knowing whether it ought to be turned over to his family and which will be sent to Monsieur the Governor for him to make disposition of."

Between September 2 and September 6, the personal effects, including horses and cattle, were sold at auction conducted at the house, with the purchase prices to be paid "in skins of roebucks or beavers" by the following May. Auguste Chouteau bought most of the clothing and many books. Fifteen other people also acquired books from Laclède's library.

On October 12 Leyba issued an advisory to all the people of the St. Louis area saying that the quantity of oxen, cows, and horses that Laclède had owned was believed to be considerably greater than the number that had appeared for auction. Thus he requested that people bring in any animals bearing Laclède's brand so that they could be sold. Anyone bringing in an animal would receive one-fifth the sale price.

That winter, Auguste went to New Orleans to adjust the firm's accounts with creditors. He had to borrow some money to get through short-term problems, but the fur trade had not yet encountered the setbacks that would shortly come from the American Revolution, so he was able to repay the money the following year and continue in business. In New Orleans that winter, Auguste delivered to Maxent an assortment of skins and bills of exchange with a combined value of 41,806 livres—considerably more than the 21,360 livres owed to Maxent for the supplies Laclède bought before his death.

On June 20, 1779, Leyba called a public auction to sell Laclède's farm and his mill. He described the farm as "situated on what is known as the Grand Prairie, containing one hundred arpents in width by eighty arpents in length, on which land there is a log house, covered with shingles, measuring about 80 feet in length, divided into several low rooms also some negro cabins, barns, orchard, garden, yard and whatever is now upon it at the present time, all situated about one mile from this post." The property was to be sold for deerskins or beaver skins at the prices prevalent in June 1780. Madame Chouteau bought the house and land for 2,750 livres, and the mill went to Auguste for 2,000 livres.

An expedition was sent that year to try to recover Laclède's body, but the burial site could not be located. The river, which forced the relocation of Arkansas Post several times in the post's history, had already eaten into its banks and claimed his remains. Thus the founder of St. Louis would never be laid to rest among his descendants and fellow adventurers in the little churchyard in St. Louis.

In the early summer of 1780 Auguste returned once more to New Orleans. He presented to Maxent a memorandum listing 27,891 livres in notes of various parties that were unrecoverable, 7,527 that might be collected, and a few other small notes. This made a total of 38,523 livres in outstanding notes. He delivered to Maxent the payments for the sale of the mill and farm, and Maxent took title to the lot and buildings in St. Louis, as Laclède had arranged the winter before his death, all of that apparently going against the debt Laclède owed Maxent for the start-up capital in 1763. With that, Maxent signed a release freeing Auguste from any further responsibility in Laclède's debts.

When Laclède died, Auguste was twenty-eight and Pierre was twenty. Their brother-in-law, Sylvestre Labbadie, was forty-one. The brothers, as if Laclède had prepared them for this moment, quickly and naturally assumed positions of leadership in St. Louis. Above all, they could count on their unmatched knowledge of the Indians in the area, especially the Osages, to assure them a central place in business and civic life, even as events were transpiring to put St. Louis on a larger stage.

Less than two months after Laclède's death, as war raged between England and the rebellious colonies in the East, George Rogers Clark and his band of 175 Virginians swept down the Ohio River and conquered British Illinois. Leaving the river near abandoned Fort Massac, upriver from today's Paducah, Kentucky, they marched overland to

Kaskaskia and took the town on July 4, 1778. Later they occupied Vincennes as well and claimed all the British country on the east side of the Mississippi for the state of Virginia. This was the beginning of a series of events that would draw the Upper Louisiana country and the Chouteaus into the world of the young republic claiming its independence. They would share its growing pains and, through the decisions of France and Spain to aid the struggling American colonies, its conflict with England.

One of the first things George Rogers Clark (William's older brother) and his top aides did was to visit St. Louis and get to know Leyba and some of the town's influential citizens—and do business with them. They bought goods for their men, including 150 pairs of shoes. Two surviving receipts, both dated November 19, 1778, were signed by Auguste Chouteau, one in the amount of $431 and the other $1,680 in exchange for notes or letters of credit drawn on Oliver Pollock in New Orleans for "sundries furnished to the state of Virginia." Other merchants on both sides of the Mississippi, including Gabriel Cerré at Kaskaskia, Auguste Chouteau's future father-in-law, did the same thing, to the extent of many thousands of dollars. This was a lot for the time, especially considering that neither the state that Clark represented nor the Continental Congress had currency backed by anything of value.

As George Rogers Clark traveled around both sides of the Mississippi winning friends and running up debts, one of the men from whom he found both easy friendship and support was Charles Gratiot, a young merchant in Cahokia, like Clark twenty-six years old. Gratiot's warm reception helped to confirm Clark's assumption that the French on the east side of the Mississippi, then chafing under British rule, could easily be won over to the American cause. Fluent in both French and English, Gratiot was of immense help to Clark. Gratiot's affability and communication skills would also make him a key player in some of the most important aspects of the lives of the Chouteau brothers, whose brother-in-law he would become a few years later.

Born in Switzerland in 1752 of French Protestant parents, Gratiot was sent to London at a young age to work for a maternal uncle, moving on, at age seventeen, to another uncle in Montreal. Quick-witted and ambitious, he spent five years as a clerk learning the fur trade, then headed a trading mission for his uncle to the Canadian upper country in 1774. The next year, he and a partner went into the fur trade on their own behalf, wintering among Indians in 1775–76.

In August 1777, after forming a trading connection with two Scotsmen and another Swiss, he headed for the Illinois country. Following rivers and lakes by then well used in the fur trade, his canoe carried him from Montreal up the St. Lawrence, through the Great Lakes and the Straits of Mackinac, down Green Bay to the Fox River, then by the Wisconsin River to Prairie du Chien and the Mississippi, which carried him to Cahokia, opposite St. Louis. He arrived in November and opened his store early in December. Later he opened a second trading station on the Illinois River at the eventual site of Peoria.

Despite his penchant for adventure and thirst for success, Gratiot wrote long letters to his parents in Switzerland revealing homesickness. He went into detail with them about his business affairs and the difficulties of doing business on the frontier. "I may hope, dear Father, that the period is not distant when I can fall into the arms of yourself and my dear family and prove to you my gratitude," he wrote in 1778. Having grown up an only child, he was overjoyed when they wrote him in 1779 that they had had another child, a daughter, Isabella, who was more than twenty-five years younger than he. Charles Gratiot would go home again in time to see his mother yet alive and to become acquainted with his sister, but his last sight of his father would be that of his adolescence.

In addition to providing supplies to George Rogers Clark, Gratiot became an active and vocal partisan of the cause of the Virginians and the young nation to the east, extending credit well beyond what other merchants did. In letters to Clark, Gratiot complained various times about people in the area not rallying to support the rebels.

"I cannot help regretting the Time and trouble I have lost in trying to serve a People so Destitute of Patriotic Sentiments, who are totally gided by a vile Particular Interest never doing any thing for or even caring about the General Benefit of a Country," he wrote to Clark, who was then "at the Mouth of Ohio." Expressing his own appreciation to Clark, Gratiot said he was sorry that because of "extreme scarcity," he was unable to send him a little tafia, and he signed himself "Your very obedient and humble servant and affectionate friend."

The situation along the Upper Mississippi was complicated by circumstances beyond the control of anybody in the area. France had been trying to convince Spain to formally join in a war against Britain in support of the American colonies. Instead, Spain dallied and hoped to use the threat of its war declaration to get England to cede control of Gibraltar. In January 1778, France, on its own, offered an "alliance" to the Americans. To head off congressional ratification of the alliance, England offered a conciliation package, which the Continental Congress rejected, demanding instead that the British withdraw in full and recognize American independence. The war continued, and France joined the effort. When Clark marched into the Illinois country in mid-1778, England responded by extending its attacks against the southern colonies.

After Spain finally declared war, in June 1779, the English at Michilimackinac and Detroit made preparations to drive the Spanish from Upper Louisiana and reconquer eastern Illinois from Clark. In early 1780, rumors reached St. Louis of the planned British attack. Lieutenant Governor Leyba ordered hurried construction of defenses and had a road built to Ste. Genevieve, sixty miles to the south, so militiamen there could come to the aid of St. Louis.

Convinced that the presence of Clark and his men across the river would help to relieve British pressure on St. Louis, Leyba embraced their cause. At one point he agreed to provide Clark with a hundred men and equip them with boats, arms, artillery, ammunition, and provisions, although no record could be located of that actually occurring. But when Spanish government funds for assisting the Virginians ran out, Leyba used his own money to continue helping them, and Clark maintained at least one representative in St. Louis during 1779 and 1780.

On May 26 English troops and hundreds of Indian allies attacked St. Louis, by which time only one of four projected towers had been built. Two trenches at either end of the town provided some defense

help. Many of the women and children took refuge in Laclède's former trading headquarters, now the lieutenant governor's residence.
Leyba had only 29 regular soldiers and 281 militiamen to defend the
town. Spanish artillery, however, frightened many Indians into fleeing,
and the attack was over in a few hours. Before withdrawing, the invading force got through to the common fields and killed several people
who were at work. Estimates of the total death toll in St. Louis varied
from 20 to 60, with 25 taken prisoner. The British attack on eastern
Illinois ultimately failed as well, and the force went back upriver.

Rumors of other impending British attacks surfaced several times
over the next couple of years, and each time the settlement would
rush to prepare its defenses. On one occasion, Francisco Cruzat, who
became lieutenant governor once again after Leyba's death, in June
1780, directed Auguste Chouteau to plot out the lines for a stockade
of posts to surround all the houses in the village and to erect a few
stone towers at suitable points on the line. Auguste, who had never
seen a fortified town except his native New Orleans, drew up a plan
for St. Louis with bastions, towers, *demilunes*, palisades, sally ports, es-
carpments, and counterscarps. People were put to work to execute the
plan. The palisades were planted and two or three towers built, but
when the alarm had passed, the fortifications work was abandoned.

No matter how much he shared the goals of George Rogers Clark and
the Americans, Charles Gratiot in Cahokia found that doing business
for profit during the American Revolution was difficult. "As to our paper currency it won't buy a cat at *Paincourt*," he commented to a
friend, referring to St. Louis by its French nickname. The new American government was in desperate financial straits. At the beginning of
1779 it issued $200 million in paper money—"Continentals"—which
devalued so quickly that it was withdrawn as worthless at the end of
1780.

Having sent some bills of exchange down to New Orleans with
Auguste Chouteau, Gratiot reported that Auguste had returned "with
drinkables, coffee and sugar," but no useful goods that could be used
to trade to the Indians for peltries. New Orleans merchants did not
want to accept currency or any kind of debt paper. Gratiot, like the

Chouteaus, needed goods more than cash to be able to remain in business. Traders had to continually juggle to succeed in the Indian trade—goods for peltries, peltries for more goods, perhaps throwing off a little hard currency on the side; then goods for peltries, and peltries for goods in a perpetual cycle. In any business deal, peltries were more desirable than currency because they enabled the trader to continue in business.

Instead of goods or peltries, however, Gratiot found himself with $6,000 or $7,000 in cash, and more cash was expected. He was "almost determined" to start for the East

> with all the American money which I have on hand, and expect shortly to receive, and which I cannot convert into peltries, as I had hoped—seeing that all the Bills of Exchange that Col. Clark has drawn on New Orleans have not been paid—all the vessels that the State of Virginia sent to said City were captured by Six or Seven English Frigates at Pensacola, which cruise constantly at the entrance to the river—which make us apprehensive that we shall obtain no advantages for this part of the country until that place is taken.

Even after Cornwallis's surrender at Yorktown in February 1782, followed by the change of government in England and the opening of peace negotiations with the former colonies, life along the Mississippi did not return to Creole tranquillity. Tensions arose between Spain and the new American government, largely over navigation rights on the river. In the areas where both banks of the river belonged to the Spanish, the waterway was entirely closed to Americans.

Some Americans in Kentucky and other places on the western edge of United States territory feared that their government would soon abandon claims to navigation rights. Led by General James Wilkinson, who had been a high-ranking army officer during the Revolution, they began secretly talking with Spain about an alliance. They thought their economic self-interest lay with Spain, not the United States. Some even advanced the idea of detaching some of the then-western United States, on the east side of the Mississippi, as a separate nation or as part of a new trans-Mississippi empire connected to Spain. In addition to the right to send their commerce through

New Orleans, these westerners wanted the right to freely trade with the Spanish side of the Mississippi River. Wilkinson himself at one point swore allegiance to Spain and received an annual retainer for a number of years. This issue was destined to emerge again over the next two decades, arousing great passion in the Upper and Lower Louisiana territories as well as Washington.

In the summer of 1781 Charles Gratiot moved to St. Louis and married seventeen-year-old Victoire Chouteau, youngest daughter of Madame Chouteau and Pierre Laclède. When he closed his business at Cahokia and Kaskaskia, his claims against the state of Virginia for supplies and other items furnished to George Rogers Clark and his successors totaled $8,000 to $9,000. After an attempt at collection through an agent failed, Gratiot decided in the spring of 1783 to go to Virginia in person. Leaving Victoire with their newborn daughter, he set out on horseback and traveled 1,500 miles through the "almost trackless wilds" of Illinois, Kentucky, and West Virginia, arriving safely at Richmond, the new capital of Virginia. Just as George Rogers Clark was probably the first person from the United States to travel to St. Louis, Gratiot was probably the first person from St. Louis to travel into the heart of the American nation.

Gratiot was gone more than a year, and during that time he made the acquaintance of Patrick Henry, Thomas Jefferson, and other Virginia notables. But he returned empty-handed to St. Louis in June 1784. Most of his claims had been passed from one individual or official to another in Virginia, each endorsing the claim but unable to pay. The most promising thing he obtained in Richmond was a commitment to give him lands in Kentucky as soon as land offices were established there and lands surveyed. He was eventually "saddled with a quantity of Land Warrants of the government of Virginia," including about thirty thousand acres somewhere on the Green River in Kentucky, for which he sought to establish title and sell during many years, apparently without success.

Of the five Chouteau siblings, only the eldest girl, Pélagie, married before the death of Pierre Laclède. In July 1776, at sixteen, she married Sylvestre Labbadie, who came to St. Louis from France in 1769.

Labbadie was born in Tarbes in the province of Béarn, just a few miles from the birthplace of Laclède, which suggests that other young men felt encouraged to follow Laclède to the New World in search of their fortunes. Labbadie's brothers included a lawyer, a doctor, and a priest. By 1773 he was affiliated with Joseph M. Papin, another future Chouteau spouse, in the fur trade out of St. Louis, and by 1777, as Laclède noted in his letter of instructions for his death, Labbadie was associated with his father-in-law and Auguste Chouteau in the fur trade.

Joseph Papin and the middle Chouteau sister, Marie Louise, were married on January 9, 1779. Papin was born in Montreal in 1741 to a family that had been in Canada more than a century. His mother died when he was quite young, and his father took him to France to be educated at a Jesuit school in Anjou. His father then returned to Canada, where he was governor of the Royal Arsenal at Fort Frontenac, but after all of Canada became British territory, the elder Papin returned to France and, with his son, eventually moved to St. Louis.

Typically for the time and place, the Chouteau girls were just sixteen and seventeen years old when they married, a reflection of the extreme shortage of marriageable women. In fact, some girls were wed at fifteen or even fourteen, with their parents' signed consent. St. Louis and nearby communities attracted many unmarried men in search of adventure and fortune, but young women generally settled there only as part of their parents' household, and in smaller numbers. In addition, childbirth claimed the lives of far more women in their young years than the toll exacted among men by the uncertainties of life in Indian villages and out in the wilderness. After losing a first wife to childbirth, men typically sought a second wife. As a result, women were considered ready for marriage as soon as they reached physical maturity, and it was not unusual for them to marry men twice their age, or more.

Auguste and Pierre Chouteau were both believed to have had wives from the Osage tribe before they contracted marriage with women of French descent under the strictures of the Roman Catholic Church. In 1767 or 1768, when he was seventeen or eighteen, Auguste fathered a half-Osage son who was christened Antoine Chouteau. It is not known whether Antoine grew up entirely with his mother's tribe or spent time in St. Louis as well. However, it is apparent that Antoine shared his father's life to at least some extent, because Auguste helped him to become established in the fur trade.

In 1792 Antoine Chouteau was listed among those receiving licenses from the current lieutenant governor, Zenon Trudeau, to trade with Indians. On a list of seventeen men that also included Auguste and Pierre, Antoine Chouteau was identified as a mestizo, meaning of mixed Indian and European blood, the only man on the list not identified as French. He had five people working for him.

Antoine died in New Orleans at about twenty-eight and was buried there on November 4, 1796, in the cemetery of St. Louis Cathedral. The Spanish Capuchin priest who heard his last confession and signed the death records stated that Antoine was from the "Illinois country," was the son of Auguste Chouteau, and was married to Helene Angelica Docteur. Among the reasons Antoine may have been in New Orleans when he died were business dealings or an attempt to secure medical treatment. The fact that Antoine traveled to New Orleans seems further indication that Auguste had sought to incorporate his half-Indian son into white society. The fact that Antoine was married to a woman with a French name, suggesting that she was either white or half white, further substantiates that theory.

The evidence of Pierre's ties to Indian women is less conclusive, but historians of the Osages and the fur trade generally accept as accurate the oral history of the tribe, which holds that he had at least one Osage wife. Indeed, this was a major reason for the tribe's deep trust in him. Some historians have claimed that Pierre was the father of Paul Loise, who was born in 1775 when Pierre was seventeen and living among the Osages. Loise lived until 1832 and worked throughout his life as an Osage interpreter in prominent circumstances, usually figuring on Pierre's payroll. He accompanied one Osage delegation to Washington, served as William Clark's interpreter for an Osage treaty in 1808, and accompanied an Osage delegation on a French tour in 1827–29. Although orally trilingual, he was illiterate, and he witnessed Indian treaties with an X.

Still, the records on Paul Loise are highly contradictory. The Oklahoma historian Grant Foreman uncovered an 1897 opinion by the commissioner of Indian affairs stating that Paul Loise was entirely French, the son of a Frenchman named Alexis Loise, who probably came to Fort de Chartres from France, then moved to St. Louis and married a Frenchwoman. However, a number of contemporaries of Paul Loise described him as the son of a French father and Indian mother. He was also designated a headman of the Little Osages, apparently at the request of an official in Washington, which is unlikely to have been accepted by the tribe unless he carried some Osage blood.

Adding to the confusion about Loise is the fact that he was sometimes known as Paul Chouteau or "young Chouteau," even among government officials, who apparently assumed him to be Pierre's mixed-blood son. Early St. Louis baptismal records also reveal that a "Paul Chouteau" fathered a child by an Osage woman, baptized September 5, 1803, and was also a godparent at another baptism about the same time. One possible explanation for these disparate facts is that Paul Loise may not, in fact, have been a son of Pierre Chouteau, but may have been unofficially adopted into Pierre's household because of the death of one or both parents. There are numerous known cases of various of the Chouteaus taking the children of relatives or Indian friends into their homes in times of need, without great concern for how their actions might look for posterity.

Marriage practices of French America, even after the area passed to Spanish control, were determined by the *Coutume de Paris*, the traditional matrimonial property law of north central France. Under it, family wealth was passed down more in accord with the marriage contract than with the will. In the marriage contract, it was understood that the couple would pool its wealth in an "economic community," and on the death of one of them, the community of wealth would be divided, with half going to the surviving spouse and the other half divided among all the children of the marriage. There was a prohibition on inheritance by children born outside the marriage, which provided added reason for Auguste and Pierre to marry under the auspices of the church and Spanish civil law, even if they maintained Indian marriages at the same time.

On July 26, 1783, at age twenty-four, Pierre Chouteau married sixteen-year-old Pélagie Kiersereau. Her parents were among the first settlers of St. Louis, but their deaths at an early age left her to be reared by her grandfather, Joseph Tayon, whose construction knowledge and skills created a modest fortune, which went to her. Pierre had a house built on a lot given him by Madame Chouteau—a story-and-a-half house with a portico across the front—and he and Pélagie began a family. They had three sons, Auguste Pierre, Pierre Jr., and Paul Liguest, and a daughter, Pélagie, before the elder Pélagie died on February 9, 1793, a month short of her twenty-sixth birthday.

Auguste was nearly thirty-six when he was married, on September 21, 1786, to Thérèse Cerré, sixteen-year-old daughter of Gabriel Cerré, a leading merchant in Kaskaskia, and his wife, Catherine Giard. Their second-day wedding attire, which has survived, provides an impressive example of the care taken for fine dress among the most affluent families in that remote outpost of French culture. Auguste wore an embroidered vest and pale green satin cutaway, with a wide collar and sleeves trimmed in beige lace. Thérèse wore a pink-and-green-striped taffeta dress, with ruffles trimming the sleeves and bodice and a scalloped hemline on the skirt.

About two years after his marriage, Auguste purchased from Antoine de Maxent, Pierre Laclède's former partner, the dilapidated house that had served as Laclède's business headquarters and had passed to Maxent to cover part of Laclède's debts. Laclède had shared the structure with a succession of Spanish lieutenant governors, and they continued to rent it until 1783, when a four-room stone house diagonally across the street was acquired to serve as residence and office for the governors.

Auguste bought the property for $3,000 in cash on January 6, 1789. The deed of sale described it as "a piece of ground 300 feet square, unenclosed, with a stone house 60 by 23 feet, falling to ruins, the roof rotten; another stone house, 50 by 30 feet, no floors, also in ruins, and another small house." After he and Thérèse had their first children, Auguste had the Laclède house remodeled and expanded, and they moved out of his mother's house and into it. Within a few years it grew into the grandest mansion in St. Louis.

The young Chouteaus began their married lives and families at a time when the end of the American Revolution had forced the fur traders into difficult circumstances. England reacted to Spain's support of the American cause by aggressively asserting itself in the fur trade out of Canada. With only small numbers of troops, Spain lacked the ability to defend her frontier fur posts from British encroachment. However, Governor Esteban Miró at New Orleans and Lieutenant Governor Cruzat in St. Louis had two potential aces to play. One was to calm the Osage Indians and get them to hunt and trade more. The other potential high card was the rich but almost unexploited fur country of the Upper Missouri River.

Increasing the trade volume with the Osages required nudging them into a more peaceful state of mind toward whites, as well as toward other Indian tribes. The Osages were passing through a period of particular hostility toward whites, exacerbated by the fact that after 1786, the American government began the policy in its own territory of buying title to Indian lands and slowly driving the eastern tribes toward the Mississippi. As those Indians fell back, some wanted to hunt or live permanently on the Spanish side of the river. The arrival of these immigrant tribes—the beginning of a saga that would continue for nearly a century—deeply angered the Osages, even beyond the point of their usual volatility.

Spanish authorities and the Chouteau brothers tried over the next decade and a half to help the Osages through this difficult time, while also limiting the tribe's acts of violence against whites and other tribes. But there was no obvious way in which this might be achieved. Often there was disagreement among Spanish authorities over how to proceed, especially between the lieutenant governor, who had his headquarters in St. Louis, and the governor, who was at New Orleans.

In April 1787, after some Osages murdered a hunting party of two white men and a Natchitoches woman and her daughter about sixty leagues from Arkansas Post, Governor Miró was so furious that he declared the Osages to be enemies and prohibited all trade with them under penalty of death. Lieutenant Governor Cruzat opposed the action because he feared that the Osages would go over to the British, who were penetrating Spanish-claimed lands north of the Missouri River. He thought it preferable to resume trade with them and try to use the trade as a means of controlling their behavior.

By the fall of 1787 the Osages were complaining bitterly about the denial of trade and threatening to kill or take hostage any and all Spanish subjects. An Osage delegation traveled to St. Louis and pleaded with Cruzat, trying to explain that the tribe had some braves who simply would not obey the leaders. Cruzat demanded that they turn over the murderers. This was in conformity with the long-standing Spanish policy of forcing tribes to turn over for prosecution any Indians guilty of killing or robbing. In the case of those guilty of killings, the tribes could choose to execute the guilty themselves. In practice, Spain had never executed an Indian in its North American territory. In fact, very few white settlers were killed by Indians during the entire Spanish era, but even isolated killings produced great concern among the authorities.

At that time the Little Osages and the main group of the Big Osages were still clustered fairly close together on the Upper Osage River at the western edge of the present state of Missouri. As a wandering tribe, however, the Osages were capable of showing up unexpectedly at locations hundreds of miles in any direction from their villages. They were almost continually at war with other tribes, including the Comanches on their west, the Caddos and other Texas tribes to the south of their hunting lands, and the Sacs and Foxes to the northeast.

Two things were occurring around this time to further fragment the tribe. A group known as Les Cheniers, whose leader was called Le Chenier,* had for years spent considerable time on the Arkansas River far upstream from Arkansas Post, ranging northwest into present-day Oklahoma and perhaps along the river as it crosses Kansas as well. This rebel group often refused to obey leaders of the main tribe and was a particular source of anguish for Spanish authorities. One of the things the Cheniers wanted, for instance, was the right to trade their

---

*From *chêne*, or oak, in French.

skins and furs at Arkansas Post instead of having to deal with traders sent to the main Osage villages on the Osage River.

In addition, a schism was developing within the main branch of the Big Osages still in Missouri, with two main contenders for leadership. Clermont, the hereditary chief, was a shy and retiring man whose powers were being usurped by a relative known as Cheveux Blancs, or White Hair—Pawhuska in the Osage tongue. Cheveux Blancs, who at six feet seven or eight was one of the tallest men in a race of seeming giants, acquired his name while fighting the Americans on the headwaters of the Wabash River in 1791. As the story goes, he was about to scalp a man who had fallen in battle, only to have the man's powdered wig come free in his hand. Amazed, he put on the wig and wore it ever after, including when he sat for his portrait during a visit to Washington.

The St. Louis traders, and particularly the Chouteaus, suffered from the trade ban with the Big Osages and were tempted to violate it. Although the Chouteaus probably observed the ban during the first year, in the next several years they sent boats loaded with trade goods out of St. Louis under cover of night, bound for the Osage villages. Rumors of their activities circulated widely, reaching Spanish authorities at St. Louis, who took no steps to stop them. In December 1792 a Chickasaw war party reported seeing Pierre Chouteau and about ten associates in an Osage village. Another witness said that Pierre had arrived with ten barges and pirogues of men and merchandise. Other traders complained of the Chouteaus' taking unfair advantage.

It seemed a sure sign that the Chouteau brothers had maintained warm relations with the Osages when, on March 19, 1792, Pierre concluded an agreement with both camps of the Big Osages in which they gave him a tract of 30,000 arpents of land (25,500 acres) along the Missouri River well to the west of St. Louis, where the Lamine River enters the Missouri. The idea for this concession may have come from Pierre himself. However, the tone of the document drawn up by the Osages said a lot about the nature of the relationship between Pierre and the tribe and the tribe's warm feelings toward him.

"Brother," they began,

as thou hast, since a long time, fed our wives and our children, and that thou has always been good to us, and that thou has always assisted us with thy advice, we have listened with pleasure to thy words, therefore, take thou on the Rivière la Mine the quantity of land which may suit thee and anywhere thou pleasest. This land is ours; we do give it to thee, and no one can take it from thee, neither today nor ever. Thou mayest remain there, and thy bones shall never be troubled. Thou askest a paper from us, and our [marks]; here it is. If our children do trouble thee, you have but to show this same paper; and if some nation disturbs thee, we are ready to defend thee.

The treaty was signed by the principal tribal leaders, including Cheveux Blancs, Clermont, Bel Oiseau, and Soldat du Chien, Fils.

A new Spanish lieutenant governor, Zenon Trudeau, took over in St. Louis in July 1792 and seemed to have learned quickly about clandestine trade being conducted with the Osages, but he was willing to overlook it. He saw the logic in the arguments of Osage chiefs that it would be easier for them to control their unruly members if they had more trade. Privately, Auguste Chouteau had been suggesting that he be permitted to build a trading fort among the Osages, with some troops in close proximity. He argued that the opportunity to obtain trade merchandise would keep the Osages happy, while a continual white presence would help to prevent murders and make it easier to recover stolen property.

During early 1793 a number of new Osage "depredations" occurred in Ste. Genevieve and in the Arkansas district, plus a murder on the Upper Arkansas River. In reaction, the new governor at New Orleans, Francisco Luís Hector, Baron de Carondelet, demanded that authorities and white traders in Upper Louisiana incite a war against the Osages. Finally, in May, in the face of mounting evidence and complaints from other traders, Trudeau admitted to Carondelet that Pierre Chouteau was supplying the Osages but was trying to restrict their access to guns.

An infuriated Carondelet blamed the Chouteaus for making the problem worse, and he ordered Trudeau to "incite by every means" nearby Indian nations in order to make a general attack on the

Osages. Six weeks later he ordered Trudeau to organize an expedition of hunters and militiamen to go directly to the Big Osage village and destroy it. "If the commandants, Messieurs Labbadie, Chouteau and others, had not fomented the Osages," the governor fumed, "and . . . had not already actually given them flour, [arms], and munitions a long time ago, that nation would have been reduced to begging for peace." If Pierre Chouteau and his associates continued to scorn his orders, Carondelet threatened to treat them as "true enemies."

The Osages realized it was time for negotiations. On August 9 more than a hundred Big and Little Osage riders entered St. Charles on their way to St. Louis to talk with Trudeau. The next day, thirty-one chiefs and leaders called on Trudeau, telling him that only a few tribesmen were responsible for the harm being done to whites. One chief declared, "It is true that on the Arkansas River some men were murdered and various ones taken prisoner and robbed; but what nation does not have its delinquents?"

When Trudeau finally tried to assemble a force to go against the Osages in compliance with Carondelet's orders, he found the other Indians of the area reluctant to take part, and the whites pleaded that they could not afford to leave their farms and businesses. The traders well knew that destroying the Big Osages would amount to destroying the best source of skins and pelts in the territory. Trudeau himself remained unsympathetic to the governor's demand. He believed no one could win a war against the Osages, who would simply withdraw into the prairies. While the white men dallied, September came, and it was too late to strike. The Osages had left their villages for the fall hunt.

Auguste Chouteau, meanwhile, convinced that it was foolhardy to think of exterminating the Osages, decided to take his case for a fort directly to the governor. He wrote to Carondelet in November 1793 and said that he intended to bring some Osages to New Orleans in the spring. "You will see the chiefs of the powerful and proud nation of the Osages at your feet to implore your clemency," he said, explaining that the Osages were now in a "state of distress."

After the Osages returned from their winter hunt, Auguste rounded up a delegation of four Big Osage chiefs and two from the Little Osages, plus various *considerados*, or principal men of the tribe, and they floated down the Mississippi. They were in New Orleans by the second week of May.

Perhaps swayed by Auguste's charm and confidence, Carondelet agreed to the fort proposal. Auguste was to take charge of building it at his own expense. In return, he was to receive a monopoly to trade with the Osages for six years. Auguste committed himself to build a two-story fort, with palisade, cannons, and munitions, overlooking the Big Osage village. It would have twenty militiamen, selected by the Chouteaus but paid by the Spanish crown at a cost of 2,000 pesos a year. Having forgotten his threats to treat Pierre as an enemy, Carondelet said that Pierre's "influence over said nation is such" that he was appointing him commander of the fort. Carondelet also noted Pierre's "valor, courage and the necessary qualifications."

With the agreement completed, Carondelet entertained the Osage delegation lavishly. Eager to impress the Indians with the power of white men, he staged a military parade, fired salvos in their honor, and gave them gifts and medals. The six chiefs were given Spanish coats and hats with braid to distinguish their ranks. Auguste and the Osages left New Orleans toward the end of May, and Carondelet issued a proclamation ordering other hunters and traders to stay away from the Osage River—or be fined.

While Auguste Chouteau was in New Orleans, Lieutenant Governor Trudeau was taking the first steps in St. Louis to carry out another aspect of the reinvigorated Spanish fur-trade policy. He appointed a trader named Jacques Clamorgan as trade syndic to initiate an aggressive effort to drive the English from the Upper Missouri country. Trudeau assembled all the traders of St. Louis at his residence and proposed that they "unite in co-partnership, consolidate their respective capitals, and control the trade in peltries then carried on in the Upper Missouri." Trudeau asked that they "send to the country enlightened persons, who would use every exertion to penetrate to the sources of the Missouri and beyond if possible to the Southern Oceans—take observations and heights of localities, and notices of the tribes who inhabit them, their habits and customs, the trade that might be established with them."

On May 5, 1794, at a meeting at Government House in St. Louis, articles of incorporation were drawn up for the "Company of Explorers of the Upper Missouri," known as the Missouri Company, and forwarded to Carondelet. He not only gave his wholehearted approval but offered a prize of $2,000, later raised to $3,000, to the first Spanish subject who reached the South Sea, referring to the Pacific, by way of the Missouri. Twenty merchants attended the assembly, including representation from the Chouteaus, but only nine of those assembled eventually joined the undertaking. The Chouteaus, concentrating on their new undertaking with the Osages, were among those opting out.

Jean Baptiste Truteau [sic], the town's only schoolteacher, was chosen to head the first upriver expedition. Judging by his list of challenging things to accomplish, it seems possible that the teacher was chosen because he had the skills to record what he saw and experienced. He was to proceed immediately to the Mandan villages, build a fort, and establish a trading agency. He was to collect information along the way about streams entering the Missouri and mark their distance from St. Louis or the Mandan villages. He was to amass data on the tribes he encountered and on the Rocky Mountains, which the instructions said were "located to the west of the source of the Missouri." He was to work hard to secure the friendship and help of the Mandans.

Truteau was instructed to keep records on distances and other observations. He was to learn about the Shoshones, who were on the Missouri River well above the Mandans. He was also to attempt to establish friendly contacts with the Snake Indians on the other side of the Rockies and to find out what they knew about the "Sea of the West" and whether the rivers on the other side of the mountains flowed westward. The schoolmaster was requested to send back "four well scraped skins, very large and well mottled, variegated in colors, by the first boat, of a new style altogether, from different nations if it is possible, to send to Spain." He was instructed to seek out the skins of unusual animals in order "to announce a different fashion and a more elegant mode than that of the nations whom we meet frequently."

These were ambitious goals. Had Truteau and his small team accomplished even a significant part of them, the Lewis and Clark Expedition a decade later would have been almost an anticlimax. The instructions show that the Spanish were already aware of the possibilities that Jefferson would envision later.

Truteau packed up quickly and left St. Louis on June 7, 1794, with eight men in a pirogue, bound for the Mandan villages. By August 6 they were just below the mouth of the Platte. Since the instructions were to extend the trade to the unknown tribes near the headwaters of the Missouri, Truteau tried to pass the lower tribes unbeknownst to them, but the Teton Sioux stopped him in present South Dakota and took much of his merchandise. He dropped downriver to present-day Charles Mix County, South Dakota, and built winter quarters. On March 25, 1795, he began the ascent again and eventually reached the Arikaras.

Truteau found himself relatively stranded among the Arikaras. There was little to trade because Jacques d'Église, an independent trader, had reached there ahead of him and taken the available furs. Truteau remained in the area through the summer of 1795 and wintered with the Pawnees in 1796. He was supposed to remain three years, sending furs back in the meantime. Then a new expedition would succeed him. But he was probably back in St. Louis by the summer of 1796.

The Truteau expedition and two that followed under Clamorgan's plan were eventually judged failures, apparently because the traders could not win the confidence of Indians in the Upper Missouri country and get them to hunt for furs and pelts in the quantities the company sought. The backers lost substantial sums of money, but the initiative produced some of the information provided to Lewis and Clark about the Upper Missouri country before they departed St. Louis a decade later.

Auguste Chouteau, meanwhile, encountered considerable difficulties of his own as he returned from New Orleans with the Osages. Bored with the slow passage of their vessel against the current, some of the Osages went ashore on the right bank and walked. But they were fired upon by a group of Chickasaw Indians who killed a Big Osage chief, Jean Lafon, and both Little Osage chiefs. Auguste sent the frightened survivors, including Cheveux Blancs, north through a circuitous land

and water route, and they eventually reached home safely. Auguste himself left the flotilla, loaded with trade goods, when it reached New Madrid in August 1794; he was able to reach St. Louis more quickly by land.

Despite these misfortunes, the Osages were ecstatic about the fort agreement. A group of 184 Big and Little Osages visited St. Louis in September and danced in the streets. Even before a single log was driven into the ground, the fort was having its desired effect. The Osages, always sensitive to their status in comparison to other tribes, immediately began bragging about being honored by the white traders with a fort of their own.

Auguste set about organizing the fort while Pierre selected the militiamen. Auguste sent twenty-one workmen in September 1794, with more to follow. Eventually there were ninety men at work in the construction. Like other fur-trade forts that followed, it was built to be impressive and to earn respect and confidence from the Indians when they came to trade or conduct other business with white men. The site was in present-day Vernon County, Missouri, overlooking the Osage River. Consistent with the Chouteaus' good political sense, they named it Fort Carondelet in honor of the governor.

Pierre's wife, Pélagie, died in early 1793 at the height of the crisis over Osage violence. A year later, he married fifteen-year-old Brigitte Saucier, granddaughter of the engineer who built Fort de Chartres. Once Fort Carondelet was completed, Pierre moved there with Brigitte and his children by his first wife: the three sons—Auguste Pierre, Pierre Jr., and Paul Liguest—and his daughter Pélagie. The fact that he was willing to take his family with him seemed an indication of the confidence Pierre felt in his ability to maintain a peaceful and congenial relationship with the Osages. The three boys, the eldest then eight years old, were beginning an education in Indian culture that would shape their lives and enable them to play leading roles in business and United States government policy for more than sixty years to come.

"The savages have never been seen as tranquil as they have been this year," Trudeau soon reported to Carondelet. "They are all proud of having a fort, whites, and domestic animals [among] them. They regard it all as their own property. Indians have come from very distant nations to compliment them, which has flattered their *amour propre,* they believing themselves distinguished and with preponderance over the other nations."

"It suffices to tell you that [the Osage nation] seems entirely well disposed [to do good] and that Monsieur Chouteau, just as his brother, has an authority there that no other white could have," Trudeau continued. "The former is greatly feared and the other greatly loved, a contrast which did no harm in restraining them." By the fall of 1795 Spanish Illinois had enjoyed eighteen months of relative peace. Carondelet reported that the Chouteaus, after building the fort, had "prevented all incursions and invasions which had been made in our establishments."

But by early 1797 the Osages had resumed their pillaging and assaults, and there had been one killing. Part of the reason was that Pierre became ill, probably with a hernia, and went back to St. Louis for an extended period. Brigitte also gave birth to the first of their five sons, François Gesseau, in February 1797. After authorities in New Orleans complained angrily to Auguste, Pierre arose from his sickbed and returned to the Osages, where he managed to calm them.

Defending his brother, Auguste said, "He had not hesitated to sacrifice his life to prove to your lordship how deeply he was troubled that his firmness and his threats had not prevented this murder on the Arkansas River." Explaining that Pierre had convinced the tribe to give up two men guilty in the latest violence, Auguste said, "The bearing of my brother and his firmness dismayed the tribe. His ascendancy over them convinced them to sacrifice the two guilty ones." But Auguste also expressed frustration at "the impossibility of restraining a numerous people who deem these murders an honor and who are children of nature."

Two months later, still angry about the Osages' "knavish tricks" on the Arkansas River, Auguste expressed more skepticism: "This is a tribe that will cause trouble for a long time because they are so brutal and too far away from civilization to become good people or for one to hope for this change in them except by the passage of time."

Account books of the period indicate that Pierre and Auguste were acquiring merchandise and shipping pelts and furs both north and south—to New Orleans as well as to Michilimackinac on Lake Michigan and to Montreal. The supplies they were acquiring from Andrew Todd & Company at Montreal gave an indication of what kind of work and business was being conducted at Fort Carondelet. They received two dinghies, sails, grease, items used in milling, rum, sugar, steel, and lard, plus shirts and cloth, in exchange for deerskins and "divers pelletries."

Both routes to Europe, to the south and to the north, offered challenges and inconveniences. The Chouteaus could ship most of the year to New Orleans, but the skins and furs were more likely to suffer damage from rats and infestations of bugs in the warmer climate before being forwarded. By contrast, going out the northern route meant having to contend with frequent low water levels on the rivers from Lake Michigan to Montreal. It also meant the skins and pelts had to reach Montreal in time for shipment onward to Quebec before the St. Lawrence froze for the long winter. If the pelts arrived late, they could be sold in Montreal, but at much lower prices than in Europe.

These business shipments also enabled the Chouteaus to make purchases for their own use, including things that helped them to maintain a surprisingly elegant lifestyle in their isolated location. During a business trip to London in 1794, for example, Charles Gratiot ordered for Pierre a custom-made saddle, silver-studded with Pierre's initials, plus silver stirrups.

Despite these luxurious touches, it was a struggle to make money from the trade with the Osages. In 1795 Trudeau had divided the Missouri River trade into twenty-nine shares, to be licensed to different traders, but he assigned sixteen shares to Auguste by virtue of the exclusive privileges the Chouteaus had with the Osages. However, even at relative peace with whites, the Osages were always warring with other tribes, which reduced their ability to hunt and trap. This made Auguste even more determined to resist demands from Spanish authorities that he pick up more of the cost of the fort.

"All the profits that I have been able to reap have been as if swallowed up in the foundations of the fort which I have constructed in the midst of this barbarous nation at the risk of my life and of my brother's; for of all the nations which surround us, I scarcely know one more barbarous than the Osage nation and which is more distant from civilization and more unmanageable," Auguste told Manuel Gayoso de Lemos after Gayoso succeeded Carondelet as governor in 1797. "It is only by dint of presents and by exhaustion itself that one succeeds with them. Rigor, far from softening them, renders them more ferocious."

The situation soon became worse. At the beginning of 1800 the band led by Le Chenier made a definitive break from the rest of the tribe, deciding to form its own village. The group had had its hunting season site about two hundred miles to the south on the Arkansas River for some years, perhaps as early as the 1780s, and it preferred trading downriver at Arkansas Post instead of traveling north by land to Fort Carondelet. About this time, the Chenier band probably made a permanent move to the Arkansas River. A group led by Clermont also moved to the Arkansas River during this period.

Pierre explained to Carlos Dehault Delassus, the new lieutenant governor, that the Cheniers were dissatisfied with the peaceful ways of the rest of the tribe, but population growth probably played a role as well. Reports throughout the period of Spanish rule noted the increasing numbers of young men of warrior age, and it was common for chiefs and tribal elders to complain about having large numbers of young men they could not manage. At one point Spanish authorities noted that the number of men of warrior age in the tribe had reached 1,500, an all-time high in Spanish records.

"[They] have [gone] to settle far away from [Cheveux Blancs], and have withdrawn from his authority," Pierre informed Delassus when he reported on the rupture. "The same party is doing nothing but trying to harm whites. [Cheveux Blancs] and his village intend to wage a destructive war against them, to pursue them vigorously and to chase them; so far away that [Le Chenier] can no longer cause any damage to the white man."

On July 28, 1800, however, about two hundred Osages arrived in St. Louis to tell Delassus how much they wanted peace. One of them was Le Chenier, of the dissident band, who told Delassus he wanted to reunite his group with the rest of the tribe, but the young men would not permit it. After the Indian leaders spoke, Delassus lashed out at them for their killings and other violence against peaceful people. But he did not want to offend them too much. That very night he invited Cheveux Blancs and Le Chenier to dine with him, all the St. Louis officers, and the Chouteau brothers.

The next day, before a crowd of Osage leaders and whites, and with other Osages listening outside, Delassus told them that he was on the verge of depriving them of trade, and if Le Chenier's band did not rejoin the rest of the group, the band would be destroyed. Pierre Chouteau chastised them and complained of their lying to him often. He told them that Delassus was angry with him for not controlling the "barbarous actions" of the Osages and was sending him away, to the "hot country," meaning Lower Louisiana. "You always lie to me, since you always are doing evil," Pierre shouted. "Now then, will not one speak? Where are those who in their village have so much tongue? Let them speak now."

Sending Pierre to the south was, obviously, a bluff. Delassus thought the Osages wanted so much for Pierre to remain among them that they would respond to the threat by improving their behavior. Although no individual Indian leader spoke out in response to Pierre's remarks, many of the Osages cried out with approval. Both Indian chiefs repeated their promises of the day before, and when the speeches ended, Delassus distributed presents, including muskets, powder, bullets, blankets, and white shirts. Before they left St. Louis, Pierre assembled representatives of four tribes that the Osages had been periodically fighting—the Shawnees, Abenakis, Kickapoos, and Miamis—and they reached a peace agreement. The raids subsided after the conference, but the breakaway factions did not rejoin the tribe.

In 1800 the Chouteau brothers' trade monopoly with the Osages was in its seventh year. Delassus recommended that it be extended six more years, but the new territorial governor, Sebastián Marqués de Casa Calvo, approved only a four-year extension from July 1801. While the Chouteaus very much wanted to keep the Osage monopoly, they were finding the burden of maintaining the fort extremely heavy. In June 1801 Auguste reminded Lieutenant Governor Delassus that under the 1794 contract, all of the structures at Fort Carondelet were to have passed to the control of the Spanish government in 1800.

He said the government had two choices: either garrison the fort with regular troops, or evacuate it. If evacuated, he recommended that the fort be destroyed. Otherwise he thought the Osages would be waiting to use it to obstruct trade moving along the river.

However, there was a new fur trader on the scene in St. Louis, a man driven by ambition to become wealthy. He was also something rare, a Spaniard in Spanish-ruled Louisiana Territory, and he believed he had the right to expect favors from the servants of the Spanish crown. Manuel Lisa was born in New Orleans of Spanish parents. He was in his mid to late twenties when he came upriver about 1798, first opening a trading house in New Madrid, then moving to St. Louis.

Lisa quickly focused his attention on the trade monopoly the Chouteau brothers had with the Osages. In October 1801 he launched a campaign to win the Osage trade, complaining to the new governor at New Orleans, Juan Manuel de Salcedo, about the alleged harm caused to business by concentrating trade contracts in the hands of a few. Returning to St. Louis from that first attempt, "as he walked around the billiard tables, he would boast to the clicking of the balls that he and his partners would soon have the exclusive trade with the Grand Osages," the Osage historian Mathews claimed.

When Governor Salcedo delayed in responding, Lisa with three partners made a specific proposal to cover the 2,000-peso cost of the militia at Carondelet and build a water-powered flour mill on the site in exchange for a five-year trade monopoly. Whatever the importance of Lisa's Spanish blood, the offer to cover the costs of the garrison certainly caught the governor's eye. On June 12, 1802, he canceled Auguste Chouteau's trade monopoly with the Osages in favor of Lisa.

The Chouteaus, however, read Lisa's trading license carefully and interpreted it to mean that his exclusive grant covered only the Osages on the Missouri River and its tributary, the Osage River. About that time, in a move believed to have been induced by the Chouteaus, a faction of the tribe led by a man whom the French called Grande Piste (Big Track) left the Missouri and Osage rivers and joined Clermont's group on the Arkansas River. This allowed the Chouteaus to send traders and continue doing business with several thousand Osages at their new village in the Three Forks vicinity of today's Oklahoma—where the Verdigris and Neosho rivers empty into the Arkansas. In the fall of 1802 Pierre Chouteau abandoned Carondelet as required, and the Osages ransacked it and hauled away at least four swivel guns. Despite Lisa's promises, the fort was never again garrisoned. When Zebulon Pike came through in 1806, he found only ruins at the site.

Meanwhile, in the winter of 1800, a two-page letter had reached Auguste Chouteau, written in French and signed with a confident scrawl: John Jacob Astor. It began with a matter that was entirely routine in those days of a complicated barter economy. As part of a deal with the London merchant house of Schneider & Company, Astor had acquired a debt of Auguste's in the amount of 4,000 pounds sterling. He was sending someone to receive part of the money, but the debt was not uppermost in his mind. He used it as an opening to make a proposal:

> The fur trade, in which I am engaged, obliges me to travel every year to Montreal to buy furs of various types, which are found in your country and which you buy yourself in considerable quantity, such as skins of beaver, raccoon, and otter.
>
> Last September, when I was in Montreal, I bought some skins that you had expedited. Wouldn't it be possible for you to send furs directly here [to New York]? I have no doubt that would work to our mutual advantage. Also, in such case, it would not be necessary for me to go to Montreal . . . the loss of three months' time would be avoided.
>
> The European merchandise of the type sought I have the means to bring at the most advantageous prices, and as far as the skins from you, I know how to place them for the greatest benefit.
>
> I urge you to think about this and talk about it with M. Gratiot, to whom I have sent the same proposition.

John Jacob Astor was then thirty-six years old and reasonably well established in the fur trade, though not yet the dominant figure that he would become. Born in Baden-Baden, Germany, in 1763, the year Laclède ascended the Mississippi River, Astor had gone to work in London at seventeen, then sailed for America at twenty. In 1785 he began to learn the fur trade in New York and quickly saw the immense profit potential from Europeans' love of beaver hats and other furs. A quick study, he soon began pelt-buying missions to upstate New York and beyond, eventually to Montreal, then the capital of the fur trade. One of his biographers says that Astor became aware of the Chouteaus and other St. Louis traders only in 1799.

It is quite possible, however, given the limited communications between St. Louis and the American states on the East Coast, that Auguste had not yet heard of Astor. He certainly did not act impressed by the Astor letter. He did send a note to Isaac Todd, an agent in Montreal, requesting that Todd make a partial payment of slightly more than 1,500 pounds on the note held by Astor. In the following winter he paid some more of the debt, although Todd in Montreal said the sale of Auguste's latest shipment of furs was not sufficient to cover the entire debt.

Charles Gratiot, whose name had been given to Astor by Schneider & Company in London, was much more excited by Astor's proposal than was his brother-in-law. "You are without contradiction the person who can make the most in the fur trade," Gratiot wrote Astor. "Your relations at home and abroad enable you to do what no other firm in the United States could do, and you are situated in the most lively and flourishing city that perhaps exists today on the globe, where everything from all parts of the universe abounds."

Gratiot explained, however, that it was advantageous to St. Louis traders to sell their pelts in Montreal because the goods they acquired there in exchange for the pelts could be shipped to St. Louis free of duty. By contrast, he said, merchandise from London that came through New York was subject to United States duties. He suggested that Astor use his influence in Washington to change that situation.

For the time being, Gratiot said, Auguste Chouteau found it advantageous to do business through Canada and "prefers to continue his business in that quarter."

SIX

New Rulers, New Ways

✳

At the beginning of the nineteenth century, news traveled slowly up and down the Mississippi River, whose waters washed against the soil of the American republic on the east bank and the lands of the Spanish monarchy on the west bank. In June 1802 the merchant house of Cavelier & Fils in New Orleans wrote Auguste Chouteau in St. Louis about a variety of routine matters associated with the Caveliers' role as a supplier of merchandise to the Chouteaus for the Indian trade and as a buyer of pelts in exchange. The accounts between the two firms now stood at more than $9,000 in favor of the Caveliers. As usual, the company seemed in no hurry for full payment; accounts between them and the Chouteaus had been carried forward for years.

They then turned to politics: "The news of the retrocession [to France] is supported, but until now there is nothing official."

Four months later the Caveliers had firmer information, writing Auguste on October 28: "The colony really has been retroceded; it is supposed that French troops will arrive in the course of the next month. The news is official. Our port is closed to the Americans; they do not even have warehouses for the entry and exit of their customs." But he advised Auguste that he would find "no obstacle" on his planned trip down the river to New Orleans.

Reports of decisions made nearly two years earlier were just then finding their way to the territory most affected. On October 1, 1800, the Treaty of San Ildefonso was signed in secret, beginning the process by which Louisiana was supposed to be signed over to France two years later. By a second agreement, the Treaty of Aranjuez on March 21, 1801, Napoleon Bonaparte promised to give the Grand Duchy of Tuscany, a small kingdom in Italy, to the Spanish Prince of Parma, an unemployed cousin of King Carlos IV. This was in exchange for the retrocession of Louisiana to France. Napoleon intended to resurrect the French empire in America. He would send one army to the Caribbean to put down the slave revolt on the island of St. Domingue and another, later, to New Orleans.

This "completely reverses all the political relations of the U.S. and will form a new epoch in our political course," President Jefferson fumed to Robert Livingston, minister to France, after a copy of the second treaty reached Washington. Although France was the "natural friend" of the United States, the fact that it would now possess New Orleans turned it into an enemy, Jefferson thought. "There is on the globe one single spot, the possessor of which is our natural and habitual enemy. It is New Orleans, through which the produce of three-eighths of our territory must pass to market, from its fertility it will ere long yield more than half of our whole produce and contain more than half our inhabitants." He said that the United States had been able to live with a weak Spain in control of New Orleans, but France would not be so docile.

Arguing that New Orleans was not crucial to French interests, Jefferson told Livingston to ask France to cede New Orleans and West Florida to the United States. Even if the French were initially hesitant, there would be adequate time to approach them repeatedly because he believed the French intended to send the troops then in the Caribbean to New Orleans after they had put down the slave revolt on St. Domingue. "If this were the arrangement, it will give you time to return again and again to the charge, for the conquest of St. Domingo will not be a short work."

However great the dismay of Americans along the eastern seaboard over the expected rebirth of French power in America, French hearts along the Mississippi beat a little faster at the prospect of living once more under the authority of their ancestral land. "The time is not far off when [our poor colony] will be delivered to its ancient traders,"

Charles Gratiot wrote to a friend in Ste. Genevieve. "May their arrival repair the public misery into which it has fallen; this is the hope that should come to birth under the auspices of a free government and of a brave and enlightened people."

But events destined to change forever the lives of Gratiot, the Chouteaus, and their little French Creole village were running well ahead of the rumors circulating up and down the river in 1802 and 1803—and ahead of knowledge in Washington as well. Jefferson's assessment of French intentions and possibilities was prescient.

On February 2, 1802, some two months before Jefferson wrote Livingston, an expeditionary force led by General Charles V. E. Leclerc, Napoleon's brother-in-law, appeared off the harbor of Le Cap, St. Domingue, with 5,000 men to put down the ten-year-old revolt led by Toussaint L'Ouverture. During February and March a total of 17,000 French troops landed. By April, 5,000 of them were dead and 5,000 in the hospital.

"Sickness is causing frightful havoc in the army under my command," Leclerc wrote to the Minister of the Marine on May 5, 1802. "I have at this moment 3,600 men in hospital. For the last 15 days I have been losing from 30 to 50 men a day in the colony and no day passes without from 200 to 250 men entering the hospitals, while not more than 50 come out."

Three days later he sent the names of key officers who had died of the disease. He had learned "that this sickness is that which is called Yellow fever or Siamese disease; that this sickness reigns every year in the Antilles at the time of the passage of the sun in this hemisphere . . . of those attacked not one fifth have escaped death."

Meanwhile, the projected expedition to Louisiana was held up by various problems, including ice in the Dutch harbors from which the fleet was to sail, a British blockade, and delays by Spain in ordering the handover of the colony.

Leclerc's position was becoming worse every day. On June 6 he begged for 10,000 additional men. On June 11 he again wrote the minister: "If the First Consul wishes to have an army in St. Domingue in the month of October, he must have it sent from France, for the ravages of sickness here are too great for words. Not a day passes without my being told of the death of someone whom I have cause to regret bitterly . . . Man cannot work here much without risking his life." Leclerc, too, became ill. On July 6 he begged to be replaced; his health was preventing him from carrying out his obligations.

Not wanting blacks on the island to see the decimation of the army, the French stopped normal burials and began throwing the dead into large holes during the night. Leclerc went to Tortuga to try to restore his health, improved slightly, and returned to Le Cap.

On August 6 Leclerc advised Napoleon that if he wanted to preserve the colony, he must send a new army and lots of money; otherwise the colony was lost. "What general," he asked, "could calculate on a mortality of four-fifths of his army and the uselessness of the remainder, who has been left without funds as I have, in a country where purchases are made only for their weight in gold and where with money I might have got rid of such discontent?"

Leclerc died on the night of November 2, 1802. By then most of the troops originally intended to occupy New Orleans and the Louisiana Territory had been sent to join his army and had shared its fate. Of 34,000 French soldiers who had landed, 24,000 were dead and 8,000 in hospitals. Only 2,000 exhausted men remained in arms. Thousands of former slaves were also dead from the fighting, and the colony was devastated.

Many French fortunes had been made in St. Domingue—in sugar, rum, and the slave trade. The slave rebellion on the portion that later became Haiti was a crushing blow to those influential families, some of them related by marriage to the Chouteaus and other Creole families in St. Louis and New Orleans. From Le Havre in France a relative sent encouraging words to Edouard Coursault, a future Chouteau in-law who was in Cap François trying to salvage a trade and import business. "Do not lose courage," Coursault was advised. "The efforts of the French governor to restore tranquility for you will undoubtedly be crowned with success. From all corners of the Republic troops are departing that will reach you successively, the result of which will be that the First Consul will repair your wrongs and those of French commerce."

But Coursault already knew what those in France did not: Leclerc and his expeditionary force were history. And so was the dream of a re-born French America, although the word would not reach New Or-leans or St. Louis for several months. With just the remnants of one army remaining, Napoleon would not be able to fight the new war then brewing with the English and at the same time defend a scat-tered empire on the other side of the Atlantic.

In early 1803, news of the French loss in the Caribbean began to spread along the Mississippi River. William Henry Harrison, governor of the Indiana Territory, which extended to the Mississippi, wrote the following to his friend across the river in St. Louis, the Spanish lieu-tenant governor Carlos Dehault Delassus: "The cession of Louisiana to France is confirmed beyond all doubt and nothing but the great misfortunes which have befallen the armament of that power which was sent to S'n Domingo and the reduced state of Beunaparte's [sic] finances have prevented its being taken possession of before this." Harrison believed that Spain had been greatly deceived by Napoleon Bonaparte in the transaction, and he predicted that James Monroe would try to convince the French ruler to allow the Louisiana Terri-tory to be retained by Spain.

Monroe, former governor of Virginia, sailed from New York on March 9, 1803, as President Jefferson's envoy, to join Robert Liv-ingston in Paris. Officially, they were to negotiate with the French for the opening of the Mississippi River to American commerce, but Jef-ferson hoped also to buy New Orleans and the provinces of East and West Florida. Monroe and Livingston had undoubtedly by then heard of the French failures in the Caribbean. Nevertheless, they were sur-prised at the even more dramatic news they received when the talks opened: as a result of his losses, Napoleon was ready to dispose of everything France possessed on the North American continent, except the Floridas. In a matter of days, on April 30, 1803, a treaty was con-cluded whereby the United States purchased "the colony or province of Louisiana, with the same extent that [the colony] now has in the hands of Spain."

The inhabitants of the territory were to be incorporated into the

United States, with the enjoyment of all the rights, advantages, and immunities of citizens. The purchase price was $15 million, of which $3.75 million was an assumption by the United States of claims its citizens had against France, plus stock at 6 percent, redeemable in fifteen years, which France soon sold to investors in Europe for cash.

The news reached Boston by ship from Le Havre on June 28 and circulated first in New England, where the skeptical Federalists saw it as a deal to help France. They also feared that the Mississippi Valley would become the seat of an independent confederation of states; they would have preferred to get the Floridas.

Jefferson, however, saw exciting prospects and was already making secret plans to explore the new territory and well beyond. He had sent a confidential request to Congress for $2,500 to send an exploration expedition up the Missouri with commercial, scientific, and military objectives, having intended to do this even with the territory under Spanish control.

Like many Virginians, Jefferson envisioned a western empire based on rivers. He was awed by the potential of both the Mississippi and Missouri, but most of all the Missouri. "The Missouri," Jefferson wrote, "is, in fact, the principal river, contributing more to the common stream than does the Mississippi." This was a view widely held among Frenchmen and others who explored or wrote about the rivers during the eighteenth century. Captain Philip Pittman, an English officer who had toured the Mississippi settlements in the 1760s, wrote, "The muddy waters of the Missoury [*sic*] prevail over those of the Missisippi [*sic*], running with violent rapidity to the ocean. The Missisippi glides with a gentle and clear stream, 'till it meets with this interruption."

To head the mission up the Missouri, and if possible to the Pacific, Jefferson named his private secretary, Meriwether Lewis. On June 19, 1803, Lewis asked William Clark to join him in the expedition, and Clark found the prospect "truely pleasing."

Jefferson's instructions to Lewis were "to explore the Missouri river, & such principal stream of it, as, by it's [*sic*] course and communication with the waters of the Pacific ocean, whether the Columbia, Oregan [*sic*], Colorado or any other river may offer the most direct &

practicable water communication across this continent for the purposes of commerce." He further told Lewis:

> Beginning at the mouth of the Missouri, you will take [careful] observations of latitude & longitude, at all remarkeable points on the river, & especially at the mouths of rivers, at rapids, at islands, & other places & objects distinguished by such natural marks & characters of a durable kind, as that they may with certainty be recognised hereafter . . .
>
> The interesting points of the portage between the heads of the Missouri, & of the water offering the best communication with the Pacific ocean, should also be fixed by observation, & the course of that water to the ocean, in the same manner as that of the Missouri . . .
>
> In all your intercourse with the natives, treat them in the most friendly & conciliatory manner which their own conduct will admit . . . [Inform them] of our wish to be neighborly, friendly & useful to them, & of our dispositions to a commercial intercourse with them; confer with them on the points most convenient as mutual emporiums, and the articles of most desireable interchange for them & us. If a few of their influential chiefs, within practicable distance, wish to visit us, arrange such a visit with them, and furnish them with authority to call on our officers, on their entering the U.S. to have them conveyed to this place at the public expence.

Jefferson also urged Lewis to carry "some matter of the kinepox . . . [and inform them] of it's efficacy as a preservative from the smallpox."

However, Jefferson's interest in the Indians and their territory, even at that early date, was much more complex than the explanation he gave Lewis. He was already thinking of clearing Indians from lands east of the Mississippi and moving them west to make way for white settlement. "When we shall be full on this side, we may lay off a range of States on the western bank from the head to the mouth, and so, range after range, advancing compactly as we multiply," he explained.

In August, word finally reached St. Louis that its future and that of all the vast Louisiana Territory lay not with France, but with the United States.

A business associate at Michilimackinac wrote Auguste Chouteau confirming receipt of a fur shipment and commented, "The news of the day is that the French have ceded Louisiana to the Americans for 6 million piastres, part in money, part in bad debts."

Pierre Chouteau had just returned from New Orleans when he received a letter from Pierre Clement de Laussat, French prefect there, who said that things had taken a turn he did not expect. "It seems almost certain that Louisiana has been ceded by France to the United States."

"Our Government has received official information of a treaty having been signed to that effect on the 30th of April last by our Ministers in Paris & a Minister Plenipotentiary on the part of France," Harrison in Vincennes wrote Delassus in St. Louis. "I do not know what the United States will do with upper Louisiana but think it probable that it will be annexed to this territory. Should this be the case it may give me an opportunity of serving some of your friends—if this opportunity does offer be assured my dear sire that it shall not be neglected."

The United States Senate ratified the treaty on October 19. On October 31, 1803, Jefferson signed the enabling act while the first rider waited to start the news on its way to the Mississippi Valley. Jefferson commissioned William C. C. Claiborne, governor of the Mississippi Territory, and General James Wilkinson, both at Natchez, to receive the transfer. Just a month before, the postmaster general had established an "express mail" service to Natchez and New Orleans. Riders set out from Washington and changed horses every thirty miles. After a hundred miles—a day's travel—a rider was relieved, and another took over. In this way, it was possible to reach Natchez in fifteen days.

❈

Lower Louisiana was formally transferred by Spain to France at New Orleans on November 30, 1803. On December 20, the French prefect, Pierre Clement de Laussat, transferred it to Claiborne and Wilkinson as commissioners of the United States. It took a few more months to complete the transfer at St. Louis in the midst of preparations for Lewis and Clark's voyage. As at New Orleans, the Spanish flag came down and the French flag went up in one ceremony, followed by the second ceremony passing control to the United States.

Ten weeks later, Lewis and Clark were headed upstream on the Missouri River, and Pierre Chouteau was leading his delegation of Osage Indians to meet with their new "Father" in Washington.

Fifty-three days of travel took Pierre and the Osages to Washington, where they arrived on July 11, 1804, the day of the Burr-Hamilton duel. In addition to the fourteen Osages, Pierre was accompanied by his eldest son, Auguste Pierre; his nephew, Charles Gratiot Jr.; and the two Loramier boys from Cape Girardeau, all bound for West Point. He was also bringing to Jefferson the first collection of treasured specimens and Indian cultural items from west of the Mississippi, which had been put together by Meriwether Lewis with contributions from the Chouteaus and others in St. Louis.

Jefferson first gave his attention to the Osages. "It is so long since our forefathers came from beyond the great water, that we have lost the memory of it, and seem to have grown out of this land, as you have done," he told them in a formal address a few days after their arrival.

> Never more will you have occasion to change your fathers. We are all now of one family, born in the same land, and bound to live as brothers; and the strangers from beyond the great water are gone from among us. The great Spirit has given you strength, and has given us strength; not that we might hurt one another, but to do each other all the good in our power. Our dwellings indeed are very far apart; but not too far to carry on commerce and useful intercourse. You have furs and peltries which we want, and we have clothes and other useful things which you want. Let us employ ourselves then in mutually accomodating each other.

To Pierre and the Osages, the tone of the speech said the right things: there was room in the West for everybody, and the fur trade would be the focal point of relations between the Osages and the people and government of the United States, as it had been under the French and the Spanish. Jefferson said nothing about the plans he was already advancing to push tribes from east of the Mississippi onto lands that the Osages considered theirs.

Despite the fact that he did not speak English and was forced to rely on his son and nephew and French-speaking members of the Jefferson Administration, Pierre Chouteau took on Washington with the easy confidence that he was accustomed to displaying among the French, Spanish, and Indians. He came with letters of warm endorsement from both Lewis and Clark, who were already in his debt, and he had no reason to doubt that his charm and assurance would open the way for him. It was possibly unknown to him that only a few years earlier, during the John Adams Administration, the Alien and Sedition Acts had been adopted, and in the eyes of many in the East, the French living among them were the object of that act.

Just six days after his arrival in Washington, Pierre was named "Agent of Indian Affairs for the district of upper Louisiana" at a salary of $1,500 a year, with a budget that allowed him to hire two interpreters. Secretary of War Henry Dearborn, issuing the commission in the name of "Peter" Chouteau, advised Pierre that it was his duty "to use all prudent and possible means in your power for conciliating and establishing the friendship and good will of the several Indian Nations and tribes residing in that part of Louisiana which lies to the Northward & westward of the river Arkansa—You will be particularly attentive to our friends the Osage nation."

He was to encourage them in taking up domestic pursuits such as farming and manufacturing. He could furnish them plows, hoes, axes, spinning wheels, looms, and other materials and could find a blacksmith for the Osages. He was to get the permission of the breakaway faction of Osages led by Big Track (Grande Piste) for any party sent by the President to explore the sources of the Arkansas River, and he was to "prepare the minds" of other tribes to receive American exploring parties as friends.

Based on his long experience with the Osages and other tribes in the vicinity of the Missouri River, Pierre was surely dubious about a policy of encouraging the Indians of the region to become farmers, but there is no record that he used this early opportunity to debate the assumptions on which American policy was founded. There is also no record of private conversations between Jefferson and Pierre. That was left to the French-speaking, Swiss-born Treasury Secretary, Albert Gallatin, who found Pierre too ambitious and too authoritarian in his political views. Gallatin also recognized that Pierre wielded great power and influence in an area far from Washington, about which the American governing class was largely ignorant.

"At the request of Gen. Dearborn, I had two conversations with Chotteau [sic]," Gallatin informed Jefferson.

> He seems well disposed, but what he wants is power and money. He proposed that he should have a negative on all the Indian trading licenses and the direction and all the profits of the trade carried on by Government with all the Indians of Louisiana replacing only the capital. I told him this was inadmissible, but his last demand was the exclusive trade with the Osages, to be effected by granting licenses only to his agents, but that he should not be concerned in the trade with any other nation . . . As he may be either useful or dangerous I gave him no flat denial to his last request, but told him to modify it in the least objectionable shape and to write to Gen. Dearborn from St. Louis which he said he would do.

Pierre's requests undoubtedly struck Gallatin as presumptuous. But Pierre was putting at the disposal of the American government the knowledge and influence he had developed over thirty years of fighting the currents of the Missouri River and its tributaries, sleeping in smoky Indian lodges, and sharing council meetings. Few men, if any, could match his understanding of the customs and mores of Indians in the region. As Gallatin noted, Pierre wanted wealth. He saw no reason to give up the best leverage for attaining that in exchange for nothing more than a bureaucrat's salary of $1,500 a year.

Under the Spanish, no one had found a contradiction in Pierre's trading with the Indians while also working closely with the governors to formulate policy. Now he was dealing with more rigid people.

From Washington, Pierre and the Indians traveled to Baltimore, Philadelphia, and New York, visits intended to impress the Osages with the power and might of the nation then assuming control of the lands west of the Mississippi. This concept was not original with Jefferson. The Chouteaus and the Spanish and French authorities had been practicing the art of impressing Indians with the power of white men for decades—using medals, uniforms, weapons, parades, stockaded forts, and an occasional trip to Paris and the opera.

In the eastern cities on their tour, the Osages were a big hit and were given a lot of attention by officials and the public. Hezekiah Rogers, a former Revolutionary War officer who was chief clerk in the War Department, accompanied Pierre and the Osages on their tour, which included eight days in New York before traveling to Philadelphia, which they departed on August 21 for Pittsburgh to find transportation down the Ohio River.

"During our journey the party enjoyed perfect health, and no untoward circumstance occurred to mar the pleasure of the natives, or to frustrate the object contemplated by government," Rogers informed Jefferson. "The principal villages and cities through which we passed, and individual citizens vied with each other in acts of hospitality and kindness, and I am persuaded the impressions which have been made on the minds of the Indians are most favorable to the views and wishes of the Executive."

Pierre, making his first visit to the American cities, took advantage of his time there to establish some connections. Still hoping to persuade the government to allow him to participate in the Indian trade, he made the acquaintance of a Philadelphia merchant named Samuel McKer, from whom he was thinking of ordering merchandise. His needs, he later advised McKer, would include tafia, alcohol, sugar, coffee, Bordeaux wine, French soap, beaver traps, German iron, and other small articles.

He would later call on McKer to be host to his son and nephew for their Christmas vacations from West Point. Taking advantage of the "generous offers" that McKer had made, Pierre asked him "to take them under your protection and to direct their actions. Both of them are very young and will find themselves for the first time without guides in a new world." He hoped the "severe winter season . . . can be turned to their instruction in introducing them into society and in procuring them good acquaintances."

The War Department had a boat built at Pittsburgh to carry Pierre and the Osages as far as Kaskaskia, from which they crossed the river and were back at St. Louis on October 3. Pierre sent off a four-paragraph letter to Jefferson, in French, assuring the President of the success of the trip. Despite the differences he encountered with Washington officials over his desire to continue trading with the Osages, he was delighted to have access to the White House and seemed determined to take advantage of it without delay.

"I am persuaded that the remembrance of the numberless benefactions which [the Osages] received from the government and in the United States in general will never be erased from their memories," he wrote Jefferson, "and that they will transmit the story to their remotest posterity, as well as the importance of their being punctilious in fulfilling the treaty concluded between the United States and the Osage Nation." He added: "Believe, Monsieur, that I have nothing more at heart than to fulfill exactly the duties of the mission with which the government has charged me."

While Pierre and the Osages were in the East, Auguste and other leading citizens of St. Louis were occupied with relations with their new government, about which some issues were already developing. They had three big concerns: how and by whom the Louisiana Territory was to be governed, land claims and the means to be used to verify and confirm them, and rules governing the practice of slavery.

To all appearances, the government was not pushing the idea that had been presented by Meriwether Lewis a few months earlier on behalf of Jefferson to move the whites then living west of the Mississippi to the east and create an all-Indian area in the west. It would have created great consternation among the St. Louis leaders. Rapidly growing interest by whites from the east in settling west of the Mississippi also made it impractical.

There was strong opposition in St. Louis to attaching the Louisiana Territory to the Indiana Territory as a unit of government. Indiana Territory governor William Henry Harrison, in his correspondence with people in St. Louis and during his visits, had made a good impression among the people there, but they wanted to be governed separately. Besides, Upper Louisiana was larger and more populous than the Indiana Territory.

Auguste Chouteau and Charles Gratiot were prime movers behind the formation of the Committee of the Town of St. Louis soon after the transfer of power. It organized various assemblies to which "the citizens of upper Louisiana" were invited by circular. With Harrison expected in October for his first official visit since the transfer of power, the group called a meeting to prepare for his visit and "to claim the rights which are guaranted [*sic*] to us by the treaty which conceded this territory to the United States."

On September 14, when a dozen district representatives met in St. Louis, they were smarting from what Charles Gratiot termed "calumnies being expressed against the people of Louisiana in Washington and elsewhere in America." They were particularly angered by remarks made by a Pennsylvania congressman who claimed that the people of St. Louis, having cried when they saw the Stars and Stripes raised in place of the French Tricolor at the cession ceremonies, were not friendly to the idea of control by the United States.

In a statement probably drafted by Gratiot, members of the St. Louis Committee defended their former allegiance to the Spanish monarchy and affirmed their commitment to the new government.

> On the very floor of congress, our gratitude to a government absolute in principle . . . but whose truly paternal benevolence we had uniformly experienced, and which, as virtues go hand in hand, should have been construed rather as a certain pledge of our attachment to the principles of a free government, was tortured into a satisfactory proof of our not being yet ripe to enjoy the benefits of a free government. Rumours very injurious to our general character, representing us [as] a set of covetous, rapacious land jobbers, who by false, antidated, counterfeited deeds, had monopolized the greatest quantity of the vacant lands of the district of Louisiana, were at the same time artifully circulated thro' all parts of the United States.

Auguste Chouteau, assuming the role of steady and patient patriarch of St. Louis, feared that the committee might defeat its own ends with so much anger and passion. He asked Amos Stoddard, still in St. Louis as justice of the peace, to tone down the complaints and the petition against being joined to the Indiana Territory. Auguste's moderation, with Stoddard's help, may have won the day.

When William Henry Harrison visited St. Louis in October and November, Auguste and Pierre entertained him in the same grand manner they had used to woo Lewis and Clark and Amos Stoddard, and strong bonds resulted. Harrison, who stayed in Auguste's mansion, struck the St. Louis people as affable and open, and he saw the logic of their request for a separate government. When the visit was completed, he wrote Auguste from Vincennes that Congress had already appointed a committee to take up the affairs of Louisiana, "& I doubt not but a form of Government will be adopted which will prove satisfactory to the people of that country."

Auguste set out for Washington to deliver the demands of the St. Louis Committee, but he was stricken by hip gout before reaching Vincennes and had to turn back. Instead, the case for the Louisiana Territory was made by Eligius Fromentin, a recent arrival from France, a scholar and linguist who ended up as the territory's lobbyist in Washington before moving to the future state of Louisiana, from which he was elected to the Senate.

John W. Eppes, Jefferson's son-in-law and a member of the House of Representatives, introduced the St. Louis bill to the general committee charged with Louisiana affairs at the beginning of January. Fromentin reported back to Auguste that the petition had been received without "the disdain with which hidden enemies of the cause of Louisiana had intended to frighten the settlers." He said the demands were, in general, found to be "moderate."

Two weeks later Eppes himself wrote Auguste that the committee had recommended "authorising the people of that Territory to form a Government for themselves."

"The liberal and temperate view taken in your first letter of the feelings and rights of the people of upper Louisiana induced me to lay it before Mr. John Randolph the chairman of the committee to whom the petition from upper Louisiana was referred," Eppes wrote.

> He unites with me in opinion that the view you have taken of this question is liberal and correct and that the first grade of Territorial Government ought to be extended to the people of upper Louisiana . . . A general sentiment prevails among the members of the National Legislature, that the people of Louisiana ought to stand on the footing of all other American citizens—There is no doubt also but that a liberal policy as to the land titles of your citizens will be adopted.

There is one part of the petition which I believe cannot be granted viz. the relinquishment by Congress of the right to make such future divisions of your Territory as the public convenience shall require.

On another point of concern, Auguste informed Captain Stoddard that since the transfer of power to the United States, there existed "amongst the Blacks a fermentation which may become dangerous, and which seems to be created by the reports spread by some whites, that they will be free before long." He said the St. Louis Committee believed that the government intended "to maintain each proprietor peaceably in possession of his property," in which case clarifications were needed regarding the obligations of slaves and their owners.

"In all countries where slavery exists," Auguste informed the New Englander,

> there is a Code that establishes in a positive manner the rights of the Masters, and the Duties of slaves. There is also a watchful policy, which prevents their Nocturnal Assemblies, that Subjects them to their Labour, provides for their Subsistance, and prevents as much as possible their Communication with the whites . . . Under the old French Government, and Spanish, the Black Code was our Guide, Be so kind Sir as to have it put in force, keep the slaves in their duty, according to their Class, in the Respect they owe generally to all Whites, and more especially their masters."

Stoddard said he was unfamiliar with the normal policies of slave countries and asked that the committee suggest rules and regulations "to restrain the licentiousness of the slaves and keep them more steadily to their duty." Stoddard was quick to respond to the slaveholders' suggestions, essentially allowing the continuation of the Black Code.

Landownership turned out to be the most conflictive and longest running of the three big issues with which the St. Louis Committee was concerned. The work of the various land commissions and other bodies of supposed experts that examined and ruled on the legitimacy of French and Spanish land grants dragged on until long after the deaths of many of the principals. The largely French claimants, arguing that the legitimacy of their claims was guaranteed in the Louisiana Purchase agreement, fought back with petitions to Congress and lobbying for legislation to clear titles. The first land commission began its work in St. Louis in 1805, and the last did not finish until 1833. All of the commissioners were sent from the East, and some of them came with the impression that the longtime residents of the territory were claiming land to which they had no valid right; others were sympathetic to the claimants.

Seemingly forgotten by some of the commissioners as they studied the St. Louis and Louisiana claims was the fact that land speculation was then a widespread activity throughout the western and southern parts of the existing United States, including Pennsylvania, Virginia, the future Kentucky, and the Ohio Valley. Those who were claiming the lands routinely went after immense tracts, to be sold or subdivided as settlers moved into new areas. A few decades earlier, Jefferson, Washington, and other Virginia leaders had dealt in land for speculative purposes that far surpassed in size most of the holdings at stake in Upper Louisiana.

"The first laws passed by Congress relative to the land titles in Louisiana excited much alarm and apprehension among the people of that country," recalled Amos Stoddard.

> They contended, that the United States had no right to enquire, whether the Spanish authorities had exceeded their powers in the concession of lands; because such an enquiry would militate against the treaty; and against that full faith and credit, which one nation was bound to put in the official acts and proceedings of another. They also contended that, if the Spanish authorities exceeded their powers, and we chose to remedy the evils occasioned by it, the dispute rested between the two nations, and not between the claimants and the United States.

Some of the first land commissioners suspected that during the months before the close of the Spanish government, there had been a spate of new land claims, particularly by people who had previously taken no interest in agriculture "so long as they were able to navigate the rivers, pursue the chase or the Indian trade," in Stoddard's words. The early commissioners also suspected that some boundary lines had been extended in the area around St. Louis.

Under the ground rules first established by the land commission in 1805, a title derived from the Spanish or French crown or sanctioned by the maximum authority at New Orleans was deemed "complete," and therefore legitimate. But that was a small share of the total. The titles extended by the French or Spanish lieutenant governors at St. Louis, or by the commandants, were deemed "incomplete," and these constituted 95 percent of the total. Those cases led to years of paperwork, petitioning, and litigation. Until 1795, surveying had not been done on a systematic basis in Upper Louisiana, so people with older grants made by a lieutenant governor often had to have the property surveyed before applying for ratification of ownership.

While the differences over landownership were being vetted, Pierre Chouteau returned from Washington in October and had to quickly assert himself in his new post as Indian agent for Upper Louisiana. He faced a touchy situation involving Sac and Fox Indians who had killed some more Osages while he was gone and, in a second episode, three whites. Also, there was a new ranking military officer in the region, Major James Bruff, who commanded the military cantonment, while Stoddard dealt with civil matters.

After the attack on the Osages, Bruff and Stoddard had concluded that the Sacs and Foxes were jealous of the Osages, whom they saw as receiving preferential treatment from the United States, exemplified by the trip to Washington with Pierre and the quantity of presents distributed at St. Louis. The subsequent assault on a white settlement north of St. Louis, in which three whites were killed, set off panic in the outlying white settlements. The young killers made things worse by racing back to their village and triumphantly throwing the scalps at the feet of their angry chiefs.

Bruff ordered the Sacs to surrender the warriors responsible for the killings, but they did not respond. On his return, Pierre sent a message to the chiefs of the Sacs and Foxes demanding that they bring the guilty to him. "My brothers," he began, "since the great chief of the 17 great cities of America, having chosen me to maintain peace and union between all the Red Skins and the government of the United States, I have in consequence just received the order of the great Chief of our country, which came from the post of Vincennes, to send for the chiefs of your villages with some important men, and to bring with them those of you who recently killed his children."

Some chiefs from the two closely related tribes came to St. Louis and surrendered one of the guilty braves to Pierre. William Henry Harrison, who had arrived in St. Louis in the meantime, imprisoned him. But instead of demanding the other killers, Harrison decided to take advantage of the moment, with the Sac and Fox chiefs wanting to pacify the whites, by asking for something that had been on his mind for two years. He offered to seek a presidential pardon for the imprisoned brave, and at the same time he broached to the chiefs the idea of a treaty and cession of some of their lands in exchange for compensation.

As governor of Indiana, Harrison had been proposing talks to clarify the Sac and Fox boundaries and avoid problems for white settlers. Secretary of War Dearborn finally authorized him on June 27, 1804, to make a treaty to get land cessions on both sides of the Illinois River in the present state of Illinois and to grant the tribes an annual compensation of $500 to $600 in exchange. After Harrison made his proposal to the tribes, Pierre softened up the Indian delegation with a generous selection of gifts, and the talks began.

Instead of the cession proposed by Dearborn, however, in what would go down in history as one of the blackest episodes in early-nineteenth-century Indian affairs, the tribes were persuaded to give title to an immense stretch of land on both sides of the Mississippi covering 50 million acres. The ceded lands included the northeastern corner of the future Missouri, a huge piece of Illinois, lower Wisconsin, and the eastern edge of Iowa. Harrison signed the treaty on November 3, 1804, buying all that land from the tribes for a onetime payment of $2,234.50 and an annual annuity of $1,000, with the tribes to retain the right to live and hunt on it, presumably until whites settled there. The witnesses included Bruff, Stoddard, Gratiot, and the Chouteau brothers.

The surviving documents and letters do not indicate who proposed expanding the size of the cession. Pierre was eager to take credit for his role in facilitating the treaty, writing later to Jefferson that he saw "with satisfaction that my credit and influence with these two nations have finally brought these chiefs to conclude a treaty which I dare believe you will find advantageous." Harrison, however, was known throughout his life for aggressively seeking Indian land concessions. But Auguste Chouteau, who was then Harrison's gracious host, probably had the most to gain because the cession of lands on the west side of the Mississippi in present-day Iowa encompassed the huge Dubuque lead mines, of which he claimed half.

In 1788 Julien Dubuque had acquired from the Sacs and Foxes approximately 145,000 French arpents (about 125,000 acres or 195 square miles) of lead-mining land fronting on the Mississippi five hundred miles above St. Louis. The terms of the acquisition were expressed vaguely, both by the tribe and by the Spanish governor when he was asked to approve the cession. The Sacs and Foxes, to whom Dubuque was close, said they were granting him the hill and contents of the land to mine "as he saw fit." In November 1796, when Dubuque petitioned Governor Carondelet for "peaceable possession" of the mines and lands, Carondelet scrawled a note at the bottom of the request stating that "grant is as asked." These various terms and phrases created subsequent confusion as to whether the land had been given outright to Dubuque, with Carondelet's approval, or whether the Indians had only given him the right to use and mine it, also with Carondelet's approval.

Dubuque had very limited working capital, but he did have a friendly relationship with Auguste Chouteau and may have turned to him for assistance over the years. On October 20, 1804, just two weeks before Harrison and the chiefs signed the land cession treaty, Auguste bought half of Dubuque's rights to the mine site for $10,848, again without any document that clarified whether Dubuque actually owned it.

When Harrison negotiated the treaty with the Sacs and Foxes, he had a clause inserted in the agreement noting "that nothing in this treaty contained shall affect the claim of any individual or individuals who may have obtained grants of land from the Spanish government, and included within the general boundary line laid down in this treaty, provided that such grants have at any time been made known to the Indian tribes and recognized by them."

Harrison later said that he was shown papers on the Dubuque grant after the treaty was made, and he found that without the insertion of this clause, the mine site would have been considered part of the territory passing to control of the U.S. government. He said the Indians were shown the claim of Dubuque, "the validity of which they acknowledged."

But the 1804 Sac and Fox Treaty did more than raise questions about the ethics of those who negotiated the accord. It deeply angered the celebrated Sac warrior Black Hawk, who was not part of the Indian delegation and who contended that the chiefs who negotiated the treaty had not been authorized by their tribes to cede the entire area, rather just to "pay" for the whites killed. The chiefs, returning to their villages wearing elegant coats and medals provided by Pierre, were also accused by fellow tribesmen of having been drunk during most of their stay in St. Louis.

In their favor, it might be said that the chiefs who negotiated the treaty saw it as a means of gaining the protection of the United States government against their longtime enemies, the Osages. In fact, the affair was followed by years of distrust between the Sacs and Foxes and the American government and people. It created an atmosphere that contributed to attacks on Americans in the War of 1812 and eventually erupted into the Black Hawk War of 1832.

Aside from the immediate crisis with the Sacs and Foxes, Pierre Chouteau was trying to establish the ground rules for his dealings with all Indian tribes and for his relations with Washington. He used every opportunity to press his case for engaging in Indian trade, at least with the Osages. The breadth of his responsibility as Indian agent for Upper Louisiana was almost overwhelming. In his letter book in November 1804 Pierre listed twenty-two separate tribes in the Louisiana Territory, ranging from the nearly extinct Missouris with just 80 warriors, to the Sioux with 12,000, and a tribe he called the "Laulanne who skirt the Spanish border" at 15,000 men.

The size of his challenge was clear in an experience that Lewis and Clark had recorded within a few days of setting out from St. Charles earlier in the year. Near the Osage River, they met a raft carrying a Frenchman and an Indian couple who reported that Osages on the Arkansas River had tossed into the fire the letter Pierre had sent them announcing the Louisiana Purchase. They did not want to hear that the United States now had possession of the country. The Osages were probably the tribe most loyal to the French and Spanish, but they were certainly not the only tribe that distrusted the government from east of the Mississippi.

Before Pierre left Washington, Jefferson and Secretary of War Dearborn told him to give priority to healing the breach between the main part of the Osage nation and the group led by Grand Piste, or Big Track, and to persuade the dissidents to rejoin the central group. Pierre, of course, had been partly responsible for the split, which occurred when the Spanish authorities had canceled the Chouteaus' exclusive trading agreement in favor of Manuel Lisa. With the Americans now in control, Lisa's license was a dead issue.

Pierre repeatedly made the point to Dearborn, Gallatin, and Jefferson that he could better control and influence the Osages if he had the leverage of being able to trade with them — and to cut off trade as necessary to keep them in line. If others were to be allowed to trade with them, he wanted the authority to issue the licenses, and he particularly wanted to restrict traders from going to the Arkansas River, because that would encourage the dissident Osages to remain there and not move back to the Osage homelands.

He told Jefferson that Cheveux Blancs had been distressed on returning from Washington to learn that merchandise was getting across the Arkansas River to the village of Grand Piste: "He expected that the village would be completely deprived of merchandise, that being, according to Cheveux Blancs, the surest means of bringing a revolting chief back to obedience."

Pierre pressed Dearborn for clarification of how far he could go in regulating the Indian trade. He wanted to know in a clear manner the qualifications which I should require from those who are in a position to ask me for permits to go and trade with the tribes of savages; complete freedom is certainly harmful to the interests of the United States . . . It is, it seems to me, very dangerous to permit all sorts of people to enter the territory of the savage tribes, being well convinced that there would be found among this number of strangers several who are able to poison the minds of these Indians, who are easy to seduce.

Dearborn must have been slow or vague in his responses, because Pierre's complaints grew stronger. He said too many whites were moving among the tribes, some of them trying to stir up Indians on the east side of the Mississippi to launch war against their eternal enemies, the Osages. "The savage, left to himself, knowing that he would displease the American government, whose power he knows, would not resort to such procedures unless incited by restless and dangerous minds," Pierre told the Secretary. "This observation leads me to insist . . . that nobody shall gain admittance to the nations of the District of Louisiana either for commerce, or to travel or under any other pretext whatsoever, without a permit from the general agency, and I believe it would be my duty to refuse it to everyone whose character, intentions and prudence were not perfectly known to me."

Wanting more authority for himself to control who could trade and mix with the Indians, he said, "These reflections are dictated to me by the purest zeal for the interest of the United States and the tranquility of its citizens, and by my fear of seeing the good will, the efforts I have put forth, and my credit among the savage nations become, so to speak, useless, because of the false steps and the imprudent and even seditious proposals of the whites who traffic with them."

He worried that the British, or traders they licensed, coming down from the north, would seek to gain advantage in this uncertain situation. He asked for a ruling against introducing liquor among the tribes. Under the Spanish, he said, "there were severe regulations which absolutely prevented its entry. I have not as yet received any orders regarding this, but I believe it most necessary that the government take vigorous measures to avoid the incalculable miseries which a longer tolerance of this article could occasion."

As Cheveux Blancs had requested in Washington, Pierre hired a blacksmith for the Osage village, providing him with a forge of iron and steel, and hired an interpreter for the nations of the Mississippi. He also sent Dearborn an estimate for the amount of merchandise traded with the Indians of the district in recent years. He put the total at $216,000 a year. The breakdown included $35,000 for the Big Osages, $40,000 for Sacs, $20,000 for Foxes, $8,000 for Little Osages, $12,000 for Iowas, $40,000 for Sioux, and smaller amounts for others.

Pierre told Dearborn that he normally had kept a capital of "about 30,000 piastres in the Indian trade" and would like to continue his trading activities.

> I ask you to grant me a private license for the Osage nation; if I make this request, Monsieur, it is only in order to separate my interests from those of the public and to bring together again the two villages, that of Grand Piste and Cheveux Blancs. This separation being one of the most harmful to the true interests of the United States, it is of the greatest importance that their reunion be effected, but as long as this nation has an influx of traders such as one has seen this year, it will be very difficult to maintain harmony, as it is the concern of all these traders to prevent it.

He wrote to Gallatin at the same time: "I dare hope that you will use your interest with the secretary of war for me in order that I may obtain a private license for a post in Missouri so that I could invest the funds there, which I have always had in trade; nevertheless, if I thought that the thing would be contrary to the views of the government I would give it up because I never wish to ask anything which would in any manner be objectionable to it."

Pierre was making plans to go to the Osages on the Arkansas River on what was becoming his perpetual quest to reunite them with White Hair's band, when personal disaster struck. On the night of February 15, 1805, his magnificent home—the second showplace of St. Louis after his brother's house—was destroyed by fire. The family, plus various relatives and slaves, fled into the cold. Less than a month later, his flour mill on the Mississippi was flooded and destroyed by a tornado.

"In the space of one hour I saw the flames devour the fruits of 25 years of unremitting work," Pierre wrote Jefferson.

> I was hardly able to save my family and a small part of my papers; all the rest is gone. This loss, which I shall never be able to recoup, has affected me keenly, rather on account of my wife and my children than for myself, but, full of confidence in the interest which you have always been pleased to show me and which I shall endeavor to merit all my life, I flatter myself that my children will find in you a protector and that they can, by your help, found for themselves a fortune which I have no longer the hope of leaving them.

It may seem strange that Pierre would turn directly to the President after a personal calamity such as a fire, but he came of age under a system in which good relations with the representatives of the monarchy had been considered a guarantee of success and happiness. Having made Jefferson's personal acquaintance, it made sense to him to turn to the most powerful man he knew at a time of loss.

Noting that newspapers arriving from the East had brought the news of Jefferson's reelection, Pierre added, "Happy are the United States, happy am I myself, even in my misfortune, to have had the honor of knowing you and of prompting in you an interest which is at this moment my only resource."

Shortly, Pierre wrote Dearborn, and sent a copy to Jefferson, saying he had learned that one of his slaves was responsible for the fire. He said he felt the loss "more acutely because I believe that I can, without injustice, impute it to the vengeance of one of my slaves, whom, nevertheless, I need not reproach myself with having mistreated. She is now in prison and the first general court will decide her fate, but not her innocence, because, if there are not sufficient proofs to condemn her, yet I am not the less certain that she lighted with her own hands the fire that devoured my property and that of the United States which I had."*

The fire, however, did not diminish Pierre's determination in his new job. Within a short time he and Major Bruff were locking horns. Bruff

---

*Historians have been unable to find any record of the outcome of the proceeding against the slave.

behaved in the affair like an arrogant white man and military officer, ignorant of Indian ways but determined to be obeyed. Pierre behaved like an arrogant, snobbish French Creole, confident he could use his knowledge and influence to outmaneuver a simple military officer.

The Sac warrior whom the chiefs had turned over to Pierre before negotiation of the 1804 land cession treaty was in prison, in irons, on the murder charges, under the authority of Major Bruff. About 120 men from the Sac and Fox tribes showed up in April 1805 and came to Pierre with a request to see the prisoner. Pierre asked Bruff to permit this because otherwise it might "create in the minds of that savage nation a dissatisfaction against the government of the U.S. which may afterward be the cause of the destruction of many innocent men of our frontiers if they should be ill-disposed against us." He proposed that the prisoner be escorted out of the garrison by twenty soldiers to meet with the tribe.

Bruff refused, saying that only the highest chief and the nearest relative of the prisoner could enter the fort to see him. That did not satisfy the Indians, so Pierre convened the Indian leaders together in council with fifty town militiamen, then proposed that the prisoner be brought out of the fort and turned over to him while he was surrounded by militamen, who would prevent any attempted escape. Pierre pledged to return the prisoner to the garrison.

Meanwhile, never reluctant to go over the head of an obstinate man, Pierre wrote Harrison at Vincennes that Major Bruff "is very jealous of his just rights and also ready to anticipate some rights which are, I think, without any ground."

Bruff finally relented. The meeting went off peacefully, and the large Indian group left St. Louis. But the next day Pierre heard by rumor that the prisoner had escaped in the night; Bruff had not informed him. Pierre's normally warm and engaging personality was now giving way to his occasional temper and volatility. He was fed up and on the verge of an explosion, believing that he could have captured the Indian had he been told of the flight when it occurred.

Reporting the events to Dearborn, he said, "Permit me, Sir, to observe to you how unfortunate and even harmful it is to the interests of the United States that the different heads to whom authority is confided are not always disposed to aid each other; circumstances can arise when I will need help from the commandant of the garrison, or others when I can be of help to him."

It must have given Pierre great satisfaction a few days later to send over to Bruff the presidential pardon for the escaped Indian, which arrived soon after the prisoner broke free. However, it was not of much use to the Sac, because there was one more thing Bruff had not told Pierre: the Indian prisoner had been killed by buckshot to the neck the night of the escape.

Occasionally Pierre received word from Indians or traders on the Missouri of the progress of Lewis and Clark. He passed along to Jefferson any tidbit of information he picked up. "The rivers being still frozen have until now interrupted all communication, except that by the hearsay of some of the savages I have been informed that Captain Lewis, after a successful journey, wintered about fifty leagues above the village of the Mandanes; that is, a little more than 450 [leagues] in the upper part of the Missoury," Pierre wrote in January 1805, eight months after the expedition set off.

"The news which I have received indirectly of Captain Lewis and which I announced to you in my last letter has been found to be true," he wrote a month later. "A merchant from this village who wintered at the village of the Mahas wrote by an express that Captain Lewis had arrived about 50 leagues above the Mandans before things had frozen up, and without any disagreeable incident."

The other news about Captain Lewis was that, in his enthusiasm for making friends along his travel route, he was sending group after group of Indian chiefs and other leaders downriver to St. Louis with the promise that someone would take them to Washington to see the President. A group of Iowa chiefs arrived in November 1804 and told Pierre that Lewis had promised them a trip to Washington. Shortly, seven Sioux chiefs arrived with the same story.

Pierre informed Jefferson of their arrival and said that he thought such a trip could be worthwhile but he had received no authorization from Dearborn or anyone else to arrange such visits. Some Sacs had also approached him about sending two or three leaders. "These chiefs, who all belong to important tribes, would transmit to their people the immensity of the forces that they saw in the United States, and from the evidence of this physical superiority, it will be much easier to maintain them in that subordination from which they are always ready to emerge," he told Jefferson.

To Dearborn, Pierre complained that Captain Stoddard had just told him the day before that he and Lewis had previously agreed that Stoddard would escort the Sioux chiefs to Washington: "I was expressly opposed to it, as my orders were not to permit the departure of any chiefs for the seat of government without having first obtained special permission."

"The different savage nations which surround us are disposed to be jealous of one another," he continued.

> Supposing that the government thought it well to have the chiefs of some nations come to Federal City, I think it would be at the same time economical and prudent to unite in a single journey several chiefs of different nations; secondly, to undertake this journey in autumn, since the season of cold is the best and healthiest for the northern [Indian] nations, and, finally, to take the most prudent measures to keep within bounds on a long and difficult route these insubordinate savages, whose spirit must be thoroughly understood in order to keep them in order without nevertheless arousing their ill-will, a skill which is acquired only by long acquaintance with them.

He added that if any more of the chiefs showed up in St. Louis before specific orders arrived from Dearborn, he would give them some presents and send them away, telling them to return in the fall. He soon sent the Sioux chiefs home with gifts and the understanding that they would wait until fall for the trip to Washington.

When the weather warmed, Pierre organized anew for his long-planned and often delayed trip to visit the Arkansas River Osages to try to convince them to return to the main tribe. In late April he dispatched his boat up the Missouri, with a plan to catch up to it by land. The boat had gone about fifteen leagues up the river, but Pierre had not yet left St. Louis on horseback when a barge sent by Lewis reached St. Louis at the end of a sixteen-hundred-mile voyage from the Mandan villages. It carried forty-five chiefs and principal men of the Sioux, Poncas, Arikaras, Mahas, Otoes, and Missouris, all expecting to be escorted to Washington and received by the President.

Pierre advised Governor Harrison in Vincennes that he did not plan to take any of the Indians to Washington without express instructions. He repeated that summer was the wrong time to take them, because they would "fall victims to so long and tiring a journey in a climate so different from their own." He planned to keep them in St. Louis until fall, by which time he estimated that the delegation to Washington would grow to sixty or more.

In addition to the Indians being sent to St. Louis by Meriwether Lewis, a delegation of forty Sioux arrived, bringing to Pierre one of their men who had killed two Frenchmen on the St. Peter's River coming from Canada, a move probably calculated to win favor with the new power in the region. And of course, the four chiefs in the new Sioux group wanted to go to Washington. They also returned to Pierre their old flags and medals, presumably from the Spanish or English, and demanded some from the United States.

Harrison agreed with Pierre's decision not to take the Indians to Washington during the summer. While they waited to depart for Washington, Pierre planned to amuse them — "I shall equip a suitable wagon carriage to convey them from time to time to places where they can hunt without danger." Within a short time, however, some of the chiefs were suffering from dysentery in St. Louis, and they decided to go home and return in September for the trip to Washington.

Indian chiefs were not the only living creatures making the forty-five-day journey downriver as guests of Meriwether Lewis. The same barge brought "two magpies, one pheasant, a prairie-dog and two trunks," all consigned to Pierre to care for and forward securely to the President. Inside the trunks was a collection of skins, horns, and bones of a number of animals, including pronghorn, mule deer, prairie dogs, white-tailed jack rabbits, coyotes, weasels, badgers, elk, and bighorn sheep.

It took about three weeks for Pierre to find the means to send the

shipment on its way, addressed to Governor Claiborne at New Orleans, a trip of another three weeks. Claiborne put everything on the
ship *Comet* bound for Baltimore; then it was transported by land to
Washington. On August 12 it reached the majordomo at the White
House, who wrote Jefferson, at Monticello, that he had put it all in the
room where he received callers.

SEVEN

Intrigues and Possibilities

✳

In late June 1805 General James Wilkinson, newly appointed governor of the Louisiana Territory, was slowly ascending the Mississippi River toward St. Louis against what he described as "an impetuous current, a burning Sun and myriads of musquetoes." As his boat neared Kaskaskia, on the east bank, it was met by a vessel carrying Pierre Chouteau and three chiefs from the Sac and Fox tribes. The encounter was vintage Chouteau style and audacity.

Knowing that Wilkinson was en route, Pierre had summoned eight or ten chiefs of the two closely connected tribes to St. Louis in order to allow Wilkinson the honor of informing them of the presidential pardon that had been extended to the Sac brave shot and killed as he escaped prison two months earlier. Instead, about 160 members of the two tribes showed up, hoping for presents from the new governor. Pierre took control of the situation by taking the three most important chiefs downriver to an early meeting with Wilkinson.

Pierre's thinking, no doubt, was that everybody benefited: the Indian chiefs felt honored at being able to meet Wilkinson ahead of others, especially their dreaded Osage enemies; Pierre looked good in the eyes of both Wilkinson and the chiefs; and Wilkinson received a showy and enthusiastic welcome to his new post.

The larger group of Sacs and Foxes was waiting for Wilkinson when he reached St. Louis on July 2 in the company of the three chiefs. He immediately went into council with all of them. He produced the President's pardon of the warrior who had been shot, gave the pardon to the brother of the deceased, and told him to preserve it in remembrance of his brother. Although they parted in good humor, the chiefs told Wilkinson that they regretted having sold so much of their land to Governor Harrison the year before and thought they had made a bad bargain.

Pierre himself had made a good first impression on Wilkinson. That night, Wilkinson dined at the home of Auguste with other members of the town's magistracy, and the Chouteaus were well on the way to working their magic on the new governor.

"I consider after close examination the appointment of Pere [*sic*] Chouteau a very judicious one," Wilkinson soon wrote Secretary of War Dearborn,

> not only on account of his capacity for the Conduct of Indian affairs, and his general influence among the Nations acquainted with this place, but for the universal confidence which himself and his Brother enjoy, with all ranks and distinctions of People in this Country—whatever may have been his anterior attachments, the respect with which he has been treated by You and the President, and the trust with which he is honoured, have disposed him to serve the United States with the Zeal, which is inseparable from his ardent temperament, and upon us he has fastened all his hopes of Honor and Emolument.

He added that Pierre might have to be reined in a bit on expenditures. "The force of Spanish habits and his inexperience of our modes of Business, may have involved Some improper expences, but I must in justice observe, that I have not remarked any disposition to extravagance."

James Wilkinson owed his appointment as governor to an act passed by Congress on March 26, 1805, creating the territory of Louisiana. The new territory, with its capital at St. Louis, embraced all of the Louisiana Purchase lands north of the Arkansas River nearly to the Canadian border. The territory of Orleans was created from the lands to the south of the Arkansas River, including New Orleans. Wilkinson, a senior army officer and veteran of the Revolutionary War, was sent from Natchez to govern the new northern territory.

Then forty-eight years old, Wilkinson had been commanding general of the army during the Administration of John Adams. Afterward, he moved to Kentucky and engaged in commerce and land speculation. For more than a decade Wilkinson's name also had been linked with rumored efforts to separate the area west of the Appalachians into an independent republic affiliated in some manner with Spain. Although it had not yet become public knowledge, Wilkinson had been on the Spanish payroll, identified as Agent 13, since 1787. Even in 1805, with the Louisiana Purchase in the hands of the United States, Spain still held most of the territory westward from the Rocky Mountains, so the possibility remained of further contact—and intrigue.

It is something of a mystery why Jefferson and other national leaders of the time tolerated Wilkinson. He seems to have been a curious choice for the sensitive post overseeing a new territorial acquisition whose leading residents had an emotional attachment to another culture and might have been susceptible to Wilkinson's importuning. Some historians believe that Jefferson, because of his fears that the Federalists in the East were secretly monarchists, shared some of Wilkinson's notions about launching an independent republic west of the Mississippi. An independent republic in the West may have been seen as a potential refuge for Jefferson and others of strong republican views if they concluded that those in the East were too conservative.

Even this man destined to go down in history as one of the great masters of political intrigue found his new home "raging with personal animosities in all quaters [sic]." Wilkinson told Dearborn, "I publicly avowed my abhorrence of Civil fueds [sic], declared my determination to resist the Sympathies and antipathies of all parties."

St. Louis, in his words, was rife with "bitter animosities, and vindictive Personal Factions which rend several districts of this Territory, excited I have cause to beleive [sic], by a few impatient, abitious [sic] and perhaps sordid Spirits."

"Attempts have been made to introduce here, the political distinctions of the union and to excite national prejudices, but without effect: the French are not able to distinguish between republicanism and federalism, and our fugitive countrymen, who sought asylum here during the Spanish Government, wear their Political Morality as loosely as they do their cloaths."

Wilkinson, however, quickly added to the heated political climate in St. Louis, becoming deeply involved in local issues and the disputes over confirmation of Spanish and French land claims. His doings added zest to the agenda of rumor and gossip at William Christy's smoky city tavern, the new gathering place favored by the movers and shakers of St. Louis.

William Christy had arrived in 1804 from Jefferson County, Kentucky, being among the first English-speaking Americans to cross the Mississippi and settle in St. Louis. Bringing slaves and capital, he opened a "public house" in the old government headquarters diagonally across from Auguste Chouteau's home.

In addition to billiards, Christy offered "liquors of the best kind, and good pasture for horses, with corn, oats and green clover." The tavern provided a setting for the arriving Anglophones and old French to mix and wager. Gambling was the favorite pastime of St. Louis men, who would sometimes play for thirty hours straight. The new tavern also served as the locale for big dinners and other notable public social events.

In St. Louis, two cultures were meeting—and sometimes conflicting. On one level, there was a conflict between those accustomed to the ways of a monarchy and those who believed in the democratic experiment of the daring young government in the East. But idealism and political principle were not what motivated most, if any, of them. It was almost impossible to distinguish the public officials appointed and sent by the Jefferson Administration from the adventurers and speculators arriving from Kentucky, Pennsylvania, Virginia, and New England. Everybody wanted to protect or advance his own interests. As Wilkinson noted, dealings were replete with animosities and vindictiveness. But fortunes were to be made. This was the birth of America's Great West, and nobody was attending it with much gentility.

Rules governing the behavior of public officeholders were not clear or did not exist, and the great distance to Washington meant long delays in learning of important decisions, at times creating a power vacuum. Lewis and Clark were barely halfway through their voyage, and no one in St. Louis knew what roles they would play when—and if—they returned.

Despite their outer graciousness, the Chouteaus were determined to protect and advance their own interests. They mixed affably with everyone because that seemed the surest way of defending their turf. With little understanding of the politics of the United States, they sought to gain favor and achieve business success by ingratiating themselves with the territory's new rulers. Their goals were advanced by the fact that they had more to offer than others—especially knowledge about and influence with the tribes, and the respect of other traders and landowners.

At the time Wilkinson arrived, Pierre Chouteau was preparing to lead a second Indian delegation to Washington, this one to represent twelve tribes, including the Kansa, Sioux, and Little Osage. Some of them had arrived in St. Louis the previous spring in response to Meriwether Lewis's promise that they would be taken to Washington, and they had been sent back home by Pierre with instructions to return in the fall.

Like officials in Washington, Wilkinson was concerned about the cost of everything. Partly for that reason he decided that Amos Stoddard would escort this group of Indians. Stoddard was due for leave and would be going east anyway. Wilkinson told Dearborn, "If Cadet Chouteau can be prevailed on to abandon his wish to go in, without hazarding such disgusts as may impair his Zeal, and finally oblige us to turn him off, the Captain will have charge of them." Each of the chiefs making the next trip would be provided "a course Capot, two shirts, a Hat, leggins & Clout, a blanket, handkerchief for the head, and mocassins, on the cheapest terms."

The group left in October, reached Washington in January, and remained until spring. The Indians caused quite a stir when they appeared before Congress in traditional dress, and again at a theater on Pennsylvania Avenue, where they danced, whooped, and pretended to scalp one of their group. They requested half of their pay in rum for the theater appearance, and the next morning one of the Indians was found dead in his bed. Contemporary news accounts attributed his death to drinking too much rum.

Although Pierre did not protest being left behind on this trip, he did write Secretary Dearborn to recommend that he limit the number of medals handed out to the Indian travelers and not be too quick to accede to other requests from members of the group. "A multiplicity of medals spread around a [tribe] only stirs up jealousies which often become dangerous," he told Dearborn. "You must expect to be continually importuned by demands from the savage bands conducted by Capt. Stoddard; but most of these demands are suggested to them by the interpreters, or are even made solely by them."

As could be seen in the letter to Dearborn, Pierre showed no hesitation in lecturing American officials about the handling of Indian affairs, and some of them must have felt threatened by his knowledge of Indian customs and culture. Pierre was trying to straddle a line between siding totally with the Indians, who trusted him, and representing purely the interests of the United States, which paid him. The Jefferson Administration wanted to take advantage of his knowledge and skills without opening the door wide enough for him to gain personal advantage. This probably contributed to the contentious relationship he was developing with Secretary Dearborn, whose most frequent advice to Pierre was to exercise the "greatest prudence" in spending government money.

Coming back from a visit to Osage country to find that merchandise had arrived for the annual payments to the Sac and Fox nations in accord with the 1804 treaty, Pierre promptly informed Dearborn that it was of poor quality. "This merchandise, both because of its selection and the damages it has suffered, seems to me unfit to fulfill the object for which it is destined," he wrote. He had already warned Wilkinson "that if this merchandise was offered to the savages they would be not at all satisfied and, I dare add, with just reason, being in no way suited to their needs nor of a quality comparable to that which these nations draw each year from the English firms."

Over the next few months Pierre repeatedly made his case for increasing expenditures. In a lengthy report to Wilkinson that revealed Pierre's broad knowledge of geopolitics and the strategy involving the Indians, he explained: "When Spain took possession of Louisiana, she felt the necessity of attaching to herself the savage nations of these parts, who . . . seemed to regret the [departure of the] French and not to be as attached to their successors. The means which [the Spanish] employed to gain their affections, and which succeeded, was to act with more generosity toward them than the old government."

He estimated the maximum annual expenditures for presents during the forty-year reign of the Spanish at $30,000 and the minimum at $8,000. He said the gifts probably averaged $13,500 a year during the period. But he pointed out that the U.S. government was establishing contact with more Indian nations than those with which the Spanish authorities had had relations, suggesting that this called for a higher level of expenditures.

"The journey of Capt. Lewis," he wrote,

> drew several [Indian] nations to St. Louis who had never been here before. The ties of commerce and friendship did not formerly extend higher up the Mississippi than the Des Moines River. The nations of the Upper Mississippi and of the River St. Pierre, although dwelling in the territory included within the Spanish limits, had no commercial or friendly connections except with the English nations established at Prairie du Chien, or directly with Canada. Lastly, the nations established on the Arkansas River had no connection with St. Louis. The nations which received presents and provisions from the lieutenant-governor of upper Louisiana were, accordingly, the Loups, the Chavanons (Shawnees), the Peorias, a little band of Machecoux, the Great and Little Osages, the Cances (Kansas), Ottos (Otoes), Ayouas (Iowas), Sacs and Foxes, Kickapoo.

He pointed out that the still uncompleted Lewis and Clark Expedition had already produced visits to St. Louis by leaders of additional tribes, including Arikaras, Sioux of the Des Moines River, Sioux of the Upper Missouri, Mandans, Mahas, and Pawnees. Pierre concurred, however, in the need to win the affections of those northern tribes if the United States hoped to attract to eastern ports or New Orleans the fur commerce that had formerly gone to Canada.

The Chouteaus soon developed good relations with Wilkinson, connections good enough to be seen in a sinister context by some critics, including John B. C. Lucas, a friend of Treasury Secretary Gallatin and member of the first St. Louis Land Commission. Lucas, a major land speculator himself, was the lone dissenter on the commission when the other members recommended confirmation of the 125,000-acre mine claim by Auguste Chouteau and Julien Dubuque recognized in the 1804 Sac and Fox Treaty.

Sometimes, however, Wilkinson gave off mixed signals about his views of Pierre Chouteau, on the one hand praising him, on the other planting doubts about him. At one point Wilkinson told Dearborn that Pierre was "ambitious in the extreme" and "by no means regardless of his private interests." Then he added, "Yet his Zeal is as ardent as his ambition, & his principles rather more chaste than those of three fourths of his Country Men."

Zebulon M. Pike, who was dispatched on his exploring missions by Wilkinson during this time, was critical of Pierre and passed his opinions along to Wilkinson, who sometimes passed them along to Washington. "Mr. Pike considers our Agent C. S. (Pierre Chouteau) as an Imposter in all things, and at heart our Enemy," Wilkinson commented to Dearborn.

But while he was raising tempers and passions at Christy's Tavern and elsewhere in St. Louis, Wilkinson was also intriguing with bigger fish. Aaron Burr, Jefferson's first-term Vice President and the man who mortally wounded Alexander Hamilton in their 1804 duel, talked with Governor Wilkinson in 1805. Some versions say the meeting occurred in St. Louis in September that year; others place it at Fort Massac in southern Illinois at about the same time.

"No doubt the whole situation was canvassed, the probability of war with Spain; the ease with which the Floridas might be overrun; the matter of the equipping of an army which should sail for Vera Cruz to light the torch of insurrection in Mexico," wrote Walter F. McCaleb in one of the early histories of the conspiracy. In addition to Wilkinson and Burr, those rumored to be involved included William Henry Harrison, Henry Clay, and Attorney General John Breckinridge, all prominent Jefferson men well regarded by the Chouteaus and others in the St. Louis leadership.

Pike, meanwhile, was crossing the future state of Kansas to explore the headwaters of the Arkansas and Red rivers on instructions from

Wilkinson. This took him directly into Spanish territory, making the motives for this trip a subject of debate in St. Louis and Washington.

Word of the meeting between Burr and Wilkinson reached Jefferson in Washington at the beginning of December, and the mail on Christmas Day brought word to St. Louis that the President was unhappy. In reaction to rumors that Wilkinson might be removed from office, Auguste Chouteau circulated a petition stating that the residents were "perfectly satisfied" with Wilkinson. Auguste and nine other prominent men signed a letter to Jefferson defending and supporting Wilkinson against "a Contemptible cabal, of which some are goaded by avarice & others by ambition."

Nevertheless, in May 1806 Dearborn ordered Wilkinson to leave St. Louis to take command of military forces in the Orleans Territory, based at Natchitoches. Jefferson and Dearborn wanted Wilkinson out of the politicized environment of St. Louis, but they did nothing to publicly bring him down, and they showed their confidence in him by giving him an important new post. Natchitoches was then the southwestern frontier of the United States facing Spanish territory, providing Wilkinson with continuing opportunities to plot.

Paradoxically, he was soon joined there by a Chouteau—Auguste Pierre, the promising eldest son of Pierre. Auguste Pierre finished the two-year West Point program in July 1806, graduating fourth in a class of fifteen, and was named an ensign in the Second Regiment of Infantry and assigned as Wilkinson's aide-de-camp. Wilkinson was undoubtedly happy to have the assistance of a young man who was heir to his father's superb knowledge of Indian ways and culture and who also spoke good English.

Pierre may have had a role in his son's assignment. A couple of months before Auguste Pierre finished at West Point, his father wrote Secretary Dearborn reminding him that promises had been made when his son entered military school. "The interest which you then evinced for him is so precious to me and I regard it as so necessary to his advancement and his happiness that I beg you urgently please to maintain it. I hope that by his conduct and his application he will render himself always worthy of it." When Dearborn wrote young Auguste Pierre informing him of his assignment, he said that President Jefferson was "pleased" to make it.

Wilkinson, for his part, soon turned on Burr, revealed the conspiracy, and publicly disavowed his own participation. Burr was arrested in Alabama in early 1807 and tried for treason in Richmond, where he was acquitted. Wilkinson continued to hold various public posts until his death in Mexico in 1826.

Even with Wilkinson out of the picture, there was a growing chasm between Pierre Chouteau and Dearborn. Dearborn did not trust Pierre, and Pierre surely found the New England farmer to be excessively rigid, as well as ignorant about Indians. After hearing allegations that Pierre was conducting trade for his personal profit, Dearborn warned him against trading with the Indians while serving as a government agent, saying he had "received information that you have so far deviated from the spirit and letter of your instructions, as to pay, in goods, what ought to be paid in money. I hope the information is not correct."

"Any trade carried on by you, directly or indirectly, with the Indians, which shall, in the most trifling degree, affect the United States, will be considered as sufficient ground for your removal from Office," the Secretary continued. "I am thus explicit that you may have no possible excuse in future, for any kind of impropriety of conduct; and you may rest assured that any complaint hereafter will be closely investigated."

Pierre replied that he was trying to "conform with the most rigid exactitude to the instructions which you have given me and to the orders which I have since received." He claimed that Dearborn had received false allegations about him from his enemies, without naming them. The allegation of his trading with the Osages, he said, may have resulted from the fact that he had allowed Noel Mongrain, an interpreter working for him, to assist some traders as an interpreter.

"When I was appointed by the government as agent of the Indian Department for Louisiana Territory I had a considerable mercantile establishment whose principal relations were with the Indian nations; on my arrival in St. Louis [from the visit to Washington] I yielded this establishment to Mr. D. Delaunay and since then have undertaken no business," Pierre wrote Dearborn. "Perhaps you have been told that I give preference to my debtors or old employees in employing people for government service, and it is true that I employ as interpreters and *engagés* the people whom I believe the most capable and faithful. For the same reasons, I believe I should hire them again for the Indian Department."

The reference to debts due him undoubtedly meant debts that the Osages, and possibly other tribes, had run up with Pierre before he became a government agent, debts he would normally have expected to recover from the skins and furs brought in by the tribe in future hunts. Noel Mongrain, the interpreter, and David Delaunay, to whom he had entrusted his business, had both worked for Pierre in the past, so there was a certain logic in Dearborn's concern that they were fronting for Pierre.

As this exchange occurred, Lewis and Clark were on the last leg of their epic journey, the fast, thrilling downstream trip on the Missouri River. On September 6, as they passed the Niobrara River, they met a trading boat of Auguste Chouteau's bound for the James River to trade with the Yankton Sioux. They bought a gallon of whiskey from the leader with a promise to pay in St. Louis. A few days earlier they had met another trading boat and learned about the fire at Pierre's house.

On September 12 they met two pirogues from St. Louis bound for the Platte River, one belonging to one of the Chouteaus. Two days later, a little below the former Kansa village near present-day Kansas City, they met three large boats bound to the Yanktons and Mahas. The boatmen provided whiskey, biscuits, pork, and onions, and spent two hours with them, imparting the news. Everybody in the Lewis and Clark party received a dram of whisky and spent the evening singing. By September 17 they had reached the big bend of the river at its junction with Grand River, north of present-day Boonville, nearly halfway across the future state of Missouri.

In St. Louis, plans were being laid for their return and for their onward trip to Washington. Pierre Chouteau was going to accompany them. Despite the differences between him and Dearborn, the Secretary had agreed to his suggestion to bring a delegation of the rebellious Arkansas River Osages, the only faction of Osages that had not yet been to the capital. Accompanied by seventeen-year-old Pierre Jr., Pierre Chouteau had gone to Grande Piste's village on the Verdigris River in present-day Oklahoma to ask the chief to come to St. Louis and travel onward to Washington. Grande Piste was on his deathbed, "without hope," but he finally agreed to permit his son, who was in line to succeed him, to make the trip as part of a delegation of six leaders of the tribal faction.

Lewis and Clark reached St. Louis on Tuesday, September 23, 1806. They brought with them the Mandan chief Shahaka, who was also going to the capital, along with his wife and son, and an interpreter and his wife and child. The Mandans held a special place in the hearts of Lewis and Clark as well as that of Jefferson, in part because the friendly tribe had provided assistance and hospitality during the winter the explorers spent among them in 1804–05.

The Mandans were also the tribe associated with the long-held theory that Welsh voyagers had arrived in the New World several centuries earlier, ahead of other European settlement, and had made their way upriver until, becoming lost, they were gradually absorbed into an Indian group. Jefferson found some credibility in these reports, which were substantiated by various travelers who claimed that the Mandans were lighter skinned than most Indians and had a variety of hair colors. The Mandans also lived in permanent villages, cultivating maize and vegetables that could have been introduced by whites.

After storing their belongings at Christy's Tavern, Lewis and Clark accepted Pierre's invitation to stay at his rebuilt house. There is no record of where the Mandan group was lodged, or the six Osages either—perhaps in the Indian guesthouse Pierre had talked earlier of building on his square-block estate.

That evening, Lewis and Clark visited Auguste Chouteau and "some of our old friends." The next night, they dined with "Mr. Choutoux"—presumably meaning Pierre this time—then went to a store, bought some fabric, and took it to a tailor to be made into new clothing. The next day, they put their skins in the sun to dry, then stored them at Pierre's place. That evening, they were entertained at a grand dinner and ball at Christy's Tavern, where a round of toasts was drunk to "the fair daughters of Louisiana" and to Lewis and Clark for "their perilous services to the nation."

All ears in St. Louis were tuned to the tales Lewis and Clark brought back of the promise of the upriver and mountain country for the fur trade. Although the French had been navigating the upriver areas for more than a century, they had not yet tried to establish permanent sites north of the Platte. Manuel Lisa, the aggressive Spanish competitor of the Chouteaus, was working on that idea at the very moment Lewis and Clark returned. With William Morrison and Pierre Ménard from Kaskaskia, Lisa was organizing a company that would push off early the following spring to ascend the Missouri River to the Yellowstone River, building forts, storage, and rendezvous points along the way.

Lewis and Clark left for Washington on October 21, accompanied by Pierre Chouteau, Shahaka's party, the Osages, several members of the expedition team, and Clark's slave, York. The two main elements of the party separated at Frankfort, Kentucky. Pierre and the Osages went through Lexington, then onward to Washington. Lewis and Clark and the others went through various Virginia communities to visit friends and family. Lewis's group arrived at Washington on December 28 after being feted at numerous locations in Virginia; Pierre's group was already there. Clark arrived later, having spent time in Fincastle, Virginia, where he proposed to his future wife, Julia Hancock.

A festive atmosphere greeted the travelers. Jefferson formally welcomed Shahaka on December 30 and received the Osages the next day, urging them to reunite with the main branch of the tribe. There were numerous receptions and dinner parties. The visitors were invited to Jefferson's New Year's Day reception, and Pierre was among the guests at a White House banquet on January 14 in honor of Lewis. The Osages and Mandans went to various theater events and, like previous Indian visitors, went onstage, danced and whooped, brandished tomahawks, and beat drums. In the words of one observer, a "frightful yell was uttered by all."

The President honored Lewis by naming him the new governor of the Louisiana Territory. At Lewis's request, he then named Clark as Indian agent for the entire area west of the Mississippi. Pierre's responsibilities were reduced to cover only the Big and Little Osages, who were excluded from Clark's area of responsibility.

Although Pierre was surely disappointed at the diminution of his authority and the reduction in his annual salary to $1,200, it did not produce a rupture between him and Lewis and Clark. As would become clear in the coming months, the effectiveness of both Lewis and Clark would depend to a considerable degree on the continuing advice and assistance of Pierre and his extended family.

Lewis remained in Washington, staying with Jefferson at the White House through the winter. He went to Philadelphia for several months, then home to Virginia. During this time, he and Jefferson presumably held long talks about what he had seen on the expedition, and then he worked on arranging the publication of his journals. Lewis's tendency to drink too much, plus the continuing public adulation, which occupied much of his attention, interfered with preparing his journals for publication. Jefferson was eager for that to be done, but he also wanted Lewis to take up his new post in St. Louis. Eventually the journals were put aside, and Lewis went to St. Louis in March 1808, nearly eighteen months after his triumphant return from the voyage.

Clark had moved to St. Louis a full year earlier, in March 1807, and he set to work arranging the return of Mandan chief Shahaka and his party to their village near today's Bismarck, North Dakota. Nathaniel Pryor, an army veteran of the expedition, was assigned to lead it. To hold down costs, Dearborn suggested that private traders be allowed to accompany the expedition in exchange for trading rights with the Mandans. One of the trading parties was organized by Pierre's son, twenty-one-year-old Auguste Pierre Chouteau, who had wearied of his career as an army officer after just six months, resigned, and returned to St. Louis.

The expedition departed St. Louis near the end of May 1807 with ninety-five people, including Indians, traders, and military escorts. Two noncommissioned officers and eleven privates under Ensign

Pryor escorted Chief Shahaka. A deputation of Sioux Indians—eighteen men and women and six children returning home after a visit to St. Louis—had its own escort of soldiers.

The trading party under Auguste Pierre, who would soon establish his name as A. P. Chouteau, consisted of thirty-two men going to trade with the Mandans. In the other trading group were ten men led by trader and interpreter William Dorion, going to the Sioux trade. After the Sioux delegation and its military escort and Dorion's trading party dropped off in Sioux country, the others continued upriver. On September 9 they reached the lower Arikara village, about six miles above the mouth of Grand River near present-day Mobridge, South Dakota, and were met by an angry crowd of about 650 Arikaras waving weapons.

Some of the Arikaras, joined by a few Sioux, opened fire as A. P. Chouteau's barge pulled into view. It turned out that they were upset about several things. For one thing, they had recently learned of the death of one of their chiefs during the Stoddard-led visit to Washington in April 1806, and they blamed the whites. They had also recently been at war with the Mandans and were angered by the fact that the trading group was bound for the Mandan villages and did not want to trade with them. Further, Manuel Lisa had built up the Arikaras' expectations of trade when he passed through the area a short time earlier. They had allowed him to proceed only after he told them that another trading group was on the way.

Ensign Pryor met with the Arikaras in council and hung a medal on one of the chiefs. The boats then continued a short distance to the upper village, where the Indians ordered the traders to stay and trade. They seized hold of A.P.'s barge, which contained merchandise and no soldiers. Fighting broke out; A.P. and some of his men were on the beach. Pryor soon decided they were overwhelmed and ordered a retreat, but A.P.'s boat became stuck on a sandbar, and his men had to get into the water and drag the boat while exposed to continual fire from the shore.

For about an hour the two boats struggled to get away through a narrow channel, with firing coming from both banks. When the boats were finally free, the men lashed them together and checked for dead and wounded. One of A.P.'s men had been killed on the beach, another in a pirogue that accompanied the barge, and a third died nine days later of wounds. Six of A.P.'s men were badly wounded; three of Pryor's men were wounded, and one Sioux was killed.

At this point Pryor proposed continuing north by land to deliver Chief Shahaka to his home, but the chief would not agree, so they raced back to St. Louis as fast as the current would carry them, and Pryor reported to Clark.

"If my opinion were asked 'What number of men would be necessary to escort this unhappy chief to his nation," he told Clark, "I should be compelled to say, from my own knowledge of the association of the upper band of the Sieux [Sioux] with the Ricaras [Arikaras] that a force of less than 400 men ought not to attempt such an enterprize. And surely it is possible that even one thousand men might fail in the attempt."

When Clark passed the news of the failed mission along to Secretary Dearborn, he commented that "young Mr. Choteau behaved verry [sic] well."

Pierre was with the Osages on the Osage River when his son had his close escape on the Upper Missouri. Clark had apparently organized the expedition without Pierre's direct involvement, in the light of the recent reduction in his responsibilities, but Pierre was quick to offer his future help, doing so in a letter directly to Jefferson:

> The unfortunate event which forced Mr. Pryor and my son Auguste to return to St. Louis confirms the opinion I have held for a long time, that the savage nations are almost all influenced by [English] traders or the English government, which has great interest in preventing frequent communication between the Americans and the nations of the Upper Missoury. It is not my place to think in advance what means you will judge best to return the Mandan chief back to his nation, but whatever they are, if I can contribute to their success in any manner I beg you to be assured that I will use the greatest exactitude in the execution of the orders of the government.

Winter was coming, however, and other issues had to be dealt with in St. Louis and the territory. It would be some time before another effort could be made to return Shahaka to his home.

The St. Louis landowners, particularly the Chouteaus and other old French settlers, continued to chafe at the demands and rulings of the three-member Land Commission. The St. Louis Town Committee, still led by Auguste Chouteau, sent a petition to Congress complaining that the "court established to decide the validity of our titles grants to-day what to-morrow it refuses."

Struggling to express themselves in English, the petitioners wrote:

> Almost all our titles following the customs and usages of the Spanish Government . . . consist ordinarily in simple decree of the Lieutenant Governor and survey certificate . . . We do not find in the laws of Congress any article which may be adopted to our position and when we present these titles to the court the single objection and one so oft repeated [by] the Agent of the United States is enough that such title is not an act in good faith, that it is antedated or even only suspected of being so that this title is entirely rejected.

It was almost impossible to furnish other proofs of the titles, because the officers who granted them were dead or absent, they said, arguing that if American officials suspected a fraudulent title, it was their obligation to furnish the proof. "The title presented ought to be considered in good faith in conformity with the usages and customs of the government which granted them." They complained that landowners in Upper Louisiana were subject to the capriciousness of a single individual who often demanded witnesses to title impossible to produce. (They were referring to Judge Lucas, the friend of Secretary Gallatin who had come west as a member of the Land Commission and was setting out to amass extensive landholdings of his own.) They further charged that the court was lax about returning documents of title that inhabitants presented, creating great inconvenience to people who might want to buy or sell lands. "We beg you to order that every title of lands granted by the Spanish government when it was in possession of Louisiana be recognized and sanctioned by law unless it be proved to be antedated or fraudulent."

Despite their dissatisfaction, the Chouteaus and the other long-time residents of the territory continued to file required documents with the commission and, from time to time, to receive rulings in their favor. Sometime in 1806 Auguste Chouteau filed in the record office in St. Louis a stack of copies of land sales, deeds, and grants, including the bill of sale for his purchase of Laclède's water mill at auction at the church door after high mass on July 4, 1779, for 2,000 livres' worth of beaver or deer skins. There was also a translation of a land grant to Laclède by St. Ange de Bellerive, when St. Ange was de facto lieutenant governor, on August 11, 1766, just two years after the settlement was begun. The tract, measuring eight arpents in front and eighty arpents deep, was on a small stream and probably became the site of the water mill. About the same time, the Land Commission reviewed a 1796 survey of 2,160 arpents of land (1,836 acres) belonging to Auguste and found it to be a "compleat Spanish title."

Pierre and Auguste were both selling land regularly from their holdings. Some of the dealings were with Lewis or Clark, reflecting both business and personal interdependence that would last for decades in the case of Clark, and in Lewis's case until his early death.

On August 3, 1808, for example, soon after Lewis arrived in St. Louis, Pierre and his wife, Brigitte, deeded to him a tract of 30.93 arpents (26.3 acres) described as "adjoining the town lots of the town of St. Louis," which suggested that it was on the edge of the most populated area. The transfer was made for $248 "in hand." Two weeks later Pierre and Brigitte sold to Clark 1,400 arpents (1,190 acres) of land two and a half leagues northwest of St. Louis for $800. On May 26, 1808, Pierre bought at public auction some land at Portage des Sioux being sold by William Clark.

An act of the Territorial Legislature on June 18, 1808, "authorized the people of any village in the territory on petition of two-thirds of their taxable inhabitants to be incorporated into a town on application to the proper court." Less than three weeks later, eighty residents of St. Louis presented a petition in French and English asking to become a town. That was quickly followed, on July 23, with the first election. People gathered at the courthouse and elected five trustees to set up the new government: Auguste Chouteau, Bernard Pratte, Edward Hempstead, Pierre Chouteau, and Alexander McNair.

It turned out that they had acted too soon. The town had not yet been legally incorporated. So on December 11, 1809, interested residents met at Auguste's place to incorporate. The trustees were elected again, and Auguste was also elected town treasurer.

The first newspaper published in St. Louis made its appearance on July 12, 1808. From a stone building on the east side of Main Street, Irish-born Joseph Charless published the first issue of the *Missouri Gazette* on a sheet of foolscap 8 by 12 inches, there being no other suitable paper in town. The original subscription base was 170; some people paid in farm products or peltries.

A post office was established in the spring of 1808, but an early article in the *Gazette* complained of poor mail service. Letters from Philadelphia and New York usually took about six weeks and those from Europe three months.

Although population growth was slow in the first two or three years after cession, by 1807 the area seemed to be taking off. Every house was crowded, and rents were rising. Six or seven new houses were built that year, and twice that many were expected to be built the following year. St. Louis now had a dozen mercantile establishments, which were handling about $250,000 worth of merchandise a year.

Governing the growing territory required additional officials. Jefferson appointed Frederick Bates, a Virginian, to be secretary of the territorial government, recorder of land titles, and member of the Board of Land Commissioners. Bates arrived on April 1, 1807, and doubled as acting governor until the arrival of Meriwether Lewis a year later.

Bates commissioned Silas Bent, an arrival from the East and son of a leader of the Boston Tea Party, as justice of the Common Pleas Court. Auguste Chouteau and Bernard Pratte, who had married a daughter of one of the Chouteau sisters, were among the three men commissioned as associate justices.

For protection, Cantonment Bellefontaine was constructed on a site that General Wilkinson had selected on the south bank of the Missouri River twelve miles by land from St. Louis. Wilkinson judged it a good setting for the small fort, on elevated ground "richly ornamented by fields and forests, groves and Meadows." It had both spring and river water, of which the Missouri River water was better, in his view. Before his departure Wilkinson had also done some organizing of the militia and defense. He appointed Auguste Chouteau as lieutenant colonel in the militia and Pierre a captain in the militia cavalry, positions they held through the War of 1812, during which they were promoted.

Despite all the attention they had received from Pierre and the Jefferson Administration, including three trips to Washington and many gifts, the Osages continued to be unhappy and edgy. They were seeing a lot of movement within their traditional lands—white settlers arriving and attacks or hunting incursions by longtime enemy tribes from the Ohio Valley. Returning from a trip to the Big Osage villages on the Osage River, Pierre reported to Bates in October 1807 that the area was in a state of turmoil.

Entering the Osage River, Pierre had heard shots, leading him to believe he was followed by Indians of another tribe wanting to go to war against the Osages. After reaching White Hair's village, he went to bed early in a lodge at the end of the village, but he was awakened by a discharge of gunshots nearby. In the lodge next to him, two Osage men were found slain and a woman was mortally wounded. The Osages were angry with Pierre, thinking he had led the hostile Indians into the village. They felt that "the Indians who actually live in the bosom of the United States continually strike them," and that the United States, while preaching peace to the Osages, did not prevent attacks on the Osages. Pierre gave presents to the families of the dead, and the tribe sent 130 warriors in pursuit of the killers, whom they thought to be Potawatomis and the Sacs and Foxes.

The Osages stepped up their own attacks on whites and other Indians during this time, and the attack on White Hair's village by another tribe may have been in response. By 1808 the Osages were once again at war with virtually every other tribe in the Louisiana Territory.

In April 1808 Pierre used the opportunity of letters he sent to Grande Piste and White Hair about some horse thefts and plundering of families on the St. Francis River to warn the chiefs that Americans were fed up with the behavior of the Osages. He said that Americans who had had their horses stolen were asking permission from Lewis to incite other tribes to go to war against the Osages. He also urged Grande Piste to reunite with White Hair and move back to "the land where you saw the light of day and which serves as cover for the bones of your ancestors." If they didn't listen to his counsel, he said, they could expect to be deprived of trade and other help from the whites.

President Jefferson, meanwhile, had begun to question the wisdom of a tolerant attitude toward the Osages. He and Secretary of War Dearborn talked about wiping out the Osages by organizing a large war party of tribes from east of the Mississippi to launch war against them. Jefferson went so far as to instruct Dearborn to provide logistical support to the friendly Indians.

Meriwether Lewis, after his arrival in St. Louis, began involving himself actively in Indian decisions, apparently consulting with Clark but often cutting Pierre out of the deliberations, even those involving the Osages. Lewis became convinced that a generalized Indian war was imminent, instigated by the Spaniards, who were said to be holding councils with disaffected Osages and the Kansas and Pawnees. But after considering, as Jefferson had done, backing eastern Indians in a war against the Osages, he proposed something different: a trading fort in the heart of Osage country along the same concepts as Fort Carondelet. It had been nearly fifteen years since Pierre and Auguste Chouteau had built Carondelet for the Spanish near the headwaters of the Osage River. It had succeeded, at least for a few years.

Lewis wrote Dearborn on July 1, proposing a fortified trading post for the Osages. He wanted to build it at a place known as Fire Prairie, about twenty miles east of present-day Kansas City on the right bank of the Missouri River. During their expedition, Lewis and Clark had taken note of the advantages of the site, a high bluff with a view for several miles up and down the river. Clark judged it an "elegant" situation, in which the river could be "completely defended." It was near the Big Osage villages, but not directly adjacent to them, and it was not far from the hunting grounds of the Kansa and Iowa tribes. Lewis's plan was to control the tribes through the traders by exercising "the power of withholding merchandise from them at pleasure." It was the same logic the Spanish regime had followed and the concept that Pierre had been trying to explain to Dearborn for four years.

The installation, initially called Fort Clark but better known as Fort Osage, was an early expression of a government policy of establishing trading posts called "factories," to be run by factors, or government agents, rather than by private traders. Jefferson had promised this to White Hair in Washington in 1804; Lewis and Clark had promised the same to other tribes during their expedition. George C. Sibley, whose name would eventually be given to the small town that arose nearby, was named factor of the new fort to be built at Fire Prairie. He and the factor appointed to serve Fort Bellefontaine near St. Louis went east for goods to stock the trading rooms of the forts.

Clark had the job of building the fort. On the morning of August 25 he rode out of St. Charles at the head of a column of eighty dragoons. He was then thirty-eight years old, six feet tall, slender and erect; he had fiery red hair. Riding beside him as "pilot" was twenty-six-year-old Nathan Boone, youngest son of Daniel. The handsome Sylvestre Labaddie Jr., twenty-nine-year-old nephew of Auguste and Pierre Chouteau, was his aide-de-camp. A road took them west for about twenty miles; then the column had to ford streams or make bridges of trees. Clark saw no settlement of white families west of Charette, except for a few around the mouth of the Osage River at Cote sans Dessein.

When they reached the site on September 4, Clark noted in his journal that the group had traveled 247 miles, adding that the route could be "stratened" to 230 miles. The men sharpened their axes and went to work building a structure of irregular shape with four blockhouses, a two-story officers quarters, and soldiers barracks. The site stood seventy-two feet above the high-water mark.

It is not clear whether what occurred next was entirely Clark's idea or whether he was acting on instructions from Lewis. Mathews, the Osage historian, said that Jefferson himself had earlier directed Lewis and Clark to obtain a large land concession from the Osages, but Mathews gives no source for the claim, and there appears to be no written record of it. At any rate, while the construction was under way, Clark sent Nathan Boone and Paul Loise, the interpreter, to the Big

and Little Osage villages to tell them that "if they wished to take protection under this fort to come."

The Indians gathered on September 12 and met with Clark in
council for the next two days. He expressed dismay over Osage "habits
of committing Theft Murder and Robory on the Citizens of the U.S.
in this Territory" and said that to stop such acts he was proposing "a
line to be run between the U S & the Osage hunting lands."

The Osages had probably been informed by Pierre Chouteau of
the threat by Lewis and the President to back eastern tribes in a war to
annihilate them. As usual, they were regretful about the plunder and
stealing by their young men and were eager to placate the whites.
What Clark demanded was that they give up their rights to all the
lands south of the Missouri River, as far as the Arkansas River, and east
of a line extending due south from Fire Prairie, the location where
they were meeting. The cession was a huge tract of land, amounting
to about half of each of the present states of Missouri and Arkansas.
Clark estimated it to be nearly 50,000 square miles of "excellent country." In fact, it was considerably more than that, with later estimates
ranging from 60,000 to 90,000 square miles—certainly larger than the
state of Virginia.

Within the present state of Missouri, their ancestral homeland, the
Osages were left with only a narrow plank of land twenty-five miles
wide running the length of the west side of the state. They still had
rights to hunting lands extending well across Kansas, into the northeast corner of Oklahoma and the northwest corner of Arkansas. In
essence, they were no longer to set foot east of the new fort unless invited. In return, Clark told them the United States government would
reimburse its citizens for the property "their bad men had stolen" and
for the inconvenience caused to white people who had been
"Robbed, plundered & Sent naked in cold weather without the means
of procuring food."

Clark said the chiefs agreed to all of this, "telling me they would
do it with pleasure, &c and informing me that I was doing them a
great Service." He spent the night writing up a treaty and fighting
dysentery while the Indians "danced hollered and Sung."

The next day, they signed the treaty. Clark gave a rifle to each principal chief and to the two tribes 12 fuses, 100 pounds of gunpowder, 200 pounds of lead, 14 "carrots" of tobacco, some paint, knives, and blankets, for a combined value of $317.74. "This unexpected present pleased those people greatly," Clark reported. They painted themselves, and again danced and sang all night while he continued to suffer dysentery.

When Clark returned to St. Louis on September 22, however, seventy-four disgruntled Osages were waiting. They had missed the treaty negotiations because they had been in the city returning some stolen horses. In line with their complaints, Lewis rewrote the treaty and sent Pierre Chouteau to Fort Osage with a special commission "to restore peace and friendship between our People and the Great and Little Osage."

"It is our unalterable determination, that if they are to be considered our friends and allies, they must sign that instrument, conform to its stipulations, and establish their permanent villages, near the Fort erected a little above the Fire Prairie," Lewis instructed Pierre. He said those who failed to do so could not obtain merchandise from the factor or from individual traders. Furthermore, he warned that he would have troops ready in St. Louis for an expedition against the Osages if the treaty talks did not succeed.

Pierre traveled to the fort, then still under construction, and met with the tribal representatives on November 10, 1808. The draft treaty he brought was somewhat sweeter for the Osages than the version that Clark had written. It limited government responsibility for claims of individual whites for Osage damages to $5,000, but it also provided for the Big Osages to receive $1,000 worth of merchandise and $800 in cash annually, and for the Little Osages to receive half of each of those sums. In addition, it promised the nation a blacksmith, a horse or water mill, and agricultural implements.

Possibly concerned that the tribe would resist signing after realizing how much land it was relinquishing, Pierre delivered strong words to his assembled friends. "You have heard this treaty explained to you," he said. "Those who now come forward and sign it shall be considered the friends of the United States and treated accordingly. Those who refuse to come forward and sign it shall be considered enemies of the United States and treated accordingly."

White Hair, the chief with whom Pierre had counciled and traded for decades, was the first of the Osages to sign, marking his X after the signatures of Pierre, two army officers, and Reuben Lewis, Meriwether's brother, who had been appointed an Indian subagent. More than 125 Osages signed. Later, in St. Louis, sixteen representatives of the Arkansas River Osages signed the treaty, led by Chiefs Clermont and Grande Piste.

Some of the Big and Little Osages responded to the treaty by moving north a hundred miles to the area near the fort, but the majority remained in their villages on the Osage River. Nor did the Arkansas Osages leave their river. Before the year was out, White Hair died and was buried at the Osages' historic village site.

At some point in the negotiations, whether at the initiative of Pierre or the Osages, a statement was inserted in the draft that recognized Pierre's rights to the tract of 25,500 acres of land where the Lamine River flows into the Missouri, granted to him by the Osages in 1792, during Spanish rule. A tract on the Saline River given to Noel Mongrain, the interpreter who worked for Pierre, was similarly recognized.

However, when Pierre went back to St. Louis with the treaty, he ran into opposition from both Lewis and Clark, who thought the private land claims were invalid. Clark, who complained for the next couple of years about his treaty being replaced, dismissed as "a mear [sic] come off" the Osage claim that they had been misled about the extent of the land cession to the United States. He seemed to think that Pierre had manipulated the Osages to oppose the first version of the treaty in order to have an opportunity to insert recognition of his own claim into the treaty.

Antagonism between Pierre and Clark over this issue reached the point where Lewis told Jefferson that his work was being impeded by the "want of cordiality" between his two associates. The references to the land claims of Pierre and Noel Mongrain were removed, presumably by Lewis, before the treaty was forwarded to Washington for Senate ratification, which did not occur until April 28, 1810.

However, Pierre defended his right to the land directly, writing to Jefferson, to whom he also made clear his important role in winning tribal approval. Telling Jefferson that Lewis had sent him to get the "malcontents" to sign, he explained, "I had the good fortune to succeed, and you have acquired for the United States a territory which is very valuable, for its adjacent position, for its immense extent, which I estimate without exaggeration at more than 90,000 or 100,000 square miles, and for the quality of the land, almost all of which is suited for agriculture." Then he proceeded to raise the matter of his land claim within the ceded area, using these words:

> At this moment I dare to ask your protection and help in an affair which is of great interest to me. At the time when I was passing half of my life with the Osages the nations gave me a bit of land, as they did to Noel [Mongrain], of the lands which belonged to them. Not content with the customary title which they gave me, I had this title ratified and confirmed by the Spanish authorities of whom we were then dependents, and I never doubted the validity of my rights. Now these lands, which so long belonged to me, are comprised in those ceded to the United States. I did not want to have them mentioned in the treaty which the Governor gave me, but at this council which I held and of which a copy has surely been sent you, the Osages recognized my rights and those of Noel [Mongrain] and declared that those earlier ceded to us were not included in those ceded to the United States. My entire confidence in the government makes me hope that I will not experience any difficulty in obtaining a complete title to these lands which were acquired by me so long ago and so legitimately, and it is on this subject that I claim your protection.

This put a strong tint of self-interest on Pierre's role in the treaty negotiations. However, he has been credited by various historians with gaining Osage adherence to a treaty that the tribe probably would have not respected for very long otherwise. Many years of dealings between the Osages and the United States lay ahead before the government would finally subdue them, but Pierre's influence in the years following 1808 kept them loyal to the United States when the War of 1812 erupted. It took Pierre more than three decades to finally win government approval of his land claim on the Lamine River, but it is significant that those who disputed his ownership were never the Osages.

His relations with Clark were eventually repaired, although Pierre grew increasingly frustrated at the tendency of Lewis and Clark to decide questions about Osage affairs between themselves, without consulting him. Nevertheless, all three men needed each other, and this interdependence often put them in the position of having to defend and support one another in dealings with Washington officials ignorant of the problems associated with life at the outer edge of the American republic.

EIGHT

Enveloped in a Cloud of Miseries

❉

Except for his trip to Washington in the fall and winter of 1806–07 and the tragic foray up the Missouri River during the summer of 1807, the unlucky Mandan chief Shahaka whiled away his long days in St. Louis for about two and a half years. Meanwhile, Manuel Lisa returned in the summer of 1808 from his own trading expedition to the Upper Missouri with a large cargo of pelts, impressing the other traders with the riches of the upper country and making them jealous. As entertaining as political intrigue had been for a while, what really motivated the men of St. Louis was making money, and they now saw great possibilities opening before them. There were fortunes to be made, and in that scenario Meriwether Lewis also found the means of seeing Chief Shahaka to his home.

This led to a two-pronged venture, commanded by Pierre Chouteau, intended to take the chief home while blazing a wide, new trail in the fur trade that would unite some of the most prominent businessmen—and Lewis and Clark as well. The businessmen formed a partnership called the St. Louis Missouri Fur Company, which in turn signed an agreement with Lewis to safely escort Shahaka home before proceeding with a trading expedition above and to the west of the Mandan villages.

It did not occur to any of the men organizing this venture that government employees—including Lewis and Clark and Pierre Chouteau—might be violating ethical standards or government rules by mixing their government functions with personal business ventures. They were on the frontier, where they were making the rules, and they gave little thought to the possible reactions of men in Washington whose own fortunes and financial well-being had already been secured. They faced a challenging assignment from Washington of finding a way to return Shahaka to his home. In their view, combining the two ventures made success more likely because the fur-trade portion attracted a far larger number of men than the army alone could provide.

Pierre Chouteau was appointed by Lewis to run what was deemed the "military" portion of the operation—the return of Shahaka. Pierre was also an investor in what became known as the Missouri Fur Company, or simply the M.F.C.*

On February 24, 1809, articles of agreement for the return of Shahaka were signed between Meriwether Lewis, as governor of the Louisiana Territory, and the Missouri Fur Company. Three of the ten partners in the fur company were from the Chouteau clan: Pierre, his son A.P., and his nephew Sylvestre Labbadie Jr.; a fourth, Pierre Ménard of Kaskaskia, was Pierre's brother-in-law. Other partners were Manuel Lisa, William Morrison, William Clark, Andrew Henry, Benjamin Wilkinson, who was a nephew of the former governor, and Reuben Lewis, the governor's brother. It was widely assumed that Meriwether Lewis himself was a silent partner in the venture.

The business group agreed to raise a force of 125 men, of whom 40 were to be Americans and expert riflemen, acting in a "military capacity . . . for the safe conveyance and delivery of the Mandan Chief his Wife and Child to the Mandan nation." The company would furnish the detachment "with good and suitable Fire arms, of which Fifty at least shall be Rifles, and a sufficient quantity of good ammunition."

Pierre Chouteau was to command the detachment "until the said expedition shall arrive at the Mandan nation or Villages." The company was to take good care of the chief and his party and "defend them from all War like and other attacks, by force of arms, and every other means to the extent of their power, and at the [risk] of the lives

*The name had been used by various groups in the past, starting in 1794 with the company formed at the urging of Spanish lieutenant governor Zenon Trudeau.

of the said detachment." The company was to be paid $7,000 for the safe delivery of the chief, half before leaving St. Louis, the other half when a messenger reached St. Louis and informed Lewis that the chief was safely home.

Under the articles of association and copartnership signed by the ten men in the fur venture, each partner was obliged to accompany the expedition in person or to send someone approved by the majority to act in his behalf. None could "traffic or trade for his own separate or individual interest" upriver from the Mandan nation during the existence of the agreement. The partners also agreed to buy from Manuel Lisa, Pierre Ménard, and William Morrison some horses and merchandise they had left in their fort at the mouth of the Bighorn River on the Yellowstone during their previous expedition. Each member had to act in accord with the decisions of the majority and had to share equally in all costs. Capitalization was understood to be $40,000.

Once Pierre led the party safely to the Mandan villages, Manuel Lisa and Benjamin Wilkinson were to take over as "factors" to handle trade with the Indians and manage men employed by the M.F.C., keeping accounts, buying peltries, hiring men, and performing other functions. William Clark was appointed agent at St. Louis, where he was to receive all peltries and money and hold them until it was time to divide them. For subsequent years, there was a rotation agreement. Three partners would return to St. Louis each fall, then go back upriver in the spring.

The field of operations of the new Missouri Fur Company embraced the entire watershed of the Missouri River from the mouth of the Platte upward. The partners knew that they might encounter Indian hostility, but they thought that liberal trade policies would secure the tribes' friendship.

Neither Lewis nor Clark nor Pierre Chouteau had provided much information to people in Washington about what was being organized. Pierre sent a brief letter, in English, on May 28, 1809, to William Simmons, accountant for the War Department, stating that he was leaving in a few days to escort the Mandan chief to his nation.

The previous summer, on August 24, 1808, President Jefferson had written Lewis asking what had been done about returning Shahaka home and apparently authorizing in advance any measures Lewis considered necessary. Jefferson told Lewis that getting the chief safely home "is an object which presses on our justice and our honour." But by the time the expedition was ready to push off nearly a year later, Jefferson was out of office. James Madison was President, and most of his Cabinet Secretaries were new to matters concerning the West, and probably not as supportive as the Jefferson Administration would have been.

Although the contract with the government specified that the Missouri Fur Company would provide a force of 125 men for the military portion of the trip, estimates of the total size of the expeditionary force when it set out range as high as 350 men. In addition to the armed men called for by the agreement with Lewis, there were men to operate each of the thirteen barges and keelboats, plus the traders themselves, Shawnee and Delaware Indian hunters to go ashore and hunt for food every day, and Shahaka's party.

The expedition left St. Louis in two groups. The first, consisting of ten barges with 160 men, set out on May 17, and the rest of the expedition, including Pierre and the Mandan chief's party, left in the first days of June. The two flotillas met at the mouth of the Osage River, just east of present-day Jefferson City, Missouri, and then continued up the Missouri to Fort Osage. They announced their arrival at the fort with several blasts from guns on the ordnance barges, and they were answered back with the same number.

In the less than a year since its construction, Fort Osage had become a magnet not only for the Osage Indians but for other tribes as well. When the huge expeditionary group from St. Louis arrived, visitors were already at the fort from the Maha, Pawnee, Kansa, and Sac and Fox tribes. One of the arriving travelers thought the mingling Indians served "to render this quarter a most discordant portion of the continent." After two weeks at the fort, during which time they laid in a large supply of fruits and vegetables, the upriver travelers departed on July 11.

Among those who had signed on with the expedition were a surgeon whose name was listed only as "Dr. Thomas" and a young but seasoned frontiersman named Thomas James. Both recorded their first-person accounts of the voyage. Dr. Thomas was included in many of the activities of Pierre Chouteau and the other partners in the M.F.C. The twenty-seven-year-old James, who was born in Maryland but had moved to Missouri with his parents, was assigned as steersman, or captain, of a boat of twenty-four men; he shared the harsh conditions of the boatmen.

For the boatmen, the trip meant days on end of "rowing, pushing with poles, cordelling, warping, and sailing." Allotted provisions gave out in six weeks, and the men had to live on boiled corn, without salt, while "the gentlemen proprietors in the leading barge were faring in the most sumptuous and luxurious manner," James recalled. Some of the hands became disgusted and left to return home. At one point James had a struggle to keep men from breaking into a barrel of pork that belonged to the company.

In conditions that were probably typical of such trade missions, there was a lot of feuding, threatening, and name-calling among the men and between them and the partners, often over food and equipment. Liquor provided the only relief from hard work and miserable accommodations. Once, young A. P. Chouteau intervened to prevent his father from having one of the men put in irons the day after some men got into a drunken argument.

On August 1 they reached the half-mile-wide mouth of the Platte River. Above there, vegetation became scarce, and the soil was sandy. James described the scene: "As you ascend the river, the woods diminish in number and extent. Beyond Council Bluffs, about 700 miles above the mouth, they entirely disappear, except on the river bottoms, which are heavily timbered. The prairies were covered with a short thick grass, about three or four inches high. At this time the game was very abundant. We saw Elk and Buffalo in vast numbers, and killed many of them. Prairie dogs and wolves were also very numerous."

When the group reached the Maha village on August 11, Shahaka was invited to parade on horseback in the regalia he had brought back from Washington.

"Having put on an elegant full dress suit of regimentals, with his horse covered with the most showey ornaments, he set out accompanied by thirty Maha chiefs on horse back, in their best dress," Dr. Thomas recalled. "The whole nation were lost in astonishment at the [splendid] figure of the Mandan, so much superior to anything their chiefs could display. Before dinner a council was held with Mr. Chouteau for the purpose of requesting a trader to reside among them, and to beg presents, in which the Mandan preserved the dignity of the superior; indeed Shehekeh's manners would grace any circle; he took great pains to copy the manners of the first characters of the United States whom he was acquainted with."

On August 18 the travelers arrived at the Yankton Sioux village, which contained 300 lodges. As Dr. Thomas described the arrival, "50 warriors arranged themselves on the shore, and discharged their pieces loaded with ball into the water at the bows of our barges. Having brought to near the shore, the officers landed and were carried to the council, by six Indians in Buffaloe [sic] robes; in the council their demands were similar to the Maha's. They were given to understand that no trader could be left with them, and they could have no presents. Menace took the place of supplication."

The principal chief told Pierre Chouteau that the Missouri would be "made to run blood" if their demand was not met. Faced with this level of insistence, the traders agreed to leave one man with the Yanktons. They did the same with virtually every tribe that the expedition later encountered.

As the voyagers pushed deeper into the wilderness, conditions of survival became worse. There was bad food or no food for the boatmen, and at times men were near starvation. If the trappers and boatmen wanted whiskey, they had to buy it from the Missouri Fur Company at $12 a gallon, running up debts at the rate of $1.50 against each of the beaver skins they expected to get by trapping. James said the same whiskey cost $6 in St. Louis. "Their prices for every thing else were in about the same proportion. Even at this price some of the men bought whiskey by the bucket full, and drank."

Meanwhile, all was not settled and calm in St. Louis. Since Lewis's arrival in the spring of the previous year, he had had difficult relations with Frederick Bates, who served as territorial secretary and had been acting governor before Lewis's arrival. Their tense and explosive dealings were open knowledge within the small circle of people who governed and influenced St. Louis and the territory. Lewis and Bates disagreed on appointments and Indian policy, and even on petty things. Lewis canceled some of Bates's appointments to public positions. Bates was complaining to people in Washington about Lewis's behavior.

"I never saw, after his arrival in this country, anything in his conduct towards me, but alienation and unmerited distrust," Bates told his brother Richard. Bates claimed that during his own period as acting governor, he "had acquired . . . a good portion of the public confidence," for which Lewis could not forgive him. Lewis displayed a "supercilious air" toward him, Bates claimed.

"He has fallen from the Public esteem & almost into the public contempt," Bates wrote on another occasion.

> He is well aware of my increasing popularity . . . and has for some time feared that I was at the head of a party whose object it would be to denounce him to the President and procure his dismission. The Gov. is greatly mistaken in these suspicions; and I have accordingly employed every frank & open explanation which might have a tendency to remove that veil with which a few worthless fellows have endeavoured to exclude from him the sunshine. He called at my office & personally demanded this explanation . . . As a Citizen, I told him I entertained opinions very different from his, on the subject of civil government, and that those opinions had, on various occasions been expressed with emphasis; but that they had been unmixed with personal malice or hostility.

Lewis asked that they maintain a display of cordiality in public, and Bates agreed. Still, in an encounter at a ball, they came close to blows. Only the intervention of William Clark prevented a duel.

"I attended early, and was seated in conversation with some Gentlemen when the Governor entered," Bates recounted.

> He drew his chair close to mine—There was a pause in the conversation—I availed myself of it—arose and walked to the opposite side of the room. The dances were now commencing.—*He* also rose—evi-

dently in passion, retired into an adjoining room and sent a servant for General Clark, who refused to ask me out as he foresaw that a Battle must have been the consequence of our meeting. [Lewis] complained to the general that I had treated him with contempt & insult in the Ball-Room and that he could not suffer it to pass. He knew my resolutions not to speak to him except on business and he ought not to have thrust himself in my way.

After several weeks went by, Clark asked Bates to make an overture to Lewis, but Bates refused. "I replied to him, 'NO, the Governor has told me to take my own course and I shall step a *high* and a *proud* Path. He has *injured* me, and he must *undo* that injury or I shall succeed in fixing the stigma where it *ought* to *rest*. You come' added I 'as *my* friend, but I cannot separate you from Gov Lewis—You have trodden the *Ups* & the *Downs* of life with him and it appears to me that these proposals are made solely for *his* convenience.' "

Later, when Bates had business in Lewis's office, Lewis "made very handsome explanations" about their differences. Bates insisted that someone else be brought in as a witness, and the lawyer William C. Carr was summoned. They then "adjusted" the misunderstanding to Bates's satisfaction.

Lewis was perpetually short of money. He was borrowing small sums from Clark, from Auguste Chouteau, and even from Bates. He was drinking in excess and seemed to be bothered by health problems, possibly including recurring malaria, for which he was taking opium and other medication. He was also lonely. At an age when his friends and contemporaries, including Clark, had found wives, he had not. And he had a major case of writer's block, having done nothing about preparing his expedition journals for publication. The disappointed Jefferson gently reminded him of this from time to time.

Lewis's woes were exacerbated by the actions of bureaucrats in Washington who often questioned even minor expenses. A clerk in the State Department, for instance, rejected Lewis's claim for $18.50 to cover the cost of translating the laws of the territory into French. This upset Lewis tremendously because he foresaw that other expenditures to which he was already committed would likewise be rejected, and his personal assets were not enough to cover them.

In this already unsettled atmosphere, a letter arrived from Secretary of War William Eustis that shook Lewis like a thunderbolt and reverberated around the town. The letter, arriving on August 18—the day that Pierre Chouteau and the other members of the upriver expedition were in a tense encounter with the Yankton Sioux—was strongly critical of Lewis for combining commercial and government interests in the expedition. Eustis also complained that some of the expenditures had not received prior approval from Washington; he disallowed them.

Eustis said that his department had understood that the $7,000 expenditure the government had authorized in exchange for the fur company's organizing, arming, and equipping a security force would be sufficient to cover all costs, and "it was not expected that any further advances of any further agency would be required on the part of the United States."

> Your Excellency will not therefore be surprised [*sic*] that your Bill of the 13th of May last drawn in favor of M. P. Chouteau for five hundred dollars for the purchase of Tobacco, Powder, &c. intended as Presents for the Indians, through which this expedition was to pass and to insure its success, has not been honored. It has been usual to advise the Government of the United States when expenditures to a considerable amount are contemplated in the Territorial Governments. In the instance of accepting the volunteer services of 140 [*sic*] men for a military expedition to a point and purpose not designated, which expedition is stated to combine commercial as well as military objects, and when an Agent of the Government appointed for other purposes is selected for the command, it is thought the Government might, without injury to the public interests, have been consulted.

Eustis went on to say that this expedition could not be considered as having government sanction. And he said the government was thinking of replacing Pierre Chouteau as Osage agent because he had left his post to command the expedition. Eustis closed by saying that President Madison approved of the things said in his letter.

"I have never received a penny of public Money," the angry and wounded Lewis responded, "but have merely given the Draft to the person who had rendered the public service, or furnished articles for public use." He told Eustis the feelings incited by the letter were "truly painful" because he had always accompanied drafts on public moneys with letters explaining the expenditures.

He found it impossible from such a great distance to explain and defend himself, so he said he was coming to Washington to see officials in person, bringing all his papers. He also denied the allegations floating about that the Upper Missouri expedition was intended to cross into British territory, creating diplomatic problems for the United States or even inciting war.

"I do most solemnly aver, that the expedition sent up the Misoury under the Command of Mr. Pierre Chouteau, as a military Command has no other object than that of conveying the Mandane Chief and his Family to their Village—and in a commercial point of view, that they intend only, to hunt and trade on the waters of the Misoury and Columbia Rivers within the Rockey-Mountains and the Planes bordering those Mountains on the east side—and that they have no intention with which I am acquainted, to enter the Dominions, or do injury to any foreign Power."

"Be assured Sir," Lewis continued, "that my Country can never make 'A Burr' of me—She may reduce me to Poverty; but she can never sever my Attachment from her."

He said his credit had been "effectually sunk" by the protested bills from the Departments of War and Treasury, which had caused all his private debts to be called in. These amounted to about $4,000, for which he was compelled to deposit with his creditors, as security, the property he had purchased in Missouri. The best proof the government could have of his integrity in the future, he said, would be "the poverty to which they have now reduced me."

He justified his authorization to Pierre Chouteau of additional expenditures on the basis of information he had received, after making the $7,000 contract, that the Cheyennes and the Arikaras intended to stop all boats ascending the river. Pierre was given the additional presents and other supplies to enable him to engage "an auxiliary Force among the friendly Nations through which they would pass," if that became necessary.

He urged that Pierre not be removed from his position as Osage agent, saying that he was to return to St. Louis as soon as the chief was in his home village. Meanwhile, he claimed, Auguste Chouteau was acting as agent in his half brother's place. In a postscript he added that removing Pierre before ratification of the 1808 Osage treaties would be a major mistake because it would probably lead the unhappy Osages to declare war on the United States.

In those anguished days after receiving the letter from Eustis, Lewis also spoke with twenty-year-old Pierre Chouteau Jr., who was running the family office in the absence of his father and older brother. Lewis told him something of the contents of Eustis's letter.

The knowledge that his father was being criticized in Washington deeply angered Pierre Jr., who took up his own pen in defense. Filling up several pages in French, young Pierre told Eustis that the mission of returning Shahaka to his village would have had little chance of success without his father's leadership. He charged that Lewis and Clark had cut Pierre Sr. out of Indian policy—except when they had no one else on whom they could rely to get the job done. He also implied that Lewis and Clark were treating the Osages with less tolerance than other tribes and were willing to have them wiped out, using these words:

> A short time before the arrival of Governor Lewis in St. Louis there were some complaints from some of the settlers in the Territory against an Osage party which had stolen some horses. From this moment, I may say, the Governor took upon himself the entire direction of the department even up to the last detail, which until then had been intrusted to the care of my father. This offense of the Osages, which previously among all other [Indian] nations was made good by the mere punishment of the guilty individuals, served as a pretext to declare openly that the Osage nations were outside the protection of the United States. The Lorimier's Delawares and Shawnees, which had always been the enemies of the Osages, were called and invited to make war against the Osages. In a public council it was promised that the militia of the territory would join their warriors in annihilating the Osages. The time for this expedition was fixed; my father, merely a spectator of all these proceedings, was not consulted. A little

later the Osages brought back the stolen horses and the Governor abandoned his project of war.

Recalling Clark's effort to negotiate the 1808 land cession treaty with the Osages, he said that Governor Lewis was eventually "forced to have recourse to my father to get this treaty ratified, or rather to have another made toward the same ends. My father solved all difficulties, succeeded in appeasing the thwarted spirits of the Osages and made them acquiesce in all the desires of the Governor."

But after Fort Osage was completed, he said, the governor appointed an agent for the Indian Department who took instructions directly from him, and cut Pierre Sr. out of all correspondence and discussions.

These facts, the son wrote, "prove to you that for a long time my father has been agent in name only, and that the direction of the Osage nations has been entirely in the care of the Governor and of his subagents; my father, who has never sought to penetrate into the conduct of his superiors, but only to give them continual proof of his fidelity, has seen with pain but without complaint that the Osage nations have ceased to be under his direction."

Pierre Jr. said that his father for several years had had "irreparable" financial losses because of his work for the government and, as a result, became interested in this new company. He thought there was no conflict with his duty because he had seen General Clark also joining the company as a partner. "His intention was never to be one of the directors of this society, as his oldest son was charged to watch his interests and to work harmoniously with the other associates."

After all of this was set up, Pierre Jr. wrote, Lewis decided to name Pierre as chief of the expedition. "My father joyfully accepted this proposition," he said, "with the idea of being useful to the Government, and of getting away from the inactivity to which he found himself reduced by the action of the Governor in regard to himself."

Young Pierre's comments about his father's finances alluded to the pressures the elder Pierre had felt since assuming the post of Indian agent and being unable to engage in the fur trade. Nor had he been able to collect pelts or money due him from earlier trading enterprises, because it was traditional in the fur trade for accounts to be continually carried forward. Indian tribes that owed furs to Pierre for goods extended to them on credit were not likely to pay him at a time when they knew he could extend them no more credit. Pierre, at the same time, was still being pressed by creditors and suppliers to pay for merchandise ordered in earlier years.

It is logical to wonder why Pierre continued in his government role when it so hampered him in pursuing his dreams of riches. But he also enjoyed the prestige and influence it gave him, including access to the White House, which he believed might be turned to his advantage. He had absorbed well a lesson from his father, Pierre Laclède, to serve one's monarch when asked, and had transferred this philosophy to the republican government.

It is also logical to ask why Lewis and Clark did not entirely pursue their own paths in handling Indian affairs. The answer seems to lie in comments indicating the extent to which they relied on Pierre's knowledge of Indians. He knew like the back of his hand many of the things Lewis and Clark needed to understand in order to run the territory and direct Indian policy. Finally, the three men had many joint dealings in land and, now, the fur trade.

While these issues were being aired in St. Louis, the voyagers on the Upper Missouri were encountering various Sioux bands. At the mouth of the Jacques River, they agreed to go to a Teton Sioux village. When the boats anchored, Indians carried the partners of the company on individual litters of buffalo skins to a feast of dog meat. On August 26 they arrived at another Teton Sioux camp, consisting of about a hundred lodges, near White River, below present-day Pierre.

Above there, the wind became brisk, and they were able to use sails every day, which made the voyage less arduous for the boatmen. On September 12 they reached the villages of the Arikaras, who had attacked the previous party in 1807. Pierre sent for the chief to come down to his camp and hold a council, which the tribe agreed to do only after the cannon on the expedition barges were turned in the opposite direction.

After lecturing the Arikaras for their attack on the barges and the killings two years earlier, Pierre said that unless they wanted to be destroyed on the orders of the President of the United States, they must allow the safe passage of the Mandan chief. Pierre related later what happened next: "The chiefs of the [Arikaras] then took the Mandan chief by the hand, saying, if they fired upon him the first time, it was because the principal chief of the nation was then absent, that the death of their chief in the United States had been the cause of great dissatisfaction in their nation, but that he might with great safety now pass in their villages without fearing anything."

When the expedition finally approached the first of the Mandan villages on September 21, a salute was fired off from its cannon, and the Mandans answered from shore. As the barges docked, the travelers ran up the American flag, and the waiting Mandans thronged aboard the barges, congratulating those who had accomplished the safe voyage. Thrilled to have their chief among them again, they invited Pierre and the other leaders to a feast with a stew of meat, corn, and vegetables. A horse was brought to the chief, who dressed the animal in scarlet and gold-laced housings and mounted it. Some thirty or forty members of the tribe followed as he pranced about the village.

In a few days, with his mission peacefully accomplished, Pierre Chouteau turned back downriver toward St. Louis. The rest of the group proceeded to a point above the upper Mandan villages to erect a trading fort. Some of the group made it to the area of the Gros Ventres, near the Milk River in the northern part of the future Montana, and others reached the mouth of the Bighorn, probably toward the end of October, where they settled in for the winter in the fort that Lisa's group had built in 1807.

A few days before Pierre started down the Missouri, Meriwether Lewis had set out from St. Louis to go down the Mississippi and get a ship for Washington, intending to defend himself with regard to his use of government moneys. He had told Eustis he would be leaving a week after he wrote him on August 18, but his preparations actually took more than two weeks. He carried in his bags the precious journals from the 1804–06 expedition.

Before going, he turned over for sale his personal holdings, mainly land and the warrant for 1,600 acres that Congress had given him. He put most of his titles and deeds in the hands of the lawyer William C. Carr, who had recently arrived in St. Louis from Virginia via Kentucky. Lewis also returned to Auguste Chouteau land he was buying from him on credit.

Shortly before his departure, Lewis spent a day with William Clark, who was planning to depart soon by the land route to take up some of his own issues with Washington, and to visit Virginia. He and his wife, Julia, wanted to show her family their first child, Meriwether Lewis Clark, born in January 1809.

Clark wrote his brother Jonathan that he had "not Spent Such a day as yesterday for maney years." His friend was in a great deal of distress, "ruined" by the government's decision to protest some of his expenditures. Clark was convinced that Lewis had done nothing dishonorable. "I do not beleve [sic] there was ever an honest er [sic] man in Louisiana nor one who had pureor motives than Govr. Lewis," Clark wrote. "If his mind had been at ease I Should have parted Cherefuly."

Clark thought Meriwether Lewis would eventually return to his post in St. Louis, but another player in the events of those days saw the situation differently.

"Our governor left us . . . with his private affairs altogether arranged," Will Carr, the lawyer, wrote to his brother.

> He is a good man but a very imprudent one. I [perceive] he will not return. He has drawn on the general government for various and considerable sums of money which have not been paid; of course his bills have been protested. He has vested Judge Stuart of Kaskaskia, General Clark & myself with full powers to adjust and liquidate all demands against him and left in my hands all his land titles, to be sold for that purpose. Some of these lands, situated about 10 miles from this place near a little village called St. Ferdinand will be sold. The title is complete and the quality of the land excellent. It is also situated on the bank of the Missouri. If I had the money I would give it for the land instantly.

When Lewis had been gone about three weeks, Acting Governor Bates wrote Eustis complaining that Lewis had not left him records or correspondence, so he had little to guide him in carrying out the conduct of public affairs. Also, with Clark gone to Virginia, he had no access to Clark's office for Indian matters, of which Bates was also supposed to be in charge. He raised the question of Pierre's status as Osage agent, making points and raising questions that seemed to suggest that Pierre Jr. may have had some input into the shaping of the letter. He wrote in part:

> May I be permitted to enquire whether Peter Chouteau esquire the Agent for the Osage Nations of Indians has been so unfortunate as to lose the confidence of the President? Insinuations have been made to this effect tho' I have heard nothing alledged against him, except his absence by order of the Superintendent. Mr. Chouteau must have presumed that Gov Lewis acted in this affair under the orders of the President; and surely sufficient time had elapsed after the commencement of the preparations to have obtained his sanction or his censure. Previously to his acceptance of the command of the Mandan Escort, the Osage business had from time to time and under various pretexts been almost entirely taken out of his hands, and I am very certain . . . that his principal inducement in undertaking this distant charge, was, to escape from the official degradation into which he had fallen. It is greatly to be feared that the character of Mr. Chouteau has not been entirely understood at Washington. I do not fear to hazard the assertion that he possesses a respectability and weight in this country, beyond any other person employed in the transaction of Indian business. —And this reputation, together with the influence of an extensive family connection, has, on all proper occasions, been thrown into the American Scale, when the policy of our government has been in collision with the prejudices of former times.

By the time Meriwether Lewis sailed from St. Louis, he was in a deranged state, twice trying to kill himself, according to the boat crew. At Chickasaw Bluffs, the future Memphis, the fort commander, Captain Gilbert Russell, put him under suicide watch. On September 29 Russell decided that Lewis's mental state had improved and turned him over to Major James Neely, the government agent to the Chickasaw nation. Neely agreed to travel to Washington with Lewis, who had decided that he should proceed by land because if he took a ship from New Orleans, the British might capture it.

Proceeding along the Natchez Trace, Neelly and Lewis crossed into Tennessee and camped. When two of the horses strayed from camp, Neelly went to look for them, and Lewis continued on with his servant and Neelly's servant until they reached an inn seventy-two miles from Nashville, where he took a room. Neelly was to join him there.

But Lewis passed an anguished evening, and in the early morning hours of October 11 he took out his pistols and shot himself, first with one, then the other. When the owner of the house heard the shots, she summoned the two servants, but they arrived too late to save Lewis. Death came shortly after daybreak.

Pierre Chouteau, then making his way down the Missouri River, reached St. Louis on November 20 to learn of the death of the man who had been his frequent houseguest, collaborator, friend, and nemesis. Coming off an exhausting five-month trip that tested his knowledge of Indian culture and required all his skills at managing men, Pierre now found himself in a city in turmoil. Many people in St. Louis blamed Bates for upsetting Governor Lewis to the point of driving him to suicide. Most of them probably had no insight into his precarious mental state.

Bates's correspondence indicates that the news of Lewis's death had reached St. Louis by at least November 9. On that date, Bates wrote one of his brothers, Richard, about the "premature and tragical death of Gov. Lewis." Bates admitted having "had no personal regard . . . and a great deal of political contempt" for Lewis, but he said that he could not "but lament that after all his toils and dangers he should die *in such a manner.*"

Bates thought Lewis had been "spoiled" by the "elegant praises" and "so many flattering caresses" of the powerful and prominent to the extent that "like an overgrown baby, he began to think that everybody about the House must regulate their conduct by his caprices."

"Gov. Lewis, on his way to Washington became *insane,*" Bates concluded.

A more sympathetic view of Meriwether Lewis and his problems poured forth from the anonymous pen of a writer in the *Mis-*

souri Gazette. The tribute, signed by "Z" and dated November 19, said that Lewis had recently undergone a change — "his mind enveloped in a cloud of miseries, distilled unhappily from a deranged imagination."

"Some secret cause he might have had," the writer continued,

> yet none was evidently known to friends why thus he seemed so changed — he lost all confidence in man, and thought himself in the midst of enemies . . . his reason at last became dethroned, and he coolly did his own quietus make, with the cruel mean of pistols — he aim'd too well — the trigger drawn, ere a friendly hand could arrest his purpose, the horrid deed was done! — Oh fortune! Where are thy boasted trophies for those who deserve well of these — is it thus the brave must die? . . . Oh spirits of departed heroes, return to earth and give to men a nobler fortitude! What serves it otherwise to brave the storms of howling ocean, the horrid dangers of a savage realm, to scale the rugged tops of flinty mountains, hungry, thirsting, fainting! To be thus sped to an untimely grave!!

For Pierre Chouteau, not the least of concerns after the death of Lewis were his own tightly stretched financial affairs. Much of what the government had protested against Lewis, and refused to pay, now fell back on him. Pierre was also left with nothing but his own word to back up his claims of what Lewis had instructed him to do during the final year of Lewis's life.

The Philadelphia merchant house of Bryan & Schlatter, which had supplied some of the goods purchased with drafts from Lewis, wrote Pierre Jr. as soon as it learned of "the Melancholy fate" of Lewis. It urged Pierre Jr. to have his father "take the necessary steps to secure Himself by an attachment of [Lewis's] property etc." In almost the next sentence, the firm hastened to request that Pierre "make us as early a remittance as possible."

Nowhere in his own papers did Pierre preserve anything to help historians interpret his reaction to Lewis's death. Rare for him, he seems to have kept his emotions under control, writing tersely to Eustis two days after his return that "the late transactions in the indian department of Louisiana have been of so Extraordinary a character, that I am impelled, by the Strongest motives to solicit an opportunity of Explaining Personaly the Share which I have had in them."

That was not to be. Bates insisted that there was too much need for Pierre in St. Louis at a time when Clark was away in the East.

Pierre wrote Eustis that he still hoped to come to Washington as soon as practicable, then proceeded to relate some details of the expedition, seeming determined to impress upon Eustis the danger of the mission he had undertaken. After describing several encounters and events along the route, including the safe and happy return home of the Mandan chief, he said, "I have thus given you a faithful and I trust satisfactory detail of a voyage in which I have encountered many difficulties and dangers, and which was by me undertaken with [nothing more than] pure motives."

He said he hoped that the government's confidence in him had not been diminished, and he complained about having been cut out of the loop on management of Indian affairs prior to his departure.

"For a considerable time previous to my departure on the expedition with the Mandan chief, I could not be considered in any other light, than as a mere nominal agent, without Powers to exercise or duties to perform, subagents for the particular tribes for which I was appointed, were made without my knowledge or consent; they assumed my powers without reporting to me or having any communication with me. Measures were taken without my advice, or if perchance I was spoken to, it was only to approve of measures already adopted, and the execution of them perhaps begun."

Clark, who had learned of the death of Lewis from a newspaper article when he reached Frankfort, Kentucky, continued to Washington and met with officials before settling in with family in western Virginia for a stay that would keep him away from St. Louis until the following summer. From Fincastle he wrote Pierre in a bland and reassuring tone that the "Government were not as favorably impressed with the objects and correct intentions of the [Missouri Fur] Company as they were intitled to. I explained to them the real views of the Company, and have obtained their approbation and some assurance in support of Missouri . . . I will explore this subject when I see you, which I hope will be in a few weeks." He added that the Secretary of War had promised to retain Pierre as Osage agent.

Before receiving Clark's letter, Pierre wrote Eustis that he had sold to the fur company for $754.50 most of the goods that Lewis had authorized him to acquire and give to friendly tribes in case their help was needed during the upriver trip. Most had not been needed. In a later letter he seemed to be growing irritated with the financial obligations that were falling back on him, and he wanted to know whether he was going to be reimbursed, explaining:

> These goods had been bought in different stores in St. Louis by myself on express orders from the governor, who gave me two of his drafts to pay for them. One of these drafts, in the sum of $40 came back protested, and since I had endorsed it, Mr. Lewis having made it payable to my order, I was obliged to immediately reimburse the full amount, as well as the expenses, interest and charges caused by the protest, and apparently the second letter of exchange which was to pay likewise for these goods will come back protested and I shall again be obliged as endorser to pay it. I venture to observe to you, Sir, that it is very unfortunate for me to be the victim of my obedience to the orders of Mr. Lewis, moreover a small portion of this merchandise was used to obtain the free passage of the Mandan chief and to replace the presents announced and promised to his nation, which had not been forthcoming, and the rest of these goods were sold for the benefit of the U. S., which will receive the total in August 1810. I venture to flatter myself, Sir, that now that you are well informed of the circumstances, you will not consider it just that this loss should fall upon me and that you will authorize me to draw on you for the amount that I have paid.

Not hearing from Eustis, Pierre wrote him two months later that he was still hoping to receive an answer to his letter about the protested letters of exchange drawn by Governor Lewis. Eustis finally agreed, in a letter that probably crossed in the mail with Pierre's latest letter, to honor the letters of exchange.

There was little to celebrate when the leaders of St. Louis gathered for their Independence Day dinner at William Christy's tavern in 1810.

In fact, the event added to the prevailing sense of gloom when a cannon went off while a soldier was ramming down the charge, severely wounding him. Meriwether Lewis's "cloud of miseries" had enveloped them all, as well as the fur-trading venture that remained upriver from the ambitious and hopeful undertaking launched the previous year in collaboration with the man now gone.

NINE

Dreaming Big—and Stumbling

✳

Snow was deep as horses around the Gros Ventre village where some of the men of the Missouri Fur Company passed the winter of 1809–10. They had moved higher and westward after the delivery of the Mandan chief to his home village and the departure of Pierre Chouteau for St. Louis. When spring came, those at the Gros Ventre village, including Thomas James, joined the larger group under Pierre Ménard and Andrew Henry at the Three Forks area of present-day Montana.

Reaching the Forks on April 3, 1810, they planned to build a fort and trap for beaver. James's group agreed to trap on the Missouri, another group on the Jefferson River, and the others agreed to remain with Pierre Ménard to complete the fort between the Jefferson and Madison rivers. But on the morning of April 12 a band of Blackfeet came down on the Ménard-Henry party, killed five men, and stole their horses, guns, ammunition, traps, and furs. The men continued trying to trap, but a few days later the Blackfeet fell on them again.

"This unhappy miscarriage causes us a considerable loss, but I do not propose on that account to lose heart," Ménard wrote to Pierre Chouteau. "The resources of this country in beaver fur are immense. It is true that we shall accomplish nothing this spring, but I trust that we shall next Autumn."

Ménard's ambitious plan was to go to see the Snake and Flathead Indians, try to induce them to make war on the Blackfeet, get some Blackfoot prisoners in the course of the fighting, and then go to the

Blackfeet with peace terms, including a request for trading rights. Soon, however, some of the hunters wanted to abandon the effort, and Ménard led them to return downriver. Henry and the rest of the men remained at Three Forks.

Around the same time that spring, young A. P. Chouteau, who had also wintered in the upper country, set out for St. Louis to take down the furs that had been collected below the Mandan villages. Just before he reached Cedar Island in the future South Dakota, fire swept through the post, destroying $15,000 worth of furs that he was coming to collect.

Things were not going well for the company elsewhere, either.

Manuel Lisa, who had come downriver with Pierre Chouteau the previous November, traveled to Detroit on his way to Canada to sell the first peltries from the new firm. It was a miserable trip, taking him sixteen days from Vincennes. "We found much cold, bad roads, and unfortunately I fell into the water twice through the fault of my horse," Lisa wrote Pierre. He was riding a horse that belonged to either Pierre or Pierre Jr., and he could not help needling his old competitors a little about the quality of the animal they had provided him. It was "an excellent horse, which has held out well until here, and with which I am continuing my journey . . . It has, however, one great defect, that of being weak, particularly in its hind feet . . . it threw me and almost broke the lower part of my back, which still pains me very much."

To make matters worse, although the War of 1812 was still more than two years away, Lisa found it "impossible to get even a needle past the embargo" against trade with Britain and its possession, Canada. He was not allowed to cross the Detroit River into Canada with his pelts. "The embargo prevents communications between the two sides," Lisa told Pierre. "There are guards along the whole length of this river, who watch to see if one is carrying anything across, and the penalties are very severe, confiscation of the effects, five hundred piastres fine and twenty five days in prison."

But the St. Louis partners were not the only people attempting a daring push into the rich northern beaver areas that year. Rebuffed years

earlier in his efforts to do business with the Chouteau brothers, John
Jacob Astor was beginning his own campaign to take control of the fur
trade on the Upper Missouri and across the mountains to the Pacific.
Since his overtures to the Chouteaus in 1800, when he was hardly
known to them, Astor had become the most important figure in the
American fur trade. He had been in the business more than twenty
years. He had developed a substantial reputation and was on his way
to becoming America's first millionaire. When Jefferson made the
Louisiana Purchase, an excited Astor envisioned what could be accomplished through that huge piece of real estate.

He assumed—prematurely—that as part of the Louisiana Purchase, the United States now owned the mouth of the Columbia
River and the Pacific coastline. Coupling that assumption with the
tales brought back by Lewis and Clark of the fur and pelt potential of
the Upper Missouri and the mountains to the west of it, he quickly
grasped the magnitude of the business that could be done. In his vision, traders would avoid the laborious process of dropping down to
St. Louis with the returns of the fur trade each season, then trans-
shipping them to New Orleans or Montreal by barge. His idea was to
establish a central trading "emporium" on the Oregon coast, from
which he would take out the pelts in oceangoing vessels and circle the
globe on a regular basis.

Washington Irving, who years later became Astor's confidant and
wrote the history of the undertaking, said that under Astor's plan, "a
ship was to be sent annually from New York to this main establishment with reinforcements and supplies, and with merchandise suited
to the trade. It would take on board the furs collected during the preceding year, carry them to Canton, invest the proceeds in the rich
merchandise of China, and return thus freighted to New York."

"With China a market for furs from the Pacific Coast, with Russian
establishments on the Northwest coast which his ships might supply
as an incident to their main business, with markets at home for the
products of the Orient, with lines of trading posts along the Columbia
from the sea to its source, connected then with the Missouri, and extending down that stream to St. Louis, and from that point by way of
the Great Lakes to New York itself, Mr. Astor saw that his business

would indeed be worldwide in scope and international in importance," explained fur-trade historian Hiram Chittenden.

Irving said that Astor, already rich beyond the wildest imagination of most Americans then living, was motivated by more than the desire for further commercial success. "He now aspired to that honorable fame which is awarded to men of similar scope of mind, who by their great commercial enterprises have enriched nations, peopled wildernesses, and extended the bounds of empire."

In April 1808 Astor obtained a charter from the state of New York creating the American Fur Company. A subsidiary called the Pacific Fur Company would operate the central establishment near the mouth of the Columbia River. From there, trade was to be conducted in all directions with Indians of the Northwest interior and then along the Yellowstone, Bighorn, and Missouri rivers.

Astor launched what Irving called the "great scheme of commerce and colonization" with two expeditions: one by sea to establish the viability of the international trade route, and the other by land and river, generally along the Lewis and Clark route. Except for Charles Gratiot, none of the St. Louis traders was part of the Astor plan. The Chouteaus' brother-in-law was still enthusiastic about doing business with Astor and was included in some of Astor's correspondence on the expedition, but there is no indication that Gratiot had a stake in the company. He was in debt to Astor for trade merchandise, and he was willing to assist Astor's undertakings as much as he could. He took great pleasure, for instance, in sending Astor a rare white beaver skin and some wool made from buffalo hair, which he thought had manufacturing potential. Despite the lack of direct involvement by the St. Louis traders, however, Astor's venture would challenge them and shape their business lives for decades to come.

Astor found most of his partners in the East or among fur-trade veterans in Canada. The group handling the land expedition was led by Wilson Price Hunt, a merchant from Trenton, New Jersey, with no experience in the West or with Indians. Several of the other partners were Scotsmen, including David and Robert Stuart, who were uncle and nephew, and Donald McKenzie and Duncan McDougal, who had experience in the British Northwest Company. Twenty-three-old Ramsay Crooks, who had come to the United States from Scotland at sixteen and entered the fur trade, was soon added to the group.

The partners and managers recruited boatmen and hunters in Canada, then traveled to St. Louis via Lake Michigan, the Fox and Wisconsin rivers, and the Mississippi, arriving on September 3, 1810. Continuing out of St. Louis, they established a winter headquarters near present-day St. Joseph, Missouri. Robert McLellan, a veteran of America's Indian wars who had met Ramsay Crooks a few years earlier in St. Louis, joined the company. Hunt returned to St. Louis in the winter of 1810–11 and continued recruiting, competing with the Missouri Fur Company for men.

On September 3, 1810, the sea portion of the Astor plan got under way when the 290-ton *Tonquin* sailed from New York with twenty-two crewmen and thirty-three other men working for the fur company. Traveling south, it followed the coast of South America, sighted the Falkland Islands on December 3, reached the Pacific Ocean on December 24, and made Hawaii, then known as the Sandwich Islands, on February 11, 1811. After taking aboard twenty-four boatmen and laborers, the *Tonquin* left Hawaii on February 28. On March 22, more than six months into the voyage, it sighted land at the mouth of the Columbia.

In the process of trying to find the channel of the river, Captain Jonathan Thorn sent out several small boats, losing a boat and eight men in the effort. On March 25 the ship finally found safe anchorage. After looking about for a site to erect a post, the workmen began clearing ground on April 12 for the central trading and warehouse establishment, which was christened Astoria.

Hunt and his party, meanwhile, left St. Louis on March 12, 1811, a few days before the *Tonquin* entered the mouth of the Columbia. The overland Astoria expedition had four boats and nearly sixty people, of whom forty were Canadian *engagés* or voyageurs. Their boats all had masts and sails, which were useful when winds were strong.

Manuel Lisa was also preparing to set out anew from St. Louis on behalf of the Missouri Fur Company, leading a group to look for the missing Andrew Henry and his men. Unbeknownst to those in St.

Louis, the Henry group was under recurring Blackfoot attack. Eventually they moved across the Continental Divide and established camp on the north fork of the Snake River.

Both expeditions departing St. Louis captured the imaginations of naturalists and scholarly travelers. John Bradbury, the Scottish-born English naturalist, and Thomas Nuttall, a budding English botanist who later taught at Harvard, traveled with Hunt's party for a considerable distance up the Missouri. Henry M. Brackenridge, a young American writer who had moved to the territory a few years earlier, traveled with Lisa. Bradbury and Brackenridge eventually published accounts of the voyage.

Lisa, who did not get away until the end of March, was concerned about safety going through Sioux country, so he decided to catch up with Hunt, thinking their combined numbers would help to ward off danger. Not fully aware of the extent of Sioux hostility, Hunt thought Lisa was trying to gain competitive advantage, so he did not slow down to wait for him.

Lisa had a fast keelboat, manned by twenty men. But Hunt was nineteen days and about 240 miles ahead when Lisa left St. Charles. The resulting pursuit lasted more than two months and covered a distance of about 1,100 miles. Lisa encountered continuous storms and wind but gradually closed the gap. Exuberant in the midst of the chase, Lisa led his men in songs to stimulate them to work harder and faster. When Lisa took a rest, he and Brackenridge conversed in Spanish and read *Don Quixote.*

"Great exertions are made by Mr. Lisa," wrote an admiring Brackenridge after the trip was over. "He is at one moment at the helm, at another with the grappling iron at the bow, and often with a pole assisting the hands in impelling the barge through the rapid current."

Lisa was just sixty miles behind Hunt when he reached the Niobrara River. Feeling his group in great peril, he drove himself and his crew even harder. They frequently sailed most of the night, on one occasion covering seventy-five miles in twenty-four hours. Both managed to pass through Sioux country without incident, and Lisa overtook Hunt on June 2 after averaging more than eighteen miles a day for sixty days.

The two parties continued upriver at a leisurely pace until they met the descending Andrew Henry and his men. The Henry party had gone through a severe winter but still managed to get about forty packs of beaver before starting to descend. Having found the missing men, Lisa turned back on July 17, taking the three writers with him.

Hunt's party continued up the Missouri and then crossed the Divide to the Snake River en route to the Oregon coast to joint the seafaring group. It would be nearly two years before anyone in St. Louis, or anywhere to the east of there, would learn of their fate.

Pierre Chouteau, after returning from the Mandan villages and going through the struggle with Eustis to collect his expenses and save his position as Osage agent, was facing troubled Indian affairs in the Lower Missouri River region. He remained a partner in the Missouri Fur Company, but his son A.P. was the active participant on his behalf.

Fearful of a war between the Osages and the Shawnees, who were then living in the southeastern part of present-day Missouri, Pierre traveled back and forth several hundred miles among their villages to clear up differences between them in the summer and fall of 1810. The Osages had long hated the Shawnees, an emigrant tribe from the East that had adopted many white ways and many of whose members had intermarried with whites. The Osages used the term "Shawnee" dismissively to refer to any tribe from east of the Mississippi. The Shawnees were equally dismissive toward the Osages, calling them "buffalo Indians."

The Osages were also bitter over the fact that Congress still had not ratified the 1808 treaty in which they gave up land and were promised an annuity and other things. This led them to believe the treaty was not in force. After using all his "credit and authority" with the Osages to get them to sign the treaty, Pierre had heard nothing more about it—or the commitments made by the government—since he returned to St. Louis from Fort Osage in the fall of 1808 and gave the signed document to then-Governor Lewis. Not a cent of the annuity had yet been paid, nor had the Osages received the mill promised them to grind their grain or the forge to repair arms and tools.

In fact, the Senate had unanimously ratified the Osage treaty on

April 28, 1810, but Pierre did not learn of it until William Clark told him in the summer of 1811 that the treaty had recently been published in Washington. Pierre immediately sent for the chiefs and headmen to gather at Fort Osage for the first annuity payments.

To succeed Meriwether Lewis as governor of Louisiana Territory, the President appointed Benjamin Howard, member of Congress from Lexington, Kentucky. He arrived at St. Louis on September 17, 1810. Frederick Bates continued as territorial secretary.

Auguste Chouteau, who turned sixty in 1810, was chairman of the Board of Trustees of the town of St. Louis, as well as town treasurer. In the election for five new trustees, held at Christy's Tavern on November 27, 1810, Pierre was added to the board. Presenting the town's first full financial statement at the end of 1810, Auguste said that receipts from all sources totaled $529.68, with expenditures of $399.15 and a balance on hand of $130.53. When the tax assessment for town purposes was made in 1811, Auguste led the list of taxpayers, paying $268.10 on property assessed at $76,000.

Auguste continued to engage in the fur trade independently of the Missouri Fur Company, shipping his furs via New Orleans and Montreal. Cavelier & Son in New Orleans predicted that buffalo robes would sell well in 1812 because wool blankets were scarce. Lead, which Auguste had been shipping from the mines south of St. Louis, was also selling well.

Both Pierre and Auguste bought and sold land as opportunities arose. When the administrator auctioned the land in the estate of Meriwether Lewis, Pierre acquired rights to two tracts totaling 3,669 arpents (3,118 acres) for just $55. Pierre himself had deeded the land to Lewis on August 3, 1808. Considering that most land in the area was then going for a dollar or more an acre, it seems likely that Pierre had taken back a mortgage from Lewis and that the repurchase price of just $55 represented Lewis's equity.

On June 4, 1812, Congress passed legislation that for the first time used the name Missouri as the designation for the territory. Out of the territory previously called Louisiana, encompassing most of the lands north of the Arkansas River between the Mississippi and the Rocky

Mountains, it created the new "territory second grade" of Missouri. A month earlier, Congress had admitted the former Orleans Territory to the Union as the state of Louisiana.

Despite tough going, the Missouri Fur Company got through its first three years with a small profit, having saved its original capital in addition to the posts it built on the upper rivers. The company was reorganized on January 24, 1812, and the property of the old company sold to the new.

Charles Gratiot, who handled the paperwork on behalf of Pierre to dissolve the first partnership, suggested that Astor be included in the reorganization. He proposed that the new company have fifteen shares for a total capital of $45,000 and that Astor be offered five of the shares. He told Astor that some members liked the idea, but the majority apparently did not, and there is no record of an offer being extended to Astor.

A new expedition was fitted out that spring of 1812 with $11,000 worth of merchandise; two boats were sent up the river under the charge of Lisa. But the returns that September were not good, and in the fall of 1813, stockholders met to dissolve the company. Surviving records show that a business continued to operate under the name of Missouri Fur Company during the next few years, but with only Lisa as a principal member.

On June 19, 1812, after more than a year of rising tensions over maritime rights, Congress declared war against England. The news reached St. Louis on July 9 and immediately sapped interest from the fur trade, especially in areas close to British-held lands in Canada and on the Oregon coast, where both governments claimed sovereignty. Lisa withdrew his remaining establishments from the Upper Missouri and concentrated them at Fort Lisa, the trading post he had built at the future Council Bluffs.

The war suddenly restored Pierre Chouteau's importance to the government, making him the point man for securing the loyalty of Indian tribes up and down the Mississippi. He was key to winning complete loyalty from the Osages. Less than three weeks after news of the declaration of war reached St. Louis, Governor Howard sent him up the Mississippi to Prairie du Chien to check on the intentions of the northern tribes and learn what he could about British activities in the area.

At the same time, to head off any problems with the Osages, Pierre sent his son A.P. and a number of workers to the Osage village near Fort Osage to build the long-planned mill. When Pierre returned from Prairie du Chien on November 18, he continued to the Osage village and found that the Osages there were fearful of attack from tribes up or across the Mississippi. They wanted the government to build two blockhouses at the fort to protect them. Pierre asked permission from Eustis to appoint a subagent to the Arkansas River Osages because of their scattered locations over a vast territory. He proposed giving the job to A.P., who was respected by the Osages and understood their language. It took more than a year for this request to be approved, during which time A.P., who was then twenty-six years old, lent his services to his father and the government.

Within a short time, however, the government was asking more than just loyalty of the Osages. With the British making great efforts to incite tribes of the Mississippi and Upper Missouri against the United States, the government wanted the Osages to offer their blood as well. Frederick Bates, serving again as acting governor while Howard was gone from Missouri, told Pierre in March 1813 to go back to the Osages and ask them to send 200 to 400 warriors to "our lines." It would be their job "to watch and to oppose the Indian Nations confederated with the British." He wanted them to serve as a buffer protecting Americans from tribes sympathetic to the British.

Pierre reached the Osage towns on April 7 and had to wait for the principal men to return from hunting expeditions. He sent A.P. onward to the Arkansas Osages to ascertain their state of mind and return. The Osages and Pierre met in council on April 20 and he "found them firm in their reliance on the friendship and protection of the American Government."

"They appeared highly gratified with the proposal to establish them on our northern borders," he informed Howard, "and had made every preparation for that purpose."

The war party headed east immediately. A.P., using his military training in a way probably not contemplated by instructors at West Point, rode at the head of 260 Osage warriors. Pierre traveled by river with the supplies. But when the group reached the first white settlements on the river, near present-day Jefferson City, a message arrived from Governor Howard telling Pierre to turn the Indians back to their villages. In a subsequent message Howard told Pierre to secure the chiefs' agreement for the evacuation and closing of Fort Osage as well. He said the troops stationed there would be more useful against the British on the frontiers.

The Osages were greatly disappointed at the lost opportunity "to defend their allies and at the same time to avenge themselves of their long sworn enemies," Pierre reported. It was difficult to persuade them to go back home. Pierre had to give them the rest of the goods he had put together to win their favor, and he also promised to pay their annuities—by then two years past due—the following July. But the most damaging action was the abrupt closing of Fort Osage, which would offend and anger the sensitive tribe for years to come.

Howard later told Pierre he had thought it useful to use the Osages against the tribes allied with the English—which included the Potawatomis, Kickapoos, Winnebagos, and the Prophet's party of the Wabash—but officials in Washington did not agree.

In the midst of tensions and fears over the war, seven men floated into St. Louis from the Missouri River and created a sensation with news that tragedy had befallen the Astorian expedition. Ramsay Crooks, Robert McLellan, Robert Stuart, and four other Astorians landed at St. Louis on April 30, 1813, after traveling for ten months from the mouth of the Columbia River.

Theirs was a sobering tale, revealing the risks in a venture as broad in scope as Astor's in an era when it usually took months, or even years, to know what was occurring with another part of the operation. The effort had ended with the loss of at least sixty-five lives among the ship crews and fur company employees and more than a hundred Indians who attacked the *Tonquin*. The first attempt to open a door to global trade through the American West had been destroyed primarily by distances and lack of communication among New York, the Pacific coast, and Asia. It was, in fact, not entirely over.

Arriving in surprisingly good health, Crooks, McLellan, Stuart, and their companions were soon filling in everybody in St. Louis— through the pages of the *Missouri Gazette*—on the events that transpired after the Hunt and Lisa parties parted in July of 1811. Hunt's group had continued north and west, and Lisa's group returned downriver with Andrew Henry and the remaining trappers of the Missouri Fur Company.

While the Hunt party was still ascending the Missouri River, the *Tonquin* sailed from Astoria on June 1, 1811, leaving behind part of the company to continue organizing the trading post and open contacts with Indians in the area. Heading north, the *Tonquin* arrived after about ten days at Nootka Sound on Vancouver Island and anchored opposite a large Indian village. To Captain Thorn, the Indians coming to the boat in pirogues seemed friendly. Many of them came aboard to trade their furs. Brisk trading followed, with all the Indians requesting knives.

When the crew became fearful about the large number of knives in Indian hands and prepared to sail, the Indians launched an assault and killed most of the crew and the workers from Hawaii. The next day, a mortally wounded survivor blew the ship to bits, killing as many as a hundred of the Indians as well; only the interpreter lived to return to Astoria and tell the story.

Members of Hunt's land party, meanwhile, still trying to reach Astoria, had abandoned their horses on reaching the Snake River, thinking they could travel the rest of the way by water. But they ran into a stretch of the river that was not navigable, became confused about which route to follow, and ended up splitting into three groups. Hunt, Crooks, and McLellan each led a group along a different route. Travel conditions were rugged, food was short, many of the men became ill, and the Indian wife of the interpreter gave birth. The first of the three groups, led by McLellan, stumbled into Astoria on January 18, 1812. Hunt's group arrived on February 15, and Crooks did not appear until May 11.

During the time the land travelers were making their way to Astoria and the *Tonquin* was facing destruction, the forty-two men who had remained behind at Astoria were successfully opening trade with the Indians near there. They finished construction of some buildings and were planning to have skins and furs to put aboard the ship when it returned.

On May 12, 1812, a day after the Crooks party reached Astoria, the company's resupply ship *Beaver* arrived, sent from New York by an unaware Astor. The *Beaver* brought a large cargo of goods for trading and some clerks and other employees. So far, the people at Astoria had heard only rumors from Indians of the sad end of the *Tonquin*. But the partners present at Astoria decided that they should continue with Astor's maritime plan by sending Hunt on the *Beaver* with furs and trade goods for the Russian coast. Crooks and McLellan, meanwhile, decided to resign their shares in the venture and return to St. Louis; they left in June with Stuart and four other men, who were also abandoning the venture.

Unaware that the United States had recently declared war against Britain, thereby making American ships vulnerable to attack, Hunt sailed away from Astoria on the *Beaver* on August 4. Reaching the Asian coast of Russia, he found officials and merchants hostile, and payment methods could not be worked out. The captain of the ship wanted to make repairs, so they headed for the Sandwich Islands and were tied up there a long time before proceeding to Canton, where the captain was afraid to leave. After learning that the United States and Britain were at war, Hunt chartered another ship, the *Albatross*, and departed on June 20, 1813, bound for Astoria.

With Hunt gone to Asia and Crooks and McLellan back in St. Louis, those left at Astoria lacked leadership. They were confused about what to do when news of the war reached them on January 15, 1813. Some thought the war made the situation hopeless. Half the leaders wanted to abandon the enterprise; half wanted to continue. They were doubly torn because many of them were British subjects, and there was concern that the British might soon send war vessels to the mouth of the Columbia. Those who wanted to abandon Astoria finally won in July 1813 by arguing that the non-return of the *Beaver* from Asia had left them without supplies and that with the war under way, the vessel was unlikely to get through to them again.

Hunt, in fact, arrived in the *Albatross* the following month, but he was unable to change people's minds. They decided to try to sell the installation to a British group operating in the area. Hunt ordered work begun to shut down Astoria, and he left five days later to find a ship to remove all those remaining. The *Albatross* was not available for another charter, so he rode with it to the Sandwich Islands, where he bought a brig, the *Pedler*, and put it in charge of the captain of a supply ship that Astor had sent from New York but which had been wrecked near the Sandwich Islands. It was February 28, 1814, before Hunt returned to Astoria on the *Pedler*. By then the post had been sold to a British group, which had taken possession two months earlier.

Taking the company's records and all those who wanted to leave, Hunt sailed away from the Columbia on the *Pedler* on April 3, 1814. Russell Farnham, a young company clerk from Massachusetts, was dropped at Kamchatka. With a small backpack of provisions, he set out on foot for a perilous trek across Asian and European Russia, carrying dispatches and British sterling drafts for Astor. Battling a severe climate and suffering great deprivation, Farnham became so hungry that he cut off his boot tops and ate them. He eventually reached St. Petersburg, found a ship, and sailed to New York. He delivered the documents to Astor, who repaid him with lifetime employment, much of which occurred in or near St. Louis.

With the continuing influx of new people from east of the Mississippi, St. Louis and the Missouri Territory were becoming more and more American and Anglophone in character. While Pierre continued to concentrate on his work with Indians, Auguste Chouteau tried to remain active as a leader of the town whose first structures he had planned and helped to build with his own hands. Missouri was being prepared for statehood, and the city was growing. A Legislative Council was being established to serve as a governing body, and officials approached Auguste about being a member. He was still serving as a member of the Court of Common Pleas, from which he would have to resign in order to serve in a legislative capacity. A plea made from the chief judge, Silas Bent, for Auguste to reject the legislative posi-

tion and remain with the court sheds light on the tensions over language underlying civic life in the bilingual town and territory.

Bent told Auguste his resignation from the court would be a severe
loss for the French people and that Americans who most hated the
French would likely be appointed to replace him. Bent, whose own
roots were in Massachusetts, theorized that those people who disliked
the French were really trying to remove Auguste from the court,
where he might be effective with his vote, even while lacking the ability to speak English. In the Legislative Council, Bent warned, Auguste
would be more limited by his lack of English.

"[Those who dislike the French] know also that your Judgment
and integrity will avail nothing in the council because it is not expected that you will be a public speaker, for no Interpreter can keep
pace with the debates." He went on to say that in a legislative body, "a
silent vote against an improper act is worse than none" because the
person is unable to explain his vote.

Nevertheless, when Acting Governor Bates announced, on June 3,
1813, that the President had named nine men to the Legislative
Council for the territory, one of the nine was Auguste Chouteau. One
of the body's early acts was to adopt English common law as the basis
of jurisprudence for the territory, which had operated under Spanish
and French code law until then.

In July 1813 William Clark, who had been assigned to active militia duty at the outbreak of the war, returned to St. Louis and took up
his new position as territorial governor, replacing Benjamin Howard.
The position of territorial governor also included being superintendent of Indian affairs, so Clark continued to oversee Pierre Chouteau's
work with the Osages.

The final defeat and abdication of Napoleon in April 1814 enabled
the British to concentrate their military efforts on the war with the
United States. American forces responded to new British offensives
with decisive campaigns of their own, and both sides decided to talk
peace even while continuing to fight. John Quincy Adams opened
talks with the British in Belgium in August 1814, and on Christmas
Eve the Treaty of Ghent was signed to end the war. Among other

things, it confirmed United States ownership of the Oregon Territory, including the site of Astoria.

Along the Mississippi and Missouri Rivers, however, additional peace negotiations were needed. By the calculations of the United States government, a total of thirty-seven Indian tribes had sided with Britain in the war, and the government wanted peace treaties negotiated with them. Most of those tribes lived along the Upper Mississippi and the Upper Missouri rivers. President Madison appointed three commissioners with full power to make a treaty with all the tribes who had been at war against the United States: William Clark, Auguste Chouteau, and Governor Ninian Edwards of the Illinois Territory. Clark was the leader of the group.

"You will give immediate notice to all the tribes of Indians with whom the United States is at war on the Mississippi and the waters that discharge into it of the peace that has been concluded between the United States and Great Britain," Secretary of War James Monroe wrote each of them. "You will also invite them to be present, by a deputation of their chiefs, at the place or places that you may fix, to conclude the treaty of peace and friendship proposed between the United States and all these tribes." Monroe said they should "take advantage of this opportunity to inform the Indian leaders that the Government intended to establish military posts very high up on the Mississippi and from the Mississippi to Lake Michigan, and to open trading stations at these posts or others."

The summer of 1815 was given over to negotiations as delegation after delegation of Indian leaders arrived and set up camps at Portage des Sioux. Manuel Lisa, for example, as subagent for tribes of the Upper Missouri, arrived with forty-three chiefs and headmen of the several bands of Sioux, plus the chiefs of the Mahas and Poncas residing between the Missouri and Mississippi rivers. At Portage des Sioux, according to a *Missouri Gazette* correspondent, the Indians camped in a "handsome display of about 100 tents." The number of Indians camped there was estimated at 2,000 to 3,000, and their varied tribal dress created a colorful scene.

Although the *Gazette* described the ambience as tranquil, Clark had two fully manned gunboats stationed nearby, and 275 regular soldiers—in case of unrest. Some of the thirty-seven groups invited did not appear—notably the Winnebagos, the Iowas, the Kickapoos, and the Rock River Sacs and Foxes, who in May had been responsible for the massacre of a farm family on the Missouri River.

During most of a month, tribal leaders met with the commissioners in William Clark's council house on the southeast corner of Main and Vine streets in St. Louis. Some of the tribes resisted the terms of the treaties, in which they would have to renounce further belligerence against the United States and its citizens. To help bring them around, Clark distributed gifts from $30,000 worth of goods supplied by the government. Then everybody went to Portage des Sioux for the ceremonial conclusion of the treaties.

In the course of these negotiations, Auguste Chouteau called on his half century of experience with the Indians over a vast region in the central and upper midsections of the continent. After the treaty talks had been completed, he put all that he could remember about tribal boundaries down on paper. His report was subsequently deposited in the Office of Indian Affairs in Washington as "Notes of Auguste Chouteau on Boundaries of Various Indian Nations."

One of the points Auguste made in "Notes" was that Indian tribes often held overlapping claims to certain lands. This came from their histories. In different periods, Indian nations had splintered into tribes, which, though still part of the same nation, scattered over large areas. So two or more tribes within the same nation might end up claiming all of their ancestral lands without recognizing that the lands belonged to a number of tribes within the same nation. This situation complicated the work of the commissioners, who, in addition to negotiating cessions with the principal tribe on a piece of land, often had to persuade other tribes to renounce whatever claims they had to the lands as well.

Auguste stressed that intertribal warfare had destroyed or nearly wiped out many tribes before the white man came, or where white men were not very numerous. He cited the example of the Illinois nation, which in 1675 was more numerous than any other Indian nation in the territory comprising the future states of Illinois, Missouri, and Wisconsin. It included at least seven tribes, among them the Miamis,

Peorias, Cahokias, and Kaskaskias. Over decades, however, the Illinois were continually harassed and killed by various enemies, including the Sioux, Sacs and Foxes, Choctaws, and Cherokees. The Illinois tribes continually moved to escape these enemies.

Once the tribes gained access to alcohol from the traders, there was a new threat to their well-being. Auguste pointed out that they handled alcohol very badly and often killed each other while drunk, producing massive retaliation by entire Indian families. As a result of the intertribal warfare and family vengeance, Auguste estimated that by 1763, when he moved to the Missouri River with his stepfather, the tribes of the Illinois nation had been reduced to about a thousand fighting men. In 1780, when the Illinois moved to Ste. Genevieve, the number of men did not exceed two hundred. In 1816, when he wrote his "Notes," he said the "once great & powerful nation of Illinois" was left with only about seventy men, women, and children living near Kaskaskia and a "few Straggling Peorias about Ste. Genevieve."

By the cold and snowy winter of 1815–16, Pierre Chouteau was fifty-seven years old and not willing to bend to the government's pressures for him, and all Indian agents, to live among the tribes. He wanted to go to Washington while Congress was in session to explain why that was impossible. But his assistant, M. P. Leduc, wrote Territorial Secretary Bates that Pierre was confined by a "violent cold, and a Sciatick— and at this time such a quantity of Snow that travelling appears almost impracticable." Further, Pierre Sr. was worried about Pierre Jr., who was ill with a "disease."

"The Osages are not stationary," Leduc explained on behalf of Pierre. "Hunger compels them to follow the Herds of Buffaloes and other animals for subsistence some time at the distance of six hundred Miles, from whence they return about the time of Planting & gathering corn, Should the agent be at the village when they are gone he certainly would run the risk of being killed or at least plundered by other tribes who very often in the summer destroy the cabbins & crops of the osages."

Pierre thought it would be better for the agent to go twice a year, in April and August—because the Osages returned from their winter hunts about the middle of March to plant corn, then left on the first of May and returned again toward the end of July, abandoning the village in September after gathering the corn.

These were not peaceful days among the always unpredictable Osages. In addition to their own internal differences, they were greatly distressed by the movement of Cherokees into former Osage lands. The Osages claimed that the immigrant tribe was taking Osage lands that had not been ceded to the United States in the 1808 treaty.

At this point the Osages remained divided into what were essentially four bands. One band of the Big Osages, with about five hundred warriors, resided at its longtime village on the Osage River, just east of the eventual Kansas boundary. The other band of Big Osages, with about four hundred warrior-age men, was residing at considerable distance away, on the Arkansas River near present-day Claremore, Oklahoma. The Little Osages also had two bands. One was living in close proximity to the first band of Big Osages on the Osage River in western Missouri. The other band was on the Neosho River in present-day southeastern Kansas.

The land in dispute between the Osages and the Cherokees fell at the southern end of the the twenty-five-mile-wide strip running most of the length of the western boundary of Missouri and into Arkansas and Oklahoma, land that had been left to the Osages by the 1808 treaty. The same commissioners who had negotiated with the belligerent Indians to end the War of 1812—William Clark, Auguste Chouteau, and Ninian Edwards—looked into whether government agents had mistakenly placed the Cherokees on land still belonging to the Osages. The commissioners recommended that the line of the Osage cession be run by a surveyor to determine whether the Cherokees had been situated too far west. The commissioners noted that the Cherokees, who were in an area near the present boundary between Arkansas and Oklahoma, had made "considerable" and valuable improvements, so the government might have to buy this land from the Osages, if it belonged to them.

The War Department authorized the commissioners to make the survey, but Clark eventually dealt with it in another manner. In exchange for settling damage claims against the Osages by various individual white settlers and Cherokees, Clark persuaded the Osages to cede a circular piece of land sixty miles wide that included eventual Cherokee County in Oklahoma. Clark told Secretary of War John C. Calhoun that it was "a large body of very fine land."

Pierre Chouteau witnessed the new Osage treaty when it was signed in September 1818, but he had already ceased being the Osage agent. Six months earlier, perhaps because of his refusal to live among the tribe or perhaps because he wearied of seldom having his advice heeded, his name had been removed from the list of reappointed agents. Secretary of War Calhoun told Clark that Pierre and another agent being replaced should turn over all "public property, monies, books and papers in their possession to the nearest Indian agent."

At the signing, the Osages requested that Pierre be reappointed as their agent, and Clark passed the request along to Washington, but there was no response. Pierre Chouteau still had a long life ahead of him. Except through his sons, however, his dealings with the Osages had come to an end after more than forty years.

TEN

The Third Generation

✳

Historians have theorized that Meriwether Lewis selected two young men of the Chouteau clan—Pierre's son Auguste Pierre and Victoire's son Charles Gratiot Jr.—to form part of the West Point class of 1806 because he wanted to secure the loyalty of the social and economic elite in the newly acquired lands west of the Mississippi. If so, young Auguste Pierre, who would make his considerable reputation on the frontier as A. P. Chouteau, demonstrated in his final days at the academy that he had every intention of seeing that his stature was recognized.

A few weeks after completing his studies, but before leaving West Point, the new ensign displayed the Chouteau style—and a fine touch of Gallic self-esteem—in a run-in with the West Point commandant, Colonel Jonathan Williams, over carrying a bag of mail.

It began when A.P. was planning a personal trip into Peekskill and an aide to the commandant asked if he would carry the academy mail into town with him. "I told him I would not," A.P. informed Williams. "He then asked if I would bring your letters. I said, if there were but few I would, but if a great number I should not encumber myself with them as I went on my own account not as post man."

Before he could depart, however, A.P. tore one of his boots, so he canceled the trip. When word that A.P. was not going into town reached Williams, the disgusted commandant apparently called A.P. "fickle," and he told his aide, Mr. Wyndham, that the new graduate should not be trusted with the mail anyway. Learning of Williams's comment, A.P. was incensed.

"Your saying . . . that I was a fickle [*sic*]—something I do not understand . . . was not very pleasing to my feelings," he told Williams, reminding him "that it is not a part of my Duty as an officer to officiate as a post boy."

Not being considered trustworthy enough to carry the mail is "extremely grating to my feelings," A.P. said. How was it possible, he asked, that Colonel Williams "would recommend a man for a commission in the army and think him unworthy to take charge of his mail?" Claiming offense, he said that Williams owed him an explanation "so as to do away [with] the stigma [the words] attach to my character."

A.P.'s English was not yet as polished as it would become, which may have accounted for some of the misunderstanding. Nevertheless, his reactions and interpretations were enough to thoroughly confound and perplex Williams. The commandant wrote back that he had never expected or wanted A.P. to carry the mail but understood that he had offered to do so. He added that he did not consider it "derogatory" for an officer to carry the mail, having done so himself.

A few months after A.P.'s flap with the commandant and his subsequent departure for assignment at Natchitoches, his fourteen-year-old cousin, Auguste Aristide Chouteau, eldest son of Auguste, was thrown out of a boy's seminary in Montreal following a series of missteps that greatly embarrassed the maternal aunt and uncle who were overseeing his education in Canada. It was the third school in which he had been enrolled in the five years he had been in Montreal.

In the course of those years he had run away from school on numerous occasions; hung out in the streets for days—until hunger and cold drove him to a cousin's home; stolen a classmate's ice skates; and spent entirely too much time in the stables and kitchen among the servants, in the view of his uncle, P. L. Panet. The Panets did their best with their unruly young kinsman from the wilds, including him in special learning experiences with their own well-behaved children. During vacations each was assigned a small garden to cultivate. "In the evening we keep them busy translating fables from English into French and in reading some amusing book," Panet wrote Auguste.

The Panets also supported the boy in his desire to study drawing and painting, like his cousin Melanie, believing that art "can only add to the qualities of a well-raised man and . . . occupy him agreeably all his life in his moments of leisure."

Auguste Aristide seemed to miss the hybrid culture into which he had been born. During the first year he spent in Montreal, he wrote his father—in adequate English and good penmanship, surely gladdening Auguste's heart—to request that he send him a bow and quiver of arrows so he could "exercise," plus the "Deers horns which I forgot in the garret," and a pair of shoes decorated, Indian style, with porcupine quills.

Four years later, however, after a series of increasingly frustrated letters to St. Louis, Panet informed Auguste that the boy had been ousted from his third school because of unstated conduct problems. Further, the headmaster would not accept him for the new high school he was starting, so the prospects did not look bright for turning Auguste Aristide into the educated gentleman that his father wanted him to become.

While awaiting instructions on sending the boy back to St. Louis, Panet put him in a "common school"—his fourth institution. "He is at least kept busy for some hours of the day instead of remaining inactive at home," Panet told Auguste. "As this school is English he will improve in the language in which he is beginning to express himself rather well; as for writing, as well as for French, you will find him very ignorant, due to his lack of application and an absolutely determined distaste for study." By the following summer he was back home in St. Louis.

Marie Thérèse Bourgeois Chouteau, grandmother of both A.P. and Auguste Aristide, lived a long life after the death of Pierre Laclède, her companion of twenty years and the father of four of her five children. Just one grandchild, a daughter of Pélagie and Sylvestre Labbadie Sr., had been born by the time Laclède died, in 1778. By the time Madame Chouteau died, in 1814, however, her sons and daughters— Auguste and Pierre Chouteau, Victoire Gratiot, Pélagie Labbadie, and Marie Louise Papin—had given her fifty grandchildren, including

A.P. and Auguste Aristide. Forty-one of her grandchildren lived to adulthood, and most of them had various children each, creating an immense extended family.

This does not take into account any part-Indian children of Auguste and Pierre. Although there are indications of affection and lifetime connections between them and their mestizo children—and also on the part of several members of the cousins' generation who fathered a large number of children by Indian women—there was no place for them on the family tree in the legally rigid French culture of the time.

Although Auguste was the eldest of Madame Chouteau's family, he had been the last of the siblings to marry in the church—at nearly age thirty-six. His first two children, both girls, died in childhood. Auguste Aristide was the first of his children to grow up, by which time his brother Pierre and his sisters had various children older than Auguste Aristide. Eventually Auguste and his wife, Marie Thérèse Cerré, had nine children, of whom seven lived to adulthood. Pierre, by his two wives, produced a family of eight boys and one girl, all of whom lived to adulthood, providing him a huge crop of grandchildren for his long old age. Among the sisters, Victoire and Charles Gratiot had six girls and four boys, of whom nine lived to adulthood. Marie Louise and Joseph Marie Papin produced seven boys and six girls, eleven of whom lived to grow up. Marie Pélagie and Sylvestre Labbadie had seven girls and two boys, of whom five grew up.

As if to confuse historians for centuries to come, the family showed a distinct lack of originality in selecting names for the children, with the result that the same names were repeated over and over. The family tree during the first four generations in St. Louis is laden with Augustes, Pierres, Pauls, Sylvestres, Emilies, Julies, Thérèses, Pélagies, or some combination. Even the half-Indian descendants were often christened with the same name as a sister, brother, or cousin of the father, sometimes with interesting twists, as in the case of a son born to A.P. in Indian country. The baby was named Gesseau in honor of A.P.'s half brother François Gesseau, but spelling being what it was in the future Oklahoma, the child grew up to be known variously as Gesso, Jesse, Fesseau, or Geso.

Paradoxically, the name Laclède did not figure among the names of the cousins. The closest to recognizing his connection to the family came in the naming of Pierre's third son, who was christened Paul Liguest Chouteau, incorporating Laclède's third name as the middle name. Paul Liguest Chouteau eventually fathered seven sons by two successive St. Louis wives and gave five of them the middle name Liguest, although only two of those boys lived to adulthood. One of those who died as a toddler was Alexandre Liguest, and one of Paul Liguest's many sons by Osage women was christened Alexandre Ligeste [*sic*]. A daughter of his born to an Osage woman was christened with the classically French name Pélagie, the name of Paul Liguest's mother, sister, and an aunt.

Like most parents, the Chouteaus were concerned with the education, marriage, and future prospects of the offspring of their marriages. They expected that their children, especially the sons, would be prepared to survive and flourish in Indian country as well as in the salons of power. These expectations were complicated in a frontier community that was ruled under three different flags during the lifetimes of Auguste and Pierre and their sisters.

Before sending Auguste Aristide to Montreal for schooling, Auguste and his wife may have given him some primary education at home or in the school that Jean Baptiste Truteau had operated on and off since arriving from Montreal in 1774. For a number of years, Truteau's was the only school in St. Louis. A Madame Rigauche also had a school for a while, during the 1790s. After 1804, new teachers appeared on the scene and began to open schools, but by then the older offspring of the Chouteau siblings were beyond the age for grammar school. This meant they had been schooled at home or sent away.

Auguste and his wife began to think about sending Auguste Aristide abroad by the time he was five years old, but Auguste corresponded with his brother-in-law for several years as he tried to make up his mind whether his first son should be sent to France or to Montreal.

Three years later, in 1800, Auguste sent the Panets a gift of a keg of pecans and told them he had decided to send Auguste Aristide to

Montreal. The concerns expressed in his letter seem prescient about the problems that his son would experience as a student in Montreal:

> The education of [one's] children is the most important thing for a good father, since it concerns their happiness or unhappiness and, finding myself living in a country where it is impossible to get a good one for mine, I finally decided to separate myself from [my son] . . . I must send him away from me, from a country where he can never conform himself to the usage of the world and good society, and acquire such talents as would distinguish him in the world or at least make him the equal of all that is called good society . . .
>
> With you he will doubtless acquire that tone, that worldly manner, that distinguishes the well-born man from the one who has had the misfortune not to have had sound principles from his early youth . . .
>
> As the English language even now begins to be, and some day will become, absolutely necessary here, I desire that he learn it and that he perfect himself in it. It is an expedient that will always be open to him, and, besides, even at present it is almost in general the language of commerce. So I think that an English school where he would find himself with children of his own age . . . would be the one that would best suit him at the beginning . . .
>
> As to his character . . . you will appraise it yourself . . . You will perhaps find that his manners will not be such as are acquired amongst polished people; perhaps he is too frank, too wild, but, as I have already observed, it is the misfortune of such places as this; there is no means of procuring education.

Only a few records survive to tell us how the other children of Pierre and Auguste and their sisters were educated. Among the older members of the cousins' generation, it seems likely that they had a combination of grammar schooling with Monsieur Truteau or other teachers who gradually set up shop in St. Louis, plus the guidance of their parents, supplemented with music and dancing instruction as it became available. Among those who were known to have been sent abroad for education at a more advanced level was Sylvestre Labbadie Jr., the eldest boy among the cousins, who was in school in France when his father died, in 1794.

There is no indication of how A. P. Chouteau and Charles Gratiot Jr. were taught before going to West Point at eighteen, but both were able to finish in the top half of the academy's graduating class. Gratiot eventually rose to brevet brigadier general in the army. A.P.'s surviving letters, written over more than thirty years, show that even in early manhood, he could write and spell better in both English and French than Meriwether Lewis, William Clark, or General Wilkinson, for whom he served as aide-de-camp. His next-born brother, Pierre Jr., was equally adept at expressing himself, having shown no hesitation at the age of twenty in writing an angry defense of his father to the Secretary of War.

Paul Liguest, the third son, who began a lifetime of work in Indian country while still in his teens, told a visitor in his later years: "I wasted little of my time at school, and I completed my education at the Osage academy." Nevertheless, he, too, left an abundance of letters in both English and French to attest to his literacy and ability to express himself. Pierre Millicour Papin, who also spent his adult life among the Osages, with his cousins Paul Liguest and A.P., regularly reminded his brothers and sisters in St. Louis to forward the newspapers and magazines to which he subscribed. Some of them were from France and undoubtedly helped him stay abreast of Continental affairs.

Less evidence exists concerning the education of the girls of the family, beginning with the three sisters of Auguste and Pierre. However, a rare glimpse at their level of literacy is provided by a surviving letter from Victoire Gratiot, the youngest of the sisters, to a business associate of her husband's in 1802 while Charles Gratiot was traveling. In a neatly written note dealing with some lead that her husband had ordered from the mines south of St. Louis, Victoire expressed dismay that "lead has become so expensive" and went on to discuss instability in lead ore prices and her efforts to hire a barge to pick up the shipment at Ste. Genevieve.

With their brothers and husbands away in Indian country, New Orleans, or Montreal for months at a time, it seems likely that the sisters provided teaching for their children before schools became more common in St. Louis after 1804. Victoire's letter certainly suggests that she would have been capable of providing some of the early education of her son, the future West Point cadet.

Among the girls in the next generation, all or most had some education, however it may have been acquired. Letters survive that were written to several of them by the men in the family, indicating that they could read and respond with ease. Jules de Mun, who married Isabelle Gratiot, one of the daughters of Victoire and Charles Gratiot, wrote long letters to her while he was traveling. In one of them, he urged her not to spend too much time on needlework but to improve her knowledge by reading, and also to work on her writing skills.

In the years following the Louisiana Purchase, schools opened in St. Louis with regularity, usually small institutions run by a single teacher, most likely operating from the teacher's home. Educators arrived from the East, from France and other European countries. They offered instruction in French and English grammar, dancing, fencing and broadsword, drawing, geography, and mathematics. Most of the early focus was on education for boys, but in 1812 a Madame Pescay opened a Young Ladies' Academy and Boarding School. In 1818 the Reverend Salmon Giddings took the unusual step of opening a school for both boys and girls. A. C. Vanhertum, from Amsterdam, taught "Forte Piano and Clarionet" in a building adjoining the *Gazette* offices.

For the younger cousins in the large family, educational opportunities became available at institutions somewhat larger than the one-teacher schools the older cousins experienced. Auguste's second son, Gabriel Sylvestre, who was born in 1794, was sent to a Catholic school at Bardstown, Kentucky, for what was probably the equivalent of high school. Paul and Jean Pierre "Bunyon" Gratiot, younger sons of Victoire and Charles Gratiot, also studied at Bardstown. In 1818 St. Louis College was opened by Bishop William DuBourg, and boys of the family began to study there, including Henry Pierre Chouteau, next to the youngest of Auguste's sons. The institution eventually grew into the Jesuit-run St. Louis University.

But as late as 1811 St. Louis was still a place where a silversmith named Fred Yeizer, who also had for sale "a heap of whisky," peach brandy, linen, shoes, and other items, ran a business notice in the *Missouri Gazette* advising that he did not extend credit "as I have never learnt to write." It was a town where Joseph Charless, owner of the newspaper, threatened to sue those who had not yet brought him the flour, corn, beef, or pork with which they had promised to pay for their subscriptions.

Finding suitable mates for the Chouteau offspring was at least as challenging as educating them. Given the shortage of marriageable young women in the settlement during the town's early decades, the young men of the cousins' generation often sought wives among their cousins, either on the Chouteau side or the other side of each family, such as the Cerrés and Ménards. This helped to keep property and business affairs within the large family circle. There were also a few French families at Ste. Genevieve and Kaskaskia deemed of sufficient standing to marry the Chouteaus.

The other primary source of worthy spouses for the women were the young men arriving from France or the French Caribbean. They or their parents had fled the Revolution in France, the slave rebellion in Haiti, or the turbulent politics of the Continent after the rise of Napoleon. As a result, the Kentucky farmers and eastern lawyers pouring into St. Louis after the Louisiana Purchase found themselves rubbing shoulders with a young Frenchman who had spent time in the Bastille, with a Tyrolese who had joined the Italian army to fight the invading forces of Napoleon, and with the son of a man who had held a post in the household of Napoleon. Also, the region of Laclède's birth in the Pyrenees continued to send ambitious young men to St. Louis decades after the death of the city's founder.

The two eldest sons of Pierre Chouteau married first cousins. Less than three years after his graduation from West Point, A. P. Chouteau wed eighteen-year-old Anne Sophie Labbadie, a daughter of Pélagie and Sylvestre Labbadie Sr. A bit more than four years later, on June 15, 1813, Pierre Jr., then twenty-four, married another of the first cousins, nineteen-year-old Emilie Anne Gratiot. Earlier, on June 25, 1807, Sylvestre Labbadie Jr. had married Emilie's older sister Victoire.

In the early years after the Louisiana Purchase, marriage contracts among the young French Creoles continued to follow French tradition. These contracts, such as that of A. P. Chouteau and Sophie Labbadie, signed February 15, 1809, with Lewis and Clark among the witnesses, established a community of property that would eventually be divided among their children. Each brought to the marriage certain assets—A.P. had $1,000 in cash, provided by his father, and Sophie had the equivalent of $2,973, most of it in deerskins from her father's estate—which became joint property. A.P. also promised to give Sophie $1,000 because of the "sincere affect" he felt for her, to be used however she chose, whenever she chose. In effect, this second $1,000 provided security to the bride in the event the marriage failed.

Auguste and Pierre Chouteau and their brothers-in-law worked assiduously to introduce the next generation into the fur trade. With a few exceptions, such as Charles Gratiot Jr., who made his career in the army, and Auguste Aristide Chouteau, who was not notably successful at anything, the older male cousins found places in the business, at least at the outset of their careers. By the time the younger cousins came of age, St. Louis and the state of Missouri had grown sufficiently to provide other opportunities that attracted some of them.

There is no record as to why A. P. Chouteau, after finishing fourth in his West Point class, resigned his army commission with less than six months' service as an aide to General Wilkinson at Natchitoches, but it seems likely that he foresaw better financial prospects in the family business. After playing a leading role in the failed first attempt to escort the Mandan chief Shahaka back to his village on the Upper Missouri in the summer of 1807, A.P. oversaw his father's interests in the Missouri Fur Company and worked with him in conducting Indian affairs. It was A.P., in the spring of 1813, who gathered 260 young Osage men to march toward St. Louis to help protect white settlements up the Mississippi from Indians supporting the British—until being turned back when word came that officials in Washington did not approve of the action. In April 1813 he was appointed one of four St. Louis County judges. The next year, at his father's request, William Clark appointed him subagent for the Osages.

While Auguste's eldest son, Auguste Aristide, was to disappoint his father for the remainder of his life, the second son, Gabriel Sylvestre, was the object of his loving delight. Known throughout his life as Cerré, his mother's maiden name, he experienced his first taste of working life on the river in 1810 at age sixteen after coming home from his studies at Bardstown. Reaching Fort Osage near the future Kansas City, Cerré sent a letter back to his family before the boat continued upriver. Auguste quickly responded to *"Mon cher Cerré et bien aimé fils—."* Happy to hear of his son's good health, he said he was confident the boy would carry out his mission to deliver merchandise to the Indians. "Your mother, sisters and brother wish you good health and a prompt return."

A few years later, while his son was on another voyage upriver, Auguste wrote with encouragement and advice. "Your mother had the same pleasure as I in reading your letter—she charges me to give you her love; she and I recommend you to be exact and punctual in your job—you must know, my dear son, that your reputation and people's . . . confidence in you depends on the manner in which you comport yourself on this voyage. I dare to flatter myself that you will behave with wisdom and economy in your management."

"We long to see you with us and especially if you have finished your task and have satisfied those for whom you are working," Auguste wrote two months later. "As for me, I dare flatter myself that on this voyage you have acquired a good reputation, which will give me satisfaction in the evening of my days."

By contrast, Cerré's older brother, Auguste Aristide, was accumulating a lot of debts, some so long overdue that the sheriff of St. Louis County once ordered him held on bail the next time he showed up in St. Louis. Auguste Aristide was trying to farm at a place in rural Missouri that he called "the Bitasion," but his habit of falling into debt kept interfering. At one point an unidentified person wanted to seize the only plowing horse he had unless he came up with "64 gourdes" right away.

"My dear Papa," he wrote Auguste, "you must forgive me for not having been to see you but I cannot go to St. Louis after all I have done . . . Give Mama my love and tell her to forget all the bad things I have done to her." Then he added that he might have to go to St. Louis anyway because he needed money, and he closed with the words "Always your obedient son."

Meanwhile, Charles Gratiot Jr. was rising rapidly in the army. He made captain in 1808, and after the War of 1812, in which he commanded a post on the Canadian border, he was promoted to major and given command of all American troops in the Michigan Territory. Eventually he became a pioneer member of the army's engineering corps.

Pierre Jr., who was, like his father, known throughout his life as "Cadet," for being the second brother, began his working life as a clerk in the office of either his father or his uncle Auguste at the age of fifteen. Historians differ over which of the elder Chouteaus employed him. He received his first trading license in his name in 1807 and took two boatloads of merchandise up the Missouri to Osage villages.

At twenty-one, in early 1810, Cadet moved to the present site of Dubuque, Iowa, intending to work for Julien Dubuque and manage the substantial interest in the extensive lead mines that Auguste Chouteau had acquired in 1804. When the young man arrived, Dubuque had recently died, but Cadet remained until the start of the War of 1812, overseeing Indians who worked the mines. In return, Auguste gave his nephew a share of ownership in the property.

After his return to St. Louis, and shortly before his marriage to Emilie Gratiot, Cadet opened a store in partnership with his brother-in-law, Bartholomew Berthold, who had married Pélagie Chouteau, the only daughter of Pierre Sr., in 1811. Berthold, a Tyrolese who had joined the Italian army to fight the invading forces of Napoleon, came to the United States in 1798 as secretary to a French general who had fled after opposing Napoleon. Able to speak at least five languages, he was a combination of scholar and merchant who added worldly sophistication to the business affairs of his wife's brothers and cousins. The house of Berthold & Chouteau opened on May 1, 1813, in a two-story building at 11 North Main, with a selection of crockery, hardware, dry goods, and groceries. Fur and pelts were not part of their business plan.

Gradually, however, as almost everyone in St. Louis was wont to do, the young firm slipped into the fur trade. In 1814 it sent some traders up the Missouri and Platte rivers to deal among the Otoes, Loups, and Pawnees. By then the fur trade was becoming crowded with Chouteaus, their cousins, and their in-laws. Paul Liguest, the third of Pierre's sons, received a license to trade with the Big and Little Osages from a post he built in the southeastern corner of the future state of Kansas. Auguste's son Cerré and François Gesseau, Pierre's fourth son, obtained a license together to trade among the Osages, Kansas, and Pawnees, principally around the mouth of the Kansas River at the future Kansas City.

Eventually, three of Pierre's sons—A.P., Pierre Jr., and François— would each become a magnet around which the activities of other brothers, cousins, and in-laws would gravitate in business operations that reached outward from St. Louis, across Missouri to Kansas City, all the way up the Missouri River and beyond, southwest into present-day Oklahoma, and finally to New York and other great cities.

※

This new generation took its first big step with a venture mounted by A.P. and his cousin-in-law Jules de Mun. In 1815, with backing from Pierre Jr. and his partner Berthold, A.P. and de Mun scraped together enough capital to outfit themselves and two dozen men and buy merchandise for a daring trading expedition across the Great Plains to Santa Fe, the Spanish stronghold that had long stood as a shimmering lure to the merchants and adventurers of the western territories of the United States. They secured a license to trade along the way with the Arapahos and other tribes.

French traders had been trying to open trade with Santa Fe since 1739, when a party led by two brothers named Mallet made its way across the plains. In 1792 an expedition crossed from Santa Fe to St. Louis and returned, and after 1803 there were at least eight commercial ventures before the Chouteau–de Mun venture. But little trading had taken place, in large part because of the hostility of authorities at Santa Fe and Taos.

This was the first frontier experience for the aristocratic de Mun, who had been living just slightly more than three years in St. Louis when he joined A. P. Chouteau in the odyssey that would influence the lives of the two men for as long as they lived. Jules was from a noble family in the Bigorre area of the Pyrenees, very close to Pierre Laclède's birthplace. The family had been driven out of France by the Revolution and later out of St. Domingue, where Jules was born in 1782, by the slave insurrection. By the time Jules came to St. Louis and married Isabelle Gratiot, in 1812, most of the family fortune had been wiped out, forcing him to cast his fate with an in-law who felt at ease in the wilderness. Jules's letters to Isabelle and the journal he kept during the Santa Fe expedition left a dramatic record of suffering, deprivation, danger, and high adventure—and of the resolve, particularly on the part of Auguste Pierre Chouteau, to extract something useful from the undertaking, whatever the risk required.

Leaving St. Louis on September 10, 1815, they traveled by horseback while most of their merchandise moved by river barge. The party followed the Missouri River to the mouth of the Osage River, near today's Jefferson City, and then followed the Osage to the Marmaton River. Even in those first two weeks out of St. Louis, they often found themselves short of food; hunting expeditions by the two dozen men accompanying A.P. and de Mun produced mixed results. After a day in which they had eaten nothing but a few biscuits, they were overjoyed to see buffalo tracks. Occasionally they killed antelope and wild turkeys.

Halting at the Big Osage village, near where A.P. and his parents had lived at Fort Carondelet in the days of Spanish rule, they were welcomed with what food the Indians could offer. A young Indian woman caring for a sick husband "placed before us bowls filled with crushed corn boiled in water but barely cooked; she also sent some to our men, who had just arrived with the loads," de Mun wrote. "Having eaten nothing all day, I appeased my hunger with this sort of pap which under other circumstances I could not have looked at without its turning my stomach."

That night, they slept in a crowded Indian lodge "midst a dozen old carcasses who in order to alleviate the itching caused by the vermin, scratched their emaciated bones with corn-cobs, and it was to the sound of this sweet music that I fell asleep."

"Never did time seem so long as the time I am spending here," de Mun recorded after stormy weather delayed them in the Osage village for several days. "Just imagine a person who has never been among Indians, stuck in a lodge where one must lie down in order not to be smothered by the smoke, among old carcasses whose skin is scaly from dirt and who crunch vermin with relish; having nothing to eat but corn which is often barely cooked, and not being able to set foot outside without stepping in filth."

On October 12, a month after leaving St. Louis, they crossed into present-day Kansas, aiming for the Arkansas River. En route they crossed the Neosho River, southwest of the eventual Fort Scott, Kansas. A.P.'s brother Paul Liguest regularly visited the area to trade with a band of Osages in the area, but the village was deserted because the Indians were out on a hunt. Making their way along the Arkansas River toward the area of today's Wichita, part of the route that would become known years later as the Santa Fe Trail, they abandoned horses that succumbed to exhaustion and hunger. For the surviving horses, they peeled cottonwood bark, a favorite food of horses on the plains. A swift current on the river carried off some of their smallest canoes. Eventually de Mun and A.P. turned their own riding horses into packhorses and, with their men, made their way on foot.

In late November, struggling across the western plains into what would become southwestern Colorado, they encountered snow and ice on the river and covered their thinnest horses with robes and blankets. On November 27, a Monday, they got their first faint glimpse of the mountains, which appeared as little more than clouds on the horizon. On December 8 they reached the mountains at Huerfano Pass south of Pueblo.

There, they had expected to meet up with a group of men working for a trader with Santa Fe experience named Joseph Philibert, who had accompanied them from St. Louis. But the men had gone, so Jules proceeded to Taos in search of them. Finding them there, he remained in Taos for the better part of the winter, under the friendly care of the Spanish governor.

"Having seen on my way to Santa Fe that the rivers abounded with beaver, I asked the Governor the permission of coming, with a fixed number of hunters, to catch beaver in the rivers which empty themselves into Rio del Norte (the Rio Grande). This he could not take upon himself to grant, but had the goodness to write on that subject to the commandant General. As I could not wait for the answer, Don Alberto told me to come back, when convenient, to know the General's answer."

In late February, Jules set out to find A.P. and the rest of the men, who had remained to trap beaver on the Huerfano River, which flowed into the Arkansas in flat, arid country in the southeastern corner of the future Colorado. By then, with the addition of Philibert's men, they had more men than they had expected and not enough equipment and horses to continue to trap. It was decided that Jules would return to St. Louis for supplies and horses and then meet A.P. and the others, who would again trek cross the plains—with any luck, trapping all the way—and meet Jules at the mouth of the Kansas River.

It took Jules and his companions forty-six days to travel from the camp at the mouth of the Huerfano back to St. Louis. With new supplies and fresh horses, they departed St. Louis again on June 15, 1816.

A.P. and his men had first gone north to the South Platte River near the future Denver and traded with a large camp of Iowas, Arapahos, Kiowa-Apaches, and Cheyennes, putting together forty-four packs of furs. Then they descended to the Arkansas River and started east to meet de Mun. Coming out of the mountains and setting out across the plains, however, they were attacked by about two hundred Pawnees. They took refuge on an island in the river in present western Kansas, created a makeshift fort, and exchanged fire with the Indians until the attackers retreated.* One of A.P.'s men was killed and three wounded. Five Pawnees died. This delayed their reaching the Kansas River, where Jules waited and worried. He poured out his frustrations in letters to his wife, the beautiful Isabelle, and apologized for not being rich enough to remain at home with her.

"For the past eleven days I have been on this River, my dear Isabelle; I was unable to go higher than three miles from its mouth, the water being too low to permit my going any farther. I dispatched

---

*This event is now noted by a historical marker at the site along U.S. Highway 50 in Kearny County, Kan.

Baronet [Vasquez] with five men to go meet Auguste, they've already been gone six days and I am still waiting."

Three days later he added that his great pleasure was thinking of her:

> I love to picture my pretty Julie on your lap toying with the breast and looking at you with her sweet little smile; at your side the big Isabelle caressing her little sister and the Mamma admiring them both; how pretty you seem to me all three, dear child! Unfortunately, these are but flights of fancy, and not the reality which I enjoy.
>
> We are to be separated from each other for a long time my good Isabelle, but rest assured that I shall love you always. My love cannot alter, it is founded on esteem, I may say the respect inspired by your conduct. There are very few women who young and beautiful like you, deserving of the enjoyment of all the gifts of fortune, would stand with such patience and sweetness the embarrassing situation in which we find ourselves . . . Let us continue to endure our fate with the same patience, my friend, having no reproaches to make one another; we shall only be happy when we shall have reached the time where we need never part.

The two parties of traders found each other again on August 10, 1816. They sent some of the men back to St. Louis with the furs that A.P. had brought out of the mountains, then turned west again, convinced that they would find still more rivers rich in beavers and a friendly reception for their merchandise if they could get into Santa Fe and Taos. By now they numbered about forty-five men. They split again into two parties, with A.P. and his group planning to camp at a pass in the Sangre de Cristo Mountains, while Jules went to Taos expecting to find the same friendly governor he had met on his previous visit.

Instead, when Jules arrived at Rio Colorado, he ran up against a suspicious Spanish military commander who refused to allow him to proceed. The commander sent word into Taos about the traders, and a party of forty troops came out from Taos and forced Jules to lead them to the rest of the party, which they traced up the Rio Grande to where it emerged from the mountains. They were ordered to wait there to receive word on whether they could proceed into Santa Fe.

Twenty days later Jules received a letter from the new governor telling them to get out of Spanish dominions immediately.

"I wrote to the *alcalde* of Taos that I had just received the Governor's orders, and, in compliance with them, we were recrossing the mountains," de Mun related, "that, when on the east side of them, we should remain all Winter . . . Receiving no answer, we took it for granted that, being on [the east] side of the mountains, we gave the Spaniards no uneasiness."

In March of 1817 Jules returned to Taos, hoping that Spanish officials had changed their minds about the traders. Instead, he learned that wildly exaggerated stories were being circulated about his group, suggesting that they were an invading force of twenty thousand well-armed men and were building a fort at the first fork of the Arkansas, called the Rio de las Animas. A military unit of two hundred men forced him to accompany them back to where A.P. was camped and forced the traders to dig up all the supplies and other things they had cached. After satisfying themselves that there was no fort and no force of twenty thousand men, the Spanish troops departed.

Jules then began making plans to return to St. Louis with their furs and skins. But A.P. was determined to continue trying for a successful mission. He wanted to find a way to remain another year. Before they could resolve their differences, a new Spanish military party appeared and escorted them to Santa Fe, where they arrived on June 1, 1817.

"I was first introduced to the Governor, who inquired, in a very angry manner, why I had not obeyed him, when ordered to go out of the Spanish dominions," Jules recalled. "I replied, his orders were obeyed as soon as received; that we had been captured on American territory, where our Governor had given us a license to go. At this he got into a violent rage, saying that we should pay . . . for our own and our Governor's ignorance; using all the time very abusive language; repeating several times that he would have our brains blown up."

Both he and A.P. were thrown into dungeons in irons. The other men in their party were presumably treated in a similar manner. The irons were removed seven days later. After forty-four days of imprisonment, all the men of the Chouteau–de Mun party were presented before a court-martial presided over by the governor.

"Many questions were asked, but more particularly why we had staid so long in the Spanish dominions?" De Mun answered that,

> being on the waters of the Arkansas river, we did not consider our-
> selves in the domains of Spain, as we had a license to go as far as the
> headwaters of said river. The president denied that our Government
> had a right to grant such a license, and entered into such a rage that
> it prevented his speaking, contenting himself with striking his fist sev-
> eral times on the table, saying, gentlemen, we must have this man
> shot . . . He talked much of a big river that was the boundary line be-
> tween the two countries, but did not know its name. When mention
> was made of the Mississippi, he jumped up, saying that that was the
> big river he meant; that Spain had never ceded the west side of it.

The governor's ignorance, to an exaggerated degree, reflected the misunderstanding that long existed over how much territory had been included in the Louisiana Purchase. The western boundaries of the Purchase area had never been clearly defined. A.P. and Jules—and William Clark, who had given them the license to trap in the area—thought that as long as they remained north of the Arkansas River and on the eastern slopes of the mountains, they were safely within United States territory. That was why they were seeking Spanish permission to proceed farther.

Furthermore, Spain, which was then engaged in its ultimately un-successful wars to retain control of Mexico and most of the rest of Latin America, was always nervous about pressures from expansion-minded Americans seeking opportunity and riches west of St. Louis. This was not the first American trade party to be imprisoned for mak-ing its way to Santa Fe. One, led by Robert McKnight, spent nine years in confinement in Chihuahua after showing up at Santa Fe in 1812 with trading goods.

The governor would have felt even more justified in his fears of the Chouteau–de Mun party had he known how Pierre Chouteau Sr. reacted when word reached St. Louis about the plight of his son. Out-raged, as usual, at any mistreatment of his family, his first instinct was to turn to his old friends the Osages for help. One version of the events indicates that he threatened, and took some steps, to raise an army of a few thousand Osages and other Indians to march on the Spanish territory and free the group. "But he was informed by Col. [Thomas Hart] Benton and other friends that the government of the United States alone had the right to make war, and to avenge insults and wrongs done to her citizens; which caused Mr. Chouteau to abandon the undertaking," recalled John Darby, who moved to St. Louis from North Carolina about that time and came to know Pierre Sr.

The day after the court-martial, the prisoners were summoned back before the court in Santa Fe for the sentencing. "We were forced to kneel down . . . and forced likewise to kiss the unjust and iniquitous sentence that deprived harmless and inoffensive men of all they possessed—of the fruits of two years' labor and perils," de Mun later told Clark. Before they were allowed to leave the territory, the men were relieved of all their merchandise as well as the skins and furs in their possession. Counting the time of the court-martial, they had spent a total of forty-eight days in prison.

By then it was the middle of July, and a long, hot trek lay ahead of them. Heavy must have been their hearts and greatly dampened their dreams of fortune as they set forth on the journey home. When they stumbled into St. Louis on the first Sunday of September, they were wearing rags and down to one horse apiece. But they were warmly received by "rejoicing families and friends."

The outraged *Missouri Gazette* said that the American people "will hear with indignation and astonishment, that their fellow citizens of the oldest and most respectable families of Missouri, have, on the head waters of Arkansas, within the U. States limits, been stripped of their property by a Spanish Officer, and compelled ignominiously to kiss, upon their knees, the stupid and oppressive mandate, which consigned them to chains and a dungeon!!!"

"We know not what indemnification can be made to these gentlemen for their personal sufferings," the editorialist added, "but we are very sure that our Govern't will take prompt measures with the Spanish court for the payment of a round sum of money, equal at least in value to the property of which our merchants have been despoiled."

St. Louis not being a place where such hardships were endured

just for the sake of a great adventure, that was exactly what the Chouteaus had in mind. As soon as the welcoming celebrations were over,
they totaled up their losses, which came to the very considerable sum
of $30,380.74, and the united Chouteau clan began pressuring the
United States government to obtain compensation from authorities in
Mexico, an effort that would continue for decades.

ELEVEN

Auguste and Pierre: Men of Property

❉

On the Fourth of July in 1819 the male leaders of St. Louis gathered in the late afternoon in Pete Didier's orchard for the dinner and celebration that had grown into a tradition over the previous fifteen years. The man universally known as "Colonel" Auguste Chouteau presided. Then approaching his sixty-ninth birthday, the cofounder of St. Louis sat beneath a full-length portrait of George Washington, atop which someone had managed to affix a live eagle that periodically opened its wings over a width of about six feet.

After an elaborate feast, the guests drank toasts to Independence Day, to George Washington, to President Monroe, to the next Congress, and to the territory of Missouri, which, with a population of nearly 67,000 people, was demanding statehood. They also toasted the militia, the army and navy, the Yellowstone expedition, the American continent, Henry Clay, Secretary of War John C. Calhoun, and the entire country "free and happy"—all to ten cheers.

Even though St. Louis had become an American city, its people English-speaking in the vast majority, Auguste and Pierre Chouteau had retained their power and influence, thanks to their social skills, their business acumen, and their octopus-like family ties. They were the surviving representatives of France's last hurrah in the New World—and of the ambition that drove Pierre Laclède out of his comfortable corner of the Pyrenees and brought him and his succession to the meeting place of North America's two mightiest rivers.

As their children moved ahead with their own careers and families,

Auguste and Pierre became increasingly involved with St. Louis and Missouri civic affairs, and with their own finances and land claims. Their lives were now more settled, if no less busy. For the most part, life was good for the brothers. In addition to their showplace residences in town, both had country houses surrounded by orchards and gardens on the outskirts of St. Louis, where visitors usually found them in warm weather. They were held in high esteem by their community, often being called on to serve on legislative bodies, boards, and committees.

The two brothers and Bernard Pratte, who had married the eldest Labbadie girl, had also assumed responsibility for raising money for the new Roman Catholic cathedral. They advanced their own money for construction and sought the help of others through subscriptions and loans. They hired and paid the contractors and workers. Gabriel Paul, a son-in-law of Auguste's, was the architect for the brick structure for which the cornerstone was laid in 1818.

Auguste continued to serve as a United States commissioner in several rounds of negotiations for treaties with Indian tribes. In 1819 he and Benjamin Stephenson concluded a treaty at Edwardsville, Illinois, in which the Kickapoos gave up their last expanse of land in western Indiana and east central Illinois—between 13 million and 14 million acres. In exchange, the tribe received an annuity of $2,000 a year for fifteen years and a tract of land on the Osage River in Indian Territory, the future Kansas, to which it had to move immediately.

Between 1817 and 1819 Auguste's bankbook from the Bank of Missouri, of which he was a founder and the president, showed average balances running from $2,000 to $4,000. That was more than enough cash flow to pay for a lifestyle that included such things as four boxes of "wine coolers" sent to him from England by the Earl of Selkirk.

In 1816 Auguste announced publicly, through a notice in the *Missouri Gazette*, that he wished "to terminate all his business." He requested that anyone with a demand or claim against him present it by March 1, 1817, and that all those in debt to him make immediate payment. This, presumably, related primarily to his fur-trading affairs.

Rather than truly retiring, Auguste was making a late-life career switch. He was more deeply involved than ever in political and civic activities, and he probably wanted to make more time for that as Missouri approached statehood. In addition, even with the challenges in Washington to some of his vast land claims, he had 23,500 acres of land with clear and confirmed titles. He set out to use that to increase his fortune, provide for his family's future comfort, and foster the growth and development of St. Louis.

Until then, the town had remained confined to the three original streets on the lower plateau. With the end of the War of 1812, Auguste Chouteau and Judge John B. C. Lucas, who between them owned all of the land on the "Hill," to the west of the village, saw that there was an influx of new people who needed housing. Among other things, the army had maintained a large garrison in St. Louis for the duration of the war, and many of the soldiers decided to make St. Louis their permanent home after being mustered out.

In May 1816 Auguste and Lucas laid out an addition to the town. Auguste owned that portion of the addition south of Market Street, and Lucas owned the area north of Market. Previously there had been only two houses on the Hill. One was the residence of Judge Lucas; the other served as the living quarters for army officers at the garrison. The lots nearest Market Street sold quickly, and brick and frame houses were soon under construction. By late 1818 Auguste had sold fifty-one lots for a total of $15,393 and Lucas twenty-seven for $9,883. In all of St. Louis that year, more than a hundred houses were completed. By 1821 the total number of houses and buildings in the town of St. Louis—of brick, stone, frame, and log construction—approached 500, up from about 300 in 1815.

High construction costs, the result of labor shortages and the need to import some materials from Pittsburgh and other eastern areas, kept home construction behind demand. Caravans of settlers were now crossing the Mississippi to settle in the Missouri Territory. Most were looking for farmland, so they continued beyond St. Louis. However, the town's population had grown to 3,300 by 1818, and the federal census of 1820 found 4,598 residents, an increase of 228 percent in ten years. The county had grown to nearly 10,000, up 75 percent in a decade.

Judge Lucas announced in a paid newspaper notice that he and Auguste were also giving to the county of St. Louis "a whole square in the most central and best situation for a court house & suitable public areas, exclusive of a lot intended for the use of a jail." A new market house had already been built on the public square catercorner from Auguste Chouteau's mansion, opening on September 1, 1812. The market was sixty-four feet long by thirty feet wide and had twelve stalls, which rented for $10 to $30 a year each.

In 1818 city officials decided to undertake, for the first time since the United States had obtained possession of the territory, a survey of property lines, blocks, and streets. Joseph C. Brown, deputy federal surveyor, was given the job. The task was "difficult and tedious" because, prior to the Brown survey, the owner of every property had fixed its location on the basis of the distance from Laclède's Block, which remained the starting point for all surveys in St. Louis.

Auguste, at this time, was also developing commercial property along Main Street. He contracted with Philip Rocheblave to build a block of two-story brick buildings. According to the descriptions, the buildings had inside stairs and other facilities intended for business use. At least part of Rocheblave's work was paid for with three "town" lots that he received from Auguste. Auguste was also having remodeling and expansion work done at his mansion on Main Street. Among other things, he had five "privy" houses built on the lot behind the main structure. And the taxes Auguste paid in September 1817 included an $11 tax on a "four-wheel carriage called a coach."

Commerce grew rapidly and greatly diversified in St. Louis during the years after the war. In 1821 the city business directory listed forty-six general mercantile houses, whose wares included food and wine and household goods. Among the wide variety of artisans were twelve tailors, thirteen boatbuilders, twenty-eight carpenters, nine blacksmiths, gunsmiths, cabinetmakers, coach makers, stonecutters, bricklayers, watchmakers, and saddlers. There were about fifty saloons, five billiard halls, three hotels, six livery stables, three drugstores, and three newspapers. Light industry was beginning to appear, including a brewery, a tannery, a nail factory, a comb factory, and three soap and candle factories. More than half of the businesses had been opened after 1817.

Nothing, however, said more about the changing times than the arrival at St. Louis on July 27, 1817, of the *Zebulon M. Pike*, the first steamboat to ascend the Mississippi farther than the Ohio River. The *Pike* was not much in size compared to what steamboats would soon become. Its small engine needed a little help from old-fashioned poles in the hands of cordellers before it took its place alongside the keelboats and barges in the port of St. Louis. But onlookers cheered, and some paid the captain a dollar to go aboard.

Slightly more than two months later, a second steamboat, the *Constitution*, arrived. A day was set aside before its departure for New Orleans for people to buy tickets and take an excursion a few miles up the river to Bellefontaine. The following spring, the S.S. *Independence* fought its way into the more challenging Missouri River and got as far as Franklin, about midway across the soon-to-be state. Next, the *Western Engineer* went as far as today's Council Bluffs. By 1819, steamboats were a common sight at the St. Louis docks, but the most spectacular breakthroughs in their use on the Missouri River would fall to the next generation of Chouteaus, who would use them to expand the family's wealth and influence.

In the years following the war, St. Louis began to move from a barter economy—based on peltries, lead, and whiskey—to a money economy. The town's first bank, the Bank of St. Louis, was opened in December 1816. Auguste Chouteau was a minority stockholder, and at his insistence the bank accepted furs and lead as security for loans. Backed by those loans, it issued notes that were put into circulation as "beaver bills," featuring a sketch of a beaver. The bank, however, quickly got into trouble when the cashier made highly speculative real estate loans. Auguste and a number of other unhappy stockholders withdrew and opened the Bank of Missouri, which had its headquarters in his basement, the same foundation that Missouri Indians had dug for him in 1764.

During this time, the soldiers based at Bellefontaine began receiving their pay in notes or drafts of the Bank of the United States, and that put the first sound paper money into circulation. For a while the Bank of Missouri succeeded, becoming a depository of federal money. But a nationwide credit squeeze, accentuated by the western land boom, began in late 1818, and by 1821 the Bank of Missouri had to close. The Bank of St. Louis had already closed because of fraud. Not until 1829, when the Bank of the United States opened a branch in St. Louis, did the city have a reliable bank.

William Clark, who continued to play a prominent role in St. Louis as superintendent of Indian affairs, had regular financial dealings with Auguste Chouteau. On the strength of surviving receipts and handwritten notes, it appears that Auguste was Clark's personal banker, processing transfers from the War Department and other moneys, and often lending Clark money as well.

In 1823 Auguste's taxable properties within the city of St. Louis included four houses, three vacant lots, twenty-three slaves, two horses, three milk cows, and a wagon—with an estimated total value of $35,599. The slaves were valued at $4,500 and the houses at $30,000. Also, he possessed 18,500 arpents of land in Lincoln County, Missouri, about sixty miles northwest of St. Louis, valued at 50 cents an arpent, or $9,250; plus at least 200 arpents of land in St. Charles on which a value was not placed. This list did not include his holdings and claims in other parts of the state, nor his claim to the Dubuque mining property.

Pierre Chouteau, although he lived well, was in much tighter financial straits than his older brother—in part, no doubt, because of the many years he had devoted to the Osages and other tribes as a government Indian agent. When he needed money, he had to turn to his land holdings, some of which had been confirmed by American authorities in the years following the Louisiana Purchase while others were still in limbo. By 1814 lands for which titles had been confirmed in his name reached a total of 22,700 acres.

His trading account with the incredibly patient Caveliers in New Orleans was yet to be settled. Through Auguste, the merchant house had been prodding Pierre from time to time for many years to settle debts that dated from before the Louisiana Purchase. With the end of the War of 1812, they were optimistic about the prospects for business. Furs were scarce in France and therefore selling at top prices. The New Orleans harbor was filled with ships, with many more backed up in the river and out into the Gulf. All of them were there to do business.

"Please remind your brother of us," they wrote to Auguste the following year. "His negligence is unpardonable; we have written him several letters . . . Urge him to send us some remittances, for which we cannot often enough repeat that we have urgent need."

By the beginning of 1817 Pierre offered the Caveliers some land to settle his accounts. They wrote Auguste expressing interest in the offer but said they could not accept it until they reached a definite agreement with Pierre on the amount of the accounts and interest. They did ask the "nature" of the lands, their extent in arpents, what they could produce, if they were cleared, whether they were situated on the banks of the Mississippi or another river.

In October of that year, Pierre asked Jean Pierre Cabanné, who was married to the eldest Gratiot daughter, to take charge of settling his account with Cavelier & Son. He told him to draw on his second son's firm, then called Berthold & Chouteau, for what he owed the Caveliers, paying it over a term of six or nine months. He attributed the long-standing lack of agreement on the amount to the way the Caveliers calculated interest. He said his records showed that he owed principal of $4,180, on which he was willing to pay interest at 6 percent a year. But his older records had been lost in the fire at his house in 1805. "It is rather unfortunate for me that it has been impossible for me to honor this debt sooner without these gentlemen having to doubt my intentions and behavior toward them again," he told Cabanné.

It took six more years, but in March 1823 Antoine Cavelier Sr. agreed to accept 1,500 acres along the Missouri River to cancel the debt, which had finally been fixed at $8,274.48. Cabanné was authorized to find a buyer for the land. Cavelier still could not resist calling Pierre "your wretched brother" in a letter to Auguste a few days later. He also spoke of the "sad situation in which he finds himself," suggesting that Pierre was struggling financially.

Pierre continued to fight vigorously for the remaining land claims in his name from Spanish and French days. After statehood in 1821, he enlisted the help of Senator Thomas Hart Benton, with whom Pierre and his sons had had a friendly relationship since Benton first appeared in St. Louis in 1815, fresh from a public brawl with Andrew Jackson in Tennessee. However, Pierre's claim to more than 4,000 arpents on the Missouri River in present-day Callaway County, Missouri, was denied, despite the efforts of Benton.

Sometimes Pierre won at one level of authority only to lose in Washington. In 1822 Frederick Bates, Meriwether Lewis's old nemesis, now recorder of land titles in St. Louis, certified that Pierre's claim to 4,850 arpents (4,126 acres) had been "duly confirmed" and that he was "entitled to receive a patent for the tract," the location of which was not given. There is no record, however, of this eventually being confirmed in Washington.

In 1824 President Monroe signed a confirmation of Pierre's land title for 6,002.5 acres on Berger Creek flowing through Gasconade and Franklin counties in Missouri. The bounds of the property were marked by a white oak into which Pierre had carved his initials, plus a cottonwood and post, each of which also had "PC" etched into it.

That year, Pierre hired two St. Louis lawyers, George F. Strother and Luke E. Lawless, to institute proceedings before the federal government "to obtain the confirmation" of a long list of "claims, concessions and orders of survey" on behalf of him and his family. If they succeeded, the lawyers were to be compensated in land. The list of claims that Pierre provided to them dated from 1767. A number of cases, especially the older claims, involved concessions granted to Pierre's mother or his two sets of in-laws, the Tayons and the Sauciers, by various of the Spanish governors or lieutenant governors. They had been deeded to Pierre or his wives, possibly as part of estate settlements, and in a few cases had made their way into Auguste's hands. The process of sorting through these claims and justifying them to local and national authorities would continue for many more years.

Meanwhile, in 1818, Congress began debating Missouri's request for statehood, which turned into one of the nation's most heated political conflicts and raised the first possibility of the disunion that would come to pass nearly a half century later. Three sessions of Congress considered the matter before finally coming to agreement on the Missouri Compromise, under which Missouri entered the union as a slave state and Maine entered as a non-slave state. As part of the accord, Congress also decreed that except in Missouri, no more slavery would be permitted north of latitude 36°30', the new state's southern border.

On March 6, 1820, President Monroe signed the act authorizing inhabitants of the Missouri Territory to write a constitution and form a state government. This required the selection of a state constitutional convention. The campaign and election for that again turned into a debate over whether the right to own slaves should continue indefinitely in Missouri or be gradually eliminated.

The newspapers were filled with arguments over the issue. Taverns and other gathering places of the future state, especially St. Louis, reverberated with the rhetoric of the slavery question. Those who favored an eventual end to slavery in Missouri took the position that the first step should be to halt any further importation of slaves into the state. The *Missouri Gazette*, the newspaper Meriwether Lewis had helped finance during its start-up days, editorialized strongly in favor of electing candidates to the constitutional convention who would "take measures gradually to extinguish the evil" of slavery, instead of opting for them and their children to "be cursed with slavery, the evil and injustice of which is acknowledged by every one."

Judge Lucas, a slave owner himself who had partnered with Auguste Chouteau in real estate development, was among the candidates favoring the gradual elimination of slavery. Pierre Chouteau Jr., then thirty-one years old, was among the proslavery candidates, as was his business partner, Bernard Pratte. Lest there be any question of his position, Pierre Jr. published a notice in the *Gazette* stating: "Should I be elected a member of the convention, any attempts to prevent the introduction of slaves, or any other species of property (lawfully held in any other state of the nation) into the state of Missouri, will meet my warmest opposition."

Young Pierre was criticized by an unnamed letter writer for being unable to speak English, the writer noting that the candidate had recently given court testimony in French with an interpreter. In fact, Pierre Jr. could speak and write English, but he never felt fully at home in it, frustrating business associates throughout his life by his refusal to correspond with them in English.

When the returns were counted, Pierre Jr. had received 586 votes, the sixth highest total and more than enough to send him to the constitutional convention. The biggest vote getter, with more than 800, was Alexander McNair, a popular lawyer and state militia leader who would soon be elected Missouri's first governor.

Meeting at a hotel in St. Louis, the forty-one delegates produced the new constitution in just five weeks. Despite the intense slavery debate during the campaign, most of the differences that arose during the drafting concerned other issues, such as whether there should be property qualifications for voting and whether local officials and judges should be popularly elected. The document that emerged provided for universal white male suffrage, an independent judiciary, and a guarantee of the right to own slaves.

In December 1820 the new Missouri constitution was submitted for approval to Congress, which passed a resolution on March 2, 1821, to admit Missouri to statehood. President Monroe issued a proclamation on August 10, 1821, admitting Missouri as the twenty-fourth state of the union.

In the elections a year before the admission proclamation, William Clark stepped aside as Indian superintendent to run for governor. He was backed by the so-called St. Louis junto*—the clique of rich and powerful men, both Anglo and French, including the Chouteaus, who were then accustomed to controlling public life in the town and state. But Clark lost by a wide margin to Alexander McNair, who demonstrated skill at identifying with the small farmers and other people filling up rural Missouri. Historians usually attribute Clark's loss to the fact that he was so cozy with the power brokers of St. Louis that he did not recognize the changing demographics of the new state. Another factor, however, was that those same small farmers may have found him too soft in handling Indian matters. After his loss, Clark returned to his old position in charge of Indian affairs.

When the new state legislature met, one of its first acts was to grant a charter to the city of St. Louis. The newly incorporated city was di-

---

*The editor of the Missouri Gazette, Joseph Charless, first used this term as a derisive way of describing the power brokers of St. Louis. Its origin was probably the French junte or Spanish junta for ruling committee.

vided into three wards, with a mayor and nine aldermen. In the first city elections, in December 1822, Auguste Chouteau ran for mayor but lost to William Carr Lane by a vote of 70 to 122, with the language issue a factor. M. P. Leduc, a Chouteau in-law, came in third with 28 votes. Auguste was elected to the Board of Aldermen, as were Leduc and Bernard Pratte.

If the elections showed that the influence of the French speakers was generally on the wane, the next big event to captivate St. Louis brought them back to the forefront. In the summer of 1824 the Marquis de Lafayette returned to America for a triumphal tour that included New York, Boston, and the John Adams home in Massachusetts, then west to St. Louis and other places along the Mississippi. When word reached St. Louis that he would be coming there, Mayor Lane got on his horse and rode twenty miles out of St. Louis to the farm residence of Frederick Bates, who had been elected governor in the state's second election. Concerned about how to pay for the expenses of entertaining Lafayette, the mayor asked Bates to take part in receiving the French hero of the American Revolution, hoping the state would then appropriate money for the expenses.

Bates not only declined to take part in the event but said the state had no money to underwrite it. Lane rode back to town and made the rounds of the city aldermen, who agreed to take money out of the city treasury to cover the expenses, which eventually turned out to be $37. Bernard Pratte was appointed chairman of the arrangements committee, and Auguste Chouteau was a member.

There were few wheeled vehicles with passenger seats in St. Louis, which presented a problem in receiving the great man. Auguste Chouteau had paid taxes in recent years on a "coach," but it may not have had enough seats. Major Thomas Biddle, the army paymaster, had a four-passenger barouche and two white horses, and United States District Judge James Peck also had a barouche and two white horses. The committee borrowed Biddle's barouche and the white horses of both men so that there would be two teams pulling the carriage.

The man heralded as the "early friend of American liberty" arrived on the S.B. *Natchez* on Thursday evening, April 28, 1825, traveling upriver from Louisiana. He spent the night aboard the boat anchored at Carondelet just south of the St. Louis harbor. A delegation that included William Clark and Senator Benton went to the boat the next morning to accompany Lafayette to St. Louis. A group of other people went down the river on the S.B. *Plough Boy* to greet their hero. Returning ahead of Lafayette, the *Plough Boy* fired its engines to let everybody know he was coming. By the time the *Natchez* rounded Cahokia Bend, colors flying, and steamed up to the landing opposite Market House Square, virtually everyone in St. Louis—black, white, and brown, male and female—had made his or her way to the foot of Market Street. Cheers erupted as Lafayette stepped ashore.

After being welcomed by Mayor Lane, the sixty-eight-year-old Lafayette turned to the people who "have so many claims on my feelings" and told them, "I have once more the satisfaction to see the descendants of France, and the descendants of my American contemporaries, mingle in the blessings of republican institutions, and in a common sentiment of devotion to the confederate union."

Lafayette and Mayor Lane got into the backseat of the open carriage, and Auguste Chouteau and Stephen Hempstead, a Revolutionary War veteran, sat down facing them. The four horses, balky from never working together, pulled them along the unpaved streets of St. Louis. The town through which they passed now had eight streets running parallel to the river, intersected by twenty-three other streets. There were 651 houses by the most recent count, of which 232 were of brick and 419 of wood. The courthouse had not yet been built on the land donated by Auguste and Judge Lucas, but the pillory and the whipping post were in place. Followed by cheering people, Lafayette was driven to the mansion of Pierre Chouteau, where rooms had been prepared for him.

Pierre threw his house open to anyone who wanted to come, and Lafayette spent the next four hours receiving them. "The access to him was regulated by no etiquette," reported an observer of the events. "Everyone came that pleased and was introduced by some one at hand. Two interviews excited particular feeling; one with Mr. W. S. Hamilton, son to General Alexander Hamilton; the other, with Mr.

Alexander Bellissime, a sergeant under the Comte de Rochambeau, and the only individual who had crossed the sea with him that the General had seen in this visit to America."

After a short excursion in the carriage and a visit to William Clark's personal museum of Indian artifacts, Lafayette attended a 4 p.m. dinner for prominent citizens at Pierre's home. Then everybody went to a downtown hotel for a ball attended by more people "than had ever been seen on such an occasion west of the Mississippi," in the view of one participant. Flags and wreaths decorated the room. At midnight Lafayette departed the ballroom and returned to his boat. At dawn it pushed off into the Mississippi current and glided down to Kaskaskia, Lafayette's next stop.

✳

Despite the respect and acclaim that came to Auguste and Pierre in their later years, one issue disrupted those years and forced the brothers to defend their values and behavior. The issue was slavery. In 1824 the Missouri General Assembly passed a law allowing slaves to sue for their freedom. It also gave them the right to sue as poor people and therefore to receive free legal counsel. The law was surprisingly forward-looking for the time, especially in a state where slavery, while not as widespread as in the South, was still legal and still practiced.

The new law served to revive a festering sore that had plagued Pierre Chouteau for more than two decades regarding his rights to a part-Indian slave family that had been trying for even longer than that to be free. Auguste Chouteau, determined to permit no undermining of the principle of the rights of slave owners to their property, lent his brother firm backing through many depositions and court proceedings.

In so doing, they were asserting the strongly held views of most of their family and other slaveholders in the colony and the state. They never questioned the place of human bondage in economic life, considering it a normal state of affairs for some people to have complete authority over other people, with or without their consent. When they bought or sold a slave, the bill of sale typically carried the ominous-sounding warranty from the seller that the person being sold was "a slave for life." The Chouteaus believed that the slave owner must never let down his guard in a way that would encourage slaves to take liberties or seek rights.

Under French rule, the colony of Louisiana, including the future Missouri, had had a broader definition of who might be enslaved than that applied later under the Spanish or after the Louisiana Purchase and statehood. That definition included Indians as well as blacks, although Indian slaves were not nearly as numerous as black slaves. In most cases the Indian slaves had been captured in warfare between tribes, then sold to whites by the victorious tribe. In 1769 the Spanish governor-general at New Orleans, Alejandro O'Reilly, declared that throughout Louisiana Territory, all Indian slaves could go free at the deaths of their masters and that all those born from the date of the publication of the emancipating ordinance were free from birth. His intent was to end the practice gradually in a manner that would improve relations with Indian tribes without angering the French settlers in the region. In fact, the practice continued, and the Spanish authorities made no real effort to halt it.

Pierre Laclède and Madame Chouteau were among those who had some Indian slaves during the Spanish colonial era. When a census was done after the O'Reilly declaration, Madame Chouteau had two "savage girls" aged sixteen and thirteen, whose combined value she put at 2,000 livres in silver. Pierre Laclède owned six Indians worth more than 7,350 livres in silver.

An episode in December 1785 — in which a trusted black slave of Madame Chouteau's was accidentally killed while helping to capture two runaway Indian slaves — sheds light on the nature of the Chouteaus' relationship with their slaves, as well as the greater trouble associated with owning Indian slaves.

It seems that Madame Chouteau's trusted black slave, Baptiste, discovered two runaway Indian slaves in her barn at the rear of the village one night and ran to inform one of her sons-in-law, Joseph M. Papin, who was leading a group of militiamen that had been trying for a month to capture some runaways. The Indian slaves had apparently instigated the breakout of a number of slaves from various homesteads, taking with them some black slaves, plus guns and ammunition.

Papin gave Baptiste a bottle of rum so he could ply the runaways with drink while Papin sent for help. The militiamen gathered and divided into two groups to encircle the barn, but in the dark, the men became confused and started firing at each other as each group came around the building. Baptiste was caught in the cross fire. The two runaways were captured, but Baptiste was found dead just outside the barn door, a ball from a gun having passed through his lungs.

Madame Chouteau was so angry at the loss of this valuable man that she sued her son-in-law for damages. Testifying before Lieutenant Governor Cruzat, she said that she had not given her permission for Baptiste to be used in this manner and that Papin "acted so very hastily and inconsiderately in this matter, not appearing to reflect on the danger to which he exposed my negro man between his party and the runaways."

"His services were invaluable to me, sir; his good qualities, ability, his attachment to the family, the care he continually took of my interests, not only in his own work, but overlooking the others, so that I could safely trust him with the management of all my slaves. In the flower of his age, no money can remunerate me for his loss," she declared.

After hearing testimony from all the parties, Cruzat appointed three men to "correctly appraise the qualities, intelligence and value of Mrs. Chouteau's negro man." They unanimously decided that she was entitled to "six hundred silver dollars, as a full compensation for his loss." On May 15, 1787, Cruzat paid that sum to Madame Chouteau after having collected it from the "several owners of these runaway Indians," which apparently meant that Papin shared in the cost of the settlement to his mother-in-law but did not have to pay all of it.

As this case demonstrates, the Chouteaus generally had trust and confidence in their slaves, and probably had friendly working relations with them. They were willing to use the whip when they thought that trust had been violated, but a more common way of dealing with a difficult slave was to ship him downriver to New Orleans to be sold — or to threaten such action. The prospect of having to leave behind their families and be put to work at field labor, which was likely to be much more grueling than the working life of a slave in Missouri, usually served the purpose of getting the slaves back in line.

In the summer of 1820 Auguste Chouteau sent a troublesome black slave named Charles to New Orleans to be sold. The man had been tried and acquitted of larceny and had served thirty days in jail for some other action, costing Auguste $15 for his keep in jail.

François Ménard, a Chouteau in-law living in New Orleans, was asked to find a buyer. He soon wrote back that he was having trouble finding anyone who wanted Charles. "His manifest desire to return [to St. Louis], saying that he has seven children, his constant complaints about his bad health and the pains he says he feels in his legs do not encourage the buyers," Ménard said. Charles ran away from Ménard's home but was caught two days later when he slipped back into the house for his clothes. Ménard had him put in jail and wrote Auguste for instructions.

"Please get rid of him as soon as possible," Auguste responded,

> either at public sale or private sale, for whatever price you can; I approve in advance all you do in this regard and will be satisfied. As to the remarks he makes, they are wholly without foundation; I do not know that he has any children, and he has surely none at my place; and to my knowledge he has never complained of pains; his health is at this time very good, as I told you in my earlier letter. This negro behaved so badly here and misuses my kindness so that I decided to get rid of him. I ought to [sell him] even for the example he sets my other slaves and to maintain in them the proper subjection. I wish you, sir, in the deed that you give for his sale, to specify as an express condition that this negro may never be sent back into our territory.

Not until the following March did Ménard succeed in selling Charles at auction for $480. Before that, Charles had escaped a second time, even though shackled, and had been jailed a second time. But before Ménard could get the accounts and the money on their way to Auguste, the buyer, a Mr. Laville, demanded that Ménard take back Charles, whom he had discovered to have the habit of running away. Otherwise he said he would sue Ménard to void the sale. Long-distance negotiations ensued between Auguste and the buyer, who ended up keeping Charles at a purchase price reduced by nearly half. Auguste eventually received $238.17, after reimbursing Ménard $20 for the cost of keeping Charles in jail.

Over the years, a few slaves of the family were freed voluntarily, and there were cases of others buying their freedom. Sometimes the voluntary freeing of slaves occurred on the death of the master, whose last will and testament might include modest financial aid to the freed slave or something to help the newly freed man or woman earn a living. On her death, in 1814, Madame Chouteau freed a "female savage creature," whose name is illegible in the will. The slave, presumably Indian because of the reference to her as "savage," was bequeathed $60, a quantity of flour, one cow, and a calf. She was free to move to "wherever it seems convenient to her, being free after the decease of the said testatrix."

During the time he was lending his most determined support to Pierre in his legal battles over the part-Indian family, Auguste freed one of his own slaves. "I, Auguste Chouteau . . . from motives of benevolence and humanity, have manumitted, and hereby do manumit and set free from slavery my Mullato man François aged about forty years," Auguste declared in the document of manumission. He gave no clue to the reasons behind the action, saying only that he had purchased François from the estate of Régis Loisel.

Some slaves also bought their freedom from various of the Chouteaus. Pierre's son Paul Liguest sold a mulatta named Rosette her freedom for $250, certifying that no one else had any claim to her as the result of any of his debts and that he was forsaking his right to pass her to heirs. His cousin Theodore Papin sold a slave named Felix his freedom for an unstated sum and planned to "dictate a little moral as to how he must conduct himself in the world."

But belief in the institution of slavery began to weaken within the extended Chouteau family long before the Civil War. In 1825 Henry Gratiot and his wife, Susan Hempstead, moved to Galena, Illinois, to take part in the lead-mining business, taking with them their five children, twenty men to work in the mines, and two slaves. Soon after arriving, they liberated the slaves, stating that the practice was against their principles. In the process, they were required to put up $1,000 bond to guarantee that the former slaves would never become charges of the state of Illinois.

The case brought against Pierre Chouteau after passage of the 1824 law allowing slaves to sue for freedom had its origins in O'Reilly's declaration against continued enslavement of Indians, but it began long before that—even before Pierre's own birth—when a baby girl was born in the 1740s near Fort de Chartres to a Natchez Indian woman known as Marie or Mariette. The mother had been taken captive in warfare and sold into slavery, where she met a black slave named Scypion, who presumably fathered the child, who was given the name Marie Jean Scypion. A French priest named Guyon, who owned the mother, gave the child to his cousin, Madame Marie Boisset, whose daughter married Joseph Tayon and inherited Marie Jean. The Tayons moved to St. Louis in 1764, taking Marie Jean with them.

After moving to St. Louis, Marie Jean bore three daughters, Celeste, Catiche, and Marguerite, whose father or fathers were not recorded. Madame Tayon placed the three daughters in the households of two of her own daughters, Hélène Chevalier and Marie Louise Chauvin. After his wife died, Joseph Tayon moved in with Pierre Chouteau, whose first wife, Pélagie Kiersereau, had been the Tayons' granddaughter.

In 1799 Tayon decided to sell Marie Jean and her three daughters, provoking a row, not only with the slaves but with his own two daughters, who refused to give up the families they held. Members of the Tayon family appeared before Spanish magistrates on at least three occasions in 1799 and 1800 to argue over the matter. In the process, the issue of the slaves' part-Indian ancestry arose and the fact that O'Reilly had outlawed further Indian slavery in the territory after 1769.

At that point Pierre Chouteau had no direct involvement except his interest on behalf of his father-in-law. His brother was there to support him. Madame Chauvin testified in one trial that Auguste Chouteau had called on her in 1801 to ask whether Marie Jean Scy-

Pierre Laclède Liguest was born in 1729 in this house in the village of Bedous, in the French Pyrenees.

First home and business headquarters built by Pierre Laclède and the Chouteau family in St. Louis, 1764–65.

Marie Thérèse Bourgeois Chouteau (1733–1814), companion of Pierre Laclède and mother of Auguste and Pierre Chouteau and their three sisters.

Auguste Chouteau (1750–1829), from a miniature.

Pierre Chouteau (1758–1849), from a composite based on memories of descendants.

Thérèse Cerré Chouteau (1769–1842) married Auguste Chouteau in 1786, when she was sixteen years old.

Twentieth-century descendants of Auguste and Thérèse Cerré Chouteau model their ancestors' second-day wedding attire.

After his marriage, Auguste Chouteau expanded the original Laclède trading headquarters and home into this mansion, the grandest in early St. Louis. From a lithograph by J. C. Wild, 1840.

Cheveux Blancs (White Hair), or Pawhuska, chief of the Osages, was taken to Washington by Pierre Chouteau in 1804 and met Thomas Jefferson at the White House. Charles B.J.F. de Saint-Mémin drew the chief's portrait during the visit to Washington.

Clermont II, hereditary chief of a break-away faction of the Osage tribe, painted by George Catlin in 1834 in present-day Oklahoma.

Mo-Hon-Go, or Mihonga, shown here in a lithograph by McKinney and Hall, is believed to have been one of the Osage wives of Auguste Pierre Chouteau.

Emilie Gratiot (1793–1862), daughter of Victoire Chouteau and Charles Gratiot, wed her first cousin, Pierre Chouteau Jr.

Pierre Chouteau Jr. (1789–1865) took the reins of the American Fur Company under the tutelage of John Jacob Astor.

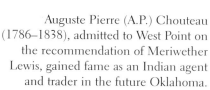

Auguste Pierre (A.P.) Chouteau (1786–1838), admitted to West Point on the recommendation of Meriwether Lewis, gained fame as an Indian agent and trader in the future Oklahoma.

Charles Gratiot Jr. (1786–1855) graduated from West Point in 1806 with his cousin A.P. Chouteau, and later rose to leadership in the Army Corps of Engineers.

Millicour Papin (1793–1849), a son of Marie Louise Chouteau and Joseph M. Papin, entertained Osage Indians with his glass eye during decades as a trader on the Neosho River.

Henry Pierre Chouteau (1805–1855), a son of Auguste Chouteau, with his wife, Clemence Coursault, in a daguerreotype ca. 1855, the year he died in the collapse of a railway bridge.

American Fur Company headquarters, built 1829–1830 in St. Louis. From an ink-on-paper drawing by Clarence Hoblitzelle, 1897.

Pierre Ménard home at Kaskaskia, Illinois, birthplace of Bérénice Ménard Chouteau (1801–1888), who, with her husband, François Gesseau Chouteau (1797–1838), founded a fur post at the future site of Kansas City.

An engraving based on a painting by Swiss artist Karl Bodmer, depicting the S.B. *Yellow Stone* as it fought currents and sunken trees on the Missouri River during an 1833 voyage.

George Catlin painted the site of J. P. Cabanné's trading post at The Bluffs, just above today's Omaha, during a trip up the Missouri River on the S.B. *Yellow Stone* in 1832 with Pierre Chouteau Jr.

pion had ever demanded her freedom on the grounds that she was an Indian, and Marie Chauvin replied in the affirmative.

"Chouteau then replied that little ought to be said about it because it might be a great injury to all those that claimed the service of Indians, and to himself," Madame Chauvin said. "He maimed some of his Indian slaves who had been disobedient and claimed their liberty. He said that he had them whipt—being tied to four sticks and they had talked no more about their liberty." In his own testimony, Auguste denied going to the Chauvin house and having the conversation that she described; he claimed he had freed Indian slaves and advanced them money.

In 1802 Marie Jean died, and in 1804 Joseph Tayon petitioned Captain Stoddard, the acting territorial governor, for permission to sell Marie Jean's children and grandchildren. Tayon's daughters objected and raised the question of whether it was possible to sell slaves of Indian ancestry. In October 1805 Celeste and Catiche filed for writs of habeas corpus in the territorial superior court. Judges John B. C. Lucas and Rufus Easton heard the case and found no cause for the detention of the sisters and issued writs to free them. Their decision was based on testimony from Madame Chevalier and her brother-in-law, Jacques Chauvin, that the two were free Indians.

Five days after the rulings, a lawyer representing Marguerite, the third daughter of Marie Jean, appeared in court asking for a writ of habeas corpus for her release from François Tayon, the son, who responded by insisting that they were Negroes, not Indians. But Lucas and Easton declared Marguerite a free person, as they had done for her sisters.

The issue over whether the Scypion offspring were Indians or blacks was further complicated by the fact that in 1804, just months after the Louisiana Purchase, the four-man Legislative Council for the territory had adopted laws governing slavery that went farther than Spanish colonial law by defining a mulatto as anyone with just one Negro grandparent. Such a person could be enslaved. It was silent about Indian slaves, but presumably an Indian with one black grandparent could have been enslaved under the American law. That would have included the Scypion descendants. But Lucas and Easton did not address that law in their 1805 rulings.

After their release in 1805 on orders of the court, the three sisters went to live in St. Charles County, where they were joined by their children. But at the next session of the territorial superior court, Joseph Tayon claimed the slaves were, and always had been, his property. The judges declined to authorize the arrest of Celeste and Catiche. By now, however, Pierre and Auguste Chouteau were becoming more active in the case, and they exerted enough pressure that the judges ordered all other members of the Scypion family apprehended, including children of the sisters. The St. Charles County sheriff placed them in Tayon's custody. Although Marguerite and her nephew Joseph were not on Tayon's warrant, Pierre had them forcibly detained and placed in Tayon's custody. Tayon was living with Pierre, so his slaves presumably lived there as well.

Through all of this, the sisters and their children were able to count on the support of a number of whites in the community, including lawyers who came forward to handle their cases. Pitting the most powerful citizens of the community against their slaves and antislavery whites, the case became more sensational with each new legal ruling or action by the various parties.

After the new detentions, Isaac Darnielle, a lawyer favoring the Scypion family, went to the superior court and demanded Marguerite's release. The judges summoned Pierre to appear in court with her the next day. The judges then gave Tayon one month to initiate a suit for any legal rights he had to Marguerite. Tayon filed petitions claiming custody of the entire Scypion family.

The two-day trial began in St. Louis on May 19, 1806, presided over by Judge Lucas. Witnesses gave conflicting accounts of the Scypions' status, whether they were slave or free, Indian or Negro. Some of them discussed such things as whether the Scypions had black "features." Since persons of color could not testify against a white person in court, the defendants had to rely on whites to make their case.

Auguste Chouteau, when he was deposed, recalled seeing Marie Jean Scypion at Fort de Chartres when he was still a boy, shortly after arriving in the area with Laclède. He recalled that her feet and hands "were of negro shape" and said he believed her to be "of Indian and negro" but knew "not which of the ancestors were Indian or negro." Auguste also told the court that he recalled hearing about O'Reilly's declaration in 1769, shortly after which he went to authorities to report on his mother's Indian slaves.

The jury, with Pierre's brother-in-law James Morrison as foreman, found that the Scypions were blacks and slaves, not free Indians. On June 5 Lucas had no choice but to grant Tayon full custody. Less than a month later Tayon sold seven members of the family—Marguerite and Catiche, four small children, and a boy of about ten—to Pierre in auction at the door of the church. The price was $1,160 in cash. The two women were described in the bill of sale as "mulattas." Normally that would have been taken to mean that their father was white or part white, although it may have referred, incorrectly in this case, to their being part Indian.

After that, the slave family remained firmly in Pierre Chouteau's hands for a number of years.

With the passage of the 1824 law, an unidentified lawyer representing Marie Scypion's descendants went to court to renew their demand for freedom. A circuit judge turned them down, so they appealed to the Missouri Supreme Court. After two such appeals, on May 15, 1826, Justice George Tompkins, who would make frequent rulings in favor of slaves during his years on the bench, overturned the lower court's findings and ordered the plaintiffs to proceed with their suit. Tompkins held that the circuit court had thwarted the intent of the 1824 statute. He also challenged the validity of the original 1806 verdict.

Several separate suits were filed in circuit court in the Scypions' behalf. One pitted Catiche, her four children, and her granddaughter Mary against Pierre. Marguerite and her children—Antoine, Baptiste, Michael, and François—also sued Pierre for their freedom. Celeste and her four children, plus two grandchildren, sued their owner, Madame Chevalier, for their freedom. All of them received free legal aid from Isaac McGirk and Hamilton R. Gamble.

According to one affidavit filed, Pierre responded violently on being taken back to court by the Scypions. On April 1, 1825, he supposedly "beat, bruised, and ill treated" Catiche, then kept her confined for thirty days. In separate suits, the slaves accused Pierre of trespass and assault and battery, and they sought damages of $500 each. The judge ordered the petitioners to court for an inspection and ordered Pierre to post a surety bond to ensure that he would not try to remove the slaves from the court's jurisdiction.

Pierre put together a top legal team that included St. Louis attorneys Luke E. Lawless, Horatio Cozzens, and Henry S. Geyer, who was elected to the United States Senate from Missouri in 1850 and became one of the attorneys who argued the Dred Scott case before the Supreme Court in 1856.

The first of the suits, *Marguerite vs. Pierre Chouteau Sr.*, went to trial in 1827. Witnesses were called who had known the three generations of the slave family. As in the 1806 proceeding, they talked about what the grandmother looked like—Indian, they said. But the daughter was lighter skinned, and the granddaughter, Marguerite, they said, had "African-like curls." The attorneys had long debates about Spanish law and policy prior to 1804. Over the strong objections of McGirk and Gamble, the judge instructed the jury "that if Marguerite's maternal grandmother had been a lawful Indian slave taken captive in war and sold as a slave before the Spaniards took possession of Louisiana, then they should consider her descendants as lawful slaves."

In late 1828 the jurors returned a verdict in Pierre's favor. Marguerite's attorneys claimed that the jury had been improperly instructed, and they appealed to the Missouri Supreme Court, which divided evenly in its opinion, so the circuit court judgment was effectively upheld. Justice Tompkins issued a dissenting opinion, which said in part: "I find nothing to induce me to think that under the French Government of Louisiana private persons had a right to reduce Indians of the Natchez tribe to slavery, and the circumstances of an Indian being transferred by sale or gift can make no difference in the case. A person held in bondage can give no assent."

Five more years went by, during which the Scypions remained

with Pierre Chouteau. In 1833 their attorney asked the Missouri high court to review its 1828 opinion. By then, Isaac McGirk's brother, Mattias McGirk, was on the court, which gave them reason for hope. By a vote of two to one, the Missouri Supreme Court declared on October 10, 1834, that the jury had been improperly instructed in the 1827 trial, and a new trial was ordered.

After the Scypions requested a change of venue, the trial was transferred first to St. Charles County, then to Jefferson County, where it came to trial on November 8, 1836, combined into one case by mutual consent. It ended quickly; the judge instructed the jury in conformity with the Missouri Supreme Court's opinion, and the twelve-member jury returned a unanimous verdict in favor of freedom for the plaintiffs. But on the assault charges, it allowed only one cent in damages in each case.

Pierre Chouteau appealed to the United States Supreme Court, which ruled in 1838 that it lacked jurisdiction, ending all his efforts to claim the family. By then it had been nearly a century since Marie Jean Scypion had been born into slavery, thirty-six years since she had died, and more than thirty years since her descendants had first set out to gain their freedom. Her daughters were in their sixties.

Time also claimed Auguste Chouteau well before the Scypion case came to a close. On February 13, 1829, Auguste drew up his will, beginning with the words, "I, Auguste Chouteau . . . knowing that there is nothing more certain than death, and nothing more uncertain than the hour of it . . ." After directing that all his debts be paid, he bequeathed to his wife, Thérèse Cerré Chouteau, the house in which they lived, with all its furnishing and goods, plus another house nearby, and a dozen slaves to be selected according to her wishes from among the fifty he possessed. He commented that she still had control of the assets she had received under their marriage contract. He directed that the remainder of his property—land, buildings, payments due him, and slaves—be disposed of or collected and divided equally among their seven living children. He named his wife as executor and requested that she use their son Henry to administer the estate and pay him "liberally" for his work.

On the morning of February 24, 1829, Auguste died, aged seventy-eight years and five months.*

The *Missouri Republican*, in that afternoon's paper, said that the "Patriarch of St. Louis" had "closed a life of singular usefulness, possessing, in every vicissitude, the esteem of his fellow citizens." It said that he had a numerous circle of friends attached to him "by his philanthropy, his . . . benevolence and the amenity of his manners." The funeral was the next day at 9 a.m., after which he was buried in the cemetery beside the still unfinished cathedral.

By all accounts, Auguste Chouteau was the richest man in St. Louis at his death. His son Henry hired three men unrelated to the family to appraise the estate. They appraised his slaves, livestock, books, furniture, housewares, and other personal effects at a total of $17,217.75. His slaves ranged in age from a hundred years to an eight-day-old baby born after Auguste's death. There were seventeen men, eleven boys, fourteen women, and eight girls. Appraised as the most valuable were three men in their early thirties, valued at $500 each. Women ages twenty-one, twenty-nine, and thirty-three were found to be worth $350 each. The century-old man was valued at nothing, the baby at $50.

Auguste had an impressive library, including fifty-five volumes of the works of Voltaire; a sixteen-volume Roman history; a six-volume Tudor history; seven volumes of the works of Montesquieu; a four-volume *History of Tom Jones*; books on botany, farming, and geography; *The Voyages of Captain Cook*; *Robinson Crusoe*; a history of the English Parliament; biographies of several French kings and Napoleon; dictionaries; books on business and finance, yellow fever, physics, and chemistry; and maps and charts of Europe and North and South America.

The inventory listed every piece of silver and crystal, napkins, gilt chairs, bedding, furniture, dining chairs, paintings and drawings, and other items found in the house, even though they remained in the possession of his widow. There were two cart horses, four pairs of red oxen, fifteen cows and calves, two steers, one bull, 600 bushels of corn

---

*There is some uncertainty about Auguste Chouteau's exact birth date, with some sources giving it as 1749 and others as Sept. 26, 1750, which is the date accepted here.

in the crib, 1,200 bushels of corn at the mill, and 300 bushels of wheat at the mill.

The estate included mortgages and promissory notes signed by about 800 people who owed money to Auguste, the total of receivables being calculated at $82,855.14. Included was a debt of $7,015.17 by Auguste Aristide, his eldest son, who had led a dissipated life of squandered opportunities and was sadly estranged from his parents.

Finally, the estate of Auguste Chouteau included enough land for a small European kingdom. At his death he owned 21,482 acres in several counties of rural Missouri, plus some in Illinois, various lots in the towns of St. Louis and St. Charles, and a big chunk of the center of St. Louis. In addition, he left claims to 39,231.5 acres whose confirmation he was still seeking from the United States government, including his share of the Dubuque mine claim.

No value was placed on the land by those who inventoried and appraised the estate. But its worth would grow and grow with the passage of years as his heirs set themselves to developing or selling the land and buildings. His heirs grew ever richer in the process and at times had to resort to the courts to settle differences among them over how to share the accumulated wealth from Auguste's lifetime.

TWELVE

Pierre Jr.: Gentle Creole, Driven Tycoon

✳

Growing up, Pierre Chouteau Jr. was a sickly child, often down with colds, fevers, and undiagnosed ailments. In a time when medications were typically limited to some combination of laudanum, opium, calomel, and vinegar, his health worried his parents enough to occasionally cause Pierre Sr. to cancel or postpone business travel in order to hover over his second son.

After a brief early experience out on the river in the fur trade and a period overseeing his uncle Auguste's interests in the Dubuque mines, Pierre Jr. settled into a seemingly routine existence in St. Louis. He displayed a knack for finances and was conscientious about his correspondence. He acquired his father's French nickname, Cadet (pronounced CAH-day), not because he was a "junior," but because he, like his father, was the second son. The voluminous correspondence he received inevitably began, "Dear Cadet." As the years passed, people inquiring about the health and affairs of Pierre Sr. referred to him as "Mr. Cadet."

Berthold & Chouteau, the store that Cadet and his brother-in-law opened in 1813, had setbacks in its early years. It suffered large losses from supplying the failed 1815–17 expedition to the Southwest led by Cadet's brother A. P. Chouteau and Jules de Mun, who came back in tatters, their pelts and merchandise confiscated by Spanish authorities. The firm lost another significant sum on an expedition to the mountains led by Manual Lisa in 1819, the year before Lisa's death. Together, the partners in Berthold & Chouteau and their relative by marriage, Jean Pierre Cabanné, who at that time had his own firm in partnership with Bernard Pratte, put about $37,000 into the Lisa expedition, most of which they lost.

The fact that so many Chouteaus, cousins, and in-laws were crowded into the fur trade undoubtedly caused tension at family gatherings. Sometimes they competed with each other, and sometimes they collaborated. But Pierre Jr. soon began to display skill—for which he would become known throughout his life—at defeating or buying out the competition. On January 30, 1819, he signed a newspaper advertisement announcing the dissolution of Cabanné & Company, having bought out his brother-in-law. Cabanné's partner, Bernard Pratte, joined Pierre Jr.'s firm right away, and Cabanné himself followed shortly.

For a while Berthold & Chouteau was timid about entering the fray of competition outside the family. Even after the death of Manuel Lisa, the Missouri Fur Company, which also included such fur-trade luminaries as Joshua Pilcher, Lucien Fontenelle, Andrew Drips, William Vanderburgh, and Charles Bent, had a strong presence on the Upper Missouri. The only early post that Berthold & Chouteau established in the upriver area where it would have to go up against the Missouri Fur Company was near Cedar Island in present South Dakota in 1819.

Most of Berthold & Chouteau's initial posts were closer to home. François Gesseau Chouteau, eldest of the five sons of Pierre Sr.'s second marriage, set up an outpost for the firm at the mouth of what the Chouteaus called the Rivière des Kans, the site of the future Kansas City. Two of François's younger brothers, Cyprien and Frederick, would eventually join him to operate branches in the same area. Uncle Auguste's son Cerré worked in partnership with François, until they decided there was not enough business at the location for all of them. South of there, along the eastern edge of the future state of Kansas, Pierre Jr.'s younger full brother, Paul Liguest, established an Osage trading post. Baronet Vasquez and Sylvestre Pratte, a son of Bernard Pratte, set up a post near the Omaha village.

The merger in 1821 of two British firms, the Hudson's Bay Company and the Northwest Company, threw a number of talented young fur-trade people out of work. Three of them—Kenneth McKenzie, William Laidlaw, and Daniel Lamont—joined Joseph Renville, James Kipp, and Robert Dickson to launch the Columbia Fur Company. In 1822–23, Columbia Fur opened several posts along the Upper Missouri River, the largest being Fort Tecumseh, creating new competition for the Chouteaus and their relatives.

The leader of this aggressive firm was the Scottish-born McKenzie. Still in his mid-twenties, Kenneth McKenzie already had the commanding presence and authoritative manner that would make him a legend on the Upper Missouri. His first move was to go after the buffalo-robe trade more actively than any trading firm had done previously.

Another stiff competitor for the young Chouteaus was the man who had been rebuffed by their elders two decades earlier: John Jacob Astor. Despite the failure of his Astoria scheme, he still had ambitions of building his business into one with continental scope. Competing against the Chouteaus while also trying to lure them into an alliance, he had bought furs on a small scale from Charles Gratiot Sr. until Gratiot's death, in 1817, then from the firm run by Cabanné, and later from Berthold & Chouteau. In 1822 Astor's New York–based American Fur Company established a western department in St. Louis to compete directly with the St. Louis traders, but it also signed a letter of agreement with Cadet's newly expanded and reorganized firm—Berthold, Chouteau & Pratte—to buy some of its pelts and supply some of its trade merchandise.

Bernard Pratte signed the accord with Astor on behalf of the partners. Ramsay Crooks, the veteran of the Astoria expedition who had risen to be Astor's trusted aide and confidant, signed for the American Fur Company. Under the agreement, Cadet's firm was to sell to the American Fur Company buffalo robes at $2.75 apiece and deerskins at 33.5¢ a pound, and to buy trade merchandise from it for a period of one year.

Within weeks of signing the agreement, the American Fur Company and Cadet's firm were doing considerable business with each other. By late summer, the joint venture looked successful enough that Astor wrote Cadet and his partners in St. Louis that "if you have not made any arrangement for your deer for next year we will thank you for the [preference] of them."

The uncertainties of the fur trade made it nearly impossible to predict from one year to the next what the profits might be, but correspondence among various principals and traders over a number of years indicates that they expected a return of anywhere from 50 to 100 percent on the capital invested to acquire the trading goods. However, there were years in which the entire investment could be lost—because of such things as smallpox among the hunting tribes, intertribal warfare, weather, the sinking of pelt-laden barges and keelboats, or fires onboard. Given the long turnaround time between the purchase of merchandise to trade to the Indians for pelts and the eventual sale of those pelts, with two trips to Europe in the process, it was also possible that the demand for a particular pelt would have fallen or even dried up by the time it was ready for sale.

However, at the end of 1822, when the profits were totaled up, it was obvious that the joint arrangement with Astor was turning out to be highly lucrative for the St. Louis firm. Of Cadet's total personal profit of $25,097.76 for the year, $16,053.65 came from his one-third share of earnings under the American Fur agreement.

By May 1823, J. P. Cabanné had joined the firm, and the name was simplified to B. Pratte & Company, for its eldest partner. Cabanné became manager of the Lower Missouri trade from what was called "the Bluffs," on the west side of the Missouri River just north of the future Omaha. Berthold created an establishment farther upriver for the Sioux trade, but he continued to spend most of his time in St. Louis. Pratte handled "external" affairs from St. Louis. John B. Sarpy ran the accounting department, and Pierre Jr. was general superintendent.

The partners were happy with their new setup and convinced it would succeed handsomely. In the fall, while Cadet and Pratte were in the East, Berthold wrote to let them know that people at home were saying good things about their firm—that it was getting off to a good start and that Cabanné was probably the best trader on the Missouri River. "Everyone congratulates me on the assured fortune we shall have," Berthold said. "I am not fooled by it, and I complain, as usual, in the face of compliments—and of the great risks, and the risks to which we are exposed."

About the same time, Berthold put together a list of furs and peltries the firm had received for all of 1823, which included these impressive numbers: 8,934 pounds of beaver skins, 898 pounds otter, 52,584 pounds shaved skins, 1,437 pounds red deerskins, 642 pounds gray deerskins, 586 pounds bearskins, 7,922 buffalo robes, 4,881 pounds raccoon, and 3,013 pounds muskrat.

"From this time forward," observed fur-trade historian Janet Lecompte, "year by year, Cadet and his associates would learn Astor's techniques: upon dissolution of a rival company, Cadet would take over its posts and men, territories and trade, allowing no fragment of the defunct company to attach to other rivals . . . Traders would work on shares, so that the company would profit both from selling them goods and buying their furs, and their territories would be carefully divided. These were the principles behind successful fur trade management, and Cadet violated them only at his peril."

In 1824 Cadet bought an elegant carriage for his trips to the East, a distance of nearly 1,000 miles on modern highways and certainly longer by the river and road routes used then. From St. Louis he normally descended the Mississippi by steamboat, then went up the Ohio to Pittsburgh. He used the carriage from Pittsburgh to Philadelphia, then onward to New York. Going home was the reverse. Such trips took at least three weeks each way, but certainly less time than it had taken for Pierre Sr. to reach Washington with the first Osage delegation in 1804, before the advent of steamboats. Without the private carriage, Cadet and his companions would have suffered the torture of public stage for the land portion.

On the first trip using the carriage, Emilie Chouteau accompanied Cadet and Bernard Pratte, beginning an unusual arrangement whereby this early-nineteenth-century wife often accompanied her husband on business trips. Her presence undoubtedly made the miles go by more quickly, for the marriage of Cadet and Emilie was the great love story of their family and circle of acquaintances. Mutual love, admiration, and friendship endured throughout their lives and was the envy of everyone who knew them.

Traveling with her husband also enabled Emilie, who enjoyed good health, to keep a concerned eye on Cadet and nurse him through sciatica, fevers, and his many other ailments. It was a sign of the crucial role Cadet played in the young firm that everyone fretted when he was ill. On Cadet's trip to the East the previous year, when Emilie was not with him and there was a long spell of no mail from him, people in St. Louis concluded that he may have taken ill. Berthold reported that it was of such concern to Emilie that she "sometimes has the vapors and no longer enjoys diversions or balls— she is completely absorbed by her Cadet."

Emilie was never described as the most beautiful of the many daughters of Victoire Chouteau and Charles Gratiot—only Cadet is known to have called her beautiful—but she was quite likely the most loved and admired. She was warm and cheerful, good and kind. A surviving portrait of her shows a woman in her thirties or forties with dark hair pulled back from a round face, large eyes, and a bow-shaped mouth. Whether her contemporaries considered her beautiful or not, she was certainly pleasant-looking.

Before she made her first trip to the East, Emilie had given birth to all their five children: Emilie, Julie, and Charles Pierre, and two sons who died at a young age—Pierre Charles and Benjamin. She had also taken into their household two motherless sons of Cadet's brother Paul Liguest, who was living in Osage country. .

Portraits of her husband in his middle years show a handsome man with crinkles at the edge of slightly smiling eyes. "At maturity he looked and acted the aristocrat he was," wrote Janet Lecompte, "tall, erect, black-eyed and black-haired. His manner was unfailingly gracious, easy and affable with everyone, from the political leaders of the country to the lowliest boatman, yet he was resolute and, when necessary, politely ruthless. He commanded deference from all who knew him and a well-founded fear from those who opposed him."

He surely inherited his grace and manner from his father. But one thing he did not inherit was Pierre Sr.'s explosive temperament. Pierre Jr. seemed always to be in control of himself. Despite the reputation

he developed as a tycoon determined to win at all costs, his correspondence and the remarks and opinions expressed by his contemporaries revealed a man who seldom allowed emotions to get in the way
of common sense and reasonable behavior—or a good business deal.

During Cadet and Emilie's visit to the East in the fall and winter of
1824–25, two courtships were under way. One, although perhaps
more accurately termed a flirtation at this point, was between Cadet
and Astor. Cadet sensed the opportunities to be found under the tutelage of the successful man his father and uncle had ignored. He was
ready to work more closely with Astor, but Astor was now delaying. He
thought B. Pratte & Company was not as aggressively competitive as it
ought to be. He wanted all of the firm's traders to have the advantage
in each of their territories before he was willing to risk his interests in
the hands of Cadet and his associates. Only the firm's trading operation among the Osages—now run by A. P. Chouteau with his brother
Paul Liguest and cousin Millicour Papin—was without serious competition, but good furs and skins were scarcer in their territory.

The other courtship that winter in New York had fewer ups and
downs. Astor's man Ramsay Crooks had been smitten by a daughter of
Bernard Pratte's, also named Emilie, during a visit to St. Louis two
years earlier. Now he was seeking her hand in marriage. Her father
may have given his permission during this visit to New York, because
a spring wedding in St. Louis was planned. Acceptance from Emilie
herself may have come through Cadet and his Emilie, who were in
Philadelphia when Crooks wrote Cadet that the letter he had received
from them on Christmas Day "enclosed the best New Year's gift your
good Lady could have possibly sent me at the present time."

Although Cadet wanted to talk business with Crooks, not much
could be accomplished with a thirty-eight-year-old man who was
"proud to confess that my mind is much occupied by reflections of the
most interesting and pleasing nature." Too atwitter to even spell out
his intended's name, he identified her as "E——" and referred to her
letters as "communication from Missouri." Making plans to travel to
St. Louis with Cadet and Emilie, or to follow soon after, he begged
them to "keep secret until we arrive at St. Louis the new character I

am then to assume." Crooks told Astor of his marriage plans and looked for a house to lease in New York.

Crooks enlisted the help of Emilie Chouteau to select gifts for his future bride, fearing that his own lack of taste in such matters "might create embarrassment." They settled on a plaid cloak from the firm of Berard & Mondon in New York, for which Crooks paid $8. He also bought a yard of cashmere for $2.25.

The New York trip gave Emilie Chouteau a taste of new luxuries, and Cadet enjoyed them at her side. They paid a bill for $44 from St. John & Ogle, which included $12 for a pair of pantaloons for Cadet. Their bill from "Widow Goudain" for fifteen days' lodging in New York came to $30. They paid $4 for two bottles of Madeira and $6 for three extra dinners for guests. Emilie paid $22 to Mrs. Goudain for "making and finding a silk coat."

Emilie's brother and Cadet's cousin Charles Gratiot Jr., by now a lieutenant colonel in the army, joined them in New York, and he and Cadet traveled together to Old Point Comfort, in Virginia. As he rose through the army ranks and gained influence in Washington, Gratiot would become an important connection for his relatives. Emilie and Cadet introduced Gratiot to Crooks and invited Crooks to make the trip to Virginia that winter, but he declined because of the pressures of tying up business and housing matters before his marriage. However, Crooks and Cadet were forming a personal and business relationship that would last for years and produce, through their correspondence, a substantial piece of the history of America's first big business. For the moment, however, all the flustered bridegroom-to-be could offer Cadet in the form of reassurance was a challenge to play whist at the first opportunity.

During his months in the East, Cadet was peppered with requests from men in the field to acquire merchandise for them to sell or trade for pelts. Many such requests were waiting, or soon arrived, when he traveled to Philadelphia in January and began his buying. After he finished business in Philadelphia and had the merchandise ready to ship, he would continue by carriage to Pittsburgh to be ready to travel west by steamboat as soon as spring navigation opened on the Ohio River.

J. P. Cabanné advised from the Bluffs that trading was going to be very competitive in his area. The Missouri Fur Company was working there, and Joseph Robidoux, a feisty competitor well-known to the Chouteaus and their associates, was headed west to the mountains. "So we need cheap merchandise to withstand the struggle; direct yourself accordingly," Cabanné admonished his younger kinsman.

From Fort Atkinson, above the Bluffs, James Kennerly asked Cadet to acquire items for him to sell to army officers, their wives and daughters, and some things for him personally, including a "first rate violin, with a case, bow, strings, etc." and "6 pair of the most fashionable & elegant white spurs." He told Cadet to ship things that would appeal to fifty young officers — "such as fishing & hunting apparatus, fine knives, hunting shirts, hunting dresses, plated or steel bridles, silver bands and tassels, sword cases, fancy suspenders, gloves etc. etc. and for our women many articles of finery, such as shoes, stockings of cotton . . . garters, corsetts, worked ruffles, inserting trimmings, thread lace, silk lace, ready made dresses, bonnets and even artificial flowers." He wanted the merchandise as early in the spring as possible because the troops would be going upriver and would be paid, on the last day of April, before leaving.

Emilie and Cadet's return to St. Louis that spring was met with a series of family concerns. There was the happy wedding of Ramsay Crooks and Emilie Pratte, but there were also deaths. J. P. Cabanné and his wife, Julie, who was Emilie Chouteau's older sister, were grieving over the loss of their sixteen-year-old son, grief that was made worse because Cabanné was far upriver. He asked Cadet to comfort his wife "for I know that, far from calming her, I would sharpen her grief." Pierre Jr., he wrote, might help her because "you are a father and you are kind."

Cabanné's concerns about his wife's state of mind and his own loneliness did not go away. It was sharpened by his anguish over what he saw as a difficult competitive situation at his post. "My wife wants to come up here," he wrote Cadet. "Alas! Can I contemplate her leaving the children after our recent loss? If it were possible, I would doubtless wish it; she must be crushed with grief; guide her, my friend, and do what you think best." He went on to pour out his heart and problems to Cadet. "When I began this letter I was far from wishing to make it a general exposition, but I like to chat with my friend and I believe that it would not be praiseworthy to hide from him that which his remoteness does not allow him to know, or hides it from his knowledge."

By June, Cabanné's wife had joined him for an extended visit, assisted in her travels, no doubt, by Cadet. Her husband was trying to find workers to finish a more comfortable house. He had housewares shipped to the post, including fine stemware and silver flatware. "My wife is pretty well, although she suffered much from the fears that this dangerous voyage often causes," he wrote Cadet. He apologized for writing so often and spilling out his feelings, but he said, "It is needful for a man to talk, as it is for him to write."

Julie Cabanné had hardly arrived at the Bluffs, however, when her mother, Victoire Gratiot, last of the sisters of Auguste and Pierre Chouteau, died in St. Louis at age sixty-one. After receiving word, Cabanné delayed telling her and asked Pierre Jr. to take care of her interests in the estate.

At fifty-two, Jean Pierre Cabanné brought to the new venture years of experience in the fur trade and other businesses. Born in the same area of the Pyrenees as Pierre Laclède, he had moved to New Orleans as a young man, then upriver to St. Louis in 1798, where he married Julie Gratiot and entered the fur trade. His experience and maturity, however, made him impatient with the shortcomings of the less-experienced people hired by the firm. He also grumbled about the aches and pains that came with aging and worried about whether the firm was taking the right steps to succeed against the competition. He had a biting sense of humor that he turned on himself as often as on others. His flood of letters to Cadet back in St. Louis brought alive the routine and loneliness of life on the frontier before the large-scale invasion of white settlers, and before army posts became ubiquitous.

Despite his obvious devotion to his wife and children, Cabanné followed the custom of white men serving for long periods at fur-trade outposts by sharing his bed with a succession of young Indian women. Back in St. Louis, these young women were referred to as "country

260 BEFORE LEWIS AND CLARK

wives." After he had been at the Bluffs a few years, Cabanné reported to Cadet that he had been treating himself with "Syphilitic of Swaim's Panacea" for an unstated illness, suggesting that he had contracted one of the sexual diseases that were rampant among the tribes and traders in the field.

Cabanné also complained about the work habits and lack of responsibility of the clerks and *engagés*, including their poor attention to details such as which items of merchandise were most appealing to Indian clients. "Much more merchandise than I had carried on the inventory has been returned to me from the different posts. I have [received] almost all the hunting knives [back]; battle axes and peace-pipes would sell better. I have 30 green coats; the Indians like only red ones."

When Cadet suggested they try to work with the troublesome trader Joseph Robidoux instead of treating him as a rival, Cabanné exploded. "I ask you in the name of the friendship that is between us, no more Robidoux! This man will bring about our ruin. His competition is no more to be feared than any other's. Disabuse yourself, my friend, it is buying him at too high a price."

Pierre Jr. must have worked out something with Robidoux over the objections of Cabanné, although Cadet, too, had his misgivings. After Robidoux and his brothers did a season's work as *engagés* of Pratte & Company, Robidoux wrote Cadet: "Although you told me I was like a snake that maneuvers to get engaged—you were wrong, my friend, but I love your way of joking." Sounding upset and sad, he pleaded against "declaring war" against each other.

The company debated whether to make another effort at trading and trapping in the Southwest, even though memory was still strong of the losses suffered from A. P. Chouteau's expedition to Taos and Santa Fe. But the region remained a lure for the traders of the Missouri River, who continued to believe that there must be riches to be made somewhere out across the High Plains. Cabanné was one of those seduced by the idea of the Southwest, in part because he saw it as a logical extension of his post at the Bluffs. He thought the Bluffs did not have enough trade to justify a large operation, unless it could expand its reach to the mountains and the Southwest. Berthold, who had been Cadet's partner when they backed A.P.'s expedition, was adamantly opposed to trying the Southwest again.

The expedition of A. P. Chouteau and Jules de Mun had followed the Arkansas River all the way to the Rockies, then dropped south to Taos and Santa Fe. Other traders crossed the future state of Nebraska along the Platte River to the future site of Denver, then proceeded south along the eastern slope of the mountains. For that route, Cabanné's post would be the point of departure and return, and probably the place to unload pelts and acquire merchandise.

"This post is unimportant unless it is supported by other means," Cabanné told Cadet. "We must cast our sights toward the mountains. 38 to 40 wagons left in the early days of last May from Franklin [Missouri] and took more than 4 months to reach Santa Fe, and they brought back, I am told, a profit of 50 percent." A few months later he apologized for harping so much on the mountain business: "I know how much I annoyed you."

This new interest in the Southwest was piqued in part by a purchase that B. Pratte & Company made in the fall of 1824 of 1,500 pounds of pale-colored beaver trapped around Santa Fe. Seeing that it sold better than darker furs, the partners bought a one-third interest in a small outfit in New Mexico owned by Ceran St. Vrain, a former clerk for Bernard Pratte. It earned little, however. So in the summer of 1826 they sent Sylvestre S. Pratte, Bernard's son, to Taos to take charge of about 120 independent trappers who were to work for two years.

Ramsay Crooks cautioned against this enthusiasm for the Southwest. "The Beaver of that region seems to be a great favorite with the folks of your country," he wrote Pierre Jr. "I doubt whether your competition will be materially increased after all the fuss they make. There is more smoke than fire in all this uproar."

The next winter, 1825–26, Astor was in Europe, where he became aware of "the unprecedented scarcity of money" and of the strong probability that the prices of skins would fall. He told his son to hold purchases of skins and furs to a minimum and not to sign any contract whatsoever with B. Pratte & Company or Ménard & Vallé, the Kaskaskia firm led by close allies and in-laws of the Chouteaus. Bill Astor even reported that his father was thinking of closing the business in a year or two.

Meanwhile, B. Pratte & Company was experiencing what Cadet would eventually write off as a "disastrous year." Many skins were arriving at St. Louis in bad shape, and competition in the field was fierce. The Santa Fe/Taos operation proved costly in both money and lives. "As for the unfortunate business at Taos I do not dare to think of it," Cadet wrote Bernard Pratte from New York. "If it were not for these inexhaustible fur-drafts I would be of a mind to await with resignation the sad end of this expedition, but these drafts, who can know where they will lead us?" This was before he learned of the truly sad outcome of the venture. One party of hunters was massacred by Indians, and later, in October 1827, young Sylvestre Pratte himself died of an undiagnosed illness—some historians said he was bitten by an infected dog—in the Rockies around the headwaters of the Platte River.

Both the American Fur Company and B. Pratte & Company were badly bruised by the time Crooks traveled to St. Louis in June 1826 and proposed to all the partners—Pratte, Cabanné, Berthold, and Pierre Jr.—a merger with the American Fur Company. In the fall, Cadet went to New York to negotiate with Astor. By early December the negotiations had broken off, but they were revived a few days later by the smooth intervention of Crooks.

Cadet, for his part, agonized over whether he was doing the right thing by his partners and associates. To add to other woes, when he was on the point of signing the agreement with Astor, a letter arrived from St. Louis telling him of the loss of the barge *Lafayette* and 93 packs of buffalo robes. The market possibilities for the remaining 107 packs did not look good.

"I ask myself, will all our enterprises meet with ill success this year? I have a presentiment of this," he wrote his partners. "This instant of passing weakness makes me believe and hope [the agreement with Astor] is perhaps the only means that remains to us of relieving this disastrous year."

After his momentary indecision, however, Cadet signed an agreement under which B. Pratte & Company became the sole western agent of the American Fur Company. The two firms agreed to combine their St. Louis fur companies into a joint effort and share equally in profit and loss. The American Fur Company would furnish all supplies, receiving a commission, and would continue to make disbursements on behalf of the St. Louis operation, charging interest of 7 percent.

Pierre Jr., then approaching his thirty-eighth birthday, was named agent of the American Fur Company, general superintendent of the business, and director of affairs in Indian country, with a salary of $2,000 a year and travel expenses. Pratte would act in his place in time of illness or absence. Berthold would continue in charge of the Sioux country and Cabanné of the Bluffs, each to be paid $1,200. All of the partners shared in the profits as well. This arrangement took effect on July 1, 1827, to run for four years, after which it could be renewed.

Thanks to Cadet's drive, dedication, and organizational skills, his onetime little family business was now in partnership with the country's richest man.

✳

Now officially called the Western Department of the American Fur Company, Cadet's firm quickly expanded its reach far beyond its existing trading posts, pushing much farther upriver. The initials A.F.C. became universally recognized throughout the region, and some people simply called it "the Company." The effort to make inroads farther upriver was aided by the failure of the Columbia Fur Company in the summer of 1827. The American Fur Company took over Columbia Fur intact, renaming it the Upper Missouri Outfit, which was to cover the area from the mouth of the Big Sioux River, near the future Sioux City, northwesterly to the mountains.

Kenneth McKenzie was the big prize in that deal, which was struck between Crooks and McKenzie, fellow Scotsmen, in a meeting on July 6. In addition to receiving a share of the profits, McKenzie was paid the handsome sum of $2,000 a year to be chief agent of the Upper Missouri Outfit, the same salary Pierre Jr. was receiving as general superintendent of the entire Western Department. William Laidlaw and Daniel Lamont also joined from the Columbia Fur Company, with Laidlaw designated as *bourgeois* at Fort Tecumseh in Sioux country.

The *bourgeois* performed a role as unique to the fur trade as *engagés, voyageurs*, and cordellers, and as important as the captain of a ship at sea. Above all, he was expected to maintain control of an outpost that was usually far from company headquarters in St. Louis, and also far from government or military authority. It fell to the *bourgeois* to maintain order on the strength of his own self-confidence and demeanor. He had to keep employees, usually numbering between fifty and a hundred, happy, and he had to maintain good relations with surrounding Indian tribes in order to keep the trade flowing and not arouse hostilities. He also had to be an able businessman. He was responsible for the supply of trade goods and provisions and the safeguarding of the pelts, which had to reach St. Louis in good condition. He was even expected to know something about medicine and to guard the supply of remedies.

In return, he was provided the best comforts that could be had on the frontier: a spacious wood-frame house, probably shared with an Indian wife; fine imported furnishings and linens; good wines, brandies, and cigars; and his own racehorses.

Despite the name, fur-trading posts were not "forts" in the military sense, at least not in the years when the fur trade was the main economic activity of the region between the Mississippi and the Rocky Mountains and there were few white settlers engaged in other work. During that period, there were virtually no army troops around these posts, even though they were laid out like military forts, with palisades and bastions.

The fur trade, especially as it was developing under Pierre Jr. and the American Fur Company, was set up as a hub system in which a series of smaller trading posts fed into a larger one. The smaller posts were generally those nearest to Indian camps. All of them were built in the style of a stockaded fort, even the small ones, and were given the names of forts. With McKenzie and the other experienced Columbia Fur Company people in the fold, Cadet could push that concept even farther into the rich fur areas of the north.

After signing the agreement with the American Fur Company in St. Louis in the summer of 1827, McKenzie set out in August with Cabanné, headed upriver. They were barely two-thirds of the way across Missouri, near where the French had once operated the military post of Fort Orléans, when Cabanné reported back, "The Missoury is high and muddy; we are making little headway. Many men are sick aboard the two barges and two American *engagés* have deserted Mr. McKenzie's barge."

They reached the Bluffs just before the end of September to find that the post had been robbed while Cabanné was away. "I found the place completely stripped of merchandise, food, horses, etc. Our loss cannot be evaluated at less than $3000—25 horses in the worst condition is all that can be rounded up . . . The negro Cirus . . . drowned in crossing the Platte."

Revealing some of the realities of life for ordinary workers, he said one of the "winterers" with the Otoes had gone back to St. Louis ill and had done no work during the voyage. So the St. Louis office should give him no more payments and should charge him $12 for equipment, $7 for a bottle of whiskey, and $1 for two medicines. Another man was to receive $40 for "his ascent" but was in debt to the firm $45.31 for his equipment, two bottles of whiskey, medicine, and tobacco.

While McKenzie continued up the river, bound for Fort Tecumseh and the rich hunting and trapping grounds beyond, Cabanné agitated about the competition, especially the annoying Robidoux and a man named Roy. "They give whiskey; they cart it into the [Indian] lands and I hope to accumulate enough proof to convict them of it. I myself refrain from giving any even to my *engagés*, and, after having considered it well, I believe it is the best decision I ever made." Twice in the same letter he told Cadet to complain to William Clark about the use of whiskey in the Indian trade.

Cabanné had reluctantly advanced about $2,000 worth of merchandise to the Otoes, Mahas, and Iowas; otherwise they would not hunt. He said the peltries he had been receiving were "rubbish," which explained "the need for stimulating the Indians to get them to go to the hunting grounds. If they do not do so, they [will have to] spread out over the Missouri [River Valley] and live on beans." All the trade terms seemed to go against him. The tribes did not have enough horses to trade with him to compensate for the cost of the powder, lead, and guns he advanced them.

In January the Indians near the Bluffs were hunting only the abundant muskrat. The Mahas, who had traded to Cabanné a good number of beaver packs the previous year, would have only a few this year because they were short of horses. The problems were causing him to think about not returning to the Bluffs after his planned trip back to St. Louis over the spring and summer. "It is not even an existence, it is really a tomb; at my age even a fortune would be a feeble recompense." Finally he asked Cadet to "remember me upon occasion to those who believe me still among the living."

These letters among the A.F.C. posts and between the posts and the St. Louis headquarters were aided by a form of "express" communication that served fur traders along the Missouri Valley. Coming down the valley, the route was generally by canoe, except in winter, when dog trains were used above the Bluffs, and saddle horses below. The upbound express was always overland above the Bluffs. Even with these extraordinary efforts, it typically took several weeks for a letter to reach its intended recipient.

The winter of 1828 was terrible along the Missouri River. The few existing roads were covered with ice. Horses were dying or going lame. Three mules that Cabanné sent to the Republican River froze on the way. Despite his opposition to providing liquor to Indians around the Bluffs, Cabanné told Cadet that McKenzie would need it as he explored possibilities in the mountains to the west of the mouth of the Yellowstone. "Drink will be indispensable to him [for the Indian trade] and I see no means of his getting any," he said. "And it would be in vain, I think, to hope to transfer any to Fort Levinwarths [sic]; I will manage to save two barrels for him."

In May, Cabanné had something else to worry about. The Pawnees had suddenly appeared at the Bluffs with an unusually large number of buffalo robes, which he could not buy for lack of merchandise. "I would have needed 5–6,000 [dollars worth of goods]." But he was "without a single article in the store with the exception of several pounds of vermilion. The Panis [Pawnees] had had more than $1,000 worth [of robes] . . . The Mahas still have almost 2 packs of beaver, quite a few otter and about 30 packs of robes, which I cannot trade for." He was convinced that the infernal Robidoux would end up getting them.

But he was cheered by the fact that McKenzie was sending down a bumper harvest of robes—more than two thousand packs from the Sioux. "That is assuredly very good business."

He had stopped talking about not returning to the post after his coming trip to St. Louis with the pelts, at least for the time being.

The business expansion following the merger with American Fur Company kept Cadet busy hiring *engagés* and *voyageurs* to go upriver, winter among the tribes, gather skins and furs, and do the other work of the fur trade. Contracts from the period reveal that in 1827 he was paying $70 for someone to winter in the area for a year, then return to St. Louis, or in another case $141 to spend a year among the Sac and Fox Indians. Under the date of July 5, 1827, he signed eighteen boatmen, *voyageurs*, and winterers with the Otoes.

A contract signed in April 1830 with Jacques Bowdeau, who marked it with an X, called for Bowdeau to spend a year on the Upper Missouri as a *voyageur* and "winterer" for $200, plus a blanket, soap, and tobacco. On May 24, 1830, Pierre Jr. hired Louis Dorion as a *voyageur interprète* for $160 for eleven or twelve months on the Upper Missouri. Twenty more *voyageurs* were signed during this period for pay ranging from $150 to $170 a year. A list dated May 10, 1830, contained the names of fifty-six men to be employed. During June and July 1830 he signed up yet more men, paying $700, $500, and $300 for "comis," or clerks, and $130 for *un bon voyageur hivernant*. On July 20, 1830, he added sixty-four Americans and five foreigners going to work on the Upper Missouri. On July 28, 1830, he hired forty-seven more men to trade among the Otoes, Mahas, and Pawnees around

Cabanné's post. More hires came in August and September, some of them for the Mississippi and others for the Black Snake Hills region of northwestern Missouri.

As weaker operations failed, Cadet and his partners continued to pick up other highly regarded expedition leaders. One of them was William H. Ashley, who had been Missouri's first lieutenant governor and was a future congressman. He had been in partnership with Andrew Henry, primarily in the upper Rocky Mountains. In September 1828 the Missouri Fur Company fell apart, and some of its key men—Lucien Fontenelle, Andrew Drips, and William Vanderburgh—also signed up with the Western Department of the American Fur Company. Sometime in the fall of 1828 Cadet managed to buy out Joseph Robidoux, paying him $1,000 a year to remain in St. Louis for two years and not bother A.F.C. people in the field. This was Cabanné's idea.

There was some expansion up the Mississippi as well, although the influx of white settlers into Iowa and Illinois reduced the potential for hunting and trapping there. The best prospects for the A.F.C. in those areas lay in trading posts to sell merchandise to Indians who could pay with cash from the government annuities that some tribes were beginning to receive.

Russell Farnham, the Astoria Expedition survivor who had crossed Siberia on foot, set up a trading post on behalf of the American Fur Company at the future Rock Island, Illinois, with his friend George Davenport, a former army officer.

The Western Department of the A.F.C. was also opening a wholesale store in St. Louis. Cadet planned to build it at his own expense and lease it to the firm. Crooks sent ideas for the layout from Wheeling on the Ohio River as he waited for a steamboat to Pittsburgh.

> There should be 2 counters running nearly the whole length of it, leaving the receiving room between them and the shelves, and a moderate passage between the counters, underneath which there should be a platform raised 8 to 10 inches from the floor, to lay goods on. At the end of one of the counters there ought to be a trap-door large enough to throw down into the packing room by a slide (the same as you have seen in auction stores at the eastward). The most

bulky kind of goods you usually have open, say blankets and cloths. In your place I would have at the end of the store over the packing room a counter running 1/3 across the store, where the scales should be placed, and I would keep there the groceries you give out in small quantities, medicines etc.

They would need a couple of wheelbarrows for transporting packages within the store, which Crooks offered to buy in Pittsburgh. He also found some bargain saddles in Wheeling for the store.

Cadet hired René Paul, husband of one of his cousins, to draw up plans for the new building. The construction firm of Laveille and Morton estimated the structure would cost $12,000 as Paul had designed it, with "walls of stone, two fronts similar to basement of Court House with all the cut stone required by the plan." The builders said Paul's plans combined "considerable beauty with many conveniences," but that they could build something for less—$10,800 or even $9,000—while still presenting "a very handsome exterior." Pierre Jr. may have opted for one of the less costly versions, because he bought $9,000 worth of coverage from Farmers' Fire Insurance of New York for a "2-story stone building on east side of Main St. between Vine & Locust St." with walls of "hewn stone." It was a significant addition to the growing city.

In the early 1820s St. Louis had begun gradually paving its streets with stones, starting with the former Rue Royale, by then known as Main Street. In 1826 the French names of the three principal north–south streets were abandoned in favor of English names, although the French names had been dropped in general usage earlier. After an economic recession in the early 1820s, economic activity revived in 1825 and construction took off anew. The brick courthouse on land donated by Auguste Chouteau and Judge Lucas was finally completed in 1832 at a cost of $14,000. Economic expansion and industrial activity were also creating health and environmental concerns. A pall of sulfurous smoke hung over the city, caused by burning coal and brickmaking. A hospital was needed, and free schools were finally being organized. By 1835 the city of St. Louis alone had grown to 8,316 people, with at least double that in the surrounding county and more in nearby St. Charles.

In late 1828, in a note beginning "Cher Cousin," Ramsay Crooks advised Pierre Jr. that Astor had instructed him to say that he was "much inclined to sell out his interest in the American Fur Company and that if you preferred it, he would sell you the Western Department, and try to dispose of the Northern Department to [Robert] Stuart and some others. I immediately said you would at once doubt his sincerity, but he said I might assure you that at present he was seriously inclined to sell out."

The note did not produce a flurry of negotiations, however. Astor was then sixty-five years old, and he would spend the next several years ruminating about whether it was time for him to get out of the business. His son Bill Astor told Cadet that business was terrible. "Many of our hat manufactorers have suspended payment, and we shall no doubt lose something in bad debts as well as by the want of demand for goods, which has never been so bad as now."

Pierre Jr. continued his efforts to dry up the competition. He bought out P.D. Papin & Company, a small firm run by some of his cousins, paying them $21,000. The firm's stock was turned over to American Fur Company at three locations: at Fort Tecumseh, at the post serving the Poncas, and at the mouth of the Niobrara River.

The most promising aspect for growth of the business of Cadet and his partners and associates in the autumn of 1829 lay in work under way far upriver, where the resourceful Kenneth McKenzie was directing gangs of men in the construction of Fort Union. The site was at the mouth of the Yellowstone River at what became the border of Montana and North Dakota, just sixty miles south of the Canadian border and close to the richest beaver area in the country. Although the fort would be rebuilt on a grander scale almost as soon as it was completed, the original version was substantial. Stretched out on a commanding bluff directly above the Missouri River, it measured 178 feet along the north and south walls and 198 feet along the east and west walls. Early in 1830, about 120 men were hired in St. Louis to ascend the Missouri and finish it.

Kenneth McKenzie was a busy man in those years, and filled with ideas. At the same time that he was supervising the construction of the fort that would become the center of his virtual empire, he was laying plans to push farther west and open trade with the often hostile Blackfeet Indians. In the summer of 1830, during his visit downriver, he suggested to Pierre Jr. that a steamboat might be useful for transporting goods to the Upper Missouri and carrying furs and skins on the return. Cadet leaped at the idea and started shopping for people to build it.

On November 24, 1830, Cadet signed agreements with two firms in Louisville to build a steamboat, which he named the *Yellow Stone*, for a combined cost of $8,950. The carpenter, William Crane, was to be paid $4,000 to build a boat 120 feet in length on deck, with a 20-foot beam, and a hold 6 feet deep. "The boat must have good sway under every beam with diagonal braces in the center and sides under the boilers and shafts . . . From the stern to the main hatch [beams] may be made of pine or yellow poplar and the balance of them of white oak," the agreement said. The main deck was to be laid with two-inch-thick pine plank not more than six inches wide. The forecastle was to be fitted for the crew to live in, was to have cabins, staterooms, and officers' rooms with berths made of materials and workmanship "of the best kind." Crane agreed to have the boat ready to receive the engine by March 1, 1831, and all the work completed by April 1.

For $4,950, engine maker Beatty Curry of Louisville agreed to build an engine with four boilers sixteen feet long and thirty-six inches in diameter of quarter-inch-thick iron, with cast-iron heads and flues. The engine was to be of "the best materials and [built] in a good workmanlike manner." He also agreed to furnish the waterwheel, shaft, and chains to support the waterwheel beams.

The winter of 1830–31 was brutal along the upper reaches of the Mississippi and all along the Missouri as well, including St. Louis. From the eastern part of the future state of Iowa, Farnham reported three feet of snow. Many of the Indians were in "a state of starvation." He feared that some of his horses would die of the same. But most of the Sacs and Foxes were having a good hunt and would be able to pay that year's credits. Only one small band was not doing well, he said, because it had become too involved in drinking and begging around the fort and was late getting to the hunt.

"Nearly everywhere our horses have died," Cabanné reported from the Bluffs. One man had also died, and another was near dying of a mysterious illness that included vomiting. This "snow-sickness" was creating shortages of manpower. The Poncas were emaciated by hunger, reduced to a cup of flour a day. Cabanné asked for gardening and farming tools and seeds—to plant turnips, cabbage, lettuce, onions, and pumpkins in the spring.

Regardless of the bad winter, as word about *l'estimboat* filtered up the Missouri, the men there could hardly contain their excitement. Cabanné wanted Cadet to bring him "several gallons of good Madeira wine or port" and "two or three gallons of brandy" when the boat made its first trip. Continuing to lament his rustic and solitary state, with his wife back in St. Louis, he said he had heard that "yours . . . is a house of pleasure, where good society assembles. The young people find there amusement suitable to their age, and those of middle age play wisik [*sic*], etc. It is without contradiction a way to pass one's time agreeably; life is short and if you do not profit by it now, at what happier time will you be able to enjoy it? As for me, my time is past; my feelings now are only ephemeral—provided I have enough food and slumber on a chair, it is all I need."

Until then, steamboats had ascended the Missouri River only as far as the Bluffs. Now the plan was to push through to the mouth of the Yellowstone, where McKenzie was completing Fort Union, a distance of about two thousand river miles from St. Louis. As long as there was enough depth to the water, a steamboat could travel faster than the keelboats, barges, and mackinaws then used in the fur trade. It could also carry much more cargo and probably cut down on the number of men required to do the work of pulling and poling more primitive boats up and down the river.

Cabanné promised to have plenty of wood cut above and below the Bluffs to supply the engines of the mechanical marvel. "If you come here and if I am here," he told Cadet, "you can count in advance on the hearty reception you will receive, a good cup of coffee, some pancakes, some nymphs, etc. This last word is superfluous—I forgot that you had become chaste." He reminded Cadet of his request for 1,500 to 2,000 pounds of tobacco. He reported himself reasonably well off, with good "company" and adequate food, though his intestines were still not right. "I have the smokehouse full of deer-legs . . . If I only had the skill of a magician, I would quickly metamorphose them into so many packs of beaver."

From farther upriver, at Fort Tecumseh in Sioux country, the news was better, even though the weather had been no better. Daniel Lamont reported that "the season has been altogether without a parallel . . . and the returns I think will fully equal if not surpass all made in the river last year. Our mountain [group] . . . passed the winter at the forks of the Yellow Stone from where they will commence their spring hunt, but in consequence of the great depth of snow it will be sometime [before] they can commence operations."

As the April 1 deadline for delivery of the steamboat approached, Cadet was planning its first journey within two weeks of taking possession. He visited Louisville in March, and by the time he was back in St. Louis, the engine makers had put steam to the engine and found that "some small alterations" were necessary, requiring a new casting of one of the mechanical parts. "Everything [else] works up to expectations," he was informed in a letter dated April 1. "The boilers are as good as any I have ever seen; they leaked very little after we got steam up; the carpenters will be done by Saturday evening, and [I] will have all my painting done by that time." The small changes would hold back delivery only until the fourth of April.

Once again, success lay before Cadet. He had gathered into his hands many pieces of the fur trade by acquiring or defeating competitors, and he had the approving eye and guidance of John Jacob Astor. Now he was about to undertake a venture intended to push the fur trade ever deeper into the richest pelt areas while increasing the volume of the trade and making it more efficient.

Life was good in other ways, too, as was apparent by the account that Ramsay Crooks sent from New York for personal purchases he had made for Cadet and Emilie. At a cost of $469.31, Crooks bought them two quart-size decanters and two dozen matching wineglasses, a dozen and a half champagne glasses, sets of engraved silver tableware, and other luxury housewares. He had been unable to find the "porte caraffe" Cadet wanted, the only thing he had seen so far being "altogether too common."

For tax purposes in 1831, Pierre Jr.'s property in St. Louis was valued at $50,700, including a square block in the middle of St. Louis valued at $45,000, sixteen slaves valued at $4,000, four horses at $250, one carriage at $300, furniture worth $1,000, and two watches worth $150.

Julie and Emilie, the daughters of Emilie and Cadet, studied in St. Charles with Mother Philippine Duchesne, one of the earliest educators of women west of the Mississippi. Young Emilie, despite frequent illnesses, then moved on to the Visitation Convent school in Georgetown, near Washington, D.C. Julie, two years younger, followed her there.

Ramsay Crooks dropped by to see the fifteen-year-old Julie in the summer of 1831 during a business trip to Washington. He relayed to Cadet a "very favorable opinion" of the convent, which he understood to be "very good, both for ornamental and practical purposes." Crooks added, "Your daughter I found very much grown, and of a most interesting appearance, and you have very fervent prayers that the 'Ladies of the Visitation' may succeed in adorning her mind as liberally as nature has her outward form."

Cadet and Emilie's son, Charles Pierre, went at age six to Mr. Savare's school in St. Louis, transferring two years later to the newly founded Jesuit Seminary at Florissant. By the time Cadet prepared for his historic trip up the Missouri in 1831, he and Emilie had done their grieving for Pierre Charles, who died a baby, and for Benjamin, whom they coddled and adored until he was taken from them at age five.

On April 16, 1831, the S.B. *Yellow Stone* left St. Louis on its maiden voyage. In addition to Pierre Jr., it carried ninety-seven hired men, about thirty of them listed as boat crew, the others "to assist in the trade with different tribes of Indians on the Upper Missouri." It carried an assortment of merchandise valued at $50,385.79, including 1,000 pairs of blankets of sizes ranging from one and one-half points to three and one-half points; fabrics in bright colors and plaids; 200 dozen mirrors; 126 dozen knives; 995 dozen scalping knives; 75 dozen combs; 50 dozen corn hoes; 100 gross of coat buttons; 4,500 pounds of blue and white round beads; 25 pounds of fine seed beads; 300 beaver traps with chains; 1,000 half axes; 300 tomahawks; 48 American felling axes; 20 battle axes; 600 pounds of vermilion; 200 pounds of verdigris; 16 gross of clay pipes; 10,000 pounds of Dupont's gunpowder; 20,000 pounds of lead, and 12,000 pounds of tobacco.

As the *Yellow Stone* fought its way northwest across Missouri, Daniel Lamont reported from Fort Tecumseh that the "returns" were coming in as plentifully as he had predicted. "All possible precautions are and will be taken to expedite the Steam Boat, and be assured your presence in her will be very gratifying," he wrote Cadet.

The joy and anticipation of this first attempt to take a steamboat to the Upper Missouri was dampened by the death, just four days after the vessel departed St. Louis, of Bartholomew Berthold, Cadet's sister's husband and one of the four principal partners of the firm. Berthold, who died at fifty, was credited with providing experienced guidance to Pierre Jr. in the firm's early years. His loss was balanced somewhat for the traveling executive by the delight of surprising his half brother François Gesseau and sister-in-law Bérénice and their family with a visit at their trading post near the mouth of the Kansas River on the last day of April, after a mere two weeks of travel from St. Louis.

The next day, the boat reached Leavenworth, but the river that could be a raging terror when the water level was high was now another problem. "The Missouri is getting very low," Cadet wrote back to Pratte by courier, "and we draw . . . too much water. At noon we had just met the *S. B. Missouri* and some instants later, because of the current and the snags, with a strong wind . . . the left crossbar of the anchor was carried away."

The *Yellow Stone* safely reached Cabanné's place at the Bluffs, but two days after leaving there, it began to drag along sandbars. "Still hoping for rising water or that we might reach the settlement of the Poncas, we continued for 8 days making use either of a log or the anchor to help us pass the flat lands," Pierre Jr. wrote Pratte. "Finally, on the 20th, 6 miles below *l'Eau qui Court* [Niobrara River], where the trading house is, we found only 3 feet 9 inches or 4 feet of water."

Cadet bought a horse from the Poncas and sent a man overland to Fort Tecumseh, about 240 miles away, to request a barge to take off some of the heavy merchandise and give the *Yellow Stone* a better chance to pass through low water. On May 31 the boat had been stuck for twelve days and was still waiting for the barge. Cadet had given up on the idea of traveling all the way to the Yellowstone River, but he still had hopes of reaching the Arikara villages near the future border of South and North Dakota. The lightened boat first had to fight its way to Fort Tecumseh.

"It is a painful situation to drag along the beach with 72 persons, which is how many we have aboard," he told his partner. "All these obstacles, General, do not change my favorable opinion of the S. Boat. Only, I am convinced one must make many improvements."

The same day, Cadet wrote Cabanné at the Bluffs. "I am exasperated to see that your unfavorable [prediction] as to the length of our voyage was only too true. But at that time it was not to be supposed that we would find only 4 to 4½ feet of water . . . This extraordinary lowering at this season has not had its like in the remembrace of old *voyageurs*. Two or three days after we left you, we began to drag, and only with the aid of logs or the anchor did we succeed in passing." He found the inaction distressing—"with so many people to feed and satisfy." He also told Cabanné, if he reached St. Louis ahead of him, to tell his "good and beautiful wife" that he would behave himself in the future. This seemed to suggest he had committed some indiscretion or foolishness that he feared Emilie might hear about before his return.

In the early days of June, Kenneth McKenzie arrived at Fort Tecumseh, bringing the pelts collected at Fort Union and Fort Clark, the trading post being built for the Mandans. Finding that Lamont had left with two keelboats to go to the aid of the *Yellow Stone*, he sent off an "express" letter to St. Louis telling Pratte that "the returns of

Fort Union have turned out much better than I had any right to expect" and that the prospects for the next year were even better. Then he set off in a skiff with John Sanford, an Indian agent and Cadet's future son-in-law, to see what they could do to aid the struggling steamboat. William Laidlaw sent nine horses downriver in case any of those on the boat wanted to come overland.

On June 19 the *Yellow Stone* finally reached Fort Tecumseh, which was crumbling into the eroding banks of the river and would be replaced by the new fort the following summer. All thought of continuing farther upriver was forgotten at that point. Instead, the merchandise for trading was unloaded and the pelts wrapped and packed for the trip back to St. Louis. Besides buffalo robes, furs, and pelts, on its return voyage the *Yellow Stone* carried 10,000 pounds of buffalo tongues, a delicacy appreciated by both whites and Indians. On June 30 it shoved off for the expected smooth downriver trip.

To add to the tribulations of that summer, Cabanné had departed the Bluffs for St. Louis on a barge laden with deerskins and furs, and the barge capsized. He left a letter at Leavenworth for Cadet's return, lamenting that he could not understand "how we could have lost our barge in the least dangerous spot on the Missouri, and no matter how much I am resigned to bear patiently life's reverses, it will be difficult for me to hide the pain I feel." His men had removed the deerskins from the water and dried them one by one. Nevertheless, the skins had shriveled up, and he feared they had lost their value and could not be sold. He left them at Leavenworth. Explaining that the people around Leavenworth "overwhelm me with kindness," he asked Cadet to leave some buffalo tongues for them.

With the river rising on the return voyage, the steamboat glided downriver in slightly more than two weeks, arriving back at St. Louis on July 15. Shrugging off the setbacks, Pierre Jr. immediately put the *Yellow Stone* back to work. On August 3 he sent it to Fort Osage with supplies for his three brothers running trading operations. A.P., with the Osages, was sent the largest amount of food, household, shipping, and hunting supplies; Paul Liguest and François Gesseau also received shipments. All told, he sent his brothers about 40,000 pounds of goods. At the same time, he began planning for a second attempt to take his steamboat to its namesake river the following spring and summer.

On the Upper Missouri, the remainder of the summer of 1831 and the following winter were busy and productive times for strengthening the position of the Western Department of the American Fur Company. Construction was under way at several posts, including the new fort to replace Fort Tecumseh. Forts Union and Clark were being finished, and a new post was being built at the mouth of the Marias River, well up the Missouri from the mouth of the Yellowstone and just east of the future Great Falls, Montana.

In August that year, Kenneth McKenzie sent a twenty-five-man delegation headed by James Kipp from Fort Union to build the fort on the Marias. Called Fort Piegan, it was an immediate success with the Blackfeet and Assiniboines, who brought in 2,400 beaver skins to trade during the first ten days after the fort was raised. But when Kipp left in the spring of 1832, the men he put in charge abandoned it, and Indians, angry that there was no one there to trade, burned it down. The next summer, it was rebuilt six miles up the Marias River and named Fort McKenzie.

Exact construction dates for Fort Union are uncertain, but historians have generally concluded that a post existed there from 1828 or 1829 onward. McKenzie was in residence at least part of each year beginning in 1830. The name Fort Floyd also appears in journals of the time and place, suggesting that it existed before Fort Union in the same area, or that it was the first name of Fort Union.

Fort Union was built on a grassy plain stretching to the north a mile from the Missouri River, providing ample surrounding space for Indian camps at trading time. Bastions for defense, three feet thick, were erected on the northeast and southwest corners of the palisades. But the bastions were intended more to awe Indians than to fight them off, a need that seldom arose at fur posts. Against the palisades, in addition to a separate house for the *bourgeois*, was a row of small apartments for other traders and workers and their families, with a fireplace shared by every two apartments.

Meanwhile, Fort Clark was being completed on the west side of the Missouri River fifty-five miles north of present-day Bismarck, North Dakota, in a layout and style that John Audubon later described as "a poor, miniature representation" of the fort being built downriver to replace Fort Tecumseh. Like most of the upriver posts, Fort Clark sat on the edge of a high bluff overlooking the Missouri. A creek ran along one side.

The scarcity of trees along the Upper Missouri hampered construction because crews had to be sent some distance to find wood. From Fort Tecumseh, men ascended the river as much as fifty or sixty miles to forested areas, chopped down the trees, and floated them down the river. William Laidlaw told Cadet he would very much like to have "a man who understands making brick," but he still promised to be ready for Cadet's visit in the spring. "I assure you that you will not break your head on the beams of our houses, as you did when you was here last. I shall have a comfortable room prepared for you."

After his two-year exile in the comforts of St. Louis, Joseph Robidoux had moved back to northwest Missouri to take over a tumbledown post at the area the French called Serpent Noir, which would later be named St. Joseph in honor of Robidoux and his saint. He found the return to a rustic life tough going. "I do not sleep well," he complained to Cadet, "as I fear that any moment the cabin will fall down. I need a house, and I am without men, without tools and absolutely without a screw; only 5 lbs of nails that you reminded me not to forget; a minot of corn." He was pessimistic about making money at the post, because the Indians demanded everything in advance of going out to hunt. "What a difference from the situation at St Louis—I had a seraglio, I was like a small sultan. Nothing here of all that, for good reasons—Enough of Prattling—One must expiate his sins in this purgatory."

From the Bluffs, Cabanné informed Pierre Jr. that he was doing all he could to help Robidoux get organized. He sent the interpreter Louis Dorion, who spoke Sac, and four men to help with construction.

Robidoux complained that the help Cabanné had sent him was "4 little boys he would better have kept." And he had more complaints:

"I have come out of purgatory to enter into Hell, this spoiled wilderness where you have nested me." He was practically besieged in his cellar because the Indians wanted to take things on credit. He had advanced them all his carbines and guns. He complained that the price list he had inherited at the post was too low for the returns he could expect. He had been accustomed to charging the Otoes and Panis double the price. "The Indians show me their blankets, which are thread-bare—saying that they are going hunting for me—how can they pass the winter thus? Actually they are rather right—but they are rascals—and I do not think them honest fellows—nor do you, I suppose."

The following January, Cabanné turned sixty, and he was feeling his age. "Two days ago I was seized by a pain in my left foot. I fear that, to add to my good fortune, it may be the gout; isn't it enough to have it in the head without its being in the feet!"

But then something happened that reduced such problems to the insignificant. Smallpox reappeared in the fall of 1831. Brought to North America by early Europeans, the disease was first recorded in the region west of the Mississippi in the period 1799–1801. Primitive inoculation, using smallpox pustules, was already known to Europeans and to whites in the New World, so many of them were protected. However, it had a devastating impact on Indian tribes throughout the region and nearly wiped out several of them, including the Mahas. The disease first hit St. Louis in 1799 and killed forty-nine people, after which Auguste Chouteau concerned himself with warning people and encouraging inoculation.

"There is a cruel sickness here, one we have not formerly known, the smallpox," Auguste wrote to a relative in Montreal in 1800. "If any of your household have been exposed, I hope that when you find it suitable you will have them inoculated. It is a precaution that should be taken. It is an operation that is neither painful nor dangerous and it can save you some day."

The improved technique of vaccination with cowpox lesion material was developed in England in 1796 and by 1802 was available in the region around St. Louis. The Chouteaus tried to obtain the new vaccine from abroad almost as soon as they heard about it. One of the things that Thomas Jefferson instructed Meriwether Lewis to do during his expedition up the Missouri with Clark was to tell the Indian tribes about the new vaccine, also known as kinepox vaccine.

When Cabanné reported the outbreak of smallpox around the Bluffs in the fall of 1831, he said the Pawnees were already ravaged by the disease; two-thirds of them were expected to die. The disease was perilously close to his post. It had reached the area of the Mahas, but many of them had been vaccinated after the tribe's previous experience with the disease. Robidoux wrote: "I hear that the Panis [Pawnees] have almost all died of smallpox, the Mahas too—the Ottos [Otoes] also have it. If our Indians also catch it, it will do us considerable harm."

"The smallpox is preventing all communication," Cabanné reported a few weeks later. "The smallpox is ruining all our hopes, & I truly do not know where our returns are to come from to cover our expenses."

It appears, however, that the disease was contained within a relatively small area at that time, probably where the corners of the state of Missouri and the future states of Nebraska and Iowa met. Smallpox was typically spread by infected travelers on river vessels, and perhaps because the Missouri River was shortly frozen to winter traffic, the disease had no opportunity to go farther upriver or downriver.

As had become his custom, Pierre Jr. spent that winter in the East, buying trade merchandise in New York and Philadelphia and mixing with people who could be useful in furthering his business affairs. He did not want to remain long, because he was eager to set out once more to go up the Missouri on the *Yellow Stone*. "There is an epidemic here of colds and fever," he reported from Philadelphia; he had caught something while crossing the mountains, but the resilient Emilie was holding up. By December he was feeling "homesick." He was worried about his aging father, and he told himself this was the last trip he was making to the East. A month later he was suffering with a toothache, which ended when a dentist pulled the tooth. Then his daughter Emilie became ill at her school in Washington, and he decided to combine a visit to her with discussions with government officials about the difficulty of competing with British firms in the northern areas without access to liquor.

Use of liquor in the Indian trade had been a sensitive issue since French and Spanish days. Authorities and traders decried its use but fell back on it as the thing the Indians most wanted—besides weapons—in exchange for their furs and skins. Historically, it had been used less among the Osages and other tribes on the Lower Missouri and the Arkansas River than in the upper country. The reason was that there was less competition in the lower region, and as a result, traders had been able to limit its use there. Now, as Cadet's firm moved into the areas closer to the Canadian border, the British firms operating out of Canada had an advantage because they used liquor freely in the trade.

Even a decade earlier, liquor had been so prevalent in the fur trade above the mouth of the Kansas River that a visiting European nobleman, Paul Wilhelm, Duke of Württemberg, recounted seeing a full barrel of whiskey washed up on the bank of the Missouri at about the present Kansas-Nebraska line. The duke, traveling upriver in July 1823, also saw men coming downriver in canoes who "had fished up brandy and were for the most part drunk." Apparently the liquor had come from a boat that hit a snag.

During his visit to Washington in the winter of 1831–32, Cadet tried, and failed, to convince Secretary of War Lewis Cass to allow the introduction of alcoholic beverages among Indians at the posts nearest the Canadian border. Frustrated, and finding Washington "a place well suited for the exercise of patience," Cadet hired a steamboat to take him, George Davenport, and John Sanford straight through from Pittsburgh to St. Louis.

Crooks, from New York, assured Cadet that he would go to Washington soon and pursue the liquor matter. He would work toward

> obtaining permission to introduce some spiritous liquor for the posts of the Yellow Stone and Marias River, where you actually come in contact with the Hudson's Bay Company—But if practicable I think it will be much better for an arrangement between the two governments to exclude it entirely—If however this prohibition cannot be immediately effected, please inform me what quantity you deem nec-

essary for the 2 posts above named, so as to put you on a fair footing with the people of Hudson's Bay—Don't tell me how much you would like to have, but what will really be required for protection and for that only.

Crooks also said he had not found the inkstand and the bronze cigar stand that Cadet wanted.

Finally, Mr. Astor would be leaving soon for Europe but would probably want to "end the matter" concerning sale of the company before leaving. Crooks wanted to know what arrangements Cadet desired to make for the future.

As Astor contemplated selling his business, the Western Department under Cadet's direction then had hundreds of men divided into outfits. The license that William Clark, as superintendent of Indian affairs, issued that year to Pierre Jr. as agent for the American Fur Company specified that his men had the right to trade with Indians at the following places: "Ponca Village, Fort Lookout, the forks of the White River, the mouth of the Teton River, Hollow Wood on the Teton River, Cherry River, River Jacques, the mouth of the Big Cheyenne, Arickara Village, Heart River, Mandan villages, the mouth of the Yellow Stone, and the mouth of the River Maria." It did not list some other posts, including the Bluffs and others downriver or to the south of there, primarily posts that Berthold & Chouteau had possessed before merging with American Fur Company.

For this huge undertaking, Cadet and his partners needed more and more men, plenty of food, and other supplies, as he admonished John Sarpy while still in the East. "I want to remove all idea of competition by engaging all those who would be able to do the work," he wrote, telling his cousin to pay higher salaries as necessary to get the best men, conditioning the higher salaries on the men signing up for periods longer than a year. "With so many men we will need a great deal of corn . . . Make sure it is good. Examine the kernels to make sure they are not blackened or eaten by worms. Get some barrels of white lard. We will also need ten barrels of good hominy grits."

❋

On March 26, 1832, the S.B. *Yellow Stone* left St. Louis on its second attempt to conquer the Upper Missouri River.

Earlier that day, Pierre Jr. and Bernard Pratte sat down and wrote a letter to Ramsay Crooks. In seven short paragraphs they said that if Crooks and associates in New York bought from Astor the Northern Department of the American Fur Company, which did business in the Northeast, then they wished to continue the same arrangement with Crooks that they had had with Astor. Crooks's firm would supply them merchandise, and they would continue sending their skins and furs to him for sale—with Crooks to collect 10.5 percent both on the merchandise he sold to them and the peltries he sold for them. Crooks's firm would be obliged to continue to honor all the notes and other monetary instruments of their firm.

This time, when the *Yellow Stone* departed St. Louis, in addition to Pierre Jr., John Sanford, and the usual contingent of *voyageurs* and other fur-trade workers, it carried the artist George Catlin. After establishing his reputation as a portrait painter in Philadelphia, Catlin had been captivated by his first view of Plains Indians, and he decided to devote years to traveling and painting them. He arrived in St. Louis in the spring of 1831 and made contact with William Clark, who took him up the Mississippi to Prairie du Chien for an Indian council. The following year, Catlin made arrangements with Cadet to ascend the Missouri on the second upriver voyage of the *Yellow Stone*.

Like his father and uncle before him, Cadet demonstrated a natural sense of public relations long before the concept had become a standard part of business life. Auguste and Pierre Sr. had both made a practice of extending courtesies and providing information to visitors from Europe and the East, Lewis and Clark not having been the first men to avail themselves of the Chouteau network. Cadet himself had first been host to a distinguished visitor a decade earlier when he helped in the travel arrangements—and advanced some money—for Paul Wilhelm, Duke of Württemberg. The amateur naturalist ascended both the Missouri and the Mississippi during his 1822–24 travels in North America, and he made a return visit over the summer of 1830, spending time at Fort Tecumseh. As time passed, more and more people would turn to Cadet or the American Fur Company for

assistance in traveling in the area, and most of them ended up praising the company and its top executive in articles, interviews, and
books, if for no other reason than gracious hospitality.

Catlin's travels on the *Yellow Stone* were doubly useful to historians because, in addition to sketching and painting events and people,
he wrote letters and articles that were published in newspapers and
magazines. Through these, he left a lively firsthand description of
events deep within the North American continent well ahead of white
settlement—or the arrival of the telegraph.

Even though this was the vessel's second voyage up the Missouri,
the *Yellow Stone* and the men aboard were destined to be challenged
all along the route.

"The Missouri is, perhaps, different in appearance and character
from all other rivers in the world; there is a terror in its manner which
is sensibly felt, the moment we enter its muddy waters from the Mississippi," Catlin reported. "From the mouth of the Yellow Stone River
. . . to its junction with the Mississippi, a distance of 2000 miles, the
Missouri, with its boiling, turbid waters, sweeps off, in one unceasing
current; and in the whole distance there is scarcely an eddy or resting-
place for a canoe. Owing to the continual falling in of its rich alluvial
banks, its water is always . . . muddy and yellow."

Like no other river, the Missouri refused to stay in one place, but
followed an ever-changing serpentine path. Later writers would find
the capricious river as uncertain as "the state of a woman's mind"
or the "action of a jury." It was a river "that goes traveling sidewise,
that interferes in politics, rearranges geography, and dabbles in real
estate."

For a thousand miles above St. Louis, the shores were filled with
snags and branches from large trees, undermined by the falling banks
and cast into the river, their roots becoming fastened to the bottom.
The surface was covered with floating limbs and driftwood. Catlin
found the Missouri to be a "Hell of Waters," but there was also "a re-
deeming beauty in the green and carpeted shores, which hem in this
huge and terrible deformity of waters." Much of the lower river was
lined with mighty cottonwoods, which fell into the river when the
mud and soil washed out from beneath them. The upper river had al-

most no timber, but "beautiful prairies . . . gracefully sloping down to the water's edge, carpeted with the deepest green."

Catlin observed that "the almost insurmountable difficulties which continually oppose the *voyageur* on this turbid stream, have been by degrees overcome by the indefatigable zeal of Mr. Chouteau, a gentleman of great perseverance, and part proprietor of the boat."

Cadet was "vexed," however, because not enough wood had been cut at various places to keep the boat steaming. "The water has lowered and lowers daily; the weather is generally fine and we will make good way if we do not lose part of the day in cutting wood," he reported to Pratte. "Robidoux had some cut at Camp Leavenworth & at his place, but the cottonwoods make a considerable part, together with the box elder reckoned half. We did not touch the former and took a few cords of the latter, not being able to do better. Cabanné had had some cut in three places . . . Mr. Laidlaw has had none cut below the Poncas, and the Lord only knows whether we shall find any above."

Along the route, Indians came to the shore to stare in amazement at what was passing upriver. "If anything did ever literally and completely 'astonish (and astound) the natives,' it was the appearance of our steamer, puffing and blowing, and paddling and rushing by their villages," Catlin wrote. "We had on board one twelve-pound cannon and three or four eight-pound swivels, which we are taking up to arm the Fur Company's Fort at the mouth of Yellow Stone; and at the approach to every village, they were discharged several times in rapid succession, which threw the inhabitants into utter confusion and amazement—some of them laid their faces to the ground and cried to the Great Spirit."

From the Ponca village, along the present-day Nebraska–South Dakota line, the steamer made uninterrupted progress for a few days. "From day to day we advanced, opening our eyes to something new and more beautiful every hour that we progressed, until at last our boat was aground; and a day's work of sounding told us at last, that there was no possibility of advancing further, until there should be a rise in the river, to enable the boat to get over the bar," Catlin wrote. "After laying in the middle of the river about a week, in this unpromising dilemma, Mr. Chouteau started off twenty men on foot, to cross the plains for a distance of 200 miles to Laidlaw's Fort."

Catlin went along on the march of six or seven days across "a verdant green turf of wild grass of six or eight inches in height; and most of the way enamelled with wild flowers, and filled with a profusion of strawberries." When Catlin and his companions reached the new fort, which was to be christened in honor of Pierre Jr. when he managed to get there, Kenneth McKenzie, who had come from Fort Union for the occasion, assembled a team of men and left in a keelboat to meet the stranded vessel.

Catlin set up his easel and went to work. The plain on which Fort Pierre was built stretched eight miles along the Missouri River beneath hills of clay and slate near the mouth of the Bad (Teton) River. The site was just two or three miles from the point to which the Vérendrye brothers had traveled downriver on the Missouri in 1742. It was the trading center for the Teton, Yankton, and Yanktonai Sioux Indians, whose hunting grounds covered the future South Dakota and some adjacent territory.

Exaggerating somewhat on the size of the fort as it was then built, Catlin said that William Laidlaw, the *bougeois*, "has a finely-built fort . . . two or three hundred feet square, enclosing eight or ten of their factories, houses and stores, in the midst of which he occupies spacious and comfortable apartments, which are well supplied with the comforts and luxuries of life and neatly and respectably conducted by a fine looking, modest, and dignified Sioux woman, the kind and affectionate mother of his little flock of pretty and interesting children." The fort was "in the centre of one of the Missouri's most beautiful plains, and hemmed in by a series of gracefully undulating, grass-covered hills, on all sides; rising like a series of terraces, to the summit level of the prairies, some three or four hundred feet in elevation." He painted the spot from atop the bluffs, showing an encampment of six hundred Sioux tents.

Eight days after Catlin's arrival, while he was busy with his paintbrush "and pretty well used to the modes of life in these regions," word went out that at long last the *Yellow Stone* was arriving on the river below the fort. "All ears were listening; when, at length, we discovered the puffing of her steam; and, at last, heard the thundering of her cannon, which were firing from her deck."

"The excitement and dismay caused amongst 6000 of these wild people, when the steamer came up in front of their village, was amusing in the extreme," he noted. "The steamer was moored at the shore, however . . . and the whole village gathered in front of the boat."

It was about 5 p.m. on May 31, 1832, when the *Yellow Stone* steamed up beneath the new fort. Flags were hoisted on the vessel and were run up the towering flagpole in the center of the fort compound, visible for many miles around. There were warm embraces and friendly greetings between those on the boat and those onshore.

The new fort was christened and formally named Fort Pierre Chouteau Jr. A few days later the Sioux gave a great feast for the visiting white dignitaries. The two Sioux chiefs formed their tents into a giant semicircle to accommodate 150 men. The guests of honor were Pierre Jr., Sanford, McKenzie, and Catlin. In the center, the hosts ran a white flag up a staff to which a calumet was also tied. A feast of dog meat was cooking in six or eight kettles that would be served in wooden bowls.

Catlin saw "thousands climbing and crowding around, for a peep at the grand pageant." The head chief spoke. Noting the presence of Pierre Jr., he addressed himself to McKenzie with these words: "Our friend who is on your right-hand we all know is very rich; and we have heard that he owns the great medicine-canoe; he is a good man, and a friend to the red men." He went on to say, "We have killed our faithful dogs to feed you — and the Great Spirit will seal our friendship."

The whites kept up a brave front but had difficulty partaking of the meal, tasting from the bowls a few times, then passing them to their hosts.

On June 5, after crewmen had spent several days chopping wood, the *Yellow Stone* departed on its continuing voyage to Fort Clark near the Mandan villages and Fort Union at the mouth of the Yellowstone River. Catlin, like Pierre Jr., was back on board. A few days later the boat approached Fort Clark among the Mandans about noon, firing a twenty-gun twelve-pound salute as it came to within three or four miles of the first village. Thinking they were hearing thunder, crowds of Mandans gathered to wait for much-needed rain. Instead, they soon saw "the steam-boat ploughing its way up the windings of the river below; puffing her steam from her pipes and sending forth the thunder from a twelve-pounder on her deck!"

Most of those in the village climbed to the tops of their lodges or ran to the riverbank for a better view. Confused about what was happening, they decided to arm themselves for defense, then disappeared from view as the steamer moored. "Three or four of the chiefs, soon after, walked boldly down the bank and on to her deck, with a spear in one hand and the calumet or pipe of peace in the other," Catlin said. "The moment they stepped on board they met (to their great surprise and joy) their old friend, Major Sanford, their agent, which circumstance put an instant end to all their fears. The villagers were soon apprized of the fact, and the whole race of the beautiful and friendly Mandans was paraded on the bank of the river, in front of the steamer."

From Fort Clark, the steamboat took a few more days to reach Fort Union, where McKenzie and his men had put together 600 packs of buffalo robes, each pack containing 100 robes carefully dressed and softened by Indian women. The vessel then started its return voyage, arriving back at Fort Pierre on June 23. By the time it left Fort Pierre on June 25, the valuable cargo had grown to 1,300 packs of buffalo robes and beaver pelts.

On its return voyage, the *Yellow Stone* raced down the Missouri River, averaging a hundred miles a day, five times its speed on the upriver voyage. It steamed triumphantly into St. Louis on July 7. The successful voyage, establishing the viability of steamboats on the upper stretches of the country's most daunting river, drew much attention in the newspapers and elsewhere. Astor, who was in Europe, saw news of it there.

"The future historian of [the] Missouri will preserve for you the honorable and enviable distinction of having accomplished an object of immense importance," Ramsay Crooks told Cadet. "By exhibiting the practicability of conquering the obstructions of the Missouri, considered till almost the present day insurmountable to steamboats, even among those best acquainted with their capabilities—you have brought the Falls of the Missouri as near comparatively as was the River Platte in my younger days, and you deserve all the advantages your successful enterprise may produce."

"Your voyage in the *Yellow Stone* attracted much attention in Europe & has been noticed in all the Papers here," Astor wrote. He wanted to know how the boat behaved, what the Indians thought of her, how far up the river it had gone, and about the firm's prospects in the region. However, Astor also had a growing concern about the state of the markets. "I very much fear beaver will not sell well very soon unless very fine," he said, "it appears that they make hats of silk in place of beaver."

Catlin had remained behind at Fort Union to paint Indians and scenery. McKenzie gave him one of the bastions as a second-floor studio looking out over the river and prairie, and Catlin sat on the breech of a twelve-pound swivel gun in front of his easel. Like nearly everyone who observed McKenzie in operation, Catlin was impressed by the Fort Union *bourgeois*. He noted that McKenzie exerted great effort in keeping peace among the tribes. For several weeks, two belligerent tribes, the Crees and Blackfeet, were camped on different sides of the fort, in wigwams or lodges made of buffalo skins. McKenzie insisted that they give him all their guns and other weapons, which he locked up for the duration of their visit.

After painting at Fort Union for several weeks, Catlin started back down the Missouri in a canoe with two crewmen. He stopped for a while among the Mandans around Fort Clark, then continued to Fort Pierre, leaving there again on August 16. Before departing Fort Union, he was presented with an invoice for the charges he had made in the company stores, including purchases of socks, nails, elk skins, soap, ribbon, an ax, spoons, coffee, sugar, salt, a cup, shot, and a skiff. The total bill was $61.63. The American Fur Company bought two paintings from him for $30, which went against the bill, leaving a cash due amount of $31.63.

❊

The Louisiana Purchase territory had previously slipped through the cracks of the American government's policy of prohibiting liquor among Indians. Congress first prohibited it in 1802, before the lands west of the Mississippi were acquired, and the American Fur Company obtained a subsequent court ruling that the "carrying of spirituous liquors" into a territory acquired by the United States after 1802 would not subject the goods of the trader in question to seizure. However, an act passed on May 6, 1822, gave the President the power to have officers and agents search for liquor in traders' goods and to cancel trading licenses if liquor was found. This left a lot of discretion to government representatives in the field.

As superintendent of Indian affairs at St. Louis, William Clark was sympathetic to the needs of the fur traders, and he regularly issued permits to the A.F.C. and other firms for ample supplies of liquor, supposedly to be used by boatmen during their tough upriver voyages. The amount he regularly authorized for each man was many times what one boatman might reasonably consume, which left a quantity for use in the Indian trade.

Now, however, a stronger prohibition was making its way through Congress. For at least a year before the second upriver voyage of the *Yellow Stone*, the Astors had been urging Cadet and Pratte to get involved in Washington to influence the outcome of that law. Bill Astor argued that their best chance of limiting its scope lay with their congressman, William Ashley, the former Missouri lieutenant governor who had briefly worked for the A.F.C. before being elected to Congress.

"The subject is one involving very materially the interest, if not the existence of our new posts above the Mandans," Bill Astor wrote Cadet, "and I would suggest . . . you . . . take an early opportunity of pressing the matter for the attention of General Ashley . . . as he is your Representative in Congress, and you have a claim upon him as one of his constituents as well as a personal friend."

That effort had not really begun by July 1832, when a bill passed Congress excluding spirituous liquors from the Indian country, whether they were intended for boatmen and traders or for Indians. An exemption in the new law continued to allow the use of liquor by military personnel in Indian country, such as those posted at Leavenworth.

Barton H. Barbour, in his history of Fort Union, cites one government witness as saying that the *Yellow Stone*, on its April voyage upriver in 1832, had taken about 1,500 gallons of liquor, seemingly under permit from Clark. This is at least partially substantiated by a letter written by Pierre Jr. from Philadelphia in January 1832 to an associate in St. Louis directing him to contact a supplier in St. Louis "to find out at what price he would furnish us 7 to 8000 gallons" of whiskey. This was probably part of the load taken upriver on the first voyage in 1832.

As Pierre Jr. steamed back to St. Louis at the beginning of July, he heard about the new liquor prohibition. Arriving on July 7, he decided to turn the ship around and send it back to the Upper Missouri with a new load of liquor for the next season, hoping to get beyond Leavenworth before enforcement was in place. Clark authorized Cadet to take a large amount on this second voyage, on the pretense that he had not yet received positive orders regarding the prohibition. Barbour, citing Clark's correspondence in the Office of Indian Affairs, places the additional amount at 1,072 gallons. Other correspondence of the time refers to 37 barrels, which would have been about 1,147 gallons, and also to 28 barrels, about 868 gallons.

When the *Yellow Stone* docked for inspection at Leavenworth on August 2, soldiers confiscated most of the barrels of liquor onboard. Cabanné was traveling with the steamboat and reported back to Cadet. In a note that is a bit difficult to interpret, he said, "27 barrels have been unloaded and 6 barrels remain, which must have escaped inspection. In the future we will oversee better." This indicates that the total shipment was at least thirty-three barrels. But he also mentioned four barrels intended "for consumption," and said "the officer of the day offered to leave me 5 barrels of rum for drinking aboard." He said the confiscated liquor would be picked up at Leavenworth on the return voyage of the *Yellow Stone*, then stored at an A.F.C. post at Liberty, Missouri, while Cadet sought approval to take it upriver.

Back in St. Louis, William Clark, deciding not to acknowledge his authorization of the liquor shipment, complained to the A.F.C. about its attempted violation of the law. The A.F.C. responded in an un-signed one-page letter that it had had a permit from Clark to take the liquor upriver and requested a ruling from him or the Secretary of War as to whether the firm would be allowed to take the liquor into Indian country.

While this game was being played out in St. Louis, Cabanné worried that some of the smaller trading outfits would manage to slip through the inspection at Leavenworth and then have the advantage over the A.F.C. in the upper country. He was particularly concerned about an opposition trader named Narcisse Leclerc.

A month later, Leclerc's keelboat, carrying whiskey authorized by Clark, was cleared through Leavenworth with all the liquor on board. A few days later, as Leclerc's boat approached the Bluffs, Cabanné led a group of twenty armed A.F.C. men to stop it. Not knowing for certain whether the boat was carrying a large supply of liquor, Cabanné justified the action on the grounds that Leclerc was carrying three or four men who had recently deserted from his outfit. Aiming a loaded swivel gun at Leclerc's boat, he forced Leclerc to hand over the men in question. Leclerc then continued on his way upriver.

After being put in irons and interrogated, the deserters confirmed to Cabanné his suspicion that the keelboat was carrying whiskey. So a group of Cabanné's *engagés*, led by his second-in-command, Peter A. Sarpy, chased after the keelboat, catching it twelve days later. Informing Leclerc that he was there to confiscate illegal liquor on behalf of the government, Sarpy began searching the vessel and opening containers. Lacking the manpower to resist, and not wanting to lose his valuable cargo, Leclerc retreated downriver, eventually returning all the way to St. Louis, where he filed legal action to collect for his losses.

Reaction among the principals in the American Fur Company varied between indignation at the government for the actions of its agents and shocked embarrassment at Cabanné's boldness.

"Entertaining as I have always done the most favorable opinion of Mr. Cabanné for moderation and invariably correct deportment, I confess my surprise at [the Leclerc] affair," Bill Astor wrote Cadet. "It is no doubt very aggravating and provoking to see how the agents of government wilfully neglect their duty to our manifest injury; but no matter how much our opponent was in the wrong, Mr. Cabanné had certainly no right to take the law into his own hands—The effect of this unwarrantable affair cannot be otherwise than injurious to the company, and I fear the public will conclude that because we are strong, we are willing to be unjust."

Almost at the same time Cabanné was facing Leclerc over the barrel of a gun, the Astors and Ramsay Crooks were using their influence in Washington in an effort to soften the prohibition on liquor in Indian country. Kenneth McKenzie traveled from the Upper Missouri to Washington to assist them. The timing of the visits to Washington and the Cabanné-Leclerc confrontation did not help either case.

"The affair between Mssrs. Cabanné & Leclerc produced a very strong sensation at Washington," Bill Astor told Cadet. "At first the Department was inclined to revoke the license, order Mr. Cabanné & Mr. Sarpy out of the [fur] country . . . But on further reflection a more moderate course was pursued & Genl Clark was ordered to call upon the accused for their justifications."

The Secretary of War "was deaf to every thing short of complete & entire prohibition and all that could be obtained was the promise that the government would cordially exert itself to induce the Court of Great Britain to interdict the use of spiritous liquors in the territories of the Hudsons Bay Company," Astor said. Crooks found Secretary of War Cass to be "a temperance society man in every sense of the word."

Astor and Crooks had earlier failed to get the sympathetic help they had expected from William Ashley, the Missouri congressman. "We appealed to your representative Genl Ashly relying upon his knowledge of the matter to sustain us in the propriety of our reasonable request," Bill Astor wrote to Cadet,

> but instead of aiding, he was decidedly opposed to us, and as he was presumed to be intimately acquainted with the subject for his having been for years among the Indians, I have no doubt his opinion operated strongly against the modification we proposed—which was, that it might be lawful for the President, or Secretary of War to permit the

introduction of such a quantity as in their discretion was deemed necessary to enable us to cope with the Hudson's Bay Company's traders who had an unlimited supply and would now make use of that and all the other means to drive us from the country where we come into competition with them.

As the government investigation went forward, along with Leclerc's suit against the A.F.C. and Cabanné, Bill Astor told Pierre Jr. to advise Cabanné to give Clark as brief a detail as possible of the occurrence. "The strong point of defence in my opinion should be that at the time Leclerc was stopped and brought back he was violating the law of the land excluding ardent spirits entirely from the Indian country, that Genl Clark's permission was no protection after the act of 9 July 1832 was published & with its provisions Mr. Leclerc was bound to be acquainted." But that argument did not prevail. The Western Department of the A.F.C. eventually settled with Leclerc for $9,200, and Cabanné was banned from the Indian country for a year.

None of this dimmed the enthusiasm of Pierre Jr. and his partners for the use of the steamboat in the fur trade. On October 12, 1832, Bernard Pratte, on behalf of the company, signed an agreement with the craftsman Burton Hazen in Cincinnati to build a second steamboat, bigger and more commodious. This one was to be 133 feet long, with a twenty-foot beam and a six-foot hold, "with timber & planks the same as in the S. B. *Yellow Stone*, but flatter and fuller than the said boat." It was to have forty-eight spaces for beds, including six in staterooms of two beds each, and a barroom.

The boat was to be ready to receive her engine on January 20–25, 1833, and all of Hazen's work was to be completed by February 25, 1833. The cost was $4,600, payable in $500 segments, with the final one of $600, which would be forfeited if the boat was not ready on time. Pratte hired three other men in Cincinnati—Joseph Pierce, Anthony Harkness, and a Mr. Voorhees—to build a steam engine for the new boat at a cost of $5,300. This put the total cost of the vessel at $9,900.

The new vessel was christened the S.B. *Assiniboine* in honor of the Upper Missouri tribe that ceded part of its land for the construction of

Fort Union, and which McKenzie and Pierre Jr. had, by opening Fort Union, managed to wean away from dependence on British traders.

But construction of the boat quickly ran into labor difficulties caused by a dreaded killer making its way south from Canada. "Cholera here makes it difficult to procure workmen," Bernard Pratte Jr. wrote from Cincinnati, where he was overseeing the construction. "I do not think the boat will be ready within 15 days of time specified . . . About 42 citizens are dying here every day."

Cholera was ravishing areas of Canada and had come as far as "Chigou," where it killed many of the troops posted there under General Winfield Scott. Ramsay Crooks wrote from New York that the disease had brought business in the city to a standstill. John Jacob Astor found that it was sweeping Europe as well. His daughter and her husband were recovering.

This new health crisis hit the Missouri River country as the toll was still being calculated from the smallpox outbreak of the year before. Traders were telling people that 900 to 1,000 men and 1,200 to 1,500 women and children of the Pawnee tribe had died of smallpox. But it had made few inroads among the Mahas and Otoes, because they had been vaccinated.

"I do not urge you to come down this year because of the terrible illness that is visiting the entire globe at this time, whose ravages are greatest where the population is most nombrous," one of the Chouteau cousins, Pierre Didier Papin, wrote from St. Louis to warn his brother Millicour, who was among the Osages. "The newspapers that come here from all other places tell of great numbers of deaths. In Canada 10, 15 or 20 persons die every day and in all other countries the same proportion. Do not let this frighten you, for temperate people and those who lead a good life are rarely attacked . . . cholera has not yet come to our country & yet we suppose that it will make us also a visit, but in the end it does not do to be afraid; one must follow a regime, abstaining from eating every kind of vegetable."

The disease eventually made its way all over the Missouri and Mississippi river country. George Davenport, from the future site of the Iowa town that would bear his name, wrote his partner in the post, Russell Farnham, who was in St. Louis visiting his wife and child, about "the terrible disease that has broke out amongst us. The

Cholera—our island is now a burying ground. More than one sixth of the troops stationed here have died during the last 6 days. The disease is yet raging. I am not very well. If I do not see you again God Bless you."

A few days later Davenport wrote Cadet that nearly 100 out of 400 men on Rock Island had died of cholera. He warned that if the disease reached St. Louis, everyone should leave, and he recommended "salt and vinegar to stop the puking."

At the end of September Davenport advised that Rock Island was again healthy. But by then the disease had arrived in St. Louis, and medical science could offer little in the way of cures or prevention.

"We have had here for some time a sickness known by the name of Asiatic Cholera, which has made great ravages and has carried off at least two hundred persons of both sexes, every age, every condition and color," wrote another of the Papin brothers to his brother Millicour. He continued with advice:

> It is an illness whose first symptoms are loose bowels, pains in the stomach and abdomen. One must immediately go to bed and drink rice-water. If the pains continue, add 5 or 6 drops of laudanum to the rice-water, and if it continues put on the stomach, the abdomen and at the feet some mustard plasters, and put bricks or hot irons at the feet. If the pain continues apply cupping-glasses to the stomach, give some ether in a small quantity with one ounce of castor-oil as a purgative after the pains have calmed down.
>
> The ether is preferable to the laudanum. Sudorifics (to cause sweating) are effectual—drink very cold and very little—to cool the interior and warm the exterior—This is the method of treatment of a New York doctor, Mr. Berger—whose recipe has been sent here to Madame Pratte by Madame Crooks.
>
> Our doctors here treat it by administering ten or fifteen grains of calomel mixed with a grain of opium for every ten grains of calomel and three or four hours later a dose of castor-oil, and those who follow this treatment in time get well, but woe to him who waits until the appearance of cramps.

The *St. Louis Beacon* published the advice of a Cincinnati physician, Daniel Drake, M.D.: "As soon as feeling sick to the stomach, go to bed in a warm room, drink hot herb tea or just hot water and bath the feet if cold. Take a powder of 10 grains of Calomel and one gram of opium, mixed, for adults; smaller portion for children or a teaspoon of powdered rhubarb."

"May this destructive scourge not visit you," wrote another St. Louis correspondent to Millicour Papin, "but in case it does the remedy our doctors employ is ten grains of calomel (compounded used as a purgative) every two hours until movement of the bowels and change in the color of excrement. Eat nothing, drink little; for a beverage rice-water and toast-and-water; stay in bed until no longer feeble. A few drops of hartshorn in rice-water is efficacious for perspiration; the symptom of this dangerous malady is diarrhoea without pain, but rumbling in the bowels."

Charles Dehault Delassus, who had been the last Spanish governor of Upper Louisiana and was now retired in New Orleans, wrote a friend in St. Louis about the cholera's impact there:

> Here it has also made frightful ravages amongst all classes, and especially amongst the colored and unfortunately on the farms, among the workshops of the negroes where it is not yet over . . . I flatter myself that you have not had the same horrors before your eyes as we here, in regard to the dead who fell rigid in the streets on the levee and hence the great number of corpses strewn in every direction before being taken to the cemeteries, where a great part remained twelve hours before being buried. The authorities could not find for gold nor silver anyone who would come near.

In Cincinnati, where he was still watching over the construction of the *Assiniboine*, Bernard Pratte Jr. picked up a St. Louis newspaper one day and saw news of the deaths of several acquaintances and relatives, including "Madame Paul," his aunt. The thirty-three-year-old wife of Gabriel Paul, born Marie Louise Chouteau, was one of the daughters of Auguste Chouteau.

Another St. Louis victim was George Davenport's partner and card-playing friend Russell Farnham, the man who had walked across Siberia in his youth and whom Davenport had thought safe in St. Louis while death hung over Rock Island. Stricken by the disease on October 23, Farnham died within hours.

Born in Massachusetts, Farnham had taken part in the seaborne portion of the 1810–13 Astoria Expedition, traveling on the ill-fated *Tonquin* around Cape Horn and up the Pacific coast, where the ship was destroyed. Surviving the disaster, Farnham was landed at Kamchatka by another ship and entrusted to carry to Astor in New York the $40,000 worth of drafts with which the British North West Company had bought out the Astor group.

"Poor Farnham!" lamented his old friend and fellow Astoria survivor, Ramsay Crooks, on learning of Farnham's death.

> He has paid the debt of nature after a life of uncommon activity & endless exposure . . . He was one of the best meaning, but the most sanguine man I almost ever met with.
>
> During all the ravages of the pestilence here, and the unexpected rapidity with which some of my friends were hurried to their long account, I never felt anything like the sensation I experienced upon hearing of my honest friend's death—for I did not know he was at St. Louis and thought him safe in some part of the Wilderness.

THIRTEEN

A. P. Chouteau: Star-Crossed Hero

✴

From his earliest days, Auguste Pierre Chouteau, Cadet's older brother, displayed immense potential. He finished fourth in his class at West Point, was cool under fire, had a commanding presence, and was highly intelligent, brave, generous, handsome, and charming. As he matured, he had the manners of the French drawing room and the suntanned vigor of an American cowboy. Probably no one from the Chouteau family so bridged the three cultures in which they lived — French, Indian, and the American frontier's — as did Auguste Pierre.

His skill in dealing with Indians matched, and possibly exceeded, that of his father. The Osages came to consider him "our old and well tried friend." He was once ready to lead them into battle to defend the United States from the British. But any Indians prone to horse stealing and other thieving found that he could erupt into a rage and threaten eternal exclusion from the right to trade with white men.

He was a witty raconteur and spinner of stories who enchanted educated travelers to the exotic West. Women flocked to him. As a youth, he won the admiration of William Clark. Later, Sam Houston found him a great drinking and gambling buddy and fellow schemer against the ways of Washington. Andrew Jackson and his Cabinet Secretaries regarded him as a man of wisdom and reflection.

His strong handwriting, in both French and English, and his bold signature, A. P. Chouteau — distinguishing him from all the other Augustes and Pierres in the family — seemed to say that this was a man determined to leave his imprint.

By the time he turned thirty, however, he had abandoned his military career, after just six months of active duty, and tried and failed in two ventures that were supposed to put him on the road to fortune. He was so burdened with debts, particularly to Cadet and his partners, that he set forth on a new life of virtual exile from home and family in hopes of repaying his debts and salvaging dreams of success.

Coming back from the disastrous expedition to Santa Fe and Taos in 1817 with Jules de Mun, he crossed part of the area he had come to know while working for his father as Indian subagent to the Arkansas River branch of the Osages. The mountains and the Southwest having lost their attraction for him in the days he spent in the dungeons in Santa Fe, he surely found the great openness, the merciless sun, and the vast sky of the plains welcoming and soothing.

Once back in St. Louis, he and de Mun and his cousin John B. Sarpy joined the crowded business scene with their own merchant house. De Mun soon backed out to run a family property in Cuba, and the firm of Chouteau & Sarpy opened in the winter of 1819–20 in a new brick building at 94 North Main, with capital borrowed from Cadet and his partner, Bartholomew Berthold. A.P. built a two-story frame house for his wife and children a few doors away. But the business had to shut its doors in 1821, with its debts added to what A.P. already owed to Cadet's firm. Sarpy soon became a partner in Cadet's reorganized company, but A.P. still had his own dreams to follow.

One of the things A.P.'s merchant house had done during its short life was to acquire a license to trade among the Osages on the Arkansas River. The first license was issued in August 1817, while A.P. was still returning from Santa Fe, to his brother Paul Liguest Chouteau and Joseph Revoir,* a frontiersman who was part French and part Indian. They located the trading house in the northeastern corner of the future Oklahoma, where the Verdigris and Grand rivers flow into the Arkansas, in the vicinity of the eventual towns of Fort Gibson, Muskogee, and Claremore. The area was known as the Three Forks.

They chose a spot called La Saline as their headquarters and also bought an existing establishment about thirty miles to the south,

*Later generations of this family also spelled the name Rivard and Revard.

closer to the mouth of the Verdigris, from two traders named Brand and Barbour. The Saline took its name from a salt spring rising from limestone rock extending over an acre or two. The Verdigris property consisted of ten to twelve log houses, thirty acres of farmland, and a ferry.

Revoir was to run the post. Before he could get it fully operational, however, he was murdered in 1821 by a Cherokee band angry about his close ties to the Osages.

As the result, in the summer of 1822, the year after Missouri became a state, A.P. set forth from St. Louis to take over the post left vacant by the death of Revoir, intending to use Berthold & Chouteau, Cadet's firm, to supply his trade goods and sell his pelts. With the remaining Osages in Missouri expected to be pushed entirely out of the new state, he wanted to attract them to his post. He envisioned becoming the trading center for all the bands of the Osages, who would range far westward through the Arkansas River valley on their hunting expeditions and return to trade their skins and furs to him.

From its headwaters in the Sangre de Cristo Mountains in Colorado, the Arkansas flows eastward into the plains, arcs north into central Kansas, then heads southeast and crosses the corner of Oklahoma before flowing into the state of Arkansas at Fort Smith. It meanders through Arkansas to empty into the Mississippi near the spot where Pierre Laclède was buried. A. P. Chouteau reasoned that this river and its tributaries presented a potential for pelts as good as that of the Upper Missouri. Further, it was an easy route to the Mississippi and the markets at New Orleans. He judged the Arkansas to be navigable for seven hundred miles for steamboats, barges, and keelboats during four or five months of the year.

The slightly elevated country appealed to him for its natural richness, its relatively mild climate, and its abundance of game. By comparison to the Upper Missouri region, its climate was mild, winters never cold—except when the winds came sweeping out of the mountains and across the great prairies. Snowfalls were generally light and did not remain long on the ground.

"The soil is fertile; the country abounds in fresh water springs boiling either through gravel or limestone rock, and it also abounds in salt water, much of it very strong," he said years after he moved to the area. It had timber comparable to that along the Mississippi, including oak, black walnut, hickory, ash, hackberry, locust, mulberry, pine, cedar, pecan, cherry, and Osage orange. The region had indigenous fruits, and livestock feasted on its grasses. The wild game included buffalo, elk, deer, antelopes, bears, and furred animals. Wild horses were so numerous that he had seen "the face of this country covered with them as far as the eye could reach . . . The same remark is still more applicable to the buffalo."

When A.P. left St. Louis in late July 1822 to carry out this grand design, he also escorted a Belgian-born priest, Charles de la Croix, who planned visits to various Osage villages in western Missouri, on the edge of what was now Indian Territory—the future state of Kansas. Among other things, the priest would conduct baptisms of mixed-blood children. When they arrived at the village of the Big Osages, led by Young White Hair, whose father had risen to leadership of the tribe with the support of A.P.'s father, they found the principal men awaiting a visit from government agents. The agents had been pressuring the tribe to move onto lands outside the boundaries of the new state, perhaps along the Neosho River* about forty miles to the west. Statehood meant that the Osages were soon to be crowded out of the remaining strip of land, some twenty-five miles wide, running south from the Missouri River along the western border of their traditional home state. Other bands of Osages had already moved to the Neosho, where A.P.'s brother Paul Liguest traded with them and would soon open a permanent trading post.

A.P. broached to tribal leaders his plan that they select a new site farther south along the Grand River, near where it flowed into the Arkansas—and near his new trading post. The tribe was then preparing to head out to the plains for the summer hunt, but before leaving, tribal leaders decided not to return to their Missouri village after the hunt. Accompanied by a cook, traders, and wagoners, A.P. went with

---

*The Grand and the Neosho are the same river, which came to be called Neosho in Kansas and Grand after flowing into Oklahoma.

them on the hunt along the Arkansas River into the middle of the future Kansas.

In late September, after the hunt, at least part of the tribe followed A.P. to his new establishment. In mid-November, barges and keelboats loaded with trade merchandise to stock the post were seen passing Union Mission, a Protestant mission and school established in 1821 along the Grand between the Saline and the Verdigris post.

However, Young White Hair and his followers hung around the Saline for nearly a year without making or planning a more permanent settlement of their own. A.P. fed them for the duration. But late in the summer of 1823 they returned to Missouri and met with those in the tribe who had remained or had gone to the Neosho. They decided to create their new permanent village on the Neosho in present-day southeastern Kansas instead of building it farther south near A.P.'s post. They departed for the Neosho the next day.

Young White Hair and several other Big and Little Osage villages ended up being situated seventy to eighty miles by land north of A.P.'s location. The remaining group, known as Clermont's band, which had broken away years earlier from the Missouri group, kept its village near the future Claremore, Oklahoma, less than thirty miles west of the Saline.

A.P. still hoped to control trade with all of them through various branch posts. He quickly put out appeals for furs and skins from the Indians, ordered trade goods from St. Louis, and put together packets of skins and furs for shipment to New Orleans. In 1823 and 1824 he lived and did business from the Verdigris post, while his cousin Millicour Papin ran trading operations at the Saline. After A.P. moved into a two-story home at the Saline, he turned the Verdigris site into a small boatbuilding operation.

Somewhat nervous as a new entrepreneur, he warned Millicour against sleeping too much during the day and fretted about whether Paul Liguest had enough business sense to operate on his own.

"I am always fearful that he will be the dupe of others, owing to his implicit faith in everyone," A.P. said of his younger brother.

Trying to quiet Millicour's anger about coming out on the short end in a business deal with some members of Young White Hair's band, A.P. told him that he should trade with the Indians if they had skins or credits and not worry about side issues.

"It is true that vengeance is natural to all men, nevertheless, it should not cause them to lose their heads to the extent that they are forgetful of their first duty," he said. "After having displayed your resentment, you should bear in mind that my main object is fur."

Returns were hopeful in the first full season of operations. In January 1824 A.P. collected 4,445 pelts, among them beaver, otter, wildcat, bear, and fat bear cubs. A few days later he reported having 127 packs made up and 45 to 50 yet to do.

At the beginning of April he sent his "big barge" on its way south with 364 packs of deerskins, 300 bearskins, 160 bear cub skins, 387 beaver, 67 otter, 720 raccoon, and 95 wildcat and fox, in addition to 726 deerskins being shipped for another trader. He was waiting for a shipment from Paul Liguest before setting out by canoe to catch up with the barge and see it safely to the Mississippi.

But a few months later A.P. was suddenly worried that the new season would not turn out well. "The men have all been very ill," he wrote to his brother Cadet and others at what had been renamed B. Pratte & Company. "No hunting this summer; forty-five packs of red deerskin and 2,500 lbs. of buffalo tallow is all we have made." That was too little to justify the expense of sending them to New Orleans. He was already beginning to look for other ways to make money, perhaps by selling goods to the soldiers who were arriving in the area to build Fort Gibson, but he was also uncertain whether there was enough business to justify his staying in the area. "For the next year, I should let you know in good time whether it is I or another who will direct the business with the Osages," he wrote.

He continued, however. In 1825, what was called the "Osage Outfit" of B. Pratte & Company grew to four trading posts. They were located at the Little Osage village on the Marais des Cygnes River in the future Kansas, kept that year by A.P.'s half brothers François Gesseau and Cyprien; at the Saline, now kept by his cousin Auguste Aristide; on the Neosho ten miles below Young White Hair's village, kept by Millicour Papin, who had moved north from the Saline; and at the Verdigris post, where another half brother, the ailing Louis Pharamond, was helping A.P. as clerk. Paul Liguest continued on the Neosho. In 1825 the four posts handled about $30,000 worth of goods.

A routine developed that twice a year, in late spring and late fall, the peltries traded from the Indians after their twice-a-year hunts were floated down to New Orleans on barges, then shipped to New York and perhaps onward to Europe. A.P. often went to New Orleans with the spring shipment, and in later years he went to New York to oversee the sales himself.

At the same time, A.P. was creating a substantial living establishment, a primitive plantation that many visitors equated to the estate and lifestyle of a feudal lord. He built what was an impressive home for the time and place, which he shared with a family of children he fathered by four Osage or part-Osage women. By 1825 he had seven children by them. His most durable relationship was that with Rosalie Lambert, a pretty girl who bore him two sons by the time she reached sixteen. She lived with A.P. for the rest of his life and was widely viewed as his wife. Rosalie was born in 1809 to an Osage mother and what was called a *métis* French, or French-Indian, father.

A.P. brought a carriage from St. Louis for Rosalie and her older sister, Masina, who lived with them and was the mother of three of his children. He hired a tutor for the children and sent at least one of them to a Protestant mission school. He had a racecourse built on a level stretch of prairie a quarter mile from the house and put together a stable of horses. He planted two paradise trees on the lawn.

At home, and whenever he traveled, A.P. seemed always to be surrounded by crowds of admirers, retainers, slaves, children, lovers, and supplicants. Dogs and cats were at peace around him, and the dogs were given fanciful names that reflected his political views and his humor. Henry Clay was a greyhound, Jackson was a bulldog, and Mrs. Trollope was a hound.

After establishing the post at the Saline in 1822, A.P. lived principally on the frontier for the remainder of his life—without completely abandoning his legal wife, Sophie Labbadie, in St. Louis. From the time of their marriage in 1813 until he moved to the Saline, he and Sophie had nine children. Three of them died as infants and a fourth at fourteen. Two additional babies were born in St. Louis after he left, indicating that he continued to spend time with Sophie during visits to St. Louis. However, in a family where many members—including his brother Pierre Jr. and half brother François—were open about expressing their affection for wives and children, A.P.'s surviving letters are remarkable for their lack of references to his wife, suggesting that they had a far from good marriage. In fact, no letters from him to her could be found among his substantial surviving correspondence. He had some continuing contact with his St. Louis children and occasionally mentioned them in letters to his siblings or business associates. His eldest St. Louis son, Augustine A. Chouteau, joined his father on the frontier for a period after he grew up, and A.P. placed his second St. Louis son, Pierre Sylvestre, in a school in Philadelphia. A daughter from St. Louis visited him at the Saline.

The surviving records of some of the births of part-Osage children fathered by A.P., plus various of his brothers and cousins, are the result of work by Jesuits and other Roman Catholic priests, who, like Father de la Croix, began traveling into the Indian country of western Missouri and beyond in 1822. Protestant missionaries began work in the region about the same time, but the French were mostly Catholic, so they took their children by Indian women to the priests to be baptized. At times the priests would record the births as being illegitimate, but more often than not they simply stated the names of the father and godfather. Unless the mother was part French and had a European first name, she was usually not identified, or identified only as "Achinga," meaning Osage woman.

A.P.'s first known mixed-blood child was Auguste Clermont Chouteau, born to Masina. No baptismal record has been located for this boy, but he was listed as being nine years old when he was admitted to the Harmony Mission School in western Missouri on January 28, 1824. This means that Auguste Clermont would have been born in 1814 or 1815, coinciding with the period in which A.P. was working for his father as government subagent to the Arkansas River Osages. The name given the baby suggests that Masina, the mother, may have been from Clermont's village, which was within the territory of A.P.'s responsibility at the time.

After the birth of Auguste Clermont and up through the middle of

1825, A.P. had at least six other children by women of the Osage tribe, including two more by Masina—Auguste Gesseau and Paul Auguste. He had two sons by Rosalie—Henry and Auguste James. And he had two daughters, both named Amelia, by different women, one named She-me-hunga and the other named Mi-hun-ga.

Perhaps the most intriguing of A.P.'s relationships with Osage women was that with the woman named Mi-hun-ga, whom various historians have concluded was the strikingly beautiful Osage painted by Charles Bird King after her return in 1830 from a two-year trip to Paris and other European cities. That portrait became part of the historic McKenney and Hall collection of Indian paintings.

The woman, holding a baby young enough to have been conceived and born during the trip, was identified by King as "Mohongo," but others have written the name as Mihonga. Both spellings are close to Mi-hun-ga, the spelling A.P. used for the mother of one of his daughters. The baby girl was born prior to 1825—well before the woman in the painting and five other Osages departed on the tour of Europe. Thus the child in the King painting could not be A.P.'s, even if the woman was the mother of his Amelia. He apparently had nothing directly to do with the trip to Europe, but it was organized by Paul Loise and David Delaunay, two men with ties to his father. The Osages were the toast of Paris for many months, and Mohongo was received at St.-Cloud by King Charles X in August 1827. After money and hospitality ran out, they came home broke, requiring help from the Marquis de Lafayette to obtain passage.

When priests began baptisms among the Osages in May 1822, two of the first baptized were identified in the record as children of A.P.'s brother, Paul Liguest, and his half brother, François. Another child baptized in 1822 was a five-year-old boy identified by the priest only as Antoine Chouteau; no parent was recorded, but Paul Liguest was listed as godfather. In addition, the Chouteaus and their cousin Millicour Papin were the godfathers in thirteen of the May 1822 baptisms. Rosalie Lambert, soon to become A.P.'s companion, was also among those baptized; she was thirteen at the time. When Father de la Croix returned to the area with A.P. in August of that year, he baptized five more children, and members of the Chouteau family were the godfathers for four of them.

In the summer of 1827 Father Peter C. Van Quickenborne, a Jesuit, conducted another round of baptisms—eighteen on August 21, 1827, at Harmony Mission in Missouri and seventeen additional baptisms six days later at Paul Liguest Chouteau's place on the Neosho in present-day Kansas. Among them was the three-year-old son of A.P. by Masina. Although christened Auguste Gesseau, the boy would be known throughout his life as Gesso or Jesse. Also baptized were a two-year-old boy fathered by A.P.'s cousin Auguste Aristide and two sons and a daughter of Paul Liguest Chouteau. Paul Liguest was married twice in St. Louis, but both wives died following childbirth, leaving him with just two St. Louis children who grew to adulthood, both boys. He eventually accumulated a large number of children among the Osages, with one or more children baptized in 1825, 1826, 1827, 1828, and 1842.

In 1825, three years after A.P. moved to the Saline, William Clark negotiated a new treaty with the Osages under which—as had been expected—they had to give up all their remaining land in Missouri and concentrate within a strip of land running along the eastern edge of present-day Kansas and into northeastern Oklahoma. They were still to be allowed to hunt on open lands to the west of their assigned lands. In exchange for their land concessions, the Big and Little Osages were to receive an annuity of $7,000 a year for twenty years, plus 600 head of cattle, 600 hogs, 1,000 fowl, 10 yoke of oxen, and farming tools. One part of the reduced Osage area, that around Clermont's village, bumped up against areas into which Cherokees had been moving for more than ten years and would soon become the source of friction between the two tribes.

The 1825 treaty also set aside specific land allotments for more than forty people identified in the treaty as "half-breeds," a measure that was to became increasingly the custom in Indian country as full-blood Indians retained communal rights and the mixed-bloods sought to straddle both cultures. Each of those named, many of them still children, was given a section of land, or 640 acres. Included were six of A.P.'s children, plus Rosalie Lambert, and a seventh child, Anthony, thought to have been a brother of Rosalie's. Last names were not used in the treaty, but subsequent correspondence among government officials and others confirmed that this group was A.P.'s family, as did the fact that all of the allotments were around his installation at the Saline. His son Auguste Gesseau, who would have been just one year old, was not included. Among others on the list to receive land allotments were James G. Chouteau and Alexander Chouteau, presumably sons of A.P.'s brothers.

"Hunting is very poor at present," A.P. wrote Bernard Pratte at the end of 1826. "The Osages have been at war all autumn." Two months later he spoke of having another season of "great deficit," informing Pratte that, "the trade is finished and does not amount to much — 200 to 225 packs of skins, 5,000 to 6,000 deer, 300 beaver, 200 otter." He had already sold goods worth $3,500 to the Osages against their government annuities, meaning that the returns from the hunt did not pay for their needs. The Osages were edgy about the continuing arrival of emigrant tribes from east of the Mississippi, which kept them in warlike turmoil and reduced their interest in hunting.

A.P. told Pratte that he was going to have to count more on selling goods for "the annuities of the different tribes who will be settled near this place than on the furs. The deer, which was the principal business, is entirely finished. Furthermore, I hope to do better with the whites, who are beginning to surround me. The Government has just permitted the settling of all the lands recently acquired from the Osages. When I speak to you of the annuities of the Indians, I am alluding to the Creeks, who receive $200,000 a year."

A.P. acknowledged that he was in debt to B. Pratte & Company and asked whether Pratte and Cadet intended to continue to supply him the next year; if so, he hoped the advances he had to pay on the goods might be lowered. He also wanted the supplies sent to the mouth of the White River on the Arkansas instead of being left for him to bring by packhorses from the mouth of the Kansas River. Tea, he commented, was in growing demand, and he requested eight to ten pounds of it "by express."

This was during the time that Cadet and Pratte were again testing the possibilities in the the mountains of the Southwest, and Pratte proposed that A.P. return there to oversee trapping and hunting operations. A.P. was unenthusiastic. "I do not doubt that there is more to be gained at the Mountains than here, but I must acknowledge that, even with much desire for gain, there is something in me that I cannot define; whether it is fear or what, I have no desire to see that land again." He said that Paul Liguest and Millicour Papin wanted "to undertake the business of the mountains in association with me" and offered to send them on his behalf, if B. Pratte & Company was willing to "furnish us the means for it." Nothing came of this proposition; at the time, Pratte's son Sylvestre was in the mountains, where he would become ill and die ten months later.

Nevertheless, A.P.'s expectation of doing good business with tribes that had government annuities was not as certain as it appeared. In the fall of 1826, in anticipation of the arrival of the Creeks, their government agent bought some of A.P.'s buildings on the Verdigris for use as what was called the Western Creek Agency. In 1828 the Creeks began arriving in the area, in groups of a hundred or so at a time. By 1829, 1,200 Creeks were living in small farming homesteads lining the Verdigris and Arkansas rivers—all frightened of the Osages, Delawares, Shawnees, and Kickapoos surrounding them.

The Creeks were also destitute. The government delayed making the promised payments, but A.P. could not ignore the Creek's needs. He ended up feeding, clothing, and outfitting them at a cost of $5,201.94 charged against their future annuities.

With the fur trade hostage to Indian wars, and the annuities turning out to be insignificant, A.P. saw a third possibility for making money through the growing army presence in the area. The rising tensions between the Osages and the eastern tribes led to the army decision to move its garrison from Belle Point, later named Fort Smith, Arkansas, to the Three Forks area—a short ride from A.P.'s Verdigris location and a little farther from his Saline location.

The new post, Fort Gibson, was built on eight square miles of green, rolling land along the banks of the Grand River under the direction of Colonel Matthew Arbuckle, who commanded the post until 1841. Quarters for 250 soldiers were completed in 1826, to which were soon added blockhouses, individual houses for the officers, a chapel, a schoolhouse, and a store—all neatly whitewashed. There was a parade ground and a little burying ground planted with trees and shrubs. Later, a racecourse was laid out, and every year there were exciting races for high stakes. Indian ponies, fresh from running buffalo, were entered against horses of Fort Gibson.

An active social life quickly developed around the fort, with romances between soldiers and Cherokee women. Mixed-blood Cherokees maintained drinking and gambling establishments just off the reservation.

On the first Fourth of July after Fort Gibson was opened, A.P. was among the speakers at a lively, and probably drunken, dinner and celebration at the fort marking the fiftieth anniversary of the signing of the Declaration of Independence. Thirteen toasts were drunk to people ranging from the President to the "Fair Sex." A.P. offered this toast: "General Andrew Jackson—his military services, his patriotic devotion to his country and independent character, deserves approbation of his countrymen."

This was the kickoff of a lively, culturally mixed lifestyle around Fort Gibson and the rapidly growing settlements stretching from the Three Forks to the Saline. John F. Hamtramck, the Osage agent, was at Three Forks, about fifty miles below A.P.'s place at Saline. His agency was part of a collection of buildings that had originally grown up around the trading post of Joseph Bogy, who came to the Three Forks in 1807. About thirty log houses were gradually built along a clearing by the Verdigris River opposite a waterfall; visiting trappers, Indians, and off-duty soldiers mixed.

When Washington Irving traveled through the area in 1832, he saw "a sprinkling of trappers, hunters, half-breeds, creoles, negroes of every hue; and all that other rabble rout of nondescript beings that keep about the frontiers, between civilized and savage life, as those equivocal birds, the bats, hover about the confines of light and darkness."

A.P. had the largest trading store in the area. Nathaniel Pryor, who had been with Lewis and Clark, came to the Three Forks in 1819, opened his own trading post, and settled down with an Osage wife. He was also a speaker at Fort Gibson's July 4 celebration in 1826 and a frequent visitor to A.P.'s home at the Saline.

A.P.'s much younger half brother, the sickly Pharamond, and his chronically unsuccessful cousin, Auguste Aristide, both remained in the area even after the fur trade proved too unprofitable for A.P. to continue to employ them. "This climate does not suit Pharamond; he is always ill. He is not the sort to go with the hunters," A.P. commented to Pratte at the end of 1826, asking if he might be sent back to St. Louis and used as a clerk or to keep a store. Pharamond remained, however, working for a while as a clerk at the Western Creek Agency, until he died in 1831 at the age of twenty-five.

Auguste Aristide, after leaving the trading post, settled on a farm a short distance upriver from the Saline. A.P. reported to Uncle Auguste that he "seems determined to work to do himself honor in this affair." Unfortunately, the place where Auguste Aristide had settled was in the Cherokee land concession, so he could not legally work the land. A.P. told his uncle that his cousin found himself "in a very disagreeable situation and in great need of your aid," adding that he would help as much as he could but that for two years his own business had been bad.

Into this setting, in mid-1829, rode Sam Houston, former governor of Tennessee and future leader of the Texas independence battles. When he arrived at Three Forks, he was as much an exile from his past as was A.P. Chouteau. Houston had abruptly abandoned his political career in Tennessee—and his bride of a few months—to seek happiness and fortune among his beloved Cherokee Indians, who adopted him. He established himself about three miles northwest of Fort Gibson at a place he named Wigwam Neosho. He took up with a pretty Cherokee woman, Diana Rogers, and hung out with army officers and traders—especially A.P. Chouteau. Playing poker, gossiping, and drinking around Colonel Arbuckle's solid mahogany card table, Houston and A.P. soon became fast friends.

Over the three years that Houston lived in the area, he and A.P. used each other frequently to mutual benefit, or at least intended mutual benefit. Sometimes their ideas backfired. Houston admired A.P.'s vast Indian knowledge and his acceptance by the tribes, which he envisioned using to help in his own scheme at that moment of establishing an Indian Territory empire. A.P. admired Houston's Washington connections and appreciated his willingness to use them on A.P.'s behalf.

One of the attractions of Fort Gibson for Houston was the sutler's license, which he tried to obtain, without success. Sutlers held licenses to sell food, alcohol, and other items at military posts. The liquor allotment alone at Fort Gibson was 6,000 gallons of good proof whiskey, on which the sutler could turn a hefty profit. Sutlers also sold cigars, shaving boxes, soap, whisker pomatum, brushes, cologne water, toothbrushes, mirrors, razor strops, violin strings, silk purses, whalebone, suspenders, snuffboxes, necklaces, fishing lines, flasks, thimbles, combs, and much more. It was a very profitable undertaking, and there was a lot of rivalry for the licenses.

Without the sutler's license, Houston decided to compete on his own. In the summer of 1830 he had a boatload of merchandise delivered to Wigwam, including five barrels of whiskey and one barrel each of cognac, gin, rum, and wine—all, he said, intended for the accommodation of the officers and others authorized to purchase it. He said not one drop would be sold to soldiers or Indians.

Houston also used his position as a Cherokee citizen to claim the right to trade with the Cherokees without a license. Colonel Arbuckle, who sometimes found him a pain in the neck, explained to the Secretary of War:

> Genl Houston is very desirous of enjoying the privileges of a Cherokee citizen, and being rather impatient of restraint has on some occasions made remarks with regard to his intentions (in the event of his wishes in this particular not being gratified) which might be regarded exceptionable, these remarks I have considered only as the result of momentary excitement, and would not have refered to them, had the Genl. Been free from a News-paper controversy which possibly may bring all he has said or done in this country (to which exception could be taken) before the public.

Houston, who had served under Jackson in the War of 1812, used his access at the highest levels of Washington to influence events on the frontier. As soon as he arrived in Indian country, he wrote William

Clark and the Secretary of War that the government was wasting large numbers of troops guarding trade routes to the West, and that the money could be saved if treaties were negotiated with the warring tribes west of Fort Gibson that had been harassing traders and other travelers.

Suggesting that this could be accomplished by distributing "some trifling presents and medals of the President . . . to the chiefs by some man who understands the character of the Indians," he proposed A. P. Chouteau for the job. "He is a man of fine intellect, clear, vigorous, and active. He has the best practical knowledge of Indians of any man with whom I have ever been acquainted. He would execute the trust with pride, effect and fidelity." Eventually officials in Washington pursued a version of that idea, though it was not as easy as Houston predicted.

There was already bad blood between A.P. and J.F. Hamtramck, agent for the Osages, and Houston quickly joined A.P.'s side in the affair. Hamtramck complained to William Clark in the summer of 1829 that a lot of intrigue was going on involving distribution of the annuities and cattle to the various Osage bands. He mentioned that the night before the Osages were supposed to take delivery of their goods, "something was poured into their ears, which caused them to decide upon refusing the goods prepared for them—and consequently to set out on that day with Mr. A. P. Chouteau (and others), who were with them—and very soon repair to his store, near their town and receive his goods in the place of those they refused here."

Hamtramck also said that earlier, on June 1, A.P., Houston, and Nathaniel Pryor had arrived at the Osage agency with a large group of Clermont's band and informed him that Clermont's people were not ready to accept the cattle they were to receive under the 1825 treaty. They did not expect to be ready to care for the cattle for two or three years. And the Little Osages wanted to put off accepting their cattle until the fields could be fenced. Although Hamtramck did not set forth a possible motivation for this, A.P. had made no secret of the fact that he thought the Osages were not ready to settle down to farm and raise cattle.

The cattle episode was a reflection of the immense cultural gap dividing the so-called buffalo Indians, including the Osages, from the eastern tribes, principally the Cherokees and Creeks. The newcomers lived in log houses and farmed land, in some cases as much as 150 acres, with fences; they raised grains and vegetables, patches of cotton, tobacco, and rice. They used spinning wheels and looms. They owned cattle, horses, hogs, sheep, goats, and poultry. The women dressed like white women and rode horses sidesaddle. Their houses had chairs, tables, beds. They drank tea and coffee. They raised enough corn for their own use and also to sell to Fort Gibson.

The Osages, like the Comanches and Pawnees to the west and northwest of them, still lived for the hunt and the chase. Their few crops basically supplemented their hunting, as did the wild fruit and vegetables the women collected. A.P. was determined that they continue that lifestyle. He was partly motivated by the conviction that this was the life for which they were suited, but also, no doubt, because the only hope he had of reviving the fur trade along the Arkansas River was to have friendly and peaceful Indians out hunting for skins to trade to him.

Shortly after the episode over the cattle, Sam Houston embarked on a 600-mile trip through the region, gathering evidence of corruption by Indian agents. In January 1830, wearing the turban, leggings, breechclout, and blanket of the Cherokees, he went to Washington with two prominent Cherokees and presented his evidence to President Jackson. One result was that Hamtramck was dismissed as Osage agent and Paul Liguest Chouteau appointed to replace him. A.P. was also reimbursed for some money he had advanced Clermont's band the summer before.

In 1828, because of a government error, a treaty with the Cherokees ceding their country in the future state of Arkansas mistakenly moved them onto lands on the Verdigris and Neosho rivers that were already settled by Creeks and by Clermont's Osages, who would be forced to move again. As part of the plan to remove the Osages from what was now Cherokee land, A.P. was appointed by the Osages to assess the value of their property improvements within the area at issue, so they might be compensated. When he appraised the improvements of Clermont's Osages, A.P. also appraised his own improvements on the property around the Saline, which was part of the territory that was supposed to go to the Cherokees.

Then, on September 1, 1830, he sold to Sam Houston and two other men, David Thompson and John Drennan, two of the eight sections awarded to Rosalie and the children, including that area containing the potentially valuable saltworks. White men were not supposed to own this land. Nevertheless, Houston and his friends paid A.P. Chouteau $3,000 in cash and merchandise for the land and salt-works. On the strength of Houston's adoption into the Cherokee nation, they thought they could operate the saltworks and make large profits. But by 1832 the validity of Houston's Cherokee citizenship was in doubt, so the three men could not use the land. A.P. offered to return the money they had paid him, if the government bought out the Osage half-breeds for a good price.

But President Jackson soon sent Houston to negotiate with Indian tribes in Texas, where he quickly became caught up in the movement for independence. What he had wrought in the future Oklahoma was left for others to untangle, including the property rights of A.P.'s family.

A.P. struggled to keep his fur-trading operation alive and stay abreast of debts to suppliers. Returns of the buffalo hunts were highly unpredictable, and his relations with Cadet's firm were taking on a complaining edge. A.P. thought that what had then become the Western Department of the American Fur Company was charging him too much for merchandise; he could find better, cheaper merchandise in New Orleans. He also complained that the items he had requested from the Company the previous winter for delivery to him at White River had not arrived by May, when he was there to receive them.

Nevertheless, in the summer of 1829 he placed another order with Pierre Jr., consisting of 750 pounds of gunpowder, plus 10 gross of knives, and 3,000 gun flints to supply the Indians with munition for the fall hunt. At that time, he said his shipments of skins for the previous season's hunt included 4 packs of deerskins of 50 pieces each,

43 pieces of other deerskin, 124 muskrats and 49 raccoons, 5 packs of raccoons of 120 skins each, a pack of 34 beaver skins and 77 otter, and 18 pounds of bearskins. This was a modest production by comparison to what was coming into St. Louis from the Upper Missouri.

There were still occasional good seasons. In the winter of 1831 Millicour Papin, who still ran the post on the Neosho near Young White Hair's village in the corner of the future Kansas, took in what he described as the best trade in his sixteen years among the Osages. He sent twenty-three horses packed with pelts and three loaded wagons to the mouth of the Marais des Cygnes River, where pirogues were built to carry everything onward to Jefferson City, to be collected there by a steamboat. Part of the reason why Millicour could produce a good return was that the Osages around his post did not feel encroached upon by other tribes, which was the case with Clermont's band near A.P.'s location.

Even with the poor results, Cadet seemed to want to keep A.P.'s outfit connected to him and his partners. In February 1832 he agreed to obtain the new barge that A.P. had requested, but he wanted an understanding that the Osage outfit would remain with his firm. Cadet probably found something in his older brother's undisciplined lifestyle to explain his lack of business success, but Cadet knew him to be highly competent. He continued to show confidence in A.P. two years later, when he had him represent the firm in its negotiations with John Jacob Astor to complete the purchase of the Western Department of the A.F.C.

A compassionate man, A.P. was called on alternately by the Indians and the government to find a way through conflicts. His sympathies for the tribes made it impossible to decline such requests, even when the government expected that he work without compensation, as was the case with a project he undertook in 1832 at the behest of Secretary of War Lewis Cass.

After A.P. sent written testimony to the Senate Committee on Indian Affairs in July 1831, Secretary Cass wrote him with a number of questions about the declining fur trade and how to deal with Indian tribes. Cass also sounded him out about undertaking missions up the

Missouri River and to the Rocky Mountains on behalf of the government. Seeing this initiative on the part of Cass as a possible way to right old wrongs, A.P. said that he had abandoned all expeditions up the Missouri and toward the headwaters of the Arkansas and Platte rivers after his bitter experience in Santa Fe, pointing out that all his goods and other property were confiscated. He said that after he returned home, he decided not to return to such trade until the government extended its protection to citizens who risked their capital and their lives "in a trade that ultimately must produce advantage to the citizens of the United States."

A.P. also confirmed to Cass that the furs were diminishing, then offered an explanation and a proposal for dealing with the issue:

> The principal cause in my opinion is the eternal war that exists between the wild Indians near the Rocky Mountains and those who live east of them, and from my knowledge of the different tribes and the policy best calculated to remedy the evil, I would suggest that commissions should be appointed to restore peace between the different tribes in such manner as may be suggested by the department. Should peace be restored, the different tribes would turn their attention altogether to hunting. Consequently, the Arkansas River would become as valuable a highway as the Mississippi and Missouri for the transportation of furs and other articles of Indian trade.
>
> It is an acknowledged fact that the nearest and best route to Santa Fe is up the Arkansas River; the safety of navigation must, however, be secured by treaties with the Wild Indians or else the lives of traders would be in imminent danger.

The Osages went through a bad winter in 1831–32 and were in great need, particularly those of Clermont's band, which still refused to move north to lands assigned to it. Colonel Arbuckle reported Clermont's group to be in "much distress for want of food." Paul Liguest, as Osage agent, forwarded to Secretary of War Cass in April 1832 a petition from the head chiefs, counselors, and principal braves of the Big and Little Osages asking permission to send a delegation to Washington to present their grievances in person.

"They are surrounded by various tribes of Indians, upon whom they look with a jealous eye," Paul Liguest told Cass.

These Indians are now overrunning the former hunting grounds of the Osages; the Osages are cramped in their means of subsistence; in fact, hunting has become so laborious that the privations and dangers they suffer in pursuing the chase is not compensated for by the sale of their skins; and as their annuity is small (only $8,500 per annum, to upwards of 6,000 souls). They have become a poor people. Their poverty drives them to commit desperate acts upon the property of their neighbors; and they were compelled last year to pay nearly all the annuity due Clermont's band to the Creeks and Cherokees for depredations committed on their property.

Paul Liguest also explained that the Osages still harbored illusions of being powerful and able to overpower other tribes and whites. A trip to Washington, he thought, would impress them with the power of the United States.

A.P. went to Washington that spring and was probably there when Cass received Paul Liguest's letter supporting the Osage petition to travel to the capital. A.P. had gone with a power of attorney from the Creek chiefs to collect the money the government had promised them when they were uprooted and moved west. A.P. also hoped to collect the more than $5,000 he had advanced the Creeks in food and supplies when they first arrived at Three Forks.

He got nowhere with his mission, but the government had no hesitation in asking him for help, which he readily gave. Perhaps acting on the suggestions A.P. had made the previous year, Cass had decided to appoint a high-level commission to travel to Indian country and look at the causes of conflicts among tribes. A few months later Cass informed A.P. that three commissioners had been appointed to visit the territory and examine the country set apart for the emigrating Indians, with the right to adjust differences among the tribes.

"I have mentioned you to these gentlemen as one whom a long acquaintance with the Indian country, and with the Indian character and affairs, had peculiarly qualified to aid them in the discharge of duties, and assured them of your ready co-operation," Cass wrote. "I request that you will communicate freely with them, and give them the benefit of your opinions." He said nothing about payment.

As commissioners empowered to treat with the tribes, the President appointed Henry. L. Ellsworth, a Connecticut businessman and son of a former chief justice of the Supreme Court; former Governor Montfort Stokes of North Carolina; the Reverend John F. Schermerhorn of Utica, New York; and Colonel S. C. Stambaugh of Pennsylvania, a former newspaper editor who was to be the nonvoting secretary. The group was to make its headquarters at Fort Gibson. Stokes and Schermerhorn would travel to Fort Gibson by steamboat up the Arkansas River. A.P. was to be leaving from St. Louis after returning from his trip to the East, so Ellsworth made arrangements to join him.

But well before the Ellsworth group set out from St. Louis, a series of chance meetings occurred that eventually led to some classic writings on the American West. Washington Irving had recently returned to the United States after seventeen years in Europe and was looking to reconnect with his native land. During his voyage from Europe to New York, Irving met Charles J. Latrobe, a thirty-one-year-old British subject who had given up the religious ministry to see the world. Latrobe was accompanied by a nineteen-year-old Swiss nobleman, Count Albert-Alexandre de Pourtalès, whose parents wanted him to sow his wild oats. Latrobe and Pourtalès decided to tag along with Irving as he set forth to see how America had changed in his absence.

One more chance encounter put the final piece in place for their grand adventure. After arriving in New York in May, Irving and his new friends made the rounds of the big cities and scenic areas of the East. From Niagara Falls they went to Buffalo toward the end of August and boarded a Lake Erie steamer, expecting to go no farther west than Ohio before returning by the Ohio River. On the steamer, they happened to meet Henry Ellsworth, then on his way to St. Louis to meet A. P. Chouteau. He invited Irving to accompany him to Fort Gibson and agreed that the others might come as well.

The travelers quickly reversed their plans in order to take advantage of this opportunity. It was now, in Latrobe's words, "hurra! for the Far West!"

At Ashtabula, they left the steamer and crossed Ohio by road to Cincinnati, where they boarded a steamboat for Louisville, then changed to the S.B. *Illinois*, headed for St. Louis. As the *Illinois* churned its way up the Mississippi toward St. Louis on September 12, it almost collided with the *Yellow Stone*, which was making a fast run downriver after Cadet's triumphant trip to Fort Union earlier in the summer. "We were nearly wrecked and sent to the bottom by encountering another steam-boat coming with all the impetus of a high pressure engine, and a rapid current," Irving wrote to his brother, Peter.

On its earlier trip up the Missouri, of course, the *Yellow Stone* had carried George Catlin, his work encouraged and facilitated by Cadet. Now A.P. was about to play a similar role in helping another major creative figure of the time gather his own impressions of life in the West. The following year, 1833, Cadet would usher another artist, Karl Bodmer, to the Upper Missouri, and in 1834 Catlin would find his way to A.P.'s country. From those visits emerged hundreds of paintings and drawings and at least a half-dozen books, which together constitute a remarkable history of the time just before the region erupted into open conflict between whites and Indians.

The travelers out of St. Louis left on September 15, divided into three groups with the intention of meeting again at Independence to continue south together. Ellsworth and Dr. Thomas O'Dwyer, a St. Louis physician accompanying him, set out by steamboat on the Missouri. A.P. and his workers traveled overland with supplies. Irving, Latrobe, and Pourtalès also traveled overland, after buying horses and a wagon for their baggage and hiring Antoine "Tonish" Deshetres, a longtime Chouteau associate and jack-of-many-trades, to guide them.

After regrouping at Independence, which Irving considered "the utmost verge of civilization," the travelers departed again on September 27. They followed the well-worn Osage Trail, leading from the historic site of the Osage villages near the Marmaton River in the northern part of Vernon County, Missouri, southwest to the crossing on the Neosho River.

Along the way, both Irving and Latrobe quickly became admirers of A.P.'s. Like nearly everyone else, they called him "the Colonel," for no particular reason other than respect. His father and uncle had both been known as Colonel, based on their services in the militias under the Spanish regime and the United States. But A.P. had never reached that level in the militia during the War of 1812, and his highest rank in the regular army had been lieutenant.

"The Colonel, whom we considered for the time being the head of the party, generally led the van; a fine, good-humoured, shrewd man, of French descent, with claims both to fortune and family in Missouri," recorded Latrobe.

> As our conductor, we were all beholden to his courteous manners, and extensive information on every subject connected with the country and its red inhabitants, for much of our comfort and entertainment . . . he had been brought up from his early boyhood, more or less in [the Osage] camps; had hunted, feasted, fought with and for them, and was considered by them as a chief and brother. From him we were glad to take our first lessons in hunting, camping, and backwoodsman's craft, and enjoy our first peep at that kind of life, which, judging from his fine vigorous person, and the health shining on his sun-burnt features, was, with all its hardships, congenial to health and good humour.

During the first few days out of Independence, they found lodging for the night with farmers or missionaries, but as they traveled farther from settlements, they had to camp on the prairie. Latrobe described one such evening:

> While the half-breed and the black cut wood, Tonish makes a fire against some fallen tree or log, and flits to and fro in the smoke, like a goblin, while preparing his poles and spits for cookery. Meanwhile, other hands are employed in pitching the tent, and lay down the bear skins and blankets within or without, as suits convenience.
>
> By the time this is all fairly arranged, and our arms and accoutrements are carefully hung around, night has closed in; and the fire gleams bright and cheerily upon the huge trunk of the oak, butter-nut and beech, which rise from the tall jungle of towering weeds springing around us far over our heads. Tonish is now by far the most important personage, and we, in common with Henry Clay, Jackson, Mrs. Trollope, and the rest of the lick-lip fraternity, await the result of his operations . . .
>
> At length the Colonel's sonorous voice is heard, "Messieurs, le soupé est paré!" and each, rousing himself to the willing toil, contrives a seat around a tent cloth, and partakes of the banquet. And banquet

it was, for we lived at this time like princes, as coffee, biscuit, and bread were plentiful in the camp, in addition to our other luxuries, among which I would recount that despised dish, fried pumpkins.

Then follows the second table, at which the dogs think themselves entitled to partake . . .

The table withdrawn, we sit half an hour round the fire, listen to each other's tales, and, between whiles, to the distant howl of the prairie wolf, the shriek of the owl, the chirp of innumerable grasshoppers and crickets, the cry of the bustards going to sleep in the neighbouring marsh, or speculate upon some odd nondescript out-of-the-way noise in the deep forest; till in fine, growing gradually sleepy, we steal off to rest.

Stretched out under a tree at night, A.P. told his companions jokes and stories, often about Indian lore and superstition.

He generally had no use for Protestant missionaries because of their efforts to turn Indians into farmers, and one night he asked Washington Irving if he knew how to compare two "half-breeds." The answer, A.P. explained, was that, "one has been twice as long at the Mission as the other and therefore is twice as good for nothing."

Irving recounted another of A.P.'s stories: "An old squaw left alone when her party had gone hunting prayed the Great Spirit to make something to amuse her—he made the mosquito."

Hearing the hooting of a screech owl, A.P. told the travelers that the Indians believed that when an owl was heard for several nights out on the prairie, it meant that the owl was following the encampment and "forebodes the death of one of the party."

The group reached A.P.'s place at the Saline on October 6, and Latrobe found that their host's "welcome home amid a crowd of Negroes, Indians of divers tribes and of both sexes, dogs, pigs, cats, turkies, horses, ducks, all looking fat and happy, was an extremely amusing sight."

Irving noted: "White log house with Piazza, surrounded by trees. Come to beautiful, clear river, group of Indian nymphs half naked on banks—with horses near—arrival at house—old negro runs to open gate—mouth from ear to ear—group of Indians round tree in court yard . . . half breeds—squaws—negro girls running & giggling—dogs

•

of all kinds—hens flying & cackling—wild turkeys, tamed geese—Piazza with Buffalo skin thrown over railing—room with guns—rifles."

Supper that night, as captured in Irving's scrawled notes, was "venison stakes—roast beef, bread, cakes, coffee. Waited on by half-breed sister of Mr. Chouteau's concubine." Then they adjourned to another room, passing through an open hall in which Indians were seated on the floor. Three of them came into the room, two bringing chairs, the other sitting on the floor with his knees to his chin; another Indian watched from the window. The center hall had a staircase to the second floor. On the ground floor there were two beds in each room, with curtains. "In these establishments," Irving thought, "the world is turned upside down—the slaves the masters, the master the slave. The master has the idea of property, the latter the reality. The former owns, the latter enjoys it."

Two days later A.P. remained at his house when the visitors continued onward to Fort Gibson, the Western Creek Agency, and the Verdigris trading post. The two other Indian commissioners had not yet reached Fort Gibson when the group arrived from the Saline, so Ellsworth and his three companions spent the next month making a circular swing out into the prairies with a company of army rangers, traveling as far as the area of the future Oklahoma City. Along the way, Ellsworth made speeches of friendship to gatherings of Indians. In early November, Irving, Latrobe, and Pourtalès departed, and the commissioners settled down to their work.

Meetings between the commissioners and the Osages opened on February 25, 1833, at A.P.'s Saline place, but weather, food shortages, and delays in the arrival of some tribal groups led to a series of postponements and the decision to move the sessions to Fort Gibson. It was finally March 11, a Monday, before about eight hundred Osages, accompanied by their agent, subagents, and interpreters, set up camp on the west bank of the Grand River, opposite Fort Gibson.

Business began on March 13, when Commissioner Stokes reminded the Osages, as they already knew, that they had to move because some of the land on which they were situated had been ceded to the Cherokees.

"All the red men living east of the Mississippi are coming over to reside here," Ellsworth said the next day. Hunting was finished as a way of subsisting; they had to learn to farm, to spin, make cloth, plant gardens, and milk cows.

"Look at your brothers, the Creeks and Cherokees," he said. "They have good houses and large fields of corn; they are not stronger than you; are they not happier than you? They think they are, and we think so too. The Cherokees and Creeks do not depend any longer upon the buffalo and deer."

The following day, Schermerhorn submitted the government's proposal. In essence, it demanded that the Osages give up all the land reserved for them by the Treaty of 1825 and move to a tract beginning sixty miles west of the Missouri state line, at a point on the Neosho River, and extending over most of the south central portion of the future state of Kansas. For White Hair's village and the other Big and Little Osages situated near there, it would simply mean a move due west from their existing locations. For Clermont's band, which was already situated outside the existing treaty area, it meant moving north and west.

The young Clermont, his father having died in 1828, wanted time to study the proposal, and he wanted A.P.'s advice. For seventy years the Osages had been accustomed to turning to a Chouteau for guidance. One of the Indians with Clermont, whose name was Wautanego, said, "My fathers, we wish to have a friend to help us in this treaty; we can neither read nor write, but we have a friend here who can; we consider him a brother, and want him to assist us."

Stokes responded, "Brothers, you can have Colonel Chouteau to assist you; we consider him your friend and our friend."

Ellsworth urged the Osages to listen to A.P. and Paul Liguest, who was their agent. "We rejoice that there are men in this country to whom you can look with confidence; men who have never deceived you," he said. "In these you can have the fullest confidence; they know and understand all we tell you; go and ask them whether we advise you for good or evil."

What happened in the private consultations is a matter of conjecture, but it appeared, from subsequent remarks and correspondence, that A.P. urged the Osages to seek a better deal and, specifically, a different tract of land.

The Osages came back to council on March 20, saying that Clermont's band simply did not want to move. They returned on March 26 with a more specific position. Clermont reiterated that he wanted to go to Washington, while saying he was now willing to move to the area of the 1825 treaty. The commissioners refused his request to go to Washington. A few days later the Clermont Osages countered that they would move to new lands if they could have a tract extending west from their present lands, perhaps as far as Mexican territory, essentially a much larger amount of land. In what was probably a desperation tactic, they also said they were willing to learn to farm as part of such a deal.

The commissioners refused to even consider that proposal, and the council broke up after thirty days, with the commissioners suggesting that the Osages go to see the proposed new land.

When the treaty council ended in disagreement, three hundred angry Osage warriors led by Clermont went rampaging out onto the prairies in search of enemies on whom to vent their frustrations. As Grant Foreman, a leading Oklahoma historian, noted, "It was Clermont's boast that he never made war on the whites and never made peace with his Indian enemies." They detected a Kiowa war party headed northeast toward the Osage villages to the north of Clermont's town, but instead of going in pursuit, they headed to the defenseless village the Kiowas had left behind. Attacking women, children, and old men, they returned home in May, jubilant, with a hundred scalps.

This tragic episode did not change the basic issues in the negotiations between the government and the Osages. However, it increased the awareness at Fort Gibson and in Washington of the bitter tensions among Indian tribes on the prairies to the west as the arrival of the emigrant tribes pushed traditional enemies, such as the Osages, Kiowas, Comanches, and Pawnees, into closer proximity to each other.

Over the summer, sharp differences emerged within the commission and between A.P. and two of the commissioners, Ellsworth and Schermerhorn. A flood swept away A.P.'s Verdigris warehouse that spring and destroyed $10,000 to $12,000 worth of peltries and merchandise and kept him from traveling to Washington. But he wrote a pointed letter to Secretary Cass giving his opinion of the two commissioners.

"I do not believe these gentlemen act upon the principle, and endeavor to carry into effect, the liberal views of the government of the United States towards the Indians," he told Cass. "I have always been induced to believe, that the government wished to act with liberality, and had no disposition to oppress the Indians. Justice to the Indians requires me to say that Mssrs. Ellsworth and Schermerhorn act upon different principles." He went on to praise Stokes, with whom he said he would be pleased to cooperate.

Four days later Stokes followed with a letter to Cass backing up A.P.:

> I found Colonel Chouteau, upon all occasions, every thing which the instructions from the War Department had led me to expect. He possesses more correct information relative to Indians and their affairs than any person I have met with west of the Mississippi; and certainly has more influence, and enjoys the confidence not only of the Osages but of the Creeks and Cherokees, than any other man in this country. The reason is obvious. He interests himself upon all occasions to see justice done, not only between the tribes themselves, but also between them and the whites.

Stokes told Cass that A.P. "incurred the displeasure of my colleagues, because he was as unwilling as myself to have the Osages removed to a poor naked prairie, destitute of timber, and much nearer to their enemies, the [Pawnees], than they now are."

He said this was very unfair to the Osages, who had already given up a vast territory consisting of most of the state of Missouri and territory of Arkansas as well as "almost the whole country on which we are now settling the southern emigrating Indians."

"If the Osages had known at the time the value of the country they were ceding, and how important the possession of it was to the United States, and the prices other Indians were obtaining for their lands, they might have secured enough to have made them a prosperous, independent, and a happy nation," Stokes wrote. "Instead of this they are very poor."

A long standoff over the treaty ensued. A.P. told Lewis Cass in March 1834 that he had recently conveyed to the Osages a set of terms from the commission, even though his first inclination was to have nothing further to do with the commission. Deciding he had a duty to serve the government, he went to Clermont's village on the Verdigris on February 22, and the Osages informed him they had "unanimously" rejected the proposition to exchange their lands.

A.P. told Cass that the Osages were also angry that the commissioners and the government had not attended to a long-standing grievance that arose with the Treaty of 1825. He said this stemmed from the theft by the Osages of some mules from a party of Spaniards traveling from Santa Fe to St. Louis in June 1825 while the Osages were negotiating that year's treaty with William Clark. Clark promptly demanded that the Osages pay $3,000 to compensate the Spaniards, and the Osages agreed that the money be taken out of their annuity. However, the Indian agent at White Hair's town subsequently rounded up the mules and took them to Missouri. So the Osages were out both the mules and the $3,000—a wrong that had gone uncorrected for nearly ten years.

"It is my duty to say to you what I have said before that a Treaty can be made with the Osages if the proper means are taken," A.P. told Cass.

> But I must also say, in justice to the Osages, that if any nation has been heretofore deceived and oppressed it is the Osages, and the Government, which is asking them for an important session [*sic*] now of part of their last home, ought at least to be as liberal as it has been with other tribes of Indians. Nothing more is asked and indeed not as much. Only look at the immense value of country that they ceeded [*sic*] to the Government in their former treaties. The lands now occupied by the Choctaws, Cherokees, Creeks, Senecas, and [a] number of other tribes to the north was once owned by the Osages. And what have they received for that immense country? Small presents and a small annuity, of which the great part will cease in a few years.

He wondered what would become of "this noble but unfortunate nation."

The next month, A.P. went to Washington, met with Cass, and offered to undertake government service in collaboration with Governor Stokes. Apparently they made a deal, because Cass and other government officials soon began making regular requests of A.P. But he wrote Cadet from the East that his expense accounts for government service and money due him from Indian annuities for trade merchandise had been "passed, there are no appropriations for paying them."

A.P. also told Cadet that Washington officials wanted to create a "government of the Indians." He said the U.S. government was "determined to form the Indians into a territory, reserving to itself to appoint the Governor, the Senate and their agents. The Indians will choose the balance of officers which make up the Government, having the right to send a delegate to Congress and consequently to form into States. These arrangements are very pleasing to the Cherokees, and the Creeks."

In May, A.P. continued to New York, where he suffered another of his many business setbacks when his deerskins arrived damaged. He managed to sell them anyway "for my own account and at my risk" and applied $1,500 against his debts to Cadet.

The trip also showed that A.P. still had access to the highest levels of American business. He and Pierre Ménard represented the family to complete the purchase from John Jacob Astor of the A.F.C.'s Western Department by the company now called Pratte, Chouteau & Company.

Coming through Philadelphia after New York, he bought merchandise for a new trading venture that he was planning to launch with a man named Robert Payne. When A.P. had stopped in St. Louis earlier, on his way to the East, he and Payne had formed a partnership for trade with the Cherokees around the Three Forks. A.P. apparently assumed that trading with the Cherokees would not hinder any work he did for the government, which now involved primarily negotiations with the "wild" tribes. It also appeared that the government needed A.P.'s expertise so badly in the Indian negotiations that it was not inclined to limit trading on his part. But the Cherokees were now the only tribe in the area with enough money for significant shopping. The Philadelphia firm of Siter, Price & Company advanced A.P. $30,000 worth of goods and gave him a start-up loan of $10,000 for the new post.

He probably did not arrive back at the Saline and Fort Gibson from his trip to the East in time to accompany the large military expedition the government sent out across the prairies that summer to the Wichita Mountains and the Red River as a show of force among warring Indian tribes. George Catlin made the trip, leaving Fort Gibson on June 15 after painting many Indians around the fort, including Clermont II. General Henry Leavenworth was in command of a force that also included Colonel Henry Dodge and Lieutenant Jefferson Davis.

A.P. could conceivably have caught up with the expedition later. There is a record of his having recommended to Dodge that the soldiers, unaccustomed to hunting for buffalo meat, take some experienced Osage hunters to handle that task. It was a suggestion that proved somewhat prescient because, although the military command did take some Indian hunters, the leaders, including Leavenworth, could not resist the temptation to go racing across the prairies killing buffalo. In one chase, Leavenworth fell from his horse and never recovered, dying a few weeks later. Many of the men in the expedition also came down with a "bilious fever" that killed at least one hundred of the four hundred soldiers.

Still, it was clear after the Leavenworth expedition that the prairies to the west of Fort Gibson were inflamed by passions of hatred among the "wild" Indians and between them and the "civilized" tribes settling near the fort. A.P. was trying to take part in efforts to negotiate new treaties, but he was also concerned with the uncertainties surrounding the eight sections of land at the Saline allotted to Rosalie and the children by the terms of the 1825 treaty and subsequently determined to be on Cherokee lands. In Washington, on March 14, 1835, the Cherokees signed a treaty with the government with a provision extinguishing the reservation of lands for the family. In exchange for giving up legal title to the lands in question, Rosalie and the children were to receive payments totaling $15,000.

Six months later, on September 19, a group of chiefs and other

Osage leaders met in Washington and signed a document appointing A.P. to deliver the title to the lands to the United States and to receive the money on behalf of the "half-breeds." In taking the step, they said they were "reposing special trust and confidence in our old and well tried friend, Auguste P. Chouteau," without identifying him as the father of most of those sharing in the money.

Meanwhile, A.P. took part in the negotiation of the first of a series of Indian treaties. It was signed in August 1835 at a new post called Camp Holmes,* located in the future Cleveland County, Oklahoma. A.P. soon built a stockaded trading fort nearby to trade with the Comanches, Wichitas, and others. He had decided to concentrate his trading activities there among the "wild" Indians after he ran into opposition from the Cherokee agent in establishing the post he had planned for the Cherokee trade with the goods he acquired in Philadelphia.

The Kiowas had departed the treaty negotiations at Camp Holmes before the conclusion, so in December, Paul Liguest Chouteau rode out to Kiowa country to try to get the Kiowas to come to Fort Gibson to talk. He ranged over a vast part of the western country in search of them, crossing the Red River as far as the headwaters of the Colorado in Texas, and pushing his horses almost beyond their endurance. He finally found the Kiowas, and they agreed to send a delegation to Fort Gibson the following May. Paul Liguest got back to Fort Gibson in April, having spent the winter on the open prairies.

However, the Kiowas did not come to Fort Gibson as promised. Instead, reports reached Fort Gibson of war among the prairie Indians.

The following winter, Paul Liguest undertook another peace mission. He went to A.P.'s trading post near Camp Holmes accompanied by his son Edward Liguest and several others. Edward Liguest, who had been brought up in the household of his aunt and uncle, Cadet and Emilie, in St. Louis, was then twenty-two years old. From Camp

---

*This post was known by some people as Camp Mason, but for simplification only the Camp Holmes designation will be used here.

Holmes he set out to visit the Comanches and Kiowas south of Red River, returning in January to report that the Comanches were so angry that they threatened to destroy Camp Holmes.

By the spring of 1837 the War Department had become concerned enough by the murders of United States citizens and other Indians by Comanches that it asked A.P. to find out the reason behind the Comanche anger. He was also to try to obtain the release of some female captives and explain to the Comanches that the Creeks and Choctaws had the legal right to establish their homes and farms in areas previously used by the Comanches as hunting grounds.

Secretary of War J. R. Poinsett told A.P. he would be speaking for the President of the United States:

> It is the desire of the department . . . that you will seek interviews with all the Indians in that region; that you will explain to those of them, with whom treaties have been made, the provisions of those treaties; learn if they have reason to be dissatisfied with the manner in which they have been carried into effect, and lead them to perceive the advantages that would result to themselves from adhering strictly to their stipulations.
>
> To the tribes which are not bound to us by treaties, you will communicate the earnest wishes of the President for their welfare, and for the continuance of peaceable relations between themselves and others. And you are authorised to conclude a convention between them and the United States, upon the basis of that of 1835, with the Camanches [sic] and Witchetaws [sic].

As usual, the government wanted this decent man to risk life and personal financial well-being with no guarantee of remuneration—unless Congress should decide to provide it. Poinsett said that an escort of dragoons would be detailed for A.P.'s security, but there was no money in the War Department to pay him, or even his expenses.

"There is no appropriation out of which any part of your expenses can be paid," Poinsett said. "I wish, therefore, that all your pecuniary engagements should rely upon Congress for indemnification of your expenses. The Department is aware that the duties of the mission cannot be successfully executed without presents to the Indians, and you are therefore authorized, under the restrictions just stated, to provide the necessary supplies for this purpose, to an amount not exceeding five thousand dollars."

Governor Stokes told Poinsett that he was gratified that the government had finally seen the wisdom of "obtaining the services of a gentleman the best qualified of all others, West of the Mississippi, to do justice between the United States and the various Nations and Tribes of Indians in any manner connected with the government." Stokes also said that he and A.P., working together, had finally concluded a treaty of peace and friendship with the Kiowas, who came to Fort Gibson to sign it.

In November of that year, 1837, A.P. returned to Camp Holmes accompanied by a military escort from Fort Gibson. He sent the escort back, and was left with just a dozen men in the midst of warring tribes. His brother Paul Liguest was waiting for him, having completed a swing through the region to tell the tribes that A.P. would be visiting their communities. The Osages, Wichitas, and Wacos had all complained to Paul Liguest of attacks by the Pawnee-Mohawks.

But A.P. advised C. A. Harris, the Indian commissioner in Washington, that it would be impossible to accomplish any meetings before spring "as it is well ascertained that they are scattered over a vast extent of country, and are almost all at war. This has in a great measure been caused by the Agents of the Mexican and Texican [sic] governments, who, I have every reason to believe, have been for some time among them, making them the most seductive offers if they would take up arms with them in their existing war. They are consequently divided."

A month later A.P. told Harris he had decided to put off taking the tribal leaders to Washington until the fall of 1838, because spring and summer were not healthy times for them to travel. But the situation among the tribes was worsening. Meanwhile the Wichitas, a small, peaceable farming tribe, had been viciously attacked by a large party of Caddos from Texas. Later he complained again of aggressive actions by the Pawnee-Mohawks, calling them "the most lawless and mischievous tribe of the West."

About that time, Paul Liguest resigned as Osage agent—the Osages' dispute with the government over lands was still in limbo—to return to the Indian trade. He settled in at Camp Holmes to deal among the "wild" Indians with whom A.P. was trying to negotiate treaties.

They were both there in May 1838, when twenty-two principal chiefs of eight prairie tribes arrived in the expectation that A.P. was going to take them to Washington. He refused, saying that their tribes were too widely scattered and all at war. The Piankashaws were threatening war against some of the Pawnees, and the Osages were talking of joining them because Clermont II had recently died and they wanted to take some fresh scalps in his honor. A.P. tried to talk them out of doing this. He also complained that the Comanches and associated tribes still held thirty or forty white prisoners captured in Texas and Mexico, some of them women, whom he wanted released. And smallpox was sweeping a Wichita village. Finally, he gave them presents and said he would meet them at Camp Holmes again the following October.

But as he reached his fifty-second birthday that month, this man who had struck so many as the picture of vigorous health was beset with one or more ailments. That may have partly explained his decision to delay the trip to Washington by the chiefs. He wrote Harris that "a severe bruise on the thigh" made it impossible for him to ride. Meanwhile, he was worried about an attack on some Comanches by an Arapaho band, which caused many deaths.

In addition to his health concerns, A.P. could no longer avoid facing his monstrous debt. Financial obligations that had long been pushed to the background were ready to come tumbling down on him. Siter, Price & Company, the Philadelphia firm from which he bought merchandise for the ill-fated Cherokee trading venture, was threatening to sue for payment. In fact, his beloved brother Cadet was already doing that.

To preempt the Siter, Price suit, Pierre Jr. had filed his own suit in January 1838 against Auguste P. Chouteau & Company, the firm name of A.P.'s old partnership with Jules de Mun, for a total of $500,000—including $100,000 for merchandise, a loan of $100,000 from the firm of Berthold & Chouteau, plus $100,000 previously borrowed, and $200,000 for other things. The just debt, by John B. Sarpy's affidavit, was $66,000 after allowance for credits. The court found for Pierre Jr. for the sum of $66,000 and ordered the attachment of A.P.'s property and other possessions in St. Louis County.

During this process, family members sent two trusted associates, Antoine Janis and Antoine "Tonish" Deshetres, to the Saline to bring A.P. back to St. Louis to meet his creditors. He refused to go—in part, no doubt, because he was ill, as Paul Liguest reported separately to Sarpy at the same time. But he also felt an obligation to keep a date with Indians at Camp Holmes. He made out a power of attorney to the St. Louis lawyers Lewis V. Bogy and Joseph J. Spalding, which Janis and Deshetres took back with them. In a statement signed May 20, 1838, A.P. acknowledged owing the money claimed by Cadet as a debt ongoing since 1818.

On September 11, 1838, St. Louis county sheriff Marshall Brotherton auctioned at the courthouse door A.P.'s real estate in St. Louis, including the house in which his wife, Sophie, and their children lived, to satisfy his business debts to Cadet and other relatives. The property, broken into five lots, including one with the family house, had 60 feet of frontage on Main Street and extended 300 feet through to Church Street. It was within a few hundred yards of the Mississippi River and on the site of today's Gateway Arch. Pierre Jr. bought all of the property for $30,000, of which $12,000 was for the lot with the house.

On the surface, this series of events seemed to reflect a bitter rupture within the family. But Pierre Jr., with his clear head for business, knew that by taking this action, he not only protected his own interests—the debts to him being far older than the debts to Siter, Price— but he also kept within the family what assets A.P. had. In theory, Sophie and the children were put on the street by the sale of their home. In reality, it seems unlikely, considering these blood ties: Sophie was a Labbadie; her mother was a Chouteau; Pierre Jr.'s late partner, Bernard Pratte, was her brother-in-law; and John B. Sarpy, another of Cadet's partners, was her nephew.

What seems more likely is that both Cadet and A.P. understood, reluctantly, that this action could not be avoided. A letter that A.P.

wrote Cadet three months after the auction, about an unrelated matter, began, "My Dear Brother," and its general tone was amiable, suggesting that there had been no rupture between them.

By October 1838, when A.P. had promised to meet the Indian leaders again at Camp Holmes, he was reported ill at Fort Smith. By December he had managed to return to the Saline–Fort Gibson area, where he wrote the letter to Cadet on December 6. He died on Christmas Day at his home at the Saline. Like most deaths at the time, there was no clear indication of the cause, a possibility being that the thigh wound did not heal and, given the absence of antibiotics, eventually became so infected that it killed him. Another possibility seems to be the lingering effects of the same "bilious fever" that killed a hundred soldiers in the area three years earlier. Comments by contemporaries about the length of his illness varied from three months to "a long time." The best-substantiated information was Paul Liguest's comment that his brother was sick in May, seven months before he died.

Two days later he was buried at Fort Gibson with the honors of war. Six army officers were his pallbearers, and the entire command of the fort took part in the ceremony.

Gabriel R. Paul, a twenty-five-year-old grandson of Auguste Chouteau and West Point graduate in the class of 1834, was stationed at Fort Gibson at the time and attended A.P.'s funeral. The next day he wrote Pierre Sr., his great-uncle: "I have returned yesterday from the melancholy duty of performing the last rites to your son Augustus P. Chouteau. He died at the Saline, after a very protracted sickness of about three months. His body was brought to this post and buried with military honors. He appears to be very much lamented, by all who knew him. His grave was dug, next to those of Pharamond and of my uncle A. A. Chouteau."*

He added that an "express" rider had set out to inform Paul Liguest, who was on the "Grand Prairie."

———

*Auguste Aristide Chouteau, A.P.'s cousin and the eldest son of Auguste (1750–1829), had died in 1833 at the age of forty-one.

As soon as word of A.P.'s death reached St. Louis, the family and business associates acted quickly to claim for the estate all his assets in Indian country. Letters of administration were issued to Sarpy, who deputed Captain Robert E. Lee at Fort Gibson to collect the property. Captain Lee was also in charge of auditing and reimbursing A.P.'s pending expenses and other moneys due him from the government. About seventy head of mules and a few horses were gathered, taken back to St. Louis by Antoine Janis, and sold. Some merchandise, wagons, and forges were also collected. A.P. had left supplies, ox wagons, and furniture at Camp Holmes, which Paul Liguest valued at $2,936.35 for estate purposes. Even after everything was counted, the estate still owed money to other creditors, including $12,590.92 in damages awarded to Siter, Price & Company from its suit.

Rosalie and the family at the Saline were left destitute. They were supposed to vacate the property and about five thousand surrounding acres, which had been transferred to the Cherokees. A.P. had attempted to provide for them in the final months, using the $15,000 he received for the land in their behalf to purchase thirty-two black slaves from Creek Indians. He apparently viewed the slaves as an investment that would appreciate in value. But the deeds the Creeks provided him were found after his death to be invalid, and other Creeks—relatives of the sellers—reclaimed most of the slaves. A former business associate of Sam Houston's took six of them.

Governor Stokes, A.P.'s seventy-eight-year-old friend, who had recently been named Cherokee agent, tried to help. Three months after A.P.'s death, Stokes wrote to the commissioner of Indian affairs, explaining the complicated situation and defending A.P.'s behavior, which he thought was motivated by good intentions.

After recalling the series of treaties and agreements that produced the allotments around the Saline for "the Indian family of the late A. P. Chouteau," he tried to explain the circumstances, writing:

For however it may be considered as a reproach on his character, almost all Traders who continue long in an Indian Country, have Indian wives. This circumstance does not affect the justice of the claim.—The Osage Nation owned the land, and chose to bestow a part of it in this manner. These reservations are all in country ceded to the Cherokee Nation by [the Osage in] the Treaties of 6th May 1828 and Feby 14th, 1833 . . .

Now Sir, Col. Chouteau, with the best intentions, thought he was doing the best for these reservees by stipulating to give them in lieu of the fifteen thousand dollars, about thirty two very valuable negroes, well worth the money. But the title for the greater portion of these negroes was derived from Indians of the Creek Nation, the friends and relations of whom claim the most of them, and it is feared that the reservees will not be able to recover and retain any of them. Since the death of Col. Chouteau, twenty-eight of them have been stolen or enticed away, and most of them are now in the Creek Nation . . . It is ascertained . . . that Colo. Chouteau's property both here and in Missouri will not pay one fourth his debts: In the meantime a Mr. Bogy the agent of the Administrator at St. Louis has seized and sold or sent to Saint Louis almost every article of Col. Chouteau's property to be found in this country, leaving Col. Chouteau's Indian family in this Cherokee Country nearly destitute of the means of subsistence . . . I think Sir, that something ought to be done by the Government of the United States to rescue from total loss, the amount of the value of their reservations.

Before his efforts on behalf of A.P.'s family could bear fruit, Stokes was forced from office. His successor in 1841, Pierce M. Butler, took up the cause and was soon able to adjust the claims to the family's satisfaction and also to that of some of the creditors. In February 1843 Rosalie went to Fort Gibson and received funds due her and the children and paid part of the money to A.P.'s creditors. Rosalie and her children became citizens of the Cherokee nation, which owned the lands on which they still lived, and she further solved the problem of their security by marrying a Cherokee.

Another piece of A.P.'s unsettled financial picture fell into place on February 2, 1848, more than nine years after his death and more than thirty years after the ill-fated trading expedition to Santa Fe. The claim of A.P. and Jules de Mun, who had also died, was held to be valid under the 1848 treaty that settled the war with Mexico. The United States agreed to pay the claims of its citizens against Mexico as part of the treaty. On their behalf, Pierre Jr. collected $81,772—which was

$30,380 principal, the rest interest. Senator Thomas Hart Benton received a 10 percent commission on the total for his help in keeping the issue alive in Washington through the years. Pierre Jr. distributed the proceeds among the legal heirs.

By conventional measurements, A.P. Chouteau left a legacy of failed dreams and miscalculations, represented by his complicated finances and messy personal situation. In other ways, however, he left a singular and distinguished legacy, one that could be matched by few others who made their way around Indian country in the first half of the nineteenth century. This was reflected in an episode that occurred in the spring of 1839 as his relatives, friends, and creditors struggled to deal with the confusion he left behind.

The southwestern trader Josiah Gregg was traveling across the prairie en route to Chihuahua, Mexico, with fourteen heavily laden wagons pulled by teams of mules and oxen, accompanied by thirty-three traders and craftsmen from seven countries. His caravan happened on "a wild romantic spot" that had been the site of the already abandoned Camp Holmes—A.P.'s short-lived dream of a mutually beneficial relationship with the "wild" Indians.

"We had not been long at the Fort, before we received a visit from a party of Comanches," Gregg wrote, "who having heard of our approach came to greet us a welcome, on the supposition that it was their friend Chouteau returning to the fort with fresh supplies of merchandise. Great was their grief when we informed them that their favorite trader had died at Fort Gibson, the previous winter."

FOURTEEN

François and Bérénice: Together to a New Place

✳

The marriage at Immaculate Conception Church in Kaskaskia on July 12, 1819, of François Gesseau Chouteau and Thérèse Bérénice Ménard united two of the most prominent French families of the American frontier and launched the newlyweds on an adventure that helped create another brash young settlement—and future metropolis—where fur trade was the way of life.

When he gave his daughter in marriage, Pierre Ménard was lieutenant governor of the year-old state of Illinois. He was the leading citizen of Kaskaskia, the state capital and once the center of French military power on the Upper Mississippi. Kaskaskia had a population of more than 1,000 people in 1819.

Ménard—the son of a French soldier who came to Canada with Montcalm in 1755—moved to Kaskaskia as a young man in 1790, opened a store, established a plantation, and became involved in local political and civic affairs at the time the territory had recently passed from English to American control. He built a comfortable home outside Kaskaskia, with touches of elegance rare for the time and place, including hand-pressed glass windowpanes from France and solid mahogany millwork. He also entered the fur trade and had frequent and amiable business dealings with the Chouteaus over many years.

Like the Chouteaus, he got along well with Indians, who were free to come and go at his home. A temperate, respected man, he was often called on to help in the relocation of eastern Indians to the west side of the Mississippi after Illinois became a state. When the Marquis de Lafayette visited the area in the spring of 1825, Pierre Ménard was his host. His home served as the headquarters of the honored man, just as Pierre Chouteau Sr. and his home had a few days earlier in St. Louis.

François Gesseau Chouteau was born at St. Louis on February 7, 1797, the first of Pierre Chouteau's five sons by his second wife, Brigitte Saucier. Thérèse Bérénice Ménard was born at Kaskaskia on August 13, 1801. Her mother, Marie-Thérèse Godin, died when Bérénice was three years old. When her father remarried, his second wife was Angelique Saucier, a sister of Pierre Chouteau's second wife. Angelique was the woman Bérénice viewed as her mother while growing up, and later as her very good friend. Even though François and Bérénice were not related by blood, the circumstances of growing up with a mother and stepmother who were sisters surely created a sense of their being cousins.

Kaskaskia was just sixty miles south and across the river from St. Louis, but in those days of slow, complicated travel, the children of the Chouteau and Ménard families may not have seen one another often. Had they not encountered each other previously, however, Bérénice and François probably played together in the winter of 1809–10, when Angelique Ménard and her children spent several months in the home of Brigitte and Pierre Chouteau.

Both husbands had gone up the Missouri River the previous summer on the expedition of the Missouri Fur Company to return the Mandan chief Shahaka to his home and launch a trading enterprise. Pierre Chouteau returned to St. Louis in November of 1809 after Shahaka was safely delivered, but Pierre Ménard and other men pushed farther up the river to "winter over" and begin trading as soon as Indians had pelts and skins from the hunting season.

Bérénice was a month short of her eighteenth birthday when she wed the young man whom she, like most of the family, called by his middle name, Gesseau. He was twenty-two.

By the time they married, François had already been in the fur trade for several years. He began by working for his half brother Paul Liguest, but in 1816 he obtained a license in his own name with his friend and cousin Cerré Chouteau, Auguste's son. The license permitted them to trade together among the Osages, Kansas, and Pawnees.

The year he married, 1819, François and his cousin built a trading post known as Four Houses, on the north bank of the Kansas River at the mouth of Cedar Creek—twenty-six miles west of the confluence of the Kansas and Missouri rivers. It was called Four Houses because four log buildings were arranged around an enclosed courtyard, their corners meeting to create a private space in what amounted to a primitive fort design. However, François's half brother Cadet, whose firm provided their trade merchandise and handled their sales, soon said there was not enough trade at the site to justify two partners, so Cerré accepted an offer to go to the Upper Missouri for Cadet.

By 1821 François was already thinking of a more central establishment, closer to the meeting place of the two rivers. For a larger trading post and warehouse, he selected a location on the north bank of the Missouri River at a spot later known as Randolph Bluffs. The site was about three miles diagonally east across the river from present downtown Kansas City, Missouri, and about thirty miles by river from Four Houses. It was just east of where the Missouri River changes from a general east–west route to generally north–south.

When François selected the confluence of the two rivers as his future headquarters, the area was entirely covered with dense forest on steep slopes broken by deep ravines. Cottonwoods crowded the riverbanks to which François brought a team of workers from St. Louis to build the first structures in 1821–22. Peregrine falcons nested in the hilltop trees—black walnut, oak, ash, hackberry—and swooped down from the heights to snatch slower, weaker prey. When night settled along the river, deer and wild turkeys came out of the forests to cool themselves on the sandbars. Travelers saw white cranes, golden eagles with wingspans exceeding eight feet, and catfish four feet long. Black bears and turtle eggs provided good eating.

Nearby streams were rich with beaver, and Indian tribes followed the Kansas River a few days' ride to find buffalo herds roaming open prairie land. First passing through the area in 1804, Lewis and Clark had noted deer, elk, bears, and "verry [sic] troublesome" quantities of ticks, rattlesnakes, and "musquiters." Lightning and thunderstorms made spectacular though fearsome sights, as did the blazing prairies when Indians burned off old grasses. The swirling current of the Missouri turned into powerful whirlpools near the mouth of the Kansas.

Indians and traders regularly navigated the two rivers between the cavernous limestone bluffs, but almost no one — Indian or white — was living at the immediate location when François and Bérénice arrived. The Kansa Indians were concentrated more than a hundred miles to the west along their namesake river. The Osages were about an equal distance to the southeast but destined to be forced entirely out of Missouri within a few years. Except for the treacherous rivers with their submerged trees and sandbars, the only significant routes through the area at the time were two Indian trails.

Much of this would change within a few years as the white settlers then pouring into eastern Missouri from Kentucky and Virginia pushed their way farther and farther west along the Missouri River. Substantial numbers had already established homes in the Boonslick area about a hundred miles to the east, and there were tiny white communities closer, at Liberty and Fort Osage. A spot that was almost virginal when François cast his dreams along the riverbank would soon draw large numbers of American farmers and merchants, attracted by the same geographical advantages that had impressed William Clark when he first looked out over the meeting place of the Missouri and Kansas rivers.

Bérénice, meanwhile, gave birth to their first child, Edmund François, in St. Louis on January 6, 1821. Their second, Pierre Ménard Chouteau, was born April 28, 1822, also in St. Louis, presumably in the home of Pierre and Brigitte Chouteau. After the christening of their second son, in June 1822, the entire family moved up the Missouri River — some four hundred miles by its serpentine path — on keelboats loaded with trade merchandise, household goods, livestock, two baby sons, business employees, and slaves. Keelboats were rib-made boats, shaped like the hull of a steamboat and decked over. They were eight to ten feet wide across the deck and five or six feet deep below deck. They had one mast and rudder, although a long oar was usually favored for steering.

Bérénice took a daring step by accompanying her husband to the frontier instead of establishing a household in St. Louis among his family and just across the Mississippi from her own beloved family—a lifestyle more typical of wives of men in the fur trade. Like others in the Mississippi Valley French community, she loved music and dancing and beautiful things, which would be in short supply at the outpost to which she headed.

In deciding to come to such a raw spot, Bérénice displayed the grit and determination for which she would be known throughout her life. John C. McCoy, who arrived with his missionary parents a few years after the Chouteaus and came to know Bérénice well, described her as "a great woman" with force of personality and character. "She had a zest for living," he recalled in his old age, "an ability to adapt herself to her surroundings . . . She was not afraid . . . of anything in life."

It is also quite likely that even as young as she was, she knew well the customs of the fur trade and did not want to share her husband with other women as he traveled among the Indian villages and met with chiefs eager to provide him companionship from among the tribe's most appealing adolescent girls. The closer his wife was to him, the less likely that was to occur.

François had already fathered a child by an Osage girl when he was seventeen years old and working on the Neosho and Marais des Cygnes rivers with Paul Liguest. The baby boy, born January 12, 1815, was named James and christened in 1822 by a Belgian priest traveling in the area. At least some members of the Chouteau family must have kept an eye on James's well-being over the years, because a section of land along the Neosho River was reserved for him under an 1825 government treaty. A James Chouteau was admitted to the school at Protestant-run Harmony Mission, about fifty miles south of the future Kansas City, in 1823. His parents were not identified in the surviving records, but the boy was about the age of François's son.

Although Bérénice went back to St. Louis for the deliveries of the next three babies born after the family's move west, she always packed up the children and returned to her husband by pirogue or keelboat. Sometimes her husband made the trip to St. Louis to collect her and the children and to spend time with his parents and other relatives.

On one such trip, in the fall of 1824, when Bérénice was awaiting the birth of her third child, her father-in-law accompanied her and the children to St. Louis after he had visited the young family's rustic home. The sixty-six-year-old Pierre Sr. had one of his classic explosions when the boatman almost ran into a partially submerged tree. Shouting at the boatman to take the boat to shore, he pulled a gun from under his seat and was ready to shoot the man, until the pregnant Bérénice grabbed hold of the gun and kept him from pulling the trigger. Her third child, another boy, whom she named Louis Amédée, was born February 27, 1825.

That year, the returns at François's operation were enough to inspire him to continue working hard: a total of 29,666 skins of various animals, mostly deer, which brought the company $11,735.71.

About that time, Cyprien, five years younger than François, joined his older brother. A short time later, Frederick, then fifteen, the youngest boy in Pierre Sr.'s family, arrived. The three of them would work together for the remainder of their lives, gradually abandoning their St. Louis roots and casting their lot with the new community coming to life around them.

Two events soon occurred that would have a major impact on their future prospects.

First, in October 1825, a wagon train carrying a Tennessee family of thirteen rolled in from Fort Osage. With five wagons loaded with household goods, plus about twenty-five horses, thirty head of cattle, and some sheep, the family was at the vanguard of white settlement.

Six months later, in the spring of 1826, floodwaters came rolling down the Missouri and completely destroyed François's main trading post and warehouse on the water's edge. Forewarned that the angry river was bearing down upon them, his family and everyone else at the location escaped to the hills behind the post.

The Chouteau family took temporary refuge at Four Houses; then Bérénice and the children returned to St. Louis during the summer or early fall of 1826. Louis Amédée, her year-old boy, died there in October 1826 of unknown causes. She was also pregnant again, and the experience of burying one baby made her concerned that she herself might die in childbirth and leave her two remaining children motherless. If she should die, she wrote her father from St. Louis, she wanted his namesake, "little Ménard," not to "go to anyone except to your house," although she hoped that God would "allow me myself to raise my children."

Louis Sylvestre was born on February 16, 1827, apparently without major problems, because Bérénice was soon doing errands and other favors for her relatives. She also involved herself in settling the tensions between her father-in-law and his only son still at home, Charles. The demanding Pierre Sr. had lost patience with a nineteen-year-old who still had not found meaningful work. Charles's brothers had all begun working at about fifteen under the guidance of older siblings or other relatives.

With Bérénice's encouragement and prodding, Pierre Ménard agreed to put Charles to work in his store in Kaskaskia. She asked her stepmother to have the store manager "teach him the ways of behaving in the store," adding, "I assure you, dear mother, that Charles is a good boy, that he only needs to get away from the paternal house."

Before rebuilding their flooded operation, François, with his brothers, moved to the south bank of the Missouri River. They were soon back in business in a two-room log house with a separate kitchen building. After the death from cholera of Baronet Vasquez, the Kansa Indian agent, they took over the nearby buildings that Vasquez had used as his headquarters. The buildings were considered too far from Kansa tribal lands to be convenient for the new agent.

François would eventually build a spacious frame house for his family near the new location, but he first concentrated on better organizing his trading network. With two brothers to help him, François worked diligently in 1828 and 1829 to improve the reach of his business to the various tribes located within fairly close proximity to the confluence of the Kansas and Missouri rivers. The most important, from a fur-trade standpoint, were the Kansas, Shawnees, and Delawares, but there were other tribes in the wider area, some of them arriving from east of the Mississippi and headed into Indian Territory, the future Kansas. François was determined to capture all of them—as either suppliers of furs and skins in exchange for merchandise or simply as buyers of goods with their annuity credits.

As was typical with fur-trade "outfits," François was not an "employee" in the modern sense but operated more like a franchisee. He had a supplier of merchandise that also sold the pelts he took in from the Indians in exchange for the merchandise. In this case, François seems to have divided his business between his half brother Cadet's firm, then called B. Pratte & Company, and the trading house of his father-in-law. From the tone of their correspondence, Pierre Ménard appeared to have been the source of some or all of François's start-up capital as well. As a result, he had frequent business discussions with Ménard, whom he called "uncle," as well as with Pierre Chouteau Jr.

François, who at first seemed somewhat uncertain about carrying so much responsibility at considerable distance from his older associates and relatives, turned to them regularly for advice. At a time when Cadet, for example, was juggling business affairs that ranged from the upper reaches of the Missouri River to New York and beyond, including dealings with John Jacob Astor, François pleaded with him to write more often. He probably wanted moral support and relief from homesickness, as well as reassurance.

In the routine of the fur trade, Indians or independent traders arrived at the warehouse with their pelts, which the head of the post examined. Generally the Indians selected merchandise from the shelves of the trading post in exchange for their pelts. The most common trade items of appeal to Indians were fabric, knives, cooking utensils, blankets, jewelry, guns, and powder. In his later years Frederick Chouteau recalled that among the best-selling items at the family trading houses had been kettles made of copper, brass, or iron. They arrived in "nests" of ten kettles in graduated sizes, the largest holding about fifteen gallons. The copper and brass kettles sold at $1 a pound, the iron ones for less. Sometimes the Indians wanted more items than their pelts covered. That meant they might ask for credit against the next season's harvest, known as "returns." The tribes generally hunted for two periods during the year, in winter and early summer, but the winter season was more productive.

The furs and skins were packed and shipped onward, generally to St. Louis. Through the summer, the post also sold items to Indians who had annuities with which to pay or to white settlers after they began moving into the area. The Chouteau posts were on the line between the new state of Missouri and Indian Territory, so they traded with both Indians and whites after the western edge of Missouri opened for white settlement.

At the time François set up his operation, most of the Kansa Indians lived in a large village of lodges on the Kansas River a short distance east of present-day Manhattan, Kansas. In 1829 or 1830, the tribe moved eastward, divided into three groups, and occupied lands reserved for them by an 1825 treaty. The Four Houses post had never been a convenient trading location—in François's view it did not attract the tribe—so a new Kansa post was built in 1828–29 at Horseshoe Lake, on the Kansas River a few miles west of the future Lawrence.

During the same time, the Shawnees, some arriving from Cape Girardeau, Missouri, and others from Ohio, settled on lands just west of the Missouri line and south of the Kansas River in what eventually became the western suburbs of Kansas City. François set up a new trading post there to capture Shawnee business. It was open by December 2, 1828, when he wrote Pierre Ménard: "I am exactly across from the Shawnee village, [a] distance of about six or seven miles, near the Kansas River. It is a very elevated point. Water has to rise more than 40 feet to endanger us. There is a good port and a good place for the barge. On the other side [of the river] across from our establishment, it is a beautiful side, rolling low land where we gather stone when we are in need." The Shawnee post, which was located on the south side of the Kansas River, about twelve miles west of the mouth of the river, was usually called Cyprien's Post because Cyprien Chouteau ran it for many years.

It appears that the brothers also built a post around this time to trade with the Delawares on the north side of the Kansas River about five miles west of the river's mouth. François commented that he now had "three good houses," referring to his trading posts, which could have meant among the Kansas, Shawnees, and Delawares. All of the posts supplied pelts that went to his warehouse on the Missouri River, where they were packed and shipped to St. Louis.

François now felt well positioned to capture trade from many sources, not only the Indian tribes already in the area but those expected to arrive. In December of 1828 he went among the Kansa and Shawnee villages encouraging the tribes to go out to hunt and trap that season. He found the Kansas well disposed, but the Shawnees seemed more interested in planting corn. Unlike the Kansa tribe, the Shawnees had the habit of running up debts with François before they had anything to trade, and they already owed him money. He told them they would never be able to pay off their existing debt if they did not hunt, and he suggested that they go on a one-month hunt, after which there would still be time to plant corn in the spring. He also convinced the Kansas to take a group of Shawnees with them to trap beaver so the recent arrivals would learn where the best trapping areas were.

At the beginning of March 1829 François returned to his Kansa trading post to pick up the packs from the winter of hunting and trapping. He came in his keelboat, the *Beaver*, then stopped among the Shawnees to gather what they had, and returned to his headquarters on the Missouri. Then he had the keelboat loaded with the household goods of the widow of Baronet Vasquez, who was returning to her family in St. Louis.

François was satisfied with the returns from the Indians, but being in great pain from frostbite in both feet, he decided not to make the trip to St. Louis himself. In his place he sent his brother Frederick, by now twenty years old. But they were both concerned about the reliability of the only man available to pilot the vessel, "Big Baptiste" Datchurut, and his ability to prevail over a river that, as François said, "is always to be feared a little."

The events that followed underscored the tremendous financial and personal risks associated with life in the fur trade, and they left François distressed and blaming himself to the point where he did not know whether he could continue. Besides Frederick, twenty-eight people were aboard the keelboat when it departed on March 27, including Mrs. Vasquez and her four children, ten Kansa Indians, two

Indian agents, and boatmen. The forty-to-fifty-ton vessel carried about 40,000 skins tied into 400 packs. But no more than a mile or two after the *Beaver* headed into the high current of the river flowing downstream, it was pushed toward a large rock by winds blowing hard from the south. As Frederick remembered it,

> I saw that we were running towards the rock. I told the men to row away. They did, and threw the bow of the boat away out from the rock, but the [pilot] was not strong enough . . . to throw the stern out, and the boat struck its side against the rock, breaking the side in. We turned right toward the shore, but the boat began to sink fast. We threw the anchor, but it would not catch. Then seven hands and myself jumped in and swam ashore. Three of the hands . . . were drowned . . . The others all remained on the boat. The boat's anchor soon got a hold and stopped the boat.

When he reached the shore, Frederick went for a flatboat and rescued the people left on the keelboat, without further loss of lives. The next day, Frederick and a mulatto slave named Joseph Lulu went back to the boat to recover the packs of pelts. They cut a hole in the deck of the vessel and could see the packs, most of which were underwater. They pulled out the pelts on top, and then Lulu began going under the chilly waters of the river and bringing out the other packs.

"He went under water no less than 375 times, taking out a pack each time," Frederick recalled. "He was worth his weight in gold."

When word reached François about the disaster, he sent Cyprien and additional men to help. They set about drying the pelts, which were found to be in salable condition.

Nevertheless, François felt devastated by the loss of life and the realization that Mrs. Vasquez and the four children had only "escaped by a miracle." She had lost $300 that was in her cabin. François thought he had neglected his duty by not traveling on the boat himself. He poured out his anguish in a letter to Pierre Ménard, saying he hoped to travel to St. Louis and Kaskaskia in a few days to talk things over in person.

"You can judge of the terrible situation in which I find myself at present and the continual reflections that I make concerning this wretchedness," he wrote. "To sum it up, I am almost discouraged. After another long absence from my family, after so much pain, so much work, running around and having been sent hither and thither, so much trouble and vexation with the Indians in order to obtain what the boat contained, and to see, after that, all my labor lost in an instant, makes me doubt for hope in the future."

François himself, with a load of furs, eventually reached St. Louis on May 23 in a voyage that also had risky moments. He traveled most of the way by the S.B. *Duncan,* but one of the boilers burst as the vessel neared Florissant. François disembarked, got a horse, and rode the rest of the way to St. Louis, where he arrived to a house in mourning. His mother, Brigitte, had died at the age of fifty, which cast great sadness over his reunion with his father and Bérénice, who awaited him with newborn Benjamin.

"Instead of the joy that I anticipated at my arrival among my own, I find that I lament the loss of my dear and good mother," François told Pierre Ménard three days later. "I assure you I find an immense emptiness in the house in not seeing her whom I loved so much. Papa is not well. My arrival renewed his sorrow and his pain in all its force."

There was still more sorrow to come. François and Bérénice remained in St. Louis through the summer and were there for the baptism of baby Benjamin. During that same time, however, two-and-a-half-year-old Louis Sylvestre died and was buried in the new Catholic cemetery.

Once back at his trading post, François pulled himself together and returned to work. He stopped blaming himself for the *Beaver* disaster. Over the next two years he oversaw construction of a comfortable frame house to the east of the warehouse and landing. It was on higher ground than the first home across the river, so he hoped it would be safe from floodwaters. When completed, the house was a two-story structure with a wide porch around the ground floor in the expansive style of the French homes at Kaskaskia and Ste. Genevieve. He also began acquiring land around the site and developing a farm.

By October of 1829 François had "outfitted" most of the tribes for the winter hunting and trapping season. He told Cadet that the

Kansas, Peorias, Weas, and Piankashaws—the latter three small remnants of once important tribes—were "now very well outfitted to make a good hunt." And he was confident of a good season. By November all the Kansa men had left for the hunt, and François had his fingers crossed for a good harvest. He always worried, however, that the warlike Pawnees to the west of the Kansa tribal lands would stir things up and interfere with hunting and trapping.

Only the Shawnees were delaying. He was increasingly frustrated with them, calling the tribe "frankly real rascals," who "come to buy on 'charge account' with us, and . . . take their money [and] their fine pelts to Independence [to trade], so as not to pay their credits."

This reflected his new worry that, being on the line between the Indian lands and expanding white settlement, he faced competition. If the Indians did not like the terms he offered for goods, he feared they would go to Independence, a few miles to the southeast, and trade with others. Although he had a license as an Indian trader, in the free-wheeling commercial environment developing in the area, there was nothing to prevent Indians from trading elsewhere. This put him in a more difficult position than traders in areas with little or no white settlement. He commented on that to both Ménard and Cadet and speculated about whether he ought to set up a store in Independence.

In December of 1829 François moved to his post near the Kansa villages to wait for the tribe's return from the hunt. "I have given a great deal of credit to the Kans [*sic*] and I am remaining here to recover it," he wrote Cadet. "If I am paid we will do very good business at this post, because, according to the information which I have been able to get, they have lots of furs."

By February, François's decision to spend most of the winter at the Kansa villages had paid off. "I . . . remained at the post because I saw that there we would bring in more pelts. I was not mistaken in my calculation," he wrote Pierre Ménard after returning to his warehouse and home. "I have put up here 150 packs of handsome deerskins, 20 bundles of good raccoons, 3 bundles of beaver and 350 otter of the first quality." Even the irksome Shawnees had been productive. From them, he had 50 packs of deerskins, 5 of raccoons, 100 beaver, and 150 otter. And he expected the Kansa tribe to hunt some more.

"The Kansas have pretty well paid their credits and owe us about 300 dollars," he told Ménard. "I suppose they will have a good enough hunt, all being in a good mood for that. They have in mind to go to the branches of the Kansas River and they tell me that there is still a lot of beaver." He also reported talking with the chiefs of the Kansas and the smaller tribes and that all had agreed to spend their government annuities on merchandise from him. They told him his merchandise was "infinitely superior" to what they had received directly from the government agent the previous year.

It was an upbeat report from the young entrepreneur. Two months later he wrote his father-in-law that the Kansas and Shawnees were back from their second hunt with good results. "There are 236 bundles of deerskins, the weight will be roughly 25,000 lbs.; 50 packs of raccoons containing 100 skins in a pack; about 500 beaver skins, 800 otter, 500 [musk]rats, and 2 bundles of bearskins. And really, these skins are superb."

The rapidly changing nature of François's trading territory—caused by the arrival of other whites to trade with the tribes and the fact that the tribes now had government annuities with which to buy merchandise whether they hunted or not—challenged him to be more inventive and aggressive in protecting his business domain. The evolving situation put him in conflict with Marston Clark, a cousin of William Clark's, who was appointed the government agent to the Kansa tribe in 1829. Marston Clark had the authority to determine whether the tribe should receive its annuities in money or goods; to decide where they were to be paid, such as a particular trading post; and even to negotiate directly with merchants or jobbers to bring supplies from St. Louis for the tribe.

Wanting to be sure that Marston Clark would not give the business to other merchants, François took his case directly to the chiefs to persuade them to do business with him. Like other members of his family, François enjoyed a high standing with the tribes. He sought to prove to them that they could get better merchandise from him than through men invited by the agent to bring merchandise. François prodded Cadet to send him plenty of goods to show the chiefs and braves before they went out to hunt. If he had something that appealed to them, François thought, the tribe would be more likely to bring its pelts to him. When they were ready to trade, he wanted to have plenty of good merchandise on hand.

François had managed to elicit from the Kansa chiefs a criticism of the merchandise they received through Marston Clark the previous year as being "too little, and of too poor a quality." As a result, this time, "All the chiefs were on my side and no one on his side. In such a way that I believe that he is angry to see that the Indians are showing me consideration and confidence."

Both Agent Clark and François appealed for support to their relatives and superiors in St. Louis. In the summer of 1830 François complained to Ménard about the "greatest theft" of the Kansa annuities by the Indian Department at St. Louis. He said that after the chiefs had asked him in the winter to list the goods he could bring for their annuities, he ordered the merchandise from St. Louis and priced it at St. Louis prices, without markup, and that "the Indians were very pleased with the conditions." But Marston Clark decided to look for a better deal in St. Louis.

When he returned with goods for their annuities, the chiefs demanded money instead. Clark threatened to bring in as many army troops "as the blades of grass to be seen on the prairies" in order to bring the tribes around to accept his merchandise. The chiefs eventually succumbed, which was at least a temporary setback for François.

This conflict between François and Marston Clark grew so intense that Clark, according to François, claimed to have asked President Jackson to take away François's trading license. "If he did that, I promise you, he will pay for it as I can find proof to put him in the most difficult situation in the world," François wrote Ménard. He called Clark a "scoundrel." But if President Jackson received such a request, he apparently did not act on it. The Chouteau name was then well-known to Jackson, particularly through his friend Sam Houston, who regularly sang the praises of François's eldest half brother, A.P., to the President.

Marston Clark also complained to William Clark that François exerted too much influence over the tribes in general and that the

Chouteaus' Kansa post was too close to the Indian agency—a distance of just a mile and on the opposite side of the river. This meant that when Indians came to the agency for annuity payments or other business, the trading post was a convenient place to spend those credits, as well as the place to make plans for the new hunting season.

As for François's having considerable influence, that was surely true; it was the result of trust built up over three generations between his family and many tribes. It was also true that when François selected the site for the new Kansa post at Horseshoe Lake to replace Four Houses, he intentionally looked for a location that would be easily accessible for the tribe.

Marston Clark said the proximity of the trading post to the government agency meant that there were lots of Indians hanging around the agency "to the great annoyance of the few whites at this place . . . killing their stock, crowding their houses and begging for provisions." To satisfy Clark's complaints, François had a new post built on a site assigned by the government. It was located between two Kansa villages at a place called American Chief Creek, where it emptied into the Kansas River on the south side. Frederick Chouteau moved into it in the fall of 1832.

In addition to his conflicts with Marston Clark, François worried about the fact that there were now three stores—potential competitors—in the bustling village of Independence, a few miles southeast of his headquarters. All had "a little Indian merchandise." Also, some men were going out in wagons with merchandise to peddle to the Indians.

Living in an area that was quickly becoming a relatively settled part of the United States, François realized that he and his family could not live indefinitely from a trade that depended on Indians having a large open area in which to hunt and trap, and also depended on their desire to do so. He began buying pieces of land at government land sales. By the beginning of the 1830s François had put together a working farm of about twelve hundred acres of bottomland surrounding his warehouse and steamboat landing. Later he began trading land.

In other ways as well, François and Bérénice were helping to lay the groundwork for a community. Unlike his grandfather, Pierre Laclède, François did not choose the name of the city that grew up on the site of his property. During his lifetime, however, his impact and that of Bérénice was such that the area on the Missouri riverfront at the mouth of the Kansas River was commonly known as Chouteau's Landing, or Chouteau's Town. This was some three decades before English-speaking settlers would incorporate the city of Kansas City in Missouri and four decades before Wyandotte Indians would incorporate a town of the same name in Kansas.

François and Bérénice's eldest son, Edmund François, was sent to day school in St. Louis at an early age, and at age ten he transferred to St. Louis College, a Catholic boarding school for boys that eventually became St. Louis University. Their second son, whom they called Ménard, which was his middle name, was sent to St. Mary's of the Barrens at Perryville, Missouri, across the Mississippi from the Ménard home at Kaskaskia. Some of Pierre Ménard's younger sons also studied there, and Bérénice expected her father to keep an eye on her own son as well.

As for "little Benjamin," François reported in April 1830, when he was sixteen months old, that he "walks all over and begins to speak French and English."

The family had to deal with frequent illnesses of children and others who came and went in the house at Chouteau's Landing. All the children had whooping cough and pulled through it in the winter of 1831–32. Later, everybody had the measles. Fevers, some of which were probably malarial, were frequent and threw fear into the parents.

They were friendly with various members of the Boone family, particularly Daniel Morgan Boone, who was government agriculturist for the Kansa Indians from 1827 to 1831 and lived across the Missouri River from the Chouteaus. François and Bérénice had used the nickname Little Morgan for one of their sons who died, probably because of their friendship with the Boones. In 1834 Bérénice was godmother to Elizabeth Boone, the Boone granddaughter; the Chouteaus' young son Benjamin was godfather to Eulalia, another Boone grandchild, in 1835.

François's business dealings with Indian tribal leaders led to friendly relations between them and his family. Bérénice took into their home to rear a young granddaughter of the Kansa chief White Plume, who wanted his tribe to absorb more white influence. Two of White Plume's daughters had had children by the same Frenchman, Louis Gonville, and the Chouteaus brought up one of the children, a girl named Mary Josephine, known as Josette.

From some of the correspondence, it appears that Bérénice was also rearing a mixed-blood daughter of a member of the Loramier family of Cape Girardeau, probably a situation arranged by her father, who often assisted Indian and mixed-blood families with the care and education of their children. Bérénice was preparing the little girl to be sent to school.

In the 1830 census, their household also included what appeared to be a slave family—a male listed as between thirty-six and fifty-five, a female between twenty-four and thirty-six, and a female child under ten. From time to time family correspondence mentioned other slaves, although they were not numerous enough to have been carrying the main load of work at Chouteau's Landing.

Always thinking of their extended families, the young couple often sent interesting gifts, some of them things made on the frontier that were not available in relatively advanced places such as St. Louis and Kaskaskia. For example, the Cree wife of an early French settler of the area named Gabriel Prudhomme, who died in a tavern brawl in 1831, crafted soft Indian shoes, which made good gifts.

Death and illness among family in St. Louis and Kaskaskia touched them deeply from their distant location. Bérénice's half brother François took ill while attending college in New York State. He had a chest malady and was coughing up blood. He returned to his parents' home in Kaskaskia, where his health continued to decline.

Hearing, after a couple of years, that his situation was dramatically worse, Bérénice was planning to visit her family in the fall of 1830 and see twenty-four-year-old François. But her own François was also ailing, and she decided not to leave him. On January 8, 1831, her brother died. Bérénice wrote her sister, Alzire Kennerly, who had just lost a baby son, and expressed the difficulty she was experiencing in dealing with the latest deaths, which also caused her to think of the children she had buried. She was especially concerned about how her father and stepmother were handling the loss of their son.

"I do not doubt that the death of our good brother is cruel for them and for all of us because he was made to be loved by all those who knew him," she told her sister. "And when I learned the unhappy news, I tried to write to our beloved father but I was unable to finish because what consolation was I able to give him, as well as to you, my beloved Alzire. I suffered this pain twice and I know well that nature will take its course."

Bérénice, who was pregnant again, told her sister she could not travel to St. Louis for the delivery because of "the health of my poor Gesseau that is very bad which means that I couldn't resolve myself to upset him."

François wrote Ménard the next month to sympathize with the loss of Ménard's son, but did not mention his own health problems. "I know that your sorrow is very great, because I myself have some experience in that area. But our dear uncle, we have to console ourselves—for those who remain with us." It had been a hard winter around the post, he said. The Indians ran short of food, several died, and horses were also suffering, the Kansas having lost many of theirs.

In April 1831 Bérénice gave birth to her sixth baby boy, the first of her children born at their farm in the river outpost. François reported the birth of "a plump son without accident" on April 14. He was christened with the name Frederick Donatien. François did not say who had assisted in the birth, but he said he had remained at home for two weeks "to give my Bérénice the care of which she is in need." It is quite likely that by that time, there were enough women in the area to provide some aid and comfort to Bérénice as well.

The smallpox epidemic of 1831 around the junction of the Kansas and Missouri rivers caused numerous deaths among the tribes in the area, including the Shawnees, Delaware-Loups, and the Kansas, although government agents arrived with vaccine in the summer and began a vaccination campaign. François feared that the disease would largely eliminate the winter hunt that year. He said the Indians who had saved themselves by going into the wilderness had not yet returned. But in January 1832 he reported that the sickness had not been as devastating as he had expected, perhaps because of the hurried vaccination campaign, so he was hopeful for a decent season.

However, François's own health problems were becoming a matter of concern. Just thirty-five years old, he was suffering chest pains and other discomforts that limited his ability to travel among the Indian villages. When the family went to St. Louis over the following summer, François planned to continue to New Orleans by steamboat and spend the winter there in hopes that the warmer climate would help him. But he consulted his father's doctor in St. Louis, who advised him "to go farther on," meaning Cuba or somewhere else in the Caribbean. François thought about this and decided against it. "I do not like to go to distant lands where I know no one," he told Ménard, "and especially in circumstances such as these where the cholera can show up from one day to another."

He returned to his own home and trading headquarters at the mouth of the Kansas River for the winter. Just a month after his return, the seriousness of his illness became more apparent. "I am still suffering from chest pains," he told Ménard, "and that makes me almost unable to see to the business."

As fascinated by steamboats as was his brother Cadet, François had returned from St. Louis by steamboat that summer, and that produced a happy thrill even in the face of his declining health. He and Bérénice had made the trip from St. Louis in just nine days. "On board we were in a very good company of men and women," he said. "In such a way that our trip was one of the most pleasant that I have ever made."

A short time after their return, the *Yellow Stone* pulled up to his landing with merchandise for him after making the trip from St. Louis in a mere five days and ten hours. François was duly impressed. But there was a reason why the vessel was trying to break records this time. After bringing the vessel back to St. Louis in July from its spectacular voyage to the mouth of the Yellowstone, Cadet had learned about the stricter government clampdown on liquor in Indian country, and he was trying—unsuccessfully as it turned out—to get a new shipment past Fort Leavenworth before the official orders reached the military post.

Paradoxically, one of the things that greatly upset François about the Indians around his place was the extent to which they abused liquor when it was made available to them by other traders. "The Loup tribe drinks a lot at the present and often many die," he wrote Ménard in the same letter in which he marveled at the travel time of the *Yellow Stone*. "Not a day passes that at least 30 gallons of whiskey is not brought to the village. In five years from now, I presume that they will be almost all destroyed if they keep on at that pace."

"A great many of the local rascals among the inhabitants" sell whiskey to the Indians at night, he had reported earlier. "The villages of the Kickapoo were drunk from the day they received their annuities."

There is no indication in his correspondence that François was aware of Cadet's attempts to make liquor available to traders on the extreme Upper Missouri, where his outfits had to compete with British companies free to use liquor to attract tribes to their posts. However, his sense of outrage toward those who used liquor around him seems to confirm that members of the Chouteau family tried to avoid the use of liquor as a trading lure except in situations where the competition had it. He complained on one occasion of Indians going to Fort Leavenworth and obtaining liquor, apparently buying it from soldiers, who were exempt from the prohibition in Indian country.

François continued to suffer "chest trouble" or pains, which forced him to rely more and more on his two younger brothers to handle the work with the tribes from their trading posts among the Shawnees and Kansas and collect the bulk of the pelts. François concentrated on developing his farm with slaves and other hands. In 1833 he bought a mulatto slave from a departing fur trader for $550, although he considered the slave "very expensive" at that price. "He is skillful and a good farmer and we have the greatest difficulty obtaining men here," François explained. "We have only four men and this is not enough."

François also filled a modest role as unofficial banker, debt collector, and lender in the community. He traded real estate and took care of legal matters that few others were educated enough to do in the raw frontier settlement.

Their son Ménard came home after a year or so at Perryville and studied at a Protestant mission school serving the Delawares. The next fall, Ménard and the eldest boy, Edmund, whom they called Gesseau after François's own middle name, were sent back downriver to St. Louis with a lot of fatherly worries. Young Gesseau had been studying at St. Louis College, not far from Pierre Sr.'s home, but François wondered if both boys might not be better off at "the Barrens" in Perryville. François always worried about cholera, and he thought it was more of a threat in a populous river town such as St. Louis than in a smaller town away from the river, such as Perryville. He also spelled out other worries to Pierre Ménard before sending the boys on their way.

"I beg of you to place Ménard at the Barrens as soon as he arrives," he wrote. "And I do not know whether Gesseau would not be better off at the Barrens than at St. Louis where he is too much exposed to bad companionship. It appears to me that at the Barrens he could have no chance for bad companionship or debauchery. He's growing up. And I hope to make of him and his brother nice boys. It seems to me that the college in St. Louis is too near to the world and all sorts of things."

But the boys' Chouteau grandfather did not want Gesseau to be far from St. Louis, and François did not want to hurt his father, "or to distress him in any way." Pierre Ménard must have eventually prevailed over Pierre Chouteau Sr. because by December he had both of his daughter's sons enrolled at the Barrens, with his own boys. This was a matter of "great satisfaction" to François.

One more boy was born to Bérénice, on February 23, 1833, at their home, after which François reported to the family that she was well. The baby was named Benedict Pharamond, his middle name honoring François's younger brother Pharamond, who had died two years earlier at the age of twenty-five. This was the second of their children born on the frontier, but the first to be baptized there.

His baptism, in February 1834, was made possible by the arrival of the Reverend Benedict Roux, who wanted to build a church for the French Catholics in the area. Father Roux had come to America in 1831 and pestered the bishop at St. Louis until he was allowed to move farther west.

One day in November 1833 Father Roux rode up to Chouteau's Landing on horseback and was given lodging by the young Chouteaus, who quickly became enthusiastic supporters of his project. "Immediately [François] called a meeting of the Catholics of the locality to discuss means toward getting a church and supporting a priest," Roux wrote his bishop. "I found everybody well disposed and ready to make all reasonable sacrifices." François and his brother Cyprien were the "two pillars" of the effort and were asking for money from their father and Pierre Ménard.

François explained their feelings to Ménard:

> At the present we have here a Curé, Mr. Roux, who desires to remain in our country. I believe he is a worthy man. We intend to build a small church for him. All the French families here are well disposed to supply, according to their ability. Bérénice assures me she intends to put in a contribution. You, papa and Cadet, you are able to judge better than I that the thing cannot be anything but advantageous. We will then later on certainly have a small group of fine people. The riffraff perhaps will improve as this will be a cause of betterment for the area.

There was little doubt that the place soon to become Kansas City attracted plenty of "riffraff." By then it was a polyglot collection of small settlements — Independence, Westport, Chouteau's Landing, and Kawsmouth, the latter a French farming community south of the mouth of the Kansas River, which was also known as the Kaw. François's brother Cadet used the designation "Chez les Cans" to describe the area around the trading headquarters. All of those communities were within a few miles of each other in the state of Missouri, but they abutted Indian Territory in the future state of Kansas. Westport and Independence were basically English-speaking towns and were growing more rapidly than the French communities.

Everybody carried weapons; shootings and knifings had become common. When the Duke of Württemberg traveled through the area in 1822–23, he had encountered hunters and boatmen "whose inclination to drink and immorality often exceeded the bounds of all human dignity." In the early-to-mid-1830s, conflict between Joseph Smith's Mormons and arriving southern farmers produced mob violence and threats of open warfare.

Aside from the fur trade, these settlements had businesses that served farmers and outfitted wagon trains. There were also plenty of taverns and liquor dealers who plied their trade as close to the border as possible in pursuit of Indian business. "Right now, the whole eastern side is filled with whiskey salesmen," François commented to Ménard in November 1834 after some of the tribes had received government annuity payments. By "eastern side," he meant the part of his trading area that was within the state of Missouri, on the east side of the border.

François and Bérénice had in mind a more refined future for their community when they provided much of the money to build a church on forty acres atop one of the bluffs. Father Roux had purchased the site from another Frenchman. The church was completed in 1835, and a rough "street" was cleared along the south side to provide access. For the first few years the little log house of worship was called simply Chouteau's Church, and the road running beside it was Chouteau's Street. Later named St. Francis Regis, the church was the forerunner of the Cathedral of the Immaculate Conception.

In addition to the church, Bérénice tried to improve and enliven her community in other ways. One of the enduring legends about her—although historians have been unable to find evidence proving it—is that she took the first piano to western Missouri on a keelboat. There was no doubt of her love for music. She once shopped for a "music notebook" while in St. Louis. And her winter dancing parties, or "balls," with the music of fiddlers, were popular enough that they incurred the disapproval of Father Roux, who complained about the activity to the bishop in St. Louis—to no avail.

In August 1834 the couple lost another child with the death of Benedict Pharamond at eighteen months. It occurred while they were spending the summer in St. Louis, and it reinforced François's notion that the climate along the Mississippi River side of Missouri was more conducive to the mysterious killer fevers than was the western side of the state. By now they had had seven babies, all boys, and lost three of them, all while visiting St. Louis.

The two older boys also proved about the same time that there was justification for their father's worries about their education and behavior. They were both expelled from St. Mary's of the Barrens, the boarding school at Perryville. Grandfather Ménard received the news first, but before he could get word to his daughter and son-in-law, the younger of the two, twelve-year-old Ménard, was allowed back in school.

What the boys may have done that warranted dismissal was not revealed in the family correspondence, but historians who examined the school archives found only that there had been some kind of "revolt" by a large number of the students. There was a suggestion in some family letters that the older boy, Gesseau, then fourteen, may have become fed up with the disciplined school environment. He later told his grandfather Ménard that he "was lured into evil instead of luring others."

François was "pained" and "afflicted" by the news that reached him in August 1835 from the man who was both uncle and father-in-law to him. He must have known, however, that the boys were unhappy at the school, because he said he had hoped they could get through to the next vacation, "and then I would have taken appropriate measures on their behalf if it were necessary." He asked Ménard to "keep Gesseau in your house and not to allow him to go to St. Louis."

Then he reflected a bit on the misdeeds of his own youth, without specifying what they had been, and as usual, he ended up heaping blame on himself. "I am obliged to undergo this mortification as, indeed, I gave to my parents cause for sorrow," he told Ménard. "And upon reflection, I admit that I well deserve this. They are extremely happy, those who do not experience sorrow on account of their children."

He was also in "a moment of tribulation." The entire family had been ill. Six-year-old Benjamin had nearly died from "an inflammation with bilious fever," but he was better. In the miserable August heat, Bérénice was close to delivering again and anxious to get it over with. "As for me, I suffer a little from time to time with chest pains, but I am more weak than suffering. If I could treat myself for that, I think I could get myself on my feet again."

Mary Brigitte Chouteau, the couple's first daughter, was born at their home at 4 a.m. on September 17, 1835. A few months later François reported her to be "small, but plump and healthy." She was baptized the following May in Kaskaskia because the straitlaced Father Roux had already given up on the rambunctious new parish and returned to St. Louis. Construction of the church was completed soon after his departure, but a new priest had not yet come.

After Gesseau's expulsion from school he spent the remainder of 1835 and the beginning of 1836 at home with his parents, during which time he managed to chop off half of one toe with a hatchet. Ménard also came home for part of that time. By the spring of 1836 their father was thinking that they should be back in school. Both went to St. Louis on a steamboat in May with their mother and the smaller children, but only Ménard was reenrolled. Seven-year-old Benjamin was enrolled at a one-room school in nearby Westport.

The following year found Gesseau, then sixteen, at work in either the warehouse or office of his uncle Cadet in St. Louis, under the demanding tutelage of John B. Sarpy. Gainful employment must have put an end to his rebellious phase, because his father had good things to report about him to Pierre Ménard: "He always writes to me by all the steamboats, of which he has perfect knowledge. Sarpy gives me praise of him in all his letters."

The winter of 1838 was exceptionally cold around Chouteau's Landing. "The Missouri is solid like a bridge and we have hardly any snow," François noted in January. On the sixteenth of the month Bérénice gave birth to her ninth baby, another girl, who was christened Thérèse Odile, and François seemed a bit surprised to find himself with two daughters after so many sons. With that out of the way, and with spring coming, François was thinking of joining Bérénice on her planned trip down to St. Louis and Kaskaskia in April.

But on April 18, while standing along the riverbank watching some of his cattle swim across an inlet or channel, he collapsed and died.

François Gesseau Chouteau was forty-one years old when his life abruptly ended. His comments about his physical condition during several years before his death strongly suggested heart disease. The grieving Bérénice packed up her smaller children and her husband's body and took a boat home to St. Louis to bury him, an unusual action in an era before embalming. He was interred there on April 25, 1838.

His young family and young community were both left to mature without François. Had he lived longer, he might have followed the paths of his father, of his uncle Auguste, and of Pierre Jr., going into other business ventures—banking, land, property development—as his town grew and flourished. In November 1838, just months after his death, fourteen of his neighbors formed the Town of Kansas Company and laid out the first town lots on land that Gabriel Prudhomme had acquired from François in 1831. Men cut through the rock cliffs behind Chouteau's Landing and began to gradually level the terrain for homes and businesses.

Bérénice Ménard Chouteau carried the banner for the family as the settlement that she and her husband had founded grew into Kansas City. After her husband's death, she spent months among family in St. Louis and Kaskaskia, then returned to Chouteau's Landing with the children. She lost one more of them, the infant Odile, within a short time. The family was flooded out again in 1844, just after the death of Pierre Ménard.

She built her new home, a two-story colonial-style frame dwelling with a wide center hall, porches, and French windows, on much higher ground well out of reach of the river. The Santa Fe Trail passed by the deep manicured lawns of the house, where she kept a large staff and entertained lavishly. With most of the other French families having departed because of the flood and the continual decline of the fur trade, she established herself as the grande dame of a now booming American town fascinated by her charm

and taste. She rode about in a splendid carriage "drawn by two perfectly matched gray horses with tails nicked in Boston fashion and
driven by a negro driver," recalled a woman who knew her in those
years.

Cyprien and Frederick also remained in the area throughout their
long lives. Both continued in the fur trade from their posts among the
Kansas and Shawnees, but as the Indians departed for reservations in
the future Oklahoma and the brothers aged, both moved closer to
town. Frederick had a succession of at least four wives, the first three
of them part Shawnee, each of whom gave him children before dying.
He profited in the land boom that accompanied Kansas City's growth,
and he died a rich man in 1891, the last surviving of his generation of
Chouteau cousins. He had between twelve and fourteen children,
who produced countless descendants.

Cyprien was married at about age fifty to a young woman of part-
Shawnee ancestry, by whom he had three children. Until the Civil
War, he and his family lived on a farm three miles south of what had
been Chouteau's Landing. After Federal troops occupied the area and
drove many families identified with the Southern cause off their land,
Cyprien leased his farm to a Union sympathizer and built a two-story
frame home on a river bluff within the city limits, where he lived until his death in 1879.

During the Civil War and the border war that preceded it around
Kansas City, Bérénice moved to Ste. Genevieve along the Mississippi.
Later she returned to Kansas City and lived in the home of her son
Pierre Ménard Chouteau, who was "Mack" in the English-speaking
city where he cut a prominent figure. After Mack's death, in 1885, she
remained with his widow, Mary.

By then the downtown hills above what had once been her riverfront home were traversed by cable cars and covered with brick buildings, one of them eight stories high. She did not retreat from this new
world. In the last year of her life, an old friend recalled seeing her,
now an "aged" lady, "in neat sable attire, save the snowy neckerchief
at her neck, standing alone waiting for a train at the corner of Eighth
and Cherry streets."

Bérénice died at her daughter-in-law's home on November 19,

1888, at the age of eighty-seven. Although she lived into the age when photography was common, she had refused to have her photograph taken. The story handed down was that she did not want her own image preserved, because François had never sat for a portrait during his short life.

FIFTEEN

Pierre Jr.: Position, Advantage, and Perhaps Vanity

❊

In the fall of 1832, after his acclaimed voyage to Fort Union on the *Yellow Stone*, Pierre Chouteau Jr. gave his older daughter, Emilie, in marriage to Virginia-born John F. A. Sanford, who had come west as an eighteen-year-old and clerked for William Clark until being appointed an Indian agent in 1826. Following the November wedding, Cadet left, as was his custom, for the East. He made his usual journey down the Mississippi and up the Ohio by steamboat just before the rivers froze, then continued by carriage. In January, from New York, he sent a note to his cousin, friend, and partner, John B. Sarpy, saying he had been to the Italian opera.

But much more than family celebrations and high culture was on Cadet's mind. He and Kenneth McKenzie were searching for a way to evade the new, stricter prohibition on taking liquor above Leavenworth on the Missouri River. Without access to liquor, they felt they could not compete with British companies in winning Indian trade.

Ramsay Crooks and McKenzie went to Washington that winter and sought to convince Secretary of War Lewis Cass to allow the use of liquor in the Indian trade in the Upper Missouri country where the American Fur Company competed directly against British traders. "I explained fully to Gov. Cass that our sole and only wish for a partial supply was to enable us to cope with our Hudson's Bay opponents at our new posts above the Mandans," Crooks told Cadet, but it was "wholly impossible to affect [*sic*] the least modification."

Crooks had warned Cass that the Upper Missouri country was likely to be "deluged by a larger supply than usual" the coming year from British traders determined to turn back the advances the A.F.C. was making in winning the trading allegiance of additional tribes near the Canadian border. Cass responded that the law was "imperative." However, he promised to bring the matter to the attention of the President and the Secretary of State "who, he was sure, would at once enter into a correspondence with the British Government and do all in their power to induce that Government to exclude from the trade of the Hudson's Bay Company every species of spiritous liquors."

When McKenzie left Washington for St. Louis, he was "disheartened," according to Crooks, to see "prospects of the future so discouraging in relation to his trade." But Crooks and the Astors either knew or sensed that a daring and politically dangerous plan was afoot, and Crooks sought to head it off. "Every eye is upon us," he warned Cadet, "and whoever can, will annoy us with all his heart—It will therefore in my opinion be madness to attempt your Cincinnati project of the Boxes, or the *alembique*—try to struggle through the disadvantages under which we must labor in the competition with the Hudson's Bay Company."

Somewhere along his route to the Ohio River to board the company's new steamboat, the *Assiniboine*, McKenzie apparently concluded that the new law forbade only the importation of liquor into Indian country, not its use or sale as such. So he saw a solution in setting up a distillery at Fort Union and producing the firm's own spirits. During that winter he or the firm's office in St. Louis had obtained a favorable legal opinion on this interpretation of the law.

As a result, in April, when the A.F.C. sent both the *Yellow Stone* and the *Assiniboine* up the Missouri, one of them carried a still. From Crooks's reference to the "Cincinnati project," it seems likely that the still was acquired in Cincinnati while the *Assiniboine* was under construction. In addition to a large contingent of workers for the fur posts, the two boats ascending the river carried Pierre Jr., Emilie and their daughters, McKenzie, Sanford, and two distinguished Europeans: Prince Alexander Philip Maximilian of Wied-Neuwied, who had studied natural science and was assembling a collection of Indian items, and the artist Karl Bodmer, who accompanied the prince and painted many of the people and scenes they saw.

To once again test the inspection system at Leavenworth, McKenzie shipped some liquor on the *Yellow Stone*; it was discovered and duly confiscated. The next stop was Cabanné's place at the Bluffs. Prince Maximilian noted that the post had fifteen acres of corn planted on the rich adjacent land. He apparently did not realize that some of it was intended for a new distillery upriver.

"We spent a very pleasant evening with Mr. Cabanné," recalled the prince. "Sitting in the balcony of his house, we enjoyed the delightful temperature and the fine scene around us. The splendid sky was illumined by the full moon; silence reigned around, interrupted only by the noise of the frogs, and the incessant cry of the whip-poor-will, in the neighbouring woods, till the Indians assembled round the house, and, at the request of Mr. Cabanné, performed a dance." The visitors returned to their vessels late that night, and Cabanné prepared to start downriver to St. Louis to begin his year of banishment from Indian country because of his role in the Leclerc affair the summer before.

Both steamboats reached Fort Pierre a day apart in late May. The *Yellow Stone* turned back from there, and McKenzie, Maximilian, and Bodmer continued to Fort Union on the *Assiniboine*, arriving June 24, 1833. By July the distillery was in operation at Fort Union, producing its first whiskey from corn grown by Mandan Indians.

McKenzie, however, soon became the victim of his own audacity and self-confidence. On August 24 Nathaniel J. Wyeth, a Yankee traveling around the West in search of business opportunities, arrived at Fort Union with a companion named M. S. Cerré. With his usual charm and hospitality, McKenzie opened up the fort and his house to them. They dined on good meat, cheese, bread, milk, and wine—all luxuries in the Upper Missouri country. In fact, McKenzie became so enthusiastic during their visit that he showed them his secret weapon: the distillery.

Before leaving, they tried to buy some liquor from McKenzie, but he refused. He also charged them the going rates for the other supplies they bought. As a result, their attitude toward McKenzie cooled considerably as they set forth downriver. Reaching Leavenworth, they gave the Indian agent there an affidavit alleging that the A.F.C. was "making and vending whiskey in quantity" at Fort Union. The agent sent this to William Clark in St. Louis, and Clark asked Pierre Jr. for the explanation that he should "think proper to give."

Pierre Jr., probably assuming that the old family friend Clark would accept whatever explanation he gave, told him that "the company, believing that wild pears and berries might be converted into wine—which they did not understand to be prohibited—did authorize experiments to be made, and if, under color of this, ardent spirits have been distilled and vended, it is without the knowledge, authority, or direction of the company, and I will take measures by sending immediately an 'express' [message] to arrest the operation complained of, if found to exist."

Word about the uproar set off downriver by his distillery was slow to find its way back to McKenzie. Prior to that, in December, he had bragged in a letter to Cadet, "Our manufactory flourishes admirably. We only want corn to keep us going. The Mandan corn yields badly but makes a fine, sweet liquor. Do not load the boat too heavily at St. Louis, that a few hundred bushels of corn may be placed on board at the Bluffs." He also asked Joshua Pilcher, who was in charge at the Bluffs in the absence of Cabanné, to send up a good supply of corn in the spring, or "my wine vats will be idle."

Pierre Jr. ordered the still shut down, but word of it had reached Washington, where the Cabanné-Leclerc affair already had politicians and officials believing the A.F.C. was entirely too freewheeling. Now came this new effrontery, adding to the sense of outrage. Through the sympathetic Senator Benton, however, Pierre Jr. assured the Secretary of War that the company would henceforth obey the law about liquor, and the firm's license to trade was saved.

Learning that Cadet had claimed to Clark and other authorities that the still "was only intended to promote the cause of *Botany*," Crooks issued a strong note of caution from New York: "*Prenez-y-garde*—Don't presume too much on your recent escape from an accusation, which might have been attended with serious consequences—The less of this sort of business you do, the better; for the time may, and very probably will come, when you will be exposed by the endless number of spies you have around you . . . and your business so much resembles a monopoly that there will always exist strong jealousies against you."

Smarting at bearing most of the blame, McKenzie strongly defended himself and repeated his argument on the need for liquor in order to compete with British traders. Finally, he offered an explanation of the still that was something of a variation on Cadet's "botany" story, offering his boss further grounds for plausible denial. His two letters of explanation, written in March, seemed to totally contradict his December report about his flourishing "manufactory."

"It is very true I brought up a Still last season, as I would do any other article of [merchandise] by the sale whereof I expected to realize a profit," McKenzie told Cadet, and went on to argue that he had brought the still for the head of a colony of British immigrants who had settled on the Red River at Lake Winnipeg in 1815–16.

> This is the Mr. [J. P.] Rourke who visited the States last spring to purchase sheep for Red River Colony. It is also true that while the Still remained at this place until an opportunity of sending it to Mr. Rourke offered, which was not expected to occur before April next (1834) an American citizen who chanced to be at this post proposed to make some experiments therewith on the fruits of this country, which the past season were tolerably abundant; he entered into the speculation on his own account & certainly succeeded in making a very palatable article but not a single gallon of liquor has been manufactured since last fall & Mr. Rourke has apprized me he will send or come for the Still next month. If herein I have erred or infringed the laws of U.S. in spirit or in letter, I acknowledge my error, but it has been so done innocently.
>
> It is true that Mr. L. Ceré [sic] & a person who introduced himself to me as a Capt. Wythe [sic] were at Fort Union in August last, they were both very earnest in their applications to purchase liquor of one, I had none to sell them but offered them wine which they declined buying altho' they drank freely of it at my table during their stay; notwithstanding which I am informed the said Capt. Wythe was heartily drunk during his voyage down the Mo. & mortified at my refusing him liquor, & being moreover a man of such dissipated habits, it seems to me that any statement of his should be listened to with extreme caution.

Regardless of this setback to his independence and authority, Kenneth McKenzie was well on his way to making himself an unforgettable figure among both whites and Indians in the fur trade of the Upper Missouri. Variously characterized as the "ablest trader that the A.F.C. ever possessed" and the "King of the Upper Missouri," he reigned over an empire larger than that of many kings and princes. He had branch outposts hundreds of miles from Fort Union. Indians came from all directions to trade, including the Assiniboines, who occupied both sides of the nearby Canadian border; the Crows from the mouth of the Bighorn; and from farther up the Missouri the Blackfeet, who also claimed land on both sides of the border. Years later the upward and westward thrust of white settlement would push additional tribes to Fort Union's area of hegemony.

By the summer of 1833 McKenzie already had his men at work expanding the fort, which grew into a small village, including an impressive two-story house for McKenzie and his successors as *bourgeois*. Originally 178 by 198 feet, the compound grew to 220 by 240 feet in the first expansion and later to 237 by 245 feet. It had a powder magazine, a row of apartments, a smithy, a bell tower, a cemetery outside the walls, a distilling building, an icehouse, a carpenter shop, a separate kitchen building behind the house, and livestock pins. The room where buffalo robes and other pelts were pressed into compact bales held 2,800 to 3,000 packs of robes, or nearly 30,000 robes.

The flagpole sent the Stars and Stripes sixty-three feet into the air every morning, and it could be seen from a great distance by those approaching by land or water. The fort occupied a grassy plain stretching to the north a mile from the river, with ample space for Indian camps at trading time.

The sense of an isolated empire was heightened in winter, when the Upper Missouri often froze to a depth of three feet and was closed to everything except dogsleds. On the day in spring when the ice broke, there would be a mighty explosion, like thunder. The water would suddenly force the mass upward; then the ice would roll downstream for hours in a continuous roar until the river was free-flowing at last.

Befitting this domain and his position in it, Kenneth McKenzie carried himself as one born to command. He often wore a uniform at Fort Union and permitted only a select few at his table. He lavished hospitality on visitors, including the rarity of chilled wine. He received Indian leaders and other visitors seated in a high-backed thronelike chair.

In the summer of 1834 a young man named Charles Larpenteur, born in Baltimore of French immigrant parents, went to work for the American Fur Company on the Upper Missouri, reporting to Kenneth McKenzie at Fort Union. As one of several clerks, who were the principal assistants to the *bourgeois* in conducting the Indian trade, he was invited to dine at McKenzie's table. He had arrived at Fort Union with only a pair of pants, a blue-checkered shirt, and a cap to his name, but his salary was to include a decent suit of clothes. For that first night, before his suit was ready, the other clerks told him he must not appear in shirtsleeves, so one of them lent him a coat.

"On entering the eating hall, I found a splendidly set table with a very white tablecloth, and two waiters, one a negro. Mr. McKenzie was sitting at the head of the table, extremely well dressed. The victuals consisted of fine fat buffalo meat, with plenty of good fresh butter, cream, and milk for those that chose."

Further buttressing McKenzie's image as frontier royalty, while he and Crooks were together in Washington in the fall of 1832, McKenzie had asked his fellow Scotsman to obtain for him a coat of mail. Crooks sent to England for it. The ruler of the Upper Missouri also requested medals to give to Indian leaders. This had long been a custom in white-Indian relations, but the medals were normally distributed by government representatives and bore the likeness of presidents or kings. Crooks hired a diemaker to produce medals with "a good likeness *de notre estimable Grand-papa*"—John Jacob Astor. He first sought an opinion from someone in Washington about the propriety of this and was told there would be no governmental objection as long as they were considered "ornaments and not medals."

McKenzie loved fine, speedy horses and used them to join Indians in buffalo hunts. In this thrilling and dangerous sport, groups of Indians dashed across the plains at a full gallop into a herd of grazing buffalo, rapidly loading and firing their guns. Terrified bison bellowed, and men screamed amid huge clouds of dust. When it was over, and the land was littered with dead animals, Indian women did the work of cutting out the tongues, the favored meat from the bison, and skinning the carcasses and preparing the skins for trading.

Days and nights were long at Fort Union, and a variety of other entertainments helped to fill them: native games of chance, card games, horse races with betting, drinking, feasting, and love affairs. Indians, whites, and mixed-bloods shared these diversions. In 1833 McKenzie ordered a "magic lantern" and a set of glass slides from Philadelphia. This primitive picture show used a reflective plate behind an oil lamp to project images against a wall. The same year, McKenzie had three crates of fireworks shipped to Fort Union.

The liquor question did not go away with the destruction of McKenzie's still. Competitors had access to liquor, generally through Canada, and the A.F.C. somehow managed to acquire its own supply. Company correspondence over the coming two decades contains many references to various ideas on getting liquor to the upriver posts, including buying it in Canada and bringing it down the Yellowstone River or sneaking it past the military's Fort Snelling in the future Minnesota.

Charles Larpenteur, the young clerk, confirmed from firsthand experience that liquor was available. "The liquor business, which was always done at night, sometimes kept me up all night turning out drunken Indians, often by dragging them out by arms and legs," he wrote. "Although the still house had been destroyed, the Company found means to smuggle plenty of liquor."

Liquor was generally not used by the A.F.C. as an item of direct exchange for furs and skins. Rather, it served to soften up the Indians with a big party or feast of drunkenness the night before trading began at the end of a hunting season. They would camp around a fur post, enjoy a night with ardent spirits, then deliver their pelts in exchange for merchandise or to pay off credits for guns and merchandise obtained in advance of the hunt. All of the fur traders in the upper country felt they needed the attraction of the liquor to draw tribes to them and prevent their going to rival trading outfits.

One of the outcomes of the still episode was that McKenzie became friends with Prince Maximilian, and in 1834 he went to Europe, where he was a guest at the prince's estate, Chateau de Neuwied. He returned to Fort Union in the autumn of 1835 and remained until 1838, when he cashed out his share of the fur trade and opened a general merchandise store at 23 Front Street in St. Louis, with Pierre Jr. as part owner.

While McKenzie was still solidifying the upriver domain, Cadet faced the prospect, finally, of becoming the principal owner of half of the Astor empire. The Astors had fretted for several years about whether the fur trade had a future. John Jacob observed that men in Europe were beginning to wear silk hats, and Bill Astor later discovered that "long-napped hats are altogether out of fashion" in New York. They were being replaced by hats made of nutria at half the cost of beaver. But the thought of letting go the reins of his business made John Jacob Astor "supremely miserable," in Crooks's words, and "constantly in dread of dying in the Alms House."

In March of 1833 Crooks received letters from "our Bon Grandpapa" in Europe stating that he had made up his mind to sell out. However, Crooks cautioned Cadet that Astor "always leaves a door wide enough to escape by, if he chooses." Three months later, from Geneva, Astor sent this note to B. Pratte & Company: "Wishing to retire from the concern in which I am engaged with your House, you will please to take this as notice thereof, & that the agreement entered into on the 7th May 1830 between your House and me on the part of the American Fur Company will expire with the outfit of the present year on the terms expressed in said agreement."

Despite its definitive tone, the letter settled nothing. Two months later Bill Astor informed Pratte & Company that his father "intimates his intension [sic] of retiring from the trade," although "on this he had not fully determined but would probably do so in the course of a few weeks . . . I think highly probably you may think of such consequent arrangements as you may desire to make without coming to any positive conclusion."

In the spring of 1834 Astor finally retired from the A.F.C., of which he owned 90 percent of the stock. Crooks, who owned 5 percent, bought the Northern Department and retained the name American Fur Company. Cadet's firm, B. Pratte & Company, bought the Western Department and called it Pratte, Chouteau & Company.

Crooks would have preferred to be in partnership in the old Western Department with Cadet and Pratte, who was Crooks's father-in-law, but he had feared that if he did not buy the Northern Department, it would be sold to someone aggressively competitive with the St. Louis firm. "I therefore felt in some degree constrained to take up the Mackinax [*sic*] and Detroit concerns . . . for supposing that I declined arranging with Mr. Astor and joined you, the Northern business would have passed into other hands, and a ruinous competition have followed beyond all doubt; for though you might have been disposed to remain within your usual limits, the trade of the Missouri is too attractive to permit the hope of your remaining undisturbed."

In the fall, Crooks and Cadet worked out the relationship between their two firms, essentially following the arrangements that had previously existed between the St. Louis partners and Astor. Crooks's firm would import from Europe or buy in the United States all the supplies B. Pratte & Company would require for its Indian trade and would also sell all the furs, skins, and other property the St. Louis firm might send to New York, receiving a commission on both kinds of transactions.

From a personal standpoint, things were going well for Cadet and Emilie. They improved and beautified their St. Louis estate at Main and Vine and were the happy and charming hosts to many friends and visitors. Cadet's health seemed to strengthen as he reached middle age, and there was no end to Emilie's energy or her circle of admirers.

On top of the natural tendency of the Chouteaus to attract traveling scholars, writers, naturalists, and dilettantes, they now had to deal with wanderers sent their way by John Jacob Astor, who tended to collect European royalty low on cash. One was King Otto, the idle young monarch of Greece, who spent several months of 1835–36 in St. Louis. Emilie and Pierre Jr. entertained him on a regular basis.

"The king spent some time here, without any seeming object," recalled John F. Darby, a St. Louis civic leader who met Otto at parties held at the Chouteau home. "He passed nearly all the time, while in St. Louis, in Mr. Chouteau's counting-room, where he went daily, and where Mr. Chouteau, from his great politeness, was compelled to entertain him in conversation."

Jean Pierre Cabanné, after calling on Emilie one December while Cadet was away in New York, was moved to gush: "What a house of peace and happiness! All breathes of order and cleanliness, and even the temperature one finds there would make one forget the cold that is felt everywhere else. One is almost tempted to imitate you, but it is easier to wish than to do it."

A firm in Cincinnati was asked to find fruit trees for Cadet and Emilie, and it sent 110 apple trees, representing eleven varieties, from a nursery in Kentucky. The same firm had a "soda apparatus" made for Cadet. It was shipped with some whiskey. At Emilie's request, Crooks sent from New York a coffee table partly of Egyptian marble, and a mahogany spring rocking chair, which together cost $143.83.

The new cathedral, built of polished stone in Doric style at the astronomical cost of $63,000, opened in St. Louis in 1834. Pierre Jr. acquired rights to two pews, Nos. 22 and 68. Paying $14 a year rent for each pew gave him "and his legitimate offspring" the rights to the pews as long as they paid the rent.

The decade of the 1830s was one of rapid growth in St. Louis. "One might imagine that the 'world and his family' are coming here," the *Missouri Republican* reported in 1835. "We have never witnessed such crowds of people as now throng our streets . . . The hotels, boarding houses, etc. are crowded to excess." An English visitor, George Featherstonhaugh, was disappointed to find that the old Creole town he was expecting to see had become just another Yankee trading enclave.

Between 1835 and 1840 the population of St. Louis doubled, then doubled again during the next five years to 35,390, overtaking Pittsburgh, which had been twice the size of St. Louis in 1830. Between 1833 and 1845 more than thirty subdivisions were added to the city, but it was still impossible to keep up with the demand for houses. Even though Cadet and his partners continued to push the fur trade to new growth, its relative importance to the economic life of St. Louis rapidly declined, and St. Louis became one more industrial city. In this shift, it was aided by the influx of more than 6,000 German immigrants, who joined the Irish and Anglo-Americans to further overwhelm the town's French bases.

Cadet and Emilie's son, Charles Pierre, after completing lower-level schooling with the Jesuits in Florissant, was sent in 1834 at age fourteen to what was termed the "civil and military institution" operated by the Peugnet Brothers in Bank Street in New York. His cousin Frederick Berthold joined him there and, later, one of his Cabanné cousins. Three daughters of the Crookses studied with Madame Peugnet.

Louis and Hyacinthe Peugnet were two more of the daring Frenchmen who, like many of the Chouteau in-laws, had found their way to the New World after narrowly averting a sad end in their homeland. In the post-Waterloo era, they had been plotters against the Bourbons, for which they were forced to flee in 1822. After a year in Canada they moved to New York and opened their school under the patronage of the Marquis de Lafayette.

"You can safely leave the management of your son to me," Crooks wrote Cadet after Charles had been accepted by the Peugnets. "Let him know before he leaves home what he has to expect."

The following winter, Crooks assessed Charles's progress: "By the last report of the Mssrs. Peugnet you will perceive that your good son Charles makes fair progress and from the conversations I have had with them about him, I have every reason to believe the small progress he made in his studies under the Jesuits was more their fault than his; and I entertain strong hopes that the result of his application here, directed by our able friend, will be most satisfactory." Charles and Frederick were allowed to leave school to dine with him and his wife every two weeks, coming after mass and spending the afternoon with them "or walking about the City with someone of riper years." Crooks added: "At our house he may not meet with all the indulgencies he might experience at yours, but we shall treat him no worse than if he was our own."

A year later Crooks informed Cadet that "Charles' progress is certainly *fair* in all he undertakes, if it be not brilliant, and in music he will probably be quite successful—His deportment is I believe free from reproach, and his manners are genteel—I think you ought to be satisfied with your son, but perhaps you have the common failing of

most parents — that of expecting *more* than is reasonable — We all desire to see our children No 1 — though we all *know* that is impossible."

Cadet and Emilie's older daughter, Emilie, had been in fragile
health throughout her life, and this continued to be a matter of concern after her marriage. Her husband, John Sanford, left government
service to join his father-in-law's business in 1834. Emilie's health
worsened during the year following the birth of their son, Benjamin
Chouteau Sanford, in May 1835. Doctors recommended a milder climate, so she was sent to New Orleans with the intention that she continue to the West Indies. But Emilie was so ill when she reached New
Orleans that those caring for her decided to turn around and bring her
home. She died, at the age of twenty-two, aboard the S.B. *George Col-
lier* on April 25, 1836. The following winter, the family baptized her
son at St. Peter's Church in New York, and the elder Emilie took to
her heart one more motherless child.

Cadet and Emilie kept up close relations with many other members of their extended family, both in St. Louis and during their stays
in New York. Connections to the family of Uncle Auguste were maintained through Henry Chouteau, the next to the youngest of Auguste
Chouteau's children and sixteen years younger than Cadet. After his
father's death, the capable and conscientious Henry became the point
man for his six siblings in distributing and managing Auguste's sizable
assets. By his early thirties he seemed to have his hand in everything
in the growing metropolis of St. Louis. Besides administering the estate of his father, he had a substantial merchant house, held local
public office, and was involved in real estate development on land left
by Auguste.

Henry married Clemence Coursault, a niece of the Paul brothers,
husbands of two of Henry's sisters. He and Clemence eventually had a
large family, with seven children living to adulthood. In 1836 the family built a baronial house looking out over Chouteau's Pond in what
was then the outskirts of St. Louis but is today the middle of town.

Henry traveled often on business, usually to New Orleans or New
York. In New York, he always dropped in on the Crooks family and
Pierre Jr., if he was there. Improvements in the means of traveling
from St. Louis to the East were obvious in a comment that Crooks

made after Henry stopped by one January en route to Albany. "He got no sleep from Wheeling to this except what he got in the stage, or rail road car." Tiring as it must have been, rail travel had shortened the trip considerably from the amount of time Cadet had spent in a stage-coach just ten years earlier.

After the *Yellow Stone* and the *Assiniboine*, Cadet regularly contracted for additional steamboats. Their life span on the powerful rivers of the region was short, an average of five years by some estimates. Water and sun weakened the wooden structures, and fires and sinkings were frequent. The fate of the *Assiniboine* provided an example. The boat reached Fort Union on its second voyage June 26, 1834. However, low water and an early freeze forced it to remain through the winter at the mouth of Poplar River. In late spring it began its return voyage, stopping first at Fort Union, then Fort Clark, and taking aboard pelts at both locations. Below the mouth of Heart River, fire broke out on the uninsured vessel, and its valuable cargo of 1,100 packs of buffalo robes and beaver was destroyed. Prince Maximilian's precious natural history collection was also on board and was lost.

But the reason for the appeal of steamboats was obvious in a report that J. P. Cabanné sent as he crossed Missouri by steamboat en route to the Bluffs. In Boonville, he informed Cadet: "We are arriving here . . . 3 days and 3 hours since our departure from St. Louis . . . We are going like an arrow." It had taken Lewis and Clark two and a half weeks to cover the same distance.

❋

In 1836 Pierre Jr. had a third steamboat built, this one in Pittsburgh. The 139-foot, 119-ton side-wheeler, christened the *St. Peter's*, set out from St. Louis on its maiden voyage in the spring of 1837. Among those on board were two members of the extended Chouteau clan, Pierre Didier Papin and Bernard Pratte Jr., who was the captain of the vessel.

Before the boat arrived at Fort Leavenworth on about April 29, a deckhand became sick with fever. A few days later, in the vicinity of the Black Snake Hills, someone on board suggested to Captain Pratte that the man be put ashore, but Pratte did not want to condemn the sick man to starvation in the wilderness—and Pratte still hoped that the illness was not smallpox. By the time the vessel reached the Bluffs, however, it was obvious that the disease was smallpox, and it had been communicated to some others on board. In addition, three Arikara women boarded near the Bluffs and soon became ill.

These events set off one of the worst known human tragedies on the Upper Missouri, made even worse by well-meaning whites who attempted primitive inoculations of Indians. The impact of the disease was compounded by ignorance, misunderstanding, and poor hygiene among the tribes. The fact that the steamboat continued its scheduled voyage to Fort Pierre, Fort Clark, and Fort Union, then returned to Fort Clark and Fort Pierre, helped to spread the disease over a vast land area.

It was a grave misjudgment to permit the infected boat to continue its scheduled journey, but the Indians were expecting the boat and knew that it carried goods for them. Company officials on the boat and at the forts, hoping against hope that the spread of the scourge could be contained, knew that the Indians would be angry and hurt if the boat did not come, and that they would fail to understand the reason. And the slow, erratic communications made it impossible to get a ruling from superiors in St. Louis about what to do. The greatest error, however, was that vaccinations had not been available to the tribes earlier, although explaining to the Indians the reasons for such precautionary treatment would have been difficult.

When the vessel made a brief stop at Fort Pierre during the upriver voyage, Jacob Halsey, a company clerk, came aboard to travel to Fort Union, where he was to take temporary command. He became ill while on board. Having been vaccinated, he eventually recovered, but he was still able to spread the highly infectious disease for a period of time.

Francis A. Chardon, the *bourgeois* at Fort Clark, near the Mandan villages, was unsuspecting of the calamity that lay ahead as the *St. Peter's* hove into sight at 2 p.m. on June 18, 1837, a Sunday. "Capt Pratte with Messrs Papin & Halsey on Board, with two Mackinaw Boats that she was towing up as far as Fort Clark to take down the returns of that Post," Chardon noted in his journal. On the following Tuesday morning, the vessel departed for Fort Union, with Papin remaining at Fort Clark.

Charles Larpenteur was on duty at Fort Union when the *St. Peter's* arrived there. "The mirth usual on such occasions was not of long duration," he recalled later, "for immediately on the landing of the boat we learned that smallpox was on board. Mr. J. Halsey, the gentleman who was to take charge this summer, had the disease, of which several of the hands had died; but it had subsided, and this was the only case on board."

In an effort to halt the spread of the disease at Fort Union, Larpenteur consulted the fort's copy of *Dr. Thomas' Medical Book* and tried to use pus from Halsey's skin eruptions to inoculate about thirty Indian women living in the fort as wives and companions of the traders. The result was horrific. In about two weeks those who had received the inoculations began to die in agony. "It was awful—the scene at the fort," Larpenteur said, "where some went crazy, and others were half eaten up by maggots before they died." The stench from the dying could be smelled for three hundred yards around the fort.

While the epidemic was at its height at Fort Union, a party of about forty Indians came in off the plains and wanted to be admitted. The doors of the fort had been locked for days, but the Indians would not leave until they were shown a small boy covered with scabs. Larpenteur claimed that they were never allowed into the fort and that their only exposure was to seeing the boy; nevertheless, more than half of the group eventually died.

At Fort Clark, Chardon did not record when he first became aware that some men on the *St. Peter's* had smallpox, but he sent out messengers warning other Indians to stay away. Convinced that they were being misled, they came anyway. Meanwhile, the three Arikara women had left the boat and gone to join their tribe, which had moved in among the Mandans and Gros Ventres. Although the women were recovering from the disease, they, like Halsey, were still infectious.

On July 14, less than a month after the boat's visit, Chardon recorded in his journal the first grim result: "A young Mandan died to day of the Small Pox—several others has caught it—the Indians all being out Makeing dried Meat has saved several of them." From then, the tragedy grew almost daily, and Chardon kept a tally.

> Wednesday [July] 26—The 4 Bears has caught the small pox, and got crazy and has disappeared from camp—he arrived here in the afternoon . . .
>
> Thursday [July] 27—The small pox is Killing them up at the Village, four died to day—
>
> Friday [July] 28—The Mandans & Rees gave us two splendid dances, they say they dance, on account of their Not haveing a long time to live, as they expect to all die of the small pox—and as long as they are alive, they will take it out in dancing—
>
> Sunday [July] 30—An other report from the Gros Ventres to day say, that they are arrived at their Village, and that 10 or 15 of them have died, two big fish among them, they threaten Death and Distruction to us all at this place, saying that I was the cause of the small pox Makeing its appearance in this country—One of our best friends of the Village (The Four Bears) died to day, regretted by all who Knew him.

In August, Chardon was recording a half-dozen or more deaths nearly every day among the Mandans and Arikaras. He gave one group six pounds of doses of Epsom salts in hopes it would help. On August 11 he wrote: "I Keep no a/c of the dead, as they die so fast that it is impossible."

> Wednesday [August] 16—Several Men, Women, and Children that has been abandoned in the Village, are laying dead in the lodges, some out side of the Village, others in the little river not entered, which creates a very bad smell all around us.

He recorded stories of Indians committing suicide to escape the miserable death brought by smallpox, of husbands and wives killing themselves, of parents killing children, then themselves. There were cases of parents with the disease cutting scabs from their own flesh and rubbing them into open cuts on their children in an attempt to inoculate them, which Chardon said sometimes worked. Chardon had probably been vaccinated in St. Louis or the East, but he came down with a fever, from which he recovered. On August 31 he estimated that five hundred Mandans had died; later he raised the estimate to eight hundred. That would prove to be only a fraction of the toll.

Into the cooling days of September, the dying continued. On September 22 Chardon's two-year-old son died. Andrew Jackson Chardon had been born of an Indian woman who died a few months before the smallpox outbreak. By October the death rate appeared to be slowing, but Chardon continued to record scattered deaths for several months.

At Fort Union, the disease spread with equal speed and destruction.

"During the prevalence of the malady the Assiniboines were continually coming in," Halsey reported later.

> I sent our Interpreter to meet them on every occasion, who represented our situation to them and requested them to return immediately from whence they came however all our endeavours proved fruitless, I could not prevent them from camping round the Fort—they have caught the disease, notwithstanding I have never allowed an Indian to enter the Fort, or any communication between them & the Sick; but I presume the air was infected with it for a half mile . . .
>
> I do not know how many Assiniboins have already died as they have long since given up counting but I presume at least 800 and of the Blackfeet at least 700, it was introduced to that nation by a *Pied noirs* who embarked on the St. Peters at Little Missouri. The Mandans have all died except 13 young & 19 old men.

The malady was also introduced among some of the Sioux bands around Fort Pierre when the vessel stopped there and government annuity goods—infected—were unloaded and distributed to the Yankton and Santee Sioux. After his recovery, Halsey traveled back to Fort Pierre and wrote his report from there on November 2. With vaccine, he said, "thousands of lives might have been saved."

The death tolls in the epidemic were variously estimated by later travelers and historians. John J. Audubon, who traveled through the area in 1843 on a company steamboat and with an introduction from Pierre Jr., wrote an account of the epidemic largely based on conversations with Chardon. He estimated the final toll at 150,000. Chittenden, the late-nineteenth-century historian of the fur trade, considered that an impossible figure because it would have meant the total annihilation of all the tribes where it prevailed.

Chittenden thought 15,000 deaths was a more accurate estimate. "But considering the population of these several tribes—Blackfeet, Crows, Mandans, Minnetarees, and Aricaras—even this diminished estimate makes a mortality almost without parallel in the history of plagues," he wrote. Prince Maximilian commented in the preface of the English edition of his book in 1843: "The destroying angel has visited the unfortunate sons of the wilderness with terrors never before known, and has converted the extensive hunting grounds, as well as the peaceful settlements of these tribes, into desolate and boundless cemeteries."

Word on what was occurring upriver reached St. Louis and New York on a delayed and piecemeal basis, with the first information probably not arriving until late fall. It is not clear when Pierre Jr. and others in the firm's offices learned of the disaster. Cadet had spent the winter in New York, and he was in Pittsburgh on his way home when a letter informed him that a traveler had arrived in St. Louis on February 24 with "the melancholy details of plague, pestilence and devastation, ruined hopes and blasted expectations."

"We can only view it as a visitation of Providence with which, though it be vain for us to contend, it behooves us to make the best of existing circumstances; to put forth all our energies; and by pursuing a course of strict economy in our expenditures, with kind and conciliatory conduct to the Indians who have escaped this dreadful pestilence, endeavor, by prudence, fortitude, and perseverance, to support ourselves under the melancholy scourge," the unidentified company letter writer said.

In New York, Crooks received letters "confirming too fully the dreadful havoc among the Indians by the small pox . . . at Fort Union all way wretchedness and dispair—The Prairies covered with dead bodies, and the whole atmosphere tainted."

This, of course, created a bleak picture for the trade in pelts in the coming season, because so many of the hunters were gone. "Our most profitable Indians have died," Halsey reported. Surprisingly, most of the tribes did not become hostile to the whites once the disease died out in the winter cold. The survivors continued to hunt and trade within the range of their reduced possibilities. Some were so emotionally overwhelmed by the power of the strange disease as to beg the whites not to desert them.

※

Cadet's son, Charles Pierre Chouteau, completed his studies in New York in 1838 at age eighteen. Once out of school, he began a series of trips and work experiences intended to gradually incorporate him into the business that would someday be his. Unlike his father, uncles, and grandfather, Charles Pierre had not experienced the rigors of life on the rivers while growing up. His father wanted him to sample it now.

In late summer of 1838 Ramsay Crooks took on that task as a favor to the man he alternately called *Mon Cher Cousin* and Father-confessor. Part of the reason Crooks was taking Charles Pierre on the swing through his own trading areas in the eastern half of the continent along the Canadian border was that Pierre Jr. wanted his son to avoid exposure to "bilious fever," which he considered more a risk in the hotter areas where his own firm traded.

October found the travelers at La Pointe on Lake Superior, and Crooks reported that Charles "had a much larger opportunity of examining and appreciating all its beauties and the excellence of our table than I had any idea of when we landed here, almost 6 weeks ago."

"Your son is an excellent young man," Crooks told Cadet, "a gentleman in his feelings and deportment—Free from the vices of most persons of his age—industrious in his habits, and willing to learn.

"I have kept him here pretty regularly at work in the office and feel at liberty to promise he will become a useful member of the Counting House if reasonable pains are taken to give him sufficient opportunity to acquire by practice and experience what every young man is destitute of when he leaves even the very best of schools."

The continuing expedition did not go as smoothly as Crooks had forecast. They set out from La Pointe, proceeding along the shore of Lake Superior for less than thirty miles toward the mouth of the Brule River before they found the small streams frozen over and the weather "boisterous." They returned to La Pointe and made their way across the northwestern tip of today's Wisconsin and down the Mississippi shoreline.

"On this new undertaking we embarked the evening of All Saints' Day, and by the aid of the moon, and 6 good paddles, reached the Bay 18 miles distant, where our journey by land was to commence before midnight," Crooks reported.

> Here we slept, and began our march next morning. The third day in the afternoon we struck the St. Croix, but to our sore disappointment could neither find Indians, nor any canoe capable of carrying our party, and after a fruitless search we had to walk 2½ days more to the company trading house at Yellow Lake, where we obtained the means of transportation, but [the river was] so full of ice that it would have been madness to attempt navigating it. We were therefore obliged to trust to our legs again for more than 2 days to the Falls of St. Croix, where we were overtaken by a heavy snowstorm that finished the closing of, till then, the partially obstructed river, and finally we were compelled to complete the journey all the way here [to St. Peter] by land, nearly 300 miles.
>
> We arrived here 2 days ago, and are now under the hospitable roof of Mr. Sibley, and shall stay no longer than will be necessary to decide whether there is any rational prospect of the Mississippi heating up, which in my opinion is not to be expected, and are therefore preparing to go on by land in sleighs to Prairie du Chien well provided with men who know the way, and are accustomed to such undertakings.
>
> Charles proved himself a capital walker, & in most things equal to an "old *voyageur*." He has never enjoyed such health as he is now blessed with, and so far from this his first adventure doing him any harm, I am satisfied he will derive much benefit from it.

On January 8, 1838, the last surviving member of the older generation of the Chouteau family, Pierre Sr., was toasted at a Democratic Party dinner in St. Louis "as the patriarch of the city and friend of her liberties." Approaching his eightieth birthday, he maintained an active interest in St. Louis civic affairs and the management of his land and properties, despite the fact that he was now surrounded by an English-speaking world. As a former mayor of St. Louis, William Carr Lane, had commented, "Major Chouteau understands very little English and I very little French."

When Pierre Sr.'s second wife, Brigitte Saucier, died, in 1829, his eldest son, A.P., had written Cadet expressing concern for their father's emotional state. "It is one of those blows from which Papa can hardly recover. It is true to say that his good days have been of short duration; he has lived to see unhappy days." Still, surrounded by his close-knit family and his immense flock of grandchildren and great-grandchildren, he did find times of joy.

During the course of 1838 he was to lose two of his sons. François Gesseau collapsed and died of a probable heart attack at the age of forty-one while overseeing his cattle operation at the mouth of the Kansas River, where the future Kansas City was developing. A.P. died at fifty-two, possibly of an infection from a thigh wound, at his home among the Osages on the Arkansas River in the future Oklahoma. In 1838 death also claimed William Clark, with whom Pierre Sr. had gone through thirty-four years of friendship, conflict, and shared interests.

Pierre's widowed daughter Pélagie was a rock of his life, as was Pierre Jr., who remembered to write during his long travels and to inquire of other family members about his father's health. Pierre Sr. closely followed the success of his second son and observed with pleasure as Cadet and Emilie traveled the country, particularly to Niagara Falls, which he had always dreamed of seeing. He often sent short notes to the traveling Cadet about the well-being of the children and the care of his son's St. Louis property. When Charles Pierre finished his studies in New York, the elder Pierre sent Cadet a note saying he was glad "that Charles fulfilled your wishes, which must be very satisfying to you," closing with the words "Goodbye, be good so that God may have you in his holy keeping."

After the death of Cadet's daughter Emilie, her husband, John Sanford, remained a close member of the family circle. Emilie

Chouteau, with help from her younger daughter, Julie, was bringing up young Ben, while Sanford traveled from St. Louis to Washington and New York and Indian country in his role as Cadet's increasingly indispensable associate.

Bernard Pratte died on April 1, 1836, but Bernard Jr. kept his father's interest in the company for the next few years. In late 1839 or the very beginning of 1840, Cadet and Cabanné—his brother-in-law, old friend, and part owner of the firm—came to a parting of the ways. Neither left behind any explanation of their rupture. The crotchety, complaining Cabanné, by then sixty-seven years old, had also fought with John B. Sarpy, who was his son-in-law as well as a partner in the firm.

After the returns came in from the 1839 season, the partners dissolved Pratte, Chouteau & Company, with each partner entitled to one-fifth of the capital. Instead of going into retirement, Cabanné put his one-fifth of the proceeds into a new partnership with young Pratte, who shared part of his late father's capital. The new firm caused some worry to Cadet, who wrote William Laidlaw at Fort Union that it threatened them with "strong opposition in the Missouri trade." But he was inclined to think it would be "mostly talk, at least for this season."

But Cabanné died before he could get the new business under way. Suddenly very ill, he went to bed and sent for Sarpy. They resolved their differences before he passed away. Cadet was in Louisville at the time, so he had no opportunity to do the same, but John Sanford wrote him of the events. The kind and cheerful Emilie, so admired by Cabanné, was at his bedside.

Cadet then reorganized his firm under the name P. Chouteau Jr. & Company. The other principal partners were John B. Sarpy, John Sanford, and Joseph A. Sire, a steamboat captain who took over management of the Upper Missouri portion. The new firm was capitalized at $500,000, of which Cadet and his father owned a little more than half.

Sanford proved to be a man of many skills, as capable of making his way among Washington politicians as canoeing back to St. Louis from the Bluffs in six days. In 1839 alone, he dealt with the sinking of two of the firm's steamboats, both loaded with skins and merchandise. The *Pirate* was a "total loss" when it went down three miles above the Platte River in April, but the crew survived. When the *Enterprise* sank on the Ohio River in June, the loss was about $10,000 worth of skins.

Like all the other men in Cadet's circle, Sanford was enchanted with Emilie, whom he called "My Dearest Mother." During a trip to Washington, he wrote her that he longed to be back in St. Louis among those he loved. "Would that I was with you tonight, help to form a circle around the Center Table in the Front parlour—But as such can't be the case I console myself by humming whilst writing, 'Oh, take your time Miss Lucy.' "

Emilie's brother Charles Gratiot Jr. suffered a blow to his career and good name about this time. After being brevetted a brigadier general in 1828 "for meritorious service and general good conduct" as chief of army engineers, his star had seemed to be shining brightly. He was revered within the family, and Cadet and his associates did not hesitate to ask Charles to open doors or run lobbying errands for them in Washington. As a career army officer, Charles had not grown as rich as most of his cousins and siblings. Like his father, he turned to John Jacob Astor for financial help. At the beginning of 1836 he sought a loan of $5,000 from Astor, who readily agreed. Crooks told him that Astor "will allow you your own time to pay it . . . All he wants is the interest regularly, for you are among the few he takes pleasure in serving."

But at the end of 1838 Gratiot was abruptly dismissed from the army in a dispute with auditors over the handling of moneys he administered on behalf of the engineers. Relatives and supporters saw it as a political action on the part of the Van Buren Administration, and several historians have judged it unjustified.

Ramsay Crooks gave an idea of the issues involved in a letter to Pierre Jr. the following month:

> The government fairly owe him for commissions on money disbursed upward of $60,000, and he owes them in account about $31,000, and the end of all this will be that U.S. will have to pay him eventually

$30,000. It was cruel to strike him from the Rolls of the Army for that always entails disgrace in the estimation of the world at large who know nothing of the circumstances, or merits of the case—Poor Charles has been shamefully sacrificed, but he is strong . . . and in due time will triumph over the miserable Cabal at Washington that can see nothing estimable in anyone not of their own unprincipled party.

Gratiot told friends that the dispute arose because the army had refused for about twenty years to draw up a complete settlement of his expense account, making it impossible for either side to know who owed how much to whom. Hoping to force the issue, he held on to some government moneys until the government agreed to settle matters. The government reacted by stopping his pay, and President Van Buren soon dismissed him from the army.

Strong as Gratiot may have been, the loss of his position was a great blow to the self-esteem of a man who had played a leading part in designing and building four military forts and had seen tough duty in the War of 1812. Family members worried about his emotional state, especially after he decided to remain in Washington and work as a clerk in the General Land Office. "I am extremely anxious about our excellent friend Gratiot, and pray with sincerity that he may confound all his enemies," Crooks told Pierre Jr.

✳

Financial panic hit the country in May 1837, precipitated by President Jackson's farewell address in March, when he warned about the inflated economy and condemned paper currency and speculation. The ensuing crisis lasted for several years. Signs of its impact were soon apparent in the worried tone of Crooks's correspondence with Pierre Jr. In addition to their fur-trade businesses, both men were now trading in bonds and other financial instruments, which made them vulnerable to the financial crisis as well as to the price of pelts.

Not until 1841 did the crisis hit the West with force, but Pierre Jr., perhaps because of what he had seen in his frequent travels to the East, had begun pulling in the reins a couple of years earlier. That he now had a great deal of wealth to protect was attested to by a comment in the *Missouri Argus*, which reported on his election as a director of the Bank of the State of Missouri and said he was "probably the richest man in the State."

After the 1839 season Cadet terminated his firm's involvement in the fur trade in the northern Rocky Mountains, believing his traders could not compete with the Hudson's Bay Company, whose traders had duty-free goods. Beaver was growing scarce, and demand was falling because, as the Astors had noted a few years earlier, nutria and silk had become the preferred materials for tall hats. Demand for buffalo robes remained strong, but some of the best buffalo-hunting tribes had been nearly destroyed by the smallpox epidemic.

Pierre Jr. exhorted William Laidlaw at Fort Union to do more to develop the capabilities of the Crow nation in hunting and pressing buffalo robes, "which now find a much more ready market than beaver." The Crows, who had had fewer losses in the smallpox epidemic, possessed "fine" buffalo country, Pierre Jr. wrote in a rare letter in English, which demonstrated how much he wanted to impress his point on the non–French-speaking Laidlaw. "The bad times in the East and in Europe have had a very sensible effect on the price of furs and skins, but we look forward with confidence to a better state of things and for good robes we can rely on a sure and steady sale—for Beaver there is no sale in New York and the market in Europe is very much overstocked."

Ramsay Crooks had an especially difficult time dealing with the crisis. He still owed Astor money for his acquisition of half of the firm, he had health problems, and he wanted to rid himself of the western parts of his fur business because they were too remote from New York for him to effectively manage. He asked Cadet to lend him money to pay off Astor, and he proposed that Cadet take over the fur-trade area around Prairie du Chien on whatever terms he wanted.

"If I was as near Prairie du Chien as you are, I would not part with it because it can be made to yield a very handsome profit even as the trade now is," he wrote, "and if muskrats get again into general use by the hatters, it will be a grand business. The recent movement of the

Winnebagoes is calculated to bring our Western Outfit affairs too near to yours for the parties on either side to remain long at peace, and I am persuaded you will do well to obtain the control while you can."

Crooks wanted "less than $10,000" to pay what he owed Astor, adding, "I really feel mortified at being compelled to trouble you with my private affairs; but thank God I shall with your good aid get out of the *poor* old man's clutches, at last."

Finally, he told Cadet, "As you love the old gentleman so much, I have promised him you would employ somebody to procure and send here via [New] Orleans 4 wild turkeys, say 2 male & 2 female."

The records are unclear as to whether Cadet provided the help that Crooks sought. Slightly more than a month later, Crooks wrote Pierre Jr. alluding to some differences between them. Crooks said that Cadet had misunderstood him. "I trust you will think no more of this affair," he continued. "It is too late for us to differ on any subject after being of one mind for so many years, and never having our feelings alienated from one another—You have obliged me too often for me to forget your kindness, and it will be a source of pleasure to me to prove I have only appreciated your good feelings."

Crooks was "saddled" with a lot of "property" from the last season, apparently meaning unsold pelts and skins, "and a never-ending demand against us for large sums of money—The weight of these two loads have nearly crushed me, and I have been looking forward with pleasure to meeting you here that we might consult about the future."

Deciding it was time to get out of the business, Crooks attempted over the next eighteen months to find a buyer for his firm, which still carried the name American Fur Company. Before he could sell, however, he was forced to suspend payments, which was done in September 1842.

"Amer. Fur Co. suspended in order to save creditors," began the announcement in the *New York Express*. "The large business could not be carried on without large advances to Indians & traders. Heavy advances already made, and large stock of furs on hand & Co. is unable to sell them here or abroad on account of disastrous times. Creditors will not lose anything assures the pres. Ramsay Crooks. He is a large stockholder, having invested his entire fortune in the Co."

Pierre Jr. was in New York at the time and reported the suspension in letters to his partners and associates in St. Louis about two weeks before the action was taken. He bought the inventory of Crooks's firm and took over his office at 39 Ann Street in New York. While the decline in the market for beaver was harmful to his business as well, he could still rely on the voluminous trade in buffalo robes, which had long since disappeared from Crooks's northeastern trading areas.

Crooks was not the only person or entity who turned to Pierre Chouteau Jr. for help getting through the credit crunch. The state of Missouri, as well, was trying to avert financial collapse. In March 1841, the same time that Crooks's problems became acute, the Bank of the State of Missouri asked Cadet's help in selling state bonds. If that was not possible, he was asked to try to borrow on behalf of the state $100,000, $200,000 or $300,000.

Cadet was then en route to New York, but before he arrived and set to work on the sale of the bonds, John Smith of the state bank wrote again. He was worried about "imminent hazard to the bank." It was injecting cash into one of the branches to prevent suspension of operations. "If these bonds could be sold, it would make the bank easy. Otherwise, I regret to say that I feel her condition to be quite precarious. I am quite sick at heart and tired of banking."

Arriving in New York, Cadet went to work fast to save his state from economic ruin, demonstrating his skill and ability to use connections. By May 17, 1841, he had secured commitments from E. Riggs, John Jacob Astor, and Nevins Townsend & Company to take $154,000 of the $254,000 in bonds at 10 percent interest a year, with the option to take the remaining $100,000 on the same terms.

"I am happy to say I met with gentlemen who were willing to treat with me even though my authority was less satisfactory than under a regular power from the Board of Directors," he informed the bank cashier with a tone of irritation. "I have agreed to sell at par the whole $254,000, to Mr. Astor, Mr. Riggs, and Mssrs. Nevins Townsend & Co . . .

"The Bonds are to be denominated in sums of $500 each, in favour of, and guaranteed by the Bank of Missouri, interest half yearly at ten per cent p annum [*sic*], payable at the Bank of Commerce, or the Bank of America in the City of New York."

In the late fall of 1841 Pierre Jr., Emilie, and six-year-old Ben moved to New York for an indefinite stay, settling into the six-story Astor House. Crooks, despite the financial disaster he was facing, arranged for their accommodations. They were to have rooms 11, 12, and 13, with as many as they wanted of rooms 16 to 19. A door would be installed between rooms 11 and 12. They were expected near the end of November.

To construct the Astor House, which had its cornerstone-laying ceremony July 4, 1834, John Jacob Astor tore down houses from Barclay to Vesey Street on Broadway, including his own home. Considered the "marvel of the age," the Astor House had three hundred rooms and seventeen bathrooms, and the interior was finished throughout in black walnut. The $2-a-night rate included a personal door key, maid service, pitcher and bowl, and soap. The corridors were carpeted and the walls hung with pictures. The Astor House attracted the rich and the famous.

Although Charles Pierre, then twenty-two, was working in St. Louis at Kenneth McKenzie's merchant firm, he found time to spend in New York, as did his sister Julie, then twenty-five. They joined their parents in a spending spree on luxury goods probably not previously experienced by anyone from their hometown.

They shopped at the best places in New York. Cadet bought, presumably for Emilie, a $525 diamond brooch at Gelston Ladd & Company in the Astor House. A couple of months later he acquired another brooch for $800 and a pair of diamond "ear knobs" for $525 from the same firm, which gave him a 5 percent discount on the three items. Cadet kept a horse in New York, although a cab to and from a party cost only a dollar and a coach could be hired for two and a half hours for two dollars. Charles Pierre bought two pairs of white drill pants for $12 and a black dress coat for $28. He acquired a signed edition of J. J. Audubon's *Birds of America* for $96.25.

The family paid $12 to rent a pianoforte from January 1 to March 1, 1843, from Gaspero Godone at 403½ Broadway. An "extension sofa

& pillows" was purchased at 403 Broadway for $85.50. On March 1 the rental of the piano was extended for one more month at $6. Ben Sanford studied at the Classical, Mathematical & Commercial Institution. John Sanford, who joined the family for part of the stay, paid $45 for one quarter's education of his son, plus $2 for stationery and $1 for books. A "patent ottoman" was purchased for $65 from Henry Parsons, cabinetmaker, 598 Broadway. Cadet bought a French morning gown for $6 from Seary & Company, hatters at Nos. 4 & 5 Astor House, "importers & dealers in French umbrellas, caps, canes, gloves & fancy articles." And he paid $33 to rent pew No. 12 at Église de St. Vincent de Paul.

During the family's years in New York, Julie Chouteau was married, at the age of twenty-seven, to Major William Maffitt, a thirty-two-year-old army physician. They had a June wedding in 1843, with flowers from the floral firm of Niblo & Dunlap at 576 Broadway. Cadet extended his father the courtesy of asking his approval of the marriage; Pierre Sr. wrote back, in a somewhat feeble hand, agreeing to the union. Maffitt left the army, receiving an acknowledgment from the surgeon general's office of his resignation "growing out of your new relations to society," and the newlyweds established their home in St. Louis.

Two months after the wedding, Julie's brother, Charles Pierre, set out for a grand voyage to Europe that would keep him abroad for two years. He sailed from Boston via Halifax, writing a farewell note to his mother from Boston. Charles Pierre not only went to London and Paris but also obtained visas to go to Turkey, Sweden, and Russia. His Russian visa described him, at twenty-five, as being six feet tall, with dark eyes, an irregular nose, black hair, light skin, and an oval face.

Returning from his travels, Charles Pierre married his first cousin, Julia Gratiot, daughter of the disgraced but beloved Charles Gratiot Jr, on November 27, 1845. Then he went to work for P. Chouteau Jr. & Company, the plan being that he would eventually step into the leadership of the firm.

Sometime during these years, Cadet and Emilie moved into their own home in New York. John Sanford also set up a home in New York, and Ben divided his time between his father and his grandparents. The family bought elegant furniture and decorations for both places. It kept two carriages and had subscriptions to three French fashion and literary magazines.

Cadet and Emilie ordered tableware from a Paris porcelain-and-crystal store; cutlery from Sheffield; crystal and glassware from James P. Drummond, 47 Maiden Lane; and tufted rugs, stair carpeting, border carpet and other coverings, plus brass stair rods from W. W. Chester & Company, 191 Broadway. They ordered champagne and pale sherry by the cask and a canary cage from Stephen F. Nidelet in Philadelphia. From Gelston & Treadwell of No. 1, Astor House, Pierre Jr. bought asparagus tongs for $6.50 and a diamond bracelet, diamond pin, and pair of diamond "ear knobs" for a total of $2,000.

The dissolution of Ramsay Crooks's firm put a sad end to the affectionate and stimulating exchange of visits and letters between Crooks and Cadet and their families. From New York in 1850 Cadet commented to his daughter, Julie, in St. Louis, that he and Emilie seldom ran into the Crooks family anymore. Somewhat cut off as they may have become from old friends, however, the Crookses were far from destitute. At a minimum, Emilie Crooks had the right to part of her late father's share of the capital of Pratte, Chouteau & Company after it was dissolved in 1839. Within months of his comment about seldom seeing the Crookses, Pierre Jr. gave them a mortgage for $12,000, payable over five years at 7 percent interest, to build a home on Lake Ontario in Niagara, Canada.

Cadet continued to travel back to St. Louis, where his business interests knew no bounds. He frequently bought buildings or lots that became available in the city, usually from business associates or relatives, including his father. In December 1844 he signed an agreement with a firm called Brewster & Hart, which was going to manage "the five stores you contemplate erecting on Main St." About the same time, he bought a lot fronting on Market Street for $13,000.

He was also in St. Louis on February 15, 1847, to share in the celebration of the founding of the city and tribute to Pierre Laclède, with Pierre Chouteau Sr. as the most honored guest. The month and day selected, February 15, corresponded to the day Laclède and young Auguste Chouteau had landed from the Mississippi and selected the spot at which to begin the settlement. But the year of the celebration, 1847, was eighty-three years after the landing, hardly a notable anniversary. It is possible that civic leaders suddenly realized that the last living family member who had been present for those events, even though only six years old at the time, was now eighty-nine years old.

One of the few impressions of Pierre Sr. in those final years was left by Francis Parkman, who visited him the spring before the celebration while researching the murder years earlier of the Indian leader Pontiac. Parkman noted: "Rode out at the 11th hour to see old Pierre Chouteau—three miles from St. Louis. Found his old picturesque, French house in the middle of the woods—neat Negro-houses, with verandahs—bird cages hung in the porch—chickens chirping about the neat yards. The old man was not well—and could not tell me much."

On the day of the celebration, Pierre Sr. rode in an open carriage, accompanied by his sons Pierre Jr. and Paul Liguest, plus two sons of Paul Liguest's and the eldest surviving child of Auguste—Gabriel Sylvestre "Cerré" Chouteau. It was only through the naming of Paul Liguest Chouteau and his descendants that the family had publicly intimated its true connection to the man whose full name was Pierre Laclède Liguest.

After the parade, Pierre Sr. returned to the home of his daughter, Pélagie Berthold, where he lived when he was in town. At 4 p.m. civic leaders and a band escorted him from Pélagie's house to the State Tobacco Warehouse for a dinner attended by four hundred people.

When the formal speeches had ended, Pierre Sr. rose and spoke briefly of Laclède, in French, saying that he "looked upon the commemoration of this day as the greatest tribute that could be paid to [Laclède's] memory." Toasts were drunk to many men who had played a role in the creation of St. Louis and Missouri, and Pierre Sr. offered his own toast to "The Memory of Laclède."

Some in the family thought this was the moment for the patriarch to acknowledge Laclède as his father, and as the father of his sisters, but that was not to be. One local historian recorded that Sylvestre Labbadie Jr., then sixty-eight, pleaded with his uncle that day to "Give us our name." To this, Pierre was said to have responded, "No! The name you've borne must go to the end."

He again displayed his intention to go to his grave as another man's son the next day, when the satin banner with Laclède's name that had hung over the dinner was sent to him by Mayor John Darby. "Honors rendered to the dead, we know, cannot affect them—they are beyond the reach of human hands," Pierre Sr. responded in a note, "but it serves to excite the living to emulate their virtues and their worth; and, permit me on this occasion to say, that Mr. Laclède, with whom I was acquainted, although very young, was, in every sense of the word, worthy of the honors now paid to his memory."

Later that same year, on November 13, Pierre Sr. made his will. He died a year and a half later, on July 10, 1849, at the age of ninety years and nine months.

Pierre Jr., his brother Cyprien, who lived at Kansas City, and their cousin John B. Sarpy were the administrators of the estate. They were instructed to gather all of the elder Pierre's lands, goods, slaves, money, credits, bonds, notes, and other property and after one year's time pay to each of his children the sum of $5,000. The residue of the estate was to go then to Pierre Jr. The document does not explain why this was the case, although Cadet and his father had had numerous business dealings over the previous twenty years in which Cadet may have advanced his father money or handled debts for him.

It is also possible that Pierre Sr. may have provided financial aid over the years to the families of some of his children, particularly A.P. and Paul Liguest. Likewise, the family of François Gesseau probably required assistance after his early death. Pierre Sr. was particularly careful in the wording of the will to say that only the children born of the marriage of A.P. and his wife Sophie Labbadie and of the marriage of François and his wife Bérénice Ménard were to inherit—wording that excluded any claims from part-Indian children.

It was clear that Pierre Sr., although he had lived well, did not die a very wealthy man, not by comparison to his brother, Auguste. His years as an Indian agent for the government, when he was blocked from pursuing the private business dealings he considered his right, may have been a factor, although Auguste's careful countinghouse habits and his close relationship with Laclède may have given him an advantage.

An inventory of the estate filed on November 28, 1849, listed personal property, including goods and notes, in the amount of about $70,000. Much of this consisted of debts to him by other people, some of which may have been uncollectible. The inventory also listed eight parcels of real estate in various parts of Missouri. Over the years, Pierre Sr. had sold off most of his large landholdings, probably to support himself and his large household.

In 1836 Congress had finally confirmed Pierre's claim to about 25,500 acres of land on the Lamine River in north central Missouri, land the Osages had granted him in 1792 with these words: "Thou mayest remain there, and thy bones shall never be troubled. If our children do trouble thee, you have but to show this same paper, and if some nation disturbs thee, we are ready to defend thee."

But when Pierre Sr. died, his Osage friends had long since been forced out of Missouri before the onslaught of white settlement. In his campaign of more than thirty years to win confirmation from American authorities of the Spanish-era land grant, Pierre had given up one-fourth of the Lamine land to the influential St. Louis businessman and congressman William Ashley for his help in Washington. In 1837, after the title confirmation, Ashley purchased the rest of the land for $43,000.

✻

In 1849, at age sixty, Pierre Jr. stepped out of the company that bore his name, leaving active management to Charles Pierre and the reliable Sarpy. But he did not retire. He went into many other business activities, particularly railroads, forming new companies and new partnerships at a relentless pace. As Lecompte said, "Railroads were to be the playthings of his old age."

Over the next ten years Pierre Jr. put together a portfolio of investments in bonds, notes, and mortgages, mostly connected to railroads, worth more than $400,000. The largest single investment on a list he compiled in 1859 was $133,750 in first mortgage bonds of the Syracuse Binghamton & New York Railroad Company. He also invested in the Toledo & Wabash; the Toledo & Illinois; the New Orleans Great Northern; the Great Western; the Buffalo & Erie; the West Chester & Philadelphia; and the Mobile & Ohio. He helped incorporate the Ohio & Mississippi Railroad in 1851 and was eventually involved in development of several branches of the Illinois Central.

But Cadet wanted a much more active involvement in building America's rail system than passive investments in bonds and notes, however large they might be. As in the fur trade, he saw the potential for new enterprises to feed off or interact in other ways with the railroads as tracks made their way across the continent. He had applied similar concepts when he was devoted to the fur trade, including taking care of all his own shipping with his fleet of keelboats and later steamboats, which could be hired out for other uses when his firm did not need them. As former Indian lands became available around fur posts—in Minnesota and Nebraska, for instance—he bought large tracts that might one day be sold for settlement or other development. At St. Paul, which the Chouteaus referred to as the "Falls of St. Anthony," he sent a man from his New York office to look for ways of making a profit from a "Boom," a device in the river to keep logs from scattering as they moved downstream to the mill.

Cadet established a firm in New York in 1849 called Chouteau, Merle & Company to sell iron for railroad construction. His partner was a New Orleans merchant with whom P. Chouteau Jr. & Company had done business since the 1830s. Later, John Sanford joined the firm, and the New York company became Chouteau, Merle & Sanford. In 1852 Merle withdrew, and the name was changed to Pierre Chouteau Jr., Sanford & Company.

That same year, Cadet became a partner with François Vallé and James Harrison in the American Iron Mountain Company, a Missouri firm dedicated to mining Iron Mountain, located about forty miles through hills from Ste. Genevieve, Missouri. He also wanted to develop 25,000 acres around it as a summer resort—"our Saratoga or Newport."

In 1851 his partnership with Vallé and Harrison built a twelve-foot-wide plank road covering the distance between Iron Mountain and Ste. Genevieve. This was considered a remarkable achievement at the time. Iron Mountain eventually employed two thousand men, and produced millions of dollars worth of ore.

Pierre Jr. and his business associates also looked for ways to connect steamboat service with railroads. They corresponded with H. F. McCloskey of the Galena and Minnesota Steam Boat Packet Company about possibly buying his firm to create connections through St. Louis with the Rock Island Railroad and also with the Illinois Central & Eastern Railroad. This was just before railroad tracks reached the Mississippi River in 1854 at Rock Island, Illinois. Two years later, a wooden bridge spanned the river, linking the Chicago, Rock Island & Pacific Railroad to Davenport, Iowa.

Cadet and Sanford both juggled a wide range of seemingly unrelated business matters. Sanford was in London in late winter of 1851 to handle sales of skins and furs, after a voyage that had taken what he considered a short eleven days. Instead of buffalo robes and beaver furs, this time the offering reflected a changing market. "The sale is just over & upon the whole, we have cause to be well pleased with the result," he wrote Cadet. "Every thing sold well, most articles higher than we expected. The sale of mink considering the large quantity offered was a most extraordinary good one & will give large profits." He also mentioned selling furs of "otter, red and silver fox, bear, bearcubs, common wild cat and coons."

Six months later, back in New York, Sanford was in bed with rheumatism in one hip for several days, then got up to deal with the details of closing up the partnership with Merle and reopening under his and Cadet's names only. He also had to go furniture shopping with his wife-to-be, Belle. He pleaded with Cadet to get on the road to the East. "I should be sorry to be the cause of your leaving home & being separated from my good mother," he said, "but I can't alter my conviction that your presence in the East is more necessary than at any time since we have been in business here." They had to plan for the future of their iron-selling business, and Cadet "should be in Washington at least a part of the winter in order to aid in the ratification of the Sioux treaties." This referred to the opportunity to collect trading debts the Sioux owed to the fur-trade operation, which would be repaid from annuities the government would provide in exchange for the tribe's giving up lands to white settlement. P. Chouteau Jr. & Company had collected a number of old tribal debts this way over the previous fifteen years or so.

Even though Cadet spent much of his time in New York from the late 1840s into the mid-1850s, family correspondence indicates that Emilie was living primarily in St. Louis, to which she had returned after their sojourn of several years in New York in the mid-1840s. The separation did nothing to dim their affection for each other. Despite the business excitement and other lures of New York, Cadet wrote letters to Emilie and others at home that were filled with longing to be with them and a desire to remain abreast of their lives. He concerned himself with whatever had to do with Emilie, including buying her corsets and furs and worrying about the fit of her new set of teeth.

Pierre Jr. continued to correspond with everyone in the family in French, and they wrote back to him in French. Julie and Charles Pierre wrote to each other in English. Cadet also steadfastly continued to write nearly all his business associates in French, even though most wrote back to him in English. Even his brother A.P., in his later years, had written Cadet in English. After years of receiving pleas from frustrated men in the field who knew no French and had no translators nearby, he began to write to a few of them in English. Many of those men, having heard him speak fluent English, were perplexed at him for making them work so hard to understand his letters. He sometimes apologized for not keeping up business correspondence with someone who did not know French, saying it was just too much work to write in English.

From New York, Cadet kept Emilie apprised of the details of his life, telling her in a letter in 1854 that New York's Metropolitan Hotel was "full of visiting Missourians." After the telegraph became available, he sent a message to her on November 18, 1854, announcing his safe arrival. Perhaps not trusting the newest thing, he immediately wrote her a letter saying he had just telegraphed her about his arrival. This trip, he had come via Chicago and Detroit, but he had arrived at Chicago too late to catch the Detroit train, which indicated that travel from St. Louis was now down to a matter of days.

This breakthrough in travel time to the East was further apparent in a trip that twenty-one-year-old Henry A. Chouteau, a son of Cadet's first cousin Henry, made to New York during the same era. Leaving St. Louis, he traveled up the Mississippi to Galena, then spent the night in a stagecoach to arrive at Rockford the next day at 2 p.m. He got a train to Chicago, arriving safely despite the fact that the car jumped the tracks while taking a curve too fast. He took the night train to Detroit, then "the fast steamer May Flower for Buffalo. The weather was fine and the sea or lake was smooth so that the crossing was delightful . . . Next morning we were in Buffalo and it was my intention to stop a day & go to the Falls, but as it was raining I went straight to the cars for Albany. This train goes at the rate of thirty miles an hour, there were in it many fashionable gents & ladies going to Saratoga Springs." He spent the night in a hotel in Albany and at seven the next morning took a steamer descending the Hudson River at twenty miles an hour, reaching New York at 5 p.m. after about five days' travel.

One of the things occupying Emilie in St. Louis was bringing up her grandson. After a few years of schooling in New York, young Ben returned to St. Louis with Emilie and continued his studies there. This took a load off the mind of the busy John Sanford, who decided to make the change "permanent" after hearing "such good accounts" of his son from Emilie.

Ben followed the example of his uncle Charles Pierre and made the grand tour of Europe. Still in his teens when he departed, he traveled about five years, stopping to study languages and other subjects with tutors in various countries. He was soon writing the family in German and Spanish in addition to French and English.

He did Italy, especially Venice, then Nice, then Switzerland for the summer. He was on the banks of the Rhine in Germany when he wrote his father and new stepmother, Belle, that he had been in Europe three years and now spoke and understood German perfectly. Taking ill one winter, he decided to go back to Nice for the milder climate. When the pace of Ben's letters slowed, his anxious grandfather asked in his own letters to the family whether there was any recent news from Ben. After some delay Cadet received a letter in New York to learn that Ben was in Jerusalem. By June 1857 Ben was back home in St. Louis, to Cadet's relief, no doubt.

Cadet's ever-expanding business dealings produced worry within the family, especially from his daughter, Julie. His response to her concerns demonstrated, again, his remarkable ability to organize his thoughts and analyze his own actions. He reflected a bit on what was driving him, saying he would like to withdraw from his activities, but then admitted that he actually enjoyed what he was doing.

I, who would like to withdraw from it, find myself drawn in deeper than ever. Railroad, iron, bonds of the state and of the town, of the railroad, i. e. Illinois Central, coal mines; so you see, my dear Julie, that I do just the contrary of what I would like. Such is man—he thinks in one way and acts in another. He often lets himself be carried away by the opinion of others. This is just the case with me at this moment; it is true to say that probabilities are so very flattering that it is difficult not to let oneself be carried away. As long as I have been in business I have never been as sanguine of clearing as much in so few years. All the probabilities, all the contingencies are in our favor and nevertheless, God alone knows what the result will be.

You will doubtless ask me, why all these speculations, why risk the substance already won, when we have enough on which to be happy if we know how to enjoy it. This question on your part would be perfectly just and reasonable if a man had enough moderation, enough judgment to comprehend it, but whether it be ambition or advantage or even perhaps a little vanity, he lets himself be subjugated. He does not like to be stationary when everything around him seems to go forward.

Especially, my daughter, when there are children he sires and grandchildren, whose number could be stretched out greatly, if it is possible and if he believes that occasion presents, to put them at least on an equal footing with his neighbors. Because certainly dear Mama and I have enough to satisfy our tastes, which are not very expensive. But do not attribute this all to you, since I have mentioned ambition, advantage and perhaps also vanity.

From the late 1840s, the fur trade fell into quick decline, in part because of changing tastes but to a larger extent because of the spread of white settlers to traditional Indian hunting and trapping areas. Animosity was growing between whites and the army on one side and Indians on the other, and the intermittent warfare between tribes increased as more and more eastern tribes were pushed onto lands west of the Mississippi. The climate was no longer right for a business that depended on amiable working relations between Indians and whites.

The first area to be hit by the decline was the Southwest, where the fur business was ruined by the time the Mexican War ended, in 1848. Traders along the Arkansas River abandoned the territory, and those along the South Platte soon did the same. Lecompte put it succinctly: "The Santa Fe Trail was jammed with soldiers, teamsters and emigrants, all with their guns pointed at whatever moved in the brush, be it rabbit or friendly Indian. Soon there were no more friendly Indians."

Within a few more years white-Indian relations began to disintegrate in the Upper Missouri and North Platte River country. White settlers were pushing into the area much faster than the government could compensate and control the Indians being shoved aside. Soldiers assigned to the area were green at dealing with Indians.

In July 1854 these circumstances erupted in a clash that marked the beginning of thirty years of Indian wars on the Upper Plains, an episode in which P. Chouteau Jr. & Company, by then managed by Charles Pierre, was caught up through no fault of its own. It began when a hungry Sioux killed a stray cow while waiting for a late government annuity payment. The settler who owned the cow complained, and inexperienced soldiers went in pursuit of a group of Sioux, who killed them all—twenty-nine men and a lieutenant. The next day, two hundred Sioux went on a rampage and attacked Fort John, the fur trade post of P. Chouteau Jr. & Company about five miles from Fort Laramie, from which the soldiers had come. Both forts were on the North Platte River in Nebraska Territory, at the eastern edge of present-day Wyoming.

John B. Didier, the clerk at Fort John, who was in charge in the absence of "Bunyon" Gratiot, the *bourgeois*, initially estimated the losses to the company from the sacking of food and clothing on July 20–21 at $13,145.53. A few months later Gratiot said the losses would be much higher, maybe double the first estimate. Furthermore, a group of Sioux had just attacked a mail train on its way to Fort Pierre, killing the crew and stealing $10,000 in gold and $1,000 in silver. Gratiot told his associates in St. Louis that they would be reading about it in the "prints."

"This looks more like open war than ever," he added. "I fear much for the trade." But he added that the Indians had not harmed the traders personally, and he thought the Sioux were still well-disposed to them. It was the army they had been attacking.

From then on, the fur trade on the Upper Missouri was at the mercy of increasingly restless tribes and an anxious government. After the episode at Fort John, the Sioux anger quickly spread to the area around Fort Pierre, raising fear not only among whites but also among smaller tribes. Government Indian agents, unable to maintain order and fearing for their lives, began calling for troops. The government's first instinct was to turn to the knowledgeable Chouteaus and their fur-trade empire for help. Lacking good communications with the area, officials in Washington sought information from Pierre Jr. during his frequent visits to the capital. At one point it wanted P. Chouteau Jr. & Company to transport government merchandise upriver and turn Fort Pierre into a military supply depot, which Cadet's partner Sarpy blocked on the grounds that the firm would be incurring too much responsibility. At that point, any troops sent to the conflicted area had to be sent from Fort Leavenworth.

In March 1855 Cadet reported to his son that people in Washington "want us to lead a number of troops up to Fort Pierre or thereabouts to build a settlement among the Sioux." Despite his use of the term "settlement," he presumably meant some kind of military installation.

But a few days later, with the help of Charles Gratiot Jr., Cadet came up with a proposal to sell Fort Pierre to the government. Cadet reasoned that it was no longer of much use to P. Chouteau Jr. & Company because the developing Sioux war made fur trading problematic, so he might as well sell it to the government for a military post. Gratiot left New York for Washington on April 12 to present the plan to the Secretary of War and the army quartermaster. Cadet was prepared to accept $30,000 for the fort, which was in very bad shape, the main appeal being its commanding site overlooking the Missouri River. However, Gratiot managed to negotiate a price of $45,000 from a government desperate to get army operations under way and probably unaware of the dilapidated condition of Fort Pierre. By all accounts, it was a vastly inflated price. It is tempting to conclude that this was Gratiot's way of extracting vengeance for his disgrace by the government seventeen years earlier—or even for the old, unpaid debts to his father for supplying George Rogers Clark and his band of Virginians when they chased the British out of the Illinois Territory in 1778.

Almost as soon as the agreement for the sale of Fort Pierre was signed, the government began to complain about the high price. John Sanford went to Washington the following February, and after two weeks of negotiations, the two sides settled on a reduced price of $36,500, still better than Cadet had expected. Within days of the price agreement, military leaders at Fort Pierre sent out a circular ordering all people not in the employ of the government, or who had no special license, to get out of Indian country immediately. Its ominous tone was a sad forecast of what was to come.

In the midst of the crisis at Fort John and negotiations over the sale of Fort Pierre, a new financial crisis began to sweep the country. It began in August 1854 and peaked in the Panic of 1857. Railroad stocks and bonds and investments in other heavy industries were under great pressure, including the holdings of Pierre Jr. and his associates.

The weight of the growing crisis was clear in Cadet's frequently complaining letters to his son in St. Louis. Charles Pierre, now in his mid-thirties, was stepping out on his own, investing in some inventions with industrial potential, which his father saw as speculating. Cadet told Charles Pierre to economize, to reduce the debt load, and to avoid placing the firm "in an embarrassing situation." They argued over the huge investment made in building the plank road to Iron

Mountain, which Charles Pierre thought was too costly. Without it, Cadet countered, they could not have extracted, and sold, so much iron. After a fire in a brickyard owned by Charles Pierre, Cadet told him, "I regret it sincerely, but if that is what it takes to stop your speculations, I am satisfied."

In 1857, floods did an estimated $200,000 worth of damage to the plank road. But the next year, still believing in the value of Iron Mountain, Cadet helped establish the Iron Mountain and Southern Railroad, a branch of the Illinois Central, to replace the road.

Not the least of Pierre Jr.'s financial concerns had to do with his own holdings in the Illinois Central, the first major railroad built outside the Northeast. The Illinois Central bonds fell from close to 100 to 62 by August 1855. British investors took advantage of this situation to make large purchases, and by February 1856 the bonds were back to 90. There is no indication, however, that Cadet had panicked and sold before they recovered. In fact, it appears that he and Sanford, who had been one of the nine original backers of the railroad, bought additional bonds in the fall of 1854 when they had fallen to 68, and possibly common stock as well. The railroad was expected to be in full operation before January 1856, and Sanford was confident it would be successful enough to justify their risk.

As the crisis grew, Cadet, in New York, remembered that he had not written to Emilie for some time. Apologizing, he told her that when he wrote to Charles, "it was almost like writing to you, as you knew that I was well, good health being the only true treasure in this world, although I could, perhaps, except a certain class of New Yorker, who, I believe, prefers money above all else. From this come financial troubles, when one wants only to 'go ahead.' " There had been many problems in his business affairs of late, he told her, "& God alone knows if we are done."

"The embarrassment for the railroads is becoming greater and greater," he told her.

They have contracted debts, bonds can be sold only at an immense sacrifice. Imagine that when the Illinois Central is finished from Cairo to Lasalle at the end of October and the bonds will sell at only

69 cents. What enormous losses on the branches of that road that go to Galena and Dubuque on one side and to Chicagou [*sic*] on the other [and which] will not be finished until spring, and we shall have advanced eight or ten months on the time of delivery. But lack of money, and again of money to complete it all, and that is an ingredient that is very hard to find.

No crisis, however, was enough to cause him to limit his generosity to his beloved wife and daughter. As Christmas of 1855 approached, the weather in New York was springlike and the stores were filled with shoppers, including Cadet. He looked at French carpets and bought a gift for Emilie, which he had boxed and shipped on December 22.

A cape that Julie had purchased for herself proved to be too expensive for her physician husband's income, and she wrote her father that she was about to return it. He told her to keep it. "Fortunately you have a father who can cover the deficit and something more besides," he said. "I desire that you do not restrict yourself in anything. Do not return the cape. Keep it for cold weather and the mantle for more moderate weather." About the same time, Cadet had suggested that the ailing Sarpy and hard-pressed Charles Pierre could use some help from Dr. Maffitt in the office.

The half-century effort of the extended Chouteau family to win government approval for its claim to the vast lands covering the mines around Dubuque, Iowa, ended in final defeat during this time. Henry Pierre Chouteau had pursued it doggedly over the years after the death of his father, in 1829. Over time, the number of claimants to the roughly 125,000 acres had grown to at least forty as the result of the sale of various pieces of Julien Dubuque's share to pay the debts of his estate and the division of Auguste's share among his children and grandchildren following his death. Various deals were also made to gain expert advice and help in guiding the claim through Washington. These lawyers, surveyors, and lobbyists often took a percentage of the claim in exchange for their work.

The claim was largely a matter for the heirs of Auguste, not of Pierre or the sisters, but Pierre Jr. had a stake as a result of working at the mines for his uncle when he was very young, and A.P., until his death, was defending a stake as a result of assuming debts for his cousin Auguste Aristide. Meanwhile, in 1836, Congress approved the laying off into lots of the town of Dubuque, which the government sold to settlers. Much of the land lay within the Chouteau claim. In 1846 Iowa became a state, and Dubuque was developing into a small city. It was surely no surprise to Pierre Jr. when his cousin Henry Pierre wrote him in August 1854 that the claim had been definitively rejected.

The loss of the old Dubuque claim, which the family had never had the opportunity to fully develop, probably felt like nothing up against the huge sums then being lost in the financial markets. In August 1857, after a trip to Washington, Pierre Jr. told his son that "the crisis seems imminent and God knows where it will end. I find myself obliged to put out $100,000 for which I was not prepared. The crash is not exactly a bed of roses."

The debts of Chouteau, Harrison & Vallé, the firm engaged in iron mining and marketing, reached $428,000 in the midst of the crisis. The firm was forced to suspend payments when the panic reached its highest point in October 1857. Nobody wanted paper currency for payment of debts.

"Another of our largest and more important business houses suspended payment yesterday," reported the *St. Louis Republican*. "We allude to the house of Chouteau, Harrison & Vallé. Although the owners of the Iron Mountain—itself a mountain of wealth at any time—and each of the members of the firm possessed of individual wealth—they have not been able to escape the general disaster." Operations had been halted at Iron Mountain and 450 men discharged. At the Laclède Rolling Mill in St. Louis, also owned by the Chouteau firm, 460 men had been laid off.

However, Chouteau, Harrison & Vallé and P. Chouteau Jr. & Company were soon back in normal operation. Documents from later years suggest that Pierre Jr. made a personal infusion of cash into Chouteau, Harrison & Vallé, and as a result ended up the principal owner.

Under Charles Pierre, the fur-trading firm of P. Chouteau Jr. &

Company continued to sell substantial numbers of skins and furs on European and American markets. The year before the panic, the firm's offering in sales rooms in Mincing Lane in London included nearly 180,000 raccoon pelts, nearly 53,000 opossum, 46,000 muskrat, and more than 31,000 mink. It also sold thousands of furs from fox, otter, Russian sable, lynx, and wildcat. There were only 244 beaver pelts, once the focus of the trade. No buffalo robes were sold in London that year, but P. Chouteau Jr. & Company offered 16,000 buffalo robes that fall at the store it operated in its name at No. 17 Broadway in New York.

Charles Pierre also claimed for his family one more breakthrough in the Upper Missouri country. In the summer of 1859, when the company sent its crews upriver on two steamboats, Charles Pierre traveled on the *Spread Eagle*. At Fort Union, previously the uppermost point to which steamboats had traveled, he transferred some of the crews and equipment to the smaller *Chippewa* and continued to within a few miles of Fort Benton in the middle of the future Montana. By the meandering path of the Missouri River, some measured this as a three-thousand-mile voyage from St. Louis. It was lauded as the longest steamboat voyage made in the American West.

In the midst of the financial disasters and the negotiations for the sale of Fort Pierre, Cadet's own world began to crumble. His closest business associates and friends underwent crises and died over less than five years' time, and he himself soon confronted a calamity that his energy, ambition, and intelligence could not overcome: He went blind.

In 1855, less than a month after negotiating the sale of Fort Pierre for his cousin and in-law, Charles Gratiot Jr. died at the age of sixty-nine, probably of cholera. He had recently retired from his Washington desk job and returned to St. Louis to settle among family. Relatives thought he had not recognized his illness as cholera until he was too ill to be successfully treated. He went to the theater in St. Louis the night he died.

Six months later, on a day at the beginning of November, Cadet's cousin Henry Pierre boarded a train of the Pacific Railroad in St. Louis headed for Jefferson City, the state capital. About fifty miles west of St. Louis, as the train crossed a bridge over Boeuf Creek near the Missouri River, high water broke the bridge, and the train tumbled into the creek. At least twenty-nine passengers died, including Henry Pierre Chouteau. He was fifty years old and had been nearly as enthusiastic about investing in railroads as Pierre Jr.

For several years Cadet had been worried about the mental and physical health of John B. Sarpy, mainstay of the St. Louis office. He first noticed unusual behavior in 1853 and soon made his suggestion that Dr. Maffitt take on some of the office responsibilities. A couple of years later, in response to concerns expressed by Charles Pierre, Cadet said Sarpy was "without a doubt sick . . . But I think it more a sickness of the spirit than of the body."

Sarpy, whom Cadet cherished as "my old friend," died in April 1857 at the age of fifty-nine. Cadet, from New York, wrote Maffitt that he and Charles Pierre would have to carry on together. "You can take over the books, the correspondence and the office, and Charles the outside business." But within a short time Maffitt had a stroke or something else that paralyzed him. He was forced to withdraw from the firm in 1859.

Ramsay Crooks, Cadet's former business associate, friend, and confidant, died in New York on June 6, 1859.

Perhaps the most tragic of the deaths was that of John Sanford, who suffered a mental breakdown in December 1856 and entered an asylum in New York, dying the following May at the age of fifty-one. While juggling the unrelenting pressures of Cadet's appetite to expand his business interests, Sanford had been going through his own personal turmoil. By an accident of birth, he became entangled in the landmark Dred Scott case on slave freedom.

Dred Scott and his wife, Harriet, had been the property of an army physician named John Emerson before Emerson married Sanford's sister, Irene. Emerson's army assignments took the household in and out of many states, including some where slavery was legal, as in Missouri, and some where it was not legal. After Emerson died, in 1843, ownership of the Scotts passed to his wife.

The Scotts asked Irene Emerson if they could buy their freedom, and she declined. Then, aided by sympathetic lawyers and church leaders, they sued for freedom in Missouri courts on the grounds that they should have been freed when Emerson took them to states where slavery was not legal. The Scotts won in state district court, but on appeal to the Missouri Supreme Court the decision was reversed in favor of Irene Emerson.

The Scotts and their supporters, however, were looking for a way to take the issue to the federal courts. They found it in John Sanford, who had entered the case as an adviser to his sister after the death of their father in 1848. Sanford was a resident of New York, a circumstance that enabled the Scotts, claiming citizenship in Missouri, to sue him in federal court. By this path, the case eventually reached the Supreme Court, which ruled at the beginning of 1857 that Dred Scott, as a slave, was not considered a "citizen" of Missouri for purposes of suing in federal court. It essentially upheld the Missouri Supreme Court's denial of freedom.

John Sanford died within weeks of the decision and may not have known of, or understood, his victory.[*]

Pierre Jr.'s eyesight began to fail in 1858. He spent time at Hot Springs in hopes of being cured, but by early 1859 he was completely blind. As the country slid into the Civil War, Cadet slipped into darkness. His mind remained strong, and he tried to maintain an interest in his business affairs, even making at least one more trip to New York after his blindness. But he could no longer sign his own name, and there was no television and no radio to fill his ears with the events of each day.

As Cadet had wished, Charles Pierre stepped completely into his shoes. In early 1860 he took over the New York office, adding the re-

---

[*]After remarriage, however, Irene Emerson quickly arranged for the emancipation of Dred Scott and his wife, which occurred about six months after the Supreme Court decision; Scott died the following year.

sponsibility for his father's other businesses and investments to management of the remaining fur trade. When the effects of the Panic of 1857 subsided, Cadet's continued faith in the Illinois Central was borne out. A railroad official advised Charles Pierre in January 1860 that revenue for the third week of the month, for both passengers and freight, reached $50,180.02, compared to $30,566.65 in the same week the previous year.

For Cadet, the cruelest blow was that Emilie Gratiot Chouteau died on August 24, 1862, at sixty-eight. Typically, no one had any idea that she was sick in the weeks before her death. Auguste Liguest Chouteau, whom Emilie had reared after his mother died, wrote the family from his home in Alton, Illinois, that he "never was so taken in my life as I was at the announcement in your letter of the death of my dear old aunt."

"Her loss will be felt by me as long as life lasts," he said, "for she has always acted the part of a good mother toward me, and to her and uncle I feel I owe a life of gratitude, not only for the education they gave me, but for the morals and religion they infused into me."

After three years without Emilie, Cadet prepared his will. "Being advanced in age but of sound and disposing mind and knowing the certainty of death and the uncertainty of the time when it may happen . . ." he began. What followed was a fairly long document, justified by his vast and varied holdings, but composed in a clear, concise, and almost elegant manner. Even in total darkness Cadet told his final story as he wished it told. In the second paragraph he said he wanted to be buried in Calvary Cemetery beside "my beloved wife and companion." Then he began to guide his estate administrators in how to deal with some of his holdings.

> I have been engaged in the Indian and fur business I may say all my life since my earliest manhood, and although it has been my desire and aim, for many years in view of my age and of the misfortune of total blindness with which for several years I have been afflicted, to wind up and close this branch of business, yet, I have still very large interests in the Indian Country, and considerable sums of money in-

vested in this business. This business is peculiar and it might be very detrimental to my estate to close it up too suddenly or too speedily. I therefore give to my executors hereinafter named full power and authority to close up this business as in their judgment it can be done consistently with the best interest of my estate . . .

I am a member of the house or firm of Chouteau, Harrison & (Felix & Jules) Vallé, which firm is very largely engaged in the Iron Business in the City, and is the owner of the rolling mill in the upper part of this city and known as the Laclède Rolling Mill.

Cadet said that he owned one-third of the "house." He said his administrators could sell all or any portion of his interest in the rolling mill and the house of Chouteau, Harrison and Vallé. "The said house is largely in my debt," he said, because he had advanced it money at different times. The same firm also owned the property known as the Iron Mountain, which could be sold or disposed of, plus his stock in a related firm called American Iron Mountain Co.

"I am the owner of a large amount of property in the State of Minnesota and situated in the City of St. Paul and St. Anthony and their environs and also in and near the town of Hastings. As it may be to the interest of my estate not to retain this property as it pays but a poor income, I thereby authorize my executors . . . to sell any or all of this said property."

Recognizing that his grandson Ben Sanford, then about thirty years old and married, was "inexperienced in business," Cadet set up a generously funded trust for him. It included five pieces of ground in prime center-city areas of St. Louis, some with buildings, and $100,000 to improve a lot that did not have a building, plus $25,000 with which to buy a residence, and an additional $20,000 that the trustees were to use for Ben's benefit as they thought he needed.

Charles Pierre and his sister Julie were to receive "the balance of all my estate of every nature and description whatsoever, and no matter where situated, or whether it be real, or personal, or mixed, bonds, notes, credits, accounts, stocks."

Before Cadet and a witness, a man named Henry S. Turner signed for him. The will did not place values on his assets, but a complaint filed against Charles Pierre later by lawyers about payment of their fees mentioned several sums, which appeared to add up to more than $2 million in the estate.

Pierre Chouteau Jr. died at 2 a.m. on September 6, 1865, at the home of his daughter, Julie. He was approaching his seventy-seventh birthday. As he wished, he was buried beside Emilie in Calvary Cemetery.

Epilogue

�֍

By the time Pierre Chouteau Jr. died, in 1865, nearly all the members of the cousins' generation had passed from the scene. Still living were two of the Gratiot siblings; Auguste's son Gabriel Sylvestre (Cerré) Chouteau; Cadet's sister, Pélagie Berthold; and three of his younger half brothers, Cyprien, Frederick, and Charles.

A century had passed since their grandparents brought the family up the Mississippi from New Orleans. It was a century in which Pierre Laclède and the Chouteaus had tackled an expanse of land nearly as large as the entire young nation to the east. Besides launching St. Louis, they had placed their imprint on an area stretching north to the Canadian border; southwest through what became the states of Missouri, Kansas, and Oklahoma; and up the Missouri River through Nebraska, the Dakotas, Wyoming, and into Montana. In the process, they took on some of the world's mightiest and most turbulent rivers, dedicated weeks and months to getting from one place to another, and faced epidemics and other great risks far from people who might come to their aid in an emergency. And they never lost sight of the need to remain connected to the larger world, patiently and tenaciously maintaining trade ties with Montreal, London, Paris, and later New York.

Within this frontier world, they claimed positions of privilege, at first on the strength of Pierre Laclède's education, connections, and ability to lead and command respect. Over decades, they proved themselves to be people of skill whose word served as law in much of the West before authority passed to the United States government and Army and a raft of sheriffs and marshals. In a distant corner of the world where most people signed their names with an X, they assumed the responsibility of educating themselves to fulfill the roles of leaders and arbiters. They represented the framework of civil society in places where none had yet arrived. Using their precious books, they figured out how to survey land and erect structures, how to chart the flow of rivers, how to grow new crops, how to confront disease and illness, and how to keep account books and conduct business.

People today would find fault with many of the principles by which the Chouteaus lived, but most people today would be incapable of meeting, with the same grace and determination, the challenges they faced. They practiced slavery. Yet when they finally had to make a choice, they remained loyal to the government that destroyed the institution of human bondage. Straddling European and Indian culture, many of the men fathered children by the young Indian women who came to them as part of business deals with tribal leaders. With a French shrug, they decided to accept the situation that they encountered. But as observant Roman Catholics, they left a paper trail effectively acknowledging these liaisons in smoky, smelly lodges and tepees far from their legal wives. Finally, the way they made their living—the fur trade—depleted North America of much of its first great resource, its wildlife. But it was a way of life that enabled Indians to support themselves without dependence on government, the situation that would prevail under the eventual policy of concentrating them on reservations.

Seeing only the negative aspects of the Chouteaus' ways of living and doing business would be to judge their behavior by the standards of another time, one that they could not anticipate. They created the forerunner of sprawling business empires during an era when most Americans lived on subsistence farms or worked in cottage industries. They created the means of making a living for large numbers of people. They saw the potential of the American West in grand terms—its endless rivers and boundless natural resources, and its unique human resources, which were mostly Indians when the Chouteaus began operations from St. Louis.

Did the Chouteaus benefit more than was their right from their pre-eminent position in the frontier society? Did they take advantage of the Indians? And of the *voyageurs* and other laborers in the fur trade? Asking these questions ignores the extent to which there was competition for the Indian trade in most areas. And the fact that the Chouteaus and others who held dominant positions in the fur trade were themselves nearly always facing the risk of bankruptcy for their investments of money and effort. Their rewards were greater, but they shared the financial risks and also the personal risks of those lower down in the structure of the business.

The fur trade was tough. People went into it because of the potential rewards at a time when the rewards to be gained in other lines of work were few, or were available only to a few. Those who ventured west in search of the means of existence, and perhaps success, had left behind no factories and offices with job security and fringe benefits back home. The fur trade was an opportunity, one in which obtaining even basic necessities was a struggle, but which men undertook in hopes of bettering their situations. With nothing to go back to in the East or Europe, they were willing to suffer and take great risks.

In the real world of paying the bills, far from centers of population and commerce, where communications might take months, it was sometimes difficult to show compassion. The people who managed and worked in the fur trade were not employees; most of them, in a small or large way, were entrepreneurs. They put up their own capital or meager savings in hopes of succeeding in a very risky endeavor. The lonely trapper, wintering along streams rich with beaver, had staked himself to the chance. There was no mighty corporation, or government, with deep pockets behind any of them, no institution able to absorb losses and provide guarantees of social well-being. The supposedly powerful American Fur Company was mostly a network of men struggling as individuals on their own assets and personal reputations.

At the bottom of the rung in the fur trade, individual hunters and trappers had to fight hard to keep their pelts until they could deliver them to a post for sale. The fruit of their labor was often lost to overturned boats or to thefts by hostile Indians and other white trappers, or they cached pelts and could not find them again in the sameness of the wilderness. Life was harsh. Men who signed on with a fur-trade outfit were treated like military conscripts. If they attempted to leave before the end of their enlistment time, they were considered deserters, sometimes hunted down and forced back to work. In rags, sometimes even naked, they survived cruel winters or merciless sun. They often went without food. Hominy grits were the norm; pancakes and coffee were luxuries.

At a higher level, where the Chouteaus themselves operated, the risks could be equally heartbreaking. They demanded that the men who signed with them complete their contracts, because they had to have men in the field who could trap on their own or trade with the Indians for pelts, thus assuring the recovery of the capital invested in merchandise and keeping the operation going year after year.

The level of risk faced by the investors and owners was demonstrated by the experience of a Chouteau in-law, Pierre Labbadie, sailing to France in 1803 with a load of skins. He spent two months at sea and was sick the entire voyage, and as the vessel neared Bordeaux, the news arrived that France and England were at war, putting "terror into every breast." Before eventually landing, the ship was forcefully boarded and inspected by the crew of an English vessel and then put through five days of quarantine by French authorities fearing an epidemic aboard ship.

Finally, when Labbadie opened his skins, all of them had been eaten by maggots; none were good enough to sell. Adding to his dismay was the fact that he had borrowed money at 12 percent interest to pay for the goods with which he had acquired the pelts and to cover other expenses. He was in debt, with nothing to show for months of effort.

Nearly a half century later, the Swiss artist Rudolph Friederich Kurz spent several years among the fur traders and Indians of the Upper Missouri and was struck by the financial risks still associated with the business. At first finding the prices the traders placed on merchandise to be "so unreasonably high," he later concluded that the great costs involved in bringing trading goods from "9,000 miles, nay, some of them halfway round the world" justified the prices.

"Wares are shipped here from Leipzig (little bells and mirrors), from Cologne (clay pipes), beads from Italy, merinos, calicos from France, woolen blankets, guns from England, sugar and coffee from New Orleans, clothing and knives from New York, powder and shot, meal, corn, etc., from St. Louis," he wrote in 1851. The *bourgeois* at each fort or trading post, he noted, had to be expert at calculating what he could sell. He also had to have a sense of the possible returns from future hunting seasons, when he placed his orders with commission agents in St. Louis, New Orleans, or New York. Stockholders or partners in the company had to assume responsibility for any damages to goods in shipment—trade goods going upriver and skins and pelts coming downriver.

Barton Barbour, the historian of Fort Union, writing in recent years, came to similar conclusions. "Some observers view the trade as nothing more than an unsavory backwoods ripoff whereby venal white men conned unsuspecting natives. In reality, success in the chancy economics of fur trading required that interrelationships among Indian, mixed-blood, and white traders be reasonably amicable. No less vital to victory, however, were large amounts of capital, access to worldwide networks for supplies and sales, and dependable connections with allies inside the government."

It was true that the Chouteaus and their relatives wanted to grow rich in the Indian trade, and they wanted to create and protect comfortable situations for their offspring and future generations of the family. They were driven by the desire for personal gain, but they also demonstrated genuine affection and sympathy for Indians, if often frustrated by the Indians' lack of understanding of the right to private property, which young braves thought was there for the stealing.

On balance, the Chouteaus recognized in the Indians just another set of people with whom to trade and do business. For this privilege, they were prepared to respect tribal culture and learn Indian tongues. In the process of striking business deals, they experienced Indian life intimately and in depth over many decades. Their approach did far more to foster good white-Indian relations than did the policies imposed later by military men and politicians. The Stars and Stripes flying from the staff high atop Chouteau fur posts, whether small or huge fortifications, lent a commanding presence—accomplished by bargaining and haggling, not through violence.

Indians were not abstractions to the Chouteaus. They knew one tribe from another, knew their quirks, strengths, and weaknesses, and their histories. Unlike whites who poured across the Mississippi and Missouri rivers and the plains and prairies in covered wagons after the Civil War, they did not see the Indians in mythical terms in which brave white settlers were pitted against warring Indians. Nor did they hold the revisionist views of a Noble Red Man that would come later among well-intentioned whites. They neither feared nor idolized Indians. They were willing to live among them on civilized terms and do business with them in a mutually beneficial way. They were prepared to cast their lot with the Indians and to seek their interests alongside them. They brought up their children to share those views and to coexist peacefully with Indians without fear.

Starting with the Jefferson Administration and Lewis and Clark, the United States government—and later the army—piggybacked on the skills and knowledge of the Chouteaus and other fur traders in the Louisiana Purchase region. The government seemed unaware of the fact that it was stepping into the midst of relationships between Indians and whites that had existed for generations. If officials did recognize the relationships, they expected to reap benefit from them without giving anything in return.

This probably explains part of Pierre Chouteau's frustration at receiving no recognition, and little recompense, for his substantial contributions to furthering American government goals among western Indians—even those goals about which his years of experience surely caused him to have reservations. The first government officials to deal with Pierre, and to a lesser extent his brother, Auguste, seemed convinced that the brothers' cravings for wealth made them suspect when they made recommendations on Indian policy. But in the next generation Pierre had the satisfaction of seeing his three eldest sons—A.P., Pierre Jr., and Paul Liguest—held in esteem by a government that turned to them repeatedly, and often desperately, for help in understanding the tribes.

The Chouteaus' attitudes toward the blacks and mulattos in their midst varied greatly from their empathetic view of Indians. Slaves were not their principal means of building wealth, but the Chouteaus thought bonded servitude had a place in economic life. They bought and sold these human beings when it served their purposes, not questioning this as a matter of principle. Neither did the Jesuits and other Catholic priests who brought the earliest slaves to the Upper Mississippi Valley and traded in them until well after the United States took possession of the territory.

Although Auguste and Pierre Chouteau were determined defenders of the institution of slavery, their children and nieces and nephews displayed less conviction about it, or even opposed it, long before the abolition movement gained momentum. This was apparent in the decision of one of the sons of Victoire Chouteau Gratiot to liberate two slaves in 1825 on principle. There are a few other recorded cases of members of the family liberating slaves on an individual basis, perhaps as a result of unusual personal rapport between slave and master. And there are other recorded cases of slaves buying their freedom from members of the family. In general, however, the Chouteaus did not become crusaders against slavery. Rather, on this issue, they continued to demonstrate their ability to sniff the way the wind was blowing.

Pierre Jr. had campaigned for the Missouri constitutional convention in 1820 on a promise not to vote to restrict slavery in the state, but there is nothing in his surviving correspondence and receipts to suggest that slavery played a role in his business affairs as he grew to be the richest of the Chouteaus and one of the richest Americans. He did have household slaves, being listed on the 1831 tax rolls as possessing sixteen slaves. The correspondence of his half brother François reveals that François would have preferred to hire a man for wages, had one been available, than to buy a slave to make up for the shortage of hands for his farm—because the slave was more expensive than a hired hand.

The behavior of some of the grandchildren of Auguste and Pierre during the Civil War underscored even more this shift in attitude. When the Civil War began, Cadet's son Charles Pierre Chouteau was running his father's wide-ranging business interests from the headquarters in St. Louis, where loyalties were sharply divided in the years immediately before the war. The divisions extended throughout the state of Missouri, which would likely have seceded from the Union had it not been for the fact that important sites in the state were occupied by Federal troops. Charles Pierre initially sided with a St. Louis group known as "conditional Unionists," who sought a middle way to avoid secession and war. But after South Carolina left the Union on December 20, 1860, followed by other states, Charles Pierre conducted his business as a Federal loyalist.

In 1861 he painted for an associate on the Upper Missouri the sad picture he saw on the horizon. "Political troubles involving every thing in a commercial way [are] creating the utmost distress all over the country. Times are harder now than ever before in all this western country. All of [the] cotton states [have] seceded. The fact is we are in a state of revolution and the greatest fear [is] that civil war may be the result, although every feasible effort is being made to prevent it."

During most of the Civil War years, large quantities of merchandise were shipped to the Upper Missouri country by P. Chouteau Jr. & Company. In addition, the firm was shipping cotton from Memphis to the East on a regular basis and receiving a large variety of goods from New York, including coffee, raisins, nuts, sardines, shoes, sugar, kegs of pickles, and wine, all presumably for onward shipment up the Missouri. The S.B. *Yellowstone*, a successor to the first *Yellow Stone* but with the name spelled as one word, was kept busy, and other steamboats as well. P. Chouteau Jr. & Company also shipped gold dust and bullion from Fort Benton and elsewhere for deposit at the United States Assay Office in St. Louis, a role requiring the trust of the United States government.

The Chouteaus, however, had traditionally supported and maintained good relations with Democratic administrations and Democratic politicians, so when Lincoln and the Republicans took office, the St. Louis trading clan suddenly found itself without friends in high places. Problems emerged between Charles Pierre and the Upper Missouri Indian agent, a Republican appointee named Samuel N. Latta. Commissioned in August 1861, Latta reached the Upper Missouri in spring 1862 and soon began to charge that Charles Pierre was against the Lincoln Administration and a supporter of secession. Two

years later Latta's charges produced results when the government refused to renew Charles Pierre's license to trade with the Indians.

Charles Larpenteur, who had been working on the Upper Missouri for more than thirty years, mostly for the Chouteaus, was there
when Charles Pierre arrived in June 1865 to break the news that his
family firm had been dislodged from the business it had dominated for
so long. Charles Pierre landed at Fort Union on the *Yellowstone* "in
great distress," according to Larpenteur, because "having been reported as a rebel he could not obtain a license, and was obliged to sell
out all his trading-posts, except [Fort] Benton." He had already signed
the papers on May 19 to sell what had once been known as the Upper
Missouri Outfit of the American Fur Company to two Minnesota
men with Republican ties, James B. Hubbell and Alpheus F. Hawley.
The next month, Pierre Jr. himself, although blind and just two
months away from death, sold the *Yellowstone*, his last Missouri River
steamboat, for $40,000.

Auguste Chouteau, a believer—until his death in 1829—in using a
firm hand to keep slaves in line, would surely have been torn between
dismay and pride over the grandson who fought with great distinction
as a Union officer in the Battle of Gettysburg. Gabriel Paul, an 1834
graduate of West Point, was not only descended from slave owners on
the Chouteau side of his family but on the paternal side as well. His
other grandfather, Eustache Paul, was France's lieutenant governor
on the island of St. Domingue, the future Haiti, and had been forced
to flee when the slaves rebelled. The young Paul first distinguished
himself on behalf of the United States in the Mexican War, when he
led a party storming the Castle of Chapultepec. In the Civil War, he
was seriously wounded at Gettysburg and left blinded for life. At the
end of the war he was recognized "for gallant and meritorious service"
to the cause of the Union and promoted to brigadier general.

Other grandchildren of Auguste's, the offspring of his son Henry
Pierre, found themselves in a paradoxical situation a few years after
the Civil War when an uncle on their mother's side died in the office
of his medical practice in New Orleans. Dr. Louis Coursault, had,
as far as they knew, lived his entire life without marrying or having

children. He had been close to their mother, Clemence Coursault Chouteau, who set aside a room for him for his regular visits to the family's St. Louis mansion.

When Dr. Coursault died, a commission merchant house in New Orleans that did business with the family sent a letter informing Gilman Chouteau, a son of Henry Pierre, of his uncle's passing. Two days later the firm advised that Dr. Coursault's funeral had not been as well attended as it should have been because "the woman with whom he was living and had his children" had insisted on taking the lead in planning the service. "Many persons abstained themselves from attending on account of the color of the above named parties," the letter writer added. The merchant house subsequently took control of the remains, and Gilman traveled to New Orleans to claim them, as well as the estate, presumably without calling on his mulatto cousins.

From time to time in the decades after the Civil War, family members grappled with the question of why the surname was Chouteau instead of Laclède. Some descendants went through a phase of simply refusing to believe that Laclède had been the father of four of Madame Chouteau's five children. They chose to pretend that her legal husband, René Chouteau, had remained in her household long enough to father all of them. However, John Francis McDermott, the twentieth-century historian descended from the family, after diligent research on the whereabouts of René Chouteau during the years in which Madame Chouteau's four younger children were born, made clear his conclusion when he dedicated an unpublished manuscript on Laclède to "all us bastards."

"The truth had always been known to the family. The problem was how to put it to the public," McDermott wrote.

Frederick Edward Chouteau, a grandson of François and Bérénice, also made clear his conclusion when he had his last name legally changed to Laclede, minus the French accent, in the late nineteenth century. He named his own son Pierre Charles Laclede, who presumably passed the surname to his descendants. This may have been a small vindication for Pierre Laclède Liguest in return for the love and care he extended to the family that never bore his name.

The Chouteaus did not impose French culture on America. As with other ethnic and cultural groups, America absorbed them. Laclède and Madame Chouteau, the first generation of the family to stake its claim in the American West, were French through and through. The sons and daughters were brought up to be the same, but in their middle years they faced a new world dominated by people they had been accustomed to consider uncultured heretics. English was foreign to them, as were the ways of the raw frontiersmen and eastern lawyers drawn to St. Louis and the larger region.

But the Chouteaus' reaction was pragmatic. They were more interested in business success than in imposing a particular political or cultural mind-set. They seduced the Yankees and Southerners with style, charm, and hospitality, protecting their own positions in the new world being created. Their children were a bridge generation, quickly adapting to the new culture and new ways while respecting the language and ways of the parents during private times. They took advantage of the opportunities presented by the new order with less conflict than their parents had experienced. The next generation, the children of the children of Auguste and Pierre and their sisters, were probably more at ease in the English-speaking world of their peers than in the French linguistic and cultural world of their elders. Thus, Gabriel Paul wrote his great-uncle, Pierre Sr., in English in 1838 to inform him of the death of A.P., although surely knowing that Pierre would require help reading the precious letter.

The world to which Lacléde and the Chouteaus gave shape was eventually overwhelmed by the sheer numbers of settlers from east of the Mississippi. A visitor to St. Louis in 1827 observed, with regret, that "Kentucky manners" now predominated over Creole style.

These, the people we think of as pioneers, came to farm, not to engage in the global business that was the fur trade or to build a city along the French and Caribbean lines that the Chouteaus had begun. They had no practical need to interact with Indians. Yet it is these people in the covered wagons whose perspective has become the popular history of the American West. St. Louis grew up to be a polyglot midwestern city of the races and cultures that make up America. The younger Kansas City became a raucous town of cowboys and outlaws on the line between cattle country and farming country before it, too, succumbed to the influx of Germans, Irish, Jews, Slavs, South Slavs, freed slaves, and others. The Chouteaus and the other early French were just the first layer of white settlement in those communities, and the later settlers came in such large numbers that the French foundations seemed forgotten, as surely as the Indian roots were overrun.

Except for the Quixote-like A. P. Chouteau, struggling almost until the day he died to protect Indian lifestyles and prevent an explosion of violence on the prairies of the future Oklahoma, the family did not attempt to block changing times. Never nostalgists, they still wanted to make money. This could not have been more apparent than in 1841, when Auguste Chouteau's widow, Thérèse Cerré, tore down the magnificent mansion Auguste built for her. By renovation and expansion, it had grown out of Laclède's first headquarters, the stone structure that Missouri Indian women helped Auguste build in 1764. After moving to a new house on the hill west of the original town site, Thérèse Chouteau used the square block of urban land for construction of thirty-two three-story brick business buildings, which she sold or rented out.

Visible remains of the world of the Chouteaus slip back into focus at unexpected moments throughout seven or eight states. Mispronounced French names dot the landscape, especially in Missouri. Traffic along Interstate 70 in the middle of the state does not pause as it races across Chouteau Creek and the Lamine River, site of Pierre Chouteau's huge land grant from the Osages. Counties and small settlements bear the name Chouteau in several states, plus Laclede, Sarpy, Labbadie, and Papin. Land opposite the Missouri River from the site that Pierre Jr. chose for his mighty trading fort to serve the Sioux tribe eventually gave rise to the South Dakota capital city. Streets, bridges, and neighborhoods in St. Louis and Kansas City bear the names Chouteau, Gratiot, Labbadie, Demun, Soulard, Guinotte, Laclede—all speaking to a tie to the French founders.

In the late nineteenth century and throughout the twentieth, however, the family name proliferated most widely in Oklahoma among the part-Indian descendants of A.P., Paul Liguest, Auguste Aristide, Frederick, Cyprien, and François, plus their cousin Millicour Papin.

Although Cyprien and Frederick lived out their lives in Kansas City, many of their mixed-blood children moved to Oklahoma after marrying into other mixed-blood families.

The energetic mixed-blood Chouteaus became so numerous that they seemed almost a tribe in themselves. Although the Indian blood of these Chouteau descendants was basically Osage in origin, intermarriage soon brought Shawnee, Kansa, and Cherokee portions. Various members of the "Oklahoma line" of the family spent decades chasing the group's genealogy, a search complicated by the fact that— at least in the first half of the nineteenth century—it had been common for a white man or a tribal leader to father children by two or more sisters. Such was the case with A. P. Chouteau, who had children by two half sisters, both of whom shared his house at the Saline. Also, A.P. and his brother Paul Liguest both fathered children by the same third woman.

In addition, great care was not always taken on early baptism records to note the names of parents with exactitude, or ages either. Rosalie Lambert, A. P. Chouteau's principal Osage wife, demonstrated this when she baptized several children born to her in the decade after the death of A.P. She had two sons baptized in 1853, listing each as nine years old and identifying "August Chouteau" as their father, even though A.P. had been dead six years when they were born, in 1844. She also took a daughter to a priest for baptism in 1848, again listing "August Chouteau" as the father but without listing the child's age.

The willingness of the men of the family to share lodges and blankets with various Indian women was regrettable not so much for itself as for what it said about the position of women in tribal societies. They were viewed as little more than commodities to be used as necessary, or bought and sold. The women's fathers, brothers, and husbands were the primary proponents of this system. The matter-of-factness of the custom was clear in a notation that Francis Chardon made in his Fort Union journal after the 1837 smallpox epidemic. Having lost two Indian female companions to early death, he soon tired of being lonely during the long Upper Missouri winters and bought himself a fifteen-year-old virgin for $150.

Some Indian men saw such use of their girls and young women

merely as the means to short-term gain. Others, however, such as Chief White Plume of the Kansa tribe, saw this as a means of marrying up. He thought that absorbing more white culture would improve the prospects of the tribe. However it occurred, from this willingness of the Chouteaus and their kin to associate so intimately with the tribes grew the makings of a new culture, a form of mixed-blood royalty that was the linkage between the tribes and white society and government. Out of that milieu emerged Charles Curtis, who was elected to Congress from Kansas in 1892, to the Senate in 1907, and became Vice President of the United States under Herbert Hoover in 1928.

As a tribe, the proud and once powerful Osages were desperately poor by the end of the Civil War. As a result, they sold part of their land in what had now become the state of Kansas to the United States government in a treaty signed September 29, 1865. They gave up a plank-shaped piece of land thirty miles wide stretching for fifty miles along the Neosho River, and they moved farther west. Five years later Congress passed legislation requiring that the Osages remove themselves entirely from Kansas, and they ended up on a piece of land in the future Oklahoma, snug against the Kansas border.

After so many decades of miseries, the Osages now owned one and a half million beautifully rolling acres, a green and treed land. It was the kind of tract that A. P. Chouteau surely had in mind when he pleaded with the government in 1833 to give them a verdant piece of ground capable of sheltering the wild game on which they were still dependent. But in this new land to which the Osages moved after 1870, wild game became a moot issue. Osage fortunes took a dramatic leap in 1897, when the first oil well was dug in Osage County. By the 1920s, million-dollar oil leases were being auctioned beneath an elm tree in Pawhuska, the county seat named for the long-ago Chief White Hair. The Osages were soon among the richest people, per capita, in the United States. Their royalties hit a peak of $13,000 a person in 1925, and Rolls-Royces purred along the streets of Pawhuska.

This would have been of comfort to A. P. Chouteau, resting in an unmarked grave. He was buried with military honors two days after Christmas in 1838 in the cemetery at Fort Gibson beside his half brother Pharamond and cousin Auguste Aristide, but efforts in later years to locate the graves were not successful. The fort was closed as a military post in the 1850s; no one was on the grounds to care for the cemetery, and many of the old graves lost their identifying markers. In 1869, all of the known and unknown remains were moved to the Fort Gibson town cemetery, where A. P. Chouteau presumably lies among those interred as unknowns.

What the Chouteaus truly contributed to America during their time as a united dynasty was the ability to live and do business peaceably with Indians. Above all, they were practical. They were not so much interested in advancing new political philosophies and ideals as living in peace day by day. Within the context of their times, they were more tolerant than most white people. Their pragmatism and their tolerance helped them maintain a realistic view of white-Indian relations. What remained after the Chouteaus no longer played a mediating role was a confrontational attitude, on both sides.

It seems significant that just slightly more than a year after the Louisiana Purchase territory passed to the United States, a Sac Indian was shot and killed by United States Army troops when he escaped confinement in St. Louis. Pierre Chouteau worked diligently to prevent the sad outcome of the 1805 episode, locking horns with a hardheaded army officer. Even though the Indian was accused in three white killings, Pierre operated on the belief that because Indians did not understand white concepts of justice, it was wrong to execute an Indian, or to shoot one while he was escaping. He believed in demanding that the tribe itself determine the punishment to be applied.

The killing of the Sac warrior might be considered the first shot fired in the bitter Indian wars that would come in the second half of the nineteenth century. By contrast to this quick hardening of attitudes almost as soon as the United States took possession of the territory, Spanish forces are not known to have executed or otherwise killed an Indian during the entire four decades of Spanish rule preceding the Louisiana Purchase. They fumed over Indian "depredations" and threatened strong measures, but they always concluded that such steps would be counterproductive. The Chouteau brothers were key instruments in carrying out those policies, and they were conditioned to work out disputes on an individual basis without resorting to killing.

Lewis and Clark and the United States government were beneficiaries of the four decades of work to conduct Indian affairs in this manner. Without the Chouteaus, without their business acumen and deep understanding of the Indians, the Louisiana Purchase territory to which Lewis and Clark arrived would have been a different place. The Chouteaus, like Laclède, had worked to create an environment where Indians generally respected white men and believed they could be trusted. The prevailing attitude among Indians of the region, when Auguste and Pierre Chouteau welcomed Lewis and Clark to St. Louis, was that it was possible to share the vast land with the white man. Many decades of bumbling policies followed before that faith was snuffed out.

Notes

Acknowledgments

Index

Notes

❋

ABBREVIATIONS USED

AC	Auguste Chouteau
AFC	American Fur Co.
APC	Auguste Pierre (A.P.) Chouteau
CC	Chouteau Collection
LCE	Lewis and Clark Expedition
MHS	Missouri Historical Society
PC	Pierre Chouteau
PC Jr.	Pierre Chouteau Jr.
SIUE	Southern Illinois University at Edwardsville
WHMC	Western Historical Manuscript Collection—University of Missouri–Kansas City

1. AMONG A PEOPLE OF STRANGE SPEECH

3 *Seen from the river: Annals of St. Louis in its Territorial Days from 1804–1821*, Frederic L. Billon, ed. (Bowie, Md.: Heritage Books, 1997, first published 1888), 22; Amos Stoddard, *Sketches, Historical and Descriptive of Louisiana* (Philadelphia: Mathew Carey, 1812), 218–19; and Dorothy Garesché Holland, "St. Louis Families from the French West Indies," in *The French in the Mississippi Valley*, John Francis McDermott, ed. (Urbana: University of Illinois Press, 1965), 50.

4 *The population:* Stoddard, *Sketches*, 220–26.

4 *These lands:* Amos Stoddard to Phoebe Benham, June 16, 1804, Stoddard Papers, MHS; Stoddard, *Sketches*, 218–21.

5 *The "West's first:* James P. Ronda, *Finding the West: Explorations with Lewis and Clark* (Albuquerque: University of New Mexico Press, 2001), 69.

5 *Each of their homes:* Lewis F. Thomas and J. C. Wild, *Valley of the Mississippi Illustrated* (St. Paul: Minnesota Historical Society, 1967), 29–30.

5 *Auguste, courtly:* "William Clark's 1795 and 1797 Journals," *Bulletin of Missouri Historical Society*, Vol. 25, No. 4, Part 1, July 1969.

5 *Forty-five-year-old:* Delassus to Casa Calvo, Nov. 29, 1800, in *Before Lewis and Clark: Documents Illustrating the History of the Missouri 1785–1804*, Abraham P. Nasatir, ed., Vol. 2, 622–24.

6 *Pierre opened:* Clark to Croghan, May 2, 1804, William Clark Papers, Clark Family Collection, MHS.

6 *They treasured books:* John Francis McDermott, *Private Libraries in Creole Saint Louis* (Baltimore: The Johns Hopkins Press, 1938), 128–63.

7 *Protestants from the East:* Stoddard, *Sketches*, 316–17.

7 *Another early visitor:* Henry M. Brackenridge, *Views of Louisiana; Together with a Voyage up the Missouri River in 1811* (Pittsburgh: Cramer, Spear & Eichbaum, 1814), 134–35.

9 *Looking to save: Annals of St. Louis in Its Early Days Under the French and Spanish Dominations* (Bowie, Md.: Heritage Books, 1997, first published 1886), Frederic L. Billon, ed., 352–54; also Inventory, Box 3, Delassus–St. Vrain Collection, MHS.

10 *Although Lewis:* Lewis to Clark, May 2, 1804, in *Letters of the LCE with Related Documents, 1783–1854*, Donald Jackson, ed., Vol. 1 (Norman: University of Oklahoma Press, 1966), 177–78.

11 *Lewis wrote:* Lewis to Jefferson, March 26, 1804, in *Letters of LCE*, Jackson, ed., Vol. 1, 170.

11 *Pierre showed: Original Journals of the LCE*, Reuben Gold Thwaites, ed., Vol. 6 (Cleveland: Arthur H. Clark, 1904–7), 32.

12 *"I fear that the slaves:* Lewis to Jefferson, Dec. 28, 1803, in *Letters of LCE*, Vol. 1, Jackson, ed., 148–55.

13 *Lewis was:* Clark to Lewis, Feb. 18, 1804, William Clark Papers, Clark Family Collection, MHS.

14 *On the return: Pittsburgh Gazette*, June 22, 1804, p. 3, col. 2.

14 *In the first:* Public Notice, Box 3, Delassus–St. Vrain Collection, MHS.

14 *Most of:* See sketch of Government House in 1804 by descendant of Pierre Chouteau in Louis Houck, *A History of Missouri from Earliest Explorations and Settlements until the Admission of the State into the Union*, Vol. 2 (Chicago: R. R. Donnelley & Sons, 1908), 361.

15 *Nevertheless, when:* Stoddard, *Sketches*, 311.

15 *Delassus formally:* Billon, ed., *Annals of St. Louis in Early Days*, 359–60.

15 *"The flag:* Ibid.

16 *You are now:* Stoddard, *Sketches*, 104–8.

16 *"It is confidently:* Ibid., 105.

16 *As the Stars:* John F. Darby, *Personal Recollections of Many Prominent People I Have Known* (St. Louis: G. I. Jones and Company, 1880), 222–23.

17 *Stoddard's party:* Stoddard, *Sketches*, 327.

17 *The party:* Amos Stoddard to Phoebe Benham, June 16, 1804, Stoddard Papers, MHS.
17 *While Delassus: Annals of St. Louis in Early Days,* Billon, ed., 366.
17 *In their search:* For information on Antoine Chouteau, see Chapter 5 this book.
18 *There was also:* Donald Chaput, "The Early Missouri Graduates of West Point," in *Missouri Historical Review,* Vol. 72, No. 4, July 1978.
19 *On March 28:* Ibid.; *Letters of LCE,* Jackson, ed., Vol. 1, 172n.
19 *West Point:* Stephen E. Ambrose, *Duty, Honor, Country: A History of West Point* (Baltimore and London: Johns Hopkins University Press, 1966), 1–20; Chaput, "Early Missouri Graduates," in *Missouri Historical Review.*
19 *But the West Point:* Ambrose, *Duty, Honor,* 21–27.
19 *The War Department:* Chaput, "Early Missouri Graduates," in *Missouri Historical Review.*
20 *Wanting to assure:* Clark to Croghan, May 2, 1804, William Clark Papers, Clark Family Collection, MHS.
20 *Clark praised:* Ibid.
20 *On May 14: Original Journals of LCE,* Thwaites, ed., Vol. 1, 19–24.
21 *In St. Louis:* Document of Lewis, May 16, 1804, *Letters of LCE,* Jackson, ed., Vol. 1, 191.
21 *There were some:* Lewis to Jefferson, May 18, 1804, ibid., 192–94.
21 *He also sent:* Ibid.
22 *A chart:* Ibid.
22 *Amos Stoddard also:* Stoddard to Dearborn, May 7, 1804, Stoddard Papers, MHS.
22 *Clark reached: Original Journals of LCE,* Thwaites, ed., Vol. 1, 16–24.
23 *On May 19: Pittsburgh Gazette,* June 22, 1804, p. 3, col. 2.
23 *On May 20: Original Journals of LCE,* Thwaites, ed., Vol. 1, 22–25.
23 *About 1:30 p.m.:* Ibid.
24 *With both:* Stoddard to Phoebe Benham, June 16, 1804, Stoddard Papers, MHS.

2. THE FIRST GENERATION: PIERRE LACLÈDE LIGUEST

26 *Pierre Laclède's:* Author's visit to Laclède birthplace in 2002.
26 *Magdeleine:* Mary B. Cunningham and Jeanne C. Blythe, *The Founding Family of St. Louis* (St. Louis: Midwest Technical Publications, 1977), 3.
27 *He was erect:* Richard Edwards, *Great West and Her Commercial Metropolis* (St. Louis: *Edwards's Monthly,* 1860), 263; also Walter Barlow Stevens, *History of St. Louis: The Fourth City 1764–1909,* Vol. 1 (St. Louis and Chicago: S. J. Clarke Publishing Co., 1909), xv.
27 *French traders:* Seymour I. Schwartz, *This Land Is Your Land: The Geo-*

graphic Evolution of the United States (New York: Harry N. Abrams, Inc., 2000), 79–87.

28 *France and:* Ibid., 88, and Charles E. Hoffhaus, *Chez les Canses* (Kansas City: The Lowell Press, 1984), 53–63.

28 *As early as:* Carl J. Ekberg, *Colonial Ste. Genevieve: An Adventure on the Mississippi Frontier* (Tucson: The Patrice Press, 1996), 144–45.

29 *Neither France:* Stoddard, *Sketches*, 226; Gustavus A. Finkelnburg, "Under Three Flags, or the Story of St. Louis Briefly Told," in *MHS Collections*, Vol. 3, No. 3, 1911, 202–3.

29 *One of:* See John Joseph Matthews, *The Osages: Children of the Middle Waters* (Norman: University of Oklahoma Press, 1961), 164–74.

29 *The French:* Stevens, *History of St. Louis*, 18.

30 *Marie Thérèse:* See Cunningham and Blythe, *Founding Family*, 1; also record of suit, filed April 20, 1771, in *Louisiana Historical Society Quarterly*, Vol. 8, 1925, 324.

30 *Chouteau:* See birth and death records of Chouteau family from L'Hermenault, La Rochelle, Box 57, CC, MHS; Cunningham and Blythe, *Founding Family*, 2; Copies from Second Register of Baptisms at St. Louis Cathedral, New Orleans, Box 57, CC, MHS; and "Chouteau's Succession," in *Louisiana Historical Quarterly*, Vol. 2, No. 3, 513.

31 *Family tradition:* Billon, ed., *Annals of St. Louis in Early Days*, 412–14.

31 *Laclède and:* Certified copies of baptismal records of the first three children, Box 45/f.21, McDermott Collection, Bowen Archives, Lovejoy Library, SIUE; Gratiot Collection, MHS, has typed copy in French of Victoire's baptism.

32 *While Laclède:* "Fragment of Col. Auguste Chouteau's Narrative of the Settlement of St. Louis," originally published in annex to *Twelfth Annual Report of the Board of Directors of the St. Louis Mercantile Library Association*, 1858.

32 *This would:* Captain Philip Pittman, *Present State of European Settlements on the Mississippi* (Gainesville: University of Florida Press, 1973, originally published 1770), 43.

32 *The Laclède-Maxent:* Before Lewis and Clark Documents, Nasatir, ed., Vol. 1, 60.

32 *To carry out:* Stevens, *History of St. Louis*, 18.

33 *Unbeknownst:* See Fred Anderson, *Crucible of War: The Seven Years' War and the Fate of Empire in British North America, 1754–1766* (New York: Alfred A. Knopf, 2000), 503–6; and Emmanuel Le Roy Ladurie, *The Ancien Régime: A History of France, 1610–1774*, Mark Greengrass, tr. (Oxford: Blackwell, 1996), 381.

33 *Whether or not:* "Fragment of Col. Auguste Chouteau's Narrative," 1.

33 *In August:* Ibid.

33 *The Laclède group:* Stevens, *History of St. Louis*, 18.

34 *The banks:* Ibid., 19.

34 *Through August:* "Fragment of Col. Auguste Chouteau's Narrative," 1.

34 *Until he could:* Ibid.

34 *Laclède pushed:* Ibid.; also see Pittman, *Present State of European Settlements,* 46.

35 *Laclède's boatmen:* J. N. Nicollet, "Sketch of the Early History," in *The Early Histories of St. Louis,* John Francis McDermott, ed. (St. Louis: Historical Documents Foundation, 1952), 134–35; Stevens, *History of St. Louis,* 19–20.

35 *On his arrival:* "Fragment of Col. Auguste Chouteau's Narrative," 1–2, 6.

35 *Observing all of this:* Ibid.

35 *In December:* Ibid.

36 *Meanwhile:* Chronology in *Early Histories,* McDermott, ed., 32.

36 *The men:* Auguste Chouteau, "Testimony before the Recorder of Land Titles, St. Louis, 1825," in *Early Histories,* McDermott, ed., 91–97.

37 *"Immediately:* Testimony of Baptiste Riviere, July 29, 1825, Hunt's Minutes II, 102–3, typescript, Box 45/f. 16, McDermott Collection, SIUE.

37 *"In the early part:* "Fragment of Col. Auguste Chouteau's Narrative," 4.

38 *Pontiac did:* Nicollet, "Sketch of the Early History" in *Early Histories,* McDermott, ed., 142–44; "Fragment of Col. Auguste Chouteau's Narrative," 7–8.

38 *In June:* Stevens, *History of St. Louis,* 24.

38 *To young:* Auguste Chouteau, "Testimony before the Recorder of Land Titles, St. Louis, 1825," in *Early Histories,* McDermott, ed., 95–96.

39 *The next:* Billon, ed., *Annals of St. Louis in Early Days,* 20–21.

39 *Most of:* Ibid.

39 *Not until:* Stevens, *History of St. Louis,* 34.

3. HAUGHTY CHILDREN OF THE MIDDLE WATERS

41 *"Although they:* "Fragment of Col. Auguste Chouteau's Narrative," 4–6.

41 *Once Laclède:* Ibid.

42 *"I will reply:* Ibid.

42 *He warned:* Ibid.

42 *During the fifteen:* Ibid.

42 *Despite the:* See Nicollet, "Sketch of the Early History" in *Early Histories,* McDermott, ed., 146–47; Auguste Chouteau "Testimony," ibid., 94.

44 *These early:* Patrick Brophy, *Osage Autumn: The Exploration Period in Western Missouri* (Nevada, Mo.: Vernon County Historical Society, 1985), 15; Introduction to *Tixier's Travels on the Osage Prairies,* McDermott, ed., Albert J. Salvan, tr. (Norman: University of Oklahoma Press, 1940), 3.

44 *"This necessitous:* Mathews, *The Osages,* 138.

45 *But the Osages:* Ibid., 124.

46 *Archeologists:* Brophy, *Osage Autumn,* 9–11.

46 *A major element:* Ibid., 10–11.

46 *Despite the wide:* Hiram Martin Chittenden, *The American Fur Trade of the Far West* (Lincoln: University of Nebraska Press, 1986, first published 1902), Vol. 2, 858; Brophy, *Osage Autumn,* 9–11.

47 *The Osage:* Mathews, *The Osages,* 29.

47 *European and eastern:* See John Bradbury, *Travels in the Interior of America 1809–1811* (Cleveland: Arthur H. Clark Co., 1904), 66; George Catlin, *North American Indians* (New York: Penguin Books, 1996, first published 1902), 301; Washington Irving, *A Tour on the Prairies* (Norman: University of Oklahoma Press, 1956), 21–22; and W. W. Graves, *History of Neosho County,* Vol. 1 (St. Paul, Kan.: Osage Mission Historical Society, Inc., 1986, first published 1949), 95, citing Louis Cortambert in *Voyage Au Pays Des Osages.*

48 *Father Jacques:* Mathews, *The Osages,* 104.

48 *In the early:* See *Before Lewis and Clark Documents,* Nasatir, ed., Vol. 1, 12–34; and Gilbert C. Din and Abraham P. Nasatir, *The Imperial Osages: Spanish-Indian Diplomacy in the Mississippi Valley* (Norman: University of Oklahoma Press, 1983), 32–42.

48 *After a few:* Ibid.

48 *Meanwhile:* Ibid.

49 *In 1722:* Ibid.

49 *Bourgmont's:* Din and Nasatir, *Imperial Osages,* 39; and Mathews, *The Osages,* 204–7.

49 *Even before:* Brophy, *Osage Autumn,* 14.

50 *When their:* See L. V. Bogy's comments on behalf of Pierre Chouteau at 1847 testimonial dinner, Box 45/f.17, McDermott Collection, SIUE.

50 *So eager:* Brophy, *Osage Autumn,* 14.

50 *To a much:* Mathews, *The Osages,* 116.

51 *Perrin du Lac:* William E. Unrau, *Mixed-Bloods and Tribal Dissolution* (Lawrence: University Press of Kansas, 1989), 14; F. A. Chardon, *Chardon's Journal at Fort Clark, 1834–1839,* Annie Heloise Abel, ed. (Lincoln: University of Nebraska Press, 1986, first published 1902), 164.

51 *Being Roman:* Mathews, *The Osages,* 114.

51 *A number of:* See *Tixier's Travels,* McDermott, ed., 123.

51 *One white:* Charles Joseph Latrobe, *The Rambler in Oklahoma,* Muriel H. Wright and George H. Shirk, eds. (Oklahoma City and Chattanooga: Harlow Publishing Corp., 1955, first published 1835), 15–16.

51 *Adultery and:* See Mathews, *The Osages,* 308; *Tixier's Travels,* McDermott, ed., 183; and Din and Nasatir, *Imperial Osages,* 13.

52 *Some travelers:* See Bradbury, *Travels in the Interior,* 166; and *The Journals of Lewis and Clark,* Bernard DeVoto, ed. (Boston and New York: Houghton Mifflin, 1953), 76.

52 *In a reaction:* See Washington Irving, *Astoria, or Anecdotes of an Enterprise Beyond the Rocky Mountains* (Norman: University of Oklahoma Press, 1964, first published 1836), 132–33; and James E. Davis, *Frontier Illinois* (Bloomington and Indianapolis: Indiana University Press, 1998), 30–31.

52 *As Davis:* Ibid.

53 *By the time:* Din and Nasatir, *Imperial Osages,* 50.

4. THE BUSINESS OF ST. LOUIS

54 *"Religion was:* McDermott, *Private Libraries,* 17.

55 *Three British:* Chittenden, *American Fur Trade,* Vol. 1, 89–95.

55 *Laclède and those:* See Chittenden, *American Fur Trade,* Vol. 1, xxviii–xxx.

55 *"They were:* Ibid.

55 *Laclède and:* Ibid.

56 *If the traders:* Ibid.

56 *As Piernas:* Louis Houck, *The Spanish Régime in Missouri* (Chicago: R. R. Donnelley & Sons, 1909), Vol. 1, 66–75.

58 *Further, the hard:* Chittenden, *American Fur Trade,* Vol. 1, 4–5.

58 *The fur companies:* Ibid.

58 *In addition:* See Finkelnburg, "Under Three Flags," in *MHS Collections,* Vol. 3, No. 3, 1911, 201–32.

59 *At the time:* Billon, ed., *Annals of St. Louis in Early Days,* 89–91.

59 *Historians have:* See Chittenden, *American Fur Trade,* Vol. 1, 6–7.

60 *These profits:* Stevens, *History of St. Louis,* 27.

60 *As Lieutenant Governor:* Houck, *Spanish Régime in Missouri,* Vol. 1, 66–75.

60 *The profit:* Laclède to AC, Dec. 31, 1777, Laclède Collection, MHS.

61 *There is no:* Copy of notarized agreement of May 8, 1769, Laclède Collection, MHS.

62 *In addition:* See original French-language document and typescript of translation into English, St. Louis Archives, 9B, MHS.

63 *Madame Chouteau:* Ibid.

63 *"Young Chouteau:* Mathews, *The Osages,* 231.

63 *By 1775:* PC to Editor, *North American Review,* January 1826; Hoffhaus, *Chez les Canses,* 113–17; and Houck, *Spanish Régime in Missouri,* Vol. 1, 149–51.

64 *Within a short:* See Din and Nasatir, *Imperial Osages,* 78–83.

65 *In the summer:* Ibid.

65 *Governor Luis Unzaga:* Ibid.

65 *It was far:* Ibid.

65 *A brief period:* Din and Nasatir, *Imperial Osages,* 90–98, 110, citing Cruzat to Galvez, Dec. 6, 1777.

66 *The next:* Ibid.

66 *In 1774:* Billon, ed., *Annals of St. Louis in Early Days,* 124; and Stevens, *History of St. Louis,* 58.

66 *Every decision:* Billon, ed., *Annals of St. Louis in Early Days,* 140–41.

67 *On Christmas:* Ibid., 125.

67 *At the Laclède-Chouteau:* Ibid., 125–27.

67 *By that time:* See Piernas's 1773 census in Houck, *Spanish Régime in Missouri,* Vol. 1, 61; and Rev. E. H. Behrmann, *The Old Cathedral* (St. Louis: Church of St. Louis IX, 1949), 20–21.

68 *On April 19:* Billon, ed., *Annals of St. Louis in Early Days,* 128, 139.

68 *Except for:* McDermott, *Private Libraries,* 12.

68 *Despite the:* Ekberg, *Colonial Ste. Genevieve,* 302–5.

69 *Farming around:* Billon, ed., *Annals of St. Louis in Early Days,* 84–85.

69 *Even though:* Houck, *History of Missouri,* Vol. 1, 305.

69 *For amusement:* Billon, ed., *Annals of St. Louis in Early Days,* 72–73.

69 *On November 16:* Ibid., 108–9.

70 *There was no:* Ibid., 86–87.

70 *For a good:* Ibid., 85–86.

70 *Dress in St. Louis:* Ekberg, *Colonial Ste. Genevieve,* 314–17.

70 *Laclède's wardrobe:* Inventory of Laclède's room taken on Aug. 10, 1778, Laclède Collection, MHS.

71 *The first African:* Harriet C. Frazier, *Slavery and Crime in Missouri, 1773–1865* (Jefferson, N.C.: McFarland & Company, 2001), 7.

71 *In 1724:* Ibid., 8; and Ekberg, *Colonial Ste. Genevieve,* 197.

72 *The French:* Frazier, *Slavery and Crime in Missouri,* 12; and Ekberg, *Colonial Ste. Genevieve,* 204–5.

72 *He spent:* See Billon, ed., *Annals of St. Louis in Early Days,* 144–45, for deed dated Dec. 13, 1777.

73 *Finally, with:* Pierre Laclède to AC, Dec. 31, 1777, Laclède Collection, MHS.

73 *"I have also:* Ibid.

73 *"If, by the will:* Ibid.

73 *"This frank:* Ibid.

73 *Nothing of:* Ibid.

74 *"Goodbye, my dear sir:* Ibid.

74 *In 1778:* See Pittman, *Present State of the European Settlements,* 40; "Cuming's Tour of the Western Country," in *Early Western Travels,* Reuben Gold Thwaites, ed. (Cleveland: Arthur H. Clark, 1904–7), Vol. 4, 299.

74 *As his barge:* Inventory presented to Leyba July 25, 1778, Laclède Collection, MHS.

75 *The boat continued:* Photocopy of handwritten statement by Balthazar de Villiers, May 27, 1778, Box 47/f.31, McDermott Collection, SIUE.

5. AUGUSTE AND PIERRE, GREATLY LOVED AND GREATLY FEARED

76 *Nearly two months:* Statement signed by Leyba, Ricard, and two witnesses, and statements signed by Leyba, July 19, 1778, and July 29, 1778, all in Laclède Collection, MHS.

76 *Auguste Chouteau:* Ibid.

76 *Six days:* Ibid.

76 *"This is why:* Ibid.

77 *After a midday:* McDermott, *Private Libraries,* 26–27.

78 *Of particular:* Document signed Leyba, Sarpy, Duralde, Perault, Labuscieres, Blanco, Aug. 4, 1778, deposited in Illinois territorial government archives at St. Louis Aug. 10, 1778, taken from English translation in Laclède Collection, MHS.

78 *Between September:* Document signed Sarpy, Duralde, Perault, Labuscieres, Blanco, LaChapelle, Sept. 21, 1778, deposited in Illinois territorial government archives at St. Louis, taken from English translation in Laclède Collection, MHS.

78 *On October:* Document signed Leyba, Oct. 13, 1778, deposited in Illinois territorial government archives at St. Louis, taken from English translation in Laclède Collection, MHS.

78 *That winter:* William E. Foley and C. David Rice, *The First Chouteaus: River Barons of Early St. Louis* (Urbana and Chicago: University of Illinois Press, 1983), 25.

78 *On June 20:* No. 264, St. Louis Archives, MHS, translation by Nellie H. Beauregard; also see Billon, ed., *Annals of St. Louis in Early Days,* 147.

79 *An expedition:* Letter from Pierre Chouteau, great-grandson of the first PC, to MHS, Sept. 5, 1903, Laclède Collection, MHS.

79 *In the early:* Billon, ed., *Annals of St. Louis in Early Days,* 148.

80 *One of the first:* See various receipts and notes in George Rogers Clark Papers, Box 3, Clark Family Collection, MHS.

81 *Despite his:* Gratiot to father and mother, unspecified dates in 1778 and 1779, Gratiot Collection, MHS.

81 *"I cannot help:* Gratiot to G. R. Clark, May 6, 1780, George Rogers Clark Papers, Box 3, Clark Family Collection, MHS.

82 *Convinced that:* See letters of Colonel Montgomery and Lieutenant John Rogers to G. R. Clark in May and December 1780, Box 1, Clark Family Collection, MHS; also Din and Nasatir, *Imperial Osages,* 126.

82 *On May 26:* See Foley and Rice, *First Chouteaus,* 27–29; Din and Nasatir, *Imperial Osages,* 127; and Nicollet, "Sketch," in *Early Histories,* McDermott, ed., 148–49.

83 *Rumors of:* Billon, ed., *Annals of St. Louis in Early Days,* 207.

83 *No matter:* Gratiot to J. Kay, April 26, 1779, Box 1, Gratiot Papers, MHS.

83 *Having sent:* Ibid.

84 *Instead of goods:* Gratiot to William Kay, June 14, 1779, Gratiot Papers, MHS.

84 *Some Americans:* Din and Nasatir, *Imperial Osages*, 147; Davis, *Frontier Illinois*, 103.

85 *In the summer:* Billon, ed., *Annals of St. Louis in Early Days*, 214–25; also see McDermott, *Private Libraries*, 8.

85 *Gratiot was gone:* Billon, ed., *Annals of St. Louis in Early Days*, 221–25; Gratiot to St. James Beauvais, Jan. 29, 1799, Box 2, Gratiot Papers, MHS.

85 *Of the five:* McDermott, *Private Libraries*, 13–14, and Billon, ed., *Annals of St. Louis in Early Days*, 260–61.

86 *Auguste and Pierre:* See Mathews, *The Osages*, 285; and Antoine's death record from Burials Book No. 4, St. Louis Cathedral, New Orleans, La., Copy in Box 56, CC, MHS.

87 *In 1792 Antoine:* Mathews, *The Osages*, 297; Trudeau to Carondelet, Nov. 13, 1792, from General Archives of the Indies, Seville, Spain, reprinted in *Before Lewis and Clark Documents*, Nasatir, ed., 162–63.

87 *Antoine died:* Copy of death record from Burials Book No. 4, St. Louis Cathedral, New Orleans, La., Box 56, CC, MHS.

87 *The evidence:* See Foley and Rice, *First Chouteaus*, 45; Unrau, *Mixed Bloods*, 13; and Clark to Secretary of War, Dec. 2, 1808, in *The Territorial Papers of the United States*, Clarence E. Carter, ed. (Washington: U. S. Government Printing Office, 1934), Vol. 14, 242–43.

87 *Still, the records:* Grant Foreman, "Our Indian Ambassadors to Europe," in *MHS Collections*, Vol. 5, February 1928, No. 2, 125 fn.

88 *Adding to:* Baptism record dated Sept. 5, 1803, Archives of the Old Cathedral, St. Louis; Secretary of War to General Wilkinson, April 9, 1806, in *Territorial Papers*, Vol. 13, Carter, ed., 486–88.

88 *Marriage practices:* Ekberg, *Colonial Ste. Genevieve*, 185.

89 *Auguste was nearly:* Their second-day attire has survived in the collection of the MHS.

89 *Auguste bought:* Billon, ed., *Annals of St. Louis in Early Days*, 149.

90 *Increasing the trade:* Din and Nasatir, *Imperial Osages*, 190.

90 *In April 1787:* Ibid., 171–79.

92 *The St. Louis:* Ibid., 211, 235–36, and 241–43.

92 *"Brother," they:* Ibid., 224–25.

93 *A new Spanish:* Ibid., 214–17 and 233.

93 *During early:* Ibid., 237–39.

93 *An infuriated:* Ibid., 240, citing Carondelet to Trudeau May 6, 1793, and June 28, 1793.

94 *The Osages:* Ibid., 247, citing Trudeau to Carondelet, Aug. 22, 1793.

94 *When:* Ibid., 248.

94 *Auguste Chouteau:* Ibid., 256, citing AC to Carondelet, Nov. 10, 1793.

95 *Perhaps swayed:* Ibid., 258; also see copy of PC's commission, Box 2, CC, MHS.

95 *With the agreement:* Din and Nasatir, *Imperial Osages*, 261.

95 *On May 5:* Billon, ed., *Annals of St. Louis in Early Days*, 283–87, citing complaint petition filed by Joseph Robidoux, March 7, 1798; also *Before Lewis and Clark Documents*, Vol. 1, Nasatir, ed., 86–87.

96 *Jean Baptiste: Before Lewis and Clark Documents*, Vol. 1, Nasatir, ed., 86–87.

96 *Truteau was:* "Instructions Given . . . to Jean Baptiste Truteau," in Houck, *Spanish Régime in Missouri*, Vol. 2, 164–72.

97 *Truteau packed: Before Lewis and Clark Documents*, Vol. 1, Nasatir, ed., 88–89.

97 *Truteau found:* Ibid.

97 *Auguste Chouteau:* Din and Nasatir, *Imperial Osages*, 260–66.

98 *Auguste set:* Ibid., 269.

98 *"The savages:* Trudeau to Carondelet, April 18, 1795, in *Before Lewis and Clark Documents*, Vol. 1, Nasatir, ed., 320–21.

99 *Defending his:* AC to Carondelet, April 18, 1797, Box 2, CC, MHS.

99 *Two months:* AC to Gayoso de Lemos draft, June 24, 1797, and account books, all Box 2, CC, MHS.

100 *These business:* Schneider & Co. invoice, March 27, 1794, Box 2, CC, MHS.

100 *"All the profits:* AC to Gayoso de Lemos, July 22, 1798, Box 3, CC, MHS.

101 *"[They] have [gone]:* PC to Delassus, April 15, 1800, cited in Din and Nasatir, *Imperial Osages*, 310.

101 *On July 28:* Din and Nasatir, *Imperial Osages*, 315.

102 *The next day:* Delassus to Casa Calvo, Sept. 25, 1800, cited in Din and Nasatir, *Imperial Osages*, 315–17.

102 *Sending Pierre:* Din and Nasatir, *Imperial Osages*, 316–19.

102 *In 1800:* Ibid., 320, 330.

103 *Lisa quickly:* Ibid., 332; also Mathews, *The Osages*, 295.

103 *When Governor Salcedo:* Din and Nasatir, *Imperial Osages*, 335–36; Walter B. Douglas, "Manuel Lisa," in *MHS Collections*, 1911, Vol 3, No. 3, 241–44.

104 *"The fur trade:* Astor to AC, Jan. 28, 1800, Box 3, CC, MHS.

104 *John Jacob Astor:* Axel Madsen, *John Jacob Astor: America's First Millionaire* (New York: John Wiley & Sons, 2001), 96.

105 *It is quite:* Document signed AC, May 1, 1800, and Todd to AC, Dec. 1, 1800, both in Box 3, CC, MHS.

105 *Charles Gratiot:* Gratiot to Schneider & Co., May 18, 1799, and Gratiot to Astor, April 29, 1800, Gratiot Papers, MHS.

105 *Gratiot explained:* Ibid.

105 *For the time:* Ibid.

6. NEW RULERS, NEW WAYS

106 *At the beginning:* Cavelier & Fils to AC, June 18 and June 22, 1802, Box 4, CC, MHS.

106 *Four months:* Cavelier & Fils to AC, Oct. 28, 1802, ibid.

107 *This "completely:* Jefferson to Livingston, April 18, 1802, in *The Portable Thomas Jefferson*, Merrill D. Peterson, ed. (New York: Penguin Books, 1977), 485–88.

107 *However great:* Letter signed by Gratiot, March 21, 1803, Box 5, CC, MHS.

108 *On February:* C. L. R. James, *The Black Jacobins: Toussaint L'Ouverture and the San Domingo Revolution* (New York: Vintage Books, 1963), 295–97, 330–45, and 355.

108 *"Sickness:* Ibid.

108 *Three days:* Ibid.

108 *Meanwhile:* Ibid.

108 *Leclerc's position:* Ibid.

109 *Not wanting:* Ibid.

109 *On August 6:* Ibid.

109 *Leclerc died:* Ibid.

109 *Many French:* See Coursault letters dated Jan. 22–Feb. 11, 1803, Box 5, CC, MHS.

110 *In early 1803:* Harrison to Delassus, March 6, 1803, ibid.

110 *Monroe, former:* See Dumas Malone, *Jefferson the President, First Term 1801–1805* (Boston: Little, Brown, 1970), 269–70, 283–89, and 303.

111 *The news:* Ibid., 284–85; and Jefferson to Breckenridge, Aug. 12, 1803, in *Portable Thomas Jefferson*, Peterson, ed., 494–97.

111 *Jefferson, however:* Malone, *Jefferson the President, First Term*, 275.

111 *Like many:* See Ronda, *Finding the West*, 1; Jefferson, "Notes on the State of Virginia," in *Portable Thomas Jefferson*, Peterson, ed., 36; and Pittman, *Present State of European Settlements*, 2.

111 *To head:* Lewis to Clark, June 19, 1803, in *Letters of LCE*, Jackson, ed., Vol. 1, 57–60; Clark to Lewis, July 24, 1803, ibid., 112–13.

111 *Jefferson's instructions:* Jefferson to Lewis, June 20, 1803, ibid., 61–66.

112 *Jefferson also:* Ibid.

112 *However, Jefferson's:* Jefferson to Breckinridge, Aug. 12, 1803, in *Portable Thomas Jefferson*, Peterson, ed., 494–97.

112 *A business associate:* Gillespie to AC, Aug. 19, 1803, Box 5, CC, MHS.

113 *Pierre Chouteau:* Laussat to PC, Aug. 24, 1803, Box 3, Delassus–St. Vrain Collection, MHS.

113 *"Our Government:* Harrison to Delassus, Aug. 2, 1803, Box 5, CC, MHS.

113 *The United States Senate:* Malone, *Jefferson the President, First Term*, 333.

114 *Jefferson first:* See speech text in *Letters of LCE*, Jackson, ed., Vol. 1, 199–203.

115 *Just six days:* Dearborn to PC, July 17, 1804, in *Territorial Papers,* Carter, ed., Vol. 13, 31–33.

115 *He was to:* Ibid.

116 *"At the request:* Gallatin to Jefferson, Aug. 20, 1804, in *Letters of LCE,* Jackson, ed., Vol. 1, 209.

117 *"During our journey:* Rogers to Jefferson, Aug. 21, 1804, ibid., 208–9.

117 *Pierre, making:* PC to McKer, Nov. 19, 1804, PC Letterbook, Boxes 6–7, CC, MHS.

117 *He would later:* PC to McKer, Dec. 7, 1804, ibid.

118 *"I am persuaded:* PC to Jefferson, Oct. 12, 1804, ibid.

118 *Auguste Chouteau:* Circular dated July 28, 1804, in *Territorial Papers,* Carter, ed., Vol. 13, 33–35.

119 *In a statement:* "Minutes of a Meeting at St. Louis," first published in *Indiana Gazette,* Vincennes, Oct. 2, 1804, in *Territorial Papers,* Carter, ed., Vol. 13, 43–46.

119 *Auguste Chouteau:* See "Anonymous Paper re Attitude of French Inhabitants," in *Territorial Papers,* Carter, ed., Vol. 13, 68–71.

119 *When William Henry:* Typescript of Harrison to AC, Dec. 21, 1804, Box 46/f. 28, McDermott Collection, SIUE.

120 *John W. Eppes:* Fromentin to AC, Jan. 12, 1805, Box 8, CC, MHS.

120 *Two weeks later:* Eppes to AC, typescript copy in Box 46/f.28, McDermott Collection, SIUE.

120 *"The liberal:* Ibid.

121 *On another:* AC to Stoddard, Aug. 4, 1804, Stoddard Papers, MHS.

121 *"In all countries:* Ibid.

121 *Stoddard said he:* Stoddard to AC, Aug. 6, 1804, Stoddard Papers, MHS.

122 *"The first laws:* Stoddard, *Sketches,* 253.

122 *Some of the:* Ibid., 255–56.

123 *Under the ground:* Ibid., 245.

123 *After the attack:* William T. Hagan, "The Sauk and Fox Treaty of 1804," in *Missouri Historical Review,* Vol. 51, October 1956, 1–7.

123 *Bruff ordered:* PC to Sacs and Foxes, Oct. 18, 1804, PC Letterbook, Boxes 6–7, CC, MHS.

124 *Instead of:* Houck, *History of Missouri,* Vol. 2, 396; PC to Jefferson, Jan. 31, 1805, PC Letterbook, Boxes 6–7, CC, MHS; and Anthony F. C. Wallace, *Jefferson and the Indians: The Tragic Fate of the First Americans* (Cambridge: Harvard University Press, 1999), 250.

125 *In 1788 Julien:* Gallatin memorandum, Jan. 7, 1807, in *Territorial Papers,* Carter, ed., Vol. 13, 73–74.

125 *Dubuque had:* See bill of sale, Boxes 6–7, CC, MHS.

125 *When Harrison:* Houck, *History of Missouri,* Vol. 2, 396.

126 *Harrison later:* Letter and Document signed W. H. Harrison, Box 3, Lucas Papers, MHS.

126 *But the 1804:* Hagan, "Sauk and Fox Treaty of 1804," in *Missouri Historical Review*, Vol. 51, October 1956, 1–7.
127 *The size: Original Journals of LCE*, Thwaites, ed., Vol. 1, 36–37.
127 *He told:* PC to Jefferson, Nov. 7, 1804, PC Letterbook, Boxes 6–7, CC, MHS.
127 *Pierre pressed:* PC to Dearborn, Nov. 19, 1804, ibid.
128 *Dearborn must:* PC to Dearborn, March 2, 1805, ibid.
128 *Wanting more:* Ibid.
128 *He worried:* PC to Dearborn, Nov. 19, 1804, ibid.
129 *As Cheveux Blancs:* PC to Dearborn, Nov. 7, 1804, ibid.
129 *Pierre told:* PC to Dearborn, Nov. 8, 1804, ibid.
129 *He wrote to:* PC to Gallatin, Nov. 7, 1804, ibid.
130 *"In the space:* PC to Jefferson, ca. March 1, 1805, ibid.
130 *Noting that:* Ibid.
130 *Shortly, Pierre:* PC to Dearborn, March 2, 1805, ibid.
131 *The Sac:* PC to Bruff, April 17, 1805, ibid.
131 *Meanwhile, never:* PC to Harrison, April 20, 1805, ibid.
131 *Reporting:* PC to Dearborn, May 5, 1805, ibid.
132 *It must:* PC to Harrison, May 8, 1805, and PC to Dearborn, May 11, 1805, ibid.
132 *Occasionally Pierre:* PC to Jefferson, Jan. 31, 1805, ibid.
132 *"The news which:* PC to Jefferson, about March 1, 1805, ibid.
132 *Pierre informed:* PC to Jefferson, Nov. 19, 1804, and PC to Dearborn, March 11, 1805, ibid.
133 *To Dearborn:* PC to Dearborn, March 2, 1805, and April 20, 1805, ibid.
133 *"The different:* Ibid.
133 *He added:* Ibid.
133 *When the weather:* PC to Dearborn, June 12, 1805, ibid.
134 *Pierre advised:* PC to Harrison, May 1, 1805, ibid.
134 *In addition:* PC to Dearborn, May 11, 1805, ibid.
134 *Harrison agreed:* PC to Harrison, May 31, 1805, and June 12, 1805, ibid.
134 *Indian chiefs:* PC to Jefferson, June 12, 1805, ibid, and Paul Russell Cutright, *Lewis and Clark: Pioneering Naturalists* (Lincoln: University of Nebraska Press, 1969), 375–77.
134 *It took:* Ibid.

7. INTRIGUES AND POSSIBILITIES

136 *In late June:* See Wilkinson to Dearborn, July 27, 1805, in *Territorial Papers*, Carter, ed., Vol. 13, 164–72; and PC to Dearborn, July 27, 1805, PC Letterbook, Boxes 6–7, CC, MHS.
136 *Knowing that:* Ibid.
136 *The larger:* Ibid.

137 *Pierre himself:* Ibid.

137 *"I consider:* Ibid.

137 *He added:* Ibid.

138 *Then forty-eight:* Dumas Malone, *Jefferson the President, Second Term 1805–1809* (Boston: Little, Brown, 1974), 216–23.

138 *Even this:* Wilkinson to Dearborn, July 27, 1805, in *Territorial Papers,* Carter, ed., Vol. 13, 164–72.

138 *St. Louis:* Ibid.

138 *"Attempts:* Wilkinson to Madison, July 28, 1805, Ibid., 172–73.

139 *Wilkinson, however:* Billon, ed., *Annals of St. Louis in Territorial Days,* 195–96.

139 *William Christy:* Ibid.

139 *In addition: Missouri Gazette,* June 27, 1810, and Houck, *History of Missouri,* Vol. 3, 73.

140 *Like officials:* Wilkinson to Dearborn, Sept. 22, 1805, in *Letters of LCE,* Jackson, ed., 259.

140 *The group:* Charles William Janson, *The Stranger in America* (New York: Press of the Pioneers, 1935, first published 1807), 231–35.

141 *Although Pierre:* PC to Dearborn, Dec. 1, 1805, PC Letterbook, Boxes 6–7, CC, MHS.

141 *As could be:* Dearborn to PC, Feb. 10, 1806, in *Territorial Papers,* Carter, ed., Vol. 13, 443.

141 *Coming back:* PC to Dearborn, Oct. 1, 1805, PC Letterbook, Boxes 6–7, CC, MHS.

141 *Over the next:* PC to Wilkinson, April 12, 1806, ibid.

142 *He estimated:* Ibid.

142 *"The journey:* Ibid.

142 *He pointed:* Ibid.

143 *Sometimes:* Wilkinson to Dearborn, Nov. 26, 1805, in *The Journals of Zebulon Montgomery Pike with Letters and Related Documents,* Donald Jackson, ed. (Norman: University of Oklahoma Press, 1966), 251.

143 *Zebulon:* Wilkinson to Dearborn, Oct. 17, 1806, ibid, 154.

143 *"No doubt:* Walter F. McCaleb, *The Aaron Burr Conspiracy* (New York: Dodd, Mead, 1903), 27.

144 *Word of:* Petition in *Territorial Papers,* Carter, ed., Vol. 13, 329–30; and Letter signed AC and others, Jan. 6, 1806, ibid., 385–86.

144 *Pierre may:* PC to Dearborn, April 12, 1806, PC Letterbook, Boxes 6–7, CC, MHS; and Dearborn to APC, July 9, 1806, photocopy of original in Box 46/f.6, McDermott Collection, SIUE.

145 *"Any trade:* Dearborn to PC, May 12, 1806, in *Territorial Papers,* Carter, ed., Vol. 13, 510.

145 *Pierre replied:* PC to Dearborn, unspecified date in July 1806, PC Letterbook, Boxes 6–7, CC, MHS.

145 *"When I:* Ibid.
146 *As this exchange: Journals of Lewis and Clark,* DeVoto, ed., 470–71.
146 *On September 12:* Ibid., 472–73.
146 *In St. Louis:* PC to Dearborn, Oct. 14, 1806, PC Letterbook, Boxes 6–7, CC, MHS; and Din and Nasatir, *Imperial Osages,* 360.
147 *That evening:* Ronda, *Finding the West,* 121; and *Journals of Lewis and Clark,* DeVoto, ed., 478.
148 *Lewis and Clark:* PC to Dearborn, Oct. 14, 1806, PC Letterbook, Boxes 6–7, CC, MHS.
148 *A festive atmosphere: National Intelligencer and Washington Advertiser,* Jan. 16, 1807; Din and Nasatir, *Imperial Osages,* 360–61; and Augustus J. Foster, *Jeffersonian America* (San Marino, Calif.: Huntington Library, 1954), 27.
148 *The President:* Dearborn to PC and Commission dated March 7, 1807, in *Territorial Papers,* Carter, ed., Vol. 14, 107–8.
150 *The trading:* Chittenden, *American Fur Trade,* Vol. 1, 119–23.
150 *Some of:* Pryor to Clark, Oct. 16, 1807, in *Letters of LCE,* Jackson, ed., Vol. 2, 432–37.
150 *Ensign Pryor met:* Ibid.
150 *For about an:* Ibid.
151 *At this:* Ibid.
151 *"If my opinion:* Ibid.
151 *When Clark:* Clark to Dearborn, Oct. 24, 1807, William Clark Papers, Clark Family Collection, MHS.
151 *"The unfortunate:* PC to Jefferson, Nov. 14, 1807, PC Letterbook, Boxes 6–7, CC, MHS.
152 *The St. Louis landowners:* Petition to the Senate and House, Jan. 2, 1808, in *Territorial Papers,* Carter, ed., Vol. 14, 161–63.
152 *"Almost all:* Ibid.
152 *It was:* Ibid.
152 *Despite their:* Undated Statement of AC, and Documents signed "By the Board," March 27, 1806, and by the "Louisiana Commisioners," Jan. 30, 1809, all in Box 8, CC, MHS.
153 *On August 3:* Deed, Box 1, Gamble Papers, MHS; sale document, Box 9, CC, MHS; also see *The History of the Expedition Under the Command of Lewis and Clark,* Elliott Coues, ed. (New York: Francis P. Harper, 1893), Vol. 1, lxxvii.
153 *An act:* Stevens, *History of St. Louis,* 80.
154 *It turned:* Billon, ed., *Annals of St. Louis in Territorial Days,* 20–21.
154 *A post office: Missouri Gazette,* Aug. 10, 1808.
154 *Although population:* Brackenridge, *Views of Louisiana,* 123.
154 *For protection:* Wilkinson to Dearborn, July 27, 1805, in *Territorial Papers,* Carter, ed., Vol. 13, 164–72.
155 *Entering:* PC to Bates, Oct. 6, 1807, PC Letterbook, Boxes 6–7, CC, MHS.

155 *In April:* Various letters PC to Grande Piste and White Hair, early 1808, ibid.

156 *President Jefferson:* Din and Nasatir, *Imperial Osages*, 360; Wallace, *Jefferson and the Indians*, 269; and Mathews, *The Osages*, 388.

156 *Meriwether:* Din and Nasatir, *Imperial Osages*, 360.

156 *Lewis wrote:* See William Clark, *Westward with Dragoons*, Kate L. Gregg, ed. (Fulton, Mo.: Ovid Bell Press, 1937), 34; Lewis to Dearborn, July 1, 1808, in *Territorial Papers*, Carter, ed., Vol. 14, 196–203.

157 *Clark had:* Clark, *Dragoons*, 13–16.

157 *When they:* Ibid., 34, 48–49.

157 *It is not clear:* Ibid., 38–39.

158 *The Indians gathered:* Ibid.

158 *The Osages:* Wallace, *Jefferson and the Indians*, 270–73.

158 *Within the present:* Clark, *Dragoons*, 67.

158 *Clark said:* Ibid., 39.

158 *The next day:* Ibid., 41.

159 *When Clark:* Lewis to PC, Oct. 3, 1808, in *Territorial Papers*, Carter, ed., Vol. 14, 229–31.

159 *"It is our:* Ibid.

159 *Pierre traveled:* Din and Nasatir, *Imperial Osages*, 360; also see text of treaty in appendix of Clark, *Dragoons*.

159 *Possibly concerned:* Mathews, *The Osages*, 387–88, quoting recollections of George C. Sibley, the first government factor at Fort Osage.

160 *Some of:* Brophy, *Osage Autumn*, 45–46.

160 *However, when:* Clark to Secretary of War, Dec. 2, 1808, in *Territorial Papers*, Carter, ed., Vol. 14, 242–43.

160 *Antagonism between:* Lewis to Jefferson, Dec. 15, 1808, *American State Papers, Indian Affairs*, Vol. 2, 766–67.

161 *However, Pierre:* PC to Jefferson, Dec. 10, 1808, PC Letterbook, Boxes 6–7, CC, MHS.

8. ENVELOPED IN A CLOUD OF MISERIES

164 *On Feb. 24:* Thomas James, *Three Years Among the Indians and Mexicans* (Lincoln: University of Nebraska Press, 1984, first published 1846), 3.

164 *The business group:* See agreement dated Feb. 24, 1809, Box 10, CC, MHS.

165 *Under the articles:* Copy of Articles dated March 7, 1809, Box 10, CC, MHS; and Chittenden, *American Fur Trade*, Vol. 1, 140.

165 *Once Pierre:* Articles dated March 7, 1809, Box 10, CC, MHS.

165 *Neither Lewis:* PC to Simmons, May 28, 1809, PC Letterbook, Boxes 6–7, CC, MHS.

166 *The previous:* Jefferson to Lewis, Aug. 24, 1808, in *Territorial Papers*, Carter, ed., Vol. 14, 222.

166 *Although the contract:* James, *Three Years*, 3.

166 *The expedition:* "Dr. Thomas' Journal" in Appendix, ibid., 167.

166 *In the less than:* Ibid., 168.

167 *For the boatmen:* James, *Three Years*, 5–6.

167 *In conditions:* Ibid.

167 *On August 1:* Ibid., 7.

168 *"Having put:* "Dr. Thomas' Journal" in Appendix of James, *Three Years*, 168–71.

168 *On August 18:* Ibid., 172.

168 *As the voyagers:* James, *Three Years*, 52.

169 *"I never saw:* Frederick Bates to Richard Bates, Nov. 9, 1809, in *Life and Papers of Frederick Bates*, Thomas Maitland Marshall, ed., Vol. 2 (St. Louis: Missouri Historical Society, 1926), 108.

169 *"He has fallen:* Frederick Bates to Richard Bates, July 14, 1809, ibid., 67–73.

169 *"I attended early:* Frederick Bates to Richard Bates, Nov. 9, 1809, ibid., 108–10.

170 *After several weeks:* Ibid.

170 *Later, when Bates had:* Ibid.

170 *Lewis was perpetually:* Stephen E. Ambrose, *Undaunted Courage: Meriwether Lewis, Thomas Jefferson, and the Opening of the American West* (New York: Simon & Schuster, 1996), 450–55.

170 *Lewis's woes:* Ibid.

171 *Eustis said:* Eustis to Lewis, July 15, 1809, in *Letters of LCE*, Jackson, ed., 456–57.

171 *"Your Excellency:* Ibid.

171 *Eustis went on:* Ibid.

171 *"I have never:* Lewis to Eustis, Aug. 18, 1809, in *Letters of LCE*, Jackson, ed., 459–61.

172 *"I do most solemnly:* Ibid.

172 *"Be assured Sir:* Ibid.

172 *He said his credit:* Ibid.

172 *He justified:* Ibid.

173 *He urged that Pierre:* Ibid.

173 *"A short time:* PC Jr. to Eustis, Sept. 1, 1809, Box 10, CC, MHS.

174 *Recalling Clark's:* Ibid.

174 *But after Fort Osage:* Ibid.

174 *These facts:* Ibid.

174 *Pierre Jr.:* Ibid.

174 *After all of this:* Ibid.

175 *While these issues:* "Dr. Thomas' Journal" in Appendix of James, *Three Years*, 173.

176 *After lecturing:* PC to Eustis, Dec. 14, 1809, PC Letterbook, Boxes 6–7, CC, MHS.

176 *When the expedition:* "Dr. Thomas' Journal" in Appendix of James, *Three Years*, 176.

176 *In a few days:* James, *Three Years*, 12–13; and Chittenden, *American Fur Trade*, Vol. 1, 140–41.

177 *Clark wrote:* James J. Holmberg, *Dear Brother: Letters of William Clark to Jonathan Clark* (New Haven: Yale University Press, 2002), 210.

177 *"Our governor:* Will Carr to Charles Carr, Aug. 25, 1809, Carr Papers, MHS.

177 *When Lewis:* Bates to Eustis, Sept. 28, 1809, in *Life and Papers of Frederick Bates*, Marshall, ed., Vol. 2, 86–92.

178 *By the time:* Neelly to Jefferson, Oct. 18, 1809, in *Territorial Papers*, Carter, ed., Vol. 14, 332–33.

179 *Proceeding along:* Ibid.

179 *But Lewis passed:* Ibid.

179 *Bates's correspondence:* Frederick Bates to Richard Bates, Nov. 9, 1809, in *Life and Papers of Frederick Bates*, Marshall, ed., Vol. 2, 108–12.

179 *Bates thought:* Ibid.

179 *"Gov. Lewis:* Ibid.

179 *A more sympathetic: Missouri Gazette*, Nov. 23, 1809.

180 *"Some secret cause:* Ibid.

180 *The Philadelphia:* Bryan & Schlatter to PC Jr., Nov. 12, 1809, Box 10, CC, MHS.

180 *Nowhere in his:* PC to Eustis, Nov. 22, 1809, PC Letterbook, Boxes 6–7, CC, MHS.

181 *That was not:* Bates to Eustis, Jan. 12, 1810, in *Life and Papers of Frederick Bates*, Marshall, ed., Vol. 2, 122.

181 *Pierre wrote:* PC to Eustis, Dec. 14, 1809, PC Letterbook, Boxes 6–7, CC, MHS.

181 *He said he:* Ibid.

181 *"For a considerable:* Ibid.

181 *Clark, who had:* Clark to PC, Feb. 20, 1810, Box 11, CC, MHS.

182 *Before receiving:* PC to Eustis, April 12, 1810, PC Letterbook, Boxes 6–7, CC, MHS.

182 *Not hearing:* PC to Eustis, June 6, 1810, ibid; Foley and Rice, *First Chouteaus*, 147, citing Eustis to PC, June 16, 1810.

182 *There was: Missouri Gazette*, July 5, 1810.

9. DREAMING BIG — AND STUMBLING

184 *Snow was deep:* James, *Three Years*, 17–27.

184 *Reaching the Forks:* Ménard to PC, April 21, 1810, in Chittenden, *American Fur Trade*, Vol. 2, Appendices.

184 *"This unhappy:* Ibid.

184 *Ménard's ambitious plan:* Ibid.
185 *Around the same:* Chittenden, *American Fur Trade,* Vol. 1, 144–45.
185 *Manuel Lisa:* Lisa to PC, Feb. 14, 1810, Box 11, CC, MHS.
185 *To make matters:* Ibid.
186 *Washington Irving:* Irving, *Astoria,* 30.
186 *"With China:* Chittenden, *American Fur Trade,* Vol. 1, 167.
187 *Irving said:* Irving, *Astoria,* 32.
187 *Astor found:* Ibid., 164–70.
188 *The partners:* Ibid.
188 *On September 3, 1810:* Chittenden, *American Fur Trade,* Vol. 2, Appendix C, 886–87.
188 *In the process:* Ibid.
188 *Hunt and:* Bradbury, *Travels in the Interior,* 70.
189 *Lisa, who did not:* Chittenden, *American Fur Trade,* Vol. 1, 184–85.
189 *Lisa had a fast:* Ibid.
189 *"Great exertions:* Brackenridge, *Views of Louisiana,* 223.
189 *Lisa was just:* Chittenden, *American Fur Trade,* Vol. 1, 186.
190 *Hunt's party:* Ibid., 184–88.
190 *Fearful of a war:* PC to Eustis, July 19, 1810, and Oct. 13, 1810, PC Letterbook, Boxes 6–7, CC, MHS.
190 *The Osages:* PC to Howard, Oct. 14, 1810, and PC to Eustis, Jan. 17, 1811, ibid.
190 *In fact:* PC to Eustis, July 2, 1811, ibid.
191 *Auguste Chouteau:* Stevens, *History of St. Louis,* 81.
191 *Auguste continued:* Cavelier & Fils to AC, Aug. 30, 1812, Box 11, CC, MHS.
191 *Both Pierre:* See Indenture signed E. Hempstead, Nov. 23, 1812, ibid.
192 *Despite tough:* Chittenden, *American Fur Trade,* Vol. 1, 145.
192 *Charles Gratiot:* Gratiot to Astor, Dec. 14, 1811, Gratiot Papers, MHS.
192 *A new expedition:* Chittenden, *American Fur Trade,* Vol. 1, 146.
192 *On June 19:* Ibid.
192 *The war suddenly:* PC to Eustis, July 26, 1812, PC Letterbook, Boxes 6–7, CC, MHS.
193 *Within a short:* PC to Eustis, March 12, 1813, ibid.
193 *Pierre reached:* PC to Howard, May 11, 1813, ibid.
193 *"They appeared:* Ibid.
194 *The war party:* Howard to PC, April 6, 1813, in *Territorial Papers,* Carter, ed., Vol. 14, 674–75.
194 *The Osages were:* PC to Secretary of War Armstrong, May 20, 1813, PC Letterbook, Boxes 6–7, CC, MHS.
194 *Howard later:* Howard to PC, April 1813, in *Territorial Papers,* Carter, ed., Vol. 14, 674–75.
194 *In the midst:* Billon, ed., *Annals of St. Louis in Territorial Days,* 56.

194 *Theirs was a sobering:* The account of the Astoria venture in the eleven paragraphs that follow, largely based on the reports from Crooks and Stuart initially published in the *Missouri Gazette* on May 15, 1813, can also be found in Irving, *Astoria;* Chittenden, *American Fur Trade,* Vol. 1, 176–80; Darby, *Recollections,* 103; and Gabriel Franchère, *Adventure at Astoria, 1810–1814* (Norman: University of Oklahoma Press, 1967, first published 1820).

197 *With the continuing:* Bent to AC, Feb. 21, 1813, Box 12, CC, MHS.

198 *Bent told Auguste:* Ibid.

198 *"[Those who dislike:* Ibid.

199 *Along the Mississippi:* Monroe to Clark, AC, and Edwards, March 11, 1815, and copy of AC's commission, both in Box 12, CC, MHS.

199 *"You will give:* Ibid.

200 *Although the:* William E. Foley, *The Genesis of Missouri: From Wilderness to Statehood* (Columbia: University of Missouri Press, 1989), 233–34.

200 *During most: Missouri Gazette,* June 10, 1815.

200 *In the course:* "Notes of AC," in MHS *Glimpses of the Past,* Vol. 7, Nos. 9–12, October–December 1940.

200 *One of the:* Ibid.

200 *Auguste stressed:* Ibid.

201 *Once the tribes:* Ibid.

201 *By the cold:* Leduc to Bates, Dec. 30, 1815, in *Territorial Papers,* Carter, ed., Vol. 15, 98–99.

201 *"The Osages:* Ibid.

201 *Pierre thought:* Ibid.

202 *At this point:* PC to Clark, July 29, 1813, PC Letterbook, Boxes 6–7, CC, MHS.

202 *The land:* Clark, Edwards, and AC to Secretary of War, June 30, 1816, in *Territorial Papers,* Carter, ed., Vol. 15, 151–52.

202 *The War Department:* Clark to Calhoun, October 1818, ibid., 454–55.

203 *Pierre Chouteau:* Calhoun to Clark, April 22, 1818, ibid., 384.

203 *At the signing:* Clark to Calhoun, October 1818, ibid., 454–55.

10. THE THIRD GENERATION

204 *It began when:* APC to Williams, Aug. 15, 1806, photocopies of two handwritten letters in Box 46/f.6, McDermott Collection, SIUE, citing original in Jonathan Williams Collection, Lilly Library, Indiana University.

204 *Before he could depart:* Ibid.

205 *"Your saying:* Ibid.

205 *Not being considered:* Ibid.

205 *A.P.'s English:* Williams to APC, undated, photocopy of handwritten letter in Box 46/f.6, McDermott Collection, SIUE, citing original in Jonathan Williams Collection, Lilly Library, Indiana University.

205 *A few months:* Panet to AC, Dec. 28, 1806, Box 8, CC, MHS.

205 *In the course:* Panet to AC, May 18, 1804, Box 6, CC, MHS; and Panet to AC, May 18, 1805, Box 8, CC, MHS.

206 *Auguste Aristide:* Auguste Aristide to AC, Nov. 26, 1802, Box 4, CC, MHS.

206 *While awaiting:* Panet to AC, Dec. 28, 1806, Box 8, CC, MHS.

207 *As if to confuse:* See, for example, baptisms of half-Osage children of various of the Chouteaus in Louis F. Burns, *Osage Missions: Baptisms, Marriages and Interments, 1820–1886* (Fallbrook, Calif.: Ciga Press, 1986), 140–47.

208 *Paradoxically:* Ibid.

208 *Auguste and his wife:* Panet to AC, Feb. 2, 1797, Box 2, CC, MHS.

208 *Three years:* AC to Panet, May 10, 1800, Box 3, CC, MHS.

210 *Paul Liguest:* See *Tixier's Travels,* McDermott, ed., 87.

210 *Less evidence:* See Victoire Gratiot to St. Gme. Beauvais, Jan. 25, 1802, Box 4, CC, MHS.

211 *Among the girls:* See, for instance, Jules de Mun to Isabelle, Aug. 13, 1816, De Mun Collection, MHS.

211 *For the younger:* See McDermott, *Private Libraries,* 15; and Billon, ed., *Annals of St. Louis in Territorial Days,* 167 and 78–81; also receipt dated Oct. 28, 1817, Box 13, CC, MHS.

211 *But as late:* *Missouri Gazette,* July 18, 1811, and Dec. 14, 1811.

212 *In the early:* Copy of marriage contract, Feb. 15, 1809, Box 10, CC, MHS.

213 *There is no record:* Clark to John Armstrong, Aug. 20, 1814, in *Territorial Papers,* Carter, ed., Vol. 14, 786–87.

213 *While Auguste's:* AC to Cerré Chouteau, Aug. 30, 1810, Box 11, CC, MHS.

214 *A few years:* AC to Cerré Chouteau, Jan. 8, 1818, Box 13, CC, MHS.

214 *"We long to see:* AC to Cerré Chouteau, March 6, 1818, ibid.

214 *"My dear Papa:* See debt notes of 1817–18, Box 61, CC, MHS, and Auguste Aristide to AC, April 3, 1816, Box 13, CC, MHS.

214 *Meanwhile, Charles:* See Gratiot biography in *U.S. Army Index of Officers, 1789–1903;* also Francis B. Heitman, *Historical Register and Dictionary of the United States Army* (Washington: U.S. Congress, 1903), 300, 470.

215 *Pierre Jr.:* Janet Lecompte, "Pierre Chouteau, Junior," in *Mountain Men and Fur Traders of the Far West: Eighteen Biographical Sketches,* LeRoy R. Hafen and Harvey L. Carter, eds. (Lincoln: University of Nebraska Press, 1982), 25–27.

215 *After his return:* Billon, ed., *Annals of St. Louis in Territorial Days,* 127, 129, 234.

215 *Gradually, however:* See *Territorial Papers,* Carter, ed., Vol. 15, 85.

216 *French traders:* The account beginning here of the Santa Fe expedition is based on the journal and letters written by de Mun during and after his travels. See "The Journals of Jules de Mun," Thomas Maitland Marshall, ed., Nettie H. Beauregard, tr., in *MHS Collections,* Vol. 5, Nos. 2–3, February and June 1928; also de Mun to Wm. Clark, Nov. 25, 1817, in *MHS Collec-*

tions, Vol. 5, No. 2, February 1928; and Jules de Mun to Isabelle de Mun, Aug. 13, 1816, De Mun Papers, MHS. For biographical material on de Mun see Box 1, Gratiot Papers, MHS.

222 *The governor:* Darby, *Personal Recollections,* 382–83.
223 *The day after:* De Mun to Wm. Clark, Nov. 25, 1817, in *MHS Collections,* Vol. 5, No. 2, February 1928.
223 *By then:* Missouri Gazette, Sept. 13, 1817.
223 *The outraged:* Ibid.
223 *"We know not:* Ibid.

225 *On the Fourth:* Missouri Gazette, July 5, 1819.
225 *After an elaborate:* Ibid.
226 *Auguste continued:* Ibid., Aug. 11, 1819, p. 2, col. 6.
226 *Between 1817:* See AC bankbook, Box 13, CC, MHS; and Bill of Lading signed Robert Dyson, Jan. 15, 1820, Box 14, CC, MHS.
226 *In 1816:* Missouri Gazette, Nov. 23, 1816; and AC to Secretary of War and Secretary of Treasury, Jan. 25, 1821, Box 15, CC, MHS.
226 *Rather:* Lemont K. Richardson, "Private Land Claims in Missouri," in *Missouri Historical Review,* 1956, 393–94.
227 *In May 1816:* Missouri Gazette, May 18, 1816; and James Neal Primm, *Lion of the Valley* (Boulder: Pruett Publishing, 1981), 107–8.
227 *High construction:* Primm, *Lion of the Valley,* 107–8.
228 *Auguste, at this:* Accounting Records dated Nov. 13, 1820, and Surveying Request dated Oct. 31, 1820, both Box 14, CC, MHS; receipts of William Decker, Box 14, CC, MHS.
228 *Commerce grew:* Primm, *Lion of the Valley,* 111–12.
229 *In the years:* Ibid., 110.
229 *During this:* Ibid., 110–11, 141–42.
230 *William Clark:* Receipts and notes confirming their business dealings in the period 1810–20 are scattered through Boxes 11–14, CC, MHS.
230 *In 1823:* See memorandum headed *Etat des Propriétés Taxables d'Aug'te Chouteau dans la ville de St. Louis de l'Etat du Missouri pour l'année 1823,* Box 15, CC, MHS.
230 *Pierre Chouteau, although:* Richardson, "Private Land Claims in Missouri," in *Missouri Historical Review,* 1956, 393–94.
230 *His trading:* Cavelier Sr. to AC, May 12, 1815, Box 12, CC, MHS.
231 *"Please remind:* Cavelier & Son to AC, May 27, 1816, Box 13, CC, MHS.
231 *By the beginning:* Cavelier & Son to AC, Feb. 15, 1817, ibid.
231 *In October:* PC to Cabanné, Oct. 28, 1817, ibid.
231 *It took six:* Notarized document signed by Antoine Cavelier Sr., March 18, 1823, and Cavelier to AC, March 20, 1823, both in Box 16, CC, MHS.

231 *Pierre continued:* Benton to Josiah Meigs, Dec. 22, 1820, in *Territorial Papers*, Carter, ed., Vol. 15, 687.

232 *Sometimes:* Certificate dated Nov. 1, 1822, in William Clark Papers, Clark Family Collection.

232 *In 1824:* Document dated May 27, 1824, Box 17, CC, MHS.

232 *That year:* Document signed PC dated Oct. 20, 1824, ibid.

233 *The newspapers:* See *Missouri Gazette*, May 3, 1820.

233 *Judge Lucas:* Ibid., April 19, 1820.

233 *Young Pierre:* Ibid., April 26, 1820.

233 *When the returns:* Ibid., May 10, 1820.

234 *Meeting at a hotel:* Foley, *Genesis of Missouri*, 293–98.

234 *In the elections:* Ibid.; also see Paul C. Nagel, *Missouri: A History* (Lawrence: University Press of Kansas, 1988), 44–45.

234 *When the new:* Houck, *History of Missouri*, Vol. 3, 166.

235 *If the elections:* Darby, *Recollections*, 39–40.

235 *Bates not only:* Ibid., and *Missouri Republican*, Sept. 20, 1824.

235 *There were: Missouri Intelligencer*, May 21, 1825.

235 *The man heralded:* Ibid.

236 *After being:* Ibid.

236 *Lafayette and:* Darby, *Recollections*, 42–46; and *Missouri Republican*, May 2, 1825.

236 *Pierre threw: Missouri Intelligencer*, May 21, 1825.

237 *After a short:* See handwritten invitation to John B. C. Lucas, Box 11, Lucas Family Papers, MHS; and *Missouri Intelligencer*, May 21, 1825.

238 *Under French:* Frazier, *Slavery and Crime in Missouri*, 12.

238 *Pierre Laclède: Spain in the Mississippi Valley, 1765–1794*, Part 1, Lawrence Kinnaird, ed. (Washington: U. S. Government Printing Office, 1949), 173.

238 *It seems that:* See Testimony before Cruzat on Dec. 29, 1785, and ruling on May 15, 1787, in Billon, ed., *Annals of St. Louis in Early Days*, 233–42.

239 *Papin gave:* Ibid.

239 *Madame Chouteau:* Ibid.

239 *"His services:* Ibid.

239 *After hearing:* Ibid.

240 *In the summer:* Frazier, *Slavery and Crime in Missouri*, 63.

240 *François Ménard:* See letters between Ménard and AC, June–July 1820, Box 14, CC, MHS.

240 *"Please get rid:* Ibid.

240 *Not until:* Ménard to AC, March 5, 1821, and May 19, 1821, Box 15, CC, MHS.

241 *Over the years:* Will of Madame Chouteau, Jan. 13, 1813, Box 12, CC, MHS.

241 *During the time:* See Document signed AC and witnessed by Henry Chouteau, Sept. 26, 1826, Box 18, CC, MHS.

241 *Some slaves:* See Document signed P. L. Chouteau, April 11, 1831, Box 1, Gratiot Papers, MHS; Theodore Papin to Millicour Papin, June 16, 1832, Box 28, CC, MHS.

241 *But belief:* See "An Old Packet of Letters," in *Wisconsin Magazine of History*, Vol. 11, No. 2, December 1927.

242 *The case:* See William E. Foley, "Slave Freedom Suits Before Dred Scott: The Case of Marie Jean Scypion's Descendants," in *Missouri Historical Review*, Vol. 79, No. 1, October 1984, 2–3.

242 *After moving:* Ibid., 5.

242 *In 1799:* Ibid., 6.

242 *At that point:* See Lucas's 1806 Notes, Box 3, John B. C. Lucas Papers, MHS.

243 *"Chouteau then:* Ibid.

243 *In 1802:* Foley, "Slave Freedom Suits," in *Missouri Historical Review*, Vol. 79, No. 1, October 1984, 7–8.

243 *Five days:* Ibid.

243 *The issue over:* Frazier, *Slavery and Crime in Missouri*, 13 and 30–31.

244 *Auguste Chouteau:* See Lucas's 1806 Notes, Box 3, John B. C. Lucas Papers, MHS.

245 *The jury:* See Document signed Joseph Tayon, May 3, 1806, Box 8, CC, MHS.

245 *After that:* Foley, "Slave Freedom Suits," in *Missouri Historical Review*, Vol. 79, No. 1, October 1984, 12–13.

245 *With the passage:* Ibid.

245 *Several separate:* Ibid., 14–15.

246 *According to:* Ibid., 16, citing *Catiche and Others v. PC Sr.*, May 15, 1826.

246 *Pierre put together:* Ibid., 16.

246 *The first:* Ibid., 17, citing *Marguerite v. PC* (1828).

246 *In late 1828:* Ibid., 17–18.

247 *Five more years:* Ibid., 19.

247 *After the Scypions:* Ibid., 20.

247 *Pierre Chouteau:* Ibid., 21–22.

247 *Time also:* Last Will and Testament of AC, Box 21, CC, MHS.

248 *On the morning:* Missouri Republican, Feb. 24, 1829.

248 *The* Missouri Republican: Ibid.

248 *By all accounts:* See Appraisal and Inventory, May 18, 1829, Box 21, CC, MHS.

248 *Auguste had an:* Ibid.

248 *The inventory:* Ibid.

249 *The estate:* Ibid.

249 *Finally:* Ibid.

12. PIERRE JR.: GENTLE CREOLE, DRIVEN TYCOON

250 *Berthold & Chouteau:* Lecompte, "Pierre Chouteau, Junior," biographical sketch in *Mountain Men and Fur Traders,* 27–30.

251 *The fact:* Ibid., 30.

251 *Most of Berthold:* See "Trade and Intercourse" in *American State Papers, Indian Affairs,* Vol. 2, 202; and PC Jr. to G. S. Chouteau, July 19, 1822, Box 15, CC, MHS.

251 *The merger:* Barton H. Barbour, *Fort Union and the Upper Missouri Fur Trade* (Norman: University of Oklahoma Press, 2001), 11.

252 *Bernard Pratte:* Letter of Agreement dated Feb. 9, 1822, Crooks and Pratte, Box 15, CC, MHS.

252 *Within weeks:* John Jacob Astor to Berthold, Chouteau, and Pratte, Aug. 15, 1822, ibid.

253 *However, at the end:* Lecompte, "Pierre Chouteau, Junior," biographical sketch in *Mountain Men and Fur Traders,* 32.

253 *The partners:* Berthold to Pratte and PC Jr., Dec. 6, 1823, Box 16, CC, MHS.

254 *About the same:* Berthold to Pratte and PC Jr., Nov. 23, 1823, ibid.

254 *"From this time:* Lecompte, "Pierre Chouteau, Junior," biographical sketch in *Mountain Men and Fur Traders,* 32.

254 *In 1824:* See Crooks to PC Jr., Jan. 7, 1825, Box 18, CC, MHS.

255 *Traveling:* Berthold to Pratte and PC Jr., Nov. 23, 1823, Box 16, CC, MHS.

255 *Portraits of:* Lecompte, "Pierre Chouteau, Junior," biographical sketch in *Mountain Men and Fur Traders,* 24–25.

256 *During Cadet:* Ibid., 33–34.

256 *The other courtship:* Crooks to PC Jr., Dec. 26, 1824, Box 17, CC, MHS; and Crooks to PC Jr., Jan. 28, 1825, Box 18, CC, MHS.

256 *Although Cadet:* Ibid.

257 *Crooks enlisted:* Crooks to PC Jr., Jan. 7, 1825, and receipts dated Dec. 23, 1824, ibid.

257 *The New York:* Various receipts dated Aug. 31, 1824, Box 17, CC, MHS.

257 *Emilie's brother:* Crooks to PC Jr., Nov. 1, 1824, Box 17, CC, MHS, ibid.

257 *J. P. Cabanné advised:* Cabanné to PC Jr., Oct. 11, 1824, and Nov. 8, 1824, ibid.

258 *From Fort Atkinson:* Kennerly to PC Jr., Dec. 1, 1824, Box 17, CC, MHS.

258 *Emilie and Cadet's:* Cabanné to PC Jr., March 2, 1825, Box 18, CC, MHS.

258 *Cabanné's concerns:* Cabanné to PC Jr., April 28, 1825, ibid.

259 *By June:* See Cabanné to PC Jr., June 12, 1825, ibid.; also Richard E. Jensen, *The Fontenelle & Cabanné Trading Posts* (Lincoln: Nebraska State Historical Society, 1998), 25–29; and Cabanné to PC Jr., July 27, 1825, Box 8, CC, MHS.

259 *Julie Cabanné:* Ibid.

259 *Despite his:* Cabbanné to PC Jr., Dec. 7, 1829, Box 22, CC, MHS.

260 *Cabanné also:* Cabanné to PC Jr., June 5, 1825, Box 18, CC, MHS.

260 *When Cadet:* Cabanné to PC Jr., April 28, 1825, ibid.

260 *Pierre Jr.:* Robidoux to PC Jr., March 15, 1825, ibid.

261 *"This post:* Cabanné to PC Jr., Nov. 8, 1824, Box 17, CC, MHS; and March 2 and Nov. 6, 1825, Box 18, CC, MHS.

261 *This new:* Lecompte, "Pierre Chouteau, Junior," biographical sketch in *Mountain Men and Fur Traders*, 34.

261 *Ramsay Crooks:* Crooks to PC Jr., Jan. 28, 1825, Box 18, CC, MHS.

261 *The next winter:* Wm. Astor to Bostwick, Feb. 8, Feb. 22, and Feb. 25, 1826, ibid.

262 *Meanwhile:* PC Jr. to Pratte, Dec. 17, 1826, ibid.; also see Harold H. Dunham, "Ceran St. Vrain," biographical sketch in *Mountain Men and Fur Traders*, 151.

262 *Cadet, for his:* PC Jr. to B. Pratte & Co., Dec. 21, 1826, Box 18, CC, MHS.

262 *"I ask myself:* Ibid.

263 *After his momentary:* See Articles of Agreement dated Dec. 20, 1826, ibid.

263 *Kenneth McKenzie:* See Lecompte, "Pierre Chouteau, Junior," biographical sketch in *Mountain Men and Fur Traders*, 36–37, and Barbour, *Fort Union*, 121.

265 *After signing:* Cabanné to PC Jr., Aug. 26, 1827, Box 19, CC, MHS.

265 *They reached:* Cabanné to PC Jr., Oct. 11, 1827, ibid.

265 *Revealing:* Ibid.

265 *Cabanné had:* Cabanné to PC Jr., Oct. 23, 1827, ibid.

266 *In January:* Cabanné to PC Jr., Jan. 6, 1828, Box 20, CC, MHS.

266 *These letters:* Chittenden, *American Fur Trade*, Vol. 1, 40.

266 *The winter:* Cabanné to PC Jr., Feb. 10, 1828, Box 20, CC, MHS.

266 *In May:* Cabanné to PC Jr., May 10, 1828, ibid.

267 *But he:* Ibid.

267 *The business:* See contracts dated May 29–30, 1827, June 6, 1827, and July 5, 1827, Box 19, CC, MHS.

267 *A contract:* See contracts dated April 27, 1830, May 24, 1830, May 10, 1830, July 20, 1830, and July 28, 1830, all in Box 23, CC, MHS.

268 *As weaker:* See Crooks to PC Jr., July 2, 1828, and Cabanné to PC Jr., Oct. 14, 1828, both in Box 20, CC, MHS.

268 *Russell:* Davenport to PC Jr., July 23, 1828, ibid.

268 *The Western:* Crooks to PC Jr., Nov. 26, 1827, Box 19, CC, MHS.

269 *They would:* Ibid.

269 *Cadet hired:* Estimate dated July 12, 1828, Box 20, CC, MHS; and insurance document dated Feb. 20, 1830, Box 23, CC, MHS.

269 *In the early:* Primm, *Lion of the Valley*, 136–37.

270 *In late 1828:* Crooks to Cadet, Nov. 18, 1828, Box 20, CC, MHS.

270 *The note:* John J. Astor to PC Jr., July 8, 1829, and Wm. Astor to PC Jr., Aug. 15, 1829, both in Box 22, CC, MHS.

270 *Pierre Jr. continued:* See Articles of Agreement signed Oct. 14, 1830, Box 24, CC, MHS.

270 *The most:* Barbour, *Fort Union*, 39–65; also see Laidlaw to PC Jr., Oct. 26, 1829, Box 22, CC, MHS.

271 *On November 24:* Agreements dated Nov. 24, 1830, Box 24, CC, MHS.

271 *For $4,950:* Ibid.

271 *The winter of 1830–31:* Farnham to PC Jr., Jan. 10, 1831, Box 25, CC, MHS.

272 *"Nearly everywhere:* Cabanné to PC Jr., March 25, 1831, ibid.

272 *Regardless of:* Cabanné to PC Jr., Feb. 2, 1831, ibid.

272 *Cabanné promised:* Cabanné to PC Jr., Feb. 21, 1831, ibid.

273 *From farther:* Lamont to PC Jr., April 4, 1831, in Fort Tecumseh Letterbook, 33–34, Box 24, CC, MHS.

273 *As the April:* C. N. Halstead to PC Jr., April 1, 1831, Box 25, CC, MHS.

273 *Life was good:* Crooks to PC Jr., April 6, 1831, ibid.

274 *For tax purposes:* See 1831 Tax Statement, ibid.

274 *Julie and Emilie:* See Receipt from Duchesne, May 26, 1827, Box 19, CC, MHS; and Crooks to PC Jr., July 14, 1831, Box 26, CC, MHS.

274 *Cadet and Emilie's:* St. Louis *Globe-Democrat*, Jan. 6, 1901, Box 56, CC, MHS.

274 *On April 16:* See list of hires dated April 15, 1831, signed PC Jr., and duplicate of invoice dated April 12, 1831, both Box 25, CC, MHS.

275 *As the Yellow Stone:* Lamont to PC Jr., April 28, 1831, in Fort Tecumseh Letterbook, Box 24, CC, MHS.

275 *The next day:* PC Jr. to B. Pratte, May 1, 1831, Box 25, CC, MHS.

275 *The Yellow Stone:* PC Jr. to Pratte, May 31, 1831, ibid.

276 *"It is a painful:* PC Jr. to Pratte, May 31, 1831, ibid.

276 *The same day:* PC Jr. to Cabanné, May 31, 1831, ibid.

276 *In the early:* McKenzie to AFC, June 7, 1831, and Laidlaw to PC Jr., both in Fort Tecumseh/Fort Pierre Letterbook, 42–45, Box 24, CC, MHS.

277 *On June 19:* Harold H. Schuler, *Fort Pierre Chouteau* (Vermillion: University of South Dakota Press, 1990), 100.

277 *To add to:* Cabanné to PC Jr., June 17, 1831, Box 26, CC, MHS.

277 *With the river:* See Shipping Document, Aug. 3, 1831, ibid.

278 *In August:* See Chittenden, *American Fur Trade*, Vol. I, 334–35; and Barbour, *Fort Union*, 24–25.

278 *Fort Union:* Barbour, *Fort Union*, 39–60; and author's visit to Fort Union Historic Site.

279 *The scarcity:* Laidlaw to PC Jr., Oct. 14, 1831, in Fort Tecumseh/Fort Pierre Letterbook, 55–59, Box 24, CC, MHS.

279 *After his:* Robidoux to PC Jr., Sept. 24, 1831, Box 26, CC, MHS.

279 *From the Bluffs:* Cabanné to PC Jr., Oct. 5, 1831, ibid.

279 *Robidoux complained:* Robidoux to PC Jr., Oct. 8, 1831, ibid.
280 *The following:* Cabbanné to PC Jr., Jan. 12, 1832, Box 27, CC, MHS.
280 *But then:* See Din and Nasatir, *Imperial Osages,* 329; *Journals of Lewis and Clark,* DeVoto, ed., 18–19.
280 *"There is a cruel:* AC to P. L. Panet, May 10, 1800, Box 3, CC, MHS.
281 *When Cabanné:* Cabanné to PC Jr., Oct. 8, 1831, and Robidoux to PC Jr., unspecified date in October 1831, both in Box 26, CC, MHS.
281 *"The smallpox:* Cabanné to PC Jr., Dec. 3, 1831, ibid.
281 *As had become:* PC Jr. to Sarpy, Dec. 6, 1831, Box 26, and Jan. 7, 1832, Box 27, both in CC, MHS.
282 *Even a decade:* Paul Wilhelm Duke of Württemberg, *Travels in North America 1822–1824,* W. Robert Nitske, tr., Savoie Lottinville, ed. (Norman: University of Oklahoma Press, 1973), 295–99.
282 *During his visit:* PC Jr. to Sarpy, Feb. 11, 1832 Box 27, CC, MHS.
282 *Crooks, from:* Crooks to PC Jr., Feb. 26, 1832, ibid.
283 *Crooks also:* Ibid.
283 *Finally, Mr. Astor:* Ibid.
283 *As Astor contemplated:* See License dated March 26, 1832, Box 27, CC, MHS.
283 *For this huge:* PC Jr. to Sarpy, Jan. 7, 1832, ibid.
284 *Earlier that:* Pratte and PC Jr. to Crooks, March 26, 1832, Box 27, CC, MHS.
285 *"The Missouri is:* Catlin, *North American Indians,* Letter No. 3, 12–17.
285 *Like no other:* See Robert G. Athearn, *High Country Empire* (Lincoln: University of Nebraska Press, 1960), 89.
285 *For a thousand:* Catlin, *North American Indians,* Letter No. 3, 12–14.
286 *Catlin observed:* Ibid., Letter No. 2, 9.
286 *Cadet was:* PC Jr. to Pratte, April 16, 1832, Box 27, CC, MHS.
286 *Along the route:* Catlin, *North American Indians,* Letter No. 3, 16.
286 *From the Ponca:* Ibid., Letter No. 27, 215; also see Fort Pierre Letterbook, May 22, 1832, excerpted in *South Dakota Historical Collections,* Vol. 9, 1918, 156.
287 *Catlin went:* Ibid.
287 *Exaggerating:* Catlin, *North American Indians,* Letter No. 26, 202–3.
287 *Eight days:* Ibid., Letter No. 28, 220–21.
288 *"The excitement:* Ibid.
288 *The new fort:* Ibid.
288 *Catlin saw "thousands:* Ibid.
288 *The whites:* Ibid.
288 *On June 5:* Ibid., Letter No. 19, 139–40.
289 *Most of those:* Ibid.
289 *On its return:* Schuler, *Fort Pierre Chouteau,* 101; and Crooks to PC Jr., July 21, 1832, Box 28, CC, MHS.

289 *"The future:* Crooks to PC Jr., Nov. 16, 1832, ibid.
290 *"Your voyage:* J. J. Astor to PC Jr., August 1832, and Sept. 28, 1832, ibid.
290 *Catlin had:* Catlin, *North American Indians,* Letter No. 6, 36.
290 *After painting:* See invoice dated July 20, 1832, Box 28, CC, MHS.
291 *The Louisiana:* See *Chardon's Journal,* fn27, 204; and *United States Statutes at Large,* Vol. 2, 139–46, and Vol. 3, 682–83.
291 *"The subject:* Wm. B. Astor to PC Jr., April 2, 1832, Box 27, CC, MHS.
291 *That effort:* Barbour, *Fort Union,* 158.
292 *Barton H. Barbour:* Ibid., 159; and PC Jr. to William Renshaw, Jan. 6, 1832, Box 27, CC, MHS.
292 *As Pierre Jr. steamed:* Cabanné to PC Jr., Aug. 2, 4, and 11, 1832, Box 27 [the typed, translated versions of these three letters are dated in April 1832 in the files of the CC, MHS, but the author believes, after careful study of the events in question, that the dates should be in August 1832]; and William B. Astor to PC Jr., March 14, 1833, Box 29. Both in CC, MHS.
292 *When the Yellow Stone:* Ibid.
292 *Back in:* Unsigned note to Clark from AFC, dated only "1832," Box 27, CC, MHS.
293 *While this game:* Cabanné to PC Jr., Aug. 4, 1832. ibid.
293 *A month later:* See Chittenden, *American Fur Trade,* Vol. 1, 348–50; Barbour, *Fort Union,* 160, citing Leclerc letter to John Dougherty, U.S. Indian Agent, Sept. 25, 1832; and Cabanné to Clerk, March 18, 1833.
293 *After being put:* Ibid.
293 *"Entertaining:* Wm. B. Astor to PC Jr., Jan. 14, 1833, Box 29, CC, MHS.
294 *"The affair:* Wm. B. Astor to PC Jr., March 12, 1833, ibid.
294 *The Secretary:* Ibid.; and Crooks to PC Jr., Nov. 16, 1832, Box 28, CC, MHS.
294 *Astor and Crooks:* Wm. B. Astor to Cadet, Oct. 17, 1832, ibid.
295 *As the government:* Wm. B. Astor to PC Jr., March 14, 1833, Box 29, CC, MHS; and Lecompte, "Pierre Chouteau, Junior," biographical sketch in *Mountain Men and Fur Traders,* 41.
295 *None of this:* See two agreements signed Oct. 12, 1832, and unsigned letter to "Papa" in handwriting believed to be that of Bernard Pratte Jr., Nov. 10, 1832, both in Box 28, CC, MHS.
296 *But construction:* B. Pratte Jr. to PC Jr., Oct. 28, 1832, ibid.
296 *Cholera was:* Theodore Papin to Millicour Papin, July 25, 1832; Crooks to PC Jr., July 21, 1832; and J. J. Astor to PC Jr., August 1832, ibid.
296 *This new:* Theodore Papin to Millicour Papin, July 25, 1832, ibid.
296 *"I do not urge:* P. D. Papin to Millicour Papin, Aug. 27, 1832, ibid.
296 *The disease:* Davenport to Farnham, Sept. 2, 1832, ibid.
297 *A few days:* Davenport to PC Jr., Sept. 10, 1832, ibid.
297 *At the end:* Davenport to PC Jr., Sept. 29, 1832, ibid.
297 *"We have:* Hypolite to Millicour Papin, Nov. 9, 1832, ibid.

297 *The* St. Louis Beacon: *The St. Louis Beacon,* Oct. 26, 1832.

298 *"May this destructive:* M. P. Leduc to Millicour Papin, Aug. 17, 1833, Box 30, CC, MHS.

298 *Charles Dehault Delassus:* Delassus to M. P. Leduc, Nov. 23, 1832, Box 28, CC, MHS.

298 *In Cincinnati:* Unsigned letter in handwriting of Bernard Pratte Jr., Nov. 10, 1832, ibid.

298 *Another St. Louis:* Darby, *Personal Recollections,* 107.

299 *"Poor Farnham!":* Crooks to PC Jr., Nov. 16, 1832, Box 28, CC, MHS.

13. A. P. CHOUTEAU: STAR-CROSSED HERO

300 *His skill:* Comments from Osages appear in document signed by 22 Osage leaders, Sept. 19, 1835, Box 33, CC, MHS.

301 *Once back:* See J. Thomas Scharf, *History of Saint Louis City and County* (Philadelphia: L. H. Everts, 1883), Vol. 1, 150–53, 198, 582–83; and receipt dated Sept. 9, 1819, Box 14, CC, MHS.

301 *One of the:* For details of APC's start in the future Oklahoma, see Lecompte, "Auguste Pierre Chouteau," in *The Mountain Men and the Fur Trade of the Far West,* LeRoy R. Hafen, ed., Vol. 9 (Glendale, Calif.: Arthur H. Clark Co., 1972), 72–74; "Chouteaus Were Power in Indian Territory," *Tulsa Daily World,* Aug. 18, 1935; Grant Foreman, *Pioneer Days in the Early Southwest* (Lincoln: University of Nebraska Press, 1994, first published 1926), 59; and *Historical Highlights of Mayes County,* (Pryor: Mayes County Historical Society, 1973), 416–17.

301 *They chose:* Ibid.

302 *Revoir was:* Ibid.

302 *"The soil is:* APC's written testimony to Senate Committee on Indian Affairs, July 21, 1831, Records of the United States Senate, 21st Congress.

303 *When A.P.:* See Graves, *History of Neosho County,* Vol. 1, 19–20, citing *Harmony Mission Journal,* Sept. 5, 1822, and journal of relative of Croix; also see James, *Three Years,* 114.

303 *A.P. broached:* Graves, *History of Neosho County,* Vol. 1, 19–20; and James, *Three Years,* 113–14.

304 *In late September:* Graves, *History of Neosho County,* Vol. 1, 20, citing *Union Mission Journal,* Sept. 26, 1822, and Nov. 18, 1822.

304 *However, Young:* See Lecompte, "Auguste Pierre Chouteau," in *Mountain Men,* 73–74; Graves, *History of Neosho County,* 20, citing *Harmony Mission Journal,* Aug. 20, 1823.

304 *Somewhat nervous:* APC to Millicour Papin, Jan. 12, 1824, Box 17, CC, MHS.

304 *Trying to quiet:* Ibid.

305 *"It is true:* Ibid.

305 *Returns were hopeful:* Ibid.

305 *At the beginning:* APC to Millicour Papin, April 4, 1824, and April 2, 1824, both in Box 17, CC, MHS.

305 *But a few:* APC to B. Pratte & Co., Aug. 30, 1824, ibid.

305 *He continued:* Lecompte, "Auguste Pierre Chouteau," in *Mountain Men*, 76.

306 *A.P. brought:* See *The Western Journals of Washington Irving*, John F. McDermott, ed. (Norman: University of Oklahoma Press, 1944), 109; and Lecompte, "Auguste Pierre Chouteau," in *Mountain Men*, 67, fn. 14.

306 *At home:* Latrobe, *The Rambler*, 5.

307 *A.P.'s first:* W. W. Graves, *The First Protestant Osage Missions 1820–1837* (Oswego, Kan.: Carpenter Press, 1949), 171; also see Mrs. R. A. Snavely to MHS, Dec. 8, 1937, Box 58, CC, MHS.

307 *After the birth:* For substantiation of the paternity of these six children, see Foreman, *Pioneer Days*, 258–61, citing Stokes to Crawford, March 19, 1839, and affidavit made by Rosalie Lambert Chouteau, March 17, 1842; also treaty signed June 2, 1825, by Wm. Clark and Osage leaders.

308 *The woman:* See Thomas L. McKenney and James Hall, *Indian Tribes of North America* (Edinburgh: John Grant, 1933–34), Vol. 1, 44–49, for account of the Osages' European adventure. The historians John Joseph Mathews, Janet Lecompte, and Grant Foreman all concluded that the woman who sat for the portrait was the mother of one of A.P.'s children.

308 *When priests:* These baptisms were originally recorded in the parish records of St. Ferdinand in Florissant, Mo., from which the early priests traveled, and at the mission at St. Paul in the future state of Kansas. See Burns, *Osage Mission Baptisms*, 137–49.

309 *In the summer:* Ibid.

309 *The 1825 treaty:* Treaty signed June 2, 1825, by Wm. Clark and Osage leaders, cited in Mathews, *The Osages*, 519–20.

310 *"Hunting is very:* See APC to Pratte, Dec. 17, 1826, Box 18, and APC to Pratte, Feb. 8, 1827, Box 19, both in CC, MHS.

310 *A.P. told Pratte:* Ibid.

310 *A.P. acknowledged:* Ibid.

310 *This was during:* Ibid.

311 *The Creeks:* Lecompte, "Auguste Pierre Chouteau," in *Mountain Men*, 78.

311 *The new post:* Grant Foreman, *Fort Gibson: A Brief History* (Muskogee: Press of Hoffman Printing Co.), 5–12.

312 *An active:* Ibid.

312 *On the first:* Foreman, *Pioneer Days*, 167–68; and *Arkansas Gazette*, Sept. 23, 1828.

312 *When Washington:* Irving, *Tour on the Prairies*, 22.

312 *A.P. had:* Foreman, *Pioneer Days*, 196.

313 *A.P.'s much:* APC to Pratte, Dec. 17, 1826, Box 18, CC, MHS.

313 *Auguste Aristide*: APC to Auguste Sr., Aug. 14, 1828, Box 20, CC, MHS.

313 *Into this setting*: See Foreman, *Fort Gibson*, 27; and Joseph Thoburn to George W. Martin, May 28, 1912, in Manuscript Collections, Kansas State Historical Society, Topeka.

314 *Houston also*: Arbuckle to Secretary of War, July 23, 1830, copy in Box 45/f.13, McDermott Collection, SIUE.

315 *Suggesting*: Sam Houston to Secretary of War, June 24, 1829, Office of Indian Affairs, copy in Box 46/f.12, McDermott Collection, SIUE.

315 *There was*: Hamtramck to Wm. Clark, Aug. 21, 1829, ibid.

315 *Hamtramck*: Ibid.

315 *The cattle*: APC statement to Senate Committee on Indian Affairs, July 21, 1831, ibid.

316 *Shortly after*: See Lecompte, "Auguste Pierre Chouteau," in *Mountain Men*, 79; and Foreman, *Pioneer Days*, 184–91.

317 *Then, on*: Lecompte, "Auguste Pierre Chouteau," in *Mountain Men*, 80–81; also see copy of document signed Sam Houston, Nov. 22, 1831, Box 46/f.13, McDermott Collection, SIUE.

317 *A.P. struggled*: APC to Pierre Jr., July 7, 1829, Box 21, CC, MHS.

317 *Nevertheless*: APC to Pierre Jr., Aug. 24, 1829, ibid.

318 *There were*: McNair to Sarpy, March 15, 1831, Box 25, CC, MHS.

318 *Even with*: PC Jr. to Sarpy, Feb. 11, 1832, Box 27, CC, MHS; and see Lecompte, "Auguste Pierre Chouteau," in *Mountain Men*, 84.

318 *After A.P.*: APC to Cass, Nov. 12, 1831, Box 26, CC, MHS.

319 *A.P. also confirmed*: Ibid.

319 *The Osages*: See Arbuckle to John H. Eaton, May 21, 1831, copy in Box 46/f.13; and Paul Liguest Chouteau to Cass, April 6, 1832, copy in Box 46/f.15, both in McDermott Collection, SIUE.

320 *"They are surrounded*: Ibid.

320 *Paul Liguest*: Ibid.

320 *A.P. went*: Lecompte, "Auguste Pierre Chouteau," in *Mountain Men*, 81.

321 *"I have mentioned*: Cass to APC, July 14, 1832, copy in Box 46/f.15, McDermott Collection, SIUE.

321 *But well*: Washington Irving, *The Western Journals of Washington Irving*, John Francis McDermott, ed. (Norman: University of Oklahoma Press, 1944), 3–7.

321 *One more*: Ibid., 9.

322 *The travelers*: Ibid.

322 *At Ashtabula*: See Irving, *Western Journals*, 14; and Latrobe, *The Rambler*, Introduction.

322 *After regrouping*: Latrobe, *The Rambler*, fn 5.

323 *"The Colonel*: Ibid., 2–3.

323 *During the*: Ibid., 7–8.

324 *He generally*: Irving, *Western Journals*, 135.

324 *Irving recounted:* Ibid., 101.
324 *Hearing:* Ibid., 102.
324 *The group:* Latrobe, *The Rambler*, 26.
325 *Irving noted:* Irving, *Western Journals*, 108–9.
325 *Supper that:* Ibid.
325 *Meetings:* See "Journal of the Proceedings of a Council held by the United States' Commissioners with the Osage Indians, commencing at the Great Saline, upon Neosho river, on the 25th day of February 1833," 23 Cong. 1 sess. Sen. Doc. 512.
325 *Business began:* Ibid.
326 *"All the red men:* Ibid.
326 *The following day:* Ibid.
326 *The young Clermont:* Ibid.
326 *Stokes responded:* Ibid.
326 *Ellsworth urged:* Ibid.
327 *The Osages:* Ibid.
327 *The commissioners:* Ibid.
327 *When the treaty:* Foreman, *Pioneer Days*, 118–19, citing *Journal of Rev. W. F. Vaill*, American Board for Foreign Missions.
328 *"I do not:* APC to Cass, July 16, 1833, in Office of Indian Affairs, Letters Received, "Choctaws West, 1833," copy in Box 46/f.14, McDermott Collection, SIUE.
328 *Four days:* Stokes to Cass, July 20, 1833, from 23 Cong. Sen. Doc. 512, copy in Box 46/f.15, McDermott Collection, SIUE.
328 *Stokes told:* Ibid.
328 *He said this:* Ibid.
328 *"If the Osages:* Ibid.
329 *A long standoff:* APC to Cass, March 3, 1834, Office of Indian Affairs, copy in Box 46/f.16, McDermott Collection, SIUE.
329 *A.P. told Cass:* Ibid.
329 *"It is my duty:* Ibid.
330 *He wondered:* Ibid.
330 *The next month:* APC to PC Jr., May 30, 1834, Box 32, CC, MHS.
330 *A.P. also:* Ibid.
330 *In May:* Ibid., and Crooks to Pratte Chouteau, May 31, 1834, ibid.
330 *Coming through:* Lecompte, "Auguste Pierre Chouteau," in *Mountain Men*, 85.
331 *He probably:* See Foreman, *Pioneer Days*, 122–30; Catlin, *North American Indians*, 307–46; and Joseph B. Thoburn correspondence of Dec. 21, 1911, Manuscript Collections, Kansas State Historical Society.
331 *A.P. could:* Foreman, *Pioneer Days*, 130; and Catlin, *North American Indians*, 313, 346.
331 *Six months:* See document signed by 22 Osage chiefs, headmen, and warriors at Washington, D. C., Sept. 19, 1835, Box 33, CC, MHS.

332 *Meanwhile:* Foreman, *Pioneer Days,* 226–27.

332 *The Kiowas:* Ibid.

332 *The following:* Ibid.

333 *By the spring:* Poinsett to APC, April 7, 1837, Box 35, CC, MHS.

333 *Secretary of War:* Ibid.

333 *As usual:* Ibid.

333 *"There is no:* Ibid.

334 *Governor Stokes:* Stokes to Poinsett, May 30, 1837, Office of Indian Affairs, Letters Received, Copy in Box 46/f.17, McDermott Collection, SIUE.

334 *In November:* APC to Harris, Nov. 25, 1837, Records of the Office of Indian Affairs, copy in Box 46/f.17, McDermott Collection, SIUE.

334 *But A.P. advised:* Ibid.

334 *A month:* APC to Harris, Dec. 8, 1837, Office of Indian Affairs, copy in Box 46/f.17, McDermott Collection, SIUE.

335 *They were:* See Foreman, *Pioneer Days,* 234–37; and Paul Liguest to Sarpy, May 23, 1838, Box 36, CC, MHS.

335 *But as he reached:* APC to Harris, May 1, 1838, from Records of the Office of Indian Affairs, copy in Box 46/f.17, McDermott Collection, SIUE.

335 *To preempt:* Document on judgments obtained against APC, dated Sept. 14, 1838, Box 36, CC, MHS.

336 *During this:* See Lecompte, "Auguste Pierre Chouteau," in *Mountain Men,* 88, citing No. 1439, Probate Court Records, St. Louis; also Paul Liguest Chouteau to Sarpy, May 23, 1838, Box 36, CC, MHS.

336 *On September 11:* Deed from Brotherton conveying APC's property in St. Louis to Pierre Jr. on Sept. 14, 1838, Box 36, CC, MHS.

336 *What seems:* APC to PC Jr., Dec. 6, 1838, copy in Box 46/f.17, McDermott Collection, SIUE.

337 *Two days:* St. Louis Republican, Jan. 18, 1839.

337 *Gabriel R. Paul:* G. R. Paul to Pierre Sr., Dec. 28, 1838, Box 36, CC, MHS.

337 *He added:* Ibid.

338 *As soon as:* Foreman, *Pioneer Days,* fn 257; and Lecompte, "Auguste Pierre Chouteau," in *Mountain Men,* 89.

339 *After recalling:* Foreman, *Pioneer Days,* 258–61, quoting Stokes to Crawford, March 19, 1839, Indian Office, Osage Reserve File B 1463.

339 *Before his efforts:* Foreman, *Pioneer Days,* 258 fn and 290, citing Butler to Crawford, commissioner of Indian affairs, March 20, 1842; and Rosalie Chouteau affidavit, March 17, 1842, Indian Office, Osage Reserve File B 1463.

340 *Another piece:* See J. Moore, *International Arbitrations,* 1267 and 1286, Box 44, CC, MHS.

340 *The southwestern:* Josiah Gregg, "Commerce of the Prairies," in *Early Western Travels,* Thwaites, ed., Vol. 19, 232.

340 *"We had not:* Ibid.

14. FRANÇOIS AND BÉRÉNICE: TOGETHER TO A NEW PLACE

341 *The marriage: Missouri Gazette,* July 28, 1819.

341 *Ménard—the son:* See Davis, *Frontier Illinois,* 100; Pregaldin, "Genealogy of the Ménard Family" from Pierre Ménard Home historic site, Kaskaskia; and Richard E. Oglesby, "Pierre Ménard," in *French Fur Traders and Voyageurs in the American West,* LeRoy R. Hafen, ed. (Lincoln: University of Nebraska Press, 1997), 226.

341 *Like the Chouteaus:* Ibid.

342 *François Gesseau:* See Cunningham and Blythe, *Founding Family,* 62; and Pregaldin, "Genealogy of the Ménard Family."

342 *Both husbands:* See Dorothy B. Marra, Marie-Laure Dionne Pal, and David Boutros, *Cher Oncle, Cher Papa* (Kansas City: WHMC), 6; and Chapters 8–9, this book.

343 *The year:* For François's beginning career, see "Reminiscences of Frederick Chouteau," Franklin G. Adams, ed., in *Transactions of the Kansas State Historical Society* (1904), Vol. 8, 423–34; Floyd Benjamin Streeter, *The Kaw: The Heart of a Nation* (New York, Farrar & Rinehart, 1941), 28; Marra, Pal, and Boutros, *Cher Oncle, Cher Papa,* 24; and PC Jr. to G. S. Chouteau, July 19, 1822, Box 15, CC, MHS.

343 *By 1821:* See Marra, Pal, and Boutros, *Cher Oncle, Cher Papa,* 23–24; and "Reminiscences of Frederick Chouteau," 428.

343 *When François:* For an early description of the spot where the Kansas River empties into the Missouri, see Württemberg, *Travels in North America 1822–1824,* 266–75.

345 *In deciding:* See Marra, Pal, and Boutros, *Cher Oncle, Cher Papa,* 7, citing "Kansas City's Pioneer Mother Was Wife of First Settler on River Front," *Kansas City Times,* Oct. 2, 1935.

345 *François had:* See Burns, *Osage Mission Baptisms,* 138; Graves, *First Protestant Osage Missions, 1820–1837,* 171; also Chapter 13 this book for 1825 treaty terms.

346 *On one such:* "Mrs. Bernice Chouteau," *Kansas City Journal,* unspecified date in November 1888, John C. McCoy Scrapbooks, WHMC.

346 *That year:* Marra, Pal, and Boutros, *Cher Oncle, Cher Papa,* 25, citing Chouteau's Scrapbook 17.1, WHMC.

346 *About that time:* "Reminiscences of Frederick Chouteau," 423.

346 *First, in October:* "Recollections of an Old Timer Put in Print," in *Kansas City Journal,* July 22, 1888, John C. McCoy Scrapbooks, WHMC.

346 *Six months later:* "Our History," in *Kansas City Weekly Bulletin,* Feb. 22, 1871, John C. McCoy Scrapbooks, WHMC.

346 *The Chouteau family:* See Bérénice to Ménard, Jan. 25, 1827, in Marra, Pal, and Boutros, *Cher Oncle, Cher Papa,* 28.

347 *With Bérénice's:* Bérénice to Angelique Ménard, April 18, 1827, in ibid., 29.

347 *Before rebuilding:* See Interview with Nancy (Francis) Chouteau, Oct. 1, 1908, Byron Chouteau Papers, Kansas State Historical Society.

348 *François, who:* François to PC Jr., Sept. 24, 1829, Box 22, CC, MHS.

348 *In the routine:* See "Reminiscences of Frederick Chouteau," 431; additional information gathered from author's visits to three restored fur-trade posts.

349 *During the:* François to Ménard, Dec. 2, 1828, in Marra, Pal, and Boutros, *Cher Oncle, Cher Papa,* 38–39.

349 *It appears that:* Ibid.; also see "Reminiscences of Frederick Chouteau," 425.

350 *François now:* François to Ménard, Feb. 15, 1829, and March 3, 1829, in Marra, Pal, and Boutros, *Cher Oncle, Cher Papa,* 50–53.

350 *François was:* François to Ménard, Feb. 15, March 3, and March 31, 1829, in ibid., 50–55.

350 *The events:* "Reminiscences of Frederick Chouteau," 423–25.

351 *"I saw that:* Ibid.

351 *When he reached:* Ibid.

351 *"He went under:* Ibid. Frederick said that Lulu later claimed his freedom on the grounds of having some Indian blood on his mother's side and that Pierre Sr. honored his request. Frederick said Lulu went to work as a fireman on a steamboat and died in an explosion en route to New Orleans.

351 *When word reached:* Ibid.

351 *Nevertheless:* François to Ménard, March 31, 1829, in Marra, Pal, and Boutros, *Cher Oncle, Cher Papa,* 54–55.

351 *"You can judge:* Ibid.

352 *"Instead of the joy:* François to Ménard, May 26, 1829, in ibid., 57.

352 *There was still:* Ibid., 59.

352 *Once back:* Ibid., 149; also see "Reminiscences of Frederick Chouteau," 425.

352 *By October:* François to Cadet, Sept. 24, Oct. 15, and Nov. 4, 1829, Box 22, CC, MHS.

353 *This reflected:* François to Ménard, Sept. 24, 1829, in Marra, Pal, and Boutros, *Cher Oncle, Cher Papa,* 67; and François to PC Jr., Sept. 24, 1829, Box 22, CC, MHS.

353 *In December:* François to PC Jr., Dec. 12, 1829, Box 22, CC, MHS.

353 *By February:* François to Ménard, Feb. 15, and April 22, 1830, in Marra, Pal, and Boutros, *Cher Oncle, Cher Papa,* 78–80.

354 *"The Kansas:* Ibid.

354 *It was an:* Ibid.

354 *The rapidly:* William E. Unrau, *The Kansa Indians: A History of the Wind People, 1673–1873* (Norman: University of Oklahoma Press, 1971), 140–47.

355 *François had managed:* François to Ménard, April 22, 1830, in Marra, Pal, and Boutros, *Cher Oncle, Cher Papa,* 79–80.

355 *Both Agent Clark:* François to Ménard, June 6, 1830, ibid., 83–84.

355 *When he returned:* Unrau, *The Kansa Indians,* 145.

355 *This conflict:* François to Ménard, July 15, 1830, in Marra, Pal, and Boutros, *Cher Oncle, Cher Papa,* 86–87.
355 *Marston Clark also:* Unrau, *The Kansa Indians,* 143–44.
356 *Marston Clark:* Marston Clark to François, Dec. 20, 1831, in Marra, Pal, and Boutros, *Cher Oncle, Cher Papa,* 82; François to Ménard, Dec. 12, 1832, ibid., 105; also see "Reminiscences of Frederick Chouteau," 425.
356 *Living in an area:* "Our History," in *Kansas City Weekly Bulletin,* Feb. 22, 1871, John C. McCoy Scrapbooks, WHMC.
357 *François and Bérénice's:* Marra, Pal, and Boutros, *Cher Oncle, Cher Papa,* 90.
357 *As for:* François to Ménard, April 22, 1830, ibid., 79–80.
357 *They were friendly:* Ibid., 69.
358 *François's business:* See Frederick Chouteau Letters, May 6, 1880, *Kansas Historical Quarterly,* Vol. 23, 348; Unrau, *Mixed-Bloods,* 19; and Josette Gonville baptism record April 19, 1835, Folder 17.2, Native Sons Archives, WHMC.
358 *From some:* François to Ménard, Nov. 30, 1831, in Marra, Pal, and Boutros, *Cher Oncle, Cher Papa,* 96–97.
358 *In the 1830:* Ibid., 79.
358 *Death:* Bérénice to Alzire Kennerly, Feb. 3, 1831, ibid., 89.
358 *Hearing:* Ibid.
359 *"I do not:* Ibid.
359 *Bérénice, who:* Ibid.
359 *François wrote:* François to Ménard, March 20, 1831, ibid., 90–91.
359 *In April:* François to Ménard, April 16, 1831, ibid., 92–93.
359 *The smallpox:* François to Ménard, Nov. 30, 1831, and Jan. 17, 1832, ibid., 96–99.
360 *However, François's:* François to Ménard, Aug. 12, 1832, and Sept. 7, 1832, ibid., 102–4.
360 *He returned:* Ibid.
360 *As fascinated:* Ibid.
361 *Paradoxically:* François to Ménard, Sept. 7, 1832, ibid., 103–4.
361 *"A great many:* François to Ménard, June 6, 1830, ibid., 83–84.
361 *François continued:* François to Ménard, June 17, 1833, ibid., 116–17.
362 *Their son:* François to Ménard, Sept. 9, 1833, ibid., 119.
362 *"I beg of you:* Ibid.
362 *But the:* François to Ménard, Jan. 15, 1834, ibid., 125–26.
362 *One more boy:* Ibid., 112.
363 *One day in:* Roux to Bishop Rosati, Nov. 24, 1833, in Gilbert J. Garraghan, S. J., *Catholic Beginnings in Kansas City, Missouri* (Chicago: Loyola University Press, 1920), 45–47.
363 *François explained:* François to Ménard, Nov. 25, 1833, in Marra, Pal, and Boutros, *Cher Oncle, Cher Papa,* 122–23.
364 *Everybody carried:* Württemberg, *Travels in North America,* 268.

364 *Aside from:* François to Ménard, Nov. 25, 1834, in Marra, Pal, and Boutros, *Cher Oncle, Cher Papa*, 130–31.

364 *François and Bérénice:* Ibid., 123.

364 *In addition:* Garraghan, *Catholic Beginnings*, 78–80.

365 *What the boys:* Marra, Pal, and Boutros, *Cher Oncle, Cher Papa*, 140; and Edmond Chouteau to Pierre Ménard, Appendix 5, 215.

365 *François was:* François to Ménard, Aug. 30, 1835, ibid., 143.

365 *Then he reflected:* Ibid.

366 *He was also:* Ibid.

366 *Mary Brigitte:* François to Ménard, Sept. 18, 1835, and Dec. 16, 1835, ibid., 145.

366 *After Gesseau's:* François to Ménard, June 6, 1836, ibid., 156.

366 *The following:* François to Ménard, May 12, 1837, ibid., 163.

366 *The winter of 1838:* François to Ménard, Jan. 28, 1838, and March 3, 1838, ibid., 168–71.

367 *But on April 18:* Joseph S. Chick interview, Oct. 19, 1908, Kansa subgroup, Indian History, Manuscript Collection, Kansas State Historical Society.

367 *She built her new:* William L. Campbell, "Incidents of the Knob Hill or Aristocratic Residence Quarter of Kansas City of Early Days," unpublished manuscript, and Mrs. N. M. Harris in *Kansas City Star*, Sept. 17, 1922, Kansas City Scrapbook I, 117, both in Native Sons Archives, WHMC.

368 *Cyprien was married:* "Kansas City's Little Red Schoolhouse on the Old Westport and Indian Road," *Kansas City Star*, Oct. 14, 1917, Native Sons Archives, WHMC; also Marra, Pal, and Boutros, *Cher Oncle, Cher Papa*, 174–75.

368 *During the Civil:* Marra, Pal, and Boutros, *Cher Oncle, Cher Papa*, 183–87.

368 *By then:* "Jackson County History, The Recollections of an Old Timer Put in Print," *Kansas City Journal*, July 22, 1888, John C. McCoy Scrapbooks, WHMC.

15. PIERRE JR.: POSITION, ADVANTAGE, AND PERHAPS VANITY

370 *In the fall:* See Dan L. Thrapp, *Encyclopedia of Frontier Biography, Vol. 3* (Spokane: Arthur H. Clark, 1988) for Sanford biography; PC Jr. to Sarpy, Jan. 15, 1833, Box 29, CC, MHS.

370 *Ramsay Crooks:* Crooks to PC Jr., Feb. 17, 1833, Box 29, CC, MHS.

370 *Crooks had warned:* Ibid.

371 *When McKenzie:* Ibid.

371 *Somewhere along:* Chittenden, *American Fur Trade*, Vol. 1, 356.

371 *As a result:* "Maximilian's Travels," in *Early Western Travels*, Thwaites, ed., Vol. 22, 273–74.

371 *To once again:* Ibid.

372 *"We spent:* Ibid.

372 *Before leaving:* McKenzie to PC Jr., March 20, 1834, in Fort Union Letterbook, Box 31, CC, MHS; Clark to PC Jr., cited in Chittenden, *American Fur Trade,* Vol. 1, 360.

373 *Pierre Jr.:* PC Jr. to Clark, Nov. 23, 1833, ibid.

373 *Word about:* McKenzie to PC Jr., Dec. 16, 1833, in Fort Union Letterbook, Box 31, CC, MHS.

373 *Pierre Jr. ordered:* Chittenden, *American Fur Trade,* Vol. 1, 361.

373 *Learning that:* Crooks to PC Jr., Feb. 23, 1834, Box 32, CC, MHS.

373 *Smarting at:* McKenzie to PC Jr., March 18 and March 20, 1834, in Fort Union Letterbook, Box 31, CC, MHS.

374 *"It is very:* Ibid. The Red River settlement, made up mostly of Scottish farmers, was sponsored by the Earl of Selkirk and was also known as the Selkirk Colony.

375 *By the summer:* Barbour, *Fort Union,* 59.

376 *"On entering:* Charles Larpenteur, *Forty Years a Fur Trader on the Upper Missouri* (Lincoln: University of Nebraska Press, 1989), 57.

376 *Further buttressing:* Crooks to PC Jr., Nov. 16, 1832, Box 28, CC, MHS.

377 *Days and nights:* Barbour, *Fort Union,* 133.

377 *Charles Larpenteur:* Larpenteur, *Forty Years,* 60.

377 *One of the:* McKenzie to Prince Maximilian, Dec. 10, 1835, reprinted in *Chardon's Journal,* 381–82; *Missouri Argus,* Aug. 30, 1838.

378 *While McKenzie:* Wm. B. Astor to PC Jr., Oct 17, 1832, Box 28, CC, MHS; and Crooks to PC Jr., Feb. 23, 1834, Box 32, CC, MHS.

378 *In March:* Crooks to PC Jr., March 20, 1833, Box 29, CC, MHS; and Astor to B. Pratte & Co., June 25, 1833, Box 30, CC MHS.

378 *Despite its:* Wm. B. Astor to Pratte & Co., Aug. 26, 1833, ibid.

378 *Crooks would:* Crooks to Pratte and PC Jr., May 31, 1834, Box 32, CC, MHS.

379 *In the fall:* Pratte to PC Jr., Oct. 11, 1834, Box 33, CC, MHS.

379 *"The king spent:* Darby, *Personal Recollections,* 133–34.

380 *Jean Pierre Cabanné:* Cabanné to PC Jr., Dec. 22, 1837, Box 35, CC, MHS.

380 *A firm:* Irwin & Whiteman to PC Jr., March 24, 1834, Box 32, CC, MHS; and Crooks to PC Jr., June 14, 1833 Box 30, CC, MHS.

380 *The new cathedral:* See Pew Certificates, Oct. 18, 1834, Box 33, CC, MHS.

380 *The decade:* Primm, *Lion of the Valley,* 145–49.

380 *Between 1835:* Ibid.

381 *Louis and Hyacinthe:* See *l'Almanach Populaire,* Pas-de-Calais, France, 1835, Berthold Collection, MHS.

381 *"You can safely:* Crooks to PC Jr., April 10, 1834, Box 32, CC, MHS.

381 *The following:* Crooks to PC Jr., Jan. 31, 1835, Box 33, CC, MHS.

381 *A year later:* Crooks to PC Jr., Jan. 24, 1836, Box 34, CC, MHS.

382 *Cadet and Emilie's:* *Missouri Argus,* April 29, 1836; and baptismal certificate dated Feb. 12, 1837, Box 34, CC, MHS.

382 *Henry traveled:* Crooks to PC Jr., Jan 24, 1836, Box 34, CC, MHS.

383 *After the Yellow Stone: Chardon's Journal,* 37; and McKenzie to Prince Maximilian, Dec. 10, 1835, reprinted in *Chardon's Journal,* 381–82.

383 *But the reason:* Cabanné to PC Jr., May 23, 1835, Box 33, CC, MHS.

383 *Before the boat:* For sources on the succeeding narrative of the voyage of the *St. Peter's* and the spread of smallpox, see Clyde D. Dollar, "High Plains Smallpox Epidemic of 1837–38," in *Western Historical Quarterly,* January 1977, 20; Halsey to Pratte Chouteau & Co., Nov. 2, 1837, Box 35, CC, MHS; Chittenden, *American Fur Trade,* Vol. 2, 613–19; *Chardon's Journal,* 118–41; and Larpenteur, *Forty Years,* 131–33, fn. 14.

388 *"We can only:* Pratte, Chouteau & Co. to Pierre Jr., Feb. 25, 1838, cited in Chittenden, *American Fur Trade,* Vol. 2, 618.

389 *In New York:* Crooks to PC Jr., March 4, 1838, Box 36, CC, MHS.

389 *"Your son:* Crooks to PC Jr., Oct. 17, 1838, ibid.

390 *The continuing:* Crooks to PC Jr., Nov. 20, 1838, ibid.

390 *"On this new:* Ibid.

390 *"Here we slept:* Ibid.

390 *On January 8, 1838:* See J. Archdale Hamilton to Pierre Jr., Jan. 11, 1838, ibid.

391 *When Pierre Sr.'s:* APC to PC Jr., July 7, 1829, Box 21, CC, MHS.

391 *Pierre's widowed:* Pierre Sr. to PC Jr., Dec. 31, 1837, Box 35, CC, MHS.

392 *After the returns:* Memorandum by PC Jr., Dec. 16, 1850, Box 45, CC, MHS; and PC Jr. to Laidlaw, Jan. 10, 1840, Box 39, CC, MHS.

392 *But Cabanné:* Sanford to PC Jr., June 28, 1841, Box 40, CC, MHS; and Lecompte, "Pierre Chouteau, Junior," biographical sketch in *Mountain Men and Fur Traders,* 47.

392 *Cadet then:* See PC Jr.'s memorandum, Dec. 16, 1850, Box 45, CC, MHS.

392 *Sanford proved:* Sanford to PC Jr., April 26, 1839, May 18, 1839, and June 6, 1839, all in Box 37, CC, MHS.

393 *Like all:* Sanford to Emilie Chouteau, Feb. 22, 1839, ibid.

393 *Emilie's brother:* PC Jr. to Gratiot, Jan. 5, 1836, and Crooks to Gratiot, Feb. 7, 1836, both Box 34, CC, MHS.

393 *Ramsay Crooks:* Crooks to PC Jr., Jan. 31, 1839, Box 37, CC, MHS.

394 *Gratiot told:* Frederick T. Wilson, "Old Fort Pierre and Its Neighbors," in *South Dakota Historical Collections,* Vol. 1, 1902, 279–81.

394 *Strong as:* Ibid.; also Crooks to PC Jr., April 21, 1839, Box 37, CC, MHS.

394 *Financial panic:* Crooks to PC Jr., Jan. 31, 1839, and Jan. 27, 1841, Box 40, CC, MHS.

394 *Not until 1841: Missouri Argus,* Dec. 29, 1840.

395 *Pierre Jr. exhorted:* PC Jr. to Laidlaw, Jan. 10, 1840, Box 39, CC, MHS.

396 *"If I was:* Crooks to PC Jr., Jan. 27, 1841, Box 40, CC, MHS.

396 *Crooks wanted:* Ibid.

396 *Finally, he told:* Ibid.

396 *The records:* Crooks to PC Jr., March 2, 1841, Box 40, CC, MHS.

396 *Crooks was:* Ibid.

396 *"Amer. Fur Co.:* Reprinted in *Daily Missouri Republican,* Sept. 26, 1842.

397 *Pierre Jr. was:* "Memoir of H. L. Dousman," in *Minnesota Historical Society Collections,* Vol. 3, 196–97, cited in 262 fn, *Chardon's Journal;* also see B. Clapp to PC Jr., Sept. 19, 1842, Box 40, CC, MHS.

397 *Crooks was not:* Smith to PC Jr., March 24, 1841, Box 40, CC, MHS.

397 *Cadet was then:* Smith to PC Jr., May 5, 1841, ibid.

397 *Arriving:* Memo dated May 17, 1841, in handwriting of PC Jr., ibid.

397 *"I am happy:* Pierre Jr. to Shields, May 19, 1841, ibid.

398 *In the late fall:* Crooks to Pierre Jr., Oct. 7, 1841, ibid.

398 *To construct:* Madsen, *John Jacob Astor,* 250–51.

398 *They shopped:* See receipts dated Oct. 24, 1842, through March 22, 1843, Boxes 40 and 41, CC, MHS.

398 *The family paid:* Ibid.

399 *During the:* See PC to PC Jr., June 6, 1843, Box 32; receipts dated June 17, 1843, Box 41; and exchange between Maffitt and army officials, Nov. 19, 1843, Box 41, all in CC, MHS.

399 *Two months:* Charles Pierre Chouteau to Emilie Chouteau, Sept. 1, 1843, Box 41, CC, MHS; and Russian visa, Nov. 27, 1844, Box 60, CC, MHS.

400 *Cadet and:* Receipts and bills of sale dated throughout 1844, ibid.

400 *The dissolution:* PC Jr. to Julie Maffitt, April 19, 1850, and mortgage dated Sept. 21, 1850, both in Box 45, CC, MHS.

400 *Cadet continued:* Note signed Brewster & Hart, Dec. 17, 1844, Box 41, CC, MHS; and bill of sale, April 24, 1845, Box 42, CC, MHS.

401 *One of the:* *The Journals of Francis Parkman,* Vol. 2 (New York: Harper & Bros., 1847), 87.

401 *On the day:* St. Louis *Weekly Reveille,* Feb. 22, 1847.

401 *After the:* Ibid.

401 *When the:* Ibid.

401 *Some in:* Stevens, *St. Louis: Fourth City,* 1022–23.

402 *He again:* St. Louis *Reveille,* Feb. 22, 1847; and Darby to PC, Feb. 16, 1847, Box 42, CC, MHS.

402 *Later that:* Will of Pierre Chouteau Sr., dated Nov. 13, 1847, settled in St. Louis Probate Court, June term, 1854.

402 *Pierre Jr.:* Ibid.

403 *An inventory:* Ibid., also see See Foley and Rice, *First Chouteaus,* 201.

403 *In 1836:* See *American State Papers,* Vol. 6, 1828–34, Public Lands, No. 83, 839; and Richard M. Clokey, *William H. Ashley* (Norman: University of Oklahoma Press, 1980), 37–38.

403 *But when:* Clokey, *Ashley,* 37–38.

403 *In 1849:* Lecompte, "Pierre Chouteau, Junior," biographical sketch in *Mountain Men and Fur Traders,* 53.

403 *Over the:* Ibid., 54; and Memorandum of PC Jr., Dec. 14, 1859, Box 50, CC, MHS.

404 *But Cadet wanted:* John S. Prince to PC Jr., Jan. 15, 1856, Box 49, CC, MHS.

404 *Cadet established:* Lecompte, "Pierre Chouteau, Junior," biographical sketch in *Mountain Men and Fur Traders*, 53–54.

404 *That same:* See PC Jr. to Maffitt, Aug. 9, 1858, Box 49, CC, MHS.

405 *In 1851:* Lecompte, "Pierre Chouteau, Junior," biographical sketch in *Mountain Men and Fur Traders*, 53.

405 *Pierre Jr.:* McCloskey to PC Jr. & Co., Box 47, Dec. 6, 1853, CC, MHS.

405 *Cadet and:* Sanford to PC Jr., March 13, 1851, Box 46, CC, MHS.

405 *Six months:* Sanford to PC Jr., Nov. 1, 1851, ibid.

406 *From New York:* PC Jr. to Emilie, Aug. 31, 1854, and Nov. 18, 1854, Box 47, CC, MHS.

407 *This breakthrough:* Henry Chouteau to Clemence, Aug. 9, 1852, Box 46, CC, MHS.

407 *One of the:* Sanford to PC Jr., Nov. 1, 1851, ibid.

407 *He did Italy:* Ben to John and Belle Sanford, Nov. 19, 1854, Box 47, CC, MHS; Ben to PC Jr., March 19, 1855, Box 48, CC, MHS; and PC Jr. to Julie Maffitt, Feb. 10, 1857, and June 1857, both Box 49, CC, MHS.

408 *"I, who would:* PC Jr. to Julie Maffitt, July 8, 1852, Box 46, CC, MHS.

409 *The first area:* Lecompte, "Pierre Chouteau, Junior," biographical sketch in *Mountain Men and Fur Traders*, 52.

409 *In July 1854:* Affidavit given by John B. Didier, Aug. 3, 1854, and "Bunyon" Gratiot to P. Chouteau Jr. & Co., Dec. 13–14, 1854, all in Box 47, CC, MHS.

409 *John B. Didier:* Ibid.

410 *"This looks:* Ibid.

410 *In March:* PC Jr. to Charles Pierre, March 26 and March 31, 1855, Box 48, CC, MHS.

410 *But a few:* PC Jr. to Charles Pierre, April 11 and April 16, 1855, ibid.; also see Barbour, *Fort Union*, 208–9.

411 *Almost as soon:* PC Jr. to Sarpy, Feb. 9, 1856, and circular dated Feb. 20, 1856, both in Box 49, CC, MHS.

411 *The weight:* PC Jr. to Charles Pierre, July 1854, Box 47, CC, MHS; and Dec. 12, 1855, Box 48, CC, MHS.

412 *In 1857:* PC Jr. to Julie Maffitt, Feb. 21, 1857, Box 49, CC, MHS; and Lecompte, "Pierre Chouteau, Junior," biographical sketch in *Mountain Men and Fur Traders*, 53.

412 *Not the least:* Sanford to PC Jr., Oct. 7, 1854, Box 47, CC, MHS; also see Charles P. Kindleberger, *Manias, Panics, and Crashes* (New York: John Wiley & Sons, 1978), 84.

412 *As the crisis:* Cadet to Emilie, July 25, 1854, Box 47, CC, MHS.

412 *"The embarrassment:* Ibid.

413 *No crisis:* Pierre Jr. to Emilie, Dec. 24, 1855, Box 48, CC, MHS.

413 *A cape:* PC Jr. to Julie Maffitt, Dec. 20, 1855, ibid.

413 *The claim:* PC Jr. to Henry Pierre Chouteau, Aug. 14, 1854, Box 47, CC, MHS.

414 *The loss:* PC Jr. to Charles Pierre, Aug. 26, 1857, Box 49, CC, MHS.

414 *The debts:* PC Jr. to Charles Pierre, Jan. 5, 1855, Box 48, CC, MHS.

414 *"Another of:* Liberty (Mo.) Tribune, citing St. Louis Republican, Oct. 9, 1857.

414 *However, Chouteau:* See PC Jr.'s will, dated Aug. 17, 1865.

414 *Under Charles:* Sales Documents and Notices dated Feb. 29, 1856, to March 4, 1856, and Oct. 1, 1856, Box 49, CC, MHS.

415 *Charles Pierre:* St. Louis Republican, Aug. 17, 1859.

415 *In 1855:* Virginia Gratiot to Henry Gratiot, May 20, 1855, Box 1, Gratiot Papers, MHS.

416 *Six months:* Unidentified newspaper clipping, Box 48, CC, MHS.

416 *For several:* PC Jr. to Charles Pierre, March 17, 1855, ibid.

416 *Sarpy, whom:* PC Jr. to Maffitt, April 6, 1857, Box 49, CC, MHS; also newspaper announcements of May 1, 1857, and Oct. 18, 1859, Boxes 49 and 52, CC, MHS.

416 *Perhaps the most:* Louis S. Gerteis, *Civil War St. Louis* (Lawrence: University Press of Kansas, 2001), 20–63; and see Sanford entry in Thrapp, *Encyclopedia of Frontier Biography*, Vol. 3.

417 *Pierre Jr.'s eyesight:* Last Will and Testament of Pierre Chouteau Jr., Aug. 17, 1865.

418 *As Cadet:* George B. McClellan to Charles Pierre, Jan. 25, 1860, Box 51, CC, MHS.

418 *For Cadet:* Auguste Liguest Chouteau to Wm. Maffitt, Sept. 5, 1862, ibid.

418 *After three:* Will of Pierre Chouteau Jr., Aug. 17, 1865, St. Louis Probate Court records.

418 *"I have been:* Ibid.

419 *"I am the owner:* Ibid.

419 *Recognizing:* Ibid.

419 *Charles Pierre:* Ibid.

420 *Before Cadet:* Ibid.; also see Current Account submitted in appeal of Bogy and Tesson, dated Dec. 12, 1866, Box 52, CC, MHS.

420 *Pierre Chouteau Jr.:* St. Louis Republican, Sept. 7, 1865.

EPILOGUE

424 *The level:* Labbadie to AC, Sept. 10, 1803, Box 5, CC, MHS.

424 *Finally, when:* Ibid.

424 *Nearly a half:* "Journal of Rudolph Friederich Kurz," in Smithsonian Institution, *Bureau of American Ethnology Bulletin* 115, 234–37.

424 *"Wares are:* Ibid.

425 *Barton Barbour:* Barbour, *Fort Union*, 19.

427 *The behavior:* Gerteis, *Civil War St. Louis*, 225.

428 *In 1861:* Charles Pierre to Charles Primeau, Feb. 6, 1861, Box 51, CC, MHS.

428 *During most:* See variety of bills, receipts, and invoices, ibid.

428 *The Chouteaus:* Barbour, *Fort Union*, 214, 221.

429 *Charles Larpenteur:* Larpenteur, *Forty Years*, 309; and Barbour, *Fort Union*, 222.

429 *Auguste Chouteau:* Billon, ed., *Annals of St. Louis in Territorial Days*, 237–38; and Blythe and Cunningham, *Founding Family*, 10.

430 *When Dr. Coursault:* Generelly & Aleix to Gilman Chouteau, April 30, 1872, and May 2, 1872, Box 52, CC, MHS.

430 *From time:* "Laclède and the Chouteaus: Fantasies and Facts," unpublished manuscript by John Francis McDermott, Box 48/f.1, McDermott Collection, SIUE.

430 *"The truth:* Ibid.

430 *Frederick Edward:* Cunningham and Blythe, *Founding Family*.

431 *The world:* Primm, *Lion of the Valley*, 137.

432 *Except for:* See William E. Foley and C. David Rice, "Touch Not a Stone," in *Gateway Heritage*, Winter 1983–84, 15.

432 *In the late:* There were various legal efforts in Oklahoma, at least into the 1930s, by some of the part-Osage descendants of the Chouteaus to claim a share in property in St. Louis left by their fathers or more distant ancestors. Among them were the two daughters of Edward Liguest Chouteau, eldest son of Paul Liguest. Their father, who had no white wife or children in St. Louis when he died, provided a small lifetime annuity for his half-Osage daughters in his will, but their inheritance rights did not pass to their children; rather, what remained of the estate after their deaths went to the white children of his only full brother, Auguste Liguest. Efforts of the Osage women to claim part of other family estates in St. Louis failed. Lawyers for Oklahoma descendants of A. P. Chouteau also looked into the possibility of making claims to property or assets in St. Louis, through either the estate of A.P. or his father, but were rebuffed by family members who circled the wagons against the "woods colts" and "bush babies" born to "country wives."

433 *The willingness:* Chardon's Journal, 164.

433 *Some Indian:* See Unrau, *Mixed Bloods*, 108–11.

434 *After so many:* See Mathews, *The Osages*, 659, 687, 690–91, 705–6; Graves, *History of Neosho County*, 203–12.

Acknowledgments

✳

Without the Missouri Historical Society this book could not have been written. Not only did my research make ample use of the sixty-plus boxes of Chouteau family papers, portraits, and photographs in the MHS collections, but collections of many related families and other contemporaries of the Chouteaus provided additional information. These included the papers of the Papin, Gratiot, Lucas, Clark, and Bates families, plus those of Meriwether Lewis, Amos Stoddard, Hamilton R. Gamble, and, of course, Pierre Laclède.

The Missouri Historical Society's carefully assembled and maintained remnants of a time when St. Louis and the lands to the west of it were a distant and exotic place to most Americans are a priceless treasure. It is remarkable that the founders of the society had the foresight to begin to assemble these things—and recognized their importance—at a time when almost no one else in the raw and rambunctious American West was giving much thought to preserving history.

The weeks and months I spent in the beautiful converted synagogue facing Forest Park in St. Louis that serves as the MHS research library were truly a labor of love. I count it a great privilege to have been able to use it.

Also of great use to me were the first-person accounts of life west of the Mississippi River in the eighteenth and early nineteenth centuries provided by many Europeans and by Americans from the eastern states. These adventurous people included naturalists and botanists, writers and artists, military officers, titled Europeans, scholars, and plain opportunists. A surprising number of them—like Lewis and Clark—kept diaries and wrote letters as they battled the currents and submerged trees on the Missouri River and its tributaries, and as they rested after buffalo hunts and shared the spartan diets of Indians and French boatmen. When they returned home to Boston and Philadelphia, London and the Continent, their diaries and letters were often turned into published books. Many such books and journals, ranging from Charles Claude du Tisné's account of his 1719 travels among the Osages to Louis Cortambert's 1835 visits with the same tribe, were first published in France. Possibly the earliest in English was Captain Philip Pittman's book on his tour of the mid-Mississippi Valley in 1765–66. These stories represent a window on life in the Louisiana Purchase lands when white penetration was at a minimum, a century or more before the surge of pioneers from east of the Mississippi.

Like Lewis and Clark, many of these early travelers turned to the Chouteaus and their kin for help in making their way around the West. From their writings, I extracted bits and pieces of the lives of the Chouteaus as well as a broader account of the world around them.

Although the men of the fur trade themselves were not notable for literary efforts, a few of them did leave journals and other accounts that were invaluable to me. They included Francis Chardon, who recorded the number of rats he killed each month at Fort Clark with the same diligence he applied to recording the rampage of smallpox. Charles Larpenteur provided forty years' worth of detail on his life in the isolated splendor of the Upper Missouri River. And Jules de Mun, born to the genteel existence of white plantation society in the French Caribbean, left a vivid account of the harrowing trade expedition across the High Plains and Rocky Mountains that he undertook with A. P. Chouteau just three years after marrying into the Chouteau clan.

My research also benefited from the work of American historians going back a century or more who pioneered in publishing the early histories of the vast area. At the forefront of these was the Wisconsin historian Reuben Gold Thwaites. He not only edited the complete compilation of the Lewis and Clark journals in 1904–7, but during the same time period he brought out the thirty-two-volume *Early Western Travels, 1748–1846,* which gathered the writings of the earliest white travelers into the region. I am also indebted to Hiram M. Chittenden for first putting into print the incredible story of the fur trade; to Louise Barry for her huge effort to document the early history of the area that became Kansas; to Donald Jackson for compiling the letters related to the Lewis and Clark expedition and Zebulon M. Pike's letters and journals; to John Francis McDermott, a Chouteau descendant who was expert on anything having to do with the Mississippi Valley French; and to Abraham P. Nasatir for the years he spent in the Spanish and French archives to produce an English-language record of official policies and correspondence during the rule of Spain and France in the Louisiana Purchase region.

The works of many of these people were made available to me from the magnificent collection of rare Western Americana belonging to the Special Collections Department of the Miller Nichols Library at the University of Missouri–Kansas City. It was a source of continuing delight and amazement to discover that many books I expected to have difficulty in locating were easily available a fifteen-minute drive from my house. Aside from instant help in locating materials, the Special Collections research room provided a quiet place for uninterrupted reading.

The fact that this story had to be researched in three languages, French, Spanish, and English, probably helps to explain why it has previously been told only in limited form. While I was prepared to work in all three languages, I was soon pleased to learn that the Missouri Historical Society had provided for the translation, during the 1960s, of the bulk of the original French letters in the Chouteau Collection. Very recently, another breakthrough was accomplished by the Western Historical Manuscript Collection of the University of Missouri—Kansas City, which arranged for the translation of about seventy letters exchanged between François and Bérénice Chouteau, living at the future site of Kansas City, and her father, Pierre Ménard, from his home in Illinois. These letters were uncovered in the Pierre Ménard Collection of the Illinois State Historical Library.

One more work of research and translation merits special mention.

Louis F. Burns, a Chouteau descendant, dedicated years to culling from the handwritten archives kept by priests nearly two centuries ago the baptismal records of children born to Osage mothers and French fathers, principally along the western edge of Missouri, the eastern part of the future Kansas, and the northeast corner of the future Oklahoma. Among other things, Burns's *Osage Missions: Baptisms, Marriages and Interments, 1820–1886*, establishes the link between the part-Osage Oklahoma line of the Chouteaus and its French ancestors in St. Louis. Burns and his wife, Ruth, were also the donors of most of the large collection of books related to the history of the Osages, which was available at the White Hair Memorial in Osage County, Oklahoma, another quiet place of research where I found insight and inspiration.

As important as all of these people and institutions were to this book, however, none surpasses the contribution of Minnie Acker Christian, my mother, who near the end of her ninth decade still puts dinner on the table every night.

Shirley Christian
Overland Park, Kansas
August 14, 2003

Index

�֍

95, 411–13; physical appearance of, 255; and prohibition of liquor in Indian country, 282, 291–95, 360–61, 372–74; railroad interests of, 403–5, 408, 411–13, 416, 418; St. Louis estate of, 273–74, 379–80; Sanford and, 391–93, 405, 416; steamboats of, 271–78, 284–91, 295, 322, 360–61, 370–72, 383, 429; store opened in St. Louis by, 215, 250; trading operations of, 251, 260, 262–71, 283–84, 395–98, 409–11, 414–15, 432; trips East of, 254–58, 281–82, 383, 388; will of, 418–19

Chouteau, Pierre, Jr., Sanford & Company, 404, 405

Chouteau, Pierre Charles (1817–1818), 255, 274, 421

Chouteau, Pierre Ménard "Mack" (1822–1885) 344, 357, 362, 365, 368

Chouteau, Pierre Sylvestre (1819–1886), 307

Chouteau, René, 30

Chouteau, René Augustin (1723–1776), 30–31, 62, 430

Chouteau, Sophie Labbadie (1791–1862), 212–13, 306–7, 336, 402

Chouteau, Thérèse Cerré, 89, 247, 432

Chouteau, Thérèse Odile (b. 1837), 366, 367

Chouteau, Victoire, *see* Gratiot, Victoire Chouteau

Chouteau & Sarpy, 301

Christy, William, 139, 182

Civil War, 368, 417, 426–30, 434

Claiborne, William C. C., 113, 135

Clamorgan, Jacques, 95, 97

Clark, Fort, 276, 278–79, 288–90; smallpox at, 384; *see also* Osage, Fort

Clark, George Rogers, 79–85, 411

Clark, Jonathan, 177

Clark, Julia Hancock, 148, 177

Clark, Marston, 354–56

Clark, Meriwether Lewis, 177

Clark, William, 3, 6, 80, 178, 210, 300, 344; Catlin and, 284; celebrations held for, 7–8, 16, 147–48; death of, 391; duel between Lewis and Bates prevented by, 169–70; financial dealings of Auguste and, 230; first visit to St. Louis of, 5; Houston and, 314–15; and Indian delegations to Washington, 13–14, 20, 115, 148; and Lafayette's visit, 236, 237; land deals between Chouteaus and, 153; last meeting of Lewis and, 177; and Lewis's death, 181; marriage contracts witnessed by, 212; Marston Clark and, 354–56; and Missouri Fur Company, 163–65, 181–82; Osage treaties negotiated by, 120, 158–60, 162, 173, 191, 202–3, 309, 329; and prohibition of liquor in Indian country, 291–93, 295, 372–73; Sanford and, 370; and Shahaka's return home, 151; as superintendent of Indian affairs, 149, 156, 158, 173–75, 178, 234, 281, 283, 291; as territorial governor, 198, 213, 222, 223; in War of 1812, 198–200; *see also* Lewis and Clark Expedition

Classical, Mathematical & Commercial Institution, 399

Clay, Henry, 143, 225

Clermont, 65, 92, 93, 101, 160, 304, 307, 309

Clermont II, 315–20, 326, 327, 329, 331, 335

Columbia Fur Company, 252, 263–65

Columbia River, 194; fur trade on, 186–88